ROBERT
BRUCE

ROBERT BRUCE

AND THE COMMUNITY OF THE REALM OF SCOTLAND

G.W.S.BARROW

EDINBURGH
UNIVERSITY
PRESS

© G. W. S. Barrow 1976

Edinburgh University Press
22 George Square, Edinburgh

Second edition 1976
Reprinted 1982

ISBN 0 85224 307 3

First edition published in 1965 by
Eyre & Spottiswoode Ltd

Printed and bound in Great Britain by
William Collins Sons & Co. Ltd
Glasgow

Contents

APPENDIX

GENEALOGICAL TABLES

Maps

List of Abbreviations

Abbreviations conform in general to the *List of abbreviated titles of the printed sources of Scottish history to 1560*, published as a supplement to the *Scottish Historical Review*, October 1963.

In the footnotes, numerals which are set in roman capitals denote part numbers; those in lower-case roman, volume numbers; and those in arabic, page numbers, except that an arabic numeral preceded by 'No.' is the number of a document.

Abbreviations not included in the List published in the *SHR* include the following:

Annales Londonienses	*Annales Londonienses*, in vol. i of *Chronicles of the reigns of Edward I and Edward II*, ed. W. Stubbs (Rolls Ser., 1882).
BIHR	*Bulletin of the Institute of Historical Research.*
Cal. Chancery Warrants	*Calendar of Chancery Warrants: 1244–1326* (1927).
Cal. Close	*Calendar of the Close Rolls.*
Cal. Inqu. Misc.	*Calendar of Inquisitions Miscellaneous.*
Cal. Inqu. P.M.	*Calendar of Inquisitions Post Mortem.*
Cal. Pat.	*Calendar of the Patent Rolls.*
Chron. Guisb.	*The Chronicle of Walter of Guisborough*, previously edited as the chronicle of Walter of Hemingford or Hemingburgh, ed. for the Royal Historical Society by Harry Rothwell (London, 1957).
Chron. Rishanger	*Chronica Willelmi Rishanger*, ed. H. T. Riley (Rolls Ser., 1865).
Chron. Stephen etc.	*Chronicles of the reigns of Stephen, Henry II and Richard I*, ed. R. Howlett (Rolls Ser.).

Duncan, MS.	A. A. M. Duncan, Typescript of the Acts of Robert I (to be published as volume v of *Regesta Regum Scottorum*).
EHR	*English Historical Review.*
Flores Historiarum	*Flores Historiarum*, ed. H. R. Luard (Rolls Ser., 3 vols., 1890).
Gesta Edwardi de Carnarvan	*Gesta Edwardi de Carnarvan*, in vol. ii of *Chronicles of the reigns of Edward I and Edward II*, ed. W. Stubbs (Rolls Ser., 1883).
Le Bel, *Chroniques*	*Les vrayes chroniques de Messire Jehan le Bel*, ed. L. Polain (Brussels, 1863).
NLS	National Library of Scotland.
Northumberland County History	*A History of Northumberland* (Northumberland County History Committee, 15 vols., Newcastle upon Tyne, 1893–1940).
Parl. Writs	*Parliamentary Writs and Writs of Summons, Edward I and Edward II*, ed. F. Palgrave (Record Commission, 2 vols., 1827–34).
P.R.O.	Public Record Office, London.
Scimus, fili	Bull of Boniface VIII, June 27th, 1299, in Stones, *Documents*, no. 28.
SHR	*Scottish Historical Review.*
S.R.O.	Scottish Record Office, HM General Register House, Edinburgh.
Stones, *Documents*	E. L. G. Stones, *Anglo-Scottish Relations, 1174–1328: Some Selected Documents*, ed. E. L. G. Stones, 1965, 2nd edn, 1970.
TRHS	*Transactions of the Royal Historical Society.*
Vita Edwardi	*Vita Edwardi Secundi monachi cuiusdam Malmesberiensis: the Life of Edward the Second by the so-called Monk of Malmesbury*, ed. and translated by N. Denholm-Young (Nelson's Medieval Texts, 1957).
Watt, *Fasti*	*Fasti Ecclesiae Scoticanae Medii Aevi ad annum 1638*, Second Draft, ed. D. E. R. Watt (St Andrews, 1969).

For my mother
MARJORIE STEUART BARROW

Preface to the First Edition

ROBERT Bruce, the ruler of a small kingdom, is one of the big figures of history. This book was originally conceived as a study of his life, of his reign, and of his leadership in the Scottish war of independence. It soon became clear that the book must present the story not only of a man but also of an idea. It is impossible to understand the career of Robert Bruce unless he is set fully in the context of the feudal kingdom of Scotland in which he grew to manhood and learned to exercise political power. It is impossible to explain his extraordinary success solely in terms of his own qualities of courage, patience and generosity, splendid as these were. His achievement was due, in the last resort, to his understanding of the idea of the community of the realm, by which the constitutional integrity and the remarkable political toughness of the Scottish kingdom came to be expressed towards the close of the thirteenth century. At the very time that some of the most acute and radical of the political thinkers of western Europe were working out a theory of sovereignty, the community of the realm of Scotland was giving practical expression to such a theory, at first under its Guardians, finally under its king, Robert I. The political manifesto which we call the Declaration of Arbroath (1320) forms a practical counterpart to the famous work of theory which was its close contemporary, Marsiglio of Padua's *Defensor Pacis* of 1324.

The principal theme of the pages which follow is the collaboration between Robert Bruce, on the one hand, and the idea of the community of the realm on the other. Since I believe that this idea formed the dominant theme in the political history of Bruce's Scotland, I must try to explain briefly what I understand by it. The expressions *communitas regni Scotie, la commune du royaume d'Ecosse*, occur over and over again in the records of this period. Before the later nineteenth century, historians tended to suppose that this *communitas* or *commune* referred to the 'commons', the common people, the lesser folk. Not only did they fail to notice the frequency with which the phrase was employed in certain types of official documents, but on the few occasions when they did take note of it they posited – sometimes with surprise – a precocious Scottish democracy. There was, of course, an element of truth in this equation of *communitas* with 'commons'. 'Community' and 'commonalty' are doublets, and in any society whose leaders are distinguished, politically, from the common run of subjects, the collective noun for the whole body of the people will inevitably come to be used of the undistinguished generality. *Vulgus* is the 'public' but also the 'masses', even the 'mob'. A more critical and better-informed generation of scholars realized that in thirteenth-century usage, certainly in England, *communitas regni* or its alternative, *universitas regni*, was in practice used to refer to the whole body of tenants-in-chief of the Crown. At its most aristocratic, this might mean no more than the great barons and pre-lates of the kingdom; at its widest interpretation it could mean all the freeholders or even all the king's free subjects. In England, down to about 1300, the 'community of the realm' was thought of as an aristocratic body. In the opening decades of the fourteenth century the meaning of the phrase began to change markedly, until by the beginning of Edward III's reign it had come to refer to the *non-*aristocratic rather than to the aristocratic element in political society, the 'commons' of which the newly-developing 'house of commons' came to form a parliamentary focus. In contemporary Scotland, however, no house of commons came into being, and it is no coinci-dence that in Scotland the meaning of the expression *communitas regni* underwent no such rapid or radical change. As far as we can tell, it had never had such an exclusively aristocratic flavour in Scotland as it had in England, and at the same time it never acquired a positively non-aristocratic, still less an anti-aristocratic flavour. In the minds of those whose business it was to make political realities articulate, *communitas regni Scotie* remained chiefly an abstract ex-pression. It denoted, I believe, neither the feudal baronage on the one hand nor the common people on the other. It meant, rather, the totality of the king's free subjects, but also something more than this: it meant the political entity in which they and the king were comprehended. It was in fact the nearest approach to the later concept of a nation or a national state that was possible in an age when, according to older and still deeply-entrenched belief, a kingdom was, first and foremost, a feudal entity, the fief – and therefore, in a sense, the property – of its king.

For sixteen of the twenty years between the death of Alexander III and the coronation of Robert Bruce the Scottish kingdom was without an effective king. Yet these twenty years saw the first and most formative phase of the struggle for independence from English domination. The struggle could never have been waged on any plane higher than that of sporadic guerrilla warfare motivated by primitive xenophobia unless there had been some constitutional principle or ideal to inspire a sufficient number of the responsible leaders of the Scottish nation. This constitutional ideal was given consistent expression throughout the years of crisis from 1286 to 1320 and after by such terms as 'community of the realm of Scotland', 'the royal dignity of Scotland', and by the institution of guardianship. The idea of guardianship came naturally to a feudal society, for every fief had its properly appointed and responsible guardians during a vacancy or a minority. But in the hands of the Scots national leaders after 1286, guardianship achieved a wholly new and remarkable political significance.

Robert Bruce, at the start of his career, was only one of a number of the country's natural leaders to be inspired by the idea of the community of the realm. A young man driven by powerful ambition, he also possessed what he no doubt sincerely believed to be a strong claim to the Scottish Crown. On his father's death in 1304, Bruce believed that he had the strongest claim to the throne of any person then living. He was the eldest grandson of Robert Bruce 'the Competitor', who was a grandson of David earl of Huntingdon, the brother of King William the Lion. Three years before the Competitor died in 1295 he had transferred to his son Robert Bruce (the future king's father) all his hereditary claims to the throne. At about the same time the Competitor's son transferred to his own eldest son, the future king, the earldom of Carrick which since about 1272 he had held in right of his wife the countess Marjorie. The third and greatest of these Robert Bruces entered the arena of politics as an earl of Scotland – automatically one of the twelve or thirteen greatest nobles of the kingdom – and also as a rival and even an enemy of John Balliol to whom the Crown had been awarded in 1292 and of the great party of Comyns who had ranged themselves behind Balliol. When Edward I made war on Balliol in 1296, Bruce, like his father, supported the English king. But in the following year, at the age of twenty-two, he took the momentous step of rejecting his father's position and put himself among the leaders of national resistance to the Edwardian régime. He remained one of the leaders of the community of the realm for almost five years. Early in 1302, moved perhaps by a fear that the restoration of Balliol which then seemed imminent might mean the ruin of himself and his family and would certainly wreck his hopes of gaining the throne, Bruce submitted, on certain conditions, to the English king. For the next four years he remained in Edward I's peace, and took a prominent part in the settlement of Scotland which followed the general submission of the Scots leaders in 1304. In this year the death of his father made him the obvious claimant to the Scottish throne if the Balliol claims were repudiated, and from the middle of 1305 it seems that Bruce no longer enjoyed Edward I's confidence. In February 1306 Bruce and his closest adherents killed John Comyn, the principal representative of the Balliol party left in Scotland, in the Franciscan church of Dumfries, and in little more than a month Bruce was crowned king of Scots at Scone. The murder of Comyn was the starting-point of the second phase of the struggle for independence.

The purpose of this book is to set Bruce himself firmly in the context of thirteenth-century Scotland and to describe the interaction between Bruce on the one hand and the community of the realm on the other. It is not a biography in the accepted sense. This is not simply because such a biography cannot be written owing to the lack of continuous material. It is chiefly because the story of Bruce's career is almost identical with the story of the Scottish war of independence against Edward I and Edward II. It was the greatness of Robert Bruce to show a defeated nation the way to freedom; yet fundamentally it was an already free and independent Scotland which made it possible for Bruce to fulfil his ambition, which made him its king and offered him its devoted service.

The Scottish expedition to Ireland and its aftermath, from 1315 to 1318, form an omission serious enough to call for explanation in a book of this scale. The Irish affair was largely a digression as far as Bruce himself was concerned: even if it had been successful he would still have had to deal directly with English hostility. Nevertheless, Ireland was important to Bruce and the Scots, and had there been an adequate monograph on this aspect of Scoto-Irish relations it might have been possible to give it fuller treatment here. As it is, there is no such monograph, and my own knowledge of Irish history and geography is not sufficient to allow me to do justice to a complicated campaign.

I am deeply grateful for the unstinted help which has reached me from many quarters. I have had valuable information from the Astronomer Royal for Scotland (Professor H. A. Brück), Professor Robert Fawtier, Father Charles Burns, Mr Grant Simpson, Mme Kossmann-Putto, Mr Bruce Webster and Dr E. B. Fryde. Dr D. E. R. Watt read most of the work in typescript and I have been glad to incorporate many of his suggestions and profit from his corrections. In addition I have been enormously helped by being able to draw on Dr Watt's unrivalled knowledge of the educated Scottish clergy of the period, and the connexions between Scotland and the continental universities. Dr Douglas Young also read much of the book in typescript and gave extremely helpful criticism. My old friend Mr Ronald Cant, who read the whole work in typescript and proof, saved me from many errors and blunders and suggested a number of important improvements. There are, finally, two scholars whose work on the sources of the period has been so important that this book, in its present form at least, could not have been written unless I had been able to make the fullest use of the results of their research, published and unpublished. Professor E. L. G. Stones has thrown light on many of the obscurities and cleared up many of the muddles which until recently hindered the study of Anglo-Scottish relations in the time of the first three Edwards. He most kindly let me have the proofs of his valuable anthology of texts, so that in general my references to the documents which he includes could be made to his edition. At every stage of the work my friend Professor A. A. M. Duncan has discussed the sources and the problems they pose, and has furnished me with a quantity of unpublished material. With the utmost generosity, he has let me have the typescript of his forthcoming collection of the acts of Robert I, which will form Volume V of the *Regesta Regum Scottorum*. In writing the last few chapters of this book, it has proved of incalculable value to have this typescript collection at hand.

Thanks to the unfailing hospitality of my brother and sister-in-law, Mr and Mrs Jack Holmes, I am able to write these words only three or four miles from the place where Robert Bruce died, in a part of the country to which he was obviously attached. It was here that he had built for himself the house in which he spent most of the last few years of his life. It is pleasing to think that the view before me as I write, down the Clyde, past the promontory of Rosneath, to the waters of the Holy Loch and the Cowal hills, can scarcely have changed in its physical essentials from the view familiar to King Robert in his honourable retirement.

Drumhead, Cardross, 1964

Preface to the Second Edition

THE first edition of *Robert Bruce* appeared early in 1965 and has been out of print for a number of years. The chief purpose of this second edition is to make the book once more available, for there is evidence that it met and may still meet a genuinely popular need. Another purpose, almost as important, is to put right the mistakes of the first edition, whether they were slips, such as Good Friday for Maundy Thursday (p. 92), or out and out howlers, such as failing to distinguish old Robert Bruce the Competitor from his contemporary Robert de Briwes, first chief justice of King's Bench (p. 33). In fact, the opportunity has been taken to do rather more than correct simple errors, serious or trivial. In the past ten years there has been published much work of the first importance on Bruce and his age, sometimes necessitating second thoughts, often throwing additional light on obscure places and confirming or qualifying statements and opinions which appeared in the first edition. As much notice has been taken of this new work as seemed compatible with a revised and not a wholly re-cast or re-written book. At the risk of being guilty of invidious omission, I should particularly mention the first and second editions of Professor Stones's *Anglo-Scottish Relations, 1174–1328: Some Selected Documents*, Professor Nicholson's volume in the Edinburgh History of Scotland, *Scotland: the later Middle Ages*, Professor J. F. Lydon's *The Lordship of Ireland in the Middle Ages*, Dr M. C. Prestwich's *War, Politics and Finance under Edward I* and Dr J. R. S. Phillips's *Aymer de Valence earl of Pembroke*; while among shorter studies there have been the late Bruce McFarlane's critique of Edward I's policy towards his earls (*History*, vol. L), the late Sir James Fergusson's masterly piece of detection *The Declaration of Arbroath*, Professor Duncan's Historical Association pamphlet *The Nation of Scots and the Declaration of*

Arbroath, and Dr Robin Frame's thought-provoking paper on 'The Bruces in Ireland, 1315–18' in *Irish Historical Studies*, vol. XIX. Among documents newly discovered and printed, special mention should be made of Dr Patricia Barnes's edition of the news-letter of 1308 (*Scottish Historical Review*, vol. XLIX) and Dr Peter Linehan's edition of a Scottish diplomatic document from a Cordoba manuscript (*Bulletin of the Institute of Historical Research*, vol. XLVIII). On Ireland in particular, the new work, impressive alike in quantity and quality, suggests that it cannot be long before a competent scholar publishes a fresh synthesis on the topic of Scoto-Irish relations in this important period when Norse power faded from Man and the Hebrides and English power began to wane in at least three of the provinces of Ireland. Another field which has undergone minute re-examination of late is the copious resources of the English Public Record Office, in preparation for an additional volume to augment Joseph Bain's great *Calendar of Scottish Documents*. I have to thank Mr J. Galbraith for generously notifying me of relevant material from this source.

To these (and other) writers, to the discerning reviewers of the first edition, and to the many readers who wrote to me with comments and information on an almost infinite variety of points, this revision owes more than I can adequately express in a brief preface. It will still not satisfy the expert critics of the first edition, whether they wished that the book had told a different story and set forth the story it ought to have told (*Scot. Hist. Rev.*, XLV, 184–201), or felt that it might as well not have been written at all, since Dr Evan Barron had already done the job so much better (*English Historical Review*, LXXXI, 560). And yet, since in the process of scholarship it is always necessary to keep travelling hopefully even although you never arrive, I have in fact learned much from these expert critics as well as from those who were inclined, too generously perhaps, to take a more favourable view of the first edition. To all, my thanks.

Cupar, Fife, 1975

Robert Bruce

I

A Kingdom in Perplexity

ON the afternoon of Monday, March 18th, 1286, the king sat in Edinburgh Castle, dining late with the lords of his council and drinking, we may suppose, some of the blood-red wine of Gascony for whose payment a Bordeaux merchant was to sue for many years in vain. It was a wild day, overcast by equinoctial storm and evil omens. In the past twelve months a story had gone round Scotland that this would be the Day of Judgement. It must have been known to the king, for he joked about it at dinner. He was occupied with a vision more profane and less sombre than that of judgement: the young Frenchwoman, Yolande of Dreux, his wife of less than six months, whom he had left at the royal manor of Kinghorn across the Firth of Forth, twenty miles away by bad roads and the sea ferry. Forty-four years of age, a king for thirty-six, Alexander III had out-lived his first wife, Margaret of England, his two sons, and his daughter, the queen of Norway. His blood survived precariously and distantly, across the North Sea, only in his three-year-old grand-daughter Margaret, whom the magnates of Scotland had, since February 1284, accepted as heir to the throne. Doubtless nothing more than an uncomplicated desire for his young wife prompted Alexander, against his barons' advice, to set off for Kinghorn in the teeth of a snow-laden northerly gale. Yet in the nature of things politics could never be very distant from the most private life of a thirteenth-century king. The land cried out for a more auspicious heir than the little 'damsel of Norway': a boy, present and in good health, unfettered by other dynastic claims, in place of a sickly girl overseas who might one day inherit the Norwegian throne. A hus-band's uxoriousness was also a long-reigning king's duty to his people.

When Alexander reached Dalmeny the ferry master urged him to go back. The king asked if he was afraid. At once he got the answer 'I could not die better than in the company of your father's son,' and was rowed across the two miles of rough water to the royal burgh of Inverkeithing. Landing in pitch darkness, with only three esquires for escort, the king was met by one of the bailies of the town, Alexander *le Saucier*, master of the royal sauce-kitchen. As bailie it would be his duty to meet the king and offer him hospitality. He was a married man and it can be assumed that his home was one of the substantial burgess houses of the town. He assured the king that he would provide him with honourable lodging until morning. In later ages it was common enough for men of all classes in Scotland, nobles, burghers and peasants, to address their sovereign with extraordinary bluntness. Something of this familiarity shows forth in the frank rebuke which Alexander the sauce-maker addressed to Alexander the king: 'My lord, what are you doing out in such weather and darkness? How many times have I tried to persuade you that midnight travelling will bring you no good?' But the king, again in character, brushed aside rebukes and invitations. Asking only for two countrymen to guide him, he and his escort set off along the rough coast road towards Kinghorn. What happened after that no one knows, save that escort and guides lost their master in the blackness of the night and the storm. Next morning he was found dead on the shore, his neck broken. A small feudal kingdom of perhaps half a million inhabitants had now, by a whole series of unlooked for calamities, been left leaderless, in a situation for which there was no precedent. For the best part of two hundred years it had been led and held together by vigorous, warlike kings commanding the allegiance of a feudally conservative yet quarrelsome and potentially violent nobility. The new sovereign, the 'lady of Scotland', was an ailing child who had never seen her kingdom. Her name, Margaret, was a name of good hope; but her age and sex aroused on every side doubts and fears.

What was this kingdom like, which Alexander III – the last of his line to rule in Scotland – had governed peacefully and faithfully since 1249? The first thing which modern historians, especially English, French and American historians, have learned to say about medieval Scotland is that it was a Celtic country, part of what Maitland (and perhaps others before him) called the 'Celtic Fringe' of the British Isles. This emphasis on the Celtic quality of Scotland, a standard feature of modern books, derives not from Scottish historians as a whole but from a line of scholars whose chief founder and greatest figure was William Forbes Skene. Skene revolutionized the writing of Scottish history by a brilliant book which he called quite deliberately *Celtic Scotland*. Since Skene it has been impossible for serious historians to ignore the importance of the Celtic element in medieval Scottish society. But it is over a century since Skene wrote, and in the interval some of his followers have carried his theories far beyond anything he would have thought justifiable. The notion of 'Celtic Scotland' has taken hold more powerfully outside Scotland than among the Scots themselves. For some French historians the highlands begin at the English border; in the view of some English and American writers the clan system was universal from Berwick to Cape Wrath.

We must, of course, beware of this kind of exaggeration, and our picture of the Scottish past will be sadly distorted if we forget or underrate the importance of the non-Celtic element. Alexander III's kingdom was indeed a Celtic country, but saying that does not explain everything in thirteenth-century Scotland. Politically and constitutionally it explains few of the important things. Nevertheless, the Celtic features of Scotland were deeply embedded in her social structure, her language and her customs, and it is well worth considering some of those features here.

In undisputed first rank among the nobility were the earls, about thirteen in all, and their special authority and dignity were directly inherited from the Celtic kingdom of the eleventh century. Their acknowledged doyen was the earl of Fife, whose hereditary privilege it was to place a new king upon the seat of royalty at his inauguration. Although the French and English words *comte* and *earl* were applied to them, the Scottish earls were successors of the *mormaers* – literally, 'great officers' – who had been primarily provincial governors and military commanders. In this they may have resembled the earls of pre-Conquest England, but they were unlike their counterparts in Angevin England, who were essentially great landowners, lords of vast feudal estates, on whom the title of earl had been bestowed as no more than a mark of special honour. There was no one in Scotland

to compare with the English earl of Oxford whose territory was in
Essex and Suffolk, the earl of Albemarle who would be found in
Holderness, or the earl of Surrey whose lands were in Sussex, Norfolk and Yorkshire. In Scotland the arrangement was more primitive
and logical: the earl of Atholl, for instance, had his chief seat at
Moulin (near Pitlochry), most of his lands were in the surrounding
district, and it was in Atholl and only in Atholl that, as earl, he
wielded appreciable political and military authority.

Many other pieces of Celtic conservatism survived north of Forth
and in the south-west, where Galloway had its own special laws, including the archaic system of the wergild or blood-price. In these
regions, for example, there were at every court to which free men
resorted certain judges, 'doomsmen', 'dempsters', sometimes hereditary, who served as repositories of unrecorded, immemorial law
and custom. Much the same had been true of the Scandinavian parts
of England before 1066, but a great deal had happened in England in
the intervening two centuries, nowhere more than in the field of law.
In this as in many other ways Scotland had remained more conservative. The English historians who for 'conservative' tend to write
'backward' tend also in this context to forget that England was conquered by a Norman ruling class who monopolized control at the
top and eventually brought the country they had captured into a
vast trans-Channel empire. It is not surprising that the England of
Edward I was very different from the England of Edward the Confessor. Scotland, on the other hand, had had a half-hearted 'Norman
Conquest' and was never joined to the continent. At almost every
point development was slower and more gradual than in the south.

The most obvious way in which Celtic influence survived in
Alexander III's kingdom was in language and social custom, especially
in the matter of family relationships. In 1286 Gaelic had not been
driven back within the highland line: it must still have been the
language of the great majority of the peasantry north of Forth and
Clyde, as well as in Galloway. No doubt it also survived among the
gentry of these regions, but in the lowlands at least (with the probable
exception of Buchan) the greater lords and the educated clergy would
speak French or northern English, and there is little doubt that
English and French prevailed almost exclusively in the towns. Even
if Gaelic-speaking gentry survived in the north-eastern lowlands

they would certainly have been in a minority. By 1286 many families of 'Norman' or English origin had won lands in the north, and all our evidence shows that outside the highlands these new settlers kept their own languages. Yet they found Celtic custom tenacious, and in their attitude to the family they surely came under its influence. It is true that the succession of heirs by primogeniture, unknown in Celtic lands, was imported into Scotland in the twelfth century and was accepted by the entire landowning class, Normans, English and native Scots alike. But the clannishness deeprooted among the Celts can be seen in the mixed post-Celtic society of the thirteenth century and was to emerge very strongly in later medieval Scotland. The 'clan system' is one of the myths of Scottish history, but in the thirteenth century there were undoubtedly clans in the more purely Celtic parts of the country – the west highlands and Galloway – and traces of clan organization can be found elsewhere. More important than any 'clan system', with all its picturesque accompaniment of slogans, badges and tartans, was the indisputable fact that the family as a whole, rather than any single father-to-son dynasty, was the dominant social unit in Scotland. Even allowing for the small population, a remarkably small number of surnames sufficed for the landowning class.

Down to this point the written records give us clear evidence. They fail us almost completely when we seek the richer and more colourful texture of daily life, its dress, its sports and pastimes, its worship, the books read by the educated, the tales listened to in alehouses, the gossip of the village. Yet even here we can feel sure without being able to prove that Scottish society in lowlands and highlands alike retained a Celtic flavour. There was something of a conscious revival of things Celtic in the middle of the thirteenth century, which went hand in hand with an attempt to give a distinctive personality to the Scottish kingdom and nation. The name *Scotia*, the land of the Scots, which a hundred years earlier had been confined to the country north of Forth, was now applied to the whole Scottish kingdom. At the same time old chronicles and genealogies were studied in an effort to write an intelligible, acceptable history of the Scots which could compare with the better-known, more firmly established histories of neighbouring nations. To make a nation conscious of its identity you must first give it a history. Before the

thirteenth century the Scottish nation had meant the people of mixed
Scottish and Pictish descent who lived north of Forth and Clyde.
'Histories' of this nation, such as they were, related to the Scots of
the west and, to a noticeably lesser degree, to the Picts of the east.
In the thirteenth century, therefore, the only available histories (apart
from chronicles of the recent past) which were in any way suitable
for the Scottish kingdom as a whole were Celtic histories, the deeds
and feuds and sometimes doubtful genealogies of long lines of kings
with names which even then must have seemed uncouth and improbable. To make up for this there was the splendid if partly obscure story of the Scottish church, the great antiquity of the Christian
faith in Scotland, the lives of innumerable saints, the undeniable fact
that of all the missionaries who had tried to convert the English
people the Scots of Iona had had the most resounding success, and
the more questionable assumption that the Scots nation of the
thirteenth century was the sole heir of this Columban tradition.

Scotsmen of Alexander III's time might be of Pictish, British,
Gaelic, Scandinavian, English, Flemish or Norman descent. However
inappropriate, however ironical it might seem, they all took a pride
in the Celtic past of their country. At the inauguration of Alexander
III, which, by a custom already very ancient in 1249, was celebrated
at Scone, an aged highland shennachie recited the young king's
genealogy in Gaelic: 'God's blessing on the king of Scotland,
Alexander mac Alexander mac William mac Henry mac David,'
and so on, till he reached the first Scotsman, Iber Scot.[1] The string of
non-Celtic Christian names separated by the reiterated *mac* merely
serves to emphasize that the old man was rehearsing not only the
antiquity but also the Celtic character of the Scottish monarchy. And
King Alexander did not cease to be given reminders of Celtic custom
after his inauguration. He kept a harper, Master Elias, who, whether
or not himself a Celt, practised an art in which the Scots were acknowledged to excel.[2] When the king travelled by the high road
through Strathearn, it was the custom for seven women to meet him

[1] *Chron. Fordun*, i, 294-5.
[2] *Cal. Docs. Scot.*, ii, No. 131. Master Elias was a tenant of the earl of Fife, ibid., 224.
For the Scots' reputation as harpists, see Gerald of Wales, *Topographica Hibernica*
(*Giraldi Cambrensis, Opera*, ed. Dimock, v, 154-5): 'in the opinion of many, Scotland
nowadays has not only equalled her teacher Ireland in musical skill, but greatly excels
her.'

and sing before him on the way, an entertainment that seems quite in keeping with the progress of a Celtic chief, and far removed from the world of the Capetians and Plantagenets.[1] It was, indeed, a nagging reminder of Celtic habits of thought which occupied King Alexander on the day of his death. Over fifty years earlier a bastard son of Alan, lord of Galloway, by name Thomas, had been chosen as their chief by the Celtic people of that province, rather than see their land divided among Alan's three daughters and their English husbands. King Alexander's father, Alexander II, put down the Gallovidian revolt with great severity, and the bastard Thomas was shut up in Barnard Castle, in charge of John Balliol who had married Thomas's second half-sister, Dervorguilla. Now, in 1286, John Balliol's son and successor, another John, wished to release Thomas from his long imprisonment, and sought the king of Scots' permission to restore him to his native land. It was this request which came before Alexander III's council at Edinburgh on March 18th.[2] If Thomas of Galloway seemed like a ghost from the distant past, his case illustrated the gulf between feudal society which rigidly excluded bastards from inheritance and Celtic society which might prefer a man of unlawful birth to legitimate heiresses.

If Scotland was thus a Celtic country, it was also a country of non-Celtic developments and anti-Celtic tendencies. It is one of the startling paradoxes of Scottish history that the thirteenth century saw not only the first emergence of 'Scotland' in a modern sense but also the decisive defeat of the Scottish language – Gaelic – by a northern English tongue, which in the course of time coolly adopted the name 'Scots' for itself. This Scots language is now retreating fast, save in poetry and as the speech of country districts, especially the north-east. Gaelic, though confined within an ever-decreasing area, still has plenty of life left. But in the thirteenth century Scots was an aggressive tongue, slowly but surely ousting Gaelic, more than holding its own with French, confident of its future as the official and literary language of the Scottish kingdom. Why this displacement happened is not at all clear. It is true that since the tenth century there had been a sizeable population of English race and language within the Scot-

[1] *Cal. Docs. Scot.*, iv, 475.
[2] *Chron. Lanercost*, 116.

tish kingdom, concentrated in the south-east, in Lothian, Tweeddale and Teviotdale. It cannot have remained confined to this corner of the country, and there is plenty of evidence that English-speaking people could be found in the thirteenth century in Dumfriesshire and Ayrshire, in Clydesdale, and in many parts of Scotland north of Forth. It was neither lairds nor scholars but ordinary farming and fishing folk who in the first half of the thirteenth century were giving names like 'Whitefield', 'Midfield', 'Stanbrig' and 'Stinchende [Stinking] Haven' to places in Angus and Perthshire.[1]

This would explain the increase of English speaking in the northern parts of Scotland but one has still to explain the fact that no contrary movement of Gaelic into the south seems to have taken place. If the king's peace allowed Saxons to settle among Britons and Gaels, why did not the same peace allow Gaels to settle among Saxons? Perhaps the answer is to be found in the attitude of the monarchy. From David I's time there was a growing tendency for the king to treat Edinburgh as the capital, to reside there or in other southern castles like Roxburgh and Stirling, and to hunt in the great southern forest of Selkirk (or Ettrick as it is more usually called today). Here too, in the south-east, was the biggest concentration of religious houses, including some of the most famous, Holyrood, Melrose and Kelso. Agriculturally the south-east was probably the richest and most fertile part of the kingdom, and in Stirling, Edinburgh, Roxburgh and above all Berwick it could boast towns whose equal was not to be found elsewhere. Since the economic and political centre of gravity was located in Lothian, where a basic population of Anglian stock was ruled by lords who despite their 'Norman' descent were doubtless already capable of speaking English, it is not really surprising that the native language as well as the customs of Lothian were providing a model to be copied by the rest of Scotland, save for the far north, the west highlands, and Galloway.

Celtic Scotland had been rebuffed in popular devotion as well as popular speech. In ancient times the patron of the Scottish nation was Columba or Columcille of Iona, and in the thirteenth century (and for long afterwards) it was his reliquary, the *Brecbennach*, which

---

[1] Whitefield in Cargill, *ante* 1200, *BIHR*, xxix, 15–16; Midfield (1256), *Arbroath Liber*, i, No. 295; Stanbrig, ibid., No. 144; Stinchende Haven, *Panmure Registrum*, ii, 125 (probably East Haven of Panbride).

was borne by the Scots army into battle. But as early as the eighth century the cult of the apostle Andrew had been established on the east coast by a Pictish king. While Iona was ravaged by the Norsemen and fell upon evil days of obscurity and decay, Saint Andrew's shrine attracted pilgrims from Scotland, England and many other lands. In the twelfth and thirteenth centuries, in keeping with the east-ward orientation of the country, Saint Andrew, universally known and revered but also an eastern saint in an east-coast setting, became the undisputed patron of the Scottish people. Along with Andrew other saints who were specially revered or became widely popular in the thirteenth century either stood, like Ninian, for an anti-Columban tradition, or, like Nicholas, had distinct associations with the east-coast and North Sea. The cult of Margaret, Malcolm Canmore's Anglo-Hungarian queen, was significantly anti-Celtic. She was canonized in 1250, when her remains were translated with great ceremony at Dunfermline Abbey. By the end of the century Margaret had taken her place among the very small company of saints for whom all Scots felt love and reverence.

It was unquestionably in the field of government and administra-tion that the Celtic inheritance of Scotland had suffered its most permanent reverses. Royal government in the thirteenth century was based on a fairly simple structure that was imported from the feudal states of north-west Europe, especially England and France. The monarchy might be Celtic historically, possibly more Celtic in spirit than the surviving evidence would suggest, but to outward seeming there was little to distinguish it, save in opulence, from the feudal monarchies of England and France. Such central government as existed, apart from the king himself, was provided by the royal household. This was emphatically feudal, Frankish, non-Celtic in character. Its chief officers were the steward or stewart, the chancel-lor, the chamberlain, the constable, the butler and the marischal. The office of the steward had been heritable from its establishment by David I, the constable's office had been hereditary from the same period, and there was a marked tendency for the other offices (except the chancellor's) to become hereditary in the thirteenth century. The steward had general responsibility for the household and its manage-ment, and under him were senior clerks, of the Provend and of the Liverance, who had charge of the day-to-day running of the household. The chamberlain was primarily a financial officer, with a general oversight of the royal revenues. The functions of the constable and the marischal were chiefly military, the former being responsible for organizing the Crown's military resources as a whole, the latter having a more specialized role in charge of the cavalry element. The chancellor presided over the king's chapel, which in addition to being the king's personal place of worship served as his chancery or writing-office, keeping his seals, preparing letters and other written documents and issuing legal writs or 'brieves'. The chancellor, himself invariably a clergyman who could normally expect promotion to a bishopric at the end of his term of office, was assisted by numerous chaplains and clerks, some with specialized duties, for example, as custodian of the great seal. Besides these greater officers of the household, there were others, more or less important, more or less hereditary in character, such as the doorward (durward, *hostiarius*), the pantler, the foresters and hunters, and the serjeants or officers of the *dispensa* or *spence*, the sub-department of the household dealing with bread and wine.

Outside the household, the earls, as we have seen, provided a remarkable example of Celtic survival; but the role assigned to them *as earls* in the work of royal government was relatively small. The three chief administrative and judicial officers of the Crown were the justiciar of *Scotia*, responsible for Scotland proper, north of Forth and Clyde, the justiciar of Lothian, whose jurisdiction covered the whole of south-east Scotland, and the justiciar of Galloway.[1] The justiciars might happen to be earls, but their authority derived directly from the Crown. Below them were the sheriffs, some twenty-six in all, who were the principal royal officials in the local districts into which the kingdom was divided for the purposes of royal government. There was a marked tendency for the sheriff's office to become heritable, but under Alexander III the sheriff, whether hereditary or not, still constituted the pivot of royal administration, presiding over the court most in use by free men, collecting and accounting for royal revenue, and often having responsibility for the chief royal castle (or castles) in his own sheriffdom. The

[1] For these officers see G. W. S. Barrow, *The Kingdom of the Scots* (1973), 83–138.

sheriff was an English import, distinctly scotticized north of the border. Another import, less specifically English, was the royal burgh, a unit at once social, economic, political, and useful for maintaining public peace. Royal burghs and their non-royal imitators became more deeply embedded in the heart of Scottish life than perhaps any other institution imported by the kings of the twelfth century. Historically speaking, Scotland has been a land of burghs rather than villages. If the lack of true villages is a Celtic legacy, the success of burghs derives directly from the virtual absence of real town life in pre-twelfth-century Scotland, and the pioneering enthusiasm and copybook methods of the first burgesses, many of them coming from England or from across the North Sea.

Above all, Scotland was a North Sea country, looking eastward and southward to the other countries which faced the same sea and used it increasingly as the highway for their trade. However stubbornly Celtic custom might persist, Scotland under Alexander III had largely turned its back on the west and the Celtic past. There were, it is true, sea-port towns on the west coast, Renfrew, Glasgow, Rutherglen, Irvine, Ayr and Dumfries, carrying on trade with Ireland and western England, but much the larger number of rich and thriving burghs were on or near the east coast. Of these, a distinct northern group included Inverness, Elgin and Aberdeen. In the central group, the chief towns were Perth – then more of a sea-port than it is today – St Andrews, Dundee and Montrose. Lastly, there was what amounted, by Scottish standards, to an 'urban cluster', south of the Forth. Here were Stirling, Edinburgh (with its ports of Leith and Musselburgh), Haddington, Roxburgh, Berwick and others. Insofar as she was not self-supporting, Scotland lived by exporting hides, wool, timber, and fish, and it was the trade in these goods which built up the North Sea towns. Aberdeen was as close to the Elbe as to the Thames, and closer to Norway than either.

> They hoysed their sails on Monenday morn
> Wi' a' the speed they may;
> They hae landed in Noroway
> Upon a Wodensday.

Sir Patrick Spens, admittedly, was a sailor of exceptional skill. But it is a fact that when Alexander III's daughter Margaret sailed to Nor-

way to marry King Eric in 1281, her ship left Scotland on August
11th and reached Bergen early on the morning of the 15th.[1]

In the eyes of the North Sea peoples Scotland was far from being
remote, unknown or unprofitable. In 1247, for example, a ship was
built at Inverness for Count Hugh of St Pol, whose wife was a
relative of the Scottish king. This ship, designed to transport crusaders
from the Pas de Calais to the Holy Land, was so large and fine that
it caught the attention of the English historian, Matthew Paris.[2]
But the Inverness shipyards could never have built such a vessel if
Count Hugh's order had been unique. The links between Scotland
and the Low Countries went back over a century and were vitally
important for the Scottish economy. The vast flocks of sheep which
grazed on the Southern Uplands produced fine wool which was
shipped direct to Flanders from Berwick and other eastern ports. On
a certain date in 1297 Scots merchandise seized at Sluys (on its
way to Bruges) realized over £60, a fair sum for a presumably chance
haul.[3] From the time of David I Flemish immigrants had been welcome in Scotland, and under Alexander III the Flemings were almost
certainly the most numerous and important among the foreign
trading colonies. At Berwick they had their own headquarters or
'factory', the Red Hall, held directly of the Crown on condition
that they would always defend it against the king of England.[4]

The Flemings had no monopoly of Scotland's foreign trade, and
by the end of Alexander III's reign they may have been meeting
serious competition from the Germans of the Hanse towns. Various
men of Cologne, Gottschalk, Gottfried, Alexander, Ingram and
James, appear in Scottish record at the turn of the thirteenth and
fourteenth centuries,[5] and the merchants of Cologne, like the Flemings, had their own Berwick factory, the White Hall in the Seagait.[6]
A letter written eleven years after King Alexander's death, when

[1] *Chron. Lanercost*, 104–5.

[2] Matthew Paris, *Chronica Majora* (ed. Luard, Rolls Series), v, 93.

[3] *Cal. Docs. Scot.*, ii, 264.

[4] *Chron. Guisb.*, 275.

[5] Stevenson, *Documents*, ii, 96, 154; *Melrose Liber*, ii, No. 372; *Foedera*, i, 772a;
SHR, xxvii, 153.

[6] James W. Dilley, 'German merchants in Scotland, 1297–1327', *SHR*, xxvii,
153–4; Stevenson, *Documents*, ii, 154, holdings of Alexander of Cologne in the Seagait. Professor Dilley's article is a most useful survey of the evidence of German
trading activity in Scotland.

Scotland was under English rule, states that some merchants of
Lübeck, belonging to the company of merchants of that city, owed
£80 in customs duty on wool and hides exported from Dundee.[1]
The interest of this chance statement emerges in the sequel. Only a
few months after it was written, William Wallace, having driven the
English out of Scotland, wrote to the mayors of Lübeck and Hamburg explaining that his country had been liberated and that the
Scottish ports were once more open to German traders.[2] German
commercial activity in Scotland was certainly not the creation of
either Edward I or Wallace: we can be sure that before 1286 it had
come to play an essential part in the country's economy.

Apart from trade, royal marriages are a good index of a medieval
country's external relations. Since 1160, the Scottish royal family
had given brides to Brittany, Holland, England and Norway, and
had taken brides from England, France, especially north-eastern
France, and Flanders. Denmark, in fact, is the sole country bordering
the North Sea with which Scottish connections in this period are
difficult or impossible to trace. Political bonds, admittedly, are seldom
exactly the same as the ties of trade, and it was an obvious necessity
for Scotland to keep on good terms with England, not only her
closest neighbour but also the only country in a position to inflict
serious injury upon her. (As the English barons are reported to have
said in 1244, their nation was powerful enough to wipe out the
people of Scotland without the help of others.)[3] But it would be a
mistake to think that her relations with England, political, cultural
and economic, were the only ones that mattered to Scotland, or
that she counted in any way upon English protection and patronage.
Enjoying no special favours, hampered by no special prejudices or
hostility, the Scots of the thirteenth century were accustomed to
earning their own living and making their own way in the community of North Sea peoples.

If we except the northern isles of Orkney and Shetland, Britain in
1286 acknowledged two sovereignties – that of the king of England,
representing a Saxon monarchy of Wessex which had extended its

[1] P.R.O., E. 159/71, rot. 30, dorse (K.R. Memoranda Roll).
[2] Stevenson, *Wallace Docs.*, 159.
[3] Matthew Paris, *Chronica Majora*, iv, 378.

power northward, and that of the king of Scotland, representing a Pictish monarchy of the Tay Valley which had extended its power southward. Only twenty years before there had been a third sovereignty, that of the king of Norway, which made 'foreign territory' of the whole north-western seaboard of Britain from the Calf of Man to the Butt of Lewis. It was not the king of England but the king of Scotland who had annexed this Norwegian province and brought it under his rule. This had been a personal triumph for the young Alexander III in 1266, when Norwegian plenipotentiaries had come to Perth to put their seals to a treaty which gave up the Hebrides. But it was more than a personal triumph: it was the first notable alteration in the balance of power in the British Isles since the reign of Henry II, who had won back the north of England from the Scots and had taken the lordship of Ireland. Since England remained much the wealthier country, much the more homogeneous nation, much the more experienced in war, surely it would be absurd to suppose that Alexander III's acquisition of Man and the Isles made one jot of difference to English strength? It may be doubted whether contemporaries saw things in this light. Englishmen of Edward I's time, certainly less aware than we are of the great disparity of wealth between the two countries, knew only that the king of Scots had at last rid his government of its biggest single source of weakness and had become master of an island which lay only thirty miles from England, fifty from Wales, and athwart one of the principal routes to Ireland. In so doing he had added to his fighting strength an unknown number of islesmen bred to the art of sea-warfare and sea-raiding.

It is of course an over-simplification and an anachronism to speak of two 'sovereignties' partitioning Britain in 1286. Not only would the vaguer 'overlordship' be more accurate than 'sovereignty', but we must recognize that the English Crown nursed ancient claims to a 'super overlordship' over Scotland. This was in no way comparable to the harmless eccentricity of later English sovereigns in using the title 'king of France'. From 1093 to 1124 the kings of Scotland were actually or virtually vassals of the kings of England, and from 1174 to 1189 Scotland had been brought into formal feudal subjection by Henry II, It is true that in 1189 relations were as formally restored to what they had been in the time of King Malcolm IV of Scotland (1153–65) but precisely what these relations were was something which had never been defined. In consequence, the thirteenth-century kings of England, John, Henry III and Edward I, did not always behave as though they recognized the political independence of Scotland. When the Scots kings tried to get the pope's sanction for the rite of anointing in their inauguration cere-monies, the English kings lobbied successfully at the papal curia to prevent it.[1] If they married English princesses, the English kings made this a pretext for interference north of the border. When the papacy decreed that a tax should be levied to support the crusade, it seemed normal to the English kings that they should be given the right to use the proceeds of this tax from Scotland as well as England, Wales and Ireland.[2] At each change of tenure in the English throne, it was usual for the king of Scotland to do homage to the new king of England. Since homage was never performed in the opposite direc-tion, the English kings naturally regarded this usage as evidence of their feudal superiority. The practice may indeed have originated in Scottish admission of some degree of feudal dependence, but it is clear that from the time of David I the Scots kings wished to keep this so vague as to be meaningless, and that Alexander III denied it altogether. 'I become your man,' he declared to King Edward I on October 29th, 1278, 'for the lands which I hold of you in the king-dom of England for which I owe homage, saving my kingdom.' The bishop of Norwich, William Middleton – an experienced canon lawyer – intervened, saying 'And be it saved to the king of England if he have a right to homage for it.' Which gave Alexander the opportunity to reply, speaking clearly, 'No one has a right to homage for my kingdom of Scotland save God alone, and I hold it only of God.'[3]

This account of King Alexander's homage comes only from a Scottish source, but even if partisan it may be well-founded. It was copied, c. 1320–30, into the cartulary of Dunfermline Abbey by a scribe who has copied beside it two documents of Ralph of Green-

[1] P. E. Schramm, *A history of the English Coronation* (transl. L. G. Wickham Legg, 1937), 130; cf. M. Bloch, *SHR*, xxiii, 105–6; Stones, *Documents*, No. 5.

[2] A. I. Dunlop, 'Bagimond's Roll', *Miscellany* of SHS, vi, 6–7; W. E. Lunt, *Financial relations of the papacy with England to 1327*, 292, 296, 334, 338.

[3] *Dunfermline Registrum*, No. 321; Stones, *Documents*, No. 12(b) and p. 76.

law, abbot of Dunfermline from 1275 to 1296, and we know that Abbot Ralph was one of those commissioned in 1291 to make an inventory of the royal archives in Edinburgh castle.[1] Moreover, there is good evidence that King Edward employed the bishop of Norwich in confidential negotiations regarding the king of Scots' homage a few months after the ceremony on October 29th, for in February 1279 the English king sent letters-close to William Middleton, then on his way to the Scottish court, commanding him to enquire into the homage and attendant circumstances 'in as careful and confidential a manner as possible', but to attempt nothing without the king's special command.[2] Clearly King Edward took the matter seriously and had not got his own way – and indeed the much more guarded official English version of what took place might suggest as much.[3]

This personal declaration of independence was no mere posturing. King Alexander was the child of a marriage which had itself been a gesture of independence. His father's first wife, Joan of England, had been Henry III's sister. She had represented friendship with England, but also, unmistakably, the maintenance of the old tradition of Scottish dependence on England. She bore Alexander II no children, and after her death in 1238 he looked in a different direction for his second wife. On Whit Sunday 1239, at Roxburgh, Alexander was married to Marie de Couci, elder daughter of Enguerand, lord of Couci and peer of France, a great-grandson of King Louis VI. The marriage inevitably substituted French for English influence at the Scottish court. Couci adjoins the Vermandois and is not far from Vermand, and when in the year of the Couci marriage we find Master Richard 'Veirement' or 'Verment' acting for the king of Scots and a few years later holding the office of chancellor to the queen,[4] it is tempting to see in this man, who was prominent in the Scottish church for thirty years, a favoured dependant of the Couci family. Queen Marie's younger sister, Alice, married the count of Guines, in the Pas de Calais. Like their neighbour the count of St Pol, who had ordered his crusading ship from Inverness, the counts of Guines were not only near to England, they earned a useful income supplying the English king with mercenary troops. Their fief of

[1] *Dunfermline Registrum*, Nos. 320, 324; *APS*, i, 112–3.
[2] *Foedera*, i, II, 565.   [3] Stones, *Documents*, No. 12(a).
[4] Theiner, *Monumenta*, No. 100; *Cal. Papal Letters*, i, 220.

Guines, feudally dependent on Flanders, was one of those North Sea territories with which it was natural for Scotland also to have connections. The Countess Alice's younger son, Enguerand de Guines, went off to seek his fortune in Scotland where his cousin, the young Alexander III, had become king in 1249 after his father's unexpected death. Enguerand found favour in his cousin's sight.[1] He was knighted, and the marriage arranged for him by the king made him one of the foremost barons of the realm. His wife, Christian Lindsay, was heiress of the main stem of the great house of Lindsay, which held large estates in the south of Scotland, especially in Clydesdale, and a good deal of land in England also.[2] In right of this lordship, Enguerand de Guines took his place among the earls and barons of Scotland on the major political occasions of the period – the recognition of the Maid of Norway as heir to the throne in 1284,[3] and the Treaty of Birgham of 1290.[4] But he belonged to a family which had a long tradition of friendship with the king of England, and with the outbreak of war between the Scots and Edward I it is not surprising to find Enguerand taking the English part. In 1311, somewhat unexpectedly, he succeeded to the lordship of Couci, and about this time, less unexpectedly, his great Scottish estates were judged forfeit by King Robert I. The story of Enguerand de Guines is perhaps a little untypical, but it shows that we must at least distinguish as carefully as possible between nobles who were genuinely Scottish and those, like Enguerand de Guines, whose 'Scottishness' was a technicality.

Alexander III's marriages followed the same pattern as his father's. His first wife was Henry III's daughter Margaret. Bride and bridegroom, the one eleven years old, the other a few months younger, were strictly subordinated to political necessity, in other words the desire of Henry III to have some say in Scottish affairs. This desire was first clearly expressed in the Anglo-Scottish crisis of 1244, and was a continuous factor in Scottish politics from the time of the young Alexander's wedding in 1251 until 1258, when a revolution in England ruled out, for the time being, any thought of an aggressive policy towards the Scots. Margaret of England, always the object

[1] *Cal. Docs. Scot.*, ii, Nos. 209, 239, 241, 267; *Scots Peerage*, iii, 5.
[2] *Scots Peerage*, iii, 5–6. The English land was chiefly in Westmorland, part of the Honour of Kendal.
[3] *APS*, i, 424.   [4] Ibid., 441.

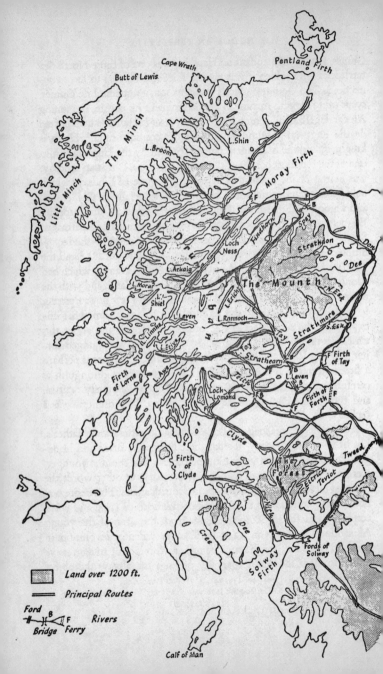

Land over 1200 ft.

Principal Routes

Ford ——B——F Rivers
Bridge Ferry

of her father's love and anxiety, recovered from the acute misery of her early days in Scotland, when she had felt herself to be imprisoned in Edinburgh Castle, that 'dreary and solitary place'.[1] She bore her husband three children and died in 1275. Ten years passed before the tragically early death of all his children forced the king of Scots to marry again. So we are brought back to Queen Yolande, her marriage to Alexander on All Saints' Day 1285, and the ill-fated ride to Kinghorn five months later. Yolande of Dreux, like Marie de Couci, belonged to one of the great noble families of France; indeed, both were descended from Count Robert I of Dreux, a son of King Louis VI. Had Alexander III lived, this second French marriage might well have seen a second influx of Frenchmen into Scotland and a strong revival of French influence. Instead there followed only disaster and uncertainty.

As things stood, the acknowledged heir to the throne was Margaret of Norway. But it was rumoured that the queen was pregnant. Should she give birth to a son, the magnates would be forced to set aside Margaret's claims in his favour. One contemporary chronicler, whose writing is too deeply imbued with a pathological misogyny to be trusted on such a point, says that for several months Yolande deliberately pretended to be pregnant, with the intention of passing off an unknown baby as the late king's son.[2] In the meantime, the peace of the kingdom must be maintained, law administered, justice done. The great men of the land, the bishops, abbots and priors, the earls and barons, assembled at Scone about April 28th, 1286.[3] No doubt it was at this 'parliament', and not at the king's funeral a month before, that the magnates swore fealty to their lady, the king of Norway's daughter, and took a solemn oath, on pain of excommunication by the bishops, to guard and preserve for her the land of Scotland and to keep the peace of her land.[4] In accordance with the oath, the main business of the Scone assembly was the setting up of a provisional government.[5] The decisions taken, which were both careful and astute, make nonsense of any belief that after King

[1] Matthew Paris, *Chronica Majora*, v, 505.

[2] *Chron. Lanercost*, 117–8.

[3] *Chron. Bower*, ii, 138, 'a fortnight after Easter'.

[4] Palgrave, *Docs. Hist. Scot.*, 42. *Chron. Lanercost*, 117, calls the Guardians *pacis custodes*.

[5] *Chron. Fordun*, 310; *Chron. Bower*, ii, 136, 138.

1. Scotland 1286–1329; physical features and communications

Alexander's death Scotland disintegrated into anarchy. The realm
was to be governed by six *custodes*, 'wardens' or (as it is usual to call
them nowadays) 'Guardians'. This body was made up of two representatives of the earls, Alexander Comyn of Buchan and Duncan of
Fife, two representatives of the bishops, William Fraser of St Andrews
and Robert Wishart of Glasgow, and two representatives of the
barons, John Comyn of Badenoch and James the Stewart. Not only
was this division very much in keeping with thirteenth-century constitutional ideas, it also met the problem posed by the traditional
division of the kingdom, since the first three magnates named above
had special responsibility for the older 'Scotia', Scotland north of
Forth, and the other three had similar responsibility for the south.[1]
In electing Duncan of Fife, a young and inexperienced man, the
assembly was really acknowledging the seniority of his earldom; in
electing the Stewart it took into account the century-old primacy of
the stewardship among the household offices. It appointed the two
leading prelates of the Scottish church, and its choice of the two
Comyns recognized the enormous influence of the most powerful
baronial family in the land. Constitutionally impeccable, the election
was also politically prudent. If the Maid of Norway should die and
Queen Yolande not bear a child, the throne would be open to
competition from a number of claimants. Of these the two strongest would be Robert Bruce, lord of Annandale, and John Balliol of
Barnard Castle. It was clearly unwise to make either of these men a
Guardian, but Bishop Fraser and the two Comyns supported Balliol
(whose sister was John Comyn's wife), while Bishop Wishart, the
Stewart, and, probably, Earl Duncan were supporters of Bruce.

According to a report preserved by Walter Bower, the Scone
parliament appointed three envoys (the bishop of Brechin, the abbot
of Jedburgh and Sir Geoffrey de Moubray) to seek out Edward I
in Gascony and ask for his advice and protection with regard to the
Scottish kingdom and the Liberty of Penrith. The envoys set off on
August 7th, found the English king at Saintes, and on November
25th, at Clackmannan, reported back to the Guardians, whom
they found dealing with the difficult and delicate problem of the

---

[1] The scheme had been foreshadowed by the arrangements to safeguard Queen
Margaret's first-born child in 1261: *Cal. Docs. Scot.*, i, No. 2229; D. E. R. Watt,
'The Minority of Alexander III of Scotland,' *TRHS*, 5th Ser., xxi, 21.

pregnancy of Queen Yolande, then lodged in Stirling Castle.[1]

The situation which faced the Guardians was full of dangers and difficulty. Scotland was a feudal kingdom and her people were feudally minded. The members of the ruling class were bound closely to the Crown by social custom and the obligations of military service in virtue of which they held their land. A great deal of land, indeed most of the more fertile land, was held by knight-service and organized into baronies and knights' fees. The majority of the men so holding were men of fairly small substance, perhaps tenants-in-chief, more often freemen who held their estates of one or other of the great magnates. Whether tenants-in-chief or sub-tenants, many were holders of only single knight's fees. As such they were not separated from the peasantry, townsmen or lesser freemen of the countryside by any unbridgeable gulf, though in Scotland the fundamental medieval class distinction between noble and non-noble birth and rank was clearly understood. The Crown acted as the linchpin of this small society of men who were free and self-sufficient, yet at the same time feudally very conservative. Nothing and no one could be an adequate substitute for the king. If for some compelling reason the throne must be left vacant, the kingdom could only resolve itself into a collective entity, into the universality of its freemen, or, in thirteenth-century language, into the 'community of the realm of Scotland' (*communitas regni Scotie*). Of course there was such a 'community' even when a king was on the throne, but in

[1] *Chron. Bower*, ii, 138. Virtual proof that such a mission reached Edward I in Gascony is found in his letter dated Saintes, September 15th, 1286, staying proceedings on the Border at the Guardians' request, Stevenson, *Documents*, i, No. 11. In Bower's text, *Sanctum Johannem Evangelistam* is perhaps a copyist's error for *Sanctum Johannem Angeliacensem*, i.e. S. Jean d'Angély. King Edward was at S. Jean d'Angély on September 11th, 1286, and at Saintes from September 13th to 16th; J. Trabut-Cussac, in *BIHR*, xxv, 168–9. Moreover, we know that Bishop Fraser and Alexander Comyn earl of Buchan, were at Stirling on November 27th, 1286; *Arbroath Liber*, i, No. 293.

This mission must be distinguished from a lesser mission consisting of two Dominicans sent by Bishops Fraser and Wishart at the time of Alexander III's funeral (March 29th, 1286: Stevenson, *Documents*, i, No. 3), presumably to give Edward the news of Alexander's death, and ask for his good pleasure. *Chron. Lanercost*, 125, seems to refer to a later mission (1289?) when it speaks of the Scots asking Edward I to assist them in their leaderless state.

The important mission sent by the Scone parliament of 1286, ignored by most if not all modern historians, shows that the Scots leaders were anxious from the start of the minority to enlist Edward's aid, but it tells against any notion that they were ready to concede, or Edward to demand, superior lordship over Scotland.

normal times, with an adult and vigorous ruler, the community would fade into the background. The king would take the initiative, would act or give orders as he thought best. In serious matters he would naturally take the advice of his council: but this council, in the theory of the time, was no other than a representation of the wider community.

Ideas of this sort had already been adumbrated in 1261 and now on Alexander III's death they sprang at once to the forefront. The Guardians invariably styled themselves 'appointed by common counsel' or 'elected by the community of the realm'.[1] The symbol of all government, the essential mark of authority, was the seal. The Guardians had a remarkable seal cut for their use, showing on one side a shield of the royal arms, on the other the figure of Saint Andrew on his cross.[2] The background or 'field' of these emblems, evenly sown with trefoils, repeated the design of the late king's seal and emphasized continuity with the immediate past. The seal bore two significant inscriptions, the first descriptive, the second emotional: 'the seal of Scotland appointed for the government of the kingdom' and 'Saint Andrew be leader of the compatriot Scots'.[3] While thus expressing the idea of the community of the realm, the Guardians were also at pains to appear as delegates or trustees of the Crown and the young queen. This we can most clearly see if we look forward a few years to the Treaty of Birgham (July 1290), entered into between Edward I and the community of the realm of Scotland led by the Guardians.[4] In this it was provided that once the Maid of Norway was made queen in the accustomed manner a seal should be cut for her with the usual arms and inscription of the name of the king of Scotland only. All relics, charters, privileges and muniments touching the Scottish 'royal dignity' and kingship were to be guarded securely within the realm of Scotland until the queen should have an heir, and in the meantime nothing pertaining to the 'royal dignity'

---

[1] For the style *de communi consilio constituti*, see Stevenson, *Documents*, i, *passim* between No. 14 and No. 123; for the less common *per communitatem ejusdem regni electi*, ibid., Nos. 15, 27 and cf. No. 89.

[2] W. de G. Birch, *History of Scottish Seals* (1905), i, 31-3 and illustrations Nos. 14 and 15.

[3] SIGILLVM SCOCIE DEPVTATVM REGIMINI REGNI; ANDREA SCOTIS DVX ESTO COMPATRIOTIS.

[4] Stevenson, *Documents*, i, No. 108.

was to be alienated or placed under subjection. But the Guardians' care for the rights and duties of the Crown had shown itself much earlier than this, especially in keeping the peace and in the defence of the realm, royal tasks *par excellence*. For example, James the Stewart, one of the Guardians, declared that public necessity had forced him to override Melrose Abbey's exemption from wapin-schaws and military aid in Kyle 'because the peace and tranquillity of the realm were disturbed after King Alexander's death and the state was threatened by conflict.'[1] This must have been in line with a general instruction, for before Whitsun (May 25th) 1287, Earl Malise of Strathearn had raised men from among the tenants of Inchaffray Abbey 'to uphold the peace and tranquillity of the realm of Scotland'.[2] A writ preserved only in a later formulary possibly gives the gist of peace-keeping orders sent out at this time by the Guardians.[3]

In 1286 the gravest threat to the peace of Scotland came from Scotsmen, especially in the south-west, where it so happened that the two noblemen with the strongest claims to the throne, Balliol and Bruce, were both very powerful. Robert Bruce, lord of Annandale, and his son Robert, who held the earldom of Carrick in right of his wife Marjorie, gathered an armed force and seized the royal castles of Dumfries and Wigtown, and the lord of Galloway's castle at Buittle.[4] The revolt can only have been meant to strengthen the Bruce position *vis-à-vis* John Balliol, whose mother's lordship of Galloway – Wigtownshire and Kirkcudbright – was already hedged in by Bruce the elder in Annandale and Bruce the younger in Carrick, and stood to be encircled completely if the Bruces controlled Dumfries and the road north through Nithsdale. It has even been argued that when on September 20th, 1286, at Turnberry (the chief castle of Carrick) the Bruces, James the Stewart, two Scottish earls, the lord of Islay and several dependants entered into a 'band' or sworn agreement to support the earl of Ulster and Thomas de Clare against their

---

[1] *Melrose Liber*, No. 396.

[2] *Inchaffray Chrs.*, No. 117.

[3] Edinburgh University Library, MS. No. 207, ff. 149–50, with the rubric *Citacio exercitus post obitum regis*. We owe the discovery of this important writ to Professor Duncan.

[4] Palgrave, *Doc. Hist. Scot.*, 42 ('Bot . . .' and 'Wygge . . .' stand for Buittle and Wigtown). Cf. *Exch. Rolls*, i, 35, 39.

adversaries, Bruce the elder made this the occasion of a deliberate claim to the Crown.[1] But the band merely saves the fealty of all parties to the king of England and to whoever shall be king of Scotland 'by reason of the blood of the late King Alexander'. With Queen Yolande possibly pregnant and Margaret of Norway not even in Scotland, still less formally enthroned, this cautious reservation is understandable. Whatever the grounds for Bruce's claim to the throne, they could not conceivably be 'by reason of the blood of King Alexander'.[2] The stir in the south west seems to have been put down peaceably, but it was an ugly contradiction of the ideas which had produced the guardianship, an ugly defiance of the 'community of the realm'. More particularly, it showed that in the troubles which lay ahead the family of Bruce would not be content to cultivate its own garden.

[1] Stevenson, *Documents*, i, No. 12. E. M. Barron, *Scottish War of Independence* (2nd edn), 112, states as a fact, and W. C. Dickinson, *Scotland from the earliest times to 1603* (1961), 144, implies, that the Turnberry Band upheld Bruce's claim to the throne. Incidentally, the band does not say 'in accordance with hereditary rights' (Dickinson, loc. cit.) but *ratione sanguinis . . . Alexandri regis*, something rather different, which points to the Maid of Norway or a possible child born to Yolande.

[2] F. M. Powicke, *The Thirteenth Century*, 598n., suggests, surely rightly, that 'some Irish enterprise was the occasion of the pact' at Turnberry. Thomas de Clare was the brother of Earl Gilbert of Gloucester and thus the nephew by marriage of Bruce the Competitor. Thomas (whose Irish interests lay in Thomond or North Munster, far from Ulster) and the new earl of Ulster, Richard de Burgh, were busy with military expeditions against the Irish of Connacht in 1285 and 1286 respectively (G. H. Orpen, *Ireland under the Normans*, iv, 73-5, 112).

2. Scotland at the end of the thirteenth century

ORKNEY
(To Norway)

CAITHNESS Ⓔ

SUTHERLAND Ⓔ

LEWIS

HARRIS

ROSS Ⓔ
Cromarty
Dingwall
Inverness
Nairn
Elgin Forres
Banff
BUCHAN Ⓔ

SKYE

MORAY

BARRA
RUM
EIGG
COLL
TIREE
MULL

GARMORAN
LOCHABER
Drumalban BADENOCH

ATHOLL Ⓔ

MAR Ⓔ
Aberdeen
The Mounth
MEARNS
Kincardine
Forfar
ANGUS Ⓔ

Perth
STRATHEARN Ⓔ
Cupar
MENTEITH Ⓔ Auchterarder
Kinross
LENNOX
Stirling
Clackmannan
DUNBAR or MARCH Ⓔ

ARGYLL
KNAPDALE
JURA
ISLAY
KINTYRE
BUTE
ARRAN
CUNNINGHAM
KYLE
Ayr
CARRICK Ⓔ
GALLOWAY
Wigtown

Dumbarton
LOTHIAN
Edinburgh
Lanark
Peebles
Selkirk
THE FOREST
Roxburgh
Berwick

Dumfries
Newcastle upon Tyne
Carlisle

ANTRIM

Seat of Sheriffdom
Earldom Ⓔ

10 20 30 40 50
Miles

MAN
(To Scotland)

2

Bruce of Annandale

FOR more than two centuries before the office and title of
Warden of the March had been thought of, the Bruce lords of
Annandale had been keeping the western march of Scotland. There
were then, as there are now, two main routes between Scotland and
England, by the east coast and by the west. Unlike its modern
counterpart, however, the western route in the middle ages did not
cross the Esk and Sark and enter Scotland at Gretna. Individuals or
small groups may have gone that way, but it was too boggy for large
numbers of men with horses and waggons, who had instead to ford
the upper Solway at low tide and reach the Scottish shore almost as
far west as Annan. Alternatively, they might strike eastward up the
River Esk to enter Scotland near its junction with the Liddel Water,
but this gave access only to difficult hilly roads through Eskdale or
Liddesdale. For any strong force coming from the south and heading for central Scotland the natural route lay up the broad dale of
Annan or further west, beyond Annandale, through Dumfries and
Nithsdale. Annandale, therefore, was a gateway to Scotland, and
its two castles of Annan and Lochmaben served as the gate.[1]

At the time the first Robert Bruce of Annandale was granted this
territory by King David I, about 1124, it formed a border zone not
only with England but also with Galloway. For King David the
Galloway border needed watching as carefully as the English – indeed
more carefully, towards the end of his reign, when he had won
control of Cumberland and Westmorland. Galloway was a wild land
which frightened and fascinated King David's French and English
followers.[2] Around it he set a ring of military fiefs, each with its

[1] R. C. Reid, 'The caput of Annandale', *Dumfriesshire Trans.*, 3rd ser., xxxii,
155-66, esp. 159 ff.
[2] R. L. G. Ritchie, *Chrétien de Troyes and Scotland* (Zaharoff Lecture, 1952), 17-24.

castle and its foreign lord:[1] Renfrew under the Breton, Walter Alan's
son, first of the Stewarts; Cunningham under Hugh de Morville the
constable; North Kyle, also placed under Walter the Stewart;
South Kyle, reserved to the Crown; Annandale under Robert Bruce.
Eastward again were Eskdale, the fief of Robert Avenel, and Liddesdale, given to Ranulf de Soules. These were men who had reason to
serve King David with skill and loyalty. Most were his vassals and
tenants on the 'Honour of Huntingdon', the great lordship sprawling
across the counties of Huntingdon and Northampton and many
other shires which King Henry I had given to David of Scotland in
1114. Bruce held manors of this Honour in Rutland, Morville and
de Soules in Northamptonshire. There was a further bond between
them: they all came from the same region of France – western
Normandy and the borders of Brittany. The first Robert Bruce –
Robert de Brus – got his name from Brus or Bruis, now Brix, a
few miles south of Cherbourg, where the family's home, 'Adam's
Castle', has disappeared long since. Morville is not far from Brix;
Soules – now Soulles – is farther south, near St Lô. The Stewart's
family came from Dol, a short distance across the border in Brittany.
The knightly families of this region supported Henry I in his early
struggles, they won great reward at his hands, and they easily attached themselves to David of Scotland who was in many ways the
most favoured of Henry's protégés.

Among those who gained a footing north of the border, this first
Robert Bruce was the oldest and much the least dependent upon
King David. He was lord of Cleveland in north Yorkshire, and he
had long served King Henry as a 'justice', that is to say a chief royal
agent, in the north of England. For all his origins in Normandy and
his lordship over Annandale, this Robert Bruce must be seen as
essentially a Yorkshireman, who on Cowton Moor in 1138, under
Saint Peter's 'Standard' and encouraged by Archbishop Thurstan,
fought stoutly even against King David to beat off a Scottish invasion. His body lies buried in the priory he founded at Guisborough.
In Cleveland he was followed by his elder son Adam and a line of
Yorkshire Bruces.

It was otherwise with his younger son, Robert, who fought

[1] G. W. S. Barrow, *The Kingdom of the Scots*, 281, 322-6, 339-51.

against his father at the battle of the Standard and took his place among the great lords of Scotland. But in general the Scottish Bruces did not sever their connections with England. They held land in County Durham and family loyalty and piety kept their love for Guisborough Priory so strong that they never tried to found a monastery of their own in Annandale. But their lordship north of the border gave them Scottish interests and ambitions. Two of them married into the royal family, and from their castles of Annan and Lochmaben they ruled over a close-knit body of knights and lesser vassals who, whatever their origins, could hardly be distinguished from the other gentry of Scotland. From Gretna up to Moffat these 'knights of Annandale' – Johnstones, Herrieses, Jardines, Kirkpatricks, Dinwiddies, Crosbies and the rest – parcelled out the land amongst themselves and settled down as country gentlemen. They were a tough, prolific stock, sharing the management of their lord's fief, making sure of the best return from their estates, and prepared if need be to restrain the diocesan officials of Glasgow when their demands grew excessive.[1] Above all, in their conventional, feudal way they were loyal to the lord of Annandale. At the turn of the thirteenth and fourteenth centuries, when such territorial-cum-feudal loyalty was dying out in southern England and perhaps could not easily be paralleled in Scotland, the lairds of Annandale survived in stubborn anachronism as a compactly united band.

At the date of Alexander III's death the Bruce lordship of Annandale, methodically divided into knight's fees and having its *caput* or legal and administrative headquarters at Lochmaben Castle, was already one of the older, more enduring features of the Scottish feudal landscape. It is against this background of five generations of Bruces and their knightly tenants that we should judge the value of the belief which even today is widely held that the Bruces were foreigners and strangers in Scotland, 'Norman' members of an alien 'Norman' baronage which had struck only shallow roots among a native Scottish population. This is the kernel of the 'Norman myth' in Scottish history, in its own small way as persistent and misleading

---

[1] Charters showing that the office of steward of Annandale was held at various times by members of different tenant families are in *Cal. Docs. Scot.*, i, Nos. 197, 706, 1,683, 1,685. For the Annandale gentry's behaviour as landlords, cf. *Chron. Lanercost*, 99–100.

as the 'Celtic myth'. A similar myth was once prevalent in books on English history also, but with a difference: a baronage which had wrested Magna Carta from the tyrant John and in the next century fought side by side with English bowmen against the French must have had its heart in the right place, even if its origins were in Normandy. Scottish historians, on the contrary, had no Magna Carta to deal with and had to explain the apparent fact that in the war of independence the nobility of Scotland were lacking in patriotism. If the nobility were not true patriots, it was some consolation to know that, after all, they were only Normans. In England, therefore, Norman ancestry was both picturesque and honourable, since the Normans had quickly effaced their defects of birth by acquiring the finest English qualities. In Scotland the Normans seemed suspect, willing to fight among themselves for the Crown and ready to betray their adopted country for the sake of estates across the border. In England the 'Norman myth' is long since dead. The Norman origin and character of the baronage of England from the Conquest to King John is never likely to be ignored or underestimated by historians, but at the same time the thorough absorption of these men of Norman and other continental stock into a distinctively English society has long been recognized, and it would occur to no English historian nowadays to describe as 'Norman' the baronage of King Edward I. It is high time the Scottish 'Norman myth' died likewise. There is absolutely no evidence whatever that families such as Murray, Olifard, Comyn, Lindsay, Stewart or Bruce – to name only the most prominent among scores with 'Norman' origin – thought of themselves or were considered by others as differing in any way that mattered from the other noble families of the Scottish kingdom. The Normans were past masters at taking on the colour of their surroundings and north of the border they had adapted themselves to a Scottish coloration some generations before the time of Alexander III.

This of course did not mean that the Scots nobility were hostile to England and had no interests south of the border. On the contrary, many a Scottish landed family had, like the Bruces of Annandale, been founded by one of the younger sons of an established English family, and many Scots lords married the daughters, sometimes the heiresses, of English barons. Not only was family feeling strong, there was no barrier to inheritance on either side of the border, and marriage itself involved the transfer of land. It is not surprising that in 1286 a large amount of land in England was held by men and women who were normally domiciled in Scotland as subjects of the Scottish king, while in Scotland a proportionately even larger amount was held by English landowners. Nothing could be further from the truth than to suppose that it was only Scotsmen of 'Norman' descent who held English land. Along with more obviously 'Anglo-Norman' barons like Balliol and Umfraville there were Scottish earls like Atholl, Buchan, Fife and Mar who either held or laid claim to estates in England. On the other hand, several Scots magnates whose continental origins were indisputable, such as Soules and the Stewart, owned little or no property south of the border.

Robert Bruce, the fifth lord of Annandale and grandfather of the future king, was born in 1210 and succeeded his father in 1245. Among the nobility of Scotland in the 1280s he may not have been a typical figure, but there was certainly nothing exotic or unnatural about the position he filled. His father was third in descent from the first Bruce of Annandale. His mother, Isabel, was the second daughter of Earl David, the youngest of King David I's three grandsons.[1] His background – it is the key to much of his grandson's conduct in the struggle with England – was at once aristocratic and royal. This Robert Bruce is known to history as the 'Competitor' or the 'Claimant', from the last phase of his career, when he staked nearly everything on a bid to become king of Scots. Contemporaries knew him as 'Robert the Noble' and before his bid for the throne he had already lived a long life rich in experience of high places, hard work and excitement. In 1237 the death of his uncle John of Scotland put his mother in possession of a third part of the vast Honour of Huntingdon and a third of the rich lordship which Earl David had held in Scotland, a lordship which included Garioch in Aberdeenshire and the growing burgh of Dundee.[2]

[1] See Genealogical Table I and *Yorkshire Archaeological Jnl.*, xiii, 226–61.

[2] *Chron. Bower*, ii, 114, gives Bruce's cognomen as *Nobilis*; *Scots Peerage*, ii, 430, wrongly attributes it to his father. The larger part of Earl David's Scottish lands are listed in the charter printed *Lindores Chartulary*, No. 1. For the events of 1237 see *Complete Peerage*, iii, 169, vi, 647; *Cal. Docs. Scot.*, i, Nos. 1,369, 1,384.

All this property came to Robert Bruce in 1252.[1]

Apparently in 1238 – if we may believe a story which comes only from a Bruce source, and sounds rather implausible – King Alexander II, still childless and not yet married to Marie de Couci, caused Robert Bruce to be designated as his heir in a formal parliament of the magnates.[2] At that date, one year after John of Scotland's death, Bruce was the man nearest to the royal line. In the uncertain state of the law of succession to the throne, it is not impossible that the Scots magnates should have declared their preference for a man rather than a woman. But in 1238 or thereabouts Hugh Balliol was born,[3] the first grandson of the eldest of Earl David's daughters and surely a clear challenger of any son of younger daughters. And in any event, within a few years of the parliament which acknowledged Bruce as heir (if it ever met) the king's second wife had given birth to a son. In the meantime, in May 1240, Bruce himself married. His wife, Isabel de Clare, 'a tocherless lass wi' a lang pedigree', brought as her dowry a single Sussex manor.[4] But she was a daughter of the earl of Gloucester, a niece of the Earl Marshal. Now, by marriage as well as by descent from his mother, Bruce belonged to the small circle of the greatest aristocratic families of England.

During the fifties and sixties of the thirteenth century Robert Bruce was deeply involved in English politics. He was for some time governor of Carlisle castle.[5] Although the belief that he served in England as a royal judge is false, being based on confusion between Bruce and a more obscure Robert 'de Briwes', the first Chief Justice of King's Bench,[6] nevertheless Bruce figured prominently in the disturbed period of baronial reform after 1258. In the relatively peaceful Scotland of Alexander III his affairs could no doubt be left to his son and other trusted agents. England was a different matter. The country was in turmoil, rent asunder for some years by a bitter civil war which brought bloodshed, disin-

[1] *Cal. Docs. Scot.*, i, No. 1,870. Much of the estate must have come to him in 1245 on his father's death, but Writtle and Hatfield Broadoak in Essex would not have passed to him until after his mother's death in 1252, *Complete Peerage*, ii, 358.

[2] Palgrave, *Docs. Hist. Scot.*, 29.

[3] *Northumberland County History*, vi, 49.

[4] *Complete Peerage*, ii, 359; *Cal. Docs. Scot.*, i, No. 1,498.

[5] *Cal. Docs. Scot.*, i, Nos. 1,994, 2,472; apparently not always a conscientious governor, ibid., No. 2,034.

[6] C. A. F. Meekings, in *Notes and Queries*, clxii (1932), 278, 436.

heritance and the countrywide destruction of property. As long as
the English baronage was largely united against Henry III, Bruce was
on their conservative wing; when they split, he became a steadfast
royalist. In April 1264 along with other Scots and northern English
lords, he led a large force of men-at-arms to Nottingham to support King Henry and his son the Lord Edward.[1] A few months
later the royalist army was smashed by Simon de Montfort at Lewes.
Along with the king and the Lord Edward, Bruce was taken
prisoner. His son, prudently left in Scotland, hurried south to arrange
for his ransom and release. There was great slaughter at Lewes, but
only (says an English chronicler) of 'insignificant men, common
folk, especially Scots'.[2] It is not hard to imagine the peasant lads
from Annandale and Nithsdale along with highlanders from
Galloway and Badenoch, unarmoured and bewildered, cut down by
Montfort's fierce young knights or, if they tried to flee through the
unfamiliar Sussex countryside, hunted down by the villagers. *Their*
ransoms would not be paid. When Scots infantry next encountered
English cavalry, more than thirty years later, Edward of England
was on the other side. Nevertheless, they were to acquit themselves
well, better, in fact, than Edward, with his memories of Lewes,
could ever have expected.

Whatever else may be said of Bruce the Competitor, his stamina was
astounding. At the age of sixty he left England in company with
the Lord Edmund, Henry III's younger son, bound for Tunis and the
Holy Land.[3] The crusade was brief and inglorious, but it acquainted
the crusaders with the great shift of power in the Near East and even
brought them into contact with the Mongol khan of Persia. It must
have impressed on all of them the place of western Christendom in
a larger world. On the one hand, Scotsmen like the knight Alexander Seton and his young esquire, who fell into Arab hands,[4]
could come from their far north-western country and take their
place beside the chivalry of Christendom. On the other hand, the
crusaders' experience of the Mediterranean with its conflicting races

[1] R. F. Treharne, *The Baronial Plan of Reform*, 140, 323, 335; *Flores Historiarum*, ii,
488.

[2] *Cal. Docs. Scot.*, i, No. 2,358; *Chron. Stephen etc.*, ii, 544.

[3] *Cal. Docs. Scot.*, i, No. 2,575.

[4] *Chron. Melrose*, 145-6.

and nationalisms, its rich, opportunist merchant states like Genoa
and Venice, its even more opportunist kings like Charles of Anjou,
must surely have given their minds some hint of social and political
patterns very different from those familiar in their own corner of
Europe.

On his way home from the east, probably in 1272, Robert Bruce
paid a visit to the great Cistercian abbey of Clairvaux in Burgundy.[1]
His purpose was to appease the anger of a man who had been dead
for 120 years and to lift a curse which, if not oppressive, must have
disturbed the lords of Annandale. The great Irish church reformer
Maelmaedoc Ua Morgair (St Malachy O'Moore), while staying at
Annan in 1140 or thereabouts as the guest of the second Robert
Bruce of Annandale, had asked that a condemned robber's life should
be spared, and was outraged when his host secretly hanged the
man after promising to reprieve him.[2] The terms of the curse which
Malachy then uttered on the house of Bruce and the town of Annan
are unknown, but it has been well said that the imprecation of an
angry Irish saint would have been 'thorough, comprehensive and
devastating'.[3] The Bruces did not wither, but it is certain that somewhere about the turn of the twelfth and thirteenth centuries their
chief castle, the Mote of Annan, was half washed away by a tremendous spate and the lords of Annandale were forced to move their
headquarters to Lochmaben.[4] St Malachy had died at Clairvaux and
he was buried in the abbey church.[5] We can picture Bruce the Competitor praying before his tomb. He gave the abbey an endowment
of land in Annandale to pay for lights to burn for ever at the shrine of
the Blessed Malachy.[6] We can only guess at Bruce's reasons for
wishing so strongly for reconciliation. On May 3rd, 1273, very soon
after he got home, he married for the second time, and the marriage
may not have been welcome to his family.[7] His second wife, twice a
widow, was Christian Ireby, daughter of a near neighbour, William

[1] Chron. Lanercost, 161; R. C. Reid, Dumfriesshire Trans., 3rd Ser., xxxii, 155-66.
[2] Chron. Lanercost, 160; cf. J. Wilson, SHR, xviii, 69-82, esp. pp. 78-80.
[3] R. C. Reid, Dumfriesshire Trans., 3rd Ser., xxxii, 157.
[4] Ibid., 163-6.
[5] Migne, Patrologia Latina, clxxxii, 1,095-6.
[6] Migne, Patrologia Latina, clxxv, 1,759-60, 'Osticroft', unidentified.
[7] G. O. Sayles, Select Cases in King's Bench, iii, 91-2; cf. SHR, xxv, 388 ff. The
Competitor's son attempted unsuccessfully to withold his step-mother's dower on
the grounds that her marriage to his father was unlawful.

Ireby, a Cumberland knight. Before taking a step which his son seems to have resented, Bruce may have thought it right to make his peace with the wrathful but holy Irishman.

Bruce's son and heir – the fifth Robert Bruce to hold the lordship of Annandale and the second of the three with whom we are chiefly concerned in this book – had meanwhile turned the family interests westward and gained a Scottish earldom. Neil, earl of Carrick – his name seems rather Celtic Niall than Norman Nigel – died in 1256, the last direct male descendant of Fergus, lord of Galloway in King David's reign. His heir was his daughter Marjorie, married to Adam of Kilconquhar.[1] Adam died at Acre on the crusade from which the elder Bruce returned safely, and about 1272 his widow married Bruce the younger who thus became, *jure uxoris*, the earl of Carrick.

This was indeed a marriage of Celtic with Anglo-Norman Scotland, though hardly in the protagonists themselves, since Marjorie was descended from Henry I,[2] her husband from Malcolm Canmore. But Annandale was thickly settled by men of English stock, and thoroughly feudalized. Carrick was historically an integral part of Galloway, and though the earls had achieved some feudalization, the society of Carrick at the end of the thirteenth century remained emphatically Celtic. In acquiring Carrick the Bruces became involved in two further commitments: a close connexion with Ireland and an ancient rivalry between Carrick and the men of Galloway

[1] There is strong though inconclusive evidence that Adam, lord of Kilconquhar, was son of Duncan of Kilconquhar, son of Adam son of Earl Duncan I of Fife (died 1154). Cf. D. W. Hunter Marshall, 'The parentage of Thomas Randolph, earl of Moray', *Scottish Notes and Queries*, 3rd Ser., vii (1940), 2–5; and for the personnel of the supposed Kilconquhar pedigree, see *St Andrews Liber*, references in index under Adam filius and frater comitis, Adam filius Duncani, Duncanus filius Ade (de Kilcunkath), Kilkuncwauch (Dunecanus de); *North Berwick Carte*, Nos. 3, 6; *Dunfermline Registrum*, Nos. 145, 179, 196. The feudal superiority of Kilconquhar vested in the bishop of St Andrews, but the fief was held of the bishop by the earls of Fife. *Chron. Bower*, ii, 152, in mentioning the Macduff appeal, gives Kilconquhar as the estate in question, this being an alternative name for Rircs.

[2] Roger Howden calls Uhtred son of Fergus of Galloway a cousin of King Henry II (*Gesta Henrici Secundi Benedicti Abbatis*, ed. Stubbs, Rolls Ser., i, 80), a relationship which is best explained on the supposition that Fergus married a bastard daughter of Henry I. The suggestion in *Scots Peerage*, s.v. 'Galloway', that Gilbert, Uhtred's brother, had a different mother is contradicted by *Cal. Docs. Scot.*, i, No. 480, where King John calls Duncan of Carrick his cousin.

proper – modern Wigtownshire and Kirkcudbright. The Turnberry Band of 1286 is to be seen as a resumption of interference in
the affairs of Ireland by which the lords of Carrick had profited
hugely ever since the Norman conquest of Ulster.[1] But naturally it
was not only the lords of Carrick who could win and exploit lands
across the North Channel. Their rivals the lords of Galloway played
the same game even more successfully.[2] The feud which went back
at least as far as the time of Gilbert and Uhtred of Galloway, the two
sons of Fergus, was still alive a hundred years later. The men of
the south-west would not have forgotten that Uhtred had been
savagely murdered on his brother's orders, nor that Gilbert had been
ousted by Uhtred's heirs from land which he believed to be right-
fully his. Marjorie of Carrick, who married Robert Bruce, was
Gilbert's great-granddaughter; the great-granddaughter of Uhtred
was the lady Dervorguilla, who married John Balliol.

Some two years after Bruce the younger's marriage to Marjorie of
Carrick, and barely more than a year after the Competitor's second
marriage, Robert Bruce the sixth, the future king, was born to
the Countess Marjorie, probably at Turnberry Castle, on July 11th,
1274.[3] He may fairly be called a Scotsman, born among Scots. He
was assuredly much more a Scotsman than his great adversary,
Edward I, was an Englishman. It has been said that the Bruces were

---

[1] R. Greeves, 'The Galloway lands in Ulster', *Dumfriesshire Trans.*, 3rd Ser., xxxvi,
115–21, esp. 116; Robin Frame, 'The Bruces in Ireland, 1315–18', *Irish Historical
Studies*, xix, 16–19.

[2] Ibid., 117–20.

[3] The cautious words in Dunbar, *Scot. Kings.*, 127, 'born – it has been supposed at
Writtle, near Chelmsford in Essex' become a categorical statement in *Scots Peerage*,
i, 7. They are based on a passage in the chronicle of Geoffrey le Baker of Swinbrook
(ed. E. M. Thompson, 1889, p. 38), which says that Alexander (III) had three daughters
but no son, that the first daughter married John Balliol, the second John Comyn and
the third Robert Bruce 'English by birth, born in Essex (at Writtle)' who later
became king. It is hard to know what to make of a statement so full of error and confusion, but there may have been a sound tradition that Bruce's father was born at
Writtle. *Chron. Guisb.*, 296, reports that Robert Bruce the future king referred to
Scotland and (probably) Carrick as his native country; and the Harcla Treaty of
1323 refers to England (under Edward II, born in Wales but clearly not Welsh by
nation) and Scotland (under Robert Bruce) each having a king of its own nation. In
1310 Bruce was absolved for his part in Comyn's murder as 'layman of Carrick in
the diocese of Glasgow' (*SHR*, xix, 325).

'not themselves bred in the Gaelic tradition',[1] but the truth seems to be that Robert Bruce's upbringing was coloured by a mixture of traditions, of which the Gaelic tradition of Carrick and the west must have been one. In what is perhaps the earliest recorded appearance of the future king, we find him witnessing a deed of Alexander Macdonald of Islay in company with his father the earl of Carrick, the bishop of Argyll, the vicar of Arran and a clerk of Kintyre, as well as various personages of the earldom of Carrick.[2]

When Alexander III died, young Robert Bruce was well on his way to manhood. His birth, and for all we know his character as a boy and a youth, may have given a special stimulus to his tough old grandfather as he prepared to put forward his claim to the throne. The Competitor would hardly have fought so keenly for his spineless, colourless son: but already in the youngest Robert Bruce he must have beheld more fiery mettle.

In 1289 the number of Guardians was reduced by death to four. Inexplicably, the young earl of Fife was murdered at Pitpollok near Brechin, by his own kinsmen the Abernethys.[3] The earl of Buchan died full of years and honour.[4] There was no breakdown in government. The four remaining Guardians, Comyn of Badenoch, the Stewart, and the two bishops, Fraser and Wishart, did not formally replace the two earls, though they may have co-opted the assistance of Sir Andrew Murray of Petty and of Matthew Crambeth, who with their approval and possibly on their nomination had become bishop of Dunkeld in 1288.[5] Apart from day-to-day administration, which seems to have gone on as usual, the Guardians began the

[1] M. McKisack, *The Fourteenth Century*, 42. Edward Bruce was educated with Domhnall Ua Neill king of Tyrone (1283–1325), Stevenson, *Illustrations*, 3.

[2] *Paisley Registrum*, 128–9.

[3] *Chron. Bower*, ii, 148 (under 1288, wrongly). *Chron. Lanercost*, 127, explains his murder by calling the earl 'cruel and greedy beyond the average'. Earl Duncan's latest appearance in record is in a brieve of August, 1289 (Stevenson, *Documents*, i, No. 69), and the murder probably took place on September 3rd or 10th of that year. The locality of Pitpollok may be established by reference to *Brechin Registrum*; and the earl seems to have been buried in Coupar Angus abbey (*Cal. Docs. Scot.*, iv, 375). See G. W. S. Barrow (ed.), *The Scottish Tradition* (1974), 37–8.

[4] *Cal. Docs. Scot.*, ii, No. 366; *Scots Peerage*, ii, 254–5.

[5] *Chron. Bower*, ii, 138, 148. They were not co-opted officially as Guardians, and Bower's statement about Murray may have been only an inference from Sir Andrew's part in bringing the earl's murderers to justice. But this is sufficiently explained on the supposition that Sir Andrew had succeeded the earl of Buchan (not Fife) as justiciar of

negotiations with England and Norway for the marriage of Queen
Margaret, now six years of age, to the five-year-old Edward of
Caernarvon, who had been King Edward's heir since the death of
his elder brother Alfonso in 1284.[1] If all went well the Crowns of
England and Scotland would both be held by the heir of this marriage. But there is no evidence, on the Scottish side at least, of any
enthusiasm for a more organic union. The whole course of the
negotiations which culminated in the marriage agreement called the
Treaty of Birgham, July 18th, 1290 (confirmed by Edward I at
Northampton on August 28th),[2] shows the Guardians anxious above
all to do nothing which might impair the 'royal dignity' of Scotland
or threaten the integrity of the Scottish kingdom. They asked that
Margaret should be given certain lands in England as dower, that the
Scottish kingdom should be 'separate, apart and free in itself without
subjection to the English kingdom', and that there should be no
fresh fortification of the English side of the border.[3] The business of
Margaret's marriage and of union (in some sense) with England was
too serious a responsibility to be borne by the four Guardians on
their own. Not only were all their documents authenticated by the
seal of regency, the 'common seal' or 'seal of Scotland' as it was
called, but the Guardians were careful to associate with themselves
the 'good men' of the realm.[4] By this they meant the men of substance and standing, the responsible men, the acknowledged leaders
of the community as a whole. The words *bone gent* (singular) and

Scotia (Scotland north of Forth), an office he certainly held *c.* 1293 (*Family of Rose*, 29).
We know, in any case, that a permanent council of magnates was associated with the
Guardians: *Aberdeen–Banff Illustrations*, ii, 129–30.

[1] For a good short account of the negotiations see F. M. Powicke, *The Thirteenth
Century*, 598–9. Bishop Fraser attempted to visit Edward I in Gascony, but it is un-
certain whether he ever reached the king. The treaty providing for the transference of
Margaret from Norway to Scotland 'free of any marriage contract' was sealed at
Salisbury on November 6th, 1289, the Scottish plenipotentiaries being the bishops of
St Andrews and Glasgow, Robert Bruce of Annandale and John Comyn of Badenoch,
Stevenson, *Documents*, i, No. 75.

[2] Ibid, No. 108.

[3] Ibid., No. 106.

[4] As in the letter of March 17th, 1290, *APS*, i, 441. Cf. also the Treaty of Salisbury
of the previous November (Stevenson, *Documents*, i, No. 75), whereby the good men
(*bona gens, la bone gent*) of Scotland promised not to arrange any marriage for the
queen without the advice and consent of Edward I and the consent of King Eric of
Norway.

bones genz (plural) which they used in French documents were translated by the Latin phrases *bona gens* and *probi homines*.[1] This last was even more of a technical term in Scotland than in England, for ever since the time of David I the kings of Scots had addressed their public pronouncements not, as did the English kings, to 'their faithful men' (*fidelibus suis*) but to 'all their good men' (*omnibus probis hominibus suis*). At its fullest the phrase no doubt covered all the king's free subjects; but essentially it referred to the king's substantial and responsible subjects, men of the landholding class, burgesses and beneficed clergy. Although these phrases, 'community of the realm' and 'good men', denoted political ideas they were not mere abstractions. The letter in which the Scots declared to King Edward their assent to the marriage and readiness to negotiate (Birgham, March 17th, 1290)[2] went in the names of the four Guardians, ten bishops, twelve earls, twenty-three abbots, eleven priors and forty-eight barons, speaking for the whole community of Scotland. This meant that the Guardians had been able to rally support from all the bishops and earls and a thoroughly representative body of barons and heads of religious houses.

The Treaty of Birgham-Northampton[3] was the high-water-mark of this common endeavour by Guardians and community, but, as we shall see, it was not the last occasion on which their voice was heard. The treaty envisaged two feudal kingdoms, England and Scotland, ruled separately though in harmony by a king and queen respectively, whose sovereignties would remain distinct. The Scottish kingdom was to remain, as the Scots had stipulated, separate, free

---

[1] *Bona gens*＝*la bone gent* in the Treaty of Salisbury (see previous note) and, in the accompanying letter of Edward I of November 6th (*Foedera*, i, 721), the words *probi homines* appear as equivalent. In a letter of King John, January 2nd, 1293, *probis hominibus* translates *as proudes hommes* once and *a la bone gent* once, *Foedera*, i, 785 (Original edn, ii, 597b, 598a, 599a). In a charter of Robert I translated into French the formal address *omnibus probis hominibus totius terre sue* becomes *a toutz les bones gentz de toute sa terre* (Duncan, MS.) In Edward I's parliament of Michaelmas, 1293, King John dared not act without consulting his *probi homines* (Stones, *Documents*, No. 21); in 1305 King Edward declared his intention of settling the government of Scotland *a les bones gentz de la terre d'Escoce* (ibid., No. 33).

[2] *APS*, i, 441. The contemporary letters-patent issued at Birgham three days earlier (Stevenson, *Documents*, i, No. 92) went in the names of the four Guardians, ten bishops, ten earls, twenty-three abbots, eleven priors and forty-eight barons . Perhaps the earls of Lennox and Ross arrived too late for the Birgham parliament.

[3] Stevenson, *Documents*, i, No. 108.

in itself and without subjection, and on certain vital points this freedom was explicitly defined. Elections of the clergy in Scotland were
to be free of external interference, tenants-in-chief of the Scots
Crown need do homage only in Scotland, persons who in Scotland
had been accused of crime or sued at law should not have to answer
in a court outside the country. The only valid symbol of Scottish
government was a seal of regency, which was to be replaced by a
new seal 'of the king of Scotland only' as soon as, but not before,
Queen Margaret had been properly installed at Scone. The customary officers of the Scottish Crown should remain, and no writ of
common law or letter of special favour should be issued save according to the accustomed process of the 'king's chapel' (i.e., the
Scottish chancery) and of the Scottish realm. The emblems of
Scottish royalty were to be kept under the seals of the great lords
until the queen had given birth to a living child. No parliament
dealing with Scottish affairs was to be held outside Scotland, and
there was to be no taxation of the Scots except for Scottish needs.
At King Edward's expense the treaty was to be confirmed by the
pope, and the papal confirmation was to be handed to the community of the realm of Scotland for safe keeping.[1] The treaty has
often been praised as a document of wise statesmanship and patriotism, but it was also something else. It was essentially a cautious,
protective document. Temporary rulers of a conservative feudal
kingdom, the Guardians were reluctant to take the full responsibility
which could be borne only by king and council; and they were sus-
picious of English encroachment.

The atmosphere in the summer of 1290 was hopeful, even joyful.
There was one shadow, but it was too faint for most Scots to notice.
On June 4th, Edward I placed the Isle of Man in the charge of Walter
Huntercombe, and took the Manx community into his protection.[2]
It may be that the men of Man, who would remember well the
great Manx revolt suppressed by Alexander III fifteen years earlier,[3]

[1] Stevenson, *Documents*, i, No. 172. The provision suggests strongly that the 'community of the realm' stood in effect for the feudal kingdom, a political entity whose properly constituted authority could arrange for the receipt and safe-custody of the treaty.

[2] Ibid., i, No. 103.

[3] *Chron. Man.*, i, 110; *Chron. Stephen etc.*, ii, 570–1 (which shows that Alexander III
was supported by Alexander Macdougall of Lorne and Alan Macruarie lord of
Garmoran).

welcomed this action. It may also be true that since 1286 they had not
enjoyed good government. It is only curious that their petition to the
English king, in which they declared unanimously that they stood in
need of protection by Edward as their lord, was made not before but
after the English king had come to the same conclusion.[1] In his
direct dealings with the Scots Edward I had not been high-handed;
he had behaved reasonably. Yet now he had seized an island which
was part of the Scottish kingdom and happened also to be strategically important to England, and he had done so apparently without
consulting or informing the Guardians of Scotland, several months
before he knew of the death of the Maid of Norway, the sovereign
lady of Man.

The bad news from the north reached the Scottish government
early in October.[2] Queen Margaret had died in Orkney on her way
to Scotland, and her body had been taken back to Bergen for burial.
There was, as we have seen, no undisputed successor and the news
of her death set in train a struggle for the throne between a number
of claimants of whom two were of outstanding importance: Robert
Bruce the elder (who now earned his title of 'the Competitor') and
John Balliol. The magnates were gathering at Perth, presumably for
Queen Margaret's inauguration at Scone. Robert Bruce, now in his
eightieth year, had arrived unexpectedly with a strong body of
armed men, and it was rumoured that his friends the earls of Mar
and Atholl were raising their forces.[3] At the same time John Balliol,
whose mother's death in the previous January had made him lord
of Galloway, was styling himself 'heir of Scotland' and making
private agreements with his friend and neighbour Anthony Bek,
the powerful and militant bishop of Durham, who at this juncture
was King Edward's chief representative in Scotland.[4] It looked as
though the guardianship would collapse and the question of succession be settled by open war between the claimants.

[1] *Foedera*, i, 739. Even this declaration seems as much concerned with the possibility of Manx disaffection from Edward I as with the desirability of having the
English king's protection.

[2] *Cal. Docs. Scot.*, ii, No. 459; Dunbar, *Scot. Kings*, 106. Margaret seems to have
died about September 26th; she died in the arms of Narfi bishop of Bergen and was
buried in Bergen Cathedral in the north aisle of the choir (Anderson, *Early Sources*,
ii, 695).

[3] *Nat. MSS. Scot.*, i, No. 70.

[4] Stevenson, *Documents*, i, No. 125.

To the Scots as a whole such a prospect must have been detestable. Bishop Fraser of St Andrews went so far as to write to the English king (October 7th, 1290) asking for his intervention[1] – an act for which later Scottish opinion has been less than fair to him. The bishop's news was that the queen might be dead, though some said she had recovered. Bruce and his friends were assembling under arms. If John Balliol should come to Edward, the king would be well advised to reach an understanding with him. If the queen died, Edward was urged to come to the border to prevent war. This would enable the lords to keep their oath[2] and the rightful heir could succeed peacefully, as long as he was ready to abide by Edward's counsel. What has really stuck in the throats of later Scottish writers is the fact that Fraser was an avowed Balliol man, but we must realize that in 1290 it was not in the least unpatriotic to be a Balliol man. Patriotism transcended the question of succession, yet if that question were not settled quickly and permanently, the kingdom, already virtually kingless for five years, might well fall apart and patriotism become meaningless.

After the winter of 1290-1 and recovery from the sorrow of his wife's death, King Edward moved swiftly. Each individual step he took may have irked or dismayed the Scots, but still they welcomed his intervention, for the alternative was civil war. As Bishop Fraser said in his letter, the community was disturbed and losing hope. After some initial sword-rattling the claimants themselves were probably not unwilling to have their case tried under King Edward's powerful supervision. Whether they would all have voluntarily submitted to his judgement as their overlord, had he not made it quite clear that no other terms would satisfy him, is something we cannot tell. Some would probably have done so, and others adhered to the community. Edward I was almost certainly less concerned about the individual competitors than about ensuring the peace of Scotland during the vacancy of the throne and obtaining an authoritative admission by the Scots of his feudal overlordship over the Scottish kingdom. Because of the subsequent turn of events the legend rapidly established itself in Scotland and survives, indeed, to the

---

[1] *Nat. MSS. Scot.*, i, No. 70.
[2] The oath of April 1286, to keep the peace of the realm, Palgrave, *Docs. Hist. Scot.*, 42.

present day that Balliol was a puppet nominated by King Edward to
the Scots kingship in defiance of a national belief that Bruce had the
better claim. There is no evidence to support the first part of this
legend, and the second part is untrue. The legend obscures the true
and therefore really damaging charge against King Edward that he
first took advantage of the leaderless state of Scotland to extract
something approaching the admissions he required, and then harried
the new king into a relationship with himself which emphasized his
new-found feudal superiority in the most humiliating manner
possible.

There is little doubt that King Edward did not get all he wanted
from the Scots in the summer of 1291. It is reasonable to infer that he
wished for recognition of his feudal suzerainty from the community
of the realm of Scotland in its fullest, most solemn, most representative character; the Guardians, prelates, earls and barons, and the
whole community, speaking with the collective voice with which
they had spoken in support of the Treaty of Birgham only ten
months earlier. Edward I reached the bishop of Durham's great castle
of Norham on the Tweed about May 10th, 1291.[1] He gave the
Guardians and other Scots leaders – *les haus hommes de Escoce* – an
assurance that if they came over the Tweed to meet him this crossing
of the border to treat of Scottish affairs should not be turned to their
prejudice or that of anyone in the Scottish realm.[2] When they appeared he confronted them with the demand for recognition of his
suzerainty.[3] The Scots asked for a delay to consider their reply. They
were given three weeks, a short time indeed, but presumably the

---

[1] *Cal. Docs. Scot.*, ii, No. 474 (where May 10th should be read for May 9th). Norham was no doubt chosen as being one of the traditional places for Anglo-Scottish
conferences. Some meetings were held at Norham, some at Upsettlington on the
Scots side of the Tweed, immediately opposite. King Edward gave an undertaking
that the award of the Crown would be made within the kingdom of Scotland,
Foedera, i, 756. The meeting of May 1291 was described in an apparently contemporary record of May 20th as 'a parliament of both England and Scotland at
Norham', showing incidentally that this joint Anglo-Scottish parliament was still in
session while the Scots were deliberating on their reply to King Edward's demands.
See *Fritz Saxl: memorial essays* (ed. D. J. Gordon, 1957), 125.

[2] Stevenson, *Documents*, i, No. 137 [May 10th]; repeated on May 31st, *Foedera*,
i, 755. Where the Latin text of May 10 speaks of 'bishops, nobles and magnates
coming as far as Norham', the French text of May 31st has *les haus hommes et une
partie de la communaute de mesme le reaume* coming 'this side of the River Tweed'.

[3] *Chron. Rishanger*, 241.

most that Edward could allow them, since he had summoned an armed force from the northern shires to meet him at Norham on June 3rd.[1] The king, framing his question characteristically as a skilled lawyer, had asked the Scots, not 'Am I the rightful suzerain of Scotland?' but 'Can you produce any evidence to show that I am *not* the rightful suzerain?' The reply of *les hauts hommes d'Escoce* to this demand came about the end of May.[2] It was the last occasion on which the voice of the community of the realm of Scotland was heard before enmity had succeeded friendship between the two countries. Couched in courteous and memorable language, the reply, delivered as a letter written in French, thanked King Edward for his great kindness towards the Scottish nation, and went on to restate the king's claim to suzerainty and his promise to adjudge the Scottish Crown to the rightful claimant. The letter continued:

Sire, to this the responsible men [*la bone gent*] who have sent us here say that they know full well that you would not make so great a demand if you did not believe that you had good right to it; yet of any such right or demand made or used by yourself or your ancestors they know nothing. They answer, with such authority as they possess, that they have no power to reply in the absence of the lord [i.e., the king of Scots] to whom such a demand should be addressed and who could reply to it. For even if they did reply it would not increase your right nor take away from the right of their liege lord. But the responsible men of the kingdom are willing that whoever shall be king shall perform to you whatever right and law require, for he and no one else will have the power to do this. Meanwhile they can only refer to the oath they took after the death of the king [Alexander III],[3] saving your faith and theirs, and [? to the treaty] confirmed in your presence at Northampton.[4]

It is known from English accounts, official and unofficial, that this reply was given to King Edward 'in the name of the community of

---

[1] *Chron. Rishanger*, 242.

[2] E. L. G. Stones, *SHR*, xxxv, 89–109, the reply itself being printed on pp. 108–9. The reply is summarized in *Chron. Rishanger*, 124–5, where it is said to have been followed by Edward's guarantee with regard to crossing the Tweed, dated May 31st. See also Stones, *Documents*, No. 16.

[3] The oath of April 1286, to keep the peace and guard the realm on Queen Margaret's behalf, Palgrave, *Docs. Hist. Scot.*, 42.

[4] Stones, *Documents*, 55, referring to the Treaty of Birgham, ratified at Northampton.

the realm of Scotland'.[1] At the same time, no answer was given to him by the Guardians, prelates, earls or barons as such, nor did the Scots furnish any evidence to rebut the English claims.[2] Consequently, Edward's advisers said that the reply contained 'nothing to the purpose',[3] and a modern historian has called it 'evasive'.[4] But this surely is to miss the whole point which the Scottish reply aimed to establish. It was a polite reminder to King Edward, an expert in such matters, that in a feudal realm the most weighty decisions affecting the very status of king and kingdom could be reached only by the lawfully constituted king, acting with the council of his lieges. As the Scots magnates said, even if they did give Edward an answer it could not validly add to his rights or detract from the rights of the king of Scotland. King Edward had been rummaging through the historical writings of England in order to produce an extremely one-sided case in favour of his claim. It had taken him a good deal longer than three weeks. Of course the Scots could have done the same, but it would have been an irrelevant waste of time. Because their answer gave no evidence, except to say that Edward's demand was unprecedented, and no doubt because it was displeasing to the English king, it was not enrolled upon the official record of the proceedings. Until recently, all that was known of the reply was a brief summary in a less official account.[5] As the Scots historian John Hill Burton wrote a hundred years ago, 'though it did not seem to King Edward . . . to be to the point, yet would many people at the present day like to know what it was that the community of Scotland had to say against King Edward's demand'.[6] Time has at last caught up with King Edward. In recent years, the late David Hunter Marshall and Professor Lionel Stones have brought to light the full text of the Scottish reply.[7] The older historians were under the impression that the 'community' meant the 'commonalty', the commons, as distinct from prelates and lords. The official record encouraged this mistake by its equivocal statement that Edward was given no answer 'by' or

[1] *Chron. Rishanger*, 242, 244–5; Prynne, *History of King John*, iii (1670), 496–7.

[2] 'Nothing at all proposed, exhibited or shown by the bishops, prelates, earls, barons, magnates and nobles', *Chron. Rishanger*, loc. cit.

[3] *Chron. Rishanger*, 245: *nihil efficax.*

[4] E. L. G. Stones, *SHR*, xxxv, 107.

[5] *Chron. Rishanger*, 124–5.

[6] J. H. Burton, *History of Scotland* (2nd ed, 1873), ii, 120.

[7] *SHR*, xxxv, 89–109.

'in the name of' the magnates. It would be unfair to accuse the record of total dishonesty here, since to the clerks who compiled it the notion of the 'community of the realm' meaning the 'commons' would scarcely have been thinkable. It is clear enough both from the tenor and contents of the reply itself, and from the sense in which the word 'community' was used in contemporary documents, that the Scottish reply was as authoritative and official as King Edward could have received at the time, and his rejection of it out of hand now emerges clearly as the first thoroughly discreditable action in his dealings with the Scottish nation.

Foiled in his attempt to obtain the fullest possible recognition, Edward was successful in getting other recognitions which he evidently felt would serve his purpose. That he put some pressure on the Guardians and the competitors to obtain them can hardly be contested. Both wanted the rightful claimant to be chosen quickly, and never was it more important that justice should not only be done but also be seen to be done. To Edward's legal and tidy mind the requirements were obvious. First, admission of his overlordship; second, physical control of Scotland, especially of the castles and strongpoints (this was both an expression of suzerainty and the necessary condition of a lawful tribunal); third, the tribunal itself, under his presidency, to decide between the claimants. During the first fortnight of June the majority of the competitors, among them Bruce and Balliol, issued formal instruments acknowledging King Edward's suzerainty and agreeing to abide by his judgement.[1] They also agreed that the king should be put in possession of the Scottish realm and especially of the royal castles. Since neither kingdom nor castles had been vested in the Competitors it is not easy to see what right they had to give them away. In any case, their concession, far-reaching though it was, had not been unconditional. King Edward, while reserving his own rights as one of the competitors, promised the rest that within two months of awarding the Crown he would restore kingdom and castles to the rightful king, and that in future on the death of a king he would demand nothing but homage and the rights incidental to it.[2]

---

[1] *Cal. Docs. Scot.*, ii, Nos. 482, 483, 488, 489.

[2] P.R.O., D.L.36/1/183. Cf. *Cal. Docs. Scot.*, ii, No. 485 and *Chron. Rishanger*, 128, which record a part of this undertaking but fail to bring out its full significance.

At what precise stage of the negotiations Edward was persuaded
into this concession, and by whose urging, is impossible to say.
Walter Bower has a story (strongly confirmed by a document lately
discovered) that when King Edward confronted the Scots with his
claim to suzerainty early in May, Robert Wishart, bishop of Glasgow, rebutted the claim in words which echoed those put into
Alexander III's mouth in 1278: 'the Scottish kingdom is not held in
tribute or homage to anyone save God alone', and went on (no
doubt to Edward's exasperation) to quote the so-called 'Prophecies of
Gildas'.[1] Now, it is a striking fact that on June 14th Bishop Wishart,
together with his close colleague Bishop Crambeth of Dunkeld,
caused to be drawn up and issued under their respective seals an
official copy or 'inspeximus' of Edward's concession.[2] Along with
this they included a copy of a declaration that the competitors'
recognition of Edward's overlordship had been made with the consent of the Guardians – all named – and of the 'responsible men' (les
bones genz) of the realm.[3] No doubt this was intended to protect the
competitors in case they had acted ultra vires. There could be no
clearer demonstration that King Edward had the Scots in a cleft
stick, and we can almost see them squirming to escape the dilemma.[4]
It was very different from the full and willing acknowledgement of
overlordship which Edward surely wished for and perhaps even expected. He had told the competitors – who, after all, were only
private men, very few of them Scotsmen – that there would be no
award unless they admitted his suzerainty. The competitors, eager
for an award, forthwith made the admission, but on certain important conditions. At the same time, they sought to indemnify
themselves with a certificate that they had acted with the consent of
the Guardians and probi homines. Robert Wishart, one of the four
Guardians (we may think that he had much to do with the Treaty of
Birgham and the community's letter of May 1291), acting with a
close colleague, saw fit to place on independent record the concession made by Edward I and the indemnification of the competitors.
From this point it was a short step for Edward to take over the

---

[1] Chron. Bower, ii, 146; P. Linehan in BIHR, xlviii, 110 and n. 2.
[2] P.R.O., D.L.36/1/183. A copy of the concessions is in Glasgow University
Library MS. Gen. 1053, fo. 6 (E. L. G. Stones, SHR, xxxv, 101).
[3] P.R.O., D.L.36/1/183.   [4] See below, p. 51.

government. The Guardians resigned their authority (June 11th)
and were reappointed by the king with the addition of Brian Fitz-
Alan of Bedale, an English baron of more reputation than fortune.[1]
They were no longer 'elected by the community' but 'appointed by
the most serene prince, the Lord Edward, by God's grace illustrious
king of England, chief (or superior) lord of Scotland'.[2] The seal of
regency, however, continued in use until judgement was given,
though it was not always available to the Guardians.[3] On November
19th, 1292, this fine symbol of independence was broken in four
pieces and these were carefully placed in the English treasury 'lest, if
the seal remained intact, doubts should arise about the authenticity of
documents, and as a sign of the king of England's full sovereign lordship in the Scottish realm'.[4] On Wednesday, June 13th, 1291, at
Upsettlington opposite Norham, in a green meadow beside the
Tweed, the Guardians and other magnates present swore fealty individually to King Edward as, according to the record, 'superior and
direct' lord of the kingdom of Scotland.[5] Besides the four Scottish
Guardians, the great men whose names were judged worthy of
record were as follows: Mark, bishop of Sodor and Man; (Alan
bishop of Caithness, chancellor of Scotland?); Robert Bruce of
Annandale, John Balliol lord of Galloway, Robert Bruce earl of
Carrick, Patrick of Dunbar earl of March, Donald earl of Mar,
John Comyn earl of Buchan, John of Strathbogie earl of Atholl,
Gilbert de Umfraville earl of Angus, Malcolm earl of Lennox,
Walter Stewart earl of Menteith, William de Soules, John de Soules,
Patrick Graham, Thomas Randolph, William Sinclair, Ralph of
Hadden, Alexander Balliol of Cavers, chamberlain of Scotland,
William Comyn, John Stewart, Ingram de Umfraville, William
Murray of Tullibardine, Henry Pinkney, Walter Burdon, Ralph
Crawford and Henry Sinclair, 'knights and barons of the realm of
Scotland'.

During the next month and a half, an appreciable number of
lords, gentry, freeholders, burgesses and heads of religious houses

[1] *Cal. Docs. Scot.*, ii, Nos. 496, 499.

[2] Stevenson, *Documents*, i, Nos. 156, 219.

[3] Ibid., No. 208, shows that the common seal was not available on February 28th,
1292.

[4] *Chron. Rishanger*, 363.

[5] *Instrumenta Publica*, 7–9.

came in person to swear fealty to the English king, including the mayor and seventy-eight burgesses of Berwick on Tweed.[1] Edward made a short progress into Scotland by way of Edinburgh, Stirling, Dunfermline, St Andrews and Perth, before returning to Berwick in time for the opening session of the court of claims on August 2nd. At Stirling on July 12th special provisions were made for the general swearing of fealty to the king throughout Scotland. 'To save everyone toil and expense,' it was ordered that the fealties should be received at Perth by the bishop of St Andrews, John Comyn of Badenoch and Brian FitzAlan, at Ayr by the bishop of Glasgow, James the Stewart and Sir Nicholas Segrave, at Inverness by the earl of Sutherland and the local sheriff and castle commander, and in Galloway by the justiciar of Galloway, Sir William Sinclair, aided by William de Boyville and by the bishop of Galloway as soon as he had himself sworn fealty. Very short notice was given, for all the fealties had to be sworn by July 27th, and strict measures were to be taken against those who neglected or refused to take the oath.

Instead, therefore, of a full and unequivocal admission of his claims in 1291, King Edward obtained three lesser things: a full but qualified admission by the competitors (not in any sense a representative body within the Scottish kingdom); *de facto* resignation of authority and power by the Guardians; and the individual fealty and homage to himself, as lord superior, of the leading men and women of Scotland from the Guardians downward.

If this was far from what Edward I required, it was also far from being a sturdy stand for independence. Within a few years, the Scots were seeking to explain it, perhaps truthfully enough, as brought about by the fear which may seize even the most steadfast. It is in any case not true that there was no gesture of resistance. When the English king commanded the earl of Angus, Gilbert de Umfraville, to surrender the castles of Forfar and Dundee the earl refused, declaring that he had not been entrusted with them by the king of England but by 'the community of the realm of Scotland' (*par la commune del reaume d'Escoce*).[2] A closely similar reply[3] was given

---

[1] *Instrumenta Publica*, 10–21; *Cal. Docs. Scot.*, ii, No. 508.

[2] *Foedera*, i, 756. Dundee was not a royal castle, but was in the hands of the Guardians presumably by reason of the death of Dervorguilla de Balliol early in 1290. The fact that her heir John was a competitor for the throne may explain why it had not been handed over to him. [3] Remaining replies in Glasgow Univ. Lib. MS. Gen. 1053, fo. 9.

by William de Soules in respect of the castle of Roxburgh entrusted to him by the community of the realm and of Inverness entrusted to him by King Alexander. The thirteen other Scots who were holding the remaining twenty royal castles entered almost identical protests. This gesture has a legalistic appearance, but it went to the heart of the matter of sovereignty and the constitution. By June 12th the commanders' scruples had been met by a compromise formula: they had taken an oath of allegiance to whoever should rule Scotland through nearness of blood to the late king, and they would now surrender the castles to King Edward simply as one of the claimants.

The dilemma was triple-horned. In the account of the meetings at Norham preserved by the Scots and produced by them in 1321,[1] King Edward's inexorable standpoint was that they could not escape one of three possible courses of action. They must concede his demand for overlordship (which he had made as an assertion, not asked as a question), or they must produce evidence to show he was not their lawful overlord, or else they must defend their independence by force of arms. Robert Wishart protested that even if the Scots nation, minus its ruler, conceded Edward's suzerainty that could not bind their ruler nor add to Edward's right; while, as to the second course of action, he reasonably objected that the Scots ought not to have to prove a negative which their rights forbade to be proved positively. On the third choice confronting the Scots, the bishop replied that it was not consonant with the honour of so great a king as Edward to invade and attack a people so divided and lacking any defender, and that such an attack would hinder the English king's declared vow as a crusader to the Holy Land. To this the indignant Edward answered that even if he had taken the Cross he would keep it with him and deflect his crusading army against the Scots.

What sort of unity could the Scots show against English invasion when the identity of their king had not even been determined? The stage was set for Scots and English, under the presidency of a king whom all now acknowledged to be the overlord (*superior dominus, soverein seignur*) of Scotland, to decide which claimant had the best right to the throne.

3

Bruce *versus* Balliol

KING Edward had gained control of Scotland without a sword being drawn. A court was at once appointed to decide which claimant had the best right to the throne.[1] Its sessions were to be held on Scottish soil, and its scale was impressive: 104 auditors, under the king, a body modelled with conscious archaism on the *centumviri*, the court of 105 used under the Roman republic to settle questions of succession to property.[2] Twenty-four auditors belonged to Edward I's council, and of the remainder forty were nominated by John Balliol of Galloway and forty by Robert Bruce of Annandale. Flattering as it might seem to the Scots, the fact that claims were lodged by no fewer than fourteen competitors, two of them kings, did not really mean that the throne of Scotland was the most coveted prize of its time in western Europe. It looks as though the field was large, but in reality, while Balliol was favourite and Bruce heavily backed, the other entries were generally non-starters. Most of the competitors, in fact, were relatively obscure men, and all but four of the claims were lodged as a formality, chiefly for the sake of being put on record so that in future they could not be said to have gone by default. From the outset the real choice lay between four claimants, Balliol, Bruce, John Hastings of Abergavenny and Florence V, count of Holland, all of them direct and legitimate descendants of Henry of Northumberland, son and heir of King David I.[3] The first three were descendants of Henry's youngest son, Earl David. Count Florence

[1] Palgrave, *Docs. Hist. Scot.*, Illustrations, No. II, 5 June, 1291.

[2] G. Neilson, *SHR*, xvi, 1–14.

[3] See Genealogical Table I. For Count Florence, the authoritative account is given by G. G. Simpson, 'The claim of Florence, count of Holland, to the Scottish throne, 1291–2', *SHR*, xxxvi, 111–24. There is a useful comment on this by Mme J. Kossmann-Putto, *Revue du Nord*, xl, 541–2.

was fourth in descent from Henry's daughter Ada. Normally a son's heirs would have a stronger claim than a daughter's, and the count's case would have carried no weight whatever had he not based it on a simple but radical allegation. He averred that in return for a grant of the Garioch (a district in Aberdeenshire) Earl David had resigned the right which he and his heirs might have in the throne to his brother King William the Lion and his heirs. At the same time (the count continued) King William had designated his sister Ada as heir, though subsequently he had had a son, the future Alexander II. Since this line had now failed and the count of Holland was Ada's great-great-grandson, the alleged resignation should have given him the Scottish Crown without further argument. But there was one snag. The count did not have copies of any of the relevant documents, especially Earl David's resignation and the record of baronial fealty to Ada as heir. It was said that they were in the treasury in Edinburgh Castle, or elsewhere in Scotland, and the count asked that a search should be made for them. With characteristic patience and thoroughness, King Edward adjourned the court for ten months, from August 12th, 1291, until June 2nd, 1292, so that the documents required by Florence of Holland might be found.[1]

The count's claim raises a host of puzzling questions. Let us, for the moment, consider only two of them. His great-great-grandmother, Ada of Scotland, who was married in 1162 to Count Florence III of Holland, had a sister Margaret, married in 1160 to the duke of Brittany.[2] Historians have usually assumed that Ada was the elder sister. There seems in fact to be no clear evidence which was the elder. In view of the girls' Christian names,[3] and the order in which they were married, it may be thought that Margaret was older than Ada. If so, her oldest direct male descendant, Humphrey de Bohun, earl of Hereford, would have had a better claim than Count Florence.[4] Yet the earl is not known to have put in a claim of any kind. Even allowing that Ada was the elder sister, it would be astonishing that the earl of Hereford had made no claim if the story

[1] *SHR*, xxxvi, 114.
[2] *Chron. Melrose*, 36.
[3] Margaret after her father's paternal grandmother, Ada after her mother or, more probably, after her mother's maternal grandmother. *Chron. Melrose*, 36, calls Ada *alia soror*, implying juniority.
[4] *Complete Peerage*, iv, Appendix H, Chart I (669).

of Earl David's resignation was widely known and believed. This brings us to what was really the crucial part of Count Florence's claim: King William's designation of Ada as heir and the Scottish barons' fealty to her. Without this, the count's claim by mere heredity would have been extremely shaky. Now, it so happens that we know on excellent authority that in 1195, three years before his son was born, King William the Lion did propose to set aside the claims of his brother Earl David in favour not of his sister but of his daughter Margaret, on condition that she married Otto of Brunswick (afterwards the emperor Otto IV).[1] Many of the Scottish nobles opposed the plan 'because' (we are told) 'it was not the custom of Scotland that a woman should have the kingdom so long as there was a brother or nephew in the family who could have the kingdom by right'. Yet in 1291 Count Florence asked the court to believe that the Scottish baronage had, before the proposal of 1195 was ever made, accepted as heir to the throne a woman who was not even the eldest daughter of the king but merely one of his sisters. Before going further with the count of Holland's claim it will be as well to take a closer look at the three descendants of Earl David, Balliol, Bruce and Hastings.

The composition of the court, with its eighty Scottish auditors chosen only by Balliol and Bruce, shows that for contemporaries these two were thought to be the really serious competitors. John Hastings, virtually unknown in Scotland, was grandson of Earl David's youngest daughter. Since he had no shadow of claim by primogeniture or by nearness of degree, it was no use his making a claim at all unless he could prove that Scotland was not a true kingdom, and that the 'royal demesne' was merely a landed estate like any other.[2] As such, by the feudal law recognized in both Scotland and England, it would be divided equally among the co-heiresses, and John Hastings would succeed to one third. This modest but destructive claim was pursued with ingenuity by Hastings' lawyers, who pointed out that the kings of Scots were neither crowned nor anointed and drew attention to other grave defects of Scottish

---

[1] *Chronica Mag. Rogeri de Houedene* (ed. Stubbs), iii, 298–9.

[2] *Chron. Rishanger*, 309–39, esp. 315–6, 'though the land of Scotland be called a "kingdom", the land itself is only a lordship, like Wales, the earldom of Chester or the bishopric of Durham'; and cf. 329–30.

kingship. The court was not convinced. It contained many of the leaders of the community of the realm of Scotland, and they were not prepared to be told by the attorneys of an English baron that the realm of Scotland had never existed.

Balliol and Bruce, the undisputed protagonists of this eighteen-month drama, each displayed the strength of his support in the body of influential sponsors which he had chosen.[1] Dr Evan Barron has said that 'apart from the clerical auditors . . . there is not much to choose between them, though Bruce's list perhaps contains more "names of fame" than does Balliol's'.[2] But it would surely be wrong to consider the clerical auditors apart from the laymen, and taking both elements together Balliol's auditors unquestionably provided a weightier, more authoritative representation of the community of the realm than Bruce's. It is true that whereas only four earls supported Balliol, five were sponsors for Bruce, to whom a sixth (his own son) might be added. But Balliol, himself lord of Galloway since his mother Dervorguilla's death in January 1290, also had on his side the lord of Argyll. Each of these lordships carried the prestige and influence of an earldom, in the south west and in the west highlands respectively. Of the bishops, Bruce had two, Glasgow and Dunkeld; Balliol six, including St Andrews and Aberdeen. Bruce, again, could count on only two heads of religious houses, Balliol no fewer than eight, including St Andrews, Dunfermline and Kelso, while one of his bishops had lately been abbot of Arbroath. Balliol's supporters were drawn evenly from the various provinces of Scotland, Bruce's show a striking but not surprising majority of notables from the south and south west. Finally, it can hardly be an accident that while Balliol preferred to nominate, almost exclusively, men of standing, earls, bishops, abbots and barons of renown, Bruce included as many

---

[1] Lists of the auditors are given in (1) Palgrave, *Docs. Hist. Scot.*, Illustrations, No. II, sections 3 and 4; (2) *Chron. Rishanger*, 262–5. The former shows the auditors formally appointed, June 5th, 1291, the latter the names of those who acted as auditors in November 1292, in some cases lesser figures representing magnates who for some reason were absent. In the second list there is larger number of *magistri*, university graduates doubtless chosen for their legal experience.

King Edward submitted the legal issues to a number of doctors of law at Paris university, whose replies are given at length in *Chron. Bower*, ii, 139–45 (also *Chron. Pluscarden*, i, 123–32). It is hard to determine what influence, if any, these opinions had; see P. Stein, *Ius Romanum Medii Aevi*, pars. V, 13b (Milan, 1968), 30–1.

[2] E. M. Barron, *The Scottish War of Independence* (2nd edn, Inverness, 1934), 110.

as eight *magistri*, university graduates whose presence probably owed
more to their legal training or experience of legal pleading than to
their status in the community at large. Balliol, too, had his *magistri*,
but he kept them in the background, as working deputies of the great
men who had lent their names to his cause. In any case, these eighty
auditors did not form a 'Bruce party' and a 'Balliol party', divided
politically, as though they were backing candidates in an election. In
reality, they were sureties or pledges, responsible witnesses that
Bruce and Balliol were themselves responsible suitors demanding
the judgement of a court.

The greater strength of Balliol's auditors surely reflected the simple
fact that Balliol had the stronger case. There is no reason to think
that Balliol's lawyers were inferior to Bruce's, but almost throughout
the proceedings they used only two arguments. First, the kingship,
the *regnum*, the 'royal dignity', of Scotland, together with all that
went with it in demesne lands, revenues and so forth, was not divisible. Secondly, Balliol, as indisputably the senior descendant of Earl
David by the strict rule of primogeniture, was the true heir to the
Crown and office of king.[1] This economy in pleading was a sign of
strength: the more numerous and various the arguments used by an
advocate the weaker his case is likely to be. And the arguments put
forward by Bruce's lawyers were indeed many and varied. Not only
did they expend every shot in the locker, but Bruce himself, outside
the court, seems to have used every possible means to bolster his
cause. Surely the only satisfactory explanation of all his ingenuity,
self-contradiction and even chicanery is that Bruce knew the
exasperating, tantalizing truth that whereas politically he could
count on powerful support, legally his case was weak.

His counsel began by taking a high line on the nature of monarchy.[2]

---

[1] The best review of the conflicting claims from a legal standpoint is by Barnaby
C. Keeney, 'The medieval idea of the state: the Great Cause, 1291-2', *University of
Toronto Law Journal*, viii, 48-71. My account owes much to this lucid and masterly
article. Curiously, Professor Keeney makes no mention of the opinions of the Parisian
jurists. For Balliol's arguments, cf. Palgrave, *Docs. Hist. Scot.*, Illustrations, No. III,
section 12, No. IV, sections 8-20, and pp. 39-51 (fragmentary); and *Chron. Rishanger*, 257 and 309-42, in rebuttal of the Hastings claim.

[2] For Bruce's pleadings, see Palgrave, *Docs. Hist. Scot.*, Illustrations, No. III,
section 13, and No. IV, sections 3-7, and pp. 23-34. 'Imperial laws' are referred to,
ibid., 20 and *Chron. Rishanger*, 345, 349. Bruce's early pleadings made frequent
reference to what was called 'the law by which kings reign'.

Succession to kingdoms was quite different from succession to landed property. It must be settled by reference to 'imperial laws' and the Natural Law. As a kingdom, Scotland was indivisible: Crown, royal honours and royal estates alike must remain in the hands of one man. They declared that according to the established customs and laws of Scotland, a living younger son, being nearer in blood to his father, had a better right to succeed than the son of a deceased elder son, who was one degree further removed. Moreover, the *son* of a younger child would take precedence of the *daughter* of an older child. Bruce maintained that these rules should be applied to the present case. He was the son of a younger daughter of Earl David, Balliol the son of a daughter of the earl's eldest daughter. In addition, Bruce claimed that Alexander II had caused him to be designated heir to the throne at a time when the king was still childless and about to lead an expedition to the western isles.[1] This can only have been after John of Scotland's death in 1237 and before King Alexander married Marie de Couci in 1239. No royal campaign in the isles is recorded for that period, and it is unfortunate that the only accounts of the incident are to be found in two documents which both come from the *milieu* of the Competitor himself.[2] The weakness of this claim was that even if Bruce's designation had been an historical fact its only justification must have been that Bruce at that particular moment was the nearest male heir. In the intervening years the king had had direct descendants down to the third generation, and John and Dervorguilla Balliol had had several sons. In any event, the facts of Scottish history for the past two hundred years were against Bruce. The succession of kings from Edgar in 1097 to the acceptance of the Maid of Norway in 1284 – in which Bruce and his son had joined – demonstrated clearly that a tendency to prefer the most senior available heir had hardened into a rule.[3] The court of 1291–2 was surely right, and not merely overawed by Edward I and English influence, when it stated that Scottish royal succession was governed by the rule of primogeniture.

[1] Palgrave, *Docs. Hist. Scot.*, 19–20, 29–30.
[2] Ibid. The Appeal of the Seven Earls seems to owe most to the earl of Mar, but Mar and Bruce were closely associated at this period.
[3] Edgar gained the throne only with the help of armed intervention by William Rufus of England, but after Edgar each successive Scottish sovereign had been the senior available heir, in marked contrast with the English succession in the same period.

At the very end of the proceedings, when it was obvious that the court was going to uphold Balliol's claim of seniority, Bruce's lawyers threw over their high-flown arguments about the Natural Law and the indivisibility of the Scottish realm. They said that if the court had agreed to apply to the Scottish Crown the lower law which governed the succession to earldoms and other feudal honours, then of course Scotland was divisible, and Bruce should be guaranteed his third share of the income and land. At the very least, he should have a third part of the Liberty of Tynedale, which was dependent on, but not an integral part of, the Crown.[1] Many historians have been scandalized by this *volte face*, calling it a piece of effrontery, a 'shameless change of position' and the like. Admittedly, Bruce's lawyers weakened their case irretrievably by arguing for the indivisibility of Scotland on the grounds that it was a true kingdom and afterwards agreeing with Hastings that Scotland was not a kingdom at all. But surely they were only doing their duty by their client, and the claim was not without logic. The court was in fact dealing with an unprecedented situation, and there is no doubt that it actually made law on this point, and did not merely apply a law already clearly established. In rejecting Bruce's desperate last claim, the court gave Balliol all that his lawyers had asked for, since they had not only awarded him the Crown, i.e., the office of king, on the principle of *ainesse* (seniority) but had coupled with this the judgement that the kingdom of Scotland in the widest sense was indivisible. Consequently, when Bruce's counsel asked at the eleventh hour that he should be allowed a third share they were hardly acting more reprehensibly than Balliol's counsel when they for their part had first of all pleaded that the succession should be determined by the common law of England with regard to subordinate fiefs, and had then argued afterwards that if the court agreed that Scotland was indivisible Balliol should take the whole.

The failure of Bruce's main arguments brings us back to Count Florence of Holland. It was not until after November 14th, 1292, only a day or two before the court finally awarded the Crown to Balliol, that the count withdrew his claim.[2] We have seen how this claim struck at the root of the claims made by Balliol, Bruce and

---

[1] *Chron. Rishanger*, 342–50 and 272.
[2] Ibid., 302, 358.

Hastings. Yet it has been said that 'there is no record of a direct contest between Bruce and the count during the pleadings'.[1] Why? We do not know for certain, and unless further evidence comes to light we shall never know. The answer suggested here, a simple answer which may perhaps be over-simple, is as follows. Although the count of Holland may have believed sincerely that he had some unsatisfied claim on the Scots, probably in connexion with his great-great-grandmother's marriage portion,[2] his claim to the Scottish throne itself was originally purely formal, not to say frivolous. As such it would have been comparable to the 'romanist' claim put in by King Eric of Norway. This harmless claim of the count's was seized on by Bruce and his supporters, and inflated for the sole purpose of defeating Balliol. This is in direct conflict with the conclusion reached by Sir Maurice Powicke that 'in [Bruce's] view his most formidable rival was the count of Holland, not Balliol'.[3] Before affirming that the exact opposite was true, we must look critically at the evidence. What, if any, are the indications that Bruce welcomed the Dutch claim because it might help him to reach the throne by the back door after he had failed to get admittance at the front?

In the spring of 1290, Bruce was apparently trying to gain complete control of the Garioch, the largest of Earl David's Scottish lordships of which Bruce, Balliol and Hastings had each inherited one third. Exactly how he proposed to oust Balliol and Hastings from their respective shares is not clear. But on April 19th, 1290, a month after they had both attended the parliament of Birgham, Bruce made an agreement with Sir Nicholas Biggar, one of the most powerful and prominent magnates of Clydesdale.[4] According to this agreement. Sir Nicholas was to bring an action in the king's court (i.e., the court held by the Guardians) against Balliol and Hastings, by a royal 'brieve of right', to 'recover' for himself all Balliol's and Hastings's lands in the Garioch. Bruce would pay the whole costs of the action. Simultaneously, however, Sir Nicholas surrendered all his rights in Garioch property to Bruce, so that the net result of the agreement, if it could have been implemented, would have been to

[1] G. G. Simpson, *SHR*, xxxvi, 115.
[2] Palgrave, *Docs. Hist. Scot.*, 20–1; cf. *Chron. Holyrood*, 130.
[3] *The Thirteenth Century*, 611, n. 1.
[4] P.R.O., D.L. 36/III/152.

make Bruce sole lord of the Garioch. In compensation, Sir Nicholas
Biggar would be given by Bruce forty merks' worth of land in
Scotland south of Forth, for the twentieth part of one knight's
service – an almost nominal rent. The scheme would mean an
appreciable addition to Bruce's Scottish estates, and more especially
it would add to his influence in the north of Scotland, where he was
the neighbour of his friend the earl of Mar.[1]

The deeper explanation of the scheme is not clear. It may have
related to the marriage arranged between Gartnait, son and heir of
Earl Donald of Mar, and Christian Bruce, sister of the future king,
who is said to have received the Garioch as her tocher or marriage
portion.[2] But this marriage can hardly have taken place so early, and
it seems more likely that the Bruce-Biggar indenture should be connected with three further pieces of evidence. The first of these, the
so-called 'Appeal of the Seven Earls', belongs to the winter of
1290–1 or spring of 1291.[3] The first part of this curious document is
in the form of an 'open letter', though since it never seems to have
borne a seal it cannot be regarded as a letter in any strict sense. This
part of the document is addressed to Bishop Fraser and John Comyn
of Badenoch, the two Guardians who supported Balliol, and also, in
the first paragraph, to Balliol himself. These three magnates are
accused of attempting to get Balliol made king of Scotland by a

---

[1] Mar's lands lay to the south and west of the Garioch. To the north-west lay
Strathbogie, the patrimony of another Bruce partisan, John earl of Atholl.

[2] Alexander, earl of Crawford and Balcarres, *The earldom of Mar in sunshine and in
shade* (1882), i, 173, states this without citing an authority. Perhaps Lord Crawford
had in mind the later grant of the Garioch to Christian Bruce on her (third) marriage
to Andrew Murray, for which see below, p. 396; but he distinctly says that her first
husband received Garioch with her.

[3] Palgrave, *Docs. Hist. Scot.*, 14–21. The document (P.R.O., E 39/89) consists of
two separate membranes of the same width, one slightly shorter than the other.
Palgrave thought they appeared to have been originally attached together at the
bottom. There is no sign that either bore a seal. Membrane 1 is composed of three
clearly separated paragraphs of closely-spaced writing (Palgrave's paras. 1–3);
membrane 2 has one similarly written closely-spaced paragraph (Palgrave's para. 4)
and two shorter paragraphs much more widely spaced, as though they had not
formed part of the document as at first written out (Palgrave's paras. 5 and 6). It
is much harder to read the document now than in Palgrave's time, for on being repaired in 1950 it was faced with muslin and backed with fresh vellum, obscuring the
endorsement. The document is a transcript, or a draft, or the transcript of a draft.
See Stones, *Documents*, No. 14, which gives only the first membrane. There is a
close connexion between the contents of the first and second membranes.

coup, aided and abetted by 'that small part (*particula*) of the community of the realm adhering to them'. There is no suggestion that Fraser and Comyn were improperly or unpatriotically using English influence; on the contrary, it is the authors of the 'Appeal' who declare that they are asking Edward I to intervene and uphold the rightful claims of Bruce of Annandale.

What gives the 'Appeal' its special interest is the fact that it calls itself the 'accusations (*appellationes*) of the seven earls of the kingdom of Scotland', and purports to state their claim in the appointment of a new king, as well as the claims of the 'community of the realm'. Some of the older historians, notably Palgrave and Skene, took the idea of the 'Seven Earls' seriously, but most were inclined to be sceptical. Nowadays the opposite is true. Most Scottish historians believe that the Seven Earls had a real existence – indeed, they have even been enumerated.[1] The truth seems to be rather that the Seven Earls were a mixture of fact and myth, and the myth surely outweighed the fact. The twelfth and thirteenth centuries were rich in the elaboration and even outright invention of ancient rights and privileges and constitutions – one is reminded of the claim of the citizens of London to elect a king of England,[2] and of the Seven Electors of Germany, with their 'ancient' claim (no older than the mid-thirteenth century) to elect a king of the Romans.[3] Indeed, Count Florence must have been well aware of the German example, for his father, William II of Holland, had been elected king of the Romans by a section of the electoral college in 1247. Bruce's allusion to 'imperial laws' referred to Roman Law, but he may have felt that the practice of the empire provided a good example of 'the law by which kings reign' when he asked King Edward as 'his sovereign lord and emperor' to award him the kingdom in accordance with this exalted law.[4] According to old chronicles, and some not so old, which were being keenly studied and rewritten in thirteenth-century

---

[1] As by F. M. Powicke, *The Thirteenth Century*, 601, no. 2. It is not clear why Sir Maurice Powicke would exclude Buchan and Fife, the latter explicitly mentioned in the 'Appeal' (Palgrave, *Docs. Hist. Scot.*, 15). Keeney, op. cit., 51, tentatively includes Bruce himself, but this is clearly out of the question.

[2] P. E. Schramm, *A History of the English Coronation*, 157.

[3] K. J. Leyser, 'A recent view of the German college of electors', *Medium Aevum*, xxiii, 76–87.

[4] Palgrave, *Docs. Hist. Scot.*, 29.

Scotland, the country north of Forth was historically divided into the magical number of seven parts, ruled first by kings, then by mormaers under a single king.[1] The earls of these provinces represented the seven mormaers, and were the recognized leaders of the kingdom. The 'Appeal' declared that they enjoyed special rights in 'making' a king and placing him on the seat of royalty. Fraser and Comyn, by prejudging the issue of succession in Balliol's favour, had gravely infringed these ancient privileges.

We need not suppose that the 'Appeal' was based on complete fiction. It was an example of that semi-antiquarian revival of things Celtic which was not uncommon in thirteenth-century Scotland. As it stands, the document is highly tendentious and, when it speaks of alleged atrocities in Moray by officers of Fraser and Comyn, it becomes charged with an emotion which smacks of propaganda.[2] It is curious that the only earls mentioned by name in the 'Appeal' are the earl of Fife – a mere infant – and the earl of Mar. Anyone in 1290 who wanted to make up a list of suitable candidates to fill the Seven Earldoms could hardly leave out the earl of Fife, whose privileges at a royal inauguration were unchallenged. The earl of Mar probably had as good a claim as any other. But so too did the earls of Angus, Buchan and Strathearn, who were all supporters of Balliol. The real suspicion attaching to the 'Appeal' lies not in the fact that it mentions Earl Donald of Mar but in its quite disproportionate emphasis on his interests and grievances.

With the internal history of the earldom of Mar we are plunged at once into a tangle of confusions, obscure genealogies and blatant forgeries. Earl Donald was son and heir of an Earl William who had sought to confirm his disputed claim to the honour with a forged charter in favour of Earl Morgan who lived in the twelfth century.[3] At the end of the 'Appeal' is a memorandum upholding this forgery as proof of Earl Donald's rights and complaining that a large part of the earldom was still unjustly withheld from him. Still more significantly,

[1] For example, the *De situ Albanie* of *c.* 1166 gives the seven divisions as 'Angus with Mearns', 'Atholl with Gowrie', 'Strathearn with Menteith', 'Fife with Fothrif', 'Mar with Buchan', 'Moray with Ross' and 'Caithness'. On this see M. O. Anderson, *Kings and and kingship in early Scotland* (1973), 139–45.

[2] Palgrave, *Docs. Hist. Scot.*, 16, 'they have cruelly slain as many men, women and little children as they could reach'.

[3] W. F. Skene, *Celtic Scotland*, iii, 441–7.

there is a memorandum that Count Florence of Holland was with
equal injustice being defrauded of the earldom of Ross which the
'old men of Scotland' declared to have been the princess Ada's
marriage portion in 1162! (It is not surprising that William earl of
Ross was a Balliol supporter). Most significantly of all, the 'Appeal'
adds that these same old men – whom it unfortunately fails to
identify – agreed that, should there be some failure in the heirs of
David earl of Huntingdon, the count of Holland was the rightful
heir by reason of King William's sister Ada.

The 'Appeal' begins by giving three quite distinct reasons why
Bruce had a better right to the throne than Balliol: he was the choice
of the Seven Earls and community, he was the male heir nearest in
blood to Earl David, he had been designated heir by Alexander II
when that king 'had nearly reached senility' (he was forty in 1238).
It ends by saying that if for some reason there was a flaw in the claim
of Earl David's heirs the rightful claimant was the count of Holland.
Even if the purpose of these arguments is not self-evident, the conjunction of Bruce and Count Florence and the story of Ada of
Scotland should put us on our guard. Well before the competitors
lodged their claims, the earl of Mar and Robert Bruce had also seen
the possibilities inherent in the Dutch claim. As yet, these possibilities
were all rather vague. The flaw in the inheritance from Earl David is
not described, and Ada's claim as next heir is based on the testimony
of the 'old men of Scotland'. But we now know that within a few
months of the 'Appeal' a document was in existence which gave to
these vital matters the precision they required.

In the second week of November 1291 two north-country prelates, the bishop of Moray and the prior of Pluscardine, formally set
their seals to copies of the resignation of Earl David which Count
Florence had made the basis of his claim in the previous summer.[1]
An early copy of these 'certified copies' still survives at The Hague in
what were formerly the count of Holland's archives.[2] The document
purports to have been issued by David, son of Henry earl of Huntingdon. It records David's resignation of all right to the throne for
himself and his posterity in exchange for the land of Garioch given
by King William. It bears no date, which is what one would expect

[1] SHR, xxxvi, 124.
[2] Ibid., 123.

for the supposed period of its issue (1165–73), but it also has no
witnesses, an omission which is scarcely credible for a twelfth-
century deed of this important nature. Moreover, the phrases in
which Count Florence's lawyers described the resignation to the
court in November 1292 are too close to the phrases in the text of the
resignation as we have it for the resemblance to be coincidence.[1]
Either the count had seen the resignation and subsequently lost it, or
he was able to 'quote' from it because he had invented it. In the present state of our ignorance it is hardly a point in favour of the count's
honesty that he told the court that the document was being wrong-
fully detained by the prior of Pluscardine, one of the two prelates
responsible for the 'certified copies' of it. We do not know whose side
the prior was on. He may have been acting against the count, but
for all we know he may have been in league with him.

Whether the bishop and prior issued their copies in good faith,
believing they had the original before them, or whether they were
art and part in a piece of deliberate falsification, is something else we
do not know. But one thing we do know is that the 'resignation' was
a forgery.[2] Obviously it would be harder to prove this from a copy
at second-hand than from the document which the forger would presumably have had to fabricate as the 'original'. The sort of criticism
by internal evidence which is nowadays applied to historical documents was only in its infancy in 1291, when the normal tests of
authenticity lay in the kind and size of parchment, in the seal, and
perhaps in the handwriting. None of this could be examined in the
copies made under the two prelates' auspices and sealed with their
seals.

Had this document been available to Count Florence and put in
by him as evidence, it is conceivable, though scarcely probable, that
the court would have upheld his claim and ruled against the three
competitors who claimed by descent from Earl David. How, then,
could this have benefited Bruce, who was one of the three? The
answer to this is contained in our third piece of evidence, the famous
agreement of June 14th, 1292, between the count and Bruce.[3] This

---

[1] Compare *Chron. Rishanger*, 275, with *SHR*, xxxvi, 124.

[2] Its authenticity is refuted by the style ascribed to Earl David, the language of the
text, and the impossibly anachronistic eschatocol *in cuius rei testimonium sigillum meum
presenti scripto est appensum*.

[3] Stevenson, *Documents*, i, No. 255.

agreement was to be effective only if one or other of the two parties gained the throne. Whichever one was successful would, within four months, grant to the unsuccessful party one third of the royal demesne as a fief to be held for five knights' service. The new king was also to have first option of taking a lease of this third if the unsuccessful party should wish to let it for a rent. Moreover, if Bruce were successful, he was to grant the count of Holland all his lands in England for the value of the third of the royal demesne of Scotland. There was no equivalent provision if Florence were to win. This hardly looks like an agreement made between competitors who were equally anxious to gain the Scottish Crown and conscious that their claims were evenly matched. Far from it meaning that in Bruce's view 'his most formidable rival was the count of Holland, not Balliol', the agreement surely means that Balliol was Bruce's only serious rival and that every device was worth using if it might help to defeat him. Hence the one-sidedness of the agreement, which seems to assume that Bruce would be successful. In that case Bruce could, at worst, take back on lease the lost third of the royal demesne, and, at best, buy it from the count of Holland by putting him in possession of a most desirable baronial estate in England. Annandale would still belong to Bruce, and if the agreement with Nicholas Biggar became effective he would also have the whole lordship of Garioch. It might still seem a heavy price for Bruce to pay, but the count's assistance was worth a good price. For his claim, if accepted, would defeat Balliol's strong single claim but could not defeat every one of Bruce's numerous claims. The expression in his agreement with the count, 'whoever shall recover the realm by judgement *or by private agreement* [*pacem*] or by any other method', may mean that Bruce still hoped to have the Great Cause settled politically rather than judicially. And the fact that there is no record throughout the pleadings of Bruce and the count being in conflict surely provides further evidence that they were in collusion.

Lastly, there is the question of timing. The court was required to decide between Bruce and Balliol, on the issue of seniority *versus* nearness of degree, before it dealt with the claims of the other competitors. It declared in favour of Balliol in pronouncements of November 5th and 6th, 1292.[1] On November 7th Bruce sealed what

[1] *Chron. Rishanger*, 261–2; cf. Keeney, *Univ. of Toronto Law Journal*, viii, 60, n. 33.

was in effect a special testament, resigning his claim to seek the Scottish throne to his son and heir and to his heirs after him.[1] The instrument of resignation was also sealed, for the sake of stronger testimony, by Gilbert de Clare earl of Gloucester, nephew of the Competitor's first wife and, since 1290, son-in-law of King Edward I. Two days later (Sunday, November 9th) the younger Bruce, to whom the claim to the throne had thus passed, himself resigned his earldom of Carrick (held in right of his wife Marjorie) to his own son and heir, the youngest Robert Bruce, the future king.[2] The precise meaning of this reshuffle of power within the three Bruce generations is not clear. Presumably the Competitor's resignation was made partly to ensure continuity of the Bruce claim in the event of his sudden death, partly to provide a formal declaration of the claim to be used as soon as a favourable opportunity arose. It certainly looks as though the Bruces had been well prepared for the court's decision in favour of Balliol on the strictly legal issue. It seems equally certain that they were determined not to abandon their 'right and claim to seek the kingdom of Scotland'. On November 10th, Bruce's lawyers made their final desperate plea for one third of the royal demesne or at least of Tynedale and the lands not comprised in the 'regality' of Scotland.[3] And it was only during this week, from Monday, November 10th, to Friday, November 14th, that Count Florence pressed his claim with all the ability and skill at his disposal.[4]

He was well aware of his disadvantages. He asked King Edward to bear in mind that he was a stranger and foreigner, against whom Balliol could range many supporters and maintainers. If a judicial enquiry were not made now into the truth of his story about Earl David's charter of the Garioch it never would be made, and the count's claim and right would be lost for ever. The count's touching picture of himself as a friendless alien among hostile natives should not be taken too seriously. The Bruce faction, far from negligible, was behind him. It hardly seems likely that the count was really anxious for the Scottish throne. If he used his claim in order to defeat

[1] British Library, Cotton Charter, xviii, 48; Stones, *Documents*, No. 18.
[2] *APS*, i, 449.
[3] *Chron. Rishanger*, 271–2.
[4] Ibid., 268–9, 272, 273–80, 302–9.

Balliol, the Bruces would reward him well. In the end, however, he seems to have withdrawn his claim in order to help Balliol. His fellow Dutchmen appear to have thought that Balliol had bribed him, presumably by offering a more tempting reward than the one provided in his agreement with Bruce.[1] But there is no certainty that Florence was bribed. In the four days or less which elapsed between the count's final statement to his claim and his withdrawal, it may have become clear for reasons now unknown that his claim would fail. After all, it depended on a document of resignation which he could not or would not produce, which in any case was undoubtedly a forgery. It was supported by vague, unverified statements that strained beyond credulity the powers of memory enjoyed by the 'old men of Scotland'. It was not difficult for Balliol's lawyers to pour scorn on the count's case, and their point about the absence of the alleged resignation must have seemed unanswerable: 'although the count has had since August 2nd [1291], over a year ago, to seek out his document and has not found it, it does not seem right that he should be heard merely because he says it exists.'[2]

The magnates and legal experts who composed the court of 1291-2, and the councillors outside the court who were consulted, 'were settling a point in law, not discussing political problems'.[3] The last occasion on which there had been a succession dispute in either kingdom was in 1199, on the death of Richard Coeur de Lion. On that occasion there had been neither court nor judgement. Backed by a few men of influence who controlled the key places and the machinery of government, Count John of Mortain, the youngest of Henry II's sons, had simply seized the throne to the exclusion of Arthur, duke of Brittany, the son of John's elder brother Geoffrey. Ninety years later, on the eve of the Great Cause in Scotland, the English rules of succession to the throne were settled by Edward I. His ordinance of April 1290 made it clear that the kingdom of England could not be partitioned and that succession to this indivisible realm would follow the strict rule of primogeniture, preference being given to males in each generation. When the king came to give judgement in the

---

[1] *SHR*, xxxvi, 117-8. Mme Kossmann, *Revue du Nord*, xl, 542, considers it likely that Balliol did bribe Count Florence.

[2] *Chron. Rishanger*, 289.

[3] F. M. Powicke, *King Henry III and the lord Edward*, ii, 790.

Scottish case, on November 17th, 1292, he and the court were apply-
ing the same rules to the northern kingdom. Scotland was a true
kingdom like other kingdoms. Since it was the peculiar property of a
kingdom that it could not be divided, the kingdom of Scotland would
be preserved intact. By the strict rule of primogeniture Balliol was
the rightful heir, and would therefore rule over what Alexander, of
happy memory, late king of Scots had ruled over – save, awkwardly,
for the Isle of Man, whose slightly belated separate restoration to
King John by Edward I (January 5th, 1293)[1] only served to highlight
the odd circumstances of its original detachment from the Scottish
realm.

The judgement in favour of Balliol was surely the triumph of law,
common sense and respect for orderly procedure in the most important public act in which a medieval nation could join. We may
regret that the Scots failed to win their point that the Great Cause
should have proceeded freely, with the English king as arbitrator and
not judge, but the two issues should not be confused, and the choice
of Balliol was not something with which most Scots had any wish to
quarrel. No doubt on personal or political grounds a number of
Bruce's auditors, men like Bishop Wishart of Glasgow and James
the Stewart, were dissatisfied. It is even possible that on more general
grounds there were misgivings that the Crown had gone to a
comparative stranger, a baron of great wealth and international
connexions who yet remained an Englishman rather than a Scotsman. Balliol's sister Eleanor, it is true, was married to the Guardian,
John Comyn of Badenoch, who was head of the senior branch – the
'Red Comyns'[2] – of the most powerful Scottish baronial family.
Moreover Balliol was lord of Galloway by descent from his mother
Dervorguilla. If Galloway was thornily separatist, regarded with

[1] *Foedera*, i, 785.
[2] On the authority of Wyntoun (*Chron. Wyntoun* [Laing], ii, 311–12), modern
historians usually call this John Comyn the 'Black Comyn' and his father and son the
'Red Comyn', as though these sobriquets had been used to distinguish three successive
heads of the family named John. Contemporary evidence, however, proves that the
John Comyn who was Balliol's brother-in-law and a competitor for the throne in
1291 was himself called the 'Red Comyn'. This, and the fact that the description
could be written as one word, support the statement in the text that the title 'Red
Comyn' was generally applied to the head of the senior branch of the Comyns,
being comparable to the titles of Red and Black Douglas. Cf. *Cal. Docs. Scot.*, ii,
Nos. 678, 822 (p. 189).

suspicion by the Scotland of east-coast lairds and burghs, there was
no denying that it was in its own way intensely Scottish. But Bruce,
for all his rich estates and long sojourns in England, was completely
at home in Scotland, where he had held a place in the first rank of the
baronage for nearly fifty years. Balliol's following in Scotland was
largely the following of the Comyns, descendants of the old 'national'
or 'patriot' party of the 1250s. Bruce's following was more of his
own making, and consisted of long-standing family or personal
alliances with neighbouring lords like the Souleses, Lindsays and
Biggars, with the powerful church of Glasgow, and with great
magnates like the Stewart and the earls of Dunbar, Lennox, Atholl
and Mar. Nevertheless, Scotland was not a tribal society in which
personal considerations were uppermost. It was sophisticated enough
to carry on a governed existence during the prolonged absence of a
ruler, but at least there had to be a ruler. What mattered most was to
end the interregnum and to inaugurate a lawful king. There is no
evidence that the enthronement of Balliol on St Andrew's Day, 1292,
failed to meet these crying needs for the generality of Scots. In the
view of the majority Balliol had been the rightful candidate: Long
live King John! The ceremony itself was respectful of national
tradition. It was held at Scone in the presence of the great men of the
realm, and though the earl of Fife was a child his right to place the
new king in the seat of royalty above the Stone of Destiny was
carefully delegated to Sir John de St John.[1]

It is true that in the following weeks and years there were some
small signs that ancient precedents were being deliberately flouted or
at least not being scrupulously followed. King John's seal styled him
'by God's grace king of Scots', where all his predecessors from the
time of King Edgar (1097-1107) had been, with pleasing allitera-
tion, 'king of Scots under God's governance' (*Deo rectore Rex
Scottorum*). This change at least was no accident, and the English
influence is obvious. King John's first chancellor was a Yorkshireman, Master Thomas of Hunsingore.[2] More often than not King
John kept to the time-honoured style 'king of Scots' in his official
documents, but sometimes he used the unfamiliar English type of
style, 'king of Scotland'. By December 1293, a treasurer of Scotland
(Master Alpin) had been appointed. Since there had never been a

[1] *Rotuli Scotiae*, i, 12a. [2] See additional note below, p. 73.

treasurer in Scotland before, it seems reasonable to regard the appointment as a deliberate imitation of English practice.[1]

If these were straws in the wind they did not amount to much. The greatest contrast of the new reign was provided squarely, if not altogether fairly, by King Edward. It is hardly a defence of the English king to say that the line he now took should have been foreseen by the Scots leaders when, in June 1291, they had been smitten by 'that fear which may strike even the stoutest-hearted'. They had taken refuge then in safeguards which now proved to be worth less than the parchment and wax of which they were composed. The Treaty of Birgham-Northampton, it is true, had not been rehearsed or confirmed, but *les haus hommes*, speaking for the community of the realm, had referred to it in their letter of May 1291. They must have had it mind when they got from Edward, on June 12th, 1291, an assurance that he would demand nothing from a new king of Scots beyond homage and its attendant rights, and a promise that the Guardians, prelates, earls, barons and the community of the realm would be secure in the rights, laws, liberties and customs of Holy Church and the laity, and that relics, charters and other muniments touching the 'royal dignity' in the kingdom of Scotland should be safely kept.[2]

For King Edward, however, the elaborately repeated homages and fealties obtained from Balliol, first after judgement had been given and then again after his enthronement, formed the concluding stage of a single process upon which he had embarked in May 1291. This was, characteristically, a process of definition, a piece of tidying up, whereby his own prejudged and highly questionable view of the relationship between the English and Scottish Crowns was to be given permanent force. It is surely somewhat naïve, somewhat unrealistic, not to see in the case – or, rather, the cases – of Roger Bartholomew an essential part of this concluding stage.[3] Definition needs demonstration. It may not have been an ideal test case from

[1] *Holyrood Liber*, No. 91 (81–2); *Reg. John de Halton, bishop of Carlisle* (1913), i, 34.
[2] P.R.O., D.L. 36/I/183.
[3] E. M. Barron, *Scottish War of Independence*, 94–5, gives his grounds for believing that Bartholomew *versus* the Guardians was a test case; *per contra*, F. M. Powicke, *The Thirteenth Century*, 608, writes, 'it so happened that at Newcastle . . . Edward in council had decided an appeal by a burgess of Berwick'. The case may conveniently be studied in Stevenson, *Documents*, i, No. 305.

Edward's point of view, but a test case of some sort was obviously necessary. It seems most unlikely that Bartholomew's appeals, the first appeals from the Scottish *curia regis* to the English, took either Edward I or the Scots leaders by surprise.

Master Roger Bartholomew was a burgess of Berwick who had been involved in litigation in the court of the Guardians. Even after their commission had been changed from an elective authority conferred by the community of the realm to a delegated authority conferred by the 'superior lord', their court still represented the Scottish *curia regis*. It was the highest secular tribunal to which Scottish litigants could have recourse. In three separate cases judgement had gone against Master Roger. He was executor of a deceased goldsmith whose widow sued him successfully for unjust detention of her dower and of money she had loaned to her late husband. He was, secondly, alleged to have deprived a fellow burgess of property in Berwick by the improper use of a brieve of right. And, finally, he was said to have frivolously accused one Gilbert of Dunbar of injuring him in the eye with a stick. Dissatisfied with the Guardians' adverse judgements, Master Roger complained to King Edward at Berwick on December 7th, 1292, one week after Balliol's enthronement. Edward had no wish to impose English law on the Scots. At Newcastle he consulted with the experienced Scotsmen in his company before giving judgement on December 22nd. In the case of the alleged assault, judgement was reversed in Roger's favour; in the property case it was confirmed, saving Roger's right to bring a further action; the case of the widow's money was settled by a compromise. That only a fortnight elapsed between the appeals and final judgement suggests strongly that if Bartholomew's case was not deliberately brought as a test case it was certainly expedited by Edward I's council in order to demonstrate the English king's right to hear appeals from Scottish litigants. On January 6th, 1293, King Edward paid £1 13s. 4d. to Bartholomew and £3 6s. 8d. to Philip of Rydale (another burgess involved in the case), which looks suspiciously like prompt settlement of expenses.[1]

The speed with which King John and his advisers reacted to the affair suggests that the Scots for their part were well prepared for a

---

[1] *Rotuli Scotiae*, i, 17a. Philip of Rydale was mayor of Berwick in 1291, *Instrumenta Publica*, 12.

test case. As soon as judgement had been given on the Bartholomew appeals, four Scots magnates and supporters of Balliol, Bishop Fraser, John Comyn earl of Buchan, Patrick Graham and Thomas Randolph, together with others unnamed, lodged a petition on behalf of their king asking that Edward should keep his promise to preserve the laws and customs of Scotland, including the promise (in the Treaty of Birgham) that Scottish lawsuits should not be dealt with outside Scotland.[1] At first, the reply was that the Scots had specially requested Edward to cut short legal delays so that justice might be done quickly; but this surely applied to outstanding business, not to the revival of cases settled and done with. It was added more plausibly that the Guardians (after June 1291) were responsible solely to Edward as overlord, who therefore had a perfect right to review their judgements. Finally, however, it was declared on Edward's behalf that any promises he had made during the interregnum were only 'for the time being', and had no binding force now that a king had been created. When on the last day of December King Edward himself, speaking personally in French, repeated that he would in no wise be bound by any promises, concessions, ratifications etc. which he might have made previously, so far as appeals were concerned, but on the contrary would hear whatever appeals might be brought and if necessary summon the king of Scotland himself, the Scots could not have been given a clearer answer to the question of what Edward understood by homage and the rights that went with it.[2] We know now that the moral shabbiness in Edward I's dealings with the Scots went back to June 1291. There was scarcely any attempt to disguise it in the pronouncements of December 1292. As if they were not enough, King John was made to issue two instruments, one in Latin, one in French, on January 2nd, 1293, by which he solemnly freed Edward from all obligations and promises which the English king might have entered into with the Guardians and responsible men (*probi homines, la bone gent*) of the Scottish realm, declaring null and void any written evidence of such promises and explicitly annulling the Treaty of Birgham-Northampton.[3] In Edward's view this was no more than a marriage contract; in Scottish eyes it had

[1] *Foedera*, i, 785 (Original edn., ii, 596–7).
[2] Ibid. (Original edn., ii, 597).
[3] Ibid. (Original edn., ii, 597–600).

been the sheet-anchor of their country's independence of the southern kingdom.

The course of events since King John's enthronement had indeed been ominous. It was not the first time an English ruler had made promises to the Scots which he afterwards repudiated. In 1149 Henry of Anjou had sworn before King David that if he became king of England he would leave Northumberland and Cumberland in Scottish hands.[1] Eight years later he went back on his word, and the Scots attempt to restore the *status quo* in 1173 led directly to an Angevin overlordship which lasted for fifteen years and saw English garrisons in Scottish castles and subjects of the king of Scots asking for the English king's direct protection. Edward I was not a man of less determination than his great-grandfather. North of the Border, on the other hand, an idea of the community of the realm had grown from experience of feudal monarchy. Concepts of legal rights, concepts of nationality, concepts of kingship had all become sharper, and there was less room for manoeuvre than in the relatively casual days of the twelfth century. The last fourteen years of Edward I's life were, in proportion, more violent, more destructive, fraught with a more bitter hostility in Anglo-Scottish relations, than the last fifteen years of Henry II's.

[1] *Chronica Mag. Rogeri de Houedene* (ed. Stubbs), i, 211; *Chron. Stephen etc.*, i, 105.

Additional Note (see above, p. 69). ·
Thomas of Hunsingore, chancellor of Scotland.
Master Thomas of Hunsingore had been an Oxford don and guarantor of good behaviour by Northerners and Scots in the university in 1274 after they had fought the Southerners and Irish [*Medieval archives of the University of Oxford*, ed. H. E. Salter, i (1920), 32]; presumably he was kinsman of Mr Richard of Hunsingore of the diocese of Glasgow, a considerable benefactor of Balliol College [Frances de Paravicini, *Early History of Balliol College* (1891), *passim*]. Hunsingore is near Wetherby in the West Riding.

4

A Lamb among Wolves

AFTER nearly seven years of uncertainty the Scots had a king again. No matter how competent or conscientious the Guardians may have been – and our evidence tells us they were both – they could not govern the feudal kingdom indefinitely nor satisfy all its needs. At best they could only be caretakers. Now, once more, 'full' parliaments could be held, charters confirmed and granted, foreign relations resumed, administrative improvements put into effect, military service performed without the suspicion of aiding private faction, vexatious lawsuits heard and determined. Vexatious lawsuits: here was the rub. The king had been regarded in former times as the very fount of justice, whose kingly duty it was, above all other duties, to punish wrongdoers and judge equitably between subject and subject. For administrative convenience or from a desire for maximum solemnity and publicity it had been usual for this ultimate jurisdiction to rest with the king and his 'full court', that is, with king and parliament. This practice, honoured by long usage, detracted nothing from the king's prerogatives. It was an entirely different matter if appeals were to be allowed from the Scottish courts to the king of England. If King John's capacity as supreme secular judge were diminished, his position was open to challenge from all sides. He might be regarded as a provincial governor or else a privileged feudatory enjoying ancient rights and revenues but possessing only the shadow of real power. He would certainly not be a king.

Modern historians sometimes suggest that in Edward I's view the Scottish kingdom resembled the duchy of Aquitaine, which he himself held as a vassal of the king of France. Whether Edward ever made the comparison we do not know; it is in any case one that cannot really be sustained. It is true that Aquitaine enjoyed almost complete independence of the Capetian kings of France as long as they were too weak to assert and exploit their rights of overlordship. At the same time the duchy had not developed for two hundred years as a self-contained kingdom with an increasingly centralized government, a distinct ecclesiastical organization, and a steady enhancement of royal authority. Power and judicial authority in Aquitaine remained stubbornly decentralized, and this made it relatively easy for Gascons to seek justice now from their duke, the king of England, now from the king of France in the *parlement* of Paris. In Aquitaine Edward I, however grudgingly, had come to accept appeals from his vassals to the French king, while at the same time offering attractively speedy and accessible justice in his own court. Even so, Anglo-French relations might be strained to breaking point over the question of appeals, despite the gradual way in which the custom of appeal had grown and despite the evident feudal subordination of the duchy to the French Crown. How much more was this likely to be true of Anglo-Scottish relations, where the practice of appeals from Scotland to England was unheard of until the case of Roger Bartholomew.[1]

The matter went far beyond a technical question of law and its administration. If King John's parliament was not to have the last word in secular causes, his authority and power in many other spheres would be called in question. How far was he free to enter into independent relations with foreign rulers, to make trade agreements with the merchants and communities upon whom Scotland partly depended for her income, to fortify and garrison castles (especially those on the Border), to harbour English fugitives, to keep in his active service subjects who might, on account of their estates in England, be required to appear in English courts or act as judges or jurors south of the Border? At every step he took, the new king would have to pause, examine its implications, and find out whether it could be allowed under the new régime. Yet there was work in plenty for a king of Scotland to do without having to look over his

---

[1] An interesting precursor of appeals from King John to Edward I was the appeal made to Henry III in 1242 by Walter Bisset, the murderer of Patrick earl of Atholl, against the judgement of Alexander II, on the grounds that Alexander was Henry's liege vassal, Matthew Paris, *Chronica Majora* (ed. Luard, Rolls Series), iv, 201–2. The king of Scotland ignored this appeal.

shoulder all the time to see what English reactions were. It was John's misfortune that he had succeeded to a kingdom which could not have been ruled by anyone forced to walk such a narrow tight-rope. At least he made a worthwhile effort at government. We must, in fairness, get behind the powerful legend of Balliol the ineffectual puppet, laughed off the throne by scornful Scots and spurned at last by his own manipulator. It is true he was not a forceful man and certainly no match for Edward I. But he was not a complete nonentity nor altogether lacking in dignity.

Far-reaching legislation can hardly be expected from a king whose effective reign lasted only three and a half years. There is, indeed, very little record of legislation of any kind. Yet there survives one brief ordinance on new sheriffdoms in the west which proves that some sensible, constructive thinking was being done in government circles and that the king possessed the will to apply it. If this ordinance had ever had the chance to take effect, it might have gone far to solve the difficult problem of governing the Hebrides and the mainland country west of Drumalban and the Great Glen. By the terms of the ordinance,[1] Lewis, Uist, Barra, Skye and the Small Isles were to be grouped with Wester Ross and Kintail to form the sheriffdom of Skye, of which the earl of Ross was to be sheriff. South of this, most of what is now Argyllshire, except for Kintyre, was to become the sheriffdom of Lorne, administered by the lord of Argyll, Alexander Macdougall, as sheriff. His castle of Dunstaffnage made an ideal headquarters for the sea-borne government of this area, reaching as it did from Ardnamurchan and Morvern in the north to Islay in the south. Finally, James the Stewart, already hereditary lord of Bute and the Cumbraes, was to be sheriff of a third new sheriffdom comprising those islands together with Kintyre and, presumably, Arran, to be known as the sheriffdom of Kintyre. This scheme, though clearly in line with the 'forward policy' followed in the west highlands and isles by the two Alexanders, was a notable advance on anything they had achieved. The names assigned to the sheriffdoms suggest that for the first time royal authority was to be firmly based in the west and government represented by royal agents stationed at local centres. To that extent, one is reminded of the three new shires of Anglesey, Caernarvon and Merioneth set up under Edward I's

[1] *APS*, i, 447.

Statute of Rhuddlan of 1284. Admittedly, two of the new highland sheriffs, the Stewart and the earl of Ross, had their chief interests outside the west. But it looks as though Alexander Macdougall – who, like Balliol, was a brother-in-law of John Comyn of Badenoch – had previously been entrusted by the king with a 'lieutenancy extending over the three sheriffdoms probably with powers wider than those of a sheriff'.[1] Within his new sheriffdom he could obviously use his hereditary power and prestige to advantage. It was Alexander whom King John commanded to bring Angus Macdonald lord of Islay and two other islesmen to do homage after Easter 1293, and to receive to the king's peace all those willing to take the king's lands in Lorne at farm.[2] Since, as far as we know, the Crown had no lands of its own in Lorne save for Loch Awe, it seems that Alexander Macdougall was to be the principal agent in a piece of forcible feudalization, by which the barons of Argyll could remain in the king's peace as long as they agreed to hold their estates of the Crown for a rent.[3]

This short excursion into the west is in no sense a digression. The interest which King John took in the west highland problem proves that he or his advisers had a good grasp of political and strategic realities. Orientated as she was towards the east, thirteenth-century Scotland could not ignore her western approaches. No able king could afford to neglect a wild terrain from which raiders might descend without warning, like a pack of winter wolves on a sleeping village, returning by trackless *bealachs* to some remote glen. No national defence was complete if it failed to provide for a coast of innumerable lochs and islands, where scores of galleys could lie hidden. For their part, the native chiefs of the west, most of them descended from Somerled, who was virtually independent lord of Argyll under David I, had been forced since 1266 to look eastward, to make unaccustomed and uncomfortable journeys to Scone or Edinburgh, to take a more active part in domestic Scottish politics. There are not many points at which it is useful to make any compari-

[1] A. A. M. Duncan and A. L. Brown, 'Argyll and the Isles in the earlier middle ages', *Proc. Soc. Antiq. Scot.*, xc, 192–220. The quotation in the text is from p. 217. This article is of the first importance for an understanding of the west highland political scene down to Robert I's reign.

[2] Ibid., 220, No. VI.

[3] For examples of the creation of military fiefs in Argyll by Alexander II and Alexander III, cf. *Highland Papers* (SHS), ii, 121 and i, 107.

son between the kingship of John Balliol and the kingship of Robert Bruce, but in his concern for Argyll Balliol foreshadowed the exploits which were to make his successor a legend in the west. It was not necessary for a king in Edinburgh to take to the heather in order to grasp the essential truth that one who was not master of the highlands was not master of Scotland.

The impression is sometimes conveyed that King John's monarchy foundered on the question of appeals, and the name of Macduff – perhaps because it is so easily memorable – has filled a disproportionately large place in Scottish history. 'Ever since the accession of John Balliol,' wrote T. F. Tout, 'there had been appeals from the Scottish courts to those of Edward ... and it looked as if, after a few years, appeals from Edinburgh to London would be as common as appeals from Bordeaux to Paris.'[1] Professor Sayles and Mr H. G. Richardson have put it even more strongly. 'Thereafter [i.e., after Balliol's accession] there was a regular stream of citations on appeals to the court of the king of England.'[2] The learned authors justify this statement with an impressive array of six separate references. When examined, however, these six references add up to no more than eleven cases, or only nine if Roger Bartholomew's three appeals be regarded as one. And our doubts about the growing popularity of appeals from Scotland to England are not dispelled but deepened when the appellants and their complaints are looked at in detail. To say that the appeals were mostly brought by foreigners and malcontents might be putting it rather strongly, but it would give a truer impression than to speak of 'a regular stream of citations on appeals'.

Three of the appellants were subjects of the king of England. John Mazun was a Bordeaux wine merchant with whom King Alexander III had run up a large bill. Both king and Guardians had attempted to settle his claims, but his wayward and intemperate behaviour, coupled with the fact that he was beset by creditors, made settlement difficult. He had certainly not improved his case by procuring the arrest in Yorkshire (1289) of Bishop Fraser of St Andrews, then a Guardian, while the bishop was on his way to Gascony to discuss

[1] *The Political History of England*, iii (*History of England, 1216–1377*), 193.
[2] H. G. Richardson and G. O. Sayles, 'The Scottish parliaments of Edward I', *SHR*, xxv, 309.

with King Edward the Maid of Norway's marriage.[1] The abbot of
Reading, William Sutton, had perhaps a stronger case. He complained that his predecessor had unlawfully sold to Bishop Fraser the
priory of May or Pittenweem, a dependency of Reading Abbey: in
making the purchase the bishop, so he alleged, had abused his
position as Guardian. Since Reading was a royal foundation, it was
only to be expected that the abbot would appeal to his patron. King
John was repeatedly summoned before the court of King's Bench
to answer the abbot's complaint. He ignored these summonses. The
case was already before his own parliament, but stood adjourned
because Bishop Fraser had himself appealed to the papal court.[2] The
other non-Scottish appellant was Anthony Bek, bishop of Durham,
a trusted servant and friend of King Edward, who presented a grotes-
quely frivolous claim to the towns of Berwick and Haddington as
being ancient possessions of his see.[3]

Of the six Scottish appellants (including Bartholomew), three were
Manx or Hebrideans. One of these, Alexander Macdonald of Islay,
was the heir of Angus Macdonald who had failed to do homage to
King John by February, 1293. He was perhaps already a supplier of
gallóglach (gallowglasses or mercenary infantry) to northern Ireland,
and he and his father had joined the Bruces in the Turnberry Band of
1286, which almost certainly presaged some Irish adventure. Although married to Alexander Macdougall's daughter, he was bitterly
opposed to the lord of Argyll, who was a loyal adherent of Balliol
and the Comyns. The dispute between the two chiefs had already
come before King Edward in 1292, when both parties had agreed to

[1] Stevenson, *Documents*, i, Nos. 53, 84.

[2] The abbot of Reading's case may be followed in *APS*, i, 445–6; *Rotuli Scotiae*,
i, 19; *Proc. Soc. Antiq. Soc.*, xc, 61–4 (the best survey, with a full account of the background).

[3] Berwick on the strength of a charter of King Edgar of 1095, yet the bishop of
Durham had not held Berwick since before 1100. Bek claimed Haddington under the
impression that 'Haedynton' (etc.) appearing in some early charters in favour of his
predecessors stood for Haddington, whereas the place intended was Edington. Cf.
A. A. M. Duncan, 'The earliest Scottish charters', *SHR*, xxxvii, 103–35, esp. 110–13.

What looks like the first stage of a further appeal by a non-Scottish appellant (not
mentioned by Richardson and Sayles in 'The Scottish parliaments of Edward I')
may be found in the complaint made to Edward I in 1294 by John de Lisle of Northumberland, to whom Balliol had granted Whitsome in Berwickshire, that the king
of Scots had refused him free possession, *Foedera*, i, 803, June 26th, 1294.

a postponement, evidently for the sake of keeping the peace in the 'isles and outlying territories'.[1] The struggle between Macdougalls and Macdonalds for land and power was the dominant feature of Hebridean 'politics' in the century from 1250 to 1350, and it was almost inevitable that Alexander of Islay should try to outflank his rival by appealing afresh to Edward I against his rival's relative and patron, King John.[2] The other Hebridean, Malcolm, had the surname 'son of the Englishman' or simply 'the Englishman' (*le fiz le Engleys, le Engleys*), and was said to be a tenant in chief in the sheriffdom of Perth, which included Argyll so long as Balliol's ordinance of 1293 was not in force.[3] Malcolm was perhaps the same man who will appear later in this book as Malcolm MacCulian, but neither origin nor identity is known. Since his appeal was an hereditary claim to Kintyre, it may be that he was related to the family of Mac Sween or Sweeney, which had held the lordship of Knapdale and lands in Kintyre until 1262, when they were dislodged by the earl of Menteith.[4] They nursed a grievance, and between 1301 and 1310 John Mac Sween was understandably active with his galleys in the English service, and still keeping alive his claim against the Menteiths.[5] In 1300 Malcolm 'le fiz le Engleys' was similarly harassing the Scots with men and galleys.[6] The third appellant from former Norwegian territory was a lady named Affrica,

---

[1] *Foedera*, i, 761.

[2] Alexander Macdonald's case can be traced in *Foedera*, i, 761; *Rotuli Scotiae*, i, 21b.

[3] *Cal. Docs. Scot.*, ii, 209, 'Maucolum le Engleys del counte de Perth'; cf. ibid., 225. *Rotuli Scotiae*, i, 22–3, prints letters from Edward I to Alexander Macdonald of Islay (Berwick, April 15th, 1296) appointing him king's bailie, empowering him to take Kintyre into his own hands, and commanding him to put Malcolm le fiz Lengleys in sasine of Kintyre. Mr G. G. Simpson has discovered Alexander's reply to a contemporary and related letter from Edward, P.R.O., S.C. 1/18/147.

The identity of Malcolm le fiz Engleys is not clear. The view taken here is that he may perhaps be identified with Malcolm MacCulian (for whom see below, p. 209), who held land in Kintyre in 1306, who had apparently been put in possession of Dunaverty by Edward I without lawful inquest, and who was evidently killed in 1307. The view that he may have belonged to the MacQuillans of Antrim, for whom see E. Curtis, *Proc. Roy. Irish Academy*, xliv, 99–113, has not been verified [K. Nicholls. *Gaelic and Gaelicized Ireland in the Middle Ages* (1972), 134].

[4] *Scots Peerage*, vi, 130–1; cf. *APS*, i, 447; A. McKerral, *SHR*, xxx, 5–6.

[5] *Cal. Docs. Scot.*, ii, No. 1,255; *Rotuli Scotiae*, i, 90.

[6] Stevenson, *Documents*, ii, No. 597.

cousin of Magnus the last king of Man, who died in 1266. Clearly, she thought the new régime an opportunity of raising an hereditary claim to Man which had probably seemed hopeless under Alexander III.[1]

The remaining three Scottish appellants were Bartholomew, whose case has been dealt with, Simon of Restalrig and Macduff of Fife. The Scots parliament had placed in wardship the barony of Restalrig because its holder was an idiot, and Simon's complaint was that during the wardship (which had not been given to him) Sir Patrick Graham had improperly persuaded Simon's mother to alienate some lands of the barony. Nothing more is known of this case.[2] Far and away the most famous appeal was that of Macduff, a younger son of Malcolm earl of Fife (died 1266). He complained that he had not been allowed peaceful possession of the lands of Creich and Rires settled on him (as he claimed) by his father, but on the contrary had been put in prison for a time by Balliol. Macduff's name, another instance of Celtic revival, seems to have puzzled at least one historian, who took it to be a surname and looked in vain for a Christian name to go with it.[3] The Fife family was evidently conscious that its members formed the 'Clan Macduff', ultimately descended from some unidentified Duf, possibly King Duf who had ruled briefly in the late tenth century. There is nothing to suggest that Macduff resorted to Edward I's superior lordship as a matter of principle. He was a man with a chip on his shoulder. In 1297 he and his sons joined Wallace,[4] and Macduff himself was killed at Falkirk the following year,[5] fighting for the very king whose judgement he had called in English help to overturn. By then he was a 'false traitor' in King Edward's eyes.

King John was summoned before King's Bench to answer for his failure to do justice in the Mazun case (May 8th, 1293)[6] and the

[1] *Rotuli Scotiae*, i, 18b.
[2] *APS*, i, 446; *Rotuli Scotiae*, i, 19–20.
[3] Sir David Dalrymple, Lord Hailes, *Annals of Scotland*, i (1776), 225; cf. index entry '[ ] Macduff' in J. H. Ramsay, *Dawn of the Constitution* (1908), 576. For the Macduff case see *APS*, i, 445; *Rotuli Scotiae*, i, 18, 20; *Rot. Parl.*, i, 110–11; *Foedera*, i, 788.
[4] Stevenson, *Documents*, ii, No. 462; *Rotuli Scotiae*, i, 42b.
[5] *Chron. Fordun*, i, 330.
[6] *Cal. Docs. Scot.*, ii, Nos. 685, 686.

Macduff appeal came before King's Bench at Trinity (May 24th) whence it was adjourned to the Michaelmas parliament.[1] The king refused to appear or defend his judgement through attorneys, and Edward's council, evidently prepared in advance for this contumacy, drew up a set of carefully worked out rules to cover these and future cases of appeal from Scotland to England.[2] The rules were drastic. They involved the personal attendance of the king of Scots to answer for his judgements, a requirement which Edward's advisers must have known would be intolerable for a ruling monarch, and, among other equally onerous terms, the forfeiture of the Scots king's lordship over an appellant's fief if its custody pending an appeal had been interfered with. Almost the only record we have of this year 1293 is official record. It shows a mixture of firmness and pliancy on King John's part which may actually reflect the king's own character but is more probably the result of occasional pressure from more forceful councillors. For example, in the John Mazun case, King Edward wrote to Balliol on the appellant's behalf, and after the case had been heard in the Scottish parliament received a reasoned answer not from Balliol himself but from the bishop of St Andrews, as principal executor of Alexander III.[3] On the other hand, humble petitions sent to Edward at this time by Balliol do not show much spirit, and the English king's gracious replies conceded very little save the news that the litigious John Mazun had died and his lawsuit was therefore void.[4]

The critical moment in this calculated oppression and provocation was reached after Michaelmas 1293, when King John at last appeared in person before the English parliament and was treated like a defaulting debtor.[5] At first he showed surprising courage and dignity. He said he neither dared nor was able to answer in an English court on a matter affecting the kingdom of Scotland without consulting the *probi homines*, the responsible men, of his realm. He could not admit any adjournment, for that would imply recognition of English jurisdiction. It is clear that so far he had been well briefed, and that

[1] *Rot. Parl.*, i, 110–11.
[2] Ibid.
[3] *Cal. Docs. Scot.*, ii, Nos. 687, 688.
[4] Palgrave, *Docs. Hist. Scot.*, 138–41.
[5] *Rot. Parl.*, i, 112–3; see also Stones, *Documents*, No. 21.

the same minds were at work here as in the Treaty of Birgham and the protestations of 1291 and 1292. But the Scots leaders had reckoned without Balliol's personal weakness, the psychological effect of a browbeating from Edward I (in the following year this was to give a dean of St Paul's heart-failure) and the humiliating high-handedness of a hostile English parliament. The king of Scots was judged to be in King Edward's mercy for contempt of court, and sentenced to lose his three chief castles and towns (presumably Edinburgh, Roxburgh and Berwick) until he made amends. Under this threat Balliol collapsed. He renewed his submission and homage in abject terms, and asked for a delay until the next English parliament.[1] 'We have no power', the Scots lords had declared in 1291, 'to reply in the absence of a king to whom such a demand should be addressed and who could reply to it.' Now, all too clearly, their king had given his reply.

Far from supporting the belief that appeals from Scotland to England became popular in King John's reign, the evidence suggests that the Scots were indifferent or hostile to the new facilities. Of course, for all we know, litigants may have been discouraged from appealing by John and his council, though if that had been so we should have expected a protest from Edward I. The historian, however, cannot have it both ways. He cannot say in the same breath that the Scots found the procedure of appeal attractive and yet regarded the practice as an unwarrantable restriction of their independence. The truth is that Anglo-Scottish relations, which on the whole had been remarkably good under the two Alexanders, were wrecked not on particular instances of appeal, not even on Edward I's stubborn insistence on his right to hear appeals, but on a wholly different principle or attitude which the English king had introduced into these relations ever since June 1291. Appeals were merely one aspect of what a Yorkshire chronicler of the time describes bluntly as the 'yoke of servitude which the Scots deserved'.[2] For there is no question that however correct and legalistic King Edward himself was, his subjects looked at the matter much less subtly. They made the inevitable comparison between what Edward had recently accomplished in Wales, which in 1284 had been

[1] *Rot. Parl.*, 113.
[2] *Chron. Guisb.*, 264.

annexed to the English Crown, and the claim of sovereign or direct
lordship which he made in Scotland. To the ordinary Englishman it
was the great glory of his king that he had defied Philip the Fair of
France and reduced the treacherous Welsh and the 'fickle and un-
stable'[1] Scots to servitude. He was mourned after his death as 'the
conqueror of lands and flower of chivalry',[2] not as a lawyer-king who
had been scrupulous about his own rights and those of others.

The Scottish leaders were clearly alarmed at the consequences of
their own weakness as early as December 1292, when they made their
formal protestation to Edward I on King John's behalf. With each of
Balliol's successive acts of defiance and subsequent surrenders their
alarm must have grown. Scotland was a small country, smaller even
than its geographical area would suggest. Its leading men formed a
correspondingly close-knit group, sub-divided of course by family
ties and by faction but still small enough for its members to know one
another well and see one another frequently. In the record of public
assemblies and acts of state the same few names occur over and over
again. After the court of Berwick had adjudged the crown to Balliol
it was only a matter of weeks before many of the auditors reassembled
at Scone for the inauguration. Around Christmas an appreciable
number were still gathered together, and just over a month later
John held his first parliament at Scone,[3] where most of the same
magnates must once again have been present. Among the auditors in
November 1292, for example, had been Bishop Fraser of St Andrews, the earl of Buchan and Sir Patrick Graham. These, with Sir
Thomas Randolph who had been Dervorguilla Balliol's executor,
were King John's spokesmen in the protest of December. Again,
Bishop Wishart of Glasgow, Sir Andrew Murray of Petty and Master
Nicholas of St Andrews (alias of Balmyle) were also auditors in
November.[4] In the following February, at John's first parliament,
they are to be found sealing or witnessing an agreement made under
the aegis of the bishop of Glasgow between his Dean and Chapter
and Sir Andrew Murray's brother, Sir William Murray of Bothwell,
'pantler of Scotland', one of the most powerful barons of the

[1] Chron. Guisb., 264. Elsewhere, 'treacherous', ibid., 294.
[2] M. Dominica Legge, SHR, xxxviii, 110-11.
[3] APS, i, 445.
[4] Chron. Rishanger, 263-4. For Master Nicholas, cf. Kingdom of the Scots, 245-7.

country and known popularly as Sir William 'le riche'.[1] Nearly all
these men played leading parts in the events of the next few years.
Nothing of their conversation has been handed down to us, but we
may be sure it was not taken up with mere pleasantries. Though they
belonged to a conventional, hierarchical society, the nobles of that
age were used to great frankness, outspoken expression of opinion,
graphic and often ribald abuse of one another. They were no fools,
and knew perfectly well that King Edward entertained, as Sir
Maurice Powicke has put it, 'no exalted ideas about the nature of
Scottish kingship'.[2] Indeed, they knew that if King John continued
to lead his subjects along the path he had taken in October 1293,
they would very soon spring the trap which Edward had set for them.

Sir Maurice believed that 'gradually the legend grew that Edward,
a foe in the guise of a friend, had struck down a trustful and defence-
less people', and cites as evidence that 'masterpiece of political
rhetoric', the Declaration of Arbroath of 1320.[3] If the legend had
really taken thirty years to gain concrete expression its growth
would indeed have been gradual. But its substance appears quite
plainly in the letter *Scimus, fili* which Pope Boniface VIII addressed
to King Edward in June 1299.[4] The contents or substance of this
letter must have been prepared, and very carefully prepared at that,
with the help of the Scots themselves, probably some while before
the formal date of its issue.[5] After summarizing the Treaty of Birg-

---

[1] *Glasgow Registrum*, No. 239. Ibid., No. 238, shows that Master William Lamberton,
future bishop of St Andrews, Master Thomas of Dundee, future bishop of Ross, and
Master William of Eaglesham, future Scottish envoy to the papal curia in 1301, were
also present at Scone at the time of King John's first parliament.

[2] *The Thirteenth Century*, 610. Nor, it may be added, about Scotland altogether.
Sir Thomas Grey (*Scalacronica*, 123) says that when King Edward, then at Newminster Abbey in Northumberland, handed over to John de Warenne the seal of
government for conquered Scotland, in September 1296, he exclaimed in jest, 'A
man does good business when he rids himself of a turd'. (Cf. *Rotuli Scotiae*, i, 35a,
instructions to obey Warenne, dated at Morpeth, September 29th, and *Cal. Close,
1288–96*, 492.)

[3] *The Thirteenth Century*, 611 and no. 2, the description of the Arbroath Declaration being cited from T. M. Cooper, Lord Cooper, *Supra Crepidam* (1951), 59.

[4] *Chron. Picts-Scots*, 216–21, Anagni, June 27th; Stones, *Documents*, No. 28.

[5] The detailed account in *Scimus, fili* of the transactions of the period 1286–92 and
later shows that the information on which the letter was based must have been supplied by Scottish informants. The grounds for believing that *Scimus, fili* was nevertheless somewhat out of date by June 1299 are that the letter, having referred to the
imprisonment of Bishop Wishart of Glasgow (1297) and of Bishop Mark of Sodor

ham and Edward's assurance of May 1291 that the visit of *les haus hommes* of Scotland to Norham should not prejudice the liberties of the realm, the bull continues:

It is said that at the time when the realm of Scotland lacked a defender, certain novel matters were, contrary to custom, introduced touching the state of that realm and the liberty it had formerly enjoyed, either by the magnates of the realm who were, so to speak, without a head and lacked the guidance of a leader and steersman, or else by him to whom the government had (though improperly) been committed by you. Nevertheless, these novel matters, exacted as it were by force and by that fear which could have smitten even the constant,[1] ought in no circumstances to remain in force by right nor redound to the prejudice of the kingdom.

Bearing in mind that this bull was expedited after King Edward's sack of Berwick and his 'abolition' of Scottish monarchy, after the battles of Stirling Bridge and Falkirk, the statement, far from embodying a legend, seems an astonishingly sober, cautious, and in the main accurate account of what happened in 1291–2.

The immediate origins of the Scottish war of independence lay in the struggle which broke out in June 1294 between Philip IV of France and Edward I over the conditions on which Gascony could continue to be held as a fief of the French Crown. If the Scots were to regain their independence they too would have to make war. They must have a specific *casus belli*, and above all they must have allies. Since the king would not take the initiative, the 'responsible men' must take it for him. It is not difficult to feel sympathy for the wretched Balliol, ground between the upper and nether millstones of an overlord who demanded humble obedience and a community of

---

(at an unknown date), speaks of them as still in prison. But Wishart was released on parole in the spring of 1298 (Palgrave, *Docs. Hist. Scot.*, 344), was evidently free in October 1299 (*Cal. Docs. Scot.*, ii, No. 1,105), and is not known to have been imprisoned again till 1306. There seems to be no record of Bishop Mark's movements between August 29th, 1296, when King Edward's bailie of Dumfries was ordered to bring him to the king at Berwick, presumably to do homage (*Rotuli Scotiae*, i, 24), and February 7th, 1302, when he was at Rushen (*Register of St Bees*, ed. J. Wilson (1915), No. 46). There is no record of the bishop's homage in 1296, and perhaps the reason for his imprisonment was his failure to perform it.

[1] This expression, derived from Roman Law, was a commonplace way of excusing acts committed under improper compulsion or duress; cf. *Collected Papers of T. F. Tout*, ii, 285–7.

the realm whose leaders insisted that he stand up manfully for their independence. A contemporary English writer, conflating Saint Luke and Isaiah, compared him to a lamb among the wolves, who dared not open his mouth.[1] The suspense which had mounted in the eighteen months from John's accession came to an end almost overnight with the outbreak of war between France and England. All at once the Scots regained their nerve.

The sequence of events which precipitated the Scottish decision to defy King Edward was as follows. On May 19th, 1294, Philip IV confiscated Edward's duchy of Aquitaine. On June 24th Edward renounced his homage as duke and sent his formal 'defiance' to the French king. He embarked upon an elaborate scheme of military alliances to encircle France. This included Germany and the northern Spanish kingdoms, especially Aragon, but concentrated, by longstanding tradition, on the principalities of the Low Countries, Holland, Brabant, Gelders, and even Flanders itself, a fief of France, which was brought in because the count, Guy de Dampierre, had a personal quarrel with King Philip. At the end of May all sea communication between England and the continent was put under strict royal control. On June 2nd King John was ordered to apply the same prohibition to Scottish shipping and report as soon as he had done so.[2] The English feudal host was summoned to be at Portsmouth on September 1st, ready to embark for overseas service. At the end of June a similar summons went out demanding the personal service of the king of Scots, ten earls of Scotland, and sixteen barons, headed by James the Stewart and Bruce of Annandale the Competitor, now eighty-four years of age.[3] Here was 'superior or direct lordship' with a vengeance. Not since 1159, when King Malcolm IV had joined Henry II's expedition to Toulouse, had a king of Scotland performed overseas military service for a king of England. On that occasion King Malcolm had come home to find the earls of Scotland angry at what he had done. They had, indeed, banded together to make sure that he would never again leave his kingdom to go on a mere adventure of chivalry. In 1294 the Scottish magnates were determined that their king should not be given the chance to perform

[1] *Chron. Rishanger*, 371.
[2] *Foedera*, i, 801.
[3] Ibid., i, 804.

military service even if he was ready to. Balliol was present at the
emergency great council convened by Edward in mid-June, and is
said to have promised to give aid.[1] In fact neither he nor any of his
barons appeared in response to Edward's repeated summons, but
instead made various excuses. In August the newly-conquered
Welsh were called on to fight in Gascony. So sure was Edward of
their loyalty that arms were distributed among them while they
were still at home. In September almost the whole of Wales broke
into fierce revolt. Local leaders were found everywhere, and in
Madog ap Llywelyn of Merioneth a national leader. The king's
castles, even great Caernarvon, were seized and destroyed. In
January 1295 a spectacularly successful ambush of Edward's baggage
train between Conway and Bangor halted the English winter campaign. Although we know of no liaison between Madog and the
Scots, his rebellion, continuing until March 1295, must have
impressed the Scots leaders profoundly. Already, before December
1294, they had apparently taken the highly significant step of obtaining from the simple-minded old Pope Celestine V absolution from
any oaths exacted from them under duress.[2]

To seek French as well as papal aid was an obvious course. It is
often said that the Franco-Scottish treaty of 1295 was the beginning
of the Auld Alliance. In fact it was nothing of the sort. Ever since
1173 (to go back no further) it had been the normal, one might
almost say the routine, practice for a French king at war with
England to call upon Scottish support, and for a Scots king at odds
with England to look for help from France. It was the inevitable
consequence both of the entry of Scotland into the community of
North Sea nations and of the development of her independent
monarchy. We do not know who took the initiative in 1295: the
first move could as easily have come from Paris as from Edinburgh.
Nor do we know the exact moment at which negotiations began. All
we can be sure of is that in March 1295 King Philip still viewed the
Scots as enemies along with the English,[3] while two months later he
held them 'not as enemies but rather as our friends'.[4] By early July

---

[1] *Handbook of British Chronology* (2nd edn, 1961), 511; *Chron. Guisb.*, 243.
[2] Ibid., 280.
[3] Stevenson, *Documents*, ii, No. 334.
[4] Ibid., No. 335.

the Scots leaders' resolve to fight for their independence, and their mistrust of Balliol, had pushed them to the point of a sober constitutional revolution. At a parliament held at Stirling the government was taken out of Balliol's hands and a council of twelve elected to manage the direction of affairs.[1] Walter of Guisborough and the Lanercost Chronicle both draw across their account the red herring of a comparison with the Twelve Peers of France, but the former adds the really significant fact that the council consisted of four bishops, four earls and four barons – a doubling of the two bishops, two earls and two barons who formed the regency council of 1286. Tout rightly compared the twelve to the council of fifteen elected to take over the government of England from Henry III in 1258,[2] but he missed the vital point of difference, namely the symmetry of representation on the Scottish council. Highly characteristic of late-thirteenth-century Scotland, this arrangement continued to express the idea of the community of the realm. So far there had been Guardians during a minority and Guardians during an interregnum. Now there were to be Guardians during the 'incapacity' or 'incompetence' of the sovereign.[3] The revolutionary nature of this step should not be underrated. In 1258, when the English baronage – not for the first time – were placing their king under constraint, the Scottish baronage, much more conservative and feudally-minded, told the Welsh leaders with whom they had concluded a treaty that they would try to persuade their king to give it his support, but that they would have to go back on their word if the king strictly ordered them to do so.[4] Unlike the English, the Scots of the thirteenth century were not habitual king-breakers. That the Scots nobles in 1295 had at last caught up with the English nobles of forty years before is proof not of the backwardness of Scotland but of the strength of Scottish hostility to Edward I.

The council of twelve had two urgent tasks, to negotiate the

[1] *Chron. Guisb.*, 264 (Scone); *Chron. Lanercost*, 161–2 (Stirling); *Chron. Fordun*, i, 327 (Scone, wrongly placed after instead of before the campaign of 1296). Though two chronicles give Scone, the true place and date of the parliament are shown to have been July 5th, 1295, at Stirling, by King John's letters to King Philip IV, *APS*, , 453. Cf. *SHR*, xxv, 304, n. 5.   [2] *History of England, 1216–1377*, 194.
[3] In *Chron. Fordun*, i, 328, the twelve are actually called Guardians.
[4] *Littere Wallie*, ed. J. G. Edwards, 184. Admittedly, this was only a section of the baronage.

French treaty and to put the country into a state of defence. At the July parliament four commissioners were appointed to go to Paris.[1] The senior commissioner was William Fraser, bishop of St Andrews, whose long experience of government included seven years as chancellor of Scotland and six years as Guardian. Uncle of Simon Fraser of Oliver Castle on the upper Tweed, who died in 1291, the bishop belonged to a baronial family of the second rank whose various branches held land in East Lothian, Stirlingshire and Tweed-dale. No doubt Fraser and the second commissioner, Matthew of Crambeth, were members of the twelve.[2] Matthew, previously dean of Aberdeen, was appointed bishop of Dunkeld at the instance of the Guardians in 1288. This see, whose diocese was composed of many separate pieces of territory dispersed across central Scotland from Drumalban almost to Berwick, ranked third in seniority after St Andrews and Glasgow. We have seen already how Bishop Matthew co-operated with Wishart of Glasgow to issue a formal copy of the guarantees obtained from Edward I in 1291. Like Wishart he was one of Bruce's auditors in the Great Cause. Despite his clerical orders, Matthew was heir to the small barony of Crambeth, now called Dowhill, whose ruined tower-house of a later date still stands on a slope of the Cleish Hills overlooking Kinross. The two lay com-missioners were younger sons of great baronial families. Sir John de Soules was brother of William de Soules, hereditary butler of Scot-land and lord of Liddesdale.[3] He had already been an envoy in Paris, in 1285, when he negotiated Alexander III's marriage to Yolande de Dreux. He too had been an auditor for Bruce. Sir In-gram de Umfraville was probably a cousin of the earl of Angus, and was related to the Balliols.[4]

These four were sent to France, and the treaty with King Philip

[1] *APS*, i, 453; and for their arrival in France, *Chron. Lanercost*, 166, where the year should be 1295, not 1294.

[2] The membership of the twelve may be deduced in part from *APS*, i, 453b, giving the names of magnates whose seals were fixed to the French treaty. There are four bishops, St Andrews, Glasgow, Dunkeld, Aberdeen; four earls, Buchan, Mar, Strathearn, Atholl; and the first four of the eleven barons named are Comyn of Badenoch, James the Stewart, Alexander Balliol and Geoffrey Moubray.

[3] For John de Soules see M. M'Michael, 'The feudal family of de Soulis', *Dum-friesshire Trans.*, 3rd ser., xxvi, 163–93, esp. 174–81.

[4] J. Hodgson, *History of Northumberland*, II, i, 31, n.b; *Cal. Docs. Scot.*, ii, Nos. 1,060, 1,696; W. Percy Hedley, *Northumberland Families*, i (1968), 211.

followed on October 23rd.[1] It provided for an offensive and defensive alliance between John and Philip, towards whose people the community of the realm of Scotland was said to be well affected. As long as hostilities continued between France and England the Scots were to wage war on the English by land and sea, not only the king but also the prelates (as far as appropriate), earls, barons, knights and the urban communities – all these groups were to notify the French in writing of their assent as soon as possible. On the other hand, if Scotland was invaded the king of France would begin diversionary activity or send suitable aid to Scotland. If Edward I left England (for the continent), the Scots were to mount a large-scale invasion by land (*bellum campestre*). Neither side would make a separate peace. The alliance was to be cemented by a marriage between King John's son Edward and Jeanne, daughter of Charles of Valois, King Philip's brother. Thus the French would be given a stake in the survival of the Balliol dynasty, since Edward, described as 'future king of Scotland', was guaranteed to be the heir by the Scottish envoys. The treaty was ratified by the Scottish king and parliament on February 23rd, 1296. From the names of those who set their seals to the ratification we may infer that the four bishops of the council of twelve were St Andrews, Glasgow, Dunkeld and Aberdeen,[2] and the four earls Buchan, Mar, Strathearn and Atholl. Of the eleven barons who sealed, it is reasonable to assume that the first two named, John Comyn of Badenoch and James the Stewart, were also of the council.

The treaty was one leg of a triangular alliance which brought together France, Scotland and Norway. It has recently been shown how some serious differences between the Scots and Norwegians were temporarily laid aside as the result of King Philip's busy diplomacy.[3] Though there was no direct Scoto-Norwegian treaty, the Scots were accessory to the Franco-Norwegian treaty completed on October 22nd, 1295, the day before their own treaty with Philip. Both countries agreed not to attack one another so long as they were helping France against England. The Norwegians could hardly invade England, so their part in the scheme was the provision of a

---

[1] *APS*, i, 451–3.

[2] Ibid., 453b.

[3] Ranald Nicholson, 'The Franco-Scottish and Franco-Norwegian treaties of 1295', *SHR*, xxxviii, 114–32.

large fleet of galleys, which would reinforce the ships Philip had both obtained direct from Genoa and was building in Normandy with skilled Genoese assistance. The French encircling alliance with Norway and Scotland seems an obvious counterpart of Edward I's encircling alliances with Germany, Spain and the Low Countries. Yet for the Norwegians it meant reversing a policy of good relations with England. The Maid of Norway's father, King Eric, had been on good terms with Edward I at the time of the treaties of Salisbury and Birgham-Northampton, and this harmony survived the rejection of Eric's far-fetched claim in the competition for the Scottish throne.

On November 9th, 1292, Robert Bruce, the Competitor's son, resigned the earldom of Carrick, which he held in right of his wife Marjorie, to their son and heir the young Robert, the future king, then eighteen years old. Next year he went to Norway by leave of Edward I to give his daughter Isabel in marriage to King Eric.[1] By refusing homage to Balliol, Bruce had kept open his father's claim to the throne; by marrying Isabel Bruce, King Eric renewed his Scottish interests and (since the Bruces were loyal friends and supporters of Edward) increased the ties of friendship which bound him to the English king.

The marriage of Isabel Bruce in particular and the position of the Bruces in general bring us to the second task confronting the council of twelve: the defence and security of Scotland. The Bruces were the most powerful of the magnatial families who were likely to be disloyal to the Balliol régime. Old Bruce, the Competitor, died at Lochmaben on Maundy Thursday 1295, before the storm broke. His last public act, characteristically, was a double defiance of Balliol. In 1294 he secured the appointment of his clerk and protégé, Master Thomas Dalton of Kirkcudbright, as bishop of Galloway.[2]

Episcopal appointments were the concern of the Crown, and King John protested against Master Thomas's election.[3] Master Thomas had been elected by the prior and canons of Whithorn, the cathedral church of the diocese. The king did not contest their right to per-

[1] *Cal. Docs. Scot.*, ii, 148 (No. 635), where the year should be 1293; cf. ibid., No. 675.

[2] J. Dowden, *Bishops of Scotland*, 359–60, Dalton doubtless from the village of that name in Annandale. He was also known as Thomas 'of Kirkcudbright'.

[3] For what follows, see R. Brentano, *York Metropolitan Jurisdiction* (1959), 94–108, esp. 98–108.

form the election, but he alleged that there had been bribery, and there can be little doubt that his accusations were really aimed at the Bruce faction. Indeed, ancient rivalries were involved in the affair. The lords of Galloway regarded themselves as special patrons of the see, and Balliol's protest had actually been addressed to the archbishop of York from Buittle, the chief residence of the lords of Galloway. Moreover, the election had taken place in an atmosphere of clerical dissension within the diocese, which itself seems to have reflected the Bruce-Balliol conflict. The chapter's right to exercise the bishop's spiritual jurisdiction during a vacancy was disputed not only by the archdeacon Henry, an elderly, blind man, but also, more vigorously and capably, by the archdeacon's nephew, Master John 'the Nephew' (*Nepos*) who had probably been for some years the most influential clergyman in the diocese. It can hardly be a coincidence that this man was one of Balliol's auditors in the competition for the throne, along with the previous bishop of Galloway.[1] Owing, presumably, to Balliol's reluctance at this stage to alienate the Bruces and their friends altogether, he climbed down in the summer of 1294, and Thomas Dalton was duly consecrated in October. But the affair had been a serious rebuff. The Competitor's family was strongly entrenched. His son succeeded to Annandale and his grandson had been confirmed in his mother's earldom of Carrick at the Stirling parliament of August 1293, sponsored by his family's friends James the Stewart and the earl of Mar.[2]

The acid test for all the nobles and gentry in Scotland who, for one reason or another, put their loyalty to Edward I before their loyalty to King John was the decision to call out the host, in accordance with the terms of the French treaty. The order went out presumably early in 1296, for a 'wapinschaw' (inspection of arms and equipment) and was followed by a summons to the host to assemble on March 11th.[3] Here, as elsewhere, we can see how much store the Scots set by the punctilious observance of tradition. The host was to meet at Caddonlee, where the Caddon Water joins the Tweed some four miles north of Selkirk. Evidently this was the correct starting-point

[1] *Chron. Rishanger*, 263, 'Magister J., nepos'.

[2] *APS*, i, 449.

[3] *Chron. Lanercost*, 169; *monstratis armis*, felicitously 'wapinschaw' in H. Maxwell's translation, *The chronicle of Lanercost* (1913), 129; *Chron. Guisb.*, 269.

for an army operating south of the march. The chronicler of an earlier Anglo-Scottish war wrote of King William the Lion in 1173,

> 'Now the king of Scotland has made ready his host,
> At Caddonlee they were assembled.'[1]

The actual writ of summons has not survived but we know from the writ probably issued by the Guardians in or after 1286[2] that a national call to arms would require 'free service' and 'Scottish service'. Free service was military service *par excellence*, performed by free men – barons, thanes, knights, serjeants and other freeholders – who according to their rank and wealth would be equipped either with a knight's full armour or the rather lighter armour of a serjeant, and would be mounted on 'barded' horses, heavily built *destriers* protected by mail, or else lighter, weaker horses wearing coats of *cuir bouillé* – leather steeped in warm oil and wax. Scottish service or 'Scottish army' was demanded from the earldoms north of the Forth. It meant the attendance of able-bodied men from the 'horseless classes' – peasant farmers, herds, drovers, shepherds and hunters, fighting on foot and wearing no body armour. Indeed, if they were highlanders they would wear an early version of the kilt, producing an effect of nakedness about the lower quarters of the body which had long struck foreign observers with amazement. The weapons used by these foot soldiers were chiefly the long spear and long-handled, pointed 'Lochaber axe'. The men from Selkirk Forest were skilled archers, but presumably they used the short bow which was soon to be outclassed by the deadly English long bow. Walter of Guisborough's words suggest that the summons of 1296 was for the landholding and propertied classes only.[3] Certainly it was only the Scottish 'host' in this narrow sense, the feudal cavalry, which the English defeated. But the speed with which Andrew Murray and William Wallace raised their infantry force in the following year

---

[1] *Chron. Stephen etc.*, iii, 242–3; likewise Alexander II in 1244, *Chron. Bower*, ii, 74.

[2] Edinburgh University Library MS. 207, fo. 149v, No. 89. This brieve was discovered by Professor A. A. M. Duncan, who kindly provided me with a transcript. For a description of the Scots army in 1244, see Matthew Paris, *Chronica Majora* (ed. Luard, Rolls Ser.), vi, 518, n. 1: '500 knights and 60,000 foot. The foot were lightly armed and suitably equipped with weapons, viz., axes sharpened to a point, spears and bows.' Cf. the Dürer drawing of 1521 reproduced in *SHR*, xxx, facing 9.

[3] *Chron. Guisb.*, 269.

suggests that the machinery for summoning and training the non-feudal 'common army' was not rusty from lack of use.

The Bruces, at all events, refused to answer the summons. In the eyes of Walter of Guisborough the Bruces (whom he knew well as the patrons of Guisborough Priory) were simply like the numerous other English nobles holding land in Scotland who remained faithful to the English king. North of the border such men had become enemies of the community. Those who had not already fled were expelled and their land given to others. Annandale was placed under the earl of Buchan, to become a base for raids on Cumberland.[1] We know too that English clergy were ejected from their Scottish livings lest they form a fifth column. In Bishop Fraser's absence the St Andrews diocese was administered by two vicars-general, Master William of Kinghorn and Master Peter de Champneys. On the orders of the council of twelve they removed twenty-six English clerks from their benefices in the diocese, and doubtless similar action was taken throughout the country. Even some English members of religious orders in Scotland were expelled.[2]

Things had gone badly for Edward in Gascony and were to go worse. The French commanders, Charles of Valois and Robert count of Artois, were more than a match for the inadequate English forces under the earl of Lincoln, John of Brittany and John de St John. First the Welsh, then the Scots, prevented Edward from leading his troops in person and sending enough men and arms. The cost of the war mounted as hopes of English success faded. But despite the Gascon failure we must not underestimate the formidable war-potential of Edward I's England. The country was rich and until 1297 was as fully united behind its king as any country in that age could be. The Welsh wars of 1277, 1282-3 and 1294-5 had revolutionized the English army, and the experience and confidence which they had given to commanders and men would prove of immense value to them in Scotland. For King Edward the years of greatest danger and difficulty were from 1297 to 1303. He rode out the storm, his will-power, force of character and relentless energy surpassing those of any of his subjects. For the last four years of his life he was back on top, master of every situation save that which broke him in

[1] *Chron. Guisb.*, 270.
[2] *SHR*, xli, 5-6 and n. 1.

the end, the rising of Robert Bruce. In 1295 neither the stubborn resistance of the Scots nor the part to be played by Bruce would have been credible to Edward. He believed he had the measure of his Scottish opponents. He had seen their commoners cut to pieces at Lewes, he had thrown their nobles into confusion at Norham. 'What matter if both Welsh and Scots are our foes?' he exclaimed at Falkirk, 'let them join forces if they please. We shall beat them both in a day.'[1] But he moved with characteristic patience. In October 1295 he demanded that the border castles of Berwick, Roxburgh and Jedburgh should be handed over till the end of the French war, and asked that no French or Flemings should be allowed to enter Scotland.[2] When the Scots replied that their country was free and they would admit whom they pleased he was astonished, and when a report reached him that some English merchants had been killed at Berwick he was shocked and indignant, saying 'Who could believe such wickedness and treachery?'[3] In February 1296 the French treaty was ratified in the Scottish parliament. It was a declaration of war; but long before this the feudal host of England had been summoned to meet at Newcastle on March 1st.[4]

[1] *Chron. Guisb.*, 325–6.

[2] Ibid., 270, where (as the editor points out) Edinburgh is a mistake for Jedburgh, *Foedera*, i, 829 (=*Rotuli Scotiae*, i, 22b, cf. ibid., 21b), October 16th, 1295. Professor Rothwell, however, is not justified in speaking of an 'agreement' to surrender the castles, despite the wording of the letters. Walter of Guisborough is clearly right in stating that the Scots refused to yield them, and in fact Edward I ordered the seizure of the English property of Scotsmen by writs of the same date, October 16th; Stevenson, *Documents*, ii, No. 342.

[3] *Chron. Guisb.*, 270.

[4] *Parl. Writs*, i, 275–7 (December 16th, 1295), the recruiting expedited by instructions of February 23rd, 1296, *Cal. Docs. Scot.*, ii, No. 727. A very large force of infantry was called up in addition to the feudal levies, for 60,000 foot were to be in pay at Newcastle at the beginning of March (P.R.O., E.159/69, m. 11d. I owe this reference to Dr E. B. Fryde). The earl of Ulster with a considerable force of Irish was ordered to be at Whitehaven on March 1st (*Parl. Writs.*, i, 277), and *Chron. Guisb.*, 279, says the earl with 400 horsemen and '30,000' foot from Ireland joined King Edward at Stirling (June 1296).

5

Two Kinds of War

CHARACTERISTICALLY, the Scots were much too confident. The border was in good hands. The earl of Buchan held Annandale, Nicholas de Soules (John de Soules' nephew) held Liddesdale, and the two most important castles of Roxburgh and Berwick were commanded respectively by the Stewart and Sir William Douglas.[1] Some of Edward I's measures against the Scots had been mere pinpricks. In October 1295 he ordered land held in England by Scots to be seized, and in April 1296, he followed this up with an order that Scotsmen in England should be arrested. The order is interesting chiefly for the light it throws on the question of nationality. Contrary to a common belief, the concept of Scottish nationality and the fact that it was distinct from English nationality were clearly understood in the late thirteenth century. At the remote north Hertfordshire village of Benington, for example, an entire colony of Scotsmen was discovered, including the rector, Henry of Adderston. They had all lived there many years.[2] At Stebbing near Dunmow the sheriff found a son of Sir William Douglas, born in England and nearly two years old. This dangerous young Scot was arrested till the king should send further instructions.[3] The difference in nationality is well shown by the story of Robert de Ros,[4] lord of Wark-on-Tweed, an Englishman who went over to the Scots because of his love for a Scotswoman whom he wished to marry. When he brought men from Roxburgh for a surprise attack on Wark they used a password to tell friend from foe – an English phrase of course, since southern

[1] *Chron. Guisb.*, 279, 275.

[2] *Cal. Docs. Scot.*, ii, 173. Adderston in Cavers, a Balliol lordship.

[3] Ibid.

[4] *Chron. Guisb.*, 271–2. *Chron. Guisb.*, and *Chron. Lanercost* are the basis of the narrative that follows. On nationality, see *Memoranda de Parliamento* (ed. Maitland), pp. 192–3.

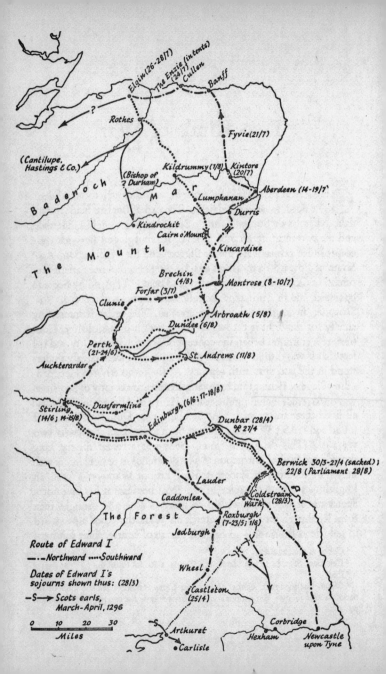

Elgin (26-28/7)
The Enzie (interns) (24/7)
Cullen
Banff
Rothes
?
Fyvie (21/7)
(Cantilupe,
Hastings & Co.)
Badenoch
Kildrummy (1/8)
Kintore (20/7)
(Bishop of ? Durham)
M a r
Lumphanan
Aberdeen (14-19/7)
Durris
Kindrochit
Cairn o' Mount
Kincardine
T h e   M o u n t h
Brechin (4/8)
Forfar (3/7)
Montrose (8-10/7)
Clunie
Arbroath (5/8)
Dundee (6/8)
Perth (21-24/6)
St. Andrews (11/8)
Auchterarder
Stirling (14/6; 14-15/8)
Dunfermline
Edinburgh (6/6; 17-18/8)
Dunbar (28/4)
R 27/4
Berwick 30/3-27/4 (sacked);
22/8 (Parliament 28/8)
Lauder
Caddonlea
Coldstream (28/3)
Wark
T h e   F o r e s t
Roxburgh (7-23/5; 1/6)
Jedburgh
Wheel
S
S
Castleton (25/4)
Corbridge
S
Arthuret
Hexham
Newcastle upon Tyne
Carlisle

Route of Edward I
—·—· Northward ······ Southward
Dates of Edward I's
sojourns shown thus: (28/3)
–S→ Scots earls,
March–April, 1296
0   10   20   30
Miles

Scots and Northumbrian English spoke the same tongue. The Northumbrians found it easy to pick up the password themselves, and so escaped. But already between the English-speaking Scot and the English-speaking Englishman, subjects of different kingdoms, a mental and emotional line of division was fixed which ran as clear as those ancient boundaries the Tweed and the Redden Burn.

The war began towards the end of March with de Ros's treachery and King Edward's rapid advance to relieve Wark. This done, he waited for the celebration of Easter (which fell this year on Lady Day) before laying siege to Berwick. Meanwhile, on Easter Monday, seven earls of Scotland and John Comyn the younger of Badenoch, the Guardian's son, crossed the fords of Solway from Annandale with a large infantry force, burning the villages from Arthuret to the suburbs of Carlisle and trying to take the city itself by storm. Ironically, the commander of Carlisle castle since October 1295 had been Robert Bruce, lord of Annandale and previously earl of Carrick, who with his young son, the future king, adhered to the English king. Although a fire started by the Scots caused great damage in the town, they lacked siege engines and made no headway against the inhabitants' stout resistance. After barely one day's 'siege' they withdrew to Annandale. Two days later (Friday, March 30th) the English army was arrayed in front of Berwick. The largest and richest town of Scotland was defended only by a ditch and timber palisade. The invaders swept over this at their first assault, taking the townsmen so much by surprise that they put up almost no fight at all. Only the thirty Flemings in the Red Hall fought to the last and were burned to death or suffocated when the building went up in flames. The castle garrison surrendered on terms, which included the condition that Douglas should be kept with the king's household till the end of the campaign.[1] Edward's magnanimity did not reach far beyond the knightly class. The men of Berwick were burgesses, merchants, artisans. By the conventions of the age, above which Edward himself never rose, such men could expect little mercy from feudal armies. Besides, they had committed outrages upon English merchants and had taunted the king himself with ribald rhymes and gestures. He gave the order that no one should be spared, and the Berwick men were killed in such numbers that their corpses became

[1] *Chron. Guisb.*, 275.

3. The Invasion of 1296

a dangerous nuisance and had to be thrown in the sea or buried in deep pits.[1] The slaughter, for which the king alone must be held responsible, went on until the frantic pleading of the clergy of the district moved him at last to pity. Their gesture was sincere enough no doubt; it was also conventional enough for Edward to understand.

In April another grim convention was observed across the hills from Berwick, in Redesdale, Coquetdale and Tynedale. The Scots earls, now based on Jedburgh, came over the Cheviots and raided purposelessly far and wide in Northumberland, burning villages, churches and monasteries. According to an English propaganda draft, they burned alive some 200 schoolboys at Corbridge,[2] a figure which seems too large to credit. Walter of Guisborough, who was not slow to relate Scottish atrocities, confines their crimes to arson.[3] Whether viewed as a reprisal or as a tactical diversion, the raid was a failure. Edward methodically set about the refounding of Berwick as an English town with English burgesses, comparable with the new towns he had built in Wales and with the *bastides* or fortified new towns of Gascony. Henceforth Berwick was to be the headquarters of the English administration of conquered Scotland, and the home of a special exchequer established for this purpose. Eventually (September 6th) a senior royal clerk, Hugh Cressingham, who had recently been chief itinerant justice in the northern counties, was put in charge of this exchequer as treasurer of Scotland.[4]

The Scots had failed to save Berwick, but their main force had not yet engaged the invaders. There is nothing to show that the Scottish leaders had any but the most conventional ideas on how to fight the war. A cavalry army must be confronted with cavalry in the open

[1] *Chron. Lanercost*, 173; Stevenson, *Wallace Docs.*, 3.

[2] Palgrave, *Docs. Hist. Scot.*, 149: 'they burned about 200 little scholars who were in the school at Corbridge learning their first letters and grammar, having blocked up the doors and set fire to the building.' This instrument (or draft) seems to have been prepared for the benefit of King Philip IV in order to demonstrate how unjust and ill-founded was his alliance with the Scots. Corbridge must be an error for Hexham. *Chron. Lanercost*, 174, says 'they collected a crowd of young schoolboys in Hexham school and, blocking the doors, set fire to the building and its inmates innocent in the sight of God.'

[3] *Chron. Guisb.*, 277. That the Scots burned the priory and town of Hexham and many other towns and villages is not in doubt, but there seems to be some uncertainty about the story of the schoolboys.

[4] *Cal. Docs. Scot.*, ii, 225. For the rehabilitation of Berwick, cf. Stevenson, *Documents*, ii, Nos. 356, 392, 406, 407, 416, 417, 418, 422, 426.

field. The rules required pitched battles and sieges, and the rules must be observed. Dunbar, the seat of the earls of Dunbar or March, was the next obstacle in Edward's path. He was in no hurry to complete the conquest of which he was confident, and it was not until April 23rd that he sent forward a cavalry force under John, Earl Warenne, to take Dunbar.[1] Earl Patrick of Dunbar was opposed to the patriots and a firm adherent of Edward. But while he was with the English king his countess, a Scottish loyalist, managed to hoodwink her husband's garrison and opened the castle to a Scottish force commanded by three other earls.[2] On Friday, April 27th, Warenne's knights, who had begun the siege of Dunbar, were attacked by the main body of King John's army, the 'feudal host' of Scotland.[3] They came up shortly after noon, a brave sight which so cheered the Scots within the castle that they raised their banners and shouted at the besiegers 'Tailed dogs, we will cut your tails off'. (The accepted way to infuriate an Englishman in the middle ages was to remind him of the popular belief that the English had tails). Warenne set his junior officers the task of preventing the garrison joining up with the main Scottish army, and with his veterans in good heart turned westward to confront it himself as it came over the brow of Spottsmuir. To reach the Scots the invaders had first to descend into the steep den cut by the Spott Burn. As they deployed to cross the burn, their ranks thinning or even out of sight altogether, the Scots thought they were fleeing. Yelling in their excitement and blowing horns loud enough to waken the dead, the Scottish horsemen left their commanding position and poured down the hill to give chase. Warenne's men were not in flight. Forming up in good order they threw themselves on the broken ranks of the Scottish host, overwhelmed them at the first onslaught and sent them swarming back across Lammermuir towards the shelter of Selkirk Forest forty miles to the west. Sir Patrick Graham stood his ground and was killed, and there were heavy casualties among the foot soldiers on the Scottish side.[4] But Dunbar is chiefly notable for the large number of dis-

---

[1] Stevenson, *Documents*, ii, 26.

[2] *Chron. Guisb.*, 277–8. For Earl Patrick, cf. Stones, *Documents*, No. 22.

[3] *Chron. Guisb.*, 278; Stevenson, *Documents*, ii, 26.

[4] Bartholomew Cotton, *Historia Anglicana* (ed. Luard, Rolls Series), 312, says the dead were, on King Edward's orders, counted under the supervision of Earl Patrick of Dunbar and Sir John Benstead, and numbered 10,052 (surely an exaggeration).

tinguished prisoners taken and for the devastating proof it had given that the feudal host of Scotland – the Crown's official military machine, on which it had depended for a century and a half – was now utterly inadequate. Viewed as a whole it was a disorderly rabble, and its members completely failed to make up for their excessive individualism by any real experience of war. With the exception of the 'battle' of Largs in 1263, in which the Scots army cannot have been numerous, there had been no serious warfare in Scotland since Alexander II's Galloway campaign in 1235.[1]

The rules of feudal warfare required that the side which had been beaten should acknowledge the fact. Then, in a gentlemanly way, terms could be discussed and ransoms arranged. There was, consequently, very little resistance to Edward I after Dunbar. The Stewart surrendered Roxburgh, Edinburgh Castle held out for only a week or so, and Stirling Castle, disgracefully, was completely abandoned, only the porter being left to hand over the keys to the invaders.[2] King John and the Comyns retired northward, without any set purpose, and at Midsummer sent messengers to Edward at Perth begging to be received to his peace and asking for surrender terms.[3] The Scots were bidden to come to Brechin Castle, where Bishop Bek of Durham told them of the harsh but surely not unexpected conditions which Edward required. John was to resign his kingdom, his seal was to be broken, and he and all his council were to renounce the French treaty.

Constitutionally or legally, Edward I was in a curious position. In his own belief he was the superior lord who had been forced to take a fief out of the hands of a tenant or vassal because the tenant had rebelled and allied himself to the lord's mortal enemy (Philip the Fair). The defaulting vassal must therefore resign the fief, which would remain in the king's hand unless he chose to grant it to another vassal. But although much that happened in 1296 can be explained by this line of reasoning, some of the king's most striking actions and one of his best-known utterances belie the notion of a feudal lord recovering possession of his fief. In the early summer of 1296 he

---

[1] The 'battle' of Ramsey, I.o.M., 1275, can hardly be reckoned a major engagement.
[2] *Chron. Lanercost.*, 178–9; *Chron. Guisb.*, 279; Stevenson, *Documents*, ii, 28.
[3] *Chron. Guisb.*, 280.

ordered the removal from Edinburgh to London of the regalia and a
mass of plate, jewellery and relics, including the Black Rood of Saint
Margaret, the holiest and most venerated relic in Scotland.[1] After he
reached 'Saint John's Town' of Perth, he commanded that the Stone
of Destiny should be moved from the abbey church of Scone and
presented to Westminster Abbey as a gift to his special patron,
Edward the Confessor.[2] The Stone of Destiny, on which the kings of
Scots had been enthroned since time immemorial, was the innermost
sacrosanct mystery among the insignia of Scottish monarchy. These
acts of plunder were the acts of a conqueror anxious for trophies and
determined to crush the pride of an independent people. His own
subjects recognized this and sang of his triumph.

> 'Their kings' seat of Scone
> is driven over down,
> to London led.'[3]

> 'I'll tell you truly what the Stone of Scotland is . . .
> Now Edward king of England has taken it,
> by the grace of Jesus and by hard fighting.
> To Saint Edward has he given it.'[4]

And the voice of Edward the Conqueror rings out in the contemp-
tuous reply with which he crushed the spineless Bruce of Annandale.
After Dunbar, Bruce put forward a plea to be allowed to take the
throne for which his father had competed in vain. 'Have we nothing
else to do,' said Edward, 'but win kingdoms for you?'[5]

Flitting aimlessly from place to place in the valleys of the north and
south Esk during the first fortnight of July 1296, King John presented
a sorry enough figure. At the old royal castle of Kincardine, on July
2nd, he confessed his rebellion in an abjectly humble document;[6] in
the kirkyard of Stracathro (July 7th) he renounced the French treaty;[7]

[1] G. Watson, 'The Black Rood of Scotland', *Transactions of the Scottish Ecclesio-
logical Society*, ii, I, 27–46, esp. 37–40.
[2] M. Dominica Legge, 'La piere d'Escoce', *SHR*, xxxviii, 109–13.
[3] *Political Songs of the English Nation*, ed. T. Wright (Camden Society, 1839), 307.
[4] *SHR*, xxxviii, 109–10.   [5] *Chron. Bower*, ii, 166.   [6] *Cal. Docs. Scot.*, ii, No. 754.
[7] Stevenson, *Documents*, ii, No. 372 (p. 60). See additional note below, p. 126.

finally at the burgh of Montrose (July 8th), he solemnly resigned his
kingdom and royal dignity to the king of England.[1] No detail
of humiliation was spared. His surcoat or tabard was embroidered
with a blazon of the royal arms. This blazon was stripped off, so that
he should suffer a total loss of face. The act gave the Scots a merciless
nickname for their wretched sovereign – Toom Tabard, the empty
surcoat which denoted King Nobody.[2] In August Balliol followed
the regalia and royal records to the Tower of London. Soon he was
moved to the relative comfort of Hertford, where he was allowed a
huntsman and ten hounds, and was not far from his own great manor
of Hitchin.[3] A few of the most prominent Scottish leaders, among
them the earl of Buchan and Comyn of Badenoch, were also sent to
England, and required to stay south of Trent.[4] Many other Scottish
barons, knights and esquires had been captured at Dunbar and were
held prisoner in various castles of the midlands, the south country and
Wales. Chief among them were the three earls (Atholl, Ross and
Menteith) who had led the force which occupied Dunbar Castle.
In recognition of their rank they went to the Tower, along with
several other noted barons and sons of barons: John Comyn the
younger of Badenoch, Richard Siward, John Moubray, John of
Inchmartin, David Graham (son of Sir Patrick), Alexander Menzies
(de Meners), and Nicholas, son of Sir Thomas Randolph. Altogether, we have the names of nearly a hundred captives whose rank
put them in the ransomable class.[5] Although most came from the
earldoms of the three earls who led them they formed a surprisingly
representative cross-section of the Scots gentry, from the Aird and
Glenurquhart west of Inverness to Nithsdale, Annandale and
Berwickshire in the south. Among the names which we have met
already was that of Sir Andrew Murray, brother of the pantler, Sir
William Murray of Bothwell. Sir Andrew was lord of Petty in
Inverness-shire, Avoch in the Black Isle and Boharm in Banffshire.[6]

---

[1] E. L. G. Stones and Margaret N. Blount, *BIHR*, xlviii, 99.

[2] *Chron. Wyntoun* (Laing), ii, 337, 'the pelure thai tuk off hys tabart (Twme-
Tabart he wes callyt efftyrwart').

[3] *Cal. Docs. Scot.*, ii, No. 1,027 (p. 256), and No. 854.

[4] Ibid., Nos. 839, 848; *Chron. Guisb.*, 284.

[5] *Cal. Docs. Scot.*, ii, No. 742. A considerable number of other documents calendared
by Bain in this volume also deal with Scots made prisoner in 1296.

[6] *Moray Registrum*, p. xxxvii; *Cal. Docs. Scot.*, ii, pp. xxix–xxx.

He had served, probably from 1289, as Justiciar of Scotia, i.e. Scotland north of Forth.[1] He went to the Tower in virtue of his office and his membership of one of the greatest Scottish baronial families. Among the names which we shall meet again was that of Sir Andrew's son and heir, Andrew Murray esquire. By chance – the sort of chance which now and again shapes the history of nations – young Andrew Murray was sent to Chester,[2] the nearest to Scotland of all the castles used to house the Scottish prisoners of war.

In July, while Thomas of Lancaster was escorting Balliol from Montrose to London, King Edward advanced steadily northward, making sure of his hold upon a conquered land and taking the homages of prominent Scots.[3] He crossed into Deeside by the Cowie Mounth, stayed for five days at Aberdeen, and then proceeded in short marches by way of Kintore, Fyvie, Banff and Cullen to the Spey.[4] Elgin, which he reached on July 26th, was the furthest point of his progress; his lieutenants – like Agricola's twelve centuries earlier – could be trusted to secure the western parts of Moray and the far north. He himself turned south to Rothes. From here a force was sent up the Spey under John de Cantilupe and John Hastings 'to search the country of Badenoch'.[5] Comyn the elder of Badenoch had submitted to the king at Montrose, but it did not follow automatically that the men of Badenoch and Lochaber, the highland districts of which he was lord,[6] would remain peaceable. The king himself crossed the hills by Invercharach at the head of the Deveron to the earl of Mar's secluded fastness of Kildrummy, and so back to the lowlands by Kincardine O'Neil and the pass of Cairn o' Mount. The bishop of Durham had accompanied or preceded Edward all the way

[1] *Chron. Bower*, ii, 148; *Family of Rose*, 29.

[2] *Cal. Docs. Scot.*, ii, 177.

[3] Ibid., *passim* between Nos. 747 and 803.

[4] Stevenson, *Documents*, ii, 28–9. During his stay of five days at Aberdeen the king seems to have gone out to Lumphanan (*Cal. Docs. Scot.*, ii, No. 787), though the fealty sworn there is puzzlingly dated July 21st. If the fealty was taken by proxy, this would affect our view of many of the fealties said to have been sworn to the king during his tour.

[5] Stevenson, *Documents*, ii, 29; under Sir John de Cantilupe, Sir Hugh Despenser and Sir John Hastings of Abergavenny.

[6] Comyn's lordship of Lochaber appears in Stevenson, *Documents*, ii, 190; note that an agreement of 1234 to which Walter Comyn lord of Badenoch set his seal was witnessed by Farquhar steward of Badenoch and Edward steward of Lochaber, *Moray Registrum*, No. 86.

to Elgin. Throughout the campaign he had behaved more like an
under-king than a prelate, with an army from St Cuthbert's Land
which is mentioned by contemporaries as quite distinct from the
king's army. From Rothes he was sent south by a different route –
probably up Stratha'an and across the upper Don into the Braes of
Mar, where at Kindrochit (now Braemar) the earl of Mar possessed
another castle.[1]

By August 22nd the king was back at Berwick. In four months he
had traversed the whole eastern part of Scotland, stayed at every
burgh and royal castle of note, and demonstrated his might to the
people. It was time to consolidate this brief summer's conquest. At
the Berwick parliament an ordinance was drawn up for the government of Scotland. Apparently the kingdom was not abolished but
remained in abeyance. Edward would rule it as direct lord, but he did
not add the title 'king of Scots' or even 'lord of Scotland' to his
royal style. The Earl Warenne, victor of Dunbar, was made lieutenant or 'keeper', Hugh Cressingham treasurer, and Walter of Amer-
sham chancellor.[2] Justices were appointed, of whom the chief was
William Ormsby, Cressingham's colleague on the northern assizes.
Sheriffs were appointed or confirmed in office, and castles were committed to a small number of trusted officials. On the English model
two escheators were appointed – officials with general oversight of
the Crown's feudal rights and revenues, Henry of Rye for north of
Forth, based apparently at Elgin, and Peter of Dunwich for the south,
entrusted with Yester in East Lothian.[3] There was a host of lesser
appointments, and different posts might be given to one official. The
clerk William de Rue (Dru), for example, had custody of the
bishopric of St Andrews because Bishop Fraser remained in France
and would not submit to Edward, and of the earldom of Fife because

---

[1] Stevenson, *Documents*, ii, 29–30. This contemporary journal (also printed in
Instrumenta Publica, 177–83, and in an early translation, P. Hume Brown, *Early
Travellers in Scotland* (1891), 2–6) states that the king stayed from July 31st to August
2nd at Kildrummy, a castle of the earl of Mar (cf. *Cal. Docs. Scot.*, ii, 196 and No.
800). The writer's form for this name, Kyndrokyn (*Instrumenta Publica*, 179), instead of Kyndromyn, suggests a confusion with Kindrochit, explicable if he had
heard that the bishop of Durham had come south through the Braes of Mar and
stayed at Kindrochit.

[2] *Rotuli Scotiae*, i, 27b; Stevenson, *Documents*, ii, 31–2; *Chron. Guisb.*, 281, 284.

[3] *Cal. Docs. Scot.*, ii, No. 853.

the earl was a minor.[1] He was also keeper of the customs of Dundee, and it was in this capacity that he encountered the Lübeck merchants who, as we have seen, were shipping hides and wool from Scotland.[2]

The more one reads or handles some of the vast quantity of records left behind by this burst of imperialist activity, the more one admires the calm ambitiousness and the extraordinary thoroughness of the thirteenth-century English monarchy as it set about governing a foreign country. Here was a feudal king, peripatetic and personally attentive to all the details of administration, ruling an empire and fighting a complex war by means of a handful of hard-working officials. It is staggering to think of the weight of responsibility that rested on such men as John Droxford, keeper of the Wardrobe, Ralph Manton, cofferer of the Wardrobe, John Sandal, Philip Willoughby, John Benstead and a few more. They had to see to the raising of vast sums of money, to the purchase of stores, weapons and equipment, to the garrisoning of castles, to a thousand and one details of day-to-day administration, for all of which they must render an exact account. There is no question that Edward I gained such success as he did enjoy in Scotland because he was able to back up his own forcefulness with the hard work of officials who in general were loyal and conscientious. Their hands were certainly not clean – corruption was more or less endemic in thirteenth-century government service – but they got the king's work done.

What of the Scots themselves? Edward was in no hurry to free the Dunbar prisoners, and with Balliol and the Comyns out of Scotland he may have thought all would be well. At all events his only major act, apart from this constraint on certain notable leaders, was somewhat legalistic, though certainly thorough. As in 1291, every substantial freeholder of land in Scotland was required to swear fealty to the king of England in his capacity – albeit unstated in his official style – of lord of Scotland. Many Scots swore fealty personally as the king made his progress to the north and back in July and August. But the vast majority of fealties, formally recorded on the 'Ragman Roll', are dated at Berwick on August 28th.[3] It is hard to believe –

---

[1] *Cal. Docs. Scot.*, ii, No. 264. William de Rue seems to have become something of a specialist in Scottish administration.

[2] P.R.O., E. 159/71, rot. 30d; above, p, 15, n. 1.

[3] *Instrumenta Publica*, 60–174; *Cal. Docs. Scot.*, ii, No. 823.

though most historians appear to believe – that all these persons were actually present together at Berwick on that or any other date. It was, to be sure, a parliament, no doubt attended by many men of substance. But to suppose that about two thousand of the gentry and clergy from every part of Scotland were assembled in such a manner not only strains credulity but seems to be based on a misunderstanding of Edward's intentions. It was not that, as Tout put it, 'a crowd of Scots of every class flocked to the victor's court and took oaths of fealty'.[1] Edward required formal, legal acknowledgement of his lordship from the appropriate persons, so that in future his subjects in North Britain should be on precisely the same footing as his subjects south of the Border.[2] Thus fealty was sworn not only by those Scots notables, such as the Bruces, who were already in his peace before war broke out, but also by certain English lay magnates and ecclesiastics who held property in Scotland. Among those doing homage, therefore, we find Brian Fitz Alan of Bedale,[3] Sir John Swinburne,[4] the abbot of Alnwick,[5] and the prior of Durham (who actually tried to do homage in place of the prior of Coldingham).[6] We even find the Italian Giacomo de Vicia, parson of Idvies in Angus and presumably a kinsman of the famous Master Bagimond – Baiamundo de Vicia – who was collector of the Crusading Tenth in Scotland in the 1280's.[7] By no stretch of the imagination can these men be regarded as defeated Scots bowing before the conqueror. The truth seems to be not that a motley gathering of 'Scots of every class' rendered homage, but that certain limited and well-defined classes of persons who held property in Scotland were required to provide written and sealed instruments of homage and fealty. Tenants-in-chief of the Crown and their heirs, substantial under-tenants and their heirs, officers and burgesses of some leading east-country burghs, heads of religious houses, a high proportion of the beneficed clergy (especially those who were university graduates) – these are the classes who make up by far the greater part of the names on the Ragman Roll. A contemporary

[1] *History of England, 1216–1377*, 198.

[2] *Cal. Docs. Scot.*, ii, 197. So in 1291: Glasgow Univ. Lib. MS. Gen. 1053, fo. 10ᵛ.
[3] Ibid., 196.   [4] Ibid., 200.   [5] Ibid., 204.

[6] Ibid., 196; *Historiae Dunelmensis Scriptores Tres* (ed. J. Raine, Surtees Soc.), 84.

[7] *Cal. Docs. Scot.*, ii, 211; cf. A. I. Dunlop, 'Bagimond's Roll', in *Miscellany* (SHS), vi (1939), 6–10.

description says that there were present at the Berwick parliament all the bishops (in fact there seem to have been only three out of a possible total of twelve), the abbots, priors, earls, barons and the 'superiors' (*souverains*) of all the common people.[1] This, if true, would make a large enough gathering, but very many fewer than two thousand.

To judge from the Roll it looks as though the names and fealties were collected on a basis of sheriffdoms, and it is likely that during July and August the sheriffs were responsible for taking the fealties and sending or bringing the instruments recording them to the English officials at Berwick. Several features of the consolidated list point to the fundamentally legalistic nature of the process. For example, a considerable number of names appear more than once. Sometimes, as in the case of Sir John Stewart of Jedburgh (the Stewart's brother), a man's name will appear once for each sheriffdom in which he held land.[2] At other times the repetition is hard to explain, but the presence of repeated names argues against the physical presence of the homagers. Again, among the Lothian names we find not only Simon of Restalrig, heir to the barony of Restalrig, but also his father John who (as we have seen) was in fact *non compos mentis*.[3] Was the idiot laird of Restalrig actually brought to Berwick to perform his homage?

One feature of the Roll has always interested historians: the absence of the name of William Wallace. In truth, a more surprising thing is the absence of the name of his brother, Malcolm, since it was he, evidently, who held land in Elderslie as a vassal of the Stewart. William Wallace may not have been judged a landholder of enough substance to justify obtaining fealty. But the list of names from the Stewart's great Lordship of Renfrew and Paisley is uncommonly full and thorough, including such apparently humble and obscure men as Thomas Brewster of the Forest of Paisley and Thomas the Wright

---

[1] Stevenson, *Documents*, ii, 31. The local inquests held at Berwick at the time of parliament, given in *Cal. Docs. Scot.*, ii, No. 824, prove that a fair number of gentry from the southern sheriffdoms of Wigtown, Ayr, Dumfries, Fife, Lothian and Berwick were present personally. In 1291 fealties were taken by sheriffdoms and the sheriff had discretion as to which freeholders should take the oath. The clerks clearly thought it odd that in the Merse Edmund of Bundington had taken the oath though only a 'simple countryman' (*simplex patriota*); Glasgow Univ. Lib. MS. Gen. 1053, fos. 10–11.

[2] *Cal. Docs. Scot.*, ii, 193, 199, 203.   [3] Ibid., 198, 201.

of Blackhall (in Paisley).[1] It is possible that the sheriff of Lanark was unable to obtain the homages of Malcolm and William Wallace because they deliberately chose not to perform them. Such a refusal would not only be in line with Wallace's whole conduct throughout the war, it would also explain why he was regarded as an outlaw when the rising of 1297 began. This, indeed, seems to be implied by Walter of Guisborough.[2]

In conquered Scotland the treasurer Hugh Cressingham quickly gained control of the occupation régime. He was the busy man on the spot, whereas Warenne, his nominal superior, disliked Scotland so much and took such a casual attitude towards his duties that he remained on his estates in Yorkshire.[3] Cressingham seems a typical enough example of his kind, though personally perhaps more obnoxious than most. Officious, smooth, with the pushfulness which often characterizes men of illegitimate birth, he had made his own way in the king's service.[4] Scotland might have been the steppingstone to higher things. As it turned out, his rich Yorkshire living of Rudby, his many prebends and his little property in Hendon and Finchley, suitable for a civil servant's retirement, were as far as he ever got.[5] The Scots despised and hated him, and dubbed him the 'treacherer'.[6] His task was to raise the Crown revenues, to oversee the English administration, and to keep the peace. We have few details of his administration. Among his measures was a proclamation that all stores of wool throughout Scotland should be seized for the king's use and sent to the nearest seaport; but there is no evidence that the government did not intend, eventually, to pay for the wool thus seized.[7] Edward believed firmly that the Scottish problem was solved. The details could be left to his ministers. He himself returned to more pressing affairs, the resumption of the war against France, the development of the Flemish alliance and the most serious political

[1] Cal. Docs. Scot., ii, 213.

[2] Chron. Guisb., 294.

[3] Ibid.

[4] Ibid., and 303, and references, passim, in Cal. Docs. Scot., ii (esp. No. 951), and in Stevenson, Documents.

[5] Chron. Guisb., 302; Cal. Docs. Scot., ii, No. 951.

[6] Chron. Guisb., 303. The pun doubtless sounded less forced in French, but it could hardly have been a piece of popular humour.

[7] F. W. Maitland, Memoranda de Parliamento (Rolls Series, 1893), 184, referring to 1296–7; Rot. Scot., i, 40b (Ayr merchants to send their wool to Berwick).

crisis of his reign, the stiff clerical, mercantile and baronial opposition which occupied his attention from the close of 1296 until after his departure for Flanders on August 22nd, 1297.

Events were to prove that the English, from their king downward, had seriously misjudged the Scottish situation, though not without good reason. Ever since the reign of Alexander II, the leadership of the community of the realm of Scotland, especially in acts of resistance to English encroachment, had rested with the prelates of the church and with a large section of the feudal nobility among whom the great family of Comyn had played a dominant role. In a sense, the war of 1296 had been their war, the war of the Comyns, assisted by the bishops of St Andrews and Glasgow. It had been fought according to their notions of warfare, and they had been decisively defeated. The Comyns themselves, the king in whose name they had fought, and a large number of the military leaders of Scotland who had adhered to them, were all *hors de combat*. The church, by contrast, was much less affected by the defeat. Fraser of St Andrews and Crambeth of Dunkeld remained in France, out of Edward's reach. Wishart of Glasgow, it is true, had been compelled to do homage. It is doubtful if he set much store by this, and it must in any case be noted that out of a possible total of twelve bishops of Scotland only three are known to have done homage to Edward – Wishart of Glasgow, Henry Cheyne of Aberdeen, and Thomas Dalton of Whithorn, who was a protégé of the Bruces and a suffragan of the archbishop of York.[1] The ageing Archibald of Moray may have done homage, though it is not recorded.[2] Three bishops were overseas, three bishoprics were vacant, nothing is known of the bishop of Argyll, and the bishop of Sodor and Man seems to have been hostile to Edward I.[3] All the same, even though the church had conspicuously not been won over to the English king,[4] a handful of bishops could not start a fresh war. At best they could fire others with courage and determination and keep the Scottish cause warm at the court

---

[1] *Cal. Docs. Scot.*, ii, 196.

[2] Ibid., No. 839, a protection for the bishop for two years from September 8th, 1296, suggests that he was in the king's peace then.

[3] He had failed to appear in time for the Berwick parliament (*Rotuli Scotiae*, i, 24), and later was put in prison.

[4] On this in general, see *Kingdom of the Scots*, 233–54.

of Philip the Fair and at the papal *curia*. The stark fact remained that many of the Scottish nobles were prisoners, and that a number of others – among them Bruce of Annandale, his son the young earl of Carrick, and the earls of Angus and Dunbar – were on the English side.

It is more than sixty years since Evan Barron, in his book *The Scottish War of Independence*,[1] showed us how big a part the north of Scotland played in the rising of 1297, taught us to see Wallace in perspective instead of regarding him as an isolated folk-hero, and stated that the Edwardian occupation, though doubtless the occasion, was emphatically not the cause of the Scottish bid for independence. It may be doubted if popular opinion has yet caught up with Dr Barron or even wishes to catch up. For his pugnacious and convincing criticism of the received view appeared to deprive Wallace of his heroic stature, and by spreading the action of the play across a wider stage he lessened the dramatic tension. There is much deeper emotional satisfaction in the story of David and Goliath than in a complex account of the community of the realm, bereft of leadership, struggling and stumbling to regain it. The popular view remains closer to that expressed by the late G. M. Trevelyan in his *History of England*.

'Deserted by her nobles, Scotland discovered herself. The governors whom Edward I left behind him were incapable and cruel and the foreign soldiery made the Scots feel their subjection. . . . A guerrilla chief of genius, a tall man of iron strength who suddenly appears on the page of history as if from nowhere, defeated at Stirling Bridge end an English army under its blundering feudal chief the earl of Warenne. . . . Edward I had thought that he was going to yoke Scotland to England through the ordinary feudal apparatus of the time. His mistake was very natural, for by the accepted standards of the day his proceedings were less abnormal than Wallace's amazing appeal to the Scottish democracy to save the Scottish nation. . . . Society was divided, not perpendicularly into nations but horizontally into feudal strata. *And Edward I had the feudal magnates of Scotland mainly on his side.* Anglo-Normans, owning estates in England as well as Scotland were excusably lukewarm in their Scottish patriotism and

[1] Evan Macleod Barron, *The Scottish War of Independence* (London: James Nisbet, 1913). In this work I have used the second edition (Inverness: Robert Carruthers, 1934).

anxious not to quarrel with England's king, from whom they held their English lands.'[1]

In this stricture on the Scots nobles, Dr Trevelyan was echoing the classical statement by Joseph Stevenson of what must surely be one of the hardest-dying half-truths of Scottish history.

'The truth is,' Stevenson wrote, 'and it must be confessed with shame and sorrow, that the Scottish nobility were not true to Scotland. . . . With few exceptions these nobles held lands in England; and their ardour was cooled and their efforts paralysed by the knowledge that their possessions in that kingdom would be forfeited to the Crown on the first moment that they exhibited any active sympathy with their countrymen in arms against Edward.'[2]

In fact, the Edwardian conquest of 1296 had been too easy and the occupation which followed it was too superficial. It may be doubted if more than a handful of leading Scots (other than those already committed to Edward I when war broke out) had resigned themselves to a permanent English occupation and overlordship. We can be certain that neither Bishop Fraser, down to his death at Auteuil near Paris on August 20th, 1297,[3] nor his colleague Matthew Crambeth of Dunkeld, had given up the struggle. In Scotland, Bishop Wishart of Glasgow had lost none of his influence or animosity towards English rule. No homage to Edward was ever done by Sir John de Soules, who perhaps remained in France and whose career shows continuous and consistent support for the Scottish cause.[4] What is often thought of as Wallace's rising in 1297 was in truth a general resumption of resistance on a national scale, but with an inevitable shift in leadership. Since the Comyns and most of the earls were temporarily discredited and not free agents, the lead was now taken

[1] Edn of 1945, 218 (my italics).

[2] Stevenson, Documents, i, pp. lii–liii.

[3] Dowden, Bishops, 21, Fordun's 'Aytuil' doubtless for Auteuil. Fraser was buried in the Dominican Priory in Paris. Cal. Docs. Scot., ii, 265, shows that the bishop was against King Edward's peace in November, 1296.

[4] Chron. Lanercost, 168–9, says that the bishops of St Andrews and Dunkeld remained in France, but the knights and esquires associated with them had to beg a lift home in a German ship trading to Scotland. Ingram de Umfraville certainly returned and did homage to Edward I (Cal. Docs. Scot., ii, 199, 224), but there is no record of any homage by or restitution to John de Soules. Moreover, a letter of Philip IV of February 25th, 1298, is evidence of continued Scottish representation at Paris (cf. Foedera, i, 861 and G. P. Cuttino, ed., Gascon Calendar of 1322 (1949), p. 41, No. 420).

largely by men who had supported the Competitor Bruce against
Balliol and the Comyns. Chief among them were Robert Wishart
and James the Stewart. Of the Guardians of 1286–92, they were the
only two left in Scotland. Although both were great lords in the
lower Clyde valley, office and connexions alike made them national
rather than local figures. Wishart belonged to an old east-country
family whose seat was Conveth in Mearns, an estate which then
gave its name to the parish now called Laurencekirk.[1] The family's
origins are unknown, but the surname – Guiscard, Wiscard, Wishart,
'cunning' – is Norman-French. Robert's uncle William, a graduate
of Oxford and perhaps of Paris also, had been archdeacon of St
Andrews, chancellor of Scotland and bishop of St Andrews. Robert
himself had become bishop of Glasgow as long ago as 1273, and by
the 1290's an unmistakably east-country and Wishart influence was
at work in the diocese. The dean of Glasgow was Thomas Wishart,
the archdeacon very possibly John Wishart, and the archdeacon of
Teviotdale was Master William Wishart. The sub-dean of Glasgow,
Master Thomas of Dundee, was a relative of Ralph of Dundee, a
prominent clerk of King Alexander III. Thomas of Dundee held the
deanery of Brechin, and in 1296, no doubt on the initiative of the
council of twelve of whom Bishop Wishart was one, he was
appointed bishop of Ross. The chancellor of Glasgow was Master
William Lamberton, almost certainly one of the Lambertons of
Linlathen near Dundee.[2] It is presumably a mark of Wishart's influence that in the last year of Balliol's rule the Official of Glasgow,
Master Alexander Kennedy, had been made chancellor of Scotland
in place of the Englishman Thomas of Hunsingore.[3] Agile, perhaps
rather plausible, fertile of ideas, Wishart was not of the stuff of
which martyrs and heroes are made, though by the close of his long
life he had suffered deeply in the cause of Scottish independence.
Again and again he bent under English pressure, but he never broke.
There was something indefatigable about the old man, and it is no
wonder that the English found him exasperating.

The Stewart presents a different problem. We cannot get as close
to James Stewart as we can to Wishart, yet something of the character

[1] *Kingdom of the Scots*, 239–40, and for what follows, 241–3.
[2] M. Ash, in *The Scottish Tradition* (ed. G. W. S. Barrow), 44.
[3] *Kingdom of the Scots*, 242; Stevenson, *Documents*, ii, 61.

of the man seems to emerge, however dimly, from his actions. Cautious and devious, possessed of a recognisably 'Stewart' canniness, he was not a man to make the first move, yet neither was he an ineffectual figure. In 1297 he seems to play a double game, but there is no doubt where his inclinations lay. He was certainly among the nobles of whom Walter of Guisborough wrote that their hearts were far from the English king, no matter where their bodies might be.[1] The distinction of his office and the size of his lordships, Renfrew, Bute and Kyle Stewart, as well as lands in Teviotdale, Lauderdale and Lothian, made him one of the greatest magnates of Scotland. In addition, his marriage to Gelis de Burgh, the earl of Ulster's sister, gave him a stake in northern Ireland. If, instead of impugning his patriotism as lukewarm, we ask what the effect would have been had he thrown his influence on the side of England, we can better appreciate the value of his part in the Scottish struggle. But there is more to it than that. William Wallace, far from being a 'man from nowhere', belonged to one of the knightly families that made up the Stewart's feudal following, and came, what is more, from the parish of Paisley which was at the very centre of the great Stewart fief. Many of the families which had composed the fief when it was founded in the twelfth century still survived at the end of the thirteenth, and the Wallaces, doubtless of Shropshire origin like so many of the others, were among them.[2] It would, of course, be absurd to set James Stewart on the stage of history beside Wallace, one of those rare immortals who tower head and shoulders above their contemporaries. But in 1297 Wallace owed such standing as he possessed in the community of the realm of Scotland to his place among the feudal vassals of James Stewart. The Lanercost Chronicle, indeed, states plainly that Wishart and the Stewart plotted the revolt and instigated Wallace to the open violence which they dared not resort to themselves.[3] This cannot be the whole story. Wallace, still a very young man, must already have performed some feats of daring and laid the foundations of his immense popular reputation. But it can hardly be doubted that Wallace was closely involved with Wishart

[1] *Chron. Guisb.*, 299; on James's career see *The Stewarts*, xii, No. 2, 77-91.

[2] *Kingdom of the Scots*, 347, 349-50, 352-3.

[3] *Chron. Lanercost*, 190; cf. also *Chron. Guisb.*, 296, calling the bishop of Glasgow and the Stewart the authors of the revolt. So also Boniface VIII. writing in 1302, *Foedera*, i, 942.

Banff
Avoch
Elgin
The Enzie
Castle
Urquhart
Inverness
M
o
r
a
y
Spey
Mar
Aberdeen
Dee
The Mounth
Argyll
Dundee
Scone
St. Andrews
11 Sep.
1297
Stirling
Glasgow
Haddington
Torphichen
Berwick
Paisley
Lanark
Irvine
Douglas-
dale
The Forest
Roxburgh
Bolton
Ayr
Ancrum
Rothbury
Rothbury
Forest
Annandale
Nithsdale
Newcastle
upon Tyne
Hexham
Corbridge
Carlisle
Cockermouth

///////// Southern limits of
Wallace's invasion
of Northern England

0 10 20 30 40 50
Miles

and the Stewart, nor that at the outset he owed much to the fact that
the Stewart was his patron and friend. His ties with Wishart are
shown by two interesting details. When the bishop surrendered in
July, Wallace was so enraged that he emerged from Selkirk Forest
to make a raid on Wishart's palace at Ancrum and carry off his
belongings, arms, horses and even his family.[1] The emotion behind
this act speaks of close relations between the two men. Later, when
Wallace had driven the English out of all but a few castles, he sent
his men to besiege Roxburgh expressly because the bishop of
Glasgow was imprisoned there, and evidently too valuable, in
Wallace's view, to be left in English hands.[2]

The rising of 1297 was partly spontaneous, partly organized. Early
in the year there were disturbances in the west highlands, not necessarily anti-English but all grist to the patriots' mill.[3] Rather later,
probably by the beginning of May, there were outbreaks of violence
in Aberdeenshire and Galloway.[4] Some time during May Wallace
slew the English sheriff of Lanark, William Hesilrig, and this gave
the signal for a general revolt.[5] Wallace's followers are supposed to
have been outlaws like himself, peasants and common folk. Perhaps
most were, but for his next much bolder exploit he must have had
horses and horsemen. The English justiciar William Ormsby was
holding his court at Scone. He was set upon by Wallace with so little
warning that he barely escaped with his life and left the Scots valu-

[1] *Chron. Guisb.*, 299. A letter of July 23rd, 1297, probably written by Cressingham,
told Edward I that Wallace lay in Selkirk Forest with a large company, Stevenson,
Documents, ii, No. 453. The raid on the *domus episcopi*, doubtless the bishop's palace at
Ancrum on the edge of the Forest, would have taken place a few weeks later.

[2] *Chron. Guisb.*, 314.

[3] *Rotuli Scotiae*, i, 40.

[4] Ibid., i, 42b; Stevenson, *Documents*, ii, No. 437. The Lancashire sheriff of Aberdeen, Henry of Lathom, went over to the Scots, *Cal. Docs. Scot.*, ii, No. 972.

[5] Stevenson, *Wallace Docs.*, 191; *Cal. Docs. Scot.*, ii, No. 418; *Chron. Fordun*, i,
328; *Chron. Bower*, ii, 170; *Scalacronica*, 123. Sir Thomas Grey, of Heaton on the Till,
no doubt preserves the true form of the sheriff's name, William de Hesilrig. A
father and son of this name witness *Laing Chrs.*, No. 16 (c. 1292–5) and occur in
another north Northumberland document, ibid., No. 14. Hesilrig is Hazelrigg, in
Chatton, north Northumberland, a few miles from Heaton. Joseph Bain, in an unhappy passage (*Cal. Docs. Scot.*, ii, pp. xxvii–xxviii), argues that the English sheriff
of Lanark or Clydesdale was really a Scot, Sir Andrew Livingstone, who was sheriff
of Lanark for the financial year ending November 1296. There is no reason to doubt
that Wallace slew an English sheriff named William Hesilrig.

4. 1297 and early 1298

able booty.[1] This daring raid had the effect of shutting up the English
north of the Forth inside a few castles. Sir William Douglas, whose
movements after the surrender of Berwick are not recorded, joined
Wallace for the raid upon Scone. Douglas was a rough and reckless
man. He had been in trouble with Edward I for abducting and
forcibly marrying an English widow while she was staying with
relatives in Scotland.[2] He had flouted the Guardians by imprisoning
three of his own men without trial, beheading one and letting another die in jail.[3] He had shown contempt for King John by keeping
the royal justiciar's officers in Douglas Castle for a night and a day
against their will.[4] Though Douglas may have been violent and unruly, there was no denying that he was also a nobleman. The lords
of Douglas had been tenants-in-chief for a century and a half and
were kin to the great family of *de Moravia* or Murray. William
Douglas himself, before he carried off Eleanor Ferrers, had been
married to Elizabeth Stewart, James the Stewart's sister. He had
therefore a natural place among the south-western magnates who
came to the fore in the summer of 1297, and his leadership in a revolt
plotted by Wishart and his former brother-in-law is quite understandable.

Less easily understandable, yet profoundly significant, was the
fact that along with Wishart, the Stewart, his brother Sir John, Sir
William Douglas, Sir Alexander Lindsay and William Wallace, we
find as a leader of the native resistance the young Robert Bruce, earl
of Carrick and king to be. He was twenty-two years old and had
lately been serving Edward I along with his father. His family had
been expelled from Scotland by the council of twelve, and it was the
English conquest which put them back in possession of their lands.
Surely young Bruce had everything to gain by loyalty to Edward,
everything to lose by supporting the hopeless and reckless enterprise
of Wishart and the Stewart, for all they were old friends of his
family? Yet he joined the Scots. It was the crucial decision of his life,
far more crucial than his similar decision in 1305 or 1306 to defy
King Edward and send the fiery cross through Scotland. Walter of

[1] *Chron. Guisb.*, 295.
[2] *Cal. Docs. Scot.*, ii, No. 357, 358, 365, 429, 431, 468.
[3] *APS*, i, 449.
[4] Ibid., i, 448.

Guisborough says that when the Scots revolt began the bishop of
Carlisle had misgivings about Bruce's loyalty and made him take a
special oath of allegiance.[1] He goes on to say that Bruce then joined
the Scots because he was a Scotsman. This explanation is too simple
for modern historians, who believe it impossible because they hold
that Scottish nationalism was the product rather than the cause of the
war of independence. Nevertheless, it seems to be no more than the
truth. After making a mock attack on Douglasdale to deceive the
English, Bruce assembled his father's vassals, the knights of Annandale, and told them that his Carlisle oath had been given under
duress. 'No man holds his own flesh and blood in hatred and I am no
exception. I must join my own people [that is, the men of Carrick]
and the nation in which I was born.' He asked the knights to follow
him, but they were unwilling. Their lord, Bruce of Annandale, remained with Edward I. As he had chosen, so would they. It was thus
that the young Bruce, who as earl could contribute the traditional
'army' of an earldom to the common cause, threw off his father's
tutelage and made the first independent political decision of his life.
It was apparently said that he already aimed at the throne. Whatever the
truth of this, there is no evidence that any such idea inspired the movement of Scottish resistance as a whole until after the collapse of 1304.

Militarily speaking, Wishart, the Stewart and Bruce were fumbling and inept. Henry Percy[2] and Robert Clifford[3] quickly recruited levies from the English border counties and moved with
great dispatch through Annandale and Nithsdale to reach Ayr by the
end of June.[4] The Scots, chiefly foot soldiers and much weaker than
the English in mounted troops, were at Irvine a few miles north. As
soon as Percy's cavalry came in sight the Stewart and Douglas sent
envoys to ask if the English were empowered to receive a formal
surrender, an act of funk which so disgusted one of the Scots,

---

[1] *Chron. Guisb.*, 295.

[2] Henry Percy the elder, grandson of John de Warenne, earl of Surrey, succeeded
his brother, *c.* 1293, and played a prominent part in the Scottish wars of Edward I
and Edward II until his death in October 1314. He was succeeded by a son of the
same name.

[3] Robert Clifford, son of Roger Clifford and Isabel de Vieuxpont, an heiress of the
great northern landowning family of Vieuxpont of Brougham, Westmorland.
Like Henry Percy, Robert Clifford played a major part in Anglo-Scottish history,
until his death at Bannockburn.

[4] *Chron. Guisb.*, 297–8.

Richard Lundie, that he promptly changed sides. But it is the Scots'
political tactics, not their lack of military skill, which are important.
The Scots leaders spun out the surrender negotiations for the best
part of a month and even then Bruce did not submit.[1] It is clear,
moreover, that Wishart, Bruce and the Stewart – one bishop, one
earl, one baron – regarded themselves as spokesmen not only for
themselves and their immediate following but also for 'the whole
community of the realm of Scotland';[2] Guardians in fact if not in
name. They talked in political terms about ancient rights and customs, and declared that the 'middle folk' of Scotland would be
ruined by Edward's demands for overseas service.[3] Although the
bishop and Douglas were imprisoned before the end of July and
although the Stewart seems to have given some assurances of good
behaviour, their attitude was not mere bravado. In the first place, the
delay was of enormous value to Wallace, who, left to his own de-
vices, was having much greater military success. Secondly, at the
very time that Wishart and the rest were beginning negotiations, on
July 10th, Hugh Cressingham, then at Bolton in Northumberland,
wrote a private letter to the deputy treasurer in London. He explained why the sum of £2,000 he had persuaded the king to send
him was needed urgently to meet expenses in Scotland. 'Not one of
the sheriffs, bailiffs or officials of the Lord King appointed within
that kingdom can at this time raise a penny of the revenues of their
bailiwicks, on account of a multitude of different perils which daily
and continually threaten them.'[4] A fortnight later he wrote to the

---

[1] Stevenson, *Documents*, ii, No. 467, shows that Wishart, Bruce and the Stewart
had not come to confirm the peace by August 5th. For the course of the negotiations,
see ibid., Nos. 447, 452, 453, 454, 462, 464; Palgrave, *Docs. Hist. Scot.*, 197-200.
Ibid., 199-200, shows that a condition of Bruce's submission was the surrender as
hostage of his only child Marjorie, who can only have been a few years old at most.
Cal. Docs. Scot., ii, 247, shows that Bruce had not submitted by early November
1297, and it is virtually certain that he neither submitted nor surrendered his daughter.

[2] Stevenson, *Documents*, ii, No. 447: '[a] Robert, counte e James Seneschal e a
tuite la comunaulte du royaume de Escoce', the context making it probable that in
this phrase the English leaders were replying in the terms used by their Scots opponents. If 'Robert' refers to Bruce, the whole of Wishart's name has been lost through
injury to the parchment.

[3] *Chron. Guisb.*, 299; Stevenson, *Documents*, ii, No. 452.

[4] P.R.O., E 159/70, rot. 29d. This letter may be said to carry even greater weight
than the better-known one mentioned in the next note, for it was a private letter
from one financial official to another.

king in even stronger terms. 'By far the greater part of your counties in the Scottish kingdom are still not provided with keepers, because they have been killed, besieged or imprisoned, or have abandoned their bailiwicks and dare not go back. *And in some shires the Scots have appointed and established bailiffs and officials.* Thus no shire is properly kept save for Berwickshire and Roxburghshire, and they only recently.'[1]

In other words, behind the high-flown stipulations of Wishart and the rest lay knowledge of a country-wide sabotage of the occupation régime and a methodical attempt to restore the independent administration of the realm. That all this was the unaided work of Wallace is impossible to believe. He was much too busy, gathering his men in the fastnesses of Selkirk Forest in July,[2] laying siege to Dundee Castle in August.[3] Barons, knights and clergy must have co-operated to get the native machinery working again. To be sure, after the capitulation of Irvine, Wallace's primacy of leadership could not be challenged. 'The common folk of the land followed him as their leader and ruler; the retainers of the great lords adhered to him; and even though the lords themselves were present with the English king in body, at heart they were on the opposite side.'[4] Wallace's audacity and success fired the people south of the Mounth with patriotic fervour, but to gather and train an army some revenue and an organized mobilization, however rough and ready, were surely needed. Hence the appointment of local officers. The 'free service' or knight-service of Scotland had largely disintegrated, but there was still the 'Scottish service' to which the able-bodied commonalty were bound.

While all this was happening in southern and middle Scotland, a strikingly similar rising broke out on the north side of the Mounth. Before the summer was over it had swept the English out of Moray and the country between Spey and Dee. This critically important revolt, the work of Andrew Murray who some time in the past winter had got away from Chester to his native heath, makes a stirring tale. Dr Barron has told it so exhaustively that we need only

[1] Stevenson, *Documents*, ii, No. 455.
[2] Ibid., No. 453.
[3] *Chron. Bower*, ii, 171.
[4] *Chron. Guisb.*, 299.

recapitulate its main features here.[1] It began in May with an assault by Andrew Murray and the townsfolk of Inverness[2] upon the Loch Ness-side stronghold of Castle Urquhart. By mid-July the insurgents had the free run of the country as far east as the Spey. By early August they had seized the English-held castles of the north, Inverness, Elgin, Banff and the rest. A number of north-country Scots lords tried, somewhat half-heartedly, to quell the rising, which seems to have been strongly popular in character although its leader was the son and heir of a prominent baron. In June King Edward sent north the two Comyns,[3] John of Badenoch and John of Buchan, to help keep the peace. Their colleagues on the spot were the bishop of Aberdeen, Henry Cheyne (a consistent supporter of the English), Countess Effie of Ross, and the heir of Earl Donald of Mar, whose ancient Pictish name of Gartnait is further evidence of the 'Celtic revival'.[4] Guisborough, writing after the event,[5] and Cressingham, writing at the time (August 5th),[6] both believed that the Comyns and most of the Scots earls were either sitting on the fence or had already jumped down on the Scottish side. The details we shall never know, but the indisputable fact is that by the end of August Andrew Murray and William Wallace, north and south of the mountains respectively, had gathered formidable armies of foot soldiers. By ancient tradition these men were accustomed to be mobilized and to serve in the 'armies' of their respective earldoms, unless they lived in districts like Moray or Gowrie where the Crown took the place of an earl. But when we find Macduff, son of an earl of Fife, joining Wallace;[7] Bruce of Carrick leading out the 'army' of his earldom; the earl of Buchan's loyalty to England at first suspect and soon proved worthless; and, finally, Cressingham writing to Edward that no one knows what is happening north of the Forth 'on

---

[1] Scottish War of Independence, 32–57.

[2] Cal. Docs. Scot., ii, Nos. 921, 922, 923.

[3] Chron. Guisb., 297, ambos illos comites Johannem de Badenaughe et Johannem de Bughan. Badenoch was not an earl, but Guisborough seems to have thought he was, cf., ibid., 366.

[4] Stevenson, Documents, ii, Nos. 456–60. For the name Gartnait in early Pictish history, cf. Anderson, Early Sources, references in index.

[5] Chron. Guisb., 297.

[6] Stevenson, Documents, ii, No. 467.

[7] Ibid., No. 462.

account of the conduct of the earls who are there',[1] it is hardly rash to guess that with a degree of connivance from some of the earls Murray and Wallace recruited what they called the 'army of Scotland' by the customary methods of raising what had been known since time immemorial as 'Scottish army'. If the earls' patriotism seems lukewarm, we must not censure them too harshly. They had much to lose if things went wrong, not because they had lands in England but because their whole way of life was geared to settled residences, regular revenues and conspicuous consumption. It was hard for them to wage a war that was not essentially a matter of cavalry and castles.

We do not know exactly when these two young men, Andrew Murray the baron's son and William Wallace the knight's son, joined forces. It must have been towards the end of August. Warenne and Cressingham had at last bestirred themselves. They advanced from Berwick to Stirling with a respectable force of cavalry and a body of infantry, many of them Welsh.[2] The castle of Stirling and the crossing of the Forth which it guarded, formed the key which would unlock the two halves of Scotland. Murray and Wallace had drawn up their men on the south-facing slope of the Abbey Craig, one mile north of the narrow bridge across the Forth which stood less than half a mile below Stirling Castle. From the north end of the bridge to the foot of the Abbey Craig ran a causeway, on either side of which lay meadow and corn fields, not necessarily swampy as is sometimes said,[3] but very probably soft ground, not suitable for deploying heavy cavalry. Beyond this, on either side, flowed the river, for Stirling Bridge was sited near the southern tip of a great horseshoe loop. The bridge itself would take only two horsemen abreast. Warenne reached Stirling in the first week of September. He was met by certain Scots lords, among them James Stewart and

---

[1] Stevenson, *Documents*, ii, No. 467, p. 226.

[2] *Chron. Guisb.*, 301, gives English strength as 1,000 cavalry and 50,000 foot, against a Scottish force of 180 horse and 40,000 foot. The numbers of both foot and horse are doubtless exaggerated.

[3] J. H. Ramsay, *Dawn of the Constitution*, 453. *Dunfermline Registrum*, No. 216, shows that the lands of Cornton, just west of the Causeway, paid teinds in oats, *c.* 1218. This record speaks of teinds of corn and fish of Airthrey and Cornton 'west of Causewayhead [*a capite de la chaucee*] next beside the Spittal as far as the peatary of Airthrey'. There was also north of the Forth an area called the 'burgh grieve's flat', part of which at least, in the direction of Airthrey and of Stirling Bridge, was regularly ploughed.

Earl Malcolm of Lennox, who suggested that if they were given a little time they might be able to pacify the Scots. They returned on September 10th empty-handed, but promised to appear with forty barded horses on the following day. As they rode off, the earl of Lennox met some English troops foraging, and after high words one of them was killed. An angry murmur of treachery arose in the army, which Warenne had difficulty in quelling. At dawn the next day many of the infantry were sent over the bridge, but were recalled because Warenne overslept. When at length he rose, they were sent over again, but again recalled, this time because the Stewart and Lennox appeared and the English thought they had come with news of a Scottish submission. The opposite was true: they explained that they could not detach any of their own men from Wallace, but it may be doubted whether they tried very hard.[1] Finally, Warenne sent two Dominican friars to Wallace to ask if he would yield. 'Tell your commander,' was his reply, 'that we are not here to make peace but to do battle to defend ourselves and liberate our kingdom. Let them come on, and we shall prove this in their very beards.'[2]

If Warenne had shown tactical skill at Dunbar, it deserted him now. Sir Richard Lundie asked the earl to send him with a detachment of horse and foot up river a little to the wide Fords of Drip,[3] where sixty men could cross the river simultaneously. 'Once we get round to the enemy's rear,' he said, 'you can cross the bridge safely.' This was sound advice, but it was overridden by the treasurer Cressingham. As if he had not done enough damage by sending home reinforcements on grounds of expense, he now urged for the same reason that no more time should be wasted, but that battle should be joined at once. So Warenne gave the order to cross. As soon as they judged that enough knights and infantry had come over, Murray and Wallace sent their spearmen rushing down the hill, along the causeway and over the meadowland, to cut the English

[1] Chron. Guisb., 300. The certainty of Chron. Lanercost, 190, that the Stewart had treacherously led the English to destruction surely exaggerates his influence with Warenne and Cressingham, of whom he was virtually a prisoner.

[2] Chron. Guisb., 300.

[3] Ibid., the vadum non longe ab hinc was obviously at Drip, the highest ford over the combined Teith and Forth, referred to as a crucial crossing in 1304, Cal. Docs. Scot., ii, Nos. 1,462, 1,470.

army in two at the bridge. The movement was brilliantly successful. The English north of the bridge were trapped, without room to manoeuvre, and their comrades south of the bridge were powerless to help them. They could only look on while a bloody massacre took place across the river, redeemed by some individual acts of presence of mind or courage, such as the escape of the Yorkshireman, Sir Marmaduke Tweng. Some of the Welsh, unencumbered by armour, swam to safety, but nearly a hundred knights were slain and a great many infantry. The treasurer rode into battle like a knight and was killed by the spearmen. The Scots flayed his body and cut the skin into small pieces to be carried about the country as tokens of liberation from a hated régime of which Cressingham had been the symbol. For their part the Scots did not get off lightly, and it seems probable that the death of their brilliant leader Andrew Murray, which occurred before the end of the year, resulted from wounds he got during the battle.[1]

Warenne himself had not crossed the bridge. When he judged that all was lost he ordered it to be broken, entrusted Stirling Castle to Sir Marmaduke Tweng, Sir William Fitz Warin and others,[2] and then, heedless of the fact that he was an elderly man, rode for the Border in such haste that his horse was reputed to have had nothing to eat between Stirling and Berwick. The waggon-teams of the English baggage train, and the rank and file trying to escape, did not fare so well. They set off down the road to Falkirk, which followed a line over higher ground with woodland to the south and, not far to the north, the area known as 'The Pows'. This was the name popularly given to the flat, boggy carse beside the Forth, intersected by countless sluggish streams called 'polles' or (in later Scots) 'pows'. James Stewart and the earl of Lennox, as soon as they saw Wallace gaining the upper hand, withdrew to their men, who were lurking in the woods which bordered The Pows. From this shelter they emerged to kill the fleeing groups of English, seizing quantities of booty and leading away the laden waggons. It proved impossible, in the lagoons and marshes of the carse, for the invaders to get any waggons or sumpter horses away.[3]

[1] *Cal. Docs. Scot.*, ii, p. xxx.
[2] Ibid., iv, No. 1,835.
[3] *Chron. Guisb.*, 303. For the 'polles', see below, pp. 303–4.

From a long-term point of view, Stirling Bridge was not a decisive battle, but it would be difficult to exaggerate its importance in the struggle for Scottish independence. It is hard to convey the sheer shock of it. For the English, the impossible had happened – not once, but twice. First, a cavalry army of gentlemen-professionals had been defeated by an infantry army of peasant-amateurs. After Courtrai (1302) such events were to become commonplace, but in 1297 it was too much to stomach. Secondly, and surely an even more bitter blow, an English army had been defeated by the Scots. Such a thing had not happened on this scale since the early eleventh century. Now the whole character of the war was changed. At Dunbar the Scots behaved as though it was all a game. Henceforth they were in grim earnest, and the stage was set for Falkirk, the most dour and bloody battle of the entire struggle. Wallace was neither so humble nor so obscure as is sometimes made out, and Murray, his colleague, belonged by birth to the great lords. But it would be absurd to deny that Stirling Bridge was a popular victory, the triumph of the inarticulate, unchronicled 'poor commons' of Scotland. The men who stood, spear in hand, on the steep slopes of the Abbey Craig, waiting for Murray and Wallace to give the signal, were no doubt mostly landless men, hardly the *probi homines* on whose collective wisdom and experience the government of Scotland depended. Some of them indeed, as Wallace later admitted, were thorough-going rascals who could not be kept in order. But they were inspired by one of the deepest and most primitive emotions known to human beings, the urge to defend their native land against a foreign invader. Led by Murray and Wallace, they had given unmistakable proof that, along with the baronage and gentry, they too had their place in the community of the realm.

Additional Note (see above, pp. 103-4).
King John's submission.

It seems that about the end of June, 1296 a 'form of peace' was proposed which would have allowed King John to make a less humiliating abdication. The substance of these terms has been published by E. L. G. Stones and M. N. Blount, *BIHR*, xlviii, 95–6, 104–5. This was presumably the first 'form of peace' mentioned in *Chron. Guisb.*, 280. Its author was possibly Balliol's friend Bishop Bek of Durham, who was Edward I's envoy charged with obtaining the Scottish king's surrender (ibid.). By July 8th, if not sooner, it had been decided to insist on unconditional surrender.

6

Experiments in Guardianship

EVEN for England as a whole, the battle of Stirling Bridge could hardly have come at a worse moment, but for the north it was an unmitigated disaster. The king was beyond the Channel, helping his ally Guy de Dampierre, count of Flanders, to conduct a futile campaign against Philip the Fair. For men in the south of England Scotland seemed very remote, and the plight of their fellow-countrymen beyond the Tees touched them scarcely at all. Those who were involved in public affairs were still preoccupied with the great quarrel between the king and 'the earls' (Norfolk and Hereford) which threatened to grow into a second Montfortian revolution. If the southern English chose at this moment of national peril to indulge in the luxury of a constitutional quarrel about the royal prerogative, so much the better for the French and the Scots. For the next seven years the guiding principle of Scottish history was the assumption that the events of the summer of 1296 should be wiped off the slate. John was still king, the community of the realm was still intact, the Franco-Scottish alliance was still in force. All this is obscured by the habit of portraying Wallace as the democratic leader in a war of precocious proletarian nationalism. In fact, the Scots, far from being in advance of the age, were intensely conservative. Unless this is understood, the events of the period make no sense whatever. Time and again we see the Scots struggling, often desperately, to maintain or restore the old, lawful order of things. Wallace was no exception in this: indeed, in some respects he was more conservative than the greater magnates.

Wallace, for one thing, made no attempt to seize the government of Scotland or set himself up as an independent ruler. Not only did he share the leadership with Andrew Murray until Murray's death in November,[1] but his consistent aim was, as he said to Warenne's envoys at Stirling Bridge, the liberation of *the kingdom*. On October 11th, Murray and he, then at Haddington, sent a letter to the mayors and communes of Lübeck and Hamburg[2] telling them that *the kingdom* of Scotland had been, by God's grace, recovered by battle from the power of the English, and that in consequence the ports of Scotland were once more open to German merchants. (No doubt this was only one of a number of similar letters to the North Sea communities whose trading activity was vitally important to the Scottish economy, especially if weapons and other munitions were to be bought abroad.) Even the English indictment against Wallace in 1305 seems to take care not to charge him with setting up a personal dictatorship.[3] It stated with evident truth that he sent out writs equivalent to writs issued by the sovereign [*superior*] of Scotland. But for Wallace the sovereign of Scotland was King John. It is yet more significant that, like the Guardians of 1286–91, like Wishart and the rest in July 1297, and like the Guardians after him, Wallace was fully aware that in the absence or incapacity of the lawful king the actual rulers must be responsible to the community of the realm and must derive their authority from its consent. This was true no matter how defective the machinery for getting that consent had become.

Only four writs and charters issued by Wallace survive. They are well written, expertly composed documents which prove, incidentally, that Wallace had clerks with him who knew something of the rules of the Scottish king's chancery.[4] The most interesting feature

---

[1] As shown by letters issued on November 7th, *Chron. Guisb.*, 306, although Murray might by then have been dead without Wallace's knowledge. An inquest of 1300 (*Cal. Docs. Scot.*, ii, No. 1,178) says that Andrew Murray was killed at Stirling against the king (of England), but probably he was mortally wounded in the battle and died some two months later. His posthumous son, the future Guardian, was not born till Whitsun, 1298.

[2] Stevenson, *Wallace Docs.*, 159 (with facsimile as frontispiece); also in K. Höhlbaum, *Hansisches Urkundenbuch*, Bd. i (Halle, 1876), No. 1251 (422). This letter was destroyed during the second world war.

[3] Stevenson, *Wallace Docs.*, 191–2.

[4] This is shown by the uniformity of the style used, by the traditional address of the only surviving charter, *omnibus probis hominibus*, and by the formulae and phraseology of the documents, which conform closely (making allowance for the unprecedented situation) with productions of the chapel during the later thirteenth century.

of the documents is the formal style which Murray and Wallace, and later Wallace alone, adopted. The letter to Lübeck and Hamburg begins, 'Andrew Murray and William Wallace, commanders of the army of the kingdom of Scotland, and the community of that realm. . . .' A month later, a letter of protection issued by them for Hexham Priory[1] begins, 'Andrew Murray and William Wallace, commanders of the army of the kingdom of Scotland, in the name of the famous prince the lord John, by God's grace illustrious king of Scotland, by consent of the community of that realm. . . .' Five months later Wallace issued a charter for Alexander Scrymgeour,[2] using this style, 'William Wallace, knight, Guardian of the kingdom of Scotland and commander of its armies, in the name of the famous prince the lord John, by God's grace illustrious king of Scotland, by consent of the community of that realm. . . .' Of course, these are all that survive of what was doubtless a large number of documents issued by Murray and Wallace. Few as they are, they are enough to prove that Wallace regarded himself as ruling on behalf of King John, and based his authority on the collective assent of the community. Just as the Guardians of 1286–91, and the Guardians of 1298–1304 held parliaments and assemblies, so also the holding of 'parliaments and assemblies' is expressly stated to have been one of Wallace's crimes in the indictment of 1305.[3] Just as the Guardians used a special seal of regency, so also did Murray and Wallace.

We know less about Wallace than we know about almost any of the great national figures of our history. Utterly fearless, violent but not lacking in compassion, possessed of a certain grim humour, Wallace impresses us most by his extraordinary singleness of mind and purpose. During the seven years of his active career he was never diverted from his aim of ridding Scotland of the English yoke. But he was not a revolutionary either in politics or as a soldier. Dr

[1] *Chron. Guisb.*, 306.

[2] Anderson, *Diplomata*, Pl. XLIII. This original is also lost, so that we now possess no original document issued by Wallace.

[3] Stevenson, Wallace Docs., 191. The Lübeck letter from Murray and Wallace was exhibited at the Glasgow Exhibition of 1911. It bore two seals, presumably of Murray and Wallace in their official capacity. Only the upper seal (Murray's?) survived in 1911, with the royal arms of Scotland on the obverse, and on the reverse possibly a personal device; compare de Soules's seal of guardianship (Stevenson and Wood, *Seals,* 25 and No. 22).

Trevelyan has called him a 'guerrilla chief of genius',[1] but in fact Wallace used guerrilla tactics only while he had no choice. As soon as possible he gathered large armies and fought pitched battles. At Stirling Bridge, with Murray at his side, he won; at Falkirk, on his own, he was badly defeated. It might have been better for Scotland if Wallace had really been a *guerrillero*. Ironically, it was not the middle-class Wallace but the aristocratic Bruce who possessed the genius for guerrilla warfare. The fact is surely that Wallace had the defects of his qualities, and one of these was lack of imagination.

The three main achievements of Wallace's régime were the invasion of Northumbria, the filling of the vacant see of St Andrews, and the successful revival of the idea of guardianship. The retaliatory raid[2] which Wallace carried out south of the Border in October and November 1297 was a savage business, marked by ghastly atrocities which seem to have been due chiefly to the lack of discipline among the Scots. At first they plundered and slaughtered at will in Northumberland, making a lair for themselves in Rothbury Forest. Many of the people, including all the clergy, fled south of the Tyne to Saint Cuthbert's Land – County Durham, as we now call it. The invaders then ravaged the country far and wide, from Cockermouth to Newcastle. The cry 'The Scots are coming', taken up from village to village, spread such panic that even in the palatinate men began to flee southwards. Yet Wallace, having no siege engines or experienced troops, had failed to capture any of the castles save Stirling.[3] Edinburgh, Roxburgh, Berwick, Alnwick, Newcastle, Durham and Carlisle – all these garrisons defied him successfully. Baffled, and demoralized by snowstorms and frost, the Scots went back to their own country about the end of November. Guisborough's statement that they first handed over to the men of Galloway their share of the plunder is doubly significant.[4] It underlines the stubbornly

---

[1] *History of England* (3rd edn, 1945), 218.

[2] *Chron. Guisb.*, 303–7; *Chron. Lanercost*, 190–1; and see p. 153 below.

[3] *Cal. Docs. Scot.*, iv, No. 1,835. Sir Richard Waldegrave, constable of Stirling in 1297, together with most of the garrison, was slain at Stirling Bridge. The castle was entrusted by Warenne to William Fitz Warin and Marmaduke Tweng, who were joined by William de Ros, brother of Robert de Ros of Wark, who had joined the Scots. They were soon forced to surrender from want of provisions. Wallace spared Ros's life because of his brother, but imprisoned him in irons in Dumbarton castle; Wallace also spared the lives of Tweng and Fitz Warin.

[4] *Chron. Guisb.*, 307.

persistent separatism of Galloway, and it at once calls to mind the Scottish incursions into Northumbria under David I, when the Gallovidians were singled out as perpetrators of especially barbarous atrocities. A story which Guisborough tells about Wallace at Hexham also recalls the campaigns of King David, and shows us, in a brief but piercing shaft of light, both the character of the great champion of Scotland and the essential weakness of his position.[1] Three of the Austin canons of Hexham Priory had plucked up courage and returned to their church. Some Scots demanded to be shown their treasures, and were told that their compatriots had already carried off everything. Wallace arrived, dismissed the intruders, and asked for mass to be celebrated. After the elevation of the Host, Wallace went out to lay down his arms. As the priest was washing his hands in readiness to take the bread and wine, the marauders returned and stole the chalice, cloths, altar ornaments and even the missal. When Wallace was told by the priest what had happened he gave orders that the thieves should be sought out and hanged, but his men made only a pretence of pursuit. 'These men are bad characters,' he said, 'they cannot be brought to justice and punished.' At the same time, he gave the priory a general letter of protection. The parallel and the contrast with King David's invasion 150 years earlier is noteworthy. In 1138 King David, in addition to giving Hexham Priory a written protection, stationed five of his officers there to see that the peace of the church was not violated.[2] When the Galloway men came in search of plunder, two of them were executed on the spot and the rest fled in terror. Wallace might have defeated the English in pitched battle, something the great King David had never achieved, but that did not make him king nor give his commands the stamp of royal authority.

A telling sentence in the English indictment against Wallace charges him with urging the prelates, earls and barons who were on his side to 'subject themselves to the lordship of the king of France and work with King Philip for the destruction of England'.[3] The appointment of a new bishop of St Andrews in place of Fraser was

[1] *Chron. Guisb.*, 305–6.
[2] John of Hexham, in *Symeonis Monachi Opera Omnia* (ed. Arnold, Rolls Series), ii, 290; and cf. *Chron. Stephen etc.*, ii, 153.
[3] Stevenson, *Wallace Docs.*, 191.

to some extent bound up with the active revival of the Franco-Scottish alliance. The Scottish Church (save for the outlying dioceses of Galloway and the Isles) formed a single province subject directly to the papacy. Consequently every new Scottish bishop had to have his election confirmed by the pope, and it was the usual practice in the thirteenth century for Scottish bishops to travel to the papal *curia* for confirmation of their appointment and for their consecration, sometimes at the hands of the pope personally, but more often by one of the cardinal bishops. The new bishop of St Andrews – and for that matter any other new bishop of a Scottish diocese – would have to run the gauntlet of a long North Sea passage to France or the Low Countries, sailing through waters patrolled by English ships on the look-out for enemy craft. Historians have not done justice to the courage of the Scots and foreign seamen and their passengers who during the long war with England undertook these perilous voyages. Sending a bishop-elect to Rome was a risky affair, and the journey was much too valuable to be devoted solely to the formalities of consecration. The new bishop would have to earn his passage by diplomatic activity in every friendly foreign court, especially at the papal *curia* itself and at Paris.

As soon as the news of Bishop Fraser's death reached Scotland, the leading clergy of the cathedral church of St Andrews entrusted the jurisdiction of the diocese (which during a vacancy belonged to the cathedral chapter) to Master Nicholas Balmyle, whom they appointed as Official.[1] Although this man keeps himself in the background of surviving historical record, we should be doing him no more than belated justice if we recognized that in these years he played a critically important part. It was of the utmost concern to the patriots that the majority they already commanded among the bishops at the start of the struggle with Edward I should be maintained and if possible increased. Glasgow and Dunkeld were already in good hands, but owing to the special pre-eminence of St Andrews in the Scottish Church it was urgently necessary that Fraser's successor should be a vigorous patriot. The five chief clergy connected with the cathedral were the prior, John of Haddington, an auditor for Balliol in the competition for the throne; the archdeacon of St Andrews, John Fraser, presumably a kinsman of the late bishop; the

1 *Chron. Bower*, i, 362.

archdeacon of Lothian, Master William Frere; the Official, Nicholas Balmyle who, under the name Nicholas 'of St Andrews,' had also been one of Balliol's auditors; and, finally, Master William Comyn, the earl of Buchan's brother.[1] He claimed a seat in the St Andrews chapter in virtue of his office as provost of the highly privileged chapel-royal of St Mary, the successor to the ancient community of 'culdees' which had been attached to the church of St Andrews in Celtic times.[2] On November 3rd, 1297, while Wallace himself was in England but acting on his instructions, the St Andrews chapter elected as their new bishop the chancellor of Glasgow cathedral, Master William Lamberton.[3] The English afterwards accused Wallace of forcing the chapter to carry out this election.[4] On the contrary, we can be sure that the two archdeacons at least were eager to elect such a staunch upholder of the national cause as Lamberton, and that although he did not actually have a vote in the election Nicholas Balmyle used his doubtless considerable influence on the same side. It may well be true that Master William Comyn also, although he was denied a vote on technical grounds, supported Lamberton's election. Already, probably, his brother the earl of Buchan had come out openly on the patriotic side,[5] and in the following year King Edward I gave Master William's valuable provostry to one of his own favoured clerks, presumably on the grounds that William was a 'rebel'.[6]

At what date and by what means we know not, Lamberton travel-

---

[1] For him, see Stevenson, *Documents*, No. 512; *Cal. Docs. Scot.*, ii, Nos. 778, 1,017, 1,574, 1,822.

[2] *Kingdom of the Scots*, 212–32.

[3] Dowden, *Bishops*, 21.

[4] Palgrave, *Docs. Hist. Scot.*, 332, 339.

[5] *Chron. Guisb.*, 297, says that when the earl was sent to pacify the north (July 1297) 'at first he pretended to repress rebellion, but in the end changed sides and became a thorn in our flesh'. *Rotuli Scotiae*, i, 50b, shows that on September 26th, 1297, the regency in London still believed that the earl was loyal, but as they held the same belief with regard to the Stewart and the earl of Lennox, who joined Wallace openly on September 11th, this is no evidence that Buchan was on the English side as late as this date. *Cal. Docs. Scot.*, ii, No. 963, orders the king's bailiff of Tynedale to resume into his own hands the lands of John Comyn (the elder) of Badenoch, November–December 1297.

[6] *Cal. Docs. Scot.*, ii, No. 1,017. Stevenson, *Documents*, No. 512, suggests that, in May 1298, William Comyn was not opposed to the election of Lamberton as such, but only to his own exclusion from participation in the election.

led to Rome, where he was consecrated on June 1st, 1298.[1] He returned to France to join the other Scots magnates staying at the French court, among them the abbot of Melrose, Sir John de Soules, and almost certainly Bishop Matthew Crambeth of Dunkeld.[2] Within two months of Lamberton's consecration Wallace had been defeated at Falkirk, and before the bishop got back to Scotland in the summer of 1299 the outlook for the patriots seemed gloomy indeed. But Lamberton and his colleagues had scored one small yet important success. As early as June and July 1298 the French king and Pope Boniface VIII both wrote to Edward I urging him to release Balliol and to cease his attacks on Scotland.[3] Now, a year later, at the very time that Lamberton and the others were waiting at Damme for a passage to Scotland, John Balliol was sent from Dover to Wissant and handed over by King Edward's officials to the bishop of Vicenza as representative of the pope.[4] At the urging of Boniface, King Edward had released Balliol on condition that he was kept in papal custody at a residence belonging to the papacy.

The Scots consistently maintained that Balliol was still their lawful king and that his enforced abdication could not be valid in the law of Scotland. But as long as Balliol was captive in England any scheme for his restoration seemed hopeless. His surrender, therefore, was a remarkable concession on Edward's part. But the pope went even further. The formal record of Balliol's transfer (July 18th, 1299) described him hopefully as 'called king of Scotland'.[5] On June 27th and 28th respectively the pope wrote to King Edward and to Archbishop Winchelsey of Canterbury condemning the English invasions of Scotland in the strongest terms, declaring that Scotland was subject to the papacy, and commanding that the dispute between Edward and the Scots should be laid before the pope for final

---

[1] Theiner, *Monumenta*, No. 362; Dowden, *Bishops*, 21–2.

[2] *Cal. Docs. Scot.*, ii, No. 1,071, shows that it was reported in England in July 1299 that the bishop of St Andrews, the abbots of Jedburgh and Melrose, and Sir John de Soules were waiting for a passage to Scotland at Damme, by Bruges. Soules was in France in 'February 1298' (=1299), *SHR*, xxvii, 139. In April 1299 King Philip had received as envoys from the Guardians in Scotland the abbot of Jedburgh and Sir John Wishart, *Cal. Docs. Scot.*, ii, 535 (for the correct dating, see Barron, *Scottish War of Independence*, 132).

[3] *Chron. Rishanger*, 185; *Foedera*, i, 897.

[4] Stevenson, *Documents*, ii, No. 574; *Cal. Docs. Scot.*, ii, Nos. 1,079, 1,080.

[5] Stevenson, *Documents*, ii, 382–3.

judgement.[1] The French king also was still taking a strongly pro-Scottish line. On April 6th, 1299, he wrote from St Germain-en-Laye to the patriot leaders in Scotland.[2] He told them that he had received their new envoys, the abbot of Jedburgh and Sir John Wishart of the Carse, with warm friendship. He applauded the constancy and perfect loyalty which they had displayed towards the illustrious king of Scotland [Balliol] and the vigour and courage of which they had given proof in defending their native land against unjust invasion. He commended to them the bishop of St Andrews, who would be able to tell them by word of mouth what plans he had in mind for implementing the Franco-Scottish alliance and the treaty of 1295, which (added the king) he had not forgotten. Apparently King Philip would not accept the proposal which Lamberton is said to have put to him that Charles of Valois should be sent to Scotland with an expeditionary force.[3] But so far as diplomacy could achieve anything for their country's cause the bishop and his colleagues had done all they could, and when they ran the English blockade and won home safely in August 1299, they did not come empty-handed.

The Scots had done better at diplomacy than in war. Stirling Bridge had caught King Edward off guard, and with winter coming on not much could be attempted before the summer of 1298. Warenne and Sir Robert Clifford, it is true, began a modest counter-attack before Christmas. Clifford raided Annandale where the local peasantry, after jeering at his cavalry with the usual shouts of 'Tailed dogs!', were trapped in a bog and suffered heavy casualties. But after burning ten townships the English withdrew.[4] Over in the east Warenne achieved no more than the relief of Roxburgh and Berwick.[5] In the middle of February a letter reached him in which Edward I announced that he was returning from Flanders directly and telling him not to attempt a major campaign until Edward arrived to take charge personally.[6] Most of the Welsh foot were sent home, and the Scots obtained five months' breathing space.

[1] *Chron. Picts-Scots*, 126; Stevenson, *Documents*, ii, No. 569.
[2] *Cal. Docs. Scot.*, ii, 535 (see above, p. 134, n. 2).
[3] Stevenson, *Wallace Docs.*, 145.
[4] *Chron. Guisb.*, 307–8.
[5] Ibid., 314.
[6] Ibid., 315.

As far as we can tell, Wallace spent this time consolidating his position and training his troops. Whether or not we accept Dr Barron's view that the impetus in the war came from the north, we cannot help noticing how important the control of Lothian, Tweed-dale and Teviotdale seemed to the Scots throughout these years and how, time and again, they placed their forces where they could most easily threaten the English-held castles of Stirling, Edinburgh, Roxburgh and Berwick. Here, the wild country of Selkirk Forest – Ettrick Forest is its rather smaller present-day successor – was enormously useful. Wallace had lurked there in 1297, and a year later the bowmen of the Forest, fine-looking men of great stature, formed a prominent *corps* in his army, fighting under James Stewart's brother, Sir John Stewart of Jedburgh.[1] It is likely that in the spring and early summer of 1298 Wallace kept to the south of Scotland,[2] though no doubt he recruited men from all parts of the country to meet the full-scale invasion which he knew could not be long de-layed. Before March 29th, one of the foremost earls of Scotland (according to a reliable English contemporary) had bestowed on him the honour of knighthood.[3] Militarily speaking he had won this at Stirling Bridge, but the important point was that the formal ceremony put Wallace, the younger son of a cadet branch of a not very prominent family, into the class of *nobiles* or *gentilhommes*, words which are scarcely translatable nowadays because in the late thirteenth century there was none of the later distinction between 'gentlemen' and 'noblemen'.

The knighting of Wallace was no doubt connected with his election as Guardian, the date of which is unknown though like the knighting it must have taken place before the end of March.[4] The whole trend of events since 1286 made it virtually certain that the guardianship would be revived. It looked like being revived in 1297, not only by Bishop Wishart and his allies, but also by Murray

<hr />

[1] *Chron. Guisb.*, 328.

[2] Wallace spent some time early in 1298 besieging Roxburgh, *Chron. Rishanger*, 184; his charter to Alexander Scrymgeour, March 29th, 1298, was issued at Torphi-chen.

[3] *Chron. Rishanger*, 384; the earl is not named, but his description as *de illa natione praecipuus* suggests a prominent earl such as Strathearn, Carrick or Lennox. For reasons given below, p. 137, n. 2, it could hardly have been Atholl or Menteith.

[4] Anderson, *Diplomata*, Pl. XLIII.

and Wallace, who actually used a seal of guardianship. The special interest and problem of Wallace's election in 1298 is that he was sole Guardian and that he was obviously chosen because he had proved himself the military champion of his country. Between Murray's death in November and the battle of Falkirk in the following July, Wallace alone was in command. The great feudal magnates, far from being, as Trevelyan believed, mainly on Edward I's side, were already mainly behind Wallace, but it is clear that if they joined fully in the common enterprise they had to submit to his commands. Edward I had taken to Flanders many of the distinguished Scots captured at Dunbar.[1] There they had served against the French, but while the king was at Aardenburg, on his way home, they reverted to their natural allegiance and joined the French king against Edward, much to his annoyance.[2] In effect, this can only mean that they joined Wallace. There may have been jealousy of Wallace among the nobles, there may have been jealousy between the Comyns on the one hand and the young earl of Carrick on the other. But the important point is that in this crucial year a large body of Scottish lords, representing both the influential Comyn faction and the friends of Bruce, were committed to the struggle against England.[3] It would

[1] Cal. Docs. Scot., ii, Nos. 937, 939, 940, 942, 944, 948, 950, 952, 953.

[2] N. Trivet, Annales (ed. T. Hog), 371; Chron. Rishanger, 185. Edward I was still at Ghent on February 25th, and at Sluys, on the point of embarking for England, on March 12th, Cal. Chancery Warrants, i, 90–91. Aardenburg, between Ghent and Sluys, was then a town of some importance (Annales Gandenses, ed. H. Johnstone, passim). We may put the date of the Scottish 'defection' about March 9th (Gascon Calendar of 1322, p. 39). Langtoft names the leaders of the party, who he says went to Paris to plead for King Philip's aid against the English, as the earls of Atholl and Menteith, and John Comyn the younger of Badenoch, the future Guardian, Stevenson, Wallace Docs., 72–3. Most of the Scots in Flanders were in the 'meinie' or following of one or other of these great men. Langtoft says that they were rebuffed by Philip IV, quickly took ship for Scotland, and reached home without being intercepted. In Cal. Docs. Scot., ii, 253, Edward I refers in a letter to Philip IV to the Scots who were in his service (in Flanders) and have deserted him.

[3] It is probably in this sense that we should view the evidence of exceptional military activity on the part of Earl Malise of Strathearn. On February 11th, 1298, he promised Sir William Murray of Tullibardine that the succour and aid in men-at-arms, horses and weapons which Sir William had rendered to the earl for the defence of the realm had been offered voluntarily, and was in addition to the 'Scottish service' which was all that Sir William strictly owed in respect of the lands he held of the earl. It seems likely that at this period Earl Malise was active on the patriotic side and meant to remain active; Moray Registrum, 470.

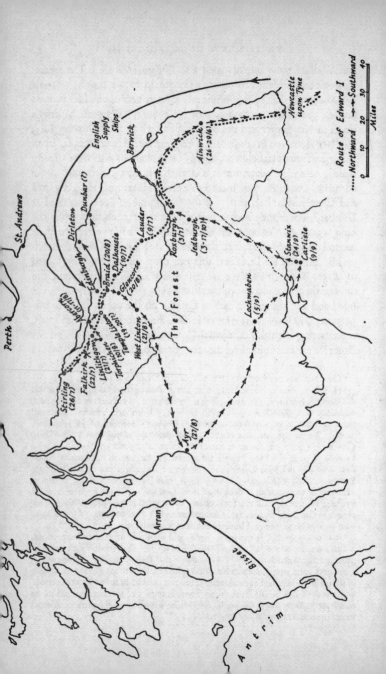

Perth

St. Andrews

Stirling (26/7)
Falkirk (22/7)
Linlithgow (21/7)
Torphichen (10/8)
Temple (19-20/7)

(18-19/11)

Newbattle

Edinburgh

Braid (20/8)
Dalhousie (10/7)
Glencorse (20/8)

West Linton (21/8)

Dirleton

Dunbar (?)

Lauder (9/7)

English Supply Ships

Berwick

The Forest

Roxburgh (3/7)
Jedburgh (3-17/10)

Lochmaben (5/9)

Stanwix (24/9)
Carlisle (9/9)

Alnwick (26-29/6)

Newcastle upon Tyne

Ayr (27/8)

Arran

Bissot

Antrim

Route of Edward I
·········· Northward   ⟶ Southward

0 10 20 30 40
Miles

be misleading, in other words, to exaggerate the difference between Wallace's war and the war fought by his successors down to 1304. In neither was there any real danger that the idea of the community of the realm would be lost. But, though many nobles were engaged in the struggle before Wallace's defeat, most of the community's natural leaders had for a time failed to give the lead or to inspire the trust which by inheritance it was their responsibility to give and inspire.

King Edward meant business in 1298. He made York the head-quarters of government. The exchequer and common law courts were moved there and remained for six years. The army he led into Scotland was formidable.[1] Of some 2,000 horse, about half were recruited by 'commissioners of array' from those who owed knight-service but were fighting for pay. The rest were brought by the great earls, who were more firmly united behind the king in the summer of 1298 than they were to be again for many years. They would bear the cost of their own contingents. There were also about 12,000 foot soldiers, a total more impressive on paper than in fact, for 10,000 were Welsh and Irish – 2,000 from Snowdon alone – and their loyalty was uncertain. The shock of the Scottish rising had at last penetrated to English minds and had aroused powerful feelings of nationalism. To the king and the nobles in particular, the victory and high position of Wallace must have been especially galling. No words were too strong for vilification. Surviving written records, which are likely to be more restrained than popular speech, call him thief, robber, master of thieves, chief of brigands, man of blood, and so forth. In the English popular imagination, Wallace had become an ogre, a monstrous bogey who would skin an Englishman to make a baldric, force nuns to dance naked in front of him and, with a heartless jest, abandon his comrades like the ignoble coward they felt he ought to be.[2] We may suspect that along with all the horror and hatred went a good deal of fascinated curiosity; but there is no hint of admiration, however grudging. We need not doubt that the

[1] J. E. Morris, *The Welsh Wars of Edward I* (1901), 286–92, 313–4, gives details of the Falkirk army. Apropos his statement, ibid., 314, that new evidence divides the cavalry into four brigades, it may be noted that Bartholomew Cotton, *Historia Anglicana* (ed. Luard, Rolls Series), 343–4, also gives four brigades.

[2] *Chron. Lanercost*, 190; *Flores Historiarum* (Rolls Series), iii, 123, 321; *Chron. Rishanger*, 385–6.

5. The Falkirk Campaign, 1298

whole of England prayed fervently for the victory of King Edward as he advanced to crush Wallace and make an end of the Scottish war.

The cavalry was ordered to assemble at Roxburgh on Wednesday, June 25th.[1] Deliberately following in the footsteps of King Athelstan, Edward made a pilgrimage to the shrine of Saint John, patron saint of Beverley,[2] and joined his army at the beginning of July. The Welshmen must have arrived at about the same time, coming across country from Carlisle. The whole army then advanced into Scotland by the road through Lauderdale,[3] burning and laying waste the countryside but finding not a soul to tell them of the enemy's whereabouts. By July 11th they had reached Braid, two miles south of Edinburgh,[4] and a week later they camped in the parish of Liston on a manor belonging to the Knights of the Temple which is now called Hallyards.[5] The Master of the English Templars, Sir Brian le Jay, had formerly been preceptor of the order in Scotland, and his presence with the English host probably accounts for the choice of site. Moreover, adjacent to Temple Liston lay the lands of Kirkliston, belonging to the 'rebel' bishop of St Andrews, and a thorough plundering of that estate would neatly kill two birds with one stone. In truth, the army was badly short of food. Wheat transports due at Leith had been held up by contrary winds and when a few ships did arrive they unfortunately carried more wine than corn.[6] At Temple Liston the king learned that Dirleton and two other castles of East Lothian were held by the Scots.[7] He sent Bishop Bek to capture them. All the castles seemed formidable, and Dirleton was newly built. Bek had no siege engines and his men no food save peas and beans they picked in the fields. He sent Sir John Fitz Marmaduke

[1] *Chron. Rishanger*, 186; *Parl. Writs*, i, 314b-15b, writs of summons for Welsh foot to reach Carlisle, and for English foot to reach Roxburgh, on Wednesday, June 25th. *Parl. Writs*, 316, alters summons so that cavalry shall gather on June 23rd; and there is also a summons for cavalry on June 25th.

[2] *Chron. Guisb.*, 324. King Edward took the banner of St John of Beverley with him on the campaign, *Cal. Docs. Scot*, ii, No. 1,177.

[3] *Cal. Chancery Warrants*, i, 94-5, shows the king at Lauder, July 9th, Fala and Dalhousie, July 10th. This route became by far the commonest to be used by large forces invading Scotland from the south.

[4] *Cal. Docs. Scot.*, ii, No. 998.

[5] *Chron. Guisb.*, 324; *Chron. Rishanger*, 186; A. Macdonald, *Place-Names of West Lothian*, 39.

[6] *Chron. Guisb.*, 325.

[7] Ibid., 324.

to the king for fresh instructions. 'Go back and tell the bishop that as bishop he is a man of Christian piety, but Christian piety has no place in what he is now doing. And as for you,' the king added, clapping his hand upon Sir John, 'you are a bloodthirsty man, I have often had to rebuke you for being too cruel. But now be off, use all your cruelty, and instead of rebuking you I shall praise you. Take care you don't see me until all three castles are burned.' 'My lord king, how shall I do what seems extremely difficult?' 'That you will know when you have done it, and you shall give me a pledge that you will do it.' Sir John returned to Bishop Bek with this inexorable message, food ships suddenly arrived, and the heartened troops renewed the assault with such vigour that Dirleton surrendered in two days and the other two castles (one of which was probably Tantallon) were abandoned and burnt.[1]

Meantime the main body of the army faced starvation and many Welsh were already dying. Edward ordered wine to be given to them to cheer their spirits, an unwise move. The wretched Welshmen got very drunk and in a serious brawl with the English several priests were slain. At this the English knights charged the Welsh, killing eighty and putting the rest to flight. Next morning the king was told that the Welsh were threatening to go over to the Scots, but he was not impressed. Angry and unappeased, the Welshmen stayed at a distance, declaring that if they saw the Scots gaining the upper hand they would desert to them at once. It looked as though the whole ambitious and hopeful expedition would end in failure, and Edward decided to fall back on Edinburgh. But at this moment Earl Patrick of Dunbar and Gilbert de Umfraville, earl of Angus, two Scottish earls[2] who were (as they had always been) on the English side, brought to Edward a scout who gave him the welcome news that the Scots were only thirteen miles away, in the Wood of Callendar beside Falkirk. The news changed everything. Ordering his men to arm themselves, the king mounted and led the host westward along the road to Falkirk. That night they bivouacked just east of Linlithgow, on the Burgh Muir,[3] each man with his horse beside

[1] *Chron. Guisb.*, 324–5. There seems to be no record of Tantallon before the fourteenth century, though the name is ancient.

[2] Ibid., 326. Umfraville was of course an Englishman, lord of Prudhoe, Redesdale and Coquetdale.

[3] Ibid., 326; *in mora citra Linlyscoch.*

him. They passed through the town at dawn. The king was slightly injured during the night when a careless groom let his horse tread on him, but he promptly mounted and quelled rumours that he was badly hurt. Not long after leaving Linlithgow they could see many lances lining the top of a hill. But the spearmen melted away as the English hurried towards them, and it was not till they had pushed further west and tents had been pitched to let the king and the bishop of Durham hear mass that they saw, in the clearer light of morning, the Scottish host making ready for battle. It was the feast of Saint Mary Magdalene, Tuesday, July 22nd. After a month of searching in an empty land on empty stomachs, the English had at last found the dragon they had come to slay in the lair which he had prepared for the encounter.

More than anything, the Scots feared the disciplined, experienced heavy cavalry of England and Gascony. They feared it with as good reason and in a sense for much the same reason as in 1939 an army of riflemen would have feared an army equipped with tanks. It was because of this fear that the Scots resistance had crumbled at Irvine in July 1297, and that two months later Murray and Wallace had stationed their spearmen on a steep hillside ringed by the Forth. It underlay the request to Philip the Fair to send the veteran Charles of Valois to Scotland with a body of knights.[1] It was this same fear which explained Wallace's tactics at Falkirk. And the English were not only immensely superior in weight of cavalry. They had archers from Sherwood and Wales and crossbowmen from Ponthieu and Guienne whose killing power was much greater than that of the Scottish bowmen. Wallace had to convert his army into a human fortress and inspire it with enough steadiness to withstand a siege. In addition, he had taught his men to attack the cavalry at its weakest spot by killing the horses. Only four years earlier, at Maes Moydog, the English had proved that skilful use of cavalry interspersed with accurate crossbowmen could outfight an army of spearmen even though they were dense-packed and strongly placed.[2] Wallace, no doubt, knew all about Maes Moydog, but given the necessity of a pitched battle he had no alternative save to do what the Welsh had

[1] Stevenson, *Wallace Docs.*, 145.
[2] Morris, *Welsh Wars*, 256–8; J. G. Edwards, *EHR*, xxxix, 1–12; ibid., xlvi, 262–5.

done on that occasion but try to do it better. He built his fortress of spearmen 'on hard ground on one side of a hill beside Falkirk',[1] facing south-east. Behind him (if my identification of the hill is correct) lay Callender Wood. In front ran the Westquarter Burn and its tributary coming down from Glen. Near their confluence there was evidently a boggy loch, lying immediately in front of the Scottish battle line. The left flank of Wallace's army, protected to some extent by the valley of the Westquarter Burn deepening away to the north-east, covered the high road to Falkirk and Stirling. His right flank may have been protected by woodland and more broken ground to the west. The position was not so strong as the Abbey Craig – why, one asks, did Wallace not repeat his movements of 1297? – but it was not badly chosen for the kind of battle he wished to fight. He arranged his spearmen in four great schiltroms, 'shield-rings', which Guisborough describes most exactly. Each was a thickly packed circle of spearmen, standing or kneeling with their spears slanting obliquely outwards towards the circumference, a hedgehog every one of whose spines was a long iron-tipped spear in the grip of a man fighting for the freedom of his country. The number of men in each schiltrom is not known; it may have been as much as one, it can hardly have been more than two, thousand. Round each schiltrom wooden stakes had been driven into the ground and roped together. In the spaces between the schiltroms Wallace placed the archers of the Forest under John Stewart. In the rear was the cavalry, contributed by the Comyns and the other earls who supported Wallace,[2] and including no doubt many of the gentry who appear in the next few years fighting against the English. Whether Robert Bruce was with them we do not know. It is virtually certain that

---

[1] *Chron. Guisb.*, 327. The *foresta de Selkyrke*, ibid., 326, is either a slip for *foresta de Falkirk*, i.e., Callendar Wood, or simply a mistake. There is remarkably complete agreement among contemporary or nearly contemporary record and chronicle sources that the battle of Falkirk was in fact fought at or beside Falkirk ('this side of Falkirk', i.e., east, *Scalacronica*, 125). One of the earliest references to the battle by name calls it *bellum varie capelle*, i.e. the battle of Falkirk (*SHR*, v, 24, a record of 1354 supplied with misleading commentary by John Edwards). Cf. also *Cal. Docs. Scot.*, ii, nos. 1007, 1011.

[2] No doubt the earls of Atholl and Menteith, who had come home from Flanders earlier in the year, together with the Stewart, the earls of Buchan, Lennox and Carrick and Comyn the younger of Badenoch, were the principal nobles contributing to the Scottish army (cf. *Chron. Rishanger*, 414).

James Stewart was one of the considerable body of knights present, most of whom fled the field, but a few of whom stayed to organize the infantry.[1]

King Edward, who could show humanity and common sense, proposed that the army should halt until men and horses had eaten, for neither had had a meal since nine o'clock the previous morning.[2] But his commanders would have none of it. A halt was dangerous, for it seemed that only a small burn separated the armies. Roger Bigod, earl of Norfolk, Humphrey de Bohun, earl of Hereford (the king's two adversaries of the year before), together with Henry de Lacy, earl of Lincoln, pressed forward with the vanguard not knowing of the loch which lay between them and the enemy. The obstacle forced them to swing westward and delayed their contact with the Scottish right. On the English right wing Bishop Bek had under him thirty-six 'bannerets' – senior commanders of cavalry – to lead the second brigade or 'battle'. They of course turned east to skirt the loch. The bishop had difficulty in restraining his knights who were eager to be the first to reach the enemy. Ralph Bassett, lord of Drayton, told him roundly, 'It's not for you, bishop, to teach us knights how to fight when you ought to be busy saying mass. Go back and celebrate mass; we shall do all that needs to be done in the way of fighting.' The two wings then made contact with the outer schiltroms. The Scottish horse, disgracefully, fled the field without striking a blow, but there is no need to put this down to treachery. The fourteenth-century historian John Fordun felt obliged to do so because, in common with all Scots of his day, he had to show the Comyns in as black a light as possible.[3] It is more likely that simple panic seized them, as at Dunbar and Irvine. Guisborough says explicitly that a few Scottish knights remained to command the schiltroms, and there is no need to doubt Fordun's statement that Macduff of Fife, indisputably a nobleman, was killed at Falkirk fighting at the head of the men of that earldom.[4]

[1] *Chron. Guisb.*, 328. Stevenson, *Documents*, ii, No. 529, shows Edward I granting away property forfeited by James 'late' Stewart of Scotland, on August 31st, 1298.

[2] Ibid., 327. The account in the text is chiefly based on *Chron. Guisb.*, which gives much the fullest account, and must have been composed by an eyewitness or from information supplied by one.

[3] *Chron. Fordun*, i, 330.

[4] Ibid.

All now turned on the steadiness of the Scots peasantry and their capacity for exhausting the repeated cavalry rushes. It must have seemed now or never, and before the battle Wallace, addressing the schiltroms, had summed up the desperateness of the hour in a homely quip, half serious and wholly memorable: 'I have brought you into the ring: now see if you can dance.'[1] They did their best. We have a list of 110 English horses killed at Falkirk and that can hardly be the full reckoning.[2] But the English knights rode first at the bowmen, and from their leader Sir John Stewart downwards they were killed almost to a man. After this the schiltroms, though still unbroken, were isolated. The Welsh archers and foreign crossbowmen got to work, pouring in a deadly rain of arrows and bolts, and heavy casualties were inflicted by lobbing stones from slings. Gradually the gaps in the dense outer circles of spearmen grew too wide to be filled up by their comrades in the centre. In each schiltrom the outer ranks fell back on the men behind. Choosing their moment, the troops of mail-clad knights charged in an irresistible mass, overwhelming the Scots by the sheer weight of their impetus. The battle, hard fought, long-drawn-out, became a slaughter, many hundreds, perhaps thousands of Scots being killed and an unknown number drowned, presumably in the loch below the battlefield. King Edward's army lost only two men of high rank: Brother Brian le Jay, the Master of the English Templars, who chased some Scots into a bog and was surrounded, and Brother John of Sawtry, the Huntingdonshire knight who had succeeded Jay as Master of the Scottish Templars.[3]

William Wallace and the other Scots magnates escaped to 'castles and woods' – no doubt at first into the great Wood of Tor which stretched between Falkirk and Stirling.[4] If Robert Bruce was on the field he must have ridden straight to Carrick, for by the end of August when Edward I reached Ayr he found the town evacuated and the castle burned down on Bruce's orders, so that they would be of no

---

[1] *Chron. Rishanger*, 187, gives what is probably one of the earliest and most authentic reports of this remark: 'I have browghte ȝowe to the ryng, hoppe ȝef ȝe kunne'. There seems no reason to doubt either that Wallace spoke, or that the greater part of his force at Falkirk would understand, Scots.

[2] *Cal. Docs. Scot.*, ii, Nos. 1,007, 1,011.

[3] *Chron. Rishanger*, 188; *Cal. Docs. Scot.*, ii, 147, 202; for Jay see *SHR*, v, 23-4.

[4] *Chron. Rishanger*, 387; cf. Bartholomew Cotton, *Historia Anglicana*, 344.

use to the English.[1] Bruce himself may have hidden in the Carrick hills or gone north, for despite the outcome of the battle the Scots remained in control of the country beyond the Tay and even between Tay and Forth the English had achieved nothing more than burning the towns of St Andrews and Perth.[2]

Like Stirling Bridge, Falkirk was not a decisive battle. But in several ways it marked a turning point in the Anglo-Scottish war. Not for another sixteen years did the Scots attempt a full-scale pitched battle against the English. Secondly, Falkirk meant the end of one experiment in guardianship and the start of another. However unfair it might be to judge a general by one defeat, Wallace could not expect to be given a second chance. He had no hereditary position as one of the natural leaders of the community, and must stand or fall on his military reputation. It seems to have been his own conservatism which led him to offer battle at all, instead of scorching the country and harassing the invaders. He gave up the guardianship, whether voluntarily or under compulsion is immaterial. Finally, though this is not a conclusion that can be proved by documentary evidence, there is little doubt that the psychological effect of Falkirk was tremendous. Just as Stirling Bridge had been a different kind of war from Dunbar, so at Falkirk the war entered yet again into a fresh phase, much grimmer than before, in which the Scots had their backs to the wall and knew it. There can hardly have been any part of the country where there were not families who mourned a father, son or husband slain in that battle. The bloody slaughter of Falkirk must have made an indelible impression on the Scottish mind and, far from discouraging the Scots, done more to stiffen the will to resist than any amount of appeals to old history, encouragement from popes and kings of France, or efforts to restore Toom Tabard to the throne of Scotland. And the nobles, the feudal magnates who are supposed not have to been true to Scotland and to have been mainly on the side of Edward I, at once put themselves at the head of a five-year struggle to frustrate his ambitions. In this they

[1] *Chron. Guisb.*, 328 (severely damaging Scone Abbey, *Scone Liber*, No. 124).

[2] Ibid. This source shows that Edward wished to proceed to Galloway but was deterred by shortage of food; Cotton (loc. cit.) says that many Scots with their forces gathered in Galloway; Bruce was well placed to lead this rallying of forces which, presumably, had had no hand in the battle of Falkirk.

were at first remarkably successful, and in any case, whether in
success or in failure, they were certainly not half-hearted. There is,
moreover, good evidence that King Edward, lacking the hindsight of
modern historians, failed to realize that the Scots landowning class
was on his side. On September 25th, 1298, after he had reached
Carlisle, the king made grants of estates 'forfeited' by Scottish
lairds. To Guy de Beauchamp earl of Warwick he gave extensive
lands belonging to Sir Geoffrey Moubray, John Stirling and Andrew
Charteris;[1] to Robert de Touny, Lochwarret (Borthwick), Megget
(in the Forest) and other lands belonging to Sir William Hay of
Lochwarret, land in Crawford belonging to the child Andrew
Murray, the son of Wallace's colleague, and land belonging to
William Ramsay (of Dalhousie).[2]

The disaster of Falkirk forced the community of the realm to fall
back once more on collective leadership. At some date between July
and December 1298, Robert Bruce earl of Carrick and John Comyn
the younger of Badenoch were elected joint Guardians, an uneasy
marriage perhaps, yet proof of the Scots determination that the
guardianship should survive.[3] Militarily the situation was grim but
not hopeless. Famine and the restlessness of the English magnates
compelled Edward I to leave Scotland in September, having taken
the elder Bruce's castle of Lochmaben, hitherto held by the Scots.[4] He
issued a summons to the host to reassemble on June 6th, 1299, but for
various reasons no campaign was possible that summer, and the king
was not in Scotland again till July 1300. From 1298 to 1303 Scotland
can scarcely be said to have been under English occupation save in
the south east where the English-held castles were much thicker on
the ground than elsewhere and the country in between much

[1] *Cal. Docs. Scot.*, ii, No. 1,009. *Chron. Rishanger*, 388, says that the king proposed
to distribute Scotland among his followers, who (if single) were to marry only
Englishwomen.

[2] British Library, MS. Add. 28024, fo. 180. For the Hays as landowners in Megget,
cf. *Origines Parochiales*, i, 223 and *Melrose Liber*, i, No. 264.

[3] S.R.O., Dudhope Muniments, Box 40, bdle 1, No. 311.

[4] *Chron. Rishanger*, 188. R. C. Reid, *Dumfriesshire Trans.*, 3rd Ser, xxxi, 60, argues
that the English could not have 'captured' Lochmaben since the elder Bruce was at
peace with Edward. But surely the younger Bruce or other Scots leaders could have
seized and garrisoned it against the English? Indeed, *Cal. Docs. Scot.*, iv, Appendix I,
No. 7, suggests strongly that Lochmaben castle was in the younger Bruce's hands
in May 1298.

easier to overawe. The Scots more than held their own in these years, yet it was to become increasingly clear that the old practice of joint or multiple guardianship would prove a failure. Apart from the transfer of Balliol to papal custody in 1299, the most hopeful features of the period were the effort, largely successful it seems, to get the normal machinery of government going again, and the ability of the patriots to keep and even extend their control over the leadership of the Scottish Church.

As far as central government was concerned, there was no break of any consequence in the guardianship between Wallace's election and the surrender of John Comyn in 1304. The Guardians recognised the legal validity of acts done by their predecessors. Bruce, for example, confirmed to Alexander Scrymgeour the constableship of Dundee 'as he held it by the grant of Sir William Wallace before I received the guardianship'.[1] All the Guardians ruled in the name of King John and associated with their rule the authority of the community. With William Wallace's style as commander and Guardian we may compare the style used by Bruce and Comyn, which we can reconstruct from the address of Philip IV's letter of April 6th, 1299: 'Robert Bruce, earl of Carrick, and John Comyn the son, Guardians of the kingdom of Scotland in the name of the famous prince, the illustrious King John, together with the bishops, abbots, priors, earls, barons and other magnates and the whole community of the realm.'[2] We know a few of the places where government documents were issued. Govan, Torwood and Inchaffray[3] may have a rustic look compared with the famous burghs and castles frequented by Alexander III, but there are also acts issued from Rutherglen, Stirling, Scone and St Andrews.[4] The justiciar of Scotland north of Forth (John Comyn, earl of Buchan) could still hold his court at Aberdeen in February 1300,[5] and in that year too we hear of two parliaments, called at properly appointed terms.[6] As for local govern-

---

[1] S.R.O., Dudhope Muniments, Box 40, bdle 1, No. 311.

[2] *Cal. Docs. Scot.*, ii, 535.

[3] S.R.O., Dudhope Muniments, Box 40, bdle 1, No. 311; *APS*, i, 454; *Hist. MSS. Comm.*, 5th Report, Appendix, 612.

[4] Sir Walter Scott, *Minstrelsy of the Scottish Border* (ed. T. Henderson, 1931), 616; *Hist. MSS. Comm.*, 5th Rep., App., 612; *Kelso Liber*, No. 397.

[5] *Arbroath Liber*, i, No. 231.

[6] *SHR*, xxiv, 325.

ment, the scanty surviving record gives us casual glimpses of sheriffs of Aberdeen, Forfar, Stirling, Lanark and even Roxburgh.[1] No doubt wherever the Scots had control of a sheriffdom, and sometimes where they had not, they would appoint a sheriff. There must also have been a more or less regular collection of revenues, however much depleted. Whenever the English won any Scottish territory the king's agents were able to use an established revenue-collecting and accounting system, and it would follow that the Scots likewise must have been able to keep this system in operation.[2]

Local government and military needs must often have gone hand in hand. The Guardians made use of, or were forced to pay attention to, local influence and local interests. We can see a clear illustration of this in the siege of Stirling, the biggest task undertaken by the Scots after they recovered from the Falkirk *débâcle*. Among the prominent landowning families of Stirlingshire were the Malherbes. One branch of this family was more commonly called Morham, from the East Lothian village which they also owned.[3] The Malherbe-Morhams held lands in the Carron valley, from Stenhouse up to Dunipace, Garth and Castlerankine.[4] In this period there were two prominent Morhams, a father, Thomas, and a son, Herbert. The elder was with Edward at Falkirk, his son on the Scottish side. Young Herbert Morham commanded the force besieging Stirling Castle in 1299,[5] a task which did not prevent him from ambushing King Edward's relative, Joan de Clare, dowager countess of Fife, as she was travelling from Stirling to Edinburgh with no better protection than an English safe-conduct.[6] Morham carried her off to his brother Thomas's house at Castlerankine and tried, without success,

---

[1] *Arbroath Liber*, i, No. 231; *Cal. Docs. Scot.*, ii, 439; *Laing Chrs.*, No. 18; *Kelso Liber*, No. 193; *Cal. Docs. Scot.*, ii, No. 1978. It is noteworthy that the sheriff of Lanark in 1301, Walter Logan, was out with Bruce in 1306. Apparently Logan was a tenant and vassal of Bruce, *Cal. Docs. Scot.*, iv, 387-8.

[2] See, e.g., the reasonably orderly accounts rendered for the years 1302-4, *Cal. Docs. Scot.*, ii, No. 1,608, implying the existence of an established revenue system.

[3] *Newbattle Registrum, passim*, contains several documents from which the descent of the Malherbe-Morham family may be traced, and refers to the property in the Carron valley which they inherited from the Colvilles.

[4] Ibid., Nos. 216-19; *Cal. Docs. Scot.*, ii, No. 1,066.

[5] *Cal. Docs. Scot.*, ii, No. 1,949 (519).

[6] Ibid., No. 1066.

to force her to marry him.[1] In a document of this period Herbert Morham's kinsman Gilbert Malherbe, lord of Slamannan and Livilands, appears as sheriff of Stirling.[2] We can be fairly certain that he already held the office in 1299, for when towards the close of the year the English garrison of Stirling was at last starved into submission it was to Gilbert Malherbe, 'Scotsman', that the English constable John Sampson handed over the castle.[3] But if it was convenient to employ local potentates it was also true that such men might rate their local interests higher than the common enterprise. The Scots leaders committed Stirling Castle to the Perthshire knight Sir William Oliphant (Olifard), thereby provoking resentment among the Malherbes.[4] At all events, after the Scots generally had made peace with Edward I in 1304 it was to Gilbert Malherbe that the goods and chattels of Sir William Oliphant, who still held out, were assigned.[5] Afterwards Malherbe seems to have recovered the sheriffdom of Stirling from Edward II, but later still he was reconciled with Bruce, only to be forfeited and executed for his part in the Soules treason-plot of 1320.[6] Trying to keep pace with every shift of power could be a perilous occupation.

Co-operation between Bruce and Comyn had begun to break down by August 1299, soon after William Lamberton's return from France. The bishop arrived just in time to join the Scots leaders in a full-scale raid south of the Forth.[7] They went first to Glasgow and from there up into the Forest,[8] at whose north-western corner they would find a good base in the bishop of Glasgow's large manor of Stobo. Many of the greatest magnates joined in the raid. Besides

[1] *Cal. Docs. Scot.*, ii, Nos. 1066 and 1108.

[2] *Laing Chrs.*, No. 18.

[3] *Cal. Docs. Scot.*, ii, No. 1,949.

[4] *Flores Historiarum*, iii, 113. It is not certain that Olifard was the first commander appointed by the Scots after they recaptured Stirling.

[5] *Cal. Docs. Scot.*, ii, No. 1,517.

[6] Ibid., iii, 433, seems to show that in 1311–12 Gilbert Malherbe, though not then sheriff of Stirling, had held the office recently. For his subsequent career, cf. *Reg. Mag. Sig.*, i, Appendix 2, No. 516; *Chron. Fordun*, i, 348; Barbour, *Bruce*, 338.

[7] Stevenson, *Documents*, ii, No. 527, a letter written by Sir John Kingston, commander of Edinburgh castle, dated August 9th. The year must be 1299, as noted by F. M. Powicke, *The Thirteenth Century*, 696, n. 1. Kingston's news was that the earl of Buchan, the bishop of St Andrews and the earls and magnates of Scotland were taking part personally in the raid.

[8] Stevenson, *Documents*, ii, No. 527.

Lamberton and the two Guardians there were the earls of Buchan and Menteith, probably the earl of Atholl also,[1] James the Stewart, Sir Ingram de Umfraville, Sir William Balliol, Sir David Graham (Sir Patrick's son), Sir David of Brechin and Sir Robert Keith, the Marischal. William Wallace was conspicuously absent, but his brother Sir Malcolm Wallace was there in Bruce's following.[2] They first planned to attack Roxburgh, but changed their minds when they learned how strongly the town was defended and how an attack would involve them in very heavy casualties – a striking illustration of the effect Falkirk had had upon Scottish strategy. Instead, Umfraville and Keith were ordered to stay in the Forest with a hundred barded horse and 1,500 foot, not counting the men of the Forest. There was a justifiable hope of winning over the most influential of the local lords, Simon Fraser of Oliver Castle, whose forebears had been sheriffs of Tweeddale, on and off, since the twelfth century. Fraser had been with the English since 1296. For a long time he dissembled his intentions, but it is virtually certain that the Scottish incursion into the Forest was made easier by the fact that Fraser was already inclined to come over to the patriotic side. The English constable of Edinburgh, advising Edward to beware of Fraser, said he had heard that Fraser, in a parley with the Scots leaders, had eaten and drunk with them and they had all been friends together.[3]

The Scots were powerful enough at this time to bring about an exchange of prisoners, and, with the help of Margaret, lady of Penicuik, and her son Hugh, to raid as far as the outskirts of Edinburgh.[4] Nevertheless, cracks had begun to show openly in the leaders' unity. Most of our knowledge of the raid into the Forest comes from a report sent to Edward on August 20th by the English constable of Roxburgh, Robert Hastings. Hastings had a spy – one of the lesser folk – among the Scots army, and

---

[1] P.R.O., C. 47/22/8 (calendared somewhat misleadingly by Bain, *Cal. Docs. Scot.*, ii, No. 1,978; there is a facsimile in *Nat. MSS. Scot.*, Pt. II, No. 8). In this document, partly illegible, the list of earls runs 'le counte de Carrik' le counte de Boghan le counte [   ]le le counte de Menethet3.' Atholl was the only carldom for which the thirteenth century form might end in the letters 'le'.

[2] P.R.O., C. 47/22/8. *Cal. Docs. Scot.*, ii, No. 1,978, omits this significant fact.

[3] Stevenson, *Documents*, ii, No. 527.

[4] *Cal. Docs. Scot.*, ii, No. 1,978; Stevenson, *Documents*, ii, No. 527.

in addition to his useful military information, he had some startling news to tell of a council which the Scots magnates held at Peebles on August 19th.[1]

At the council Sir David Graham demanded the lands and goods of Sir William Wallace because he was leaving the kingdom without the leave or approval of the Guardians. And Sir Malcolm, Sir William's brother, answered that neither his lands nor his goods should be given away, for they were protected by the peace in which Wallace had left the kingdom, since he was leaving to work for the good of the kingdom. At this, the two knights gave the lie to each other and drew their daggers. And since Sir David Graham was of Sir John Comyn's following and Sir Malcolm Wallace of the earl of Carrick's following, it was reported to the earl of Buchan and John Comyn that a fight had broken out without their knowing it; and John Comyn leaped at the earl of Carrick and seized him by the throat, and the earl of Buchan turned on the bishop of St Andrews, declaring that treason and lesemajestie were being plotted. Eventually the Stewart and others came between them and quietened them. At that moment a letter was brought from beyond the Firth of Forth, telling how Sir Alexander Comyn and Lachlan were burning and devastating the district they were in, attacking the people of Scotland (*la nacion Descoce*). So it was ordained then that the bishop of St Andrews should have all the castles in his hands as principal captain, and the earl of Carrick and John Comyn be with him as joint-guardians of the kingdom. And that same Wednesday, after the letter had been read, they all left Peebles.

The report shows us only one small eruption of rivalries which smouldered deep down below the surface. It would be hard to drive the northerners, the Balliol men *par excellence*, in the same harness as the south-westerners, Bruce and the Stewart among them, the group to which the Wallaces naturally belonged. The sinister report from the north concerned men of the Comyn faction. Alexander Comyn was the earl of Buchan's brother. Lachlan was Lachlan Macruarie, the west highland captain of galloglasses, who in 1297, in alliance with Alexander Macdougall, his son Duncan and Comyn of Badenoch, had been burning and devastating the lands and men of

---

[1] See above, p. 151, n. 1. It may be noted, in connexion with Wallace's journey abroad, that in 1300 the Lothian baron William de Vieuxpont, 'of the company of William Wallace', was arrested at Blaye near Bordeaux on suspicion of spying on English shipping movements (P.R.O., SC 1/61/32).

Edward I's friend Alexander Macdonald of Islay.[1] As yet, Lamberton was a neutral, moderating figure, supporting no faction but fighting only for the community of the realm and for the liberty of 'la nacion Descoce', to use the phrase of Hastings's spy. The bishop's career had linked him to Wishart, Glasgow, the south-west; but by family origins and now through his great bishopric, he belonged to the old Scotia north of Forth and Tay. As a result of the quarrel at Peebles and the bad news from the north, the ranks had been closed. For a little longer Bruce and Comyn would work together. Once again, the community had one bishop, one earl and one baron to rule them on behalf of their absent king. But surely there was something prophetic in the manner in which the Forest gathering broke up? While Bishop Lamberton remained at Stobo, the other great lords rode off toward their own homes. The two Comyns returned to the country beyond the Forth, Bruce and the Gallovidians headed for Annandale and Galloway – partly in order to attack the English-held castle of Lochmaben – while James Stewart and the earl of Menteith went back to Clydesdale.

[1] Stevenson, *Documents*, ii, No. 445. The 'Laclan' or 'Lohlan' 'Macrogri' of this memorandum, and his brother Roderick, are the Rolandus filius Alani and his brother Roderick of the preceding document, ibid., No. 444, and also the 'sons of Roderick' of ibid., No. 615. Lachlan and Roderick were sons of Alan son of Roderick (son of Reginald son of Somerled); hence they were 'Macalans', but also, by line, 'Macruaries'. The name Macruarie has usually been given to the family here. For Lachlan's career see *Kingdom of the Scots*, 381–2, and *Memoranda de Parliamento*, 191.

Additional Note (see above, p. 130).
Wallace's Northumbrian Raid in 1297.
According to the chronicle written at the abbey of Bury St Edmunds, which seems to be well-informed about Scottish affairs in this period, Wallace shared the leadership of the raid with 'a certain Malcis' (*Scotici, duce quodam maleis cum Willelmo Walensi . . . devastarunt*). The chronicle's editors have supposed the name Malcis to be corrupt and even a mistaken form of *de Moravia* (Murray). This seems somewhat desperate, and it looks rather as though Wallace's fellow-leader was believed to be Malise earl of Strathearn, for whose military activities before February, 1298 see above, p. 137, n. 3 (cf. V. H. Galbraith, *EHR*, lviii, 67 and n. 7, 68 and Antonia Gransden (ed.), *The Chronicle of Bury St Edmunds, 1212–1301* (1964), 142). If this identification were correct it would throw fresh light on the nature of Wallace's support in 1297–8 and tend to strengthen the argument put forward at the beginning of this chapter.

7

The King over the Water

WHETHER or not it is true that the years from 1299 to 1304 form the most obscure period in the whole struggle for independence, they are certainly the most neglected. Yet unless we try to understand the events of these years we shall miss the real significance of Bruce's bid for the throne. In order to see the period as clearly as possible some artificial divisions are unavoidable. We must deal separately with government, internal rivalries, diplomacy, war and trade. But at the time the struggle was a single national effort. Each class, nobles, merchants, clergy and lesser folk, did not pursue its own anti-English policy independently of the others. Sir Maurice Powicke has, indeed, drawn a contrast between Edward I and the Scots in this period which must be accepted as broadly true. 'The difference between the two administrations,' he has written, 'was that while Edward, in spite of his embarrassments, was master of his own household and acted through well-tried and loyal friends . . . the Scottish leaders were not thoroughly united.'[1] But from 1299 to 1302 Edward's embarrassments were formidable. He was involved in political and constitutional disputes which constantly weakened the support that the crown had a right to expect from the great feudal magnates, and he found it difficult to raise revenue. These handicaps helped the Scots materially. Master of his own household, King Edward was not in these years master of the politically responsible community of his own realm, and without that backing he could not hope to conquer Scotland and hold it in permanent subjection. The Scottish leaders, it is true, were not by any means a happy band of brothers, but for all that a dour and dogged persistence in the common enterprise distinguishes their actions from the battle of Falkirk to the submission of 1304. If this is acknowledged it becomes

[1] *The Thirteenth Century*, 696.

easier to understand the stubborn refusal of Oliphant, Soules and Wallace to surrender even then, easier to understand Bruce's decision in 1305 to resume the struggle, easier to appreciate the opinion of an observer at Forfar in 1307 that Bruce had never enjoyed the good will of the people so much as at that moment.

Bruce himself was the only leader of the first rank to desert the national cause in this period. He may well have debated for a long time whether or not to join the English, against whom he had fought consistently, if not always very effectively, since the summer of 1297. But the stages by which he reached his decision and his motives for reaching it are alike hidden from us. In November 1299 he was still Guardian with Comyn and Lamberton, waiting in Torwood for the English garrison of Stirling to surrender, and telling Edward I that, through the mediation of Philip the Fair, the Scots would agree to a truce.[1] The Guardians' constitutional position and the striking fidelity with which they adhered to the time-honoured forms of expressing it are shown in the style used in their letter to King Edward. 'William by divine mercy bishop of St Andrews, Robert Bruce earl of Carrick and John Comyn the younger, Guardians of the kingdom of Scotland in the name of the famous prince the lord John, by God's grace illustrious king of Scotland, appointed by the community of that realm, together with the community of the realm itself.'[2] The address on the seal-tag runs: 'To the lord Edward, by God's grace king of England, by the Guardians and community of the realm of Scotland.'[3]

The Scots were in a strong position and full of hope. Their great enemy was actually in Northumberland, yet he could not lift a finger to save the starving garrison of Stirling, and the castle was in Scottish hands by the end of the year.[4] The next step was to gain control of southern Scotland by wiping out pockets of native dis-affection (chiefly in Galloway) and by recapturing the border for-

---

[1] *APS*, i, 454.

[2] Ibid.

[3] This is not given in the printed text, but may be seen on the original, P.R.O., E. 39/14/14; cf. *Foedera*, i, 915.

[4] It was still holding out in August 1299, Stevenson, *Documents*, ii, No. 527, but had submitted by the end of the year when the garrison was faced by starvation, *Chron. Rishanger*, 402. They were allowed to return to England unharmed, *Flores Historiarum*, iii, 113, 310. Cf. also for this episode, *Chron. Guisb.*, 332.

tresses. It was resolved to concentrate on the south-west, where
Bruce held his earldom and where his father, firm in his English
allegiance, still held the loyalty of the knights, if not of the commoners, of Annandale. It is not rash to guess that this south-western
drive had something to do with Bruce's resignation from the
guardianship, which came some time between November 1299 and
the following May.

In that month the earl of Buchan (who was lord of Cruggleton in
Wigtownshire and sheriff of the county) went to Galloway to try to
win over the leading men to the national cause.[1] It was an uphill task.
The Gallovidians were inspired by a traditional hostility towards
Scotland in general and towards Carrick in particular. This did not
mean that they were anxious for English rule, but Edward I consistently exploited their separatism. At the outbreak of the war in
1296 Bishop Bek of Durham had brought out of his sixty years'
imprisonment in Barnard Castle the pathetic figure of Thomas of
Galloway.[2] He had been condemned as long ago as the reign of
Alexander II for his part in the Gallovidian revolt of 1235. Now the
poor old man, eighty-eight years old, was shaved, given clean clothes,
and sent back to his native province armed with a special charter of
liberties from the English Justinian which, if generously interpreted,
would have allowed the men of Galloway to do pretty much as they
liked.[3] To be sure, many Gallovidians began the war fighting against
the English: after all, Balliol was lord of Galloway. Many more
joined Wallace's raid on northern England, but this was surely
because it was traditional for Galloway men to take part in these
fearful plundering raids, not because they were heart and soul behind
the patriots. The fact is that for many years from 1297 the leading
men of Galloway, among them the MacCans and the Macdoualls,
were active on the English side.

In preparation for the campaigning season, the remaining Scots
magnates (apart from the earl of Buchan) held a parliament at
Rutherglen on May 10th.[4] Bruce must by now have resigned.

---

[1] *SHR*, xxiv, 246.

[2] *Chron. Lanercost*, 177; cf. *Cal. Docs. Scot.*, ii, Nos. 728, 729.

[3] *Cal. Docs. Scot.*, No. 728. The Gallovidians' petition to Edward I to be relieved
of the burden of 'surdit de sergaunt' (for which see *SHR*, xxxix, 170–5), may belong
to this period; *Cal. Docs Scot.*, ii, No. 1,874.

[4] *SHR*, xxiv, 246.

6. The Rule of the Guardians 1299–1302

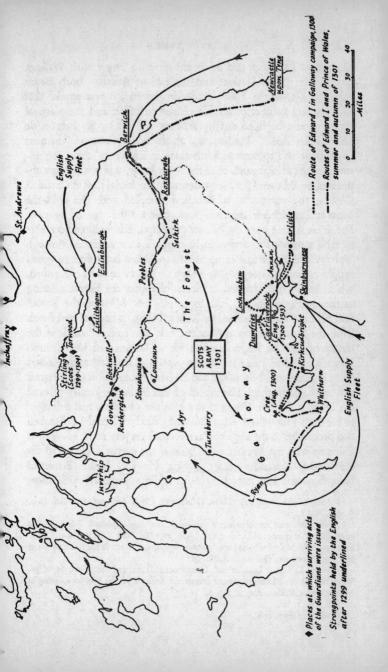

St. Andrews

Inchaffray

Stirling (Scots 1299–1304)
Torwood
Linlithgow
Edinburgh
Peebles
Selkirk
The Forest
Govan
Bothwell
Rutherglen
Stonehouse
Loudoun
Roxburgh
Barwick
Newcastle upon Tyne
English Supply Fleet

SCOTS ARMY 1301

Ayr
Turnberry
Inverkip

Galloway

Cree (Aug. 1300)
Whithorn
Kirkcudbright
Lochmaben
Dumfries
Caerlaverock (Eng. 1300–1303)
Annan
Carlisle
Skinburness
English Supply Fleet
L. Ryan

········· Route of Edward I in Galloway campaign, 1300

—··—·· Routes of Edward I and Prince of Wales,
summer and autumn of 1301

Miles
0 10 20 30 40

◆ Places at which surviving acts
of the Guardians were issued

Strongpoints held by the English
after 1299 underlined

Comyn of Badenoch said he would serve no longer with William
Lamberton. James Stewart and the earl of Atholl – both Bruce
partisans – took the bishop's side. In the end, it was agreed that
Comyn and Lamberton should remain in office, and the place of
Bruce should be filled not by another earl but by Sir Ingram de
Umfraville, Balliol's kinsman and an ally of the Comyns. The next
parliament was to meet at Rutherglen in six weeks' time, at mid-
summer. As it happened, or as the Scots knew, this was the day ap-
pointed by Edward I for the gathering of the feudal host at Carlisle.[1]
Clearly, the geography of Scotland, coupled with the hold the
Scots still retained in the south west, dictated the zone of fighting.
For the first time since the Falkirk campaign, Edward had been able
to raise a respectable army. In its support, as it advanced through
'Solwayland' to its first camp at Annan, was a large fleet to guard
supply routes and keep watch on the Galloway coast.[2] Lochmaben,
which Bruce had attacked unsuccessfully after the Forest meeting
in the previous August, had apparently not fallen to the Scots.[3]
Still held by the English, under Robert Felton, it had suffered much
from the Scots garrison at Caerlaverock, that splendid castle at the
mouth of the Nith, ten miles south-west of Lochmaben. In a skirmish
Felton's men had killed the young captain of Caerlaverock, Robert
Cunningham, and Felton had had his head hoisted aloft on the great
tower of Lochmaben. The report of this barbarity greatly grieved
the Stewart, for Cunningham was his sister's nephew and belonged
to his own following.[4] King Edward quickly relieved Lochmaben
and proceeded to the siege of Caerlaverock on July 10th, 'enraged as
a lioness who has lost her cubs' because the garrison had asked for
honourable surrender terms, saving life and limb.[5] Powerful
battering-rams and *trébuchets* (stone-lobbing engines) made short

---

[1] Morris, *Welsh Wars*, 298; *Chron. Guisb.*, 334; *Chron. Lanercost*, 194; *Cal. Docs.
Scot.*, ii, No. 1,136.

[2] *Liber quotidianus contrarotulatoris garderobae anno regni Edwardi Primi vicesimo
octavo* (Soc. Antiquaries of London, 1787), 120, 123; *Cal. Docs. Scot.*, ii, 284-5; *Chron.
Rishanger*, 439. Malcolm le fiz Lengleys was empowered to attack the Scots by sea in
July 1300, Stevenson, *Documents*, ii, No. 597.

[3] 'Edward I's pele at Lochmaben', *Dumfriesshire Trans.*, 3rd Ser., xxxi, 64, n. 36.
Bruce had attacked Lochmaben and threatened Annan after the Peebles meeting in
August 1299, *Cal. Docs. Scot.*, ii, 283-4.

[4] Ibid., No. 1,101.

[5] *Chron. Rishanger*, 440.

work of the castle, and rope tied to the nearest trees made even shorter work of some of the hapless garrison.[1]

The king then advanced westward into Galloway, brushing aside overtures of peace put forward by Thomas Dalton, bishop of Whithorn.[2] The invaders reached Bridge of Dee and turned south to Kirkcudbright. A two-day parley took place here between Edward and the Scots leaders Buchan and Badenoch. Their terms were the restoration of King John, the recognition of Edward Balliol's right to succeed his father on the throne, and the right of Scottish magnates to redeem their estates (in England) from the Englishmen to whom the king had granted them. If this was refused, the Scots would defend themselves as long as they could. These not very extravagant terms apparently filled Edward with great indignation and the Scots withdrew.

While the king was staying at Girthon and Twynholm,[3] just west of Kirkcudbright, some of his foragers, with an escort, went off in search of provender as far as the Cree,[4] beyond which the Scots were lurking in an inaccessible glen. There was a skirmish and Sir Robert Keith the Marischal was captured. Next day the whole English army reached the Cree and found the Scots facing them across the tidal estuary, presumably between Creetown and Newton Stewart. The archers on both sides exchanged shots across the river and when the tide went out the English infantry crossed over and harassed the enemy at close quarters. In each army the cavalry was grouped in three brigades. Edward, mistrusting snares and traps which the Scots were reported to have laid, wished to keep the English horse on the east side. But owing to a misunderstanding the

[1] *Chron. Rishanger*, 440; *Siege of Carlaverock* (ed. N. H. Nicolas, 1828), 82–5. The writer of the ballad on the siege says that the king spared the lives of the garrison, who numbered about sixty, ibid., 86–7. *Cal. Docs. Scot.*, ii, Nos. 1,162, 1,196, show that the constable and twenty-one of the garrison were spared and imprisoned at Newcastle and Appleby. The more laconic account in *Chron. Lanercost*, 194, says that many found in the castle were hanged.

[2] *Chron. Rishanger*, 440.

[3] Ibid., where Twynam should be read for Swynam; cf. *Cal. Docs. Scot.*, ii, Nos. 1147–50.

[4] *Chron. Rishanger*, 441 and n. 1. The MS. reads *qrend'* (British Library, MS. Cotton Claudius D vi, fo. 175ʳ); there is no doubt that this is a mistaken form of 'Crith', i.e. the River Cree; cf. *Chron. Lanercost*, 194, *usque ad aquam de Grithe* (recte *Crithe*).

earl of Hereford's brigade went over, whereupon the king and his
son Edward of Caernarvon followed in support. At this the three
Scottish cavalry brigades, commanded respectively by Buchan,
Comyn of Badenoch and Umfraville, took to flight, many knights
abandoning their horses and fleeing to the moors. The English regretted much that they had brought no Welsh troops with them to
give chase in this wild country.[1] They had got the foxes into a cairn
and now had no terriers. But in these Cree-side encounters they
had at least captured two of their 'worst enemies', Sir Robert Keith
and Robert Baird of Strathaven in Clydesdale, who were sent for
safety to Bristol and Gloucester respectively.[2]

Frustrated at not coming to grips with the enemy and exasperated
by the delivery at the hands of Archbishop Winchelsey of the pope's
rebuke of June 1299, King Edward went back to England in the
autumn of 1300, having given the Scots a truce on October 30th to
last till the following Whitsun (May 21st).[3] The Scots had made a
poor showing on the banks of Cree and had lost the castle of
Caerlaverock. But, on balance, this jubilee year of 1300, in which
their ally and patron Pope Boniface VIII reached the height of his
power and prestige, must be reckoned on the credit side. Edward I
had raised an army as large as the one he brought to Falkirk and more
representative than any he had led since he conquered Wales, nearly
twenty years earlier. Yet set beside his hopes and intentions his
achievement had been trifling. By far the greater part of Scotland
remained under the Guardians' control. The English magnates had
dispersed after a short campaign and the Scots had successfully
persuaded the pope to send his letter of rebuke to Edward personally, though it was a year late and more than a year out of date. In
their demands for a truce they had been supported by both Boniface
VIII and Philip the Fair. It is clear that they were conscious of
Edward's weakness from the conversation reported between their
envoys and the English king, presumably at Dumfries in October
when he granted the truce.[4] Edward laughed scornfully at their
offers of peace. 'Every one of you has done homage to me as chief

[1] *Chron. Rishanger*, 442, where the editor's marginal note is certainly an error.
[2] Ibid., 441-2; *Cal. Docs. Scot.*, ii, Nos. 1147, 1148, 1159.
[3] *Foedera*, i, 924; *Chron. Guisb.*, 334; *Chron. Fordun*, i, 331.
[4] *Chron. Rishanger*, 447.

lord of Scotland. Now you set aside your allegiance and make a fool of me as though I were a weakling.' To which the Scottish envoys replied, 'You should not laugh; we offer peace in all seriousness. Exert your strength and see if might will triumph over right or right over might.' 'Take care,' was Edward's answer, 'that you do not come to me again.' And he declared with an oath that he would lay the whole of Scotland waste from sea to sea and force its people into submission.[1]

The combination of Lamberton, Comyn and Umfraville lasted until the end of the year. Like their predecessors they were 'Guardians in the kingdom of Scotland appointed by the community of that realm.'[2] But their tenure of office was the last experiment in multiple or joint guardianship. It had proved impossible in turn to get Comyn and Bruce, or Comyn, Bruce and Lamberton, or Comyn, Umfraville and Lamberton, to work together. The obvious inference, that young John Comyn was an impossible man to get on with, may be too simple. We have no clear evidence to support it. But there is little doubt of one thing: the Comyn leadership of the national cause, which went far back into the thirteenth century, would no longer be accepted without challenge and discontent. This is clear from the change of régime which characterized the years 1301 and 1302, and also from Robert Bruce's desertion coming at an unknown date about the turn of these years. Yet the timing of Bruce's desertion, as we shall see, suggests that his motive was more a refusal to go on fighting for the Balliols, John or Edward, than simple dislike of the Comyns.

Between December 1300 and May 1301 – most probably, indeed, early in 1301 – Lamberton, Comyn, and Umfraville resigned office and in their place a single Guardian was elected, Sir John de Soules.[3]

[1] *Chron. Rishanger*, 447. The Scots retorted that they for their part would fight to the last to resist King Edward's schemes.

[2] Theiner, *Monumenta*, No. 368; *Cal. Papal Letters*, i, 590.

[3] Ibid., December 18th, 1300, is the last known document in which they appear as Guardians. The earliest known document in which Soules appears as Guardian is that recorded by *Chron. Fordun*, i, 332, under 1300 by mistake for 1301. The statement in one MS. of Fordun that Soules acted as 'one of the Guardians of Scotland making no mention of the other' is to be explained by reference to Fordun's earlier statement (ibid., 331) that John Comyn remained Guardian continuously from 1298 to 1304. But the other MSS. merely have 'John de Soules Guardian of the kingdom of Scotland'; and the statement about Comyn is almost certainly wrong.

Among the great men of the independence struggle Soules has been most undeservedly neglected. Fordun, writing seventy years later, calls him feeble and ineffectual.[1] This is unjust. Soules was older than Bruce, Comyn and Wallace, and though he had never been a Guardian he had a long experience in public affairs. A younger son, he was not himself a wealthy landowner, having only the upland barony of Westerkirk in Eskdale (held of Enguerand de Guines)[2] and, in right of his wife, the old barony of Ardross on the Fife coast.[3] But his family had held the lordship of Liddesdale since David I's time and their castles of Liddesdale and Hermitage controlled one of the routes from England to Scotland.[4] Soules's record of constancy in the patriot cause can stand beside that of Wallace. Perhaps his most valuable quality was that while his nephew married a Comyn and although his family were the neighbours and natural allies of the Bruces of Annandale, John de Soules himself held a neutral place. But Fordun, despite his unfair strictures, may provide the clue to the strength – and weakness – of Soules's position. He says that Soules was associated with Comyn in the guardianship by John Balliol personally.[5] This may be substantially true, though it can hardly be doubted that Soules was in fact sole Guardian and Comyn for a time resigned. Certainly Soules's term of office coincides with a marked change of policy with regard to Balliol which fits in well with Fordun's statement. If Soules was indeed appointed at the express wish of King John, the Scots may have welcomed him all the more readily as a moderator between factions. He was the much-needed secular counterpart of William Lamberton, and it is not surprising to find him working very closely with the bishop in 1301 and 1302.

Under Soules the military and diplomatic offensives were intensified, and a vigorous effort was made to restore King John to his throne. Despite the famous letter of the English barons to the pope,[6]

---

[1] *Chron. Fordun.*, i, 331.

[2] *Cal. Docs. Scot.*, ii, No. 1452.

[3] *APS*, i, 445; for identification of Ardrossan, cf. *Dumfriesshire Trans.*, 3rd Ser., xxvi, 174–81.

[4] *Cal. Docs. Scot.*, ii, 296.

[5] *Chron. Fordun*, i, 331.

[6] *Foedera*, i, 926; on the manner in which the barons were required, after the letter had been engrossed, to affix their seals, cf. *The Ancestor*, No. 6 (1903), 188–90.

which purported to come from the Lincoln parliament of January 1301, and which denied the pope's right to interfere in the Anglo-Scottish quarrel on the grounds that it was a purely domestic matter, King Edward did not in fact make light of the papal claim to arbitrate. In November 1300 a powerful delegation was appointed to go to the *curia*.[1] As in 1291, the cathedrals and monasteries were ordered to search their chronicles for evidence of English suzerainty over Scotland. One of the king's expert notaries, the Yorkshireman Master Andrew of Tong, was busy from December 1300 till February 1301 preparing an elaborate legal brief to be used at the papal court.[2] This included charges against the bishops of St Andrews and Glasgow and a copy of the thousands of oaths of fealty and homage by which in 1291 and again in 1296 the Scots had become King Edward's vassals. This work bore fruit in the king's lengthy letter to Boniface dated May 7th, 1301,[3] and was followed up by the diligent lobbying carried out at the *curia* by the Dominican, Brother William of Gainsborough, and the king's confidential clerk, Thomas Walc. These agents were still hopeful in October 1301 that they could persuade Boniface to see the justice of their master's claims.[4]

The Scots, for their part, had everything to gain from a formal trial of the dispute at the papal court. Since 1294, when Celestine V had absolved their leaders from the oaths Edward had forced upon them, the papacy had been consistently friendly towards the Scots. Boniface VIII's letter, *Scimus, fili* (Anagni, June 27th, 1299),[5] which had now been brought into the open, must have been drafted on the basis of information supplied by Scottish agents. It can hardly be a coincidence that the letter was issued the day before the consecration, at Anagni, of a new Scottish bishop who was to play an invaluable part in the national struggle. While joint Guardians, Bruce and Comyn had appointed to the bishopric of Moray (one of the more important sees) Master David Murray, parson of two old Olifard livings to which the Murrays had succeeded, Bothwell in Clydes-

[1] *Chron. Rishanger*, 451.
[2] *Cal. Docs. Scot.*, iv, 449; cf. T. F. Tout, *Chapters in Administrative History*, ii, 70, n
    Chron. Picts-Scots., 221-31; Stones, *Documents*, No. 30.
[4] *Cal. Docs. Scot.*, ii, No. 1167, which belongs to 1301, not 1300; cf. *SHR*, xxxiv, 130 and n. 5.
[5] *Chron. Picts-Scots*, 216-21; Stones, *Documents*, No. 28.

dale and Lilford in Northamptonshire.[1] It is probable that David Murray was brother of Sir William Murray of Bothwell, the Pantler, and so uncle of young Andrew Murray who had led the Moray rising and was mortally wounded at Stirling Bridge.[2] For Murray as for Lamberton, the journey to Rome must have had a diplomatic as well as a spiritual purpose. On the very day of Murray's consecration Pope Boniface issued a letter to Archbishop Winchelsey on the same lines as *Scimus, fili*, condemning English interference in Scotland.[3] Two months later, as we have seen, there was talk of William Wallace going overseas. When he left Scotland is not known, but of the fact of his going there is no doubt. He may have gone first to Orkney or Norway,[4] and we have proof that eventually he reached the French court. This confirms part of the muddled story of an English chronicler,[5] and suggests also that the Scots intended to send him on to the papal court as well. The evidence is a brief routine letter of recommendation from King Philip the Fair to his agents at the Roman *curia* telling them to assist 'our beloved William le Walois of Scotland, knight', and its date is November 7th, 1300.[6] A week earlier two high-ranking English envoys to the papacy, the earl of Lincoln and Sir Hugh Despenser, were at Canterbury on their way to Rome.[7] There is nothing to suggest that Wallace did

[1] Dowden, *Bishops*, 151; Theiner, *Monumenta*, No. 364. Instituted rector of Lilford, Northamptonshire, 1282, on presentation of Sir William Murray; resigned next year, succeeded by John Murray (*Rolls and Register of Bishop Oliver Sutton*, ed. R. Hill (Lincoln Record Soc.), ii, 16, 26). Rector of Bothwell (the principal seat of Sir William Murray of Bothwell) in 1296, *Cal. Docs. Scot.*, ii, 212.

[2] E. M. Barron, *Scottish War of Independence*, 204–5; his presentation to Lilford rectory (see previous note) would fit in well with the suggested relationship.

[3] Stevenson, *Documents*, ii, No. 569.

[4] F. Palgrave, *The Antient Kalendars and Inventories of the Treasury of His Majesty's Exchequer, etc.* (1836), i, 134, shows that the documents found with Wallace at his capture included safe-conducts issued by King Hakon of Norway as well as by the king of France.

[5] *Chron. Rishanger*, 387, which says that Wallace, crossing to France after Falkirk, was arrested by Philip IV, who offered to hand him over to Edward I.

[6] Stevenson, *Wallace Docs.*, 163 (=P.R.O., S.C.1/XXX/81). I have to thank Professor Robert Fawtier for telling me, in a letter, that Philip IV's recommendation, dated at Pierrefonds on November 7th, may be assigned to 1300, since in that year the king was at Pierrefonds on November 3rd, 8th and 9th.

[7] *Chron. Rishanger*, 451. Rishanger adds the name of the 'chancellor of Gascony', but I am assured by Dr Pierre Chaplais that there was no such official in 1300. Nevertheless, the mission was probably three in number.

not go to see the pope, and his mission may well have been the Scottish counterpart of the powerful English delegation.

Though Wallace's movements are hidden from us, we know that the principal Scottish effort at the papal court came in May 1301, when the Scots were furnished with a *processus*, or brief, designed to counter the English arguments point by point, not only on ancient history but also, and more especially, on the events of the last few years.[1] There is, of course, a great deal of fable and bad history both in Edward I's letter and in the Scottish reply, though the respect which both pay to the value of historical evidence is remarkable. There are some telling points in Edward's letter, but there is little question that the Scottish reply is the more impressive document. It is better written, its 'pre-history', though fabulous, is in some respects curiously close to the known facts about Scottish origins, its handling of events in the twelfth and thirteenth centuries, though not free from serious errors, is less tendentious than Edward's, and above all it gains strength from the emphasis which it lays upon the events of the recent past, on the importance the Scots attached to the treaty of Birgham-Northampton and on the charge that Edward had taken advantage of the Scottish dilemma of 1291. At least one statement made by Edward in these representations was plainly false. In a letter given to his delegates in November 1300 the king declared: 'My enemies the Scots have recently acknowledged that I am chief lord of Scotland by hereditary right, *by a decree of their entire nation*'.[2] Not once in the course of Edward's dealings with Scotland had their been any recognition of his suzerainty, even under duress, that could be called an act of the whole Scottish nation.

One forceful point made by the Scots was that whereas Edward I had informed the pope that he was in full possession of Scotland the truth was that of the twelve 'cities' (bishops' sees), and twelve dioceses, existing in Scotland the English king did not have complete possession of any, 'but only of certain places in the dioceses of St

---

[1] *Chron. Picts-Scots*, 232–71 (*Instructiones*); 271–84 (*processus* of Master Baldred Bisset). The date is deduced from ibid., 271, 'soon after Whitsun last past'. These Latin texts apparently survive only in *Chron. Bower* (where they were taken from a lost work attributed to Master Alan of Montrose). A very full contemporary French summary is in British Library, MS. Cotton Vespasian F. vii, fo. 15 (Stones, *Documents*, No. 31).

[2] *Chron. Rishanger*, 451.

Andrews and Glasgow'.[1] As to the rest of the Scottish pleading, there survives a summary made for King Edward at the time by one of his agents which because of its ability to convey the gist of the Scottish case in a few words deserves to be quoted in a full translation of its original French.[2]

Sire, the Scots, in the document sent from Rome, say three things. First, that your statement of claims sent to the pope ought not to have any validity since it did not reach him on the day assigned to you by summons [it was four months overdue] and if it contained anything in your favour this is already annulled and contradicted by the following contrary facts. In the second place, they deny that certain *gestes*, histories, chronicles and other matters which you have quoted are in your favour, and declare that others are in their favour. And they in turn call to witness for their side other histories and *gestes*, contrary to yours, to affirm that the condition of the kingdom of Scotland is free and not subject to you, and they have an answer to the papal bulls which you allege to be in your favour. In the third place, they attempt to prove that the kingdom of Scotland is free and in no way subject to you, and this in five ways, (i) by papal privileges, (ii) by the principle of common law that one kingdom ought not to be in any way subject to another, (iii) by prescription [i.e., independence dating back before the time of written laws], (iv) by the existence of independence at all times, and (v) by various instruments of the kings of England [especially Richard I's quitclaim of 1189 revoking the so-called 'treaty' of Falaise]. And so they pray that the pope will pronounce judgement on this affair between them and you, and that he will immediately forbid you to engage in any kind of warlike acts against them.

We know the identity of the man who was chiefly responsible for the impressive Scottish pleading at the papal court. Shortly after Whitsun (May 21st) 1301,[3] a letter was addressed to Pope Boniface by John de Soules, Guardian of the kingdom of Scotland, by the counsel of the prelates, earls, barons and other nobles of the community of the realm, giving formal authority to a delegation composed of Master William Frere, archdeacon of Lothian and professor of canon law in the university of Paris, Master William of Eagles-

---

[1] *Chron. Picts–Scots*, 239–40.

[2] British Library, MS. Cotton Vespasian F. vii, fo. 16.

[3] *Chron. Fordun*, i, 332, where the year should be 1301. For the date being after Whitsun, cf. *Chron. Picts–Scots*, 271.

ham, doctor of canon law, and Master Baldred Bisset.[1] Contemporary record and later chroniclers agree in assigning the lion's share in this business to Master Baldred, whom Andrew Wyntoun called approvingly a 'wys and cunnand clerk'.[2] In the 1280s Baldred Bisset, who seems to have belonged to the Stirlingshire branch of the Bisset family, was already a sufficiently experienced lawyer to be Official of St Andrews – president of the bishop's ordinary court and therefore enjoying a leading position in the administration of ecclesiastical law in Scotland.[3] He held the parsonage or rectory of Kinghorn, a rich living in Crown patronage.[4] After the collapse of the Scots in 1296, Edward I began to distribute to English clerks those Scottish benefices whose incumbents had not submitted to him. Bisset's name is as conspicuously absent from the Ragman Roll as Wallace's – very possibly he was abroad, at Bologna. Some time between 1296 and 1301 the English king gave the parsonage of Kinghorn to Peter of Dunwich, who was active in Scotland from 1296 as one of Edward's hated officials.[5] In 1302 or thereabouts Bisset protested formally to the bishop of Bologna against his deprivation, his protest being referred to Scottish commissioners.[6] A report made to Edward I on the situation in Scotland, which must surely have been written in 1301 or at latest 1302, gave the following news:

The bishop of St Andrews is showing the people a letter under the king of France's seal (whether counterfeit or not the writer cannot say) asserting that there will be no peace between him and the king of England unless the Scots are included. The people are putting their faith in this and in the

[1] Frere is called a regent master in canon law at Paris in a document of 1305, *Foedera*, i, 975. Some particulars of these men are given in *SHR*, xli, 11–15; much more will be found in Dr D. E. R. Watt's forthcoming work on Scottish university graduates.

[2] *Chron. Wyntoun (Laing)*, ii, 351.

[3] *Cambuskenneth Registrum*, No. 3; cf. *Newbattle Registrum*, No. 59; *Historiae Dunelmensis Scriptores Tres* (ed. J. Raine, Surtees Soc., 1839), 93; R. Brentano, *York Metropolitan Jurisdiction*, 126, 159.

[4] *Nat. MSS. Scot.*, ii, Pl. XII; NLS, MS. Adv.15.1.18, No. 43 (Sept. 1289).

[5] Ibid.; cf. *Cal. Docs. Scot.*, ii, references in index s.v. Dunwich.

[6] *Nat. MSS. Scot.*, ii, Pl. XII. Uberto was bishop of Bologna from 1302 to 1322. Baldred Bisset, 'scozzese', doctor of laws, was acting at Bologna as vicar of Bishop Uberto in an arbitration of April 15th, 1305, G. C. Trombelli, *Memorie istoriche concernenti le due canoniche di Santa Maria di Reno e di San Salvatore insieme unite* (Bologna, 1752), 71.

success which they hope will be obtained by Master Baldred, their spokes-
man at the court of Rome. They say for certain that the bishop is at the
bottom of the whole affair.[1]

The mission to the papacy caught the popular imagination. If Scotland possessed in William Wallace a military champion she could
also boast a forensic champion in Master Baldred Bisset.

In spite of the optimism of the English envoys, Bisset and his
colleagues carried the day at Rome. Since July 1299, John Balliol
had been kept in papal custody, first at Malmaison in the diocese of
Cambrai,[2] then at the Burgundian *château* of Gévrey-Chambertin.[3]
We now know that during the summer of 1301 he was released from
papal custody and installed by Philip the Fair in the ancestral *château*
of the Balliols at Bailleul-en-Vimeu, in Picardy.[4] Balliol's movements had been accompanied by increasing marks of respect in the
papal documents referring to him: 'called king of Scotland', July
1299; 'king of Scots', November 1299; and finally 'illustrious king of
Scots' by September 1300.[5] Even Edward I, by the end of 1301, had
been forced to admit the possibility either of Balliol's restoration or
of the succession of his son Edward, whom the English king had
prudently kept as a state prisoner.[6] Scottish confidence in King
John's restoration can be seen in a number of ways. Since 1297,
official acts of government had been issued in the names of the
Guardians or commanders of the army, though these officers had
consistently claimed to be acting on behalf of King John. But in
1301 such acts began to be issued directly in the name of King John
and were dated by his regnal years calculated from his accession in
November 1292.[7] John de Soules the Guardian, instead of appearing
at the head of these documents, took a more modest place as the

---

[1] P.R.O., S.C. 1/21/166, summarized in *Cal. Docs. Scot.*, ii, No. 1431. Probably
1302 is the right year, if the letter of Philip IV was brought back to Scotland by
Lamberton after his visit to France in 1301, referred to in *APS*, i, 454.

[2] Stevenson, *Documents*, ii, Nos. 579, 586.

[3] Ibid., No. 603. 'Castrum Jeuriaci in Montana', diocese Langres, belonging to the
Cf. A. I. Cameron in *Papers of the British School at Rome*, xii (1932), 36 and n. 1.

[4] *SHR*, xxxiv, 130-1.   [5] Stevenson, *Documents*, ii, Nos. 579-80, 586, 603.

[5] Stevenson, *Documents*, ii, Nos. 579-80, 586, 603.

[6] *SHR*, xxxiv, 132.

[7] A list of these acts has been made by G. G. Simpson, *Handlist of the Acts of Alexander III, the Guardians and John (Regesta Regum Scottorum*, 1960, duplicated), Appendix, Nos. 417-22.

first or only witness. A phrase in one surviving act of this type is particularly significant. 'King John', confirming (July 10th, 1301) to Alexander Scrymgeour certain rights belonging to his constableship of Dundee, concluded, 'these letters-patent to be valid at our will or that of our dearest son Edward or of John de Soules, Guardian of our kingdom'.[1] A new seal neatly symbolized the new position, with the name and title of King John on the obverse and the name and arms of 'John de Soules, knight' on the reverse.[2]

The Scrymgeour document proves that the Guardians had restored or preserved at least one ancient function of Scottish royal government: the holding of inquests about property and the formal return of their findings to the king's chancery, or 'chapel' as it was called in Scotland. The traditional head of the chapel was the chancellor, and it was in keeping with the new policy that by January 31st, 1301, a chancellor of Scotland had been appointed.[3] He was Master Nicholas Balmyle, who – for the historian – has a way of turning up unobtrusively at a number of major occasions for which written evidence survives. An auditor at the court of claims in 1292,[4] he attended King John's first parliament in 1293,[5] and was appointed Official of St Andrews during the critical vacancy of 1297 when Lamberton was elected bishop.[6] Now in 1301 he took his place with Soules and Lamberton as one of the handful of key men who directed the national struggle. Indeed, the first of the only two documents which prove that Balmyle was chancellor shows him in the company of Bishop Lamberton and of two out of the three members of the delegation to Rome, Archdean Frere and William of Eaglesham. The second document referring to Balmyle as chancellor[7] is interesting because it shows one way in which the Guardians were able to pay the salaries of high officials in a period

[1] S.R.O., Dudhope Muniments, Box 40, bdle 1, No. 309.

[2] J. H. Stevenson and M. Wood, *Scottish Heraldic Seals*, No. 22.

[3] *St Andrews Liber*, 120.

[4] As 'Master N. de Sancto Andrea', *Chron. Rishanger*, 263; *Kingdom of the Scots*, 245-7.   [5] *Glasgow Registrum*, No. 239.

[6] *Chron. Bower*, i, 362. I was wrong to say (*SHR*, xli, 14 and n. 4) that Master Nicholas could not have been appointed official after Bishop Fraser's death. As Dr D. E. R. Watt has kindly pointed out, it was clearly the prior and convent of St Andrews, claiming the spiritual jurisdiction of the church of St Andrews *sede vacante*, who appointed Balmyle Official.

[7] British Library, MS. Add. 33245, fo. 86ᵛ.

when the national revenue system had been badly dislocated. The
rich abbey of Arbroath was made responsible for paying Master
Nicholas's fee as chancellor.

The Scots had hoped that before the truce expired on May 21st,
1301, King Edward would give way under papal and French pressure and agree to a permanent peace. In fact Edward had no mind to
give way. He allowed French envoys to come to Canterbury but he
remained as stubborn as ever about his claims in Scotland and long
before the truce expired was busy planning a fresh campaign. By
contrast, the Scots attached much importance to the Canterbury
peace talks. Nicholas Balmyle, the chancellor, was one of their
four representatives, and the others were men of standing: Sir
Adam Gordon (keeper of the West March for the Guardians in
1300),[1] Sir John of Inchmartin, and Master Thomas of Bunkle, a
prominent clerk from Matthew Crambeth's diocese of Dunkeld.[2] In
1291–2 Master Thomas had been one of Bruce's auditors along with
Matthew Crambeth and Sir Alexander of Bunkle, a substantial
Berwickshire laird to whom Master Thomas was doubtless kin.
The envoys' efforts were in vain. The truce expired at Whitsun with
no sign of peace being any nearer.

In the midst of all this diplomatic activity and efforts to get Scottish government working again along its accustomed paths, Soules
did not neglect his main objective, to beat the English in the field.
He avoided pitched battles but pursued harassing tactics with
vigour. Edward I's campaign in 1301 was intended to smash the
position of strength which the Scots had built up in the south-west,
partly by direct attack, partly by severing communications with the
rest of Scotland. He was not yet strong enough to recapture Stirling.
Instead, he concentrated on seizing and holding the natural line
formed by Tweeddale and Clydesdale. The army was summoned
for midsummer in two divisions, the larger at Berwick under the
king, the smaller at Carlisle under Edward of Caernarvon, now
prince of Wales. The prince's task was direct attack upon the Scots
holding the south-west, so that, in his father's words, 'the chief
honour of taming the pride of the Scots' should fall to his son.[3] The

[1] Foedera, i, 925.
[2] Cal. Docs. Scot., ii, No. 1244 (where Balnul is in error for Balmil).
[3] Ibid., No. 1191.

king's force moved up Tweeddale, taking Selkirk and Peebles to seal off the Forest and nullify its peculiar usefulness to the Scots, and then continuing down Clydesdale to lay siege in August to the great castle of Bothwell. This castle, commanding the direct route from northern Scotland to the south-west, had been the ancient stronghold of the Oliphants (Olifards) and in 1301 was the property of the three-year-old boy, Andrew Murray, son of Wallace's colleague, who was being brought up in Moray among King Edward's enemies.

The main Scottish army was busy in Dumfriesshire and Ayrshire, highly mobile, too strong to allow the prince of Wales the share of glory his father had planned. The prince kept to the Solway coast and got no further than Whithorn and Loch Ryan. Meanwhile the Scots, under Soules and Umfraville, made a bold attack on Lochmaben (September 7th and 8th) and using Comyn of Badenoch's estate of Dalswinton as base began to recruit men from Nithsdale.[1] While they hung on to the flanks of the prince's army they also found time to menace the main English force at Bothwell. Soules and the earl of Buchan gathered at Loudoun while Simon Fraser, Alexander Abernethy and Herbert Morham were reported at Stonehouse near Strathaven.[2] At one moment they were rumoured to be threatening the English communication line by a drive towards Roxburgh, at another they were said to be heading for Galloway. Bothwell had fallen by September 24th,[3] but Soules's vigour had thwarted the English pincer movement. Instead of the king and his son meeting at Inverkip as planned, the prince withdrew to the east after some of his advance units had helped to capture Turnberry.[4] Eventually he joined his father who retired to winter at Linlithgow. The Scots could still break out of their south-western stronghold,

---

[1] *Cal. Docs. Scot.*, ii, No. 1220; Stevenson, *Documents*, ii, No. 612.

[2] Ibid., No. 611. 'Stanhouse' is clearly Stonehouse near Strathaven. Simon Fraser had been at least nominally on the English side until the capture of Caerlaverock, where he was present in the meinie of the earl of Dunbar (*Siege of Carlaverock*, ed. N. H. Nicolas, 36; 'Laonis' is of course 'Lothian', sometimes used for the title of the earls of Dunbar or March, not 'Lennox' as supposed by Nicolas). Fraser must have gone over to the Scots about the turn of the years 1300 and 1301, while at Wark on Tweed; he carried off the horses and armour of Sir William Durham, *Cal. Docs. Scot.*, ii, No. 1317. Ibid., No. 1121, reporting that 'the Guardian of the realm of Scotland' had entered Cunningham, probably belongs to this period.

[3] Ibid., iv, 449; cf. ibid., ii, No. 1235.

[4] Ibid., ii, Nos. 1224-5, 1233, 1235-6, 1239-40.

and on January 26th, 1302, Edward I agreed to a truce for nine months.[1]

One reason why the south-west was a stronghold was that the earl of Carrick had been active on the patriotic side. His castle of Turnberry held out till September 1301,[2] and as late as October its new English garrison and their comrades in the castle of Ayr were gravely threatened by a great force of Scots operating in Carrick.[3] Their infantry, significantly, were so numerous that they seemed likely to overwhelm such men of Kyle and Cunningham as were in the English peace. At least a part of this infantry must have composed the 'army' of Carrick which only Bruce, as earl, had the authority to call out. One reason why the Scots changed their strategy after 1302 was that Bruce deserted them and went over to Edward I. He changed sides before February 16th, 1302, giving himself up to Sir John de St John, English warden of Annandale and Galloway.[4] Perhaps the occasion of his surrender was the making of the truce on January 26th. Since the Scots had been led by Soules for almost a year, this drastic decision was surely not prompted by jealousy of the Comyns. It is more likely, as Professor Stones has suggested,[5] to have been due to the news from Rome that Balliol had been transferred from papal to French tutelage and to the rumour that Philip the Fair was sending him back to Scotland with a French army. It seems not to have been restoration itself that Bruce chiefly feared so much as the possibility that, with King John once more on the throne of an independent Scotland, his own paternal inheritance, Annandale, might be denied him, and perhaps even his earldom might be in danger. Yet, if he went over to Edward I, his position would be threatened by any papal arbitration or Anglo-French treaty which included the Scots. The document recording Bruce's submission is crucially important for any attempt to understand his motives and conduct. It runs as follows:

[1] Cal. Docs. Scot., ii, No. 1282; for the peace of Asnières, cf. Treaty Rolls, i (ed. P. Chaplais, 1955), 149–52; English draft in Palgrave, Docs., 241–7.

[2] Ibid., iv, 451: the news of the surrender of Turnberry reached Edward while still at Bothwell, i.e. before September 27th, and the surrender may have occurred by the end of August or beginning of September, ibid., 448.

[3] Ibid., ii, No. 1236.

[4] N. Trivet, Annales (ed. T. Hog), 397, n. 7. On the submission of Bruce, see E. L. G. Stones, in SHR, xxxiv, 122–34.

[5] SHR, xxxiv, 131.

Be it remembered that whereas Sir Robert Bruce the younger, who was in the homage and faith of the king of England for the earldom of Carrick, rose in rebellion against the said king his lord, through evil counsel, and has submitted himself to the peace and will of the same king in hope of his good grace, the king, for the sake of the good service which Robert's ancestors and family have rendered to the king and his ancestors, and the good service which Robert himself has promised to render in the future, has declared his grace and will in this manner.

That is to say, that Robert and his men and his tenants of Carrick will be guaranteed life and limb, lands and tenements, and will be free from imprisonment.

If it should happen that by a papal ordinance, or by a truce, or by a conditional peace touching the war against Scotland or the war against France, the aforesaid Robert should be at a disadvantage, so that he may not be able to enjoy his own lands, of which he has possession at present in Scotland, the king promises to take his loss into consideration so that he may have reasonable maintenance, as is proper for him.

And the king grants to Robert that, so far as it lies in his power, he will not be disinherited of any land which may fall to him by right from his father, in England or in Scotland.

And the king grants to Robert the wardship and marriage of the earl of Mar's son and heir.

And because [it is feared that][1] the kingdom of Scotland may be removed from out of the king's hands (which God forbid!), and handed over to Sir John Balliol or to his son, or that the right [le droit] may be brought into dispute, or reversed and repealed in a fresh judgement, the king grants to Robert that he may pursue his right and the king will hear him fairly and hold him to justice in the king's court. If, by any chance, it should happen that the right must be adjudicated elsewhere than in the king's court, then in this case the king promises Robert assistance and counsel as before, as well as he is able to give it.

And if, after the kingdom of Scotland is at peace in the king's hands, any persons should wish to do injury to Robert by [ ][1] the king will maintain and defend him in his right as before, as a lord ought to do for his man.

And in witness of all these points, the king has ordered these letters-patent to be made and sealed with his privy seal.[2]

The document has several points of interest and poses a difficult problem. The admission of a possible Balliol restoration is striking proof of Edward I's weakness in 1302. The chief problem, as Professor Stones has explained,[1] is to understand what is meant by *le droit*, the right which Bruce may pursue in the king's court or elsewhere. One suggestion is that it was the 'right and claim to seek the kingdom of Scotland', transmitted by the Competitor in 1292 to his son, young Bruce's father, who was to live until 1304.[2] Professor Stones, surely rightly, discounts this interpretation. It hardly seems likely that King Edward, in the circumstances of 1301–2, would calmly contemplate restoring the Scottish kingdom for Bruce, a newly surrendered rebel. The instrument of submission has, rather, to meet Bruce's practical and realistic fears. Apparently temporary measures, such as a papal ordinance or a truce or a conditional peace might oust him from his earldom of Carrick. One way or the other, he might be denied his father's lands in Annandale, Garioch and the Honour of Huntingdon. His right to these tangible and realizable properties and honours might well be disputed if John or Edward Balliol regained possession of Scotland. It might be defeated by a 'fresh judgement'. Consequently the English king promised to hear the case in his own court or uphold it in any other court. Here one is reminded of a charter which Bruce himself was to execute twenty-six years later in favour of the younger Henry Percy. Percy, a newly reconciled 'rebel', was restored to his paternal inheritance in Scotland, despite previous forfeiture, and the king granted that Henry and his heirs would not be excluded from pursuing their right, whether hereditary or otherwise, in the king's courts or in the courts of anyone else.[3] It seems inconceivable that Edward I in 1302 was envisaging a Scottish kingdom ruled by an independent Balliol and Bruce's case might have to be brought in Balliol's or in other inferior courts.

It is perhaps idle to speculate further about Bruce's motives for submission, yet there is one more fact that should be considered. 1302 was the year of Bruce's second marriage. Since his new wife was Elizabeth de Burgh, daughter of Richard de Burgh earl of Ulster, one of King Edward's staunchest supporters, it is certain that

---

[1] *SHR*, xxxiv, 126.
[2] See additional note below, p. 185.
[3] Stones, *Documents*, 171.

the wedding must have followed the submission. The marriage may possibly have been suggested by Edward himself, but for all we know it may have been arranged by Bruce for good reasons of his own. It implied a revival of the Carrick alliance with the chief magnate of Ulster.[1] Desire for this marriage may have been enough to tip the scales of Bruce's indecision, already weighted by his growing disgust and frustration with a struggle which threatened to exalt the Balliols at the expense of his family's power and position.

Winning Bruce over was a triumph for Edward I, but his change of side was more Scotland's loss than England's gain. He had not only been a Guardian, he had, as earl, time and again raised the 'army' of his earldom on the patriots' behalf although there had been no national call-up. As Bruce, then at Maybole, wrote on March 11th, 1302 to the anxious monks of Melrose Abbey, 'whereas I have often vexed the abbey's tenants on their grange of Maybole by leading them all over the country in my army of Carrick although there was no summons of the common army of the realm, troubled in conscience I shall never again demand such army service, neither of many nor of few, unless the common army of the whole realm is raised for its defence, when all inhabitants are bound to serve'.[2] It is curious, to say the least, that Bruce's conscience did not trouble him until the beginning of Lent 1302, just in time to ensure that his army would be less use to Edward than it had been to the Scots.

A much worse blow befell the Scots in 1302 than the defection of Bruce. The history of the war of independence has no greater irony than the fact that the great upsurge of proletarian nationalism in Flanders which led to the massacre of the French feudal host at Courtrai on July 11th did more to make Scotland an English province than any other single event of these years. It knocked King Philip out of the fight for a time, and his quarrel with the papacy caused an ominous change of heart in Pope Boniface, of whose fickle and fortuitous support the Scots had up till now taken every advantage. But it was nearly two years before the Scots admitted defeat. The long truce of 1302 was primarily a truce between French and English. That the Scots benefited from it seems to have been due

[1] It would have strengthened the ties between Bruce and the Stewart, since Elizabeth de Burgh was James Stewart's niece by marriage.
[2] *Melrose Liber*, i, No. 351.

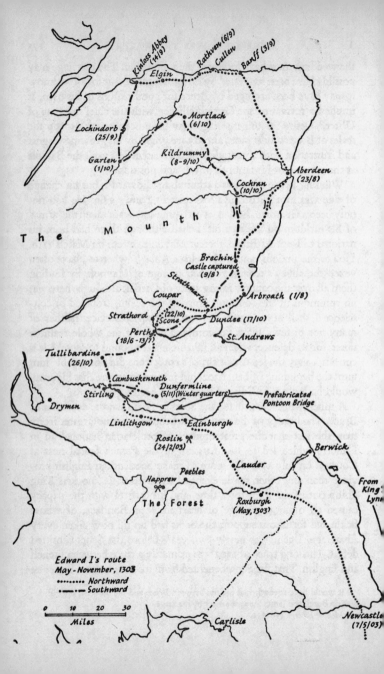

Kinloss Abbey (14/9)
Elgin
Rathven (6/9)
Cullen
Banff (3/9)

Lochindorb (25/9)

Mortlach (6/10)

Garten (1/10)

Kildrummy (8-9/10)

Aberdeen (23/8)

Cochran (10/10)

The Mounth

Brechin Castle captured (9/8)

Strathmartine

Coupar
Arbroath (1/8)

Strathord
Scone (22/10)
Dundee (17/10)

Perth (18/6 - 13/7)
St. Andrews

Tullibardine (26/10)

Cambuskenneth
Dunfermline (5/11) (Winter quarters)
Prefabricated Pontoon Bridge

Stirling

Drymen

Linlithgow
Edinburgh

Roslin (24/2/03)
Berwick

Lauder

Peebles
From King's Lynn

Happrew

The Forest
Roxburgh (May, 1303)

Edward I's route
May - November, 1303
.... Northward
—·—·— Southward

Carlisle

Newcastle (7/5/03)

0   10   20   30
Miles

to the good work of Bishop Lamberton, who went to France in
1301 and returned in time to attend a parliament at Scone in February
1302.[1] The danger of an Anglo-French peace from which the Scots
were excluded was so serious that an extraordinarily large and
powerful delegation went to Paris in the autumn of 1302, probably
with safe-conducts from King Edward. John de Soules himself was
one of the envoys. Presumably he gave up his monopoly of the
guardianship when he left Scotland, though his position as King
John's special representative may not have been affected. His
colleagues were Bishop Lamberton, the earl of Buchan, James
Stewart, Ingram de Umfraville and William Balliol. With them
was Matthew Crambeth, bishop of Dunkeld, who had possibly
served as permanent Scottish agent at Paris since as long ago as
1295.[2] The three Scottish envoys to the papal court in 1301 were
probably also with the magnates in France. At home the direction
of affairs was entrusted to John Comyn of Badenoch, who assumed
the Guardian's office for the second time.[3]

One contemporary English chronicler, who at this point seems to
know nothing of Comyn, Soules and the other leaders, states that in
1303 the Scots 'began to rebel, making William Wallace their

[1] *APS*, i, 454. *Treaty Rolls*, i (ed. P. Chaplais, 1955), 149–52, gives the English
and French versions of the agreement, showing (1) that Edward I was extremely
reluctant to concede any title of king to Balliol and (2) that Philip IV did recognize
Balliol as king of Scots. The French proposals for holding Scotland pending a final
peace treaty are of the greatest interest, and show how difficult it was for the Scots, in
shaking off English domination with French help, to avoid French domination.

[2] There is no evidence of his presence in Scotland in the intervening years, a long
period for one of the principal bishops to have left no record of his presence. On the
other hand, the dean of Dunkeld (Master Hervey of Crambeth) is found acting in
place of the bishop in a transaction of 1303, in association with John Comyn of
Badenoch (either the Guardian or less probably his father), the bishops of Glasgow
and Ross, and the abbot of Scone, *Coupar Angus Chrs.*, i, Nos. 69, 73. Moreover, the
dean of Dunkeld was functioning as Bishop Crambeth's vicar-general in 1300 and in
1302, ibid., Nos. 66, 72.

[3] *Chron. Fordun*, i, 333, 336. Ibid, 331, says Comyn was Guardian continuously
from 1298 to 1304, but we have seen reasons to suggest that he was not in office in
1301 or 1302. One must, however, note *Cal. Docs. Scot.*, iv, No. 1827 (=P.R.O.,
C. 153/1, fo. 140), which, if the regnal year is correctly stated as 31st, shows that
John de Soules was believed by an Aberdeen jury to have still been 'Guardian of the
land of Scotland on behalf of the community of that land' on November 11th, 1303.
If, however, the regnal year should be xxx instead of xxxi, this would make Soules
Guardian in November 1302, and this would square well with our other evidence of
his term of office.

7. The Invasion of 1303-4

commander and captain'.[1] It is certain that Wallace had come back
into the fray by 1303, but there is nothing to suggest that he alone
took the initiative, as though impatient of the slow peace negotiations. And it is of course absurd to speak of the Scots 'beginning to
rebel' in 1303. When the truce expired in November 1302, the
English king was not ready to campaign personally. Instead, he
summoned the host for May 1303, and in the meantime sent his
lieutenant in Scotland, Sir John Segrave, to carry out a probe in
depth into the Scottish-held territory west of Edinburgh. Segrave
was accompanied by Ralph Manton, cofferer of the wardrobe, one
of the busiest and most responsible clerks then at work for the
occupation régime. They had got as far as Roslin, south of Edinburgh, with a strong force of knights in three brigades, when on
February 24th they were caught by a surprise attack.[2] Led by Comyn
and Simon Fraser, a large party of mounted troops rode all the way
from Biggar during the night and fell upon the leading English
brigade, killing Manton and capturing many knights including
Segrave, who was badly wounded. In a short while the second
brigade rescued some of the prisoners, Segrave himself being freed
by Robert Neville of Raby. But the affair had come near to being
a major disaster for the English and the Scots were understandably
jubilant. Despite Edward's campaign of 1301 the Forest was obviously still available to the Scots, perhaps not surprisingly as long as
Simon Fraser was still active. Even the peel of Selkirk, newly built
by the English, and in the charge of Sir Alexander Balliol of Cavers,
was captured by the patriots early in 1303.[3]

It took a full-scale invasion in the following summer to avenge
Roslin and expose the essential weakness of the Scots. Edward had
three floating bridges prefabricated at King's Lynn and brought by
sea to the Firth of Forth, so that the army could cross directly into
Fife. This was in order to by-pass Stirling Castle, where Sir William
Oliphant refused to surrender. The English reached Brechin at the
end of July and laid siege to the castle there, which was held against
them with great spirit and courage by Sir Thomas Maule. When he

[1] *Chron. Rishanger*, 213.

[2] *Chron. Fordun*, i, 333–5, where *Marcii* should be read for *Augusti* in line one of
333, i.e., February 24th, 1303, Quadragesima Sunday. Cf. *Chron. Guisb.*, 351–2.

[3] H. M. Colvin and R. A. Brown, *The History of the King's Works* (1963), i, 415.
Possibly the Scots even seized Edinburgh castle in June, 1302 (Brit. Lib., MS. Cott.
Cleop. D iii, fo. 52ᵛ).

was killed on the battlements on August 9th, the garrison yielded, but its valiant resistance had made it necessary for Edward to strip the lead off Brechin Cathedral (for which he duly paid £17 18s. 4d.) and to have siege engines brought by sea to Montrose.[1] Edward continued his march northward, meeting no more recorded resistance, though later traditions, unsupported but not necessarily unfounded, claim that Urquhart and Cromarty castles were only captured after hard fighting.[2] In September the king reached Kinloss Abbey, the furthest point of his progress, and a month later he was back in Fife, having decided to make Dunfermline Abbey his winter quarters.

All this time the Scots were not idle, but they could neither bring into the field an army which was remotely equal to a pitched battle with the English nor, as yet, push to its logical conclusion their half-learned lesson that scorched earth and incessant guerrilla attacks might make it impossible for the English to stay north of Lothian. Fraser's presence at Roslin proves that the military effort in 1303, though sadly lacking in strong central control, did not consist of Comyn and the great lords fighting one war and Wallace and the commoners fighting another. For we know that while Edward wintered at Dunfermline (probably in February 1304) he sent a mounted commando (*chevauchée*) into the Forest and 'the parts of Lothian', under Segrave, Clifford and Latimer, and this force routed Fraser and Wallace together at Happrew in Stobo, a few miles west of Peebles.[3] In the autumn of 1303 John Comyn was still in southern Scotland with as many as 100 mounted men and 1,000 foot, with whom he raided the Lennox as far as Drymen.[4] But individual acts of bravery could not prop up much longer the king over the water. The writing on the wall for this ghost-king, Toom Tabard, had been seen at Courtrai. His fate was sealed absolutely on May 20th, 1303, when a peace was made between France and England from which the Scots, despite all King Philip's promises and protestations, were excluded.

Since 1297 the Scottish effort had been informed consistently by a single forceful, even if conservative, principle. Under the direction

[1] *Flores Historiarum*, iii, 113–4; *Cal. Docs. Scot.*, ii, Nos. 1687, 1386.
[2] Cf. Barron, *Scottish War of Independence*, 192–3.
[3] *Cal. Docs. Scot.*, ii, No. 1432, and ibid., iv, 474.
[4] Stevenson, *Documents*, ii, No. 645.

of properly constituted Guardians, the totality of the feudal kingdom, the community of the realm, had fought to rid their land of foreign invaders and to restore their lawful king. Political strategy had been dominated by this legitimism, by the Franco-Scottish treaty of 1295, by the belief that French military support was just round the corner, by a somewhat naïve confidence that once apprised of the facts Pope Boniface VIII would exert all the papal fullness of power to protect Scottish independence. These beliefs died very hard. On May 25th, 1303, the Scots magnates in Paris wrote to encourage Comyn the Guardian and all the faithful men of the community of the realm of Scotland.[1] It was true, they said, that firm peace had been made between France and England and the Scots had been left out. But the king of France had faithfully promised them that he would strive to bring Scotland into the peace, and was now in a better position to do so.

'Be of good heart. If the king of England agree to a truce, you should likewise agree, on the conditions to be brought to you by a man of our side who will be known to you. If the English king harden his heart, like Pharaoh, and refuse a truce, then, by the mercy of Jesus Christ, defend yourselves manfully and stay united, so that by your manful defence and with God's help you will prevail, or at least receive stronger support from us. For God's sake do not despair. If ever you have done brave deeds, do braver ones now. The swiftest runner who fails before the winning-post has run in vain. And it would gladden your hearts if you could know how much your honour has increased in every part of the world as the result of your recent battle with the English [i.e., Roslin].'

And they concluded, in striking testimony to the great part which John de Soules had played in the struggle, by asking that Soules's wife should be allowed peaceful enjoyment of the estate provided for her when the envoys went to France or else an equivalent provision in another suitable place, 'so that Sir John, who up to now has laboured loyally and diligently on the business of the realm, should not give up his efforts'.

This refusal to believe that all was lost animated the letters written by Bishop Lamberton (presumably when in France) to Wallace and

---

[1] APS, i, 454–5. Professor Stones has kindly pointed out that it is possible that this letter never reached the Scottish leaders at home, for the only extant version was intercepted. But we cannot be sure that no other copy got through.

to the officials of his own bishopric,[1] and it shows itself very clearly in the attitude of Sir William Oliphant, the young commander of Stirling Castle. Lamberton urged Wallace for the love Wallace bore him and with the bishop's blessing, to do all in his power to aid and counsel the community of Scotland, as he had done in the past, and to make war on King Edward and attack him and his men as before, as well as he knew how, and was able, to do it. To help in the good work, the bishop ordered his officers to supply Wallace with part of the revenues of his bishopric. Oliphant, when Edward I settled down to the serious siege of Stirling in May 1304, asked permission to send a messenger to his master, Sir John de Soules (by whom the castle had been committed to him), to find out whether he might surrender or whether he should defend it to the last.[2] King Edward could seldom bring himself to display towards Scottish castle garrisons the chivalrous decency which the age admired and which the Scottish Guardians had notably shown towards the starving English garrison of Stirling in 1299.[3] He rejected Oliphant's polite request, exclaiming: 'If he thinks it will be better for him to defend the castle than yield it, he will see.'[4] And when, after three tormenting months (May-July) in which every kind of siege engine and explosive material that the ingenuity of the time could devise had been used against them, the garrison at last submitted (July 20th), the king would not let them surrender with military honour but threatened them with disembowelling and hanging.[5] Only their abject basement and the sympathy of those who were with Edward mollified him at last, and they were sent, about fifty in all, to various English prisons.[6] By a piece of cold-blooded cruelty which shows Edward in a singularly unattractive light, he had refused to accept the garrison's surrender, even after it was offered unconditionally, until the castle had been bombarded for a time by one of his new engines, the 'Warwolf', while the men inside made shift to defend themselves as best they could.[7] The king's meanness of spirit and implacable,

[1] Palgrave, Docs. Hist. Scot., 333.
[2] Flores Historiarum, iii, 118.
[3] Ibid., 113; Chron. Rishanger, 388, 402.
[4] Flores Historiarum, iii, 118.
[5] Ibid., 319-20.
[6] Cal. Docs Scot.., ii, No. 1668.
[7] Ibid., No. 1560. See additional note, p. 185.

almost paranoiac hostility were not shared by his subjects, who
admired Oliphant for his courage and magnanimity. They did not
think any the worse of the young man because he refused the terms
accepted by Comyn and the rest, for as Sir Thomas Grey explained
in a phrase full of significance, Oliphant claimed to hold Stirling 'of
the Lion', that is to say, of the crown of Scotland.[1] Hence his punctilious desire to get orders from Soules, who had been a duly constituted Guardian on behalf of that crown, or (as a document of
1306 puts it) 'Guardian for the community of Scotland'.[2]

All the prominent Scots leaders save Wallace, Fraser and Soules
submitted to King Edward some five months before the fall of
Stirling. Those who had been in France returned under safe conducts,
among them the earl of Buchan, the bishops of St Andrews and
Dunkeld, James Stewart and Ingram de Umfraville.[3] On the Scottish side, the negotiations were conducted by John Comyn of
Badenoch, doubtless in his capacity of Guardian. He would not
surrender unconditionally and his demands that there should be no
reprisals or disinheritance and that prisoners on both sides should be
released free of ransom were accepted by Edward I, with some
important reservations.[4] Much the most interesting passages in the
terms set forth by Comyn are those which show the defeated
Guardian speaking, however, falteringly, the language of the Treaty
of Birgham and of his own predecessors in the days when Scotland
had powerful allies and enjoyed some success in arms. There was
more dignity in Comyn's submission than there had been in Balliol's
abject abdication eight years before. In 1304 the demands of the
defeated side were made 'on behalf of the community of Scotland'.[5]

[1] *Scalacronica*, 127.

[2] *Cal. Docs. Scot.*, iv, No. 1827.

[3] Ibid., ii, No. 1455. No. 1848 is a safe-conduct for Master Baldred (Bisset) 'the
Scot', but it seems unlikely that Bisset came to Scotland. By 1310 he was busy
defending the late Pope Boniface VIII at Avignon (*Innes Review*, xxv, 147, n. 306).

[4] Palgrave, *Docs. Hist. Scot.*, 279–285.

[5] P.R.O., C. 47/22/4. These are draft peace terms, extremely fragmentary and largely
illegible. They begin 'Les messages qui furent enuiez de part la comunaute descoce'. They
ask for Sir John de Soules to be received into King Edward's peace and faith, and the
king's answer begins, 'A ce le Roi respont qe endroit du dit Johan il ne vuet suffrir qe . . .'
There can be little doubt that some particular stiffness of Edward I towards Soules lay
behind his conduct as reported by Grey, *Scalacronica*, 127, 'Sir John refused the conditions, left Scotland and died in France.' But it seems most unlikely that Soules ever
returned to Scotland.

The Scottish people 'should be protected in all their laws, usages, customs and liberties in every particular as they existed in the time of King Alexander III, unless there are laws to be amended, in which case it should be done with the advice of King Edward *and the advice and assent of the responsible men [bones gentz] of the land*'.[1] The terms on which Comyn actually surrendered (at Strathord, north of Perth, on February 9th)[2] did not amount to a restoration of things as they had been in the good old days of King Alexander, yet they were not excessively harsh. Varying periods of exile were imposed on the leading men, and the ageing bishop of Glasgow, Robert Wishart, was at first required to stay outside Scotland for two or three years 'on account of the great evils he has caused'. But there was to be no disinheritance, and forfeited estates could be redeemed by their former owners at a cost of two, three, four or (in Umfraville's case only) five years' value.[3]

Despite this apparent generosity, King Edward was not a big enough man to forgive all his enemies, even in this hour of triumph. The humanity of the surrender terms was marred by a relentless pursuit of Wallace which could only be aimed at his extermination and which bore every mark of a personal vendetta. Had such a concept been familiar in the fourteenth century, Wallace would no doubt have been regarded as a 'war criminal'. But the special enormity of Wallace's crime lay in his steadfast refusal to submit to foreign domination and in the fact that he had become a symbol of national resistance. 'No words of peace are to be held out to William Wallace in any circumstances whatever unless he places himself utterly and absolutely in our will ['will' being here contrasted with "grace" or "mercy"].'[4] 'The Stewart, Sir John de Soules and Sir Ingram de Umfraville are not to have safe conducts nor come within

---

[1] Palgrave, *Docs. Hist. Scot.*, 287. [2] *Cal. Docs. Scot.*, ii, No. 1741; *Rotuli Parl.*, i, 212–3.
[3] Ibid.; cf. *Foedera*, i, 974–5, the terms as modified (and largely moderated) by October 1305.
[4] Stevenson, *Documents*, ii, No. 471. Cf. Palgrave, *Docs. Hist Scot.*, 284. For the contrast between 'will' and 'grace', see *Flores Historiarum*, iii, 320. The provision in the treaty of February 1304: 'as for Sir William Wallace, it is agreed that he may place himself in the will and in the grace of our lord the king, if it shall seem good to him [Wallace] to do so' is presumably the authority for Sir Maurice Powicke's statement that 'Wallace might have made his peace if he had wished' (*The Thirteenth Century*, 333). But although it may seem to contrast with the king's other provisions regarding Wallace (especially Stevenson, *Documents*, ii, No. 471; Palgrave, *Docs.*

the king's power until Sir William Wallace is given up.'[1] And, most disgracefully, 'Sir John Comyn, Sir Alexander Lindsay, Sir David Graham and Sir Simon Fraser shall exert themselves until twenty days after Christmas to capture Sir William Wallace and hand him over to the king, who will watch to see how each of them conducts himself so that he can do most favour to whoever shall capture Wallace, with regard to exile or legal claims or expiation of past misdeeds.'[2]

The capture of Wallace would only be a matter of time. Apart from him and John de Soules, who either stayed in, or returned to, France, it seemed that the Scots had been finally crushed. Even Fraser had apparently submitted. Henceforth, in Edward's view, the 'kingdom' of Scotland no longer existed. The future could be assured by a carefully planned ordinance for the 'land' of Scotland, which would be brought into line with Ireland. Once again, we should give much to have some hint of the common talk in Scotland at the end of 1304 and during 1305. There were two things which might have disturbed King Edward's peace of mind, but he was too busy to be troubled by one, John de Soules's defiant refusal to surrender, and of the other, a secret 'band' between Bishop Lamberton and Robert Bruce, he as yet knew nothing. On June 11th, 1304, at Cambuskenneth, while they were with the English army at the siege of Stirling, the bishop and Bruce entered into a solemn bond of mutual friendship and alliance against all men – that is, potential enemies – under a penalty of £10,000.[3] Nothing was said about saving their faith to the king, nor, indeed did the band explicitly mention any purpose whatever. It spoke darkly of 'rivals' and 'dangers'. But there can be no question that between its lines we may read much deep and secret conversation. It meant, first, that William Lamberton had not given up the cause of a free Scotland, secondly, that he had been forced to realize that nothing short of revolution could now save his country. For Lamberton, the friend of Wishart, Wallace and Bruce, whose episcopal seal bore the proud old title 'bishop of the Scots', the past nine years of struggle, the perilous

---

Hist. Scot., 284), this provision can hardly be taken to mean that Edward I would have extended his peace to Wallace. The indictment against Wallace at his trial declares that the king offered him peace, but this document can hardly be trusted on such a point, Stevenson, Wallace Docs., 192.

[1] Palgrave, Docs. Hist. Scot., 276.   [2] Ibid.   [3] Ibid., 323–4.

voyages to and from the continent, the strenuous diplomatic negotiations, the blood spilt at Berwick, Stirling Bridge and Falkirk, the palpable misery of a land where villages and whole towns were burned down, people homeless, churches roofless and desolate, religious houses razed to the ground, were not to go for naught, nor was their memory to be effaced by any ordinance of the conqueror, however moderate and methodical.

Additional Note (see above, pp. 172–4.)
The submission of Robert Bruce.

The discussion on pp. 172–4 above has been called 'perfunctory and misleading' (A. A. M. Duncan, *SHR*, xlv, 195), and Professor Duncan has proposed a different and far from perfunctory interpretation, which has passed into the canon of the Edinburgh history school (R. Nicholson, *Scotland: the later Middle Ages*, 63, n. 104 and 64). Briefly, this interpretation is that Edward I and Bruce feared that Edward's right as suzerain of Scotland might be challenged in a papal arbitration, while Bruce feared that his own right either to the Scottish throne or at least a share of Scottish royal demesnes might be challenged by Balliol's restoration. For most of 1301 Bruce was 'sulking' and his submission was connected to the provisions of the Anglo-French peace of Asnières.

To me, the most striking single feature of the submission document is its failure to call Bruce earl of Carrick, though it seems to admit that he is in possession of the earldom's lands. It may be that Henry Percy, in charge of Ayr and Galloway in 1296, had already staked a claim to Carrick which was in fact given to him in 1306, although in Barbour's phrase Percy 'wist that he had no richt' to the earldom in 1307 (Barbour, *Bruce*, 84). The submission document allows Bruce to sue for his right should Edward lose sasine of the Scottish kingdom, either in Edward's court or elsewhere; it is not clear whether this was Bruce's right to the earldom of Carrick (in Edward's eyes forfeited 1297–1302) or to the Scots throne (there is no other suggestion that Edward contemplated awarding this to anyone in 1302). I find it hard to believe that Edward I, no matter how parlous his plight might have been in 1302, would have casually referred to the possibility that his own overlordship of Scotland, in which he believed implicitly and fundamentally, might be in jeopardy, least of all in a document which restored his grace to a repentant vassal. Moreover, we need to know where Bruce was sulking. Presumably not in Galloway among his foes; nor in Carrick with patriot Scots holding his castle without his leave; hardly in Ulster where even if the earl was displeased with Edward I (Orpen, *Ireland under the Normans*, iv, 144) he would surely not have harboured one of the English king's chief enemies; and yet when Bruce did submit, it was to the English warden of Galloway.

Additional Note (see above, p. 181).
The use of siege engines.

This letter has been dismissed by Professor Stones as merely 'anticipatory' (*SHR*, lii, 84), yet the accounts rendered by the engineers of most of the seventeen siege engines involved show cable, rope, grease and stones ceasing to be required before July 20th by all the engines save the 'Parson', the 'Berefrey' and the 'Warwolf' (*Low de Guerre*), which were supplied continuously from July 19th to July 23rd (PRO, E 101/12/25, cited but not expounded by Professor Stones). The notarial instrument recording the surrender and listing the garrison was dated July 24th (*Foedera*, i, 966).

8

Defeat

THE fall of Stirling marked the end of an epoch and the frustration of a remarkable experiment. Guardianship had failed. It had proved more successful when the monarch was a minor or an absentee than when (as in 1291) there was no king at all or when (as in 1296) the king was present but incompetent. Restored by Wallace and given fresh life and vigour, taken over by men of higher rank, among whom John de Soules best showed what the office was capable of, guardianship on behalf of the community succumbed to the combination of military defeat, defection of allies and the chronic hopelessness of King John. But if its wardens had failed, the community persisted. It was King Edward's task to alter the character of the community, to re-shape it so that it might take its place in his dominion in an orderly manner. It must cease to be the 'community of the *realm* of Scotland' and become the 'community of the *land* of Scotland'. It must cease to look for the restoration of its king over the water and reconcile itself to the fact that its king was present at Westminster and not in any need of restoration.

In his last years Edward became a hard man who believed that it was his duty to bend the Scots to his will. It would be wrong to think of him acting in Scotland as a mere tyrant, if by tyrant we mean a ruler whose arbitrary whims are law, who pays no regard to local feeling and opinion, or for whom cruelty towards his subjects has become settled policy. If we look at the situation in 1304 as it appeared to Edward, we must in fairness admit that his attempted settlement was both mild and statesmanlike. In his view, he had to deal with a nation which had rebelled against his lordship for many years, had given aid and comfort to his enemies, and had been decisively defeated in war. How many kings or governments emerging

as the victors of long and bloody wars in the seventeenth, eighteenth
or even nineteenth centuries treated their vanquished foes as prudently and leniently as Edward I treated the Scots in 1304 and 1305?
The two main demands made by Comyn of Badenoch when he
negotiated the Scottish submission early in 1304 were, first, that there
should be an amnesty and restoration of estates for those who had
fought against Edward, and, secondly (echoing, however faintly,
the braver words of Birgham), that the Scottish people should be
assured of all their laws, customs and liberties in every respect as they
enjoyed them under King Alexander III. Such laws as must be
amended should be amended only by the counsel of the king and the
counsel and assent of the responsible men [*bones gentz*] of Scotland.[1]
Edward's dealings with the Scots at the St Andrews parliament of
March 1304,[2] and the final settlement – the Ordinance of September
1305 – were in harmony with Comyn's demands.

There was no scramble by the victors for the lands of the vanquished. Scotsmen came in and made their peace, did homage, and
had writs ordering the restoration of their property, very much as in
1296. We have no Ragman Roll for 1304, but the names of a fair
number of men who submitted are known, and we have at least two
lists, the first containing the names of some eighty-nine or ninety
landowners who did homage to the king on March 14th,[3] the second
naming forty who did homage on March 15th.[4] It is a measure of the
prejudice among historians against the Scottish nobility that Sir
Francis Palgrave (by implication)[5] and Joseph Bain (expressly)[6]
assigned the first list, dated March 14th with no year given, to 1296,
that is, some days before war had actually broken out between
England and Scotland. 'These persons,' writes Bain, apparently
without surprise, 'probably foresaw the inevitable issue of the contest.'[7] What 'these persons' had in fact seen was almost eight years of
bitter struggle, in which some of them, such as Malcolm, earl of

[1] Palgrave, *Docs. Hist Scot.*, 286–7.

[2] For the authorities for the St Andrews parliament, see *SHR*, xxv, 311, n., and
see especially Stevenson, *Documents*, ii, 471, n. 1.

[3] Palgrave, *Docs. Hist Scot.*, 194–7.

[4] Ibid., 299–301. *Foedera*, i, 955, assigns this to 1306, an impossible year.

[5] Palgrave, *Docs. Hist. Scot.*, pp. cxxii–cxxiii.

[6] *Cal. Docs. Scot.*, ii, pp. xxii–xxiii, and No. 730.

[7] Ibid., p. xxiii.

Lennox, Sir Edmund Ramsay, Sir John of Cambo and Sir John Cameron, had taken a notable part. As might be expected in a list of homages performed at St Andrews, most of the landowners recorded on it came from the north and east, especially Angus, Fife and Perthshire. There are several names on the list which are worth remembering in the light of after events: Earl Malcolm of Lennox and John of Cremannan,[1] Walter of Alyth, Walter Barclay, Sir John of Cambo, Sir John Cameron of Baledgarno, Sir William Fenton, Patrick Graham, William Gourlay, Sir John de la Hay, Sir William Mowat, Sir William Murray of Drumsargard, Sir William Murray of St Fort, Sir Adam de Valoignes, Andrew Dempster ('le Jugeor') and Sir William Wiseman. Similarly, from the second list we may select for future reference the names of Walter of Bickerton, Alan Murray of Culbin, Ralph of Dundee and Hamelin of Troup.

The 130 men and women on these lists formed, of course, only a small proportion of those who must have done homage in March 1304 or thereabouts. But there is no reason to think that the process was any different for those whose names do not happen to be recorded. Among the most interesting surviving writs issued at the St Andrews parliament are those of which the following may be regarded as typical: 'The king commands the restoration to Hugh of Penicuik, a Scottish rebel who has come to his peace, of his lands and heritage in England'.[2] It was such men whose patriotism is supposed to have been lukewarm from fear of losing their English estates. In reality, it was they who, under the Guardians' leadership, bore the brunt of the struggle against England. To the great magnates also, with some notable exceptions, King Edward was ready to be generous. As early as May 1304 the earl of Buchan had his earldom restored to him with all its appurtenances, save for the castles of Old Slains and Balvenie.[3] In the same month Bishop Lamberton had his temporalities restored,[4] and Bishop Crambeth of Dunkeld, still absent through illness, recovered not only the temporalities of his

---

[1] Cremannan, whose name survives only on the large-scale maps, was a considerable barony in Balfron, Stirlingshire. For Sir Thomas of Cremannan's grant of the patronage of Balfron church to Inchaffray abbey see *Inchaffray Chrs.*, No. 119.

[2] *Cal. Docs. Scot.*, ii, No. 1481. See above, p. 151.

[3] Palgrave, *Docs. Hist. Scot.*, 288, where the editor prints 'Glames' (!) for 'Slanes', i.e. Old Slains. 'Morthelagh' represents Mortlach or Balvenie, in Banffshire.

[4] *Cal. Docs. Scot.*, ii, No. 1529.

see but also the lands which formed his personal inheritance, Bogie (Fife), Crambeth, Cockairney and Dalqueich (Kinross) and Auchrannie in Glenisla.[1] Arbroath Abbey got back its church of Haltwhistle in Tynedale and the bishops of Brechin and Aberdeen had small grants of timber from the king.[2] James Stewart had much longer to wait: he does not seem to have got back his vast estates until after November 3rd, 1305, the date of an instrument recording his abjectly humble submission to Edward's will and pleasure.[3]

The political wisdom of King Edward is shown by his resolve to consult Scottish leaders on the new constitution to be devised for the country and to give them some measure of responsibility for making it work. It has been objected that this was neither statesmanship nor generosity but merely 'policy'. Whatever label we choose to give the decision, its author deserves credit if it was clearly designed to lessen friction, resolve tensions and frustrations, and reconcile the community of Scotland as quickly and peacefully as possible to an indefinite period of English rule. Edward, in other words, had learned part of the lesson of 1296-7. As it happened, he had not learned the most important part, but it was no small achievement for this elderly, conventional, conservative, unimaginative man that he had learned anything at all. At the Lenten parliament of 1305 Robert Wishart, Robert Bruce and John Moubray (one bishop, one earl and one baron) were commanded to advise the king on the settlement of what Edward, for the last time in his reign, called the 'kingdom of Scotland'.[4] Their reply was that ten representatives should be elected by the Scottish community to attend the next English parliament and help to draw up a constitution for Scotland. With Sir John Segrave (lieutenant in Lothian) and John of Sandal (the English chamberlain of Scotland), the three Scottish leaders assembled a parliament in May at which the ten were duly chosen.[5] The symmetry of this commission has a familiar look. It was originally meant to consist of two bishops, two abbots, two earls, and two barons, together with one

---

[1] *Cal. Docs. Scot.*, ii, Nos. 1528 and 1530 (=P.R.O., E. 39/100, 132 B, from which it appears that the name of the canon of Elgin, prebendary of Inverkeithney, was Master Geoffrey of [Dol] bodlech, i.e. Dunballoch, in Kirkhill).

[2] *Cal. Docs. Scot.*, ii, Nos. 1543, 1496, 1506.

[3] Ibid., No. 1713.

[4] F. W. Maitland, *Memoranda de Parliamento* (Rolls Series), 14.

[5] *APS*, i, 119-20; *Memoranda de Parliamento*, 293; cf. ibid, 178.

representative of the community north of the Forth and one for the south – who were, in fact, the two laymen envoys of 1301, Sir John of Inchmartin and Sir Adam Gordon.[1] The English parliament which they attended, postponed from three weeks after midsummer, met on September 15th.[2] Neither the bishop of Glasgow nor the earl of Carrick was among the ten, and (as Dr Barron has argued)[3] they both probably stayed in the north. It was at the September parliament that the Ordinance for the Government of the 'land' – no longer the 'realm' – of Scotland was drawn up and promulgated.[4]

The king's nephew John of Brittany was appointed lieutenant of Scotland. William of Bevercotes and John of Sandal remained as chancellor and chamberlain respectively, with Robert Heron as the chamberlain's comptroller. There were to be four pairs of justices (each consisting of an Englishman and a Scotsman) assigned, with sensible regard to history and geography, to the four principal zones: Lothian, Galloway (that is, the whole south-west), the country between the Forth and the Mounth, and country beyond the Mounth.[5] The sheriffs and constables appointed, some of whom were the hereditary claimants to office, were for the most part Scots. But the militarily crucial sheriffdoms and constabularies of the south-east, Edinburgh, Linlithgow, Haddington, Peebles, were kept in English hands, and the castles of Roxburgh and Jedburgh were under the lieutenant himself. Berwick, although by now almost an 'English' town, was to play a headquarters role similar to that given

---

[1] APS, i, 119 shows that Patrick earl of Dunbar (or March) failed to serve on the commission, and his place was taken by Sir John Menteith. Cf. Cal. Docs. Scot., ii, No. 1244, for Adam Gordon and John of Inchmartin. Under the Ordinance of 1305, Adam Gordon was to be one of the justices of Lothian and John of Inchmartin was to be sheriff of Perth.

[2] APS, i, 119; Handbook of British Chronology (2nd edn). 513.

[3] E. M. Barron, Scottish War of Independence, 175–8. It should be noted that Flores Historiarum, iii, 124, says that the two Scottish bishops at the September parliament were St Andrews and Glasgow; but according to APS, i, 119, they should have been St Andrews and Dunkeld, and the name in Flores Historiarum may be a mistake.

[4] APS, i, 119–22; Stones, Documents, No. 33; summarized, Cal. Docs. Scot., ii, No. 1691.

[5] The Ordinance is written in French, and gives the geographical limits as 'entre la rivere de Forth et les Montz' and 'dela les Montz'. Clearly, 'les Montz' is both a translation and an etymological equivalent of 'le Moneth', the Mounth, the ancient name given to the hills stretching from Loch Ericht to the sea between Aberdeen and Stonehaven (Kingdom of the Scots, 137–8).

it in 1296. The only castles of first-rate importance entrusted to Scotsmen were Stirling, assigned to William Bisset, and Dumbarton, placed in the charge of Sir John [Stewart] of Menteith, the younger son of Walter Stewart who from c.1260 to c.1293 had held the earldom of Menteith in right of his wife. A Scottish council was appointed to advise and assist the lieutenant.[1] If it included all those named in a surviving draft it numbered twenty-two Scots, four bishops (including Lamberton), five earls (including Bruce and Buchan), and nine barons (including Comyn of Badenoch).[2] Whether from statesmanship or expediency three former Guardians were thus brought back into the government, albeit in a restricted capacity. But certain English councillors were added to their number, and despite the conversion of old enemies into new advisers, the real power was to be vested in the lieutenant, chancellor and chamberlain. They would have authority to remove any lesser officials and replace them, as they saw fit, by Englishmen or Scotsmen. In theory, at least, they could anglicize the entire Scottish administrative system without consulting Edward I. To say therefore, as Sir Maurice Powicke has said, that the official element was derived 'mainly from Scotland'[3] is true only in the rather unreal numerical sense. There was no escaping the fact that Scotland was once more what she had been in 1296, a conquered country, occupied by foreign garrisons and governed by the foreign officials of a foreign king.

The first task of the new régime was to be the holding of an assembly of the responsible men to review the laws of Scotland. The 'laws of King David I', together with subsequent amendments and additions, were to be rehearsed and, where necessary, redressed and amended, so that they would no longer contain anything 'openly contrary to God and reason'.[4] Difficult problems were to be reserved for the king at his next parliament. In only one respect did King Edward make a decision about Scottish law without consulting the

---

[1] Palgrave, *Docs. Hist. Scot.*, 292–3. This council included all the ten commissioners elected at the Scone parliament of May 1305, including the earl of Dunbar who had failed to serve on the commission.

[2] Ibid., 293.

[3] *The Thirteenth Century*, 711.

[4] *APS*, i, 122.

community. He abolished the 'usage of Scot(s) and Bret(s)'.[1] It has been seriously suggested that by this act he destroyed the ancient Celtic law of Scotland.[2] In fact the provision referred to the custom which has come down to us in early manuscripts as the 'Law among Brets and Scots', which consisted chiefly of a tariff of wergilds or 'blood-prices' payable to the victim or his kindred in cases of wounding or slaying.[3] It is uncertain whether this archaic (and not specially Celtic) system was still in operation north of the Forth: it may perhaps have survived in the west highlands. It is most improbable that it survived anywhere south of the Forth save in Galloway, where it doubtless formed part of the 'special laws' of that province and where there were special grounds for preserving in the Gaelic cro and Welsh galnis the terms used for wergild respectively by the Scots of Galloway and the 'Brets', i.e. the Welsh or British, of Cumbria.[4] Whether operative, obsolescent or obsolete, the system was long overdue for abolition. If there had been no foreign conqueror with freedom to make drastic changes, the custom would no doubt have died out gradually. But in 1284 Edward I's Statute of Rhuddlan confirmed, by implication, the abolition of the galanas or wergild said to have been decreed by David of Wales (1240–1246). It was unthinkable that Edwardian rule would tolerate the survival north of the border of cro and galnis; it would be like expecting Lord William Bentinck to have preserved suttee in British India.

The settlement of 1305 was marked by few rewards and fewer punishments. Yet there was one punishment which, had there been no others at all, would have been more than enough. In August 1305, while King Edward was feeling his way towards a new relationship with the Scottish leaders which was surely intended to be based on mutual trust, William Wallace was captured, brought to Westminster for trial, and butchered judicially at the elms of Smithfield. Politically, it must always be a false economy to make one man pay

---

[1] APS, i, 122, 'l'usage de Scot' et de Bret' desorendroit soit defendu.'

[2] E. M. Barron, Scottish War of Independence, 210, followed by A. M. Mackenzie, Robert Bruce, King of Scots (1934), 139; cf. the latter's Scottish Pageant (1946), 173–4.

[3] APS, i, 663–5. It may have been to this 'usage of Scots and Brets' that Flores Historiarum, iii, 124, refers in saying that when Edward I approved the Ordinance in the September parliament 'he completely annulled only one single article, concerning a certain (native) Scottish judgement (de quodam judicio Scotico)'.

[4] Cf. K. Jackson, 'The Britons in Southern Scotland', Antiquity, xxix, 88.

with his blood for the deeds of a whole nation. The conspicuous leniency shown by Edward to his former enemies in 1305 gave his treatment of Wallace an unmistakably vindictive stamp. He was singled out for retribution, and what was meant, no doubt, to have been the inexorable working of justice and at the same time a fearful warning to possible imitators became instead a mark of signal honour.

The pursuit of Wallace had gone on relentlessly ever since the general Scottish surrender early in 1304.[1] His last recorded military action seems to have been a skirmish in September 1304 'below Earnside', that is below the northernmost extremity of the Ochil Hills above Bridge of Earn.[2] He was taken at last, on August 3rd, 1305, in or near Glasgow, by servants of Sir John Menteith, the keeper of Dumbarton.[3] Menteith had, during the period of guardianship, been a staunch fighter for the community of Scotland; he became a firm adherent of the English king.[4] If there was indeed treachery in the capture of Wallace it can hardly be laid at Sir John Menteith's door, for in handing Wallace over to the king he was but repaying the trust which Edward had for some time placed in him.[5] Led first to Edward, who refused to see him, Wallace was brought to London on August 22nd and lodged in the house of a well-known alderman, William de Leyre, in the parish of Fenchurch (Allhallows or St Gabriel's, Fenchurch Street).[6] Next morning, Monday, August 23rd, he was led on horseback to Westminster Hall in a procession which included the mayor of London and the other justices commissioned to try him, together with the sheriffs and

[1] Palgrave, *Docs. Hist. Scot.*, 276, 284, 295; Stevenson, *Documents*, ii, No. 633.

[2] *Cal. Docs. Scot.*, iv, 477.

[3] Stevenson, *Wallace Docs.*, 101–2, 147. Palgrave, *Docs. Hist. Scot.*, 295, has an entry 'Of land, that is £100 (worth) by [*par*, taken by the editor to mean *pour*] John Menteith', usually understood to mean that this was Menteith's reward for Wallace's capture. It is not clear beyond cavil that the entry has this meaning.

[4] The exact date of Menteith's change of sides is uncertain. Stevenson, *Documents*, ii, 453, shows him still Scottish in September 1303, while *Cal. Docs. Scot.*, ii, No. 1474 shows him in King Edward's peace and confidence by March 1304.

[5] The exceptional trust reposed in Menteith by Edward I is shown by the fact that Dumbarton castle, burgh and sheriffdom were put in his charge.

[6] Stevenson, *Wallace Docs.*, 147, 189; also in *Annales Londonienses*, in *Chronicles of the Reign of Edward I and Edward II*, ed. Stubbs, i, 139–42. For William de Leyre, alderman of Baynard's Castle Ward, 1298–1319, sheriff in 1290, and several times M.P., cf. E. Ekwall, *Two early London Subsidy Rolls* (Lund, 1951), 163, 275.

aldermen.[1] As on the previous day, immense crowds collected to gaze on the greatest spectacle of that London summer. In mockery, they put a laurel crown on Wallace's head because of his alleged boast that one day he would wear a crown at Westminster.[2] The indictment charged him with treason and many other crimes, the murder of the sheriff of Lanark, atrocities in time of war, convening Scottish parliaments, and persuading the nobles to maintain or renew the Franco-Scottish alliance. Wallace denied the treason but admitted the rest. Most of the other charges, after all, were no more than proof that he had carried out his avowed aims with great success. The charge of treason, on the other hand, meant that he had betrayed and attacked his lawful and natural lord. To Wallace it seemed plain enough that King Edward had never been his lawful and natural lord, and at no time had he ever sworn allegiance or done homage to him.

The judgement, like the trial, was a formality. It was not really a judicial proceeding but an act of simple retribution dictated by a deep desire for revenge, which might be disguised or rationalized as political necessity. William Wallace, 'a Scotsman born in Scotland', was bound to a hurdle and dragged behind a horse for more than four miles, from Westminster to the Tower, from there to Aldgate, and thence finally through the heart of the city to the Smithfield Elms. There he was hanged, cut down while still living, disembowelled and then beheaded. The law was not content to make this the limit of the butchery. The heart and entrails were burned by the executioners, and what remained of the body was cut into four pieces. The head was hoisted above London Bridge, the quarters were distributed to Newcastle upon Tyne, Berwick, Stirling and Perth, to be exposed to the public gaze probably on the bridges at those four towns.[3]

---

[1] M. H. Keen, 'Treason trials under the law of arms', *TRHS*, 5th Ser., xii, 87, 93, 103, seeks to show that Wallace's trial followed the normal pattern of treason trials under the law of arms, but his argument is unconvincing. There is no evidence that Wallace's trial was under the 'law of arms'; it was held by justices (including common law judges) acting on a commission of gaol delivery 'according to the law and the usage of our realm' (Stevenson, *Wallace Docs.*, 187). Moreover, Mr Keen ignores the principal objection to the trial, which was that Wallace was not one of King Edward's lieges, as Wallace himself was able to declare at his trial.

[2] Stevenson, *Wallace Docs.*, 189.

[3] Ibid., 193. These four towns are named in what seem to be the most authoritative sources; *Chron. Lanercost*, 203, has Newcastle, Berwick, Perth and Aberdeen.

Suddenly, seen against the whole circumstances in which Wallace was hunted down and met his death, Edward I, the greatest of the Plantagenets, a king most admired and feared and one who could show nobility of character, appears small and mean. He is measured against one of the great spirits of history and found wanting. In Wallace himself, who had fought and worked for seven years with a constancy and singleness of purpose remarkable in any age, and for a man of his time and class altogether extraordinary, who alone among the Scottish leaders had defeated a full-scale English army in the field, who had roused a nation to a new sense of its unity and freedom, all that Edward I and his subjects could see was an implacable foe (which he was) and a traitor unmindful of his fealty (which he was never).[1]

The tragedy of Wallace did not lie in the fact that he was a popular leader of proletarian nationalism betrayed by selfish aristocrats. It makes sense to call Wallace a democrat only if we mean by that description that he possessed the common touch, that he could speak to ordinary men in their own language and inspire them with courage and a sense of common purpose to which they could not normally attain. Politically and constitutionally, Wallace was a conservative, quite as much a part of the life of feudal society and breathing its air as the English king against whose might he pitted his own limited strength. Surely the real tragedy of Wallace lay in this, that he was thwarted and overthrown at last by the very same structure of society which he accepted without question. He set before himself the ideal of the community of the realm of Scotland, free and independent, owing allegiance only to its lawfully established king. If the king could not or would not act as its leader, the great feudal magnates and the prelates of the church must for the time being take his place. But if they failed, for whatever reason, to give the lead which it was their duty to give, it was for any one of the responsible men to take up the task. In a dark hour Wallace stood forth as the champion of Scotland – not in opposition to half-hearted and selfish nobles, but to do their work for them and show them that a member of one of the lesser knightly families could respond quite as well as the Comyns, Wisharts, Stewarts or Bruces to the call of the community and the

[1] J. G. Bellamy, *Law of treason in England in the later Middle Ages* (1970), which makes use, acknowledged and unacknowledged, of this work, accepts the charge of treason apparently on the ground that King John's submission of 1296 was lawfully valid and must have bound all Scots.

defence of the royal dignity. But, like Wallace himself, Scotland was conservative. In the long run, only the king and great lords could be accepted as her rulers. Defeat and, ironically, the rallying of the magnates which resulted from his defeat, removed the justification for Wallace's remaining at the top. Yet he could not return to the life of an obscure knight. From Falkirk to Smithfield Wallace's career, though obviously not negligible, was but a sad second best. The greatest achievement of this simple, single-minded man lay in the future, in his capture of the popular imagination of Scotland.

> 'Of his gud dedis and manhad
> Gret gestis, I hard say, ar made;
> Bot sa mony, I trow noucht,
> As he in till hys dayis wroucht.
> Quha all hys dedis off prys wald dyte
> Hym worthyd a gret buk to wryte
> And all thai to wryte in here
> I want bathe wyt and gud laysere'[1]

But, as it happened, this task was never to be carried out in a manner worthy of the man.

The Ordinance of September 1305 contains one chapter which because of its oddity and its rather cryptic import has always caught the eye of historians. Sandwiched between chapters which provided for the exile, for half a year and four years respectively, of Sir Alexander Lindsay and Sir Simon Fraser, are the following words: 'Also it is agreed that the earl of Carrick shall be commanded to put Kildrummy Castle in the keeping of such a man as he himself will be willing to answer for.'[2] The position of this chapter may be due to the vagaries of fourteenth-century drafting, yet the Ordinance is a methodically arranged document. The association of the earl of Carrick with two patriot leaders towards whom Edward still bore rancour, coupled with the tone of mistrust conveyed by this enigmatic provision, may point to some changes in the king's attitude to Robert Bruce. It can hardly yet have amounted to open suspicion or

---

[1] Wyntoun, *Original Chronicle* (Laing), 348–9.
[2] *APS*, i, 122. The words themselves do not necessarily imply mistrust, since ibid., 121, tells the chamberlain (whose loyalty was not in question) to commit the sheriffdom of Berwick to a man 'for whom he shall be willing to answer'.

Bruce would not have been included in the Scottish council which was to assist the lieutenant – a fact ignored by Dr Barron in his otherwise powerful arguments for believing that Bruce had 'fallen from favour'.[1] We know, of course, what Edward did not know in the autumn of 1305, that Bruce and Lamberton had entered into a secret 'band' to help each other in case of future perils. But when Wallace was captured there were found in his possession documents which included 'confederations and ordinances made between Wallace and the magnates of Scotland'.[2] These can hardly have included any agreement between Bruce and Wallace made after Bruce's change of sides in 1302, for if they had Edward would surely have taken action against Bruce at once. But there may well have been an earlier agreement. In 1299 Wallace's brother, Sir Malcolm Wallace, had been in Bruce's following,[3] a fact of some significance when it is remembered that the Wallaces' feudal superior was not Bruce but James Stewart. It was Bruce who defended Wallace in the Peebles *fracas*, and Wallace had always belonged to the southwestern group of leaders of whom Bruce, Bishop Wishart and the Stewart were the foremost figures. Other, less directly incriminating, evidence may have been found among Wallace's papers.

It is probable that after April 1305 Bruce and Bishop Wishart remained in Scotland. Since the new lieutenant could not take up his duties till the following year, the temporary custody of the country had been committed, on October 26th, to Bishop Lamberton, John of Sandal, Sir Robert Keith and Sir John Kingston.[4] Their commission was actually renewed as late as February 16th,[5] 1306 – six days after Comyn had been murdered. Clearly, Edward did not suspect that anything was seriously amiss. If he had planned Bruce's *coup d'état* himself he could hardly have arranged matters better than to allow Bruce and Wishart complete freedom in Scotland and make Lamberton chief Guardian.

The later Scottish chroniclers, Barbour, Fordun and Wyntoun, tell a romantic story about the origins of Bruce's rising which finds no confirmation in any contemporary source. Some modern historians ignore it, presumably judging it to be pure fiction. Briefly (for

[1] *Scottish War of Independence*, 172.
[2] F. Palgrave, *Antient Kalendars and Inventories*, i (1836), 134.
[3] P.R.O., C. 47/22/8. See above, p. 152. [4] *Cal. Docs. Scot.*, ii, No. 1745. [5] Ibid.

there are variations in the tale) it runs as follows.[1] Bruce and the Red Comyn, indignant at Scotland's servitude, made a pact that Bruce should take the crown with Comyn's support and Comyn in return should receive Bruce's lands. The pact was recorded in reciprocally sealed indentures. Thereupon Comyn promptly went to Edward and blabbed forth the plot. The king summoned Bruce (but not Comyn) to a parliament, confronted him with Comyn's half of the indenture and asked if the seal on it was his. Bruce asked for a night's respite, since he had foolishly forgotten to bring his seal with him. While he was at his lodgings, the earl of Gloucester (Ralph de Monthermer) sent him a messenger with a shilling and a pair of spurs – a nice touch. Bruce, tipping the messenger with the shilling (a still nicer touch), rode for Lochmaben as fast as he could go and then, finding Comyn at Dumfries, challenged him with his treachery. This tale must be regarded as a literary product, the final, satisfying version of an originally much simpler, or at least less romantic, story. There was no parliament in the period to which Bruce could have been summoned,[2] and there is no evidence that Bruce was with the king only a few weeks before Comyn's murder. The story credits King Edward with a trustfulness and simplicity which, however engaging, would have lost him his throne in a few years, while it attributes to Comyn a treacherousness which owes more to the necessity of giving the Comyns a bad name in post-Bruce Scotland than to anything we know for certain about Comyn's life and character.

But yet the tale cannot be totally fictitious. Walter of Guisborough, followed substantially by Sir Thomas Grey, gives a coherent, self-consistent account of Bruce's uprising and his dealings with Comyn of Badenoch.[3] Bruce, fearing that Comyn might hinder him in an attempt on the throne, sent two of his brothers from Lochmaben to Comyn's castle at Dalswinton asking him to come to the Franciscan convent in Dumfries to discuss certain important affairs. According to Grey, the brothers were secretly ordered to assassinate Comyn, but Guisborough says nothing of this, only that they were sent to Comyn 'treacherously'. In Grey's account, the brothers found

---

[1] Barbour, *Bruce*, 14–20; *Chron. Fordun*, i, 337–40; Wyntoun, *Original Chronicle* (Laing), 364–8.

[2] *Handbook of British Chronology* (2nd edn), 513, gives no parliament between September 1305 and May 1306.

[3] *Chron. Guisb.*, 366–7; *Scalacronica*, 129–30.

Comyn so open and friendly that they could not bring themselves to kill him – an explanation so lame that we are on safe grounds in dismissing the brother's secret commission as embroidery. Comyn duly appeared at the Greyfriars' church, whereupon Bruce himself took charge and led Comyn up towards the high altar. Here again, Guisborough and Grey diverge. The one says that Bruce, after friendly words, suddenly turned on Comyn and accused him ot treacherously reporting to Edward I that Bruce was plotting treason; the other says that Bruce spoke to Comyn of the unhappy plight ot their country prostrate beneath the heel of the conqueror. 'Help me to be king and you shall have my lands, or give me yours and I will help you to win the crown.' But Comyn, in this story the soul of uprightness, would not listen to such treason. In their essentials, shorn of the accretions which gather so readily about public events which are both dramatic and secret, the accounts of Guisborough and Grey tally with the much briefer report of the affair made to the pope by Edward I in the course of his charges against Bishop Lamberton. This report, though obviously from a potentially biassed source, is closest in time to the event of any that we have. 'When Lamberton was made chief Guardian, Bruce rose against King Edward as a traitor, and murdered Sir John Comyn, lord ot Badenoch, in the church of the Friars Minor of the town of Dumfries, by the high altar, because Sir John would not assent to the treason which Robert planned to perpetrate against the king of England, namely, to resume war against him and make himself king of Scotland.'[1]

Without more evidence than we possess at present, it is impossible to reconstruct the sequence of events leading to Comyn's murder and from there to Bruce's coronation. We can note a few certainties and suggest one of what will always be several possible interpolations between the certainties. In order to do this, it will be as well to re-capitulate some of the few known landmarks in Bruce's career since 1302, the year of his submission to Edward I.

At the time he went over to the English, Robert Bruce was twenty-eight, entering the prime of life and about to enter on his second marriage. His first wife had been Isabel, daughter of Donald, earl of Mar, his grandfather's friend and ally. The link with the Mar family

[1] Palgrave, *Docs. Hist. Scot.*, 335.

was close, for Bruce's sister Christian had married Earl Donald's son
and successor Earl Gartnait, and is said to have carried with her, as
her marriage-portion, the Bruce share in the lordship of Garioch.[1]
There was only one child of this first marriage, cut tragically short by
Isabel's death in an unknown year: this was Marjorie, born before
1297[2] and named after her grandmother who had brought the earldom of Carrick into the Bruce family. Bruce's second wife, whom he
married in 1302, obviously after his submission, was Elizabeth de
Burgh, daughter of Richard de Burgh, earl of Ulster. As we have
seen, his desire for this marriage may have been one of the reasons
which led him to desert the national cause. Yet at the same time it
strengthened his ties with James Stewart, for James's wife Egidia
(Gelis) was Elizabeth's aunt. More importantly, it preserved the
ancient connexion between the lords of Carrick and northern Ireland.
Ultimately, Marjorie Bruce was given in marriage to Walter, James
Stewart's second son, who succeeded as heir because his elder brother
Andrew died in their father's lifetime.

Between 1302 and 1304 Bruce took an active though never a
brilliant or conspicuous part in the Anglo-Scottish war. He had not
gained Edward's confidence sufficiently by the autumn of 1302 to
figure in a schedule prepared on September 20th listing senior
officers in Scotland and the men under their command.[3] Indeed, it is
a striking fact that in this list, which contains no fewer than 508
names, only the merest handful were Scotsmen. The aristocracy
which is supposed to have been supporting the English king is represented only by the earl of Dunbar (who was pro-English throughout
the war), Sir Alexander Balliol (who was more of an Englishman
than a Scotsman), and Sir Archibald Livingstone. It seems that
Bruce's first public act as an adherent of Edward I was his attendance
at the Westminster parliament in October 1302.[4] In the next year he
served for a short period as sheriff of Lanark and Ayr and had the
keeping of Ayr castle.[5] In the summer campaign of 1303 he was
ordered to call up one thousand picked footmen from Kyle, Cunning-

[1] Above, p. 60, n. 2.
[2] The English proposal of July, 1297 that Marjorie Bruce should be a hostage
(Palgrave, *Docs. Hist. Scot.*, 199) seems to be the earliest mention of her in record.
[3] *Cal. Docs. Scot.*, ii, 340–1.
[4] *SHR*, xxxiv, 127–8.
[5] *Cal. Docs. Scot.*, ii, Nos. 1420, 1437, 1658.

ham and Cumnock (which were within his sheriffdom of Ayr but not in his earldom of Carrick) and a further thousand, as he thought fit, from Carrick and Galloway.[1] These would be among the men he was accustomed to call out as his earl's army of Carrick. This, ironically, was to be done in collaboration with Gibbon MacCan and Dungal Macdouall of Galloway. They were to send their forces to join the main English army in the east, but in July 1303 we find Bruce himself still in association with Sir John de Botetourt, King Edward I's bastard son, who was then English warden of the western march.[2]

At this time Comyn, Fraser and Wallace, holding out in the forest, were still free to raid Annandale, Liddesdale and the Cumberland border with a strong force of horse and foot.[3] But by the end of the year, as we have seen, their position was hopeless. Comyn and many others were on the point of surrender and it remained only to mop up the forces still holding out under Fraser and Wallace and to await the fall of Stirling. In January 1304 Bruce was still commanding the garrison at Ayr,[4] while Botetourt planned a large-scale foray against the patriots.[5] Not long afterwards, Bruce had crossed the country to join Segrave, Clifford and William Latimer in the mounted commando which left Dunfermline about the end of February and made a rapid surprise attack on the Scots leaders near Peebles. They failed to capture Fraser and Wallace, a fact which explains a phrase in the king's letter to Bruce on this occasion (March 3rd): 'As the cloak has been made well, make the hood also.'[6] Nevertheless, it is clear that Bruce had taken a strenuous part in the main English military effort which, though it failed to shut Wallace and Fraser up in the forest did prevent them from breaking out north of the Forth in any strength.

In this same month of March, Bruce evidently had news of his father's death.[7] He must have hurried south to settle his affairs and

[1] *Cal. Docs. Scot.*, ii, No. 1356, given in full (with material omitted by Bain), Stevenson, *Documents*, ii, No. 438, where it is misdated 1297. Cf. *Scottish War of Independence* 126–8.

[2] *Cal. Docs. Scot.*, ii, No. 1385. Botetourte's relationship to King Edward appears in the Hailes Abbey chronicle (Brit. Lib., MS. Cott. Cleop. D iii, fo. 51) in an otherwise correct and detailed genealogical table. This chronicle takes the closest interest in the Plantagenet royal house and is well-informed about its relationships.

[3] Ibid., No. 1374.   [4] Ibid., No. 1437.   [5] Ibid.

[6] Ibid., No. 1465; cf. ibid., No. 1432 and iv, 474.   [7] Ibid., ii, No. 1493.

make sure of his succession to his father's large estates, mostly in the Honour of Huntingdon but including Writtle and Hatfield Broad-oak in Essex, which had been granted to the Competitor's mother in exchange for her share of the Honour of Chester. From Hatfield, on April 4th, Bruce wrote urgently requesting the necessary 'inquisitions *post mortem*' to be held without delay, so that he might return to the king and do homage for his inheritance.[1] He wrote to the king personally saying that he had been in London and Essex but could neither raise any rents nor borrow any money to buy horses and armour.[2] He was apparently back in Scotland by April 16th, when the king thanked him for sending siege engines to Stirling.[3] A fort-night later Edward issued the writs ordering the inquisitions *post mortem* on Bruce's estates. These were held about May 25th, and Bruce duly did homage for his English lands on or before June 14th.[4] Between August and October he seems to have been busy trying to recover Annandale and its liberties.[5] From November 9th, 1304, when he was at York,[6] until the Lenten parliament of 1305 his where-abouts and activities are unknown, but one fact about him at this time is clear enough: potentially he had never been richer or more favoured. Among the motives of his bid for the crown we may dis-count the desperation or bitterness of a disappointed man. He was earl of Carrick, lord of Annandale, lord of a great estate in England, a house in London and the pleasant suburban manor of Tottenham. In the far north he held part of Garioch and, as guardian of his nephew, the young Earl Donald of Mar, he had in his keeping the stoutly-built fortress of Kildrummy – which he must place in the charge of someone for whom he would be responsible. Also in the north he was keeper of at least three royal forests, Kintore, Darnaway and Longmorn.[7] He may have been financially embarrassed, but

---

[1] *Cal. Docs. Scot.*, ii, No. 1493.

[2] Ibid., No. 1495. His Essex steward bought £94 worth of clothes for him on credit, and the bills were still unpaid 10 years later (Brit. Lib., Add. Chr. 28523).

[3] Stevenson, *Documents*, ii, No. 641. This letter presents a problem, for its date allows Bruce very little time to return to Scotland from Essex and then send a letter to the king discussing the movement of siege engines.   [4] Ibid., Nos. 1540, 1546.

[5] Ibid., Nos. 1588, 1604. Ibid., iv, No. 1818, seems to refer to Bruce's father, and therefore to belong to *c.* 1302.

[6] Ibid., ii, No. 1606 (10).

[7] Ibid., Nos. 1708, 1736. Longmorn ('Launde Morgan') was a small forest south of Elgin.

with resources such as these he could surely hope for a recovery within a few years.

There is no evidence that Bruce was on bad terms with the young prince of Wales, who as all men now realized would very soon succeed his father on the English throne. Still only thirty himself, Bruce had brothers who were too young to expect to have reached a corresponding prosperity. But Edward, the eldest, was in the prince of Wales's household,[1] and for Alexander Bruce at least the future seemed bright. He had recently been a student at Cambridge[2] and the English king, probably at a date subsequent to his brother's submission and certainly before February 1304, had granted him in maintenance the living of Kirkinner ('Carnemoel') near Wigtown.[3] Alexander Bruce had had a brilliant career at the university. The Lincolnshire poet Robert Manning of Bourne, who had known him at Cambridge, wrote admiringly: 'No one who read arts at Cambridge before or since his time ever made such progress. He was a master of arts before his brother was king of Scotland.'[4] Robert Bruce himself gave the traditional feast at Cambridge when his brother 'incepted' as M.A., probably in the spring of 1303 or 1304.[5] Promotion came quickly and, probably in 1306, he was made dean of Glasgow.[6]

In the midst of all his prosperity, much of it new-found, there was one thing which Bruce could not forget. A great nobleman of royal

[1] Stevenson, Documents, ii, No. 394.

[2] On this, see Ruth Crosby, 'Robert Mannyng of Brunne: a new biography', Publications of the Modern Language Association of America, lvii (1942), 15–28, esp. 22–4. It should be added that Robert Bruce the future king cannot have been at Cambridge between May 1297 and the beginning of 1302, and he is unlikely to have been able to visit Cambridge before October 1302.

[3] Letters from Northern Registers (ed. J. Raine, Rolls Series), No. 103 (which must date not later than February 25th, 1304; cf. ibid., No. 104).

[4] The Story of England by Robert Manning of Brunne (ed. F. J. Furnivall, Rolls Series), i, 12–13; A. B. Emden, A biographical register of the University of Cambridge to 1500 (Cambridge, 1963), 99–100.

[5] It seems most improbable that Bruce was in the south as early as the spring of 1302; while his visit can hardly have been as late as 1305, since the poet Robert Manning was evidently present at the feast, and there is evidence which makes it unlikely that Manning was at Cambridge as late as that year.

[6] Alexander Bruce is called 'dean of Glasgow' in the accounts of his death. Probably he was made dean with the approval of Wishart either at the end of 1305 or in the first half of 1306; indeed, his appointment may have been in consequence of his brother's coronation.

descent, related to the greatest aristocratic family of England,
brother-in-law of the most powerful man in Ireland, he was well
aware that he inherited a claim to the Scottish throne. When put
forward by his grandfather fourteen years earlier it had proved
weaker than Balliol's. But the weakest claim may lie dormant to be
reawakened when stronger claims are extinguished, and the Bruce
claim, though weak against Balliol, was incomparably stronger than
any other. In 1292, Bruce's grandfather had carefully resigned to his
son all his possible claims to the throne, and now, since 1304, Bruce
had become the head of his family. By 1304 moreover, John Balliol
had given every proof that his was the negation of true kingship.
And Edward I was an old man, a prey to sickness, close to death.
There was something else which Bruce can hardly have forgotten,
but to which Edward was blind. The surrender at Strathord, the fall
of Stirling, Wallace's execution, the Ordinance of September, had
not abolished the Scottish kingdom or the idea of the community of
the realm. So long as men like Robert Wishart, William Lamberton
and John de Soules remained alive this powerful idea would survive
and remain articulate. This was the part of the lesson of 1296–7 which
the English king had not learned, and it was vital. But how could the
idea of the community be put once more into action? The old solution was guardianship, but a revival of guardianship – though it was
to come again in 1329, in a dangerous hour – was clearly out of the
question in 1305. The only possible answer was a revival of kingship.
The Scottish kingdom must cease to be the disembodied ghost which
it had been since Toom Tabard had been stripped of his insignia in
1296, and be turned again into a living reality. It was thus that out of
defeat was born revolution. It was, to be sure, the private revolution
of an ambitious man. Much more momentously, it was also the
political revolution of the community of the realm.

9

Revolution

BEHIND the sudden deed of violence and sacrilege in the Grey-friars' kirk at Dumfries on February 10th, 1306, lay one fact of fundamental importance. The success of any revolution would depend on the full support or else on the elimination of John the Red Comyn of Badenoch. This was true not only because of what he was himself but more precisely because of the powers and tradition he represented. John Comyn was about the same age as Robert Bruce. He was head of the senior line of his family and his estates in Nithsdale, Tweeddale, Atholl and elsewhere, as well as his two high-land lordships of Lochaber and Badenoch, placed him as a landowner in that small class which included the earls and the foremost barons. He was also lord of two large manors in Tynedale, a reminder of his descent from Waltheof of Tynedale, one of the ancient aristocracy of Northumbria, as well as from King Donald Bán (Donalbain of Shakespeare's *Macbeth*), whose daughter Bethoc married Waltheof's son. King John was his uncle, the earl of Buchan his cousin, the future earl of Pembroke his brother-in-law. The Comyns, who looked upon him as their chief, formed a powerful clan whose ramifications extended into almost every part of Scotland. Since the end of Alexander II's reign they had been peculiarly identified with leadership of the patriotic or anti-English faction among the Scots nobility. Not one of the men responsible for the conduct of the war against England had a more natural – one might say, a prescriptive – right to leadership of the community of the realm than John Comyn of Badenoch. His father had served as Guardian from 1286 to 1292 and was almost certainly one of the council of twelve in 1295–6. He himself had been Guardian from 1298 to the end of 1300, and again from 1302 until the general submission of 1304. In nearly every event of the war, save for the twenty-two months from April 1296 to February 1298, when he was King Edward's prisoner, Comyn had been in the forefront. His pedigree, connexions and career combine to make a brave story, but the harsh fact remains that he was an almost total failure. Nevertheless, revolution without or against the Comyns would be incomparably more difficult than revolution with their full support.

We can regard it as reasonably certain that in the autumn of 1305 Bruce had discussed revolution with Wishart and Lamberton.[1] In the following February he was at Lochmaben, while Comyn was at Dalswinton only nine miles away. King Edward was ill and not expected to live much longer. It was the moment for action. It is contrary to everything we know of Bruce's character that he should have called Comyn to the Greyfriars' church with the secret intention of killing him. The place of meeting, the fact that King Edward's justices were holding their session in the castle at the time, and the kiss – though it was not the kiss of peace – with which the two men greeted each other all suggest that Bruce meant only to put some such plan to Comyn as Grey and Barbour believed him to have done. Had not his grandfather proposed a similar plan to Count Florence of Holland? But no doubt Bruce would prefer to take the throne himself, and give his estates to Comyn than take Comyn's, vast as they were, and help his old rival, Balliol's nephew, to become king of Scots.

Comyn can hardly be blamed for refusing. As Bruce was to learn to his cost, there were many other great men in Scotland who could not throw over their lawfully constituted sovereign and accept Bruce. No matter how inept King John had been, he was still alive and had a full-grown son and heir. No king of Scots had been overturned in this way since 1097, when Donald Bán had been driven from the throne by Edgar with the help of an English army. This was hardly an auspicious precedent, even if it had been at all clearly remembered. But Bruce was fully committed and prepared. He would identify his own ambition with the inarticulate but nonetheless powerful desires of the community of the realm. As the two leaders stood together in front of the high altar, speaking of the future, all their old antagonism and jealousy sprang to life. Bruce urged the revival of Scottish kingship, Comyn would have none of it. It may be that Comyn called Bruce a traitor, it seems certain that Bruce struck at

[1] Wishart and Lamberton were together at Melrose on November 4th (*Melrose Liber*, No. 349).

Suggested routes taken by Robert Bruce after the murder of Comyn at Dumfries 12 Feb 1306

Suggested routes taken by Robert Bruce after the Battle of Methven, 19 June, 1306

Queen Elizabeth, Earl of Atholl & Co.

0 10 20 30 40 50
Miles

Orkney

Bishop of Moray

Tain • • St. Duthac's Sanctuary

Elgin

Kildrummy

M a r

Aberdeen

Uist

Carinish

Barra
Kisimul

Garmoran

Castle Tirrim

The Mounth

Cairnburgmore Castle

Mull

Dunstaffnage

Kenmore

Methven 19/6/06

Scone 25-27/3/06

Dail Righ
(? July, 1306)

Perth • Cupar

Scotlandwell

Stirling

Earls Ferry

Islay

Rothesay

Inverkip

Dumbarton

Kirkintilloch

Glasgow

Rutherglen

Edinburgh

Berwick

Roxburgh

Rathlin

Dunaverty

Ayr

Loch Doon

Tibbers

Dalswinton

Dumfries 12/2/06

Lochmaben

Annan

Carlisle

Newcastle upon Tyne

The Roe

Antrim

Galloway

Skinburness

Man

Comyn with his dagger. At this, Bruce's companions attacked him
with their swords. Mortally wounded, he was left for dead, lying
on the flagstones before the altar. Sir Robert Comyn, John Comyn's
uncle, rushing up to defend his nephew, was killed by a blow on the
head from the sword of Christopher Seton, the son of a Yorkshire
knight and the husband of Bruce's sister Christian. Soon the town
was in an uproar, the Scots flocking to Bruce's support as he and his
men-at-arms hurried to seize the castle. The terrified justices shut
themselves in the hall where they had been holding their session, but
surrendered when Bruce threatened to set the place on fire. It was
then reported that Comyn was still alive: the Franciscans had carried
him into the vestry to treat his wounds and administer the last sacra-
ment. According to Guisborough (who seems here to be retailing
a deliberately hostile embellishment to what was doubtless a substantially truthful account), Bruce had the dying man brought back
to the altar steps and bloodily despatched there.[1] It was enough,
surely, that Bruce had murdered him and that the deed had been
done in a consecrated place. But there was evidently a general
tradition, both in Scotland and England, that Comyn was killed in
two stages, and it is this tradition which lies behind the famous but
wholly fabulous tale of Kirkpatrick and his cry of 'I mak siccar'.

Six weeks elapsed between Comyn's murder and Bruce's coronation. It is probable that the murder itself was an act of unpremedi-
tated violence. What followed, however, must have been part of a
pre-arranged plan. The fiery cross was never to be carried more
urgently through Scotland than during February and March 1306.
Castles were seized, the kinsmen of the lord of Badenoch fled before
his murderer, and Englishmen rode as fast as they could to safe
castles or to the Border. By a piece of extraordinary good fortune,
there survives a copy of a newsletter written by an Englishman at
Berwick shortly before Bruce's coronation, which gives us an invaluable glimpse of the movements of Bruce and his supporters
during these critical weeks.[2] Since much of this information is to be

[1] *Chron. Guisb.*, 367.
[2] Best edited in Stones, *Documents*, No. 34. First edited, very badly, by H. T.
Riley, *Registra Johannis Whethamstede etc.*, (Rolls Series) ii, 347–53. Although com-
mented upon by Charles Johnson, *EHR*, xxxiii, 366–7, this highly important document seems never to have become known to Scottish historians. I have to thank
Professor Stones for drawing my attention to it.

found nowhere else, its reliability cannot be checked directly. But the writer's accuracy on points which can be checked inspires confidence in the whole of the admittedly incomplete story he has to tell. Certainly no one attempting to reconstruct the events of this period can ignore his urgent, almost breathless narrative.

Bruce's achievements in these few short weeks were remarkable, but he had not time to put himself in a commanding position militarily, save perhaps in the south-west. He and his friends seized the castles of Dumfries, Dalswinton, Tibbers and Ayr. Robert Boyd of Cunningham, who was to prove one of Bruce's staunchest companions, took Rothesay Castle by sea, and then laid siege to Inverkip.[1] At the southern extremity of the peninsula of Kintyre – the 'isle of Kintyre' as contemporaries called it[2] – stood on a sea-girt rock the castle of Dunaverty.[3] Apparently Edward I had been persuaded to grant this castle, without a proper inquest, to one Malcolm Mac-Coyllan (*alias* Malcolm MacCulian).[4] An attractive interpretation of the evidence would suggest that Malcolm MacCulian was identical with Malcolm le fiz Lengleys, to whom King Edward had given possession of at least a part of Kintyre in 1296, apparently without due process of law.[5] Malcolm MacCulian's origins are as yet a mystery. He has been claimed, doubtfully, as a MacQuillan of Antrim, and perhaps even more doubtfully as an ancestor of the Macleans. Whatever the truth of this may be, it seems that Bruce got Dunaverty from Malcolm MacCulian in exchange for another castle, and he took good care to stock Dunaverty and also his own ancestral castle of Loch Doon in Carrick with plenty of victuals.[6] Finally, before going north to Scone, Bruce tried, without success, to

[1] Rothesay belonged to James the Stewart, with whom Boyd seems to have had some connexion; G. Crawfurd, *History of the shire of Renfrew* (1710), 44. Inverkip was also in the Stewart's lordship, but whether held in demesne or not is uncertain.

[2] Palgrave, *Docs. Hist. Scot.*, 315; *Cal. Docs. Scot.*, ii, No. 1834.

[3] *Macfarlane's Geographical Collections* (SHS), 187. There is little to be seen of the castle today, and the 1-inch Ordnance Survey Map does not indicate its site.

[4] Stones, *Documents*, p. 130: 'chastel Dananerbi (de Ananorbi)', for which I should propose to read 'Donauerthi', i.e. Dunaverty. In ibid, line 13, I read (in the MS) 'ly', and would reconstruct 'en lyle de Kentir'. I suppose also that 'Mac' should be supplied before 'Coyllan' in line 15.

[5] For this identification, see above, p. 80, n. 3. The evidence that Malcolm le Fiz Lengleys was put in possession of Kintyre by King Edward without due process of law is to be found in *Rotuli Scotiae*, i, 22–3; P.R.O., S.C. 1/18/147.

[6] Stones, *Documents*, No. 34, p. 130.

persuade Sir John Menteith to surrender the castle of Dumbarton.[1]
The attention thus paid by Bruce to five of the fortresses which
commanded the Firth of Clyde is striking proof of his awareness of
the 'western approaches'. The way must be kept open for allies and
supplies to reach him from Ireland and the Outer Isles, while enemies
from the same quarter, and also English fleets based on Skinburness,
must find their approach routes barred.

Before going to Dumbarton and thence on to Scone, Bruce spent
some time at Rutherglen and Glasgow, taking individual fealties,
putting the populace on twenty-four hours' notice of mobilization,[2]
and conferring with Robert Wishart, who is known to have been at
Glasgow four days before John Comyn was killed.[3] The murder had
been committed in Wishart's diocese. Far from excommunicating
the guilty man, the bishop exhorted his flock to fight for Bruce as
though his cause were a crusade.[4] He brought out from his episcopal
wardrobe robes and vestments suitable for a new king to wear, and
also a banner bearing the arms of the last king, which the indefatigable old man had been carefully hiding in his treasury for precisely
this purpose and moment. It was a picturesque touch, and reminds
us forcefully that the mind of Wishart had most probably been behind the drafting of the Treaty of Birgham, which sixteen years
earlier had provided so elaborately that relics and muniments touching the royal dignity should be kept safely, under their seals, by the
great magnates of the realm.[5] The writer of the English newsletter
called Wishart the 'bad bishop' and considered that he was Bruce's
chief counsellor. He goes on to give a highly interesting piece of
information which though unsupported rings true enough. Wishart,
he says, not only absolved Bruce formally for his sin in being a party

---

[1] Stones, *Documents*, No. 34, pp. 133-4.

[2] Ibid., p. 131. The newsletter gives yet another example of Barbour's uncanny
accuracy in detail, for he says that after Comyn's murder 'the lord of the Bruce to
Glaskow raid', Barbour, *Bruce*, 24.

If it were not for the rubric *Summonitio exercitus post obitum regis*, the brieve referred
to above as belonging to *c.* 1286 (p. 25, n. 1) might fit the situation in February-March
1306.

[3] *Paisley Registrum*, 373-4, shows the bishop's presence at Glasgow on February
6th, 1306. It does not seem rash to guess that Wishart knew in advance approximately
when the *coup* was to be carried out.

[4] Palgrave, *Docs. Hist. Scot.*, 348; see also below, p. 266, n. 2.

[5] Stevenson, *Documents*, i, 169-70.

to the killing of John Comyn, but made Bruce swear an oath to abide under the direction and with the assent of the clergy of Scotland. Once the oath was sworn, he might do what he could to secure his inheritance. Wishart worked for the freedom of Scotland, but he would assuredly not have supported a king who would not guarantee the freedom of the Scottish Church. Barely four months before the great rising of 1297, when he was supposedly administering his diocese peaceably under the English régime of occupation, Bishop Wishart sent a mandate to the dean of Christianity of Lennox, reminding him of 'the liberties of the Scottish Church hitherto enjoyed and granted by our lord the king'.[1] We can be sure that these liberties meant much to the bishop, and when he wrote with possibly careful anonymity of 'our lord the king' it is by no means certain that it was Edward I he had in mind.[2] The oath which Robert Bruce took in Wishart's presence in March 1306 may be seen as the oath of one who was soon to be *Rex Scottorum* to preserve and defend those same *libertates ecclesie Scoticane*.

Bruce was set upon taking the throne. The die had been cast before Comyn's murder, probably long before. Perhaps the decision dated from 1304, when Bruce and Lamberton had made their secret pact. Certainly Lamberton was ready when the time came. At the crucial moment of Comyn's murder, and for some weeks afterwards, he was at Berwick, trusted by Edward I, president of the council established under the 1305 Ordinance for the government of conquered Scotland.[3] Shortly before Bruce was crowned, the bishop slipped away from Berwick under cover of darkness, crossed the Forth (no doubt by the 'earl's ferry' from North Berwick to Elie) and hurried to Scone to be present at the ceremony. We are not told how Lamberton had wind of Bruce's movements. It is clear from the newsletter that the English at Berwick realized that speedy enthronement at Scone was Bruce's objective, and there even seems to have been some communication between Bruce and the English. At

---

[1] *Paisley Registrum*, 204 (January 18th, 1297).

[2] It is possible that he was referring to Edward I's undertaking of June 1291 (of which Wishart himself had issued an inspeximus) to protect the liberties and privileges of holy church in Scotland. But the reign of King John had intervened since that date, and Edward had not renewed his undertaking after conquering Scotland in 1296.

[3] Palgrave, *Docs. Hist. Scot.*, 335–6. Barbour, *Bruce*, 21, says that Bruce at once sent a letter to Lamberton telling him of the murder of Comyn; this may be true.

this eleventh hour, Bruce made a formal demand to be recognized as king.[1] For their part, King Edward's council and his chamberlain ordered Bruce to hand over the castles he had seized, especially those belonging to the Red Comyn which had escheated to the English Crown! Bruce's answer was that he would seize castles and people and strengthen his position as fast as he could until King Edward had told him what was his will in response to his demand. If this were not granted, Bruce would defend himself 'with the longest stick that he had'.[2]

Guisborough, a hostile witness, speaks quite frankly of Bruce's coronation at Scone as a great public event, 'attended and consented to by four bishops, five earls and the people of the land'.[3] As to its full formality and solemnity there can be little doubt that he was right. He does not name the bishops and earls, and the available evidence suggests the attendance of three bishops and four earls. It seems that there were actually two separate ceremonies, and the explanation of this curious fact throws a fascinating light on the dilemma confronting the Scottish leaders: on the one hand the desperate need to have Bruce enthroned as soon as possible, on the other, the compelling arguments to make his inauguration follow the traditional pattern. He was first made king on Lady Day, Friday, March 25th, 1306 – the tenth anniversary of the outbreak of war between Edward I and the Scots. We have no details of the ceremony, but we may be sure that the bishop of St Andrews took a prominent and vitally important part.[4] The Stone of Destiny was in Westminster Abbey, but the English king had not been able to remove Scone itself, the Moot Hill, or the Augustinian abbey which acted in some sense as the custodian of what was by far the most ancient seat of royalty still in use in Britain. Apparently the abbey church was the actual scene of the coronation itself, and after Bruce's first defeat Edward I requested the pope to authorize the wholesale removal of Scone Abbey to another diocese, presumably somewhere in England.[5] Abbot Henry of Scone willingly took part in the cere-

[1] Stones, *Documents*, No. 34, p. 133.

[2] Ibid., 'il se defendroit de plus long bastoun q'il eust'.

[3] *Chron. Guisb.*, 367.

[4] Palgrave, *Docs. Hist. Scot.*, 336; *Cal. Docs. Scot.*, ii, No. 1818 (somewhat misrendered); Stones, *Documents*, No. 35; M. Ash, in *The Scottish Tradition*, 48.

[5] *Foedera*, i, 1003. The abbey, Edward declared, was 'situated in the midst of a perverse nation'.

mony along with Lamberton, Wishart and David Murray, bishop
of Moray. Maurice, abbot of Inchaffray, was almost certainly at the
coronation.[1] Three earls who are known to have been present were
John of Atholl, Malcolm of Lennox, and Alan of Menteith, and
to them we may probably add the boy Donald, earl of Mar, who
was Bruce's ward. The most conspicuous absentee among the earls
was, of course, Duncan of Fife. It might, indeed, have been denied
that any ceremony could be valid without him. In 1292 a substitute
had been carefully provided; now the earl was sixteen years of age,
but completely in King Edward's power. His sister Isabel, hardly
more than twenty, was the wife of the earl of Buchan. It does not
seem possible to tell from the surviving sources whether she was
with her husband in England when she heard of his cousin's murder,
or whether she was in Scotland. Her husband appears to have been in
England, at his Leicestershire manor of Whitwick.[2] For the countess
of Buchan, as for the countess of Dunbar in 1296, the call of patriotism and the community of Scotland was more powerful than wifely
loyalty; but English accounts of her conduct do not hesitate to say
that she was, or wished to be, Bruce's mistress.[3] She seized her husband's finest horses and set off to ride to Scone, where she arrived
too late to take part in the coronation performed by the bishops. But
her presence meant that at least a part of the ancient tradition could
be retrieved. Accordingly, a second ceremony was performed two
days after the first, on Palm Sunday, March 27th.[4] We have no
detailed account of this, but if the Countess Isabel performed the role
expected of a member of the Clan Macduff her task would have been
to place the new king on some substitute for the Stone of Destiny,
perhaps on a throne. At one, perhaps at both, of the ceremonies, a
gold coronet was placed on Bruce's head.[5] The wearing of a crown
had long been an accepted part of the inauguration of a king of
Scots, though it was hardly yet essential to it.[6]

[1] Palgrave, *Docs. Hist. Scot.*, 319.

[2] *Scalacronica*, 130, is over-concise and muddled. Stones, *Documents*, p. 131, suggests that the earl of Buchan was in the north.

[3] *Flores Historiarum*, iii, 129–30; *Proc. Soc. Antiq. Scot.*, New Ser., vii, 172.

[4] Ibid. On this day, the bishop of St Andrews celebrated pontifical high mass for
the new king, Stones, *Documents*, No. 35, p. 138.

[5] *Cal. Docs. Scot.*, ii, No. 1914 (the coronet was stolen by Geoffrey de Coigners, but
the theft was discovered and pardoned).

[6] Cf. G. W. S. Barrow, *Acts of Malcolm IV*, 27.

There was no time to call a parliament. The country must be put in a
state of defence. There may have been some proclamation, some
declaration of right, by the new king, but no formal document
issued by Bruce or on his behalf has survived from this time, or,
indeed, from earlier than the third year of his reign.[1] Bishop Wishart,
old as he was, plunged with zest into the struggle. The English had
given him timber to repair the bell-tower of his cathedral, and with
this he had siege engines made to use against the castle at Kirkintilloch. He himself seized the royal castle at Cupar in Fife 'comme
homme de guerre', as the English complained.[2] The new king
showed similar energy as he went to different parts of the country,[3]
quelling Balliol and Comyn sympathizers, taking the homage of
unwilling magnates like the earl of Strathearn (Buchan's brother-in-
law) and seizing more castles. He returned to the south-west, no
doubt to rally support, for the west-country element among his
early followers is noteworthy. His sojourn in this region included a
visit to Galloway to put hostile chiefs out of action.[4] But he could
not approach the strongly-held redoubt of Lothian, guarded as it
was by the great fortresses of Stirling, Edinburgh, Roxburgh and
Berwick. And in the mean time the English, who possessed this
enormous advantage, had not been idle.

King Edward was taken utterly by surprise, and at first he does not
seem to have been sure that it was really Bruce who had risen against
him. 'Certain Scots in malice have slain John Comyn,' he wrote, as
though unwilling to credit such a preposterous enormity as that
Robert Bruce, whom he regarded as being deeply in his debt, could
have done this deed.[5] But by April 5th he had appointed as his

[1] Palgrave, *Docs. Hist. Scot.*, 319, mentions a letter sent by Bruce to the earl of
Strathearn within a few days of his coronation. The earliest known official docu-
ment whose text has survived is a charter of inspection for Sir John of Luss, dated
Inchmahome, September 28th, 1308.

[2] Palgrave, *Docs. Hist. Scot.*, 348-9.

[3] Evidence of King Robert's movements between his coronation and the battle of
Methven is to be found in Palgrave, *Docs. Hist. Scot.*, 319-21 and *Chron. Lanercost*,
203-4. Barbour, *Bruce*, 24, is presumably covering up ignorance in saying 'and syne
went our all the land, frendis and frendschip purchesand'.

[4] *Chron. Lanercost*, 203-4. It is conceivable that this expedition to Galloway is
identical with that carried out by Bruce *before* his coronation, for which see Stones,
Documents, p. 130.

[5] *Cal. Docs. Scot.*, ii, Nos. 1747, 1748.

special lieutenant in Scotland Aymer de Valence, his own half-cousin and Comyn's brother-in-law, and had armed him with wide and drastic powers.[1] He was, in Barbour's graphic phrase, 'to burn and slay and raise dragon',[2] to raise, that is, the terrible dragon banner which meant that no mercy would be shown and that none of the accepted restraints of fourteenth-century warfare – few as these were – need be observed. This is confirmed by letters from the king congratulating Valence on burning Simon Fraser's lands in Tweeddale and admitting that he had originally ordered all prisoners to be killed.[3] He later modified these orders, partly to allow Valence to pardon the 'middling men', but partly because he wished to reserve for Bruce, Fraser and the earl of Atholl a more terrible fate than summary execution. Even in his great rage, Edward's eye for detail, his unsurpassed memory of individuals, did not desert him.

'Since we have not found in Sir Michael Wemyss' (the king wrote to Valence on June 19th), 'either good word or service, and he has now shown in deed that he is a traitor and our enemy, we command you to burn his manor where we stayed, and all his other manors, to destroy his lands and goods and to strip his gardens clean so that nothing is left, for an example to others like him. And as for Sir Gilbert de la Hay, to whom we showed much courtesy when he stayed with us in London recently, and in whom we thought we could place our trust, but whom we now find to be a traitor and our enemy, we order you to burn down all his manors and houses, destroy all his lands and goods, and strip all his gardens so that nothing is left, and if possible do worse to him than to Sir Michael Wemyss.'[4]

Armed with these extensive powers, Valence moved with speed and vigour. By June 9th, Bishop Lamberton, then at Scotlandwell in Kinross-shire, had made the first overtures of surrender,[5] though after this he apparently called out all his tenantry and sent them off to fight for Bruce, and for good measure sent him the boy Andrew, James Stewart's son and heir, who had been in the bishop's custody.[6] Wishart was captured in Cupar castle and the two bishops were sent

<hr/>

[1] *Cal. Docs. Scot.*, ii, No. 1754.
[2] Barbour, *Bruce*, 24.
[3] *Cal. Docs. Scot.*, ii, Nos. 1782, 1790. Cf. also ibid., No. 1755.
[4] *Nat. MSS. Scot.*, ii, Pl. 14 (*Cal. Docs. Scot.*, ii, No. 1787).
[5] *Cal. Docs. Scot.*, ii, No. 1781.
[6] Palgrave, *Docs. Hist. Scot.*, 328–9, 336–7.

south, along with the abbot of Scone, to be put in irons in Wessex
dungeons.[1] Only their orders saved them from hanging.[2] By midsummer Valence had secured the town of Perth and Bruce judged the
moment ripe for an attack in strength. He approached from the
mountains to the west of the town on June 18th.[3] Failing to tempt
the English out to fight, he bivouacked at Methven, in a wood on
high ground south of the Almond. Unwisely, some of his men went
off to forage, others were scattered to find sleeping quarters. Valence
seized his opportunity, coming out from Perth before daylight and
taking the Scots unawares. His men made a fierce onslaught and
there was hard fighting at first, but Methven was a rout rather than a
battle. Within three months of his coronation, King Robert was
fleeing for safety with a few hundred men. Many of his most valuable
supporters were taken prisoner, and of these very few could be saved
by Valence's clemency from the vengeful wrath of King Edward.
Yet the disaster was the saving of Bruce and his kingdom. If he had
won, as he might well have done, he would almost certainly have
met the English king in the field in a major pitched battle, eight
years before he was ready for it.

Dr Evan Barron has compiled a list of some 135 men who came out
for Bruce in the spring of 1306, most of whom were with him at his
coronation or had joined his standard before the fight at Methven.[4]
We can appreciate the great value of this list and of its author's

[1] *Cal. Docs. Scot.*, ii, Nos. 1786, 1813, 1815, 1824.

[2] Ibid., No. 1786.

[3] *Chron. Guisb.*, 368; Barbour, *Bruce*, 27–31. Palgrave, *Docs. Hist. Scot.*, 321, shows
that before Methven Bruce was at Callander, north of Crieff, and then at Kenmore
(unlocated, but a known resort of the earls of Strathearn; *Inchaffray Chrs.*, nos. 87,
118). Some sources give the date of the battle of Methven as June 26th, other sources
as June 19th. In *Chron. Holyrood*, 179, no. 2, Mrs Anderson decided in favour of
June 26th, chiefly on the strength of *Cal. Docs. Scot.*, ii, No. 1811. But there is proof
that the true date was June 19th. Malise earl of Strathearn issued an indemnifying
letter for Gilbert of Glencarnie at Perth on June 26th, Fraser, *Grant*, iii, No. 12. Apart
from the improbability of this letter's being issued on the day of the battle, it is clear
from the account of the earl's movements in *Cal. Inqu. Misc.*, i, No. 2029, that he
left his refuge at Kenmore and joined Valence only after he had heard the result of
Methven. John Sandal's Account Book for 1306–7, to be calendared in the forthcoming volume of *Cal. Docs. Scot.*, No. 492, gives June 19th as the date of Methven.

[4] *Scottish War of Independence*, 224–35. See Appendix, below, for a list of Scottish
landowners forfeited for supporting Bruce.

commentary without necessarily accepting all his conclusions or believing that his analysis is the only historically useful one that can be made. Dr Barron was primarily concerned to show two things, distinct but connected. First, that Bruce drew the bulk of his support from Scotland north of the Forth-Clyde line; secondly, that it was 'Celtic Scotland' which declared for Bruce and made possible his revolution and his ultimate success. By contrast, what Dr Barron calls 'Teutonic' Scotland, by which he means Lothian and the Merse, was hostile or indifferent to Bruce. We shall see presently whether such beliefs can be sustained, or whether the evidence may not point to a rather different and more complex conclusion. Meanwhile we must look at Bruce's supporters and try to classify them not merely geographically, as Dr Barron does, but according to their place in the community and their individual careers. We may also reflect that as far as the men of high rank are concerned a list of those who did not support Bruce would be quite as significant historically as one of those who did.

First of all, there are the men whose attitude represented and at the same time ensured continuity in the struggle for the community of the realm; the men, that is, who had been fully committed to King John and now rallied to Bruce. They were going far beyond the cautious revolution of 1295 and performing (no doubt in the community's name) nothing less than a deliberate act of deposition on-election. They were also taking a terrible risk. Foremost among these men were the three bishops, Lamberton, Wishart and Murray, and also John de Soules. Although Soules seems to have stayed or returned overseas, and died in France about 1310,[1] his support for King Robert may have counted for much among men who did not belong to the Bruce or Comyn faction. James the Stewart was another great magnate in this group who supported Bruce. He had got his lands back only at the end of 1305 and within a few months they had again been forfeited and were given to the earl of Lincoln.[2] But the Stewart was an old man. Since King Alexander's death twenty years before he had played a part which, though far from negligible, was always secondary. He would neither hang for the young king

[1] *Chron. Fordun*, i, 331; *Scalacronica*, 127; *Melrose Liber*, i, No. 391; *Dumfriesshire Trans.*, 3rd Ser., xxvi.
[2] *Cal. Docs. Scot.*, ii, No. 1857.

not take to the heather with him. On October 23rd he made a
second abject submission to Edward I and the grant to the earl of
Lincoln was rescinded.[1] But by March 1309 (the year of his death) he
was back with King Robert, taking his rightful place as the senior
officer of the royal household.[2] Simon Fraser's movements are more
obscure. The provisions for his exile suggest that he surrendered in
1304 or 1305, and in October 1305 it was agreed that he might
then recover his estates at three years' purchase.[3] Yet he faced, it
seems, a long exile.[4] He was, however, still in Scotland at the time of
Bruce's rising, apparently with the English at Berwick.[5] Landless,
deeply aggrieved, he seems to have joined the new king at or just
after his coronation. He was present at Methven, but was soon
captured, and was drawn and hanged in London on September 7th.[6]

Other leading men in this same group were the three earls, Atholl,
Lennox and Menteith. John of Strathbogie, earl of Atholl, who had
supported the common cause more or less consistently since 1296,
had nevertheless always been a close friend of the Bruces. Like Bruce
he had married a daughter of Earl Donald of Mar, and his estates in
Stratha'an and Strathbogie[7] gave him as strong an interest in the

[1] Cal. Docs. Scot., ii, Nos. 1843, 1857; cf. iii, No. 56.

[2] APS, i, 459; James the Stewart died on July 16th, 1309, Chron. Bower, ii, 242.

[3] Foedera, i, 974-5.

[4] APS, i, 122, of September, 1305, must be compared with Foedera, i, 974-5.
Sir Maurice Powicke (The Thirteenth Century, 713) believed that the later document
rescinded Fraser's sentence of exile. But although it explicitly remitted the sentence
of exile passed on John Comyn of Badenoch, David Graham and the bishop of Glasgow, it said nothing explicitly of any similar remission in favour of Fraser; merely
that in respect of redemption of his lands and amends for wrongdoing he must pay
three years' value, like Comyn.

[5] Stones, Documents, p. 132.

[6] Flores Historiarum, iii, 133-4. Proc. Soc. Antiq. Scot., New Ser., vii (1884-5),
177-8, says that he was captured at Linlithgow. His capture was the occasion of the
most sickening of the many killings ordered by King Edward in 1306. Young Herbert
Morham, son of Sir Thomas Morham, who had commanded the Scots besieging
Stirling in 1299 and had subsequently been taken prisoner with his father and lodged
in the Tower, was (along with his father) excepted from the terms of surrender in
1304, Palgrave, Docs. Hist. Scot., 281. Herbert had foolishly wagered his head that
Fraser would never be captured. On September 7th, 1306, shortly before Fraser
met his death, Herbert Morham and his esquire, Thomas du Boys, were beheaded.
Herbert Morham had the name for being the tallest and most handsome knight in
Scotland; cf. Proc. Soc. Antiq. Scot., New Ser., vii, 190-2.

[7] Inherited through descent from David, son of Duncan II earl of Fife. Cf. Moray
Registrum, Nos. 16, 30, 62; Scots Peerage, iv, 8.

north east as the lordship of part of Garioch gave to Bruce. Under the Guardians Earl John had served as sheriff of Aberdeen,[1] and in 1304, when he was Edward I's warden between Forth and Spey, he resented the fact that the Aberdeen sheriffdom had been given to Alexander Comyn, the earl of Buchan's brother.[2] He besought the king not to let Comyn have Aboyne Castle; 'Sir Alexander,' he wrote, 'already has two of the strongest castles in the north, Urquhart and Tarradale, and (as sheriff) he can use the castle at Aberdeen.'[3] He suspected that Comyn was still in league with the highlander Lachlan Macruarie, as he had been in 1299. Atholl's plea was successful, but it was not quite disinterested. When he came out for Bruce two years later the authority in the north in which Edward had confirmed him must have been of much value to the new king of Scots. Of Menteith we know only that he surrendered after Methven, to be imprisoned and deprived of his earldom.[4] Lennox escaped with Bruce, to become, along with James Douglas, Neil Campbell and Gilbert de la Hay, one of his almost inseparable companions.

The earl of Strathearn was arrested. He pleaded that after Bruce's coronation (which he had evidently not attended) Atholl, Robert Boyd and others had pursued and kidnapped him and compelled him to do homage to the new king on pain of losing his head. After Methven, he had sent his son to join in the pursuit of Bruce.[5] He was imprisoned at Rochester, but not in irons, and ultimately he recovered his earldom.[6] In truth, an appreciable number of earls were hostile, indifferent or at least not known to have been favourable to Bruce at this time: Caithness, Sutherland, Ross, Buchan, Angus, Fife and Dunbar. Of these, all but Caithness and Fife are known to have been hostile. Alexander Macdougall, lord of Argyll, and his son and heir John, respectively uncle and cousin of the murdered John Comyn, were fiercely opposed to Bruce. So, for different reasons,

---

[1] *Arbroath Liber*, i, No. 231.
[2] *Cal. Docs., Scot.* ii, Nos. 1646.
[3] Ibid., No. 1633.
[4] Ibid., No. 1849.
[5] Palgrave, *Docs. Hist. Scot.*, 319 ff., and *Cal. Inqu. Misc.*, i, No. 2029, give an exceptionally full account of the earl of Strathearn's conduct.
[6] *Cal. Docs. Scot.*, ii, No. 1854.

were the leading men of Galloway. Between them, these magnates controlled a great proportion of the wealth and military resources of Scotland in castles and manpower, especially of the country north of Forth. The majority of them opposed Bruce not because they were on principle pro-English and held English estates but because they could accept neither the overthrow of the Comyns nor the claims of Bruce, in their view a plain usurper. If Bruce, therefore, had depended solely on the men who by rank and tradition stood at the top of Scottish feudal society, his revolution would have failed.

No doubt some men joined Bruce partly because English rule threatened to leave them landless, or much poorer than they believed was just. James Douglas was one such, the son of the rough Sir William, who had died in the Tower of London about 1299, still implacably hostile to the English king.[1] His lands were given to Sir Robert Clifford.[2] James Douglas was the nephew and perhaps also (because of the great rarity of his Christian name in thirteenth-century Scotland) the godson of James the Stewart.[3] He lived to become the bravest and noblest of Bruce's comrades and subjects, with so shining a reputation for chivalry that John Barbour's great poem *The Bruce* is almost as much as the story of Douglas it is of Bruce himself.

> 'Thusgat maid thai thar aquentance
> That nevir syne, for nakyn chance
> Departyt quhill thai lyffand war.
> Thair frendschip woux ay mar and mar.'[4]

---

[1] *Cal. Docs. Scot.*, ii, Nos. 960, 1054, 1055. William Douglas was imprisoned in Berwick castle in July 1297, where he was reported 'mout sauvage e mout araillez', 'very savage and very angry', Stevenson, *Documents*, ii, 205. I consulted medieval French scholars on 'araillez', which was not familiar to them, and they suggested it might be an ill-spelled form of 'enragez'. Stevenson supposed it to be connected with *railler*.

[2] *Cal. Docs. Scot.*, iii, No. 682; Barbour, *Bruce*, 9, 22–3.

[3] *Ibid.*, 421. The name James was probably used in the Stewart family because their abbey of Paisley was dedicated to St James the Great (as well as to Mirren and Milburga of Wenlock). Probably in 1253 James the Stewart's father Alexander of Dundonald went as a pilgrim to Saint James of Compostella and his son James may have been born after his return (*Paisley Registrum*, 90; *The Stewarts*, xii, Pt. 2, 77–8). In general, James is a name of infrequent occurrence in Scottish record before 1300.

[4] Barbour, *Bruce*, 23.

Sir John, laird of Cambo in the East Neuk of Fife, was another man whom English rule threatened to deprive of property. Although his name is on the list of homagers to Edward I in 1304, he had been prevented from doing homage by Sir Henry de Beaumont, probably because he had acquired the revenues of the prosperous fishing town of Crail, to which Beaumont's sister, the lady de Vesci, claimed an hereditary right.[1] Lady de Vesci was confirmed in possession in June 1305, with reversion to her brother.[2] By the following summer Sir John of Cambo was listed among King Edward's enemies, and on August 4th he was hanged at Newcastle.[3] William Gourlay, who like John of Cambo figures on the list of homages to Edward I of March 14th, 1304,[4] was similarly frustrated by claimants supported by the English king, in his case over the land of 'Macfothel' (Pitfoddels?) in Aberdeenshire. The Aberdeen jury which rejected Gourlay's claim on December 14th, 1306, declared 'he is still an enemy of the king, adhering to Robert Bruce'.[5] How many more men among Bruce's followers had lost or were under threat of losing their lands it is impossible to say. If we look at the petitions which Scotsmen presented to King Edward at the September parliament of 1305 we find the names of Gilbert Hay, Laurence of Strathbogie, Hamelin of Troup and William Gourlay. These four men, perhaps all disappointed of achieving their desires, were out with Bruce a few months later.[6] It would certainly be wrong to suggest that the grievances of disinherited landowners formed the mainspring of Bruce's revolt. But it is beyond question that we must look to men of the class of Sir John of Cambo, Sir James Douglas and William Gourlay if we wish to know who provided the backbone of the military effort on which Bruce depended both before and after the rout at Methven.

Among such men there were many who had fought for the common cause not only when Bruce had been one of the national leaders but also for two years after Bruce had gone over to the Eng-

---

[1] *Cal. Docs. Scot.*, ii, No. 730. Cf. Nos. 704, 861, 1670 (which shows that Sir John of Cambo had rented the fishing rights of Crail for a year prior to February 1296).

[2] Ibid., No. 1676.

[3] Ibid., No. 1811.

[4] Ibid., No. 730.

[5] Ibid., iv, No. 1827.

[6] F. W. Maitland, *Memoranda de Parliamento*, Nos. 353, 381, 387.

lish. It is clear that Bruce did not rely solely on the support of men
who belonged to his own lordships or lived within his sphere of
influence. Admittedly there were many such men and they could be
important. From Kyle, Reginald Crawford and Alexander Lindsay
of Barnweill near Ayr;[1] from Carrick itself, Gilbert son of Roland
and Roland Askeloc; from Nithsdale, Stephen of Closeburn, Thomas
and Robert of Kirkconnel, and young Thomas Randolph, Bruce's
nephew on his mother's side; from upper Clydesdale, the laird of
Wiston and Simon Lockhart of the Lee; from Aberdeenshire, James
of the Garioch: none of these men of the lairds' class was insignificant,
and a few, like Alexander Lindsay and Thomas Randolph, belonged
to well-known families. The knights of Annandale, whose loyalty to
their lord we have remarked on when he was on the English side,
ran true to form and, in the main, supported the young Robert Bruce
when he made his bid for Scottish freedom. Ralph Herries, for example, was among those hanged at Newcastle on August 4th, 1306.[2]
On October 20th the earl of Hereford was granted the forfeited
lands of all those who held of Lochmaben Castle and of Annandale –
that is, the knights and other freeholders of the lordship which had
been possessed by the family of Bruce for nearly two hundred
years.[3] But there were other landowners south of the Forth who had
no territorial reason to be subject to Bruce's influence. Apart from
James Stewart, John de Soules and James Douglas, there were two
knights of Cunningham, Robert Boyd of Noddsdale and Brice
Blair. Hugh Lovel of Hawick, Simon Fraser and his brother Thomas,
and their kinsmen the Somervilles, lords of Linton in Roxburghshire and Carnwath in Lanarkshire, do not seem to have been closely
connected to Bruce. To them we may add James, son of Sir Walter
Lindsay, who held Thurston in East Lothian; William, son of Sir

---

[1] Palgrave, *Docs. Hist. Scot.*, 314. Lindsay had been a leader of the revolt in 1297
(Stevenson, *Documents*, ii, No. 454), but seems to have been in Edward I's peace
after Falkirk (ibid., No. 529). In 1305 he was regarded by Edward as having been a
prominent enemy, *APS*, i, 122.

[2] *Cal. Docs. Scot.*, ii, No. 1811. Some Annandale tenants were opposed to Bruce.
The family of Torthorald was anti-Bruce (*Reg. Mag. Sig.*, i, No. 30; *Cal. Docs. Scot.*,
iii, passim), but it is not clear that Torthorald formed part of the lordship of Annandale.
P.R.O., D.L. 36/3, fo. 87, No. 1, speaks of tolls levied 'between the barony of
Annandale and the tenement of Torthorald', which suggests that Torthorald was
separate. *Cal. Docs. Scot.*, i, No. 1683, renders this document incorrectly.

[3] Palgrave, *Docs. Hist. Scot.*, 301; *Cal. Docs. Scot.*, ii, No. 1842.

Alexander Menzies, who held Shielswood in Selkirkshire and the
neighbouring lands of Harden in Roxburghshire; and the tenants of
the royal castles and manors of Selkirk, Peebles and Traquair.[1]

It is particularly interesting to find among the middling men recorded as being with Bruce in 1306 several who had made their
peace with Edward I only two years earlier, after long years as
'rebels' or enemies. Thus, in March 1304, the following men did
homage to the king at St Andrews.[2] From Angus and Perthshire,
Walter of Alyth, Walter of Rossie, Ralph of Dundee, Sir John
Cameron of Baledgarno, Sir William Fenton,[3] Sir William Mowat,
Sir Adam de Valognes, and Andrew Dempster; from Fife, Thomas of
Balcaskie, Sir William Murray of St Fort, Alan Murray,[4] and
Walter of Bickerton, laird of Kincraig; from Banffshire, Hamelin of
Troup; from the Lennox, John of Cremannan. All these save the
last-named were reported to be out with Bruce in 1306, and though
John of Cremannan is not recorded as a rebel in that year, Thomas of
Cremannan, a well-recorded Lennox baron, forfeited his lands for
supporting Bruce, and we may suppose either that John was his
kinsman or that the name ought correctly to be Thomas.[5] The point
was in fact well put in an English memorandum of 1306: 'The king
has granted to Michael of Witton the lands *of his enemies in the first
war of Scotland*, who subsequently came to the king's peace *and have
now lately turned against the king*.'[6]

An important point which Dr Barron's analysis takes no account
of is that in Scotland at the turn of the thirteenth and fourteenth
centuries it was usual for men of knight's or esquire's rank, even
quite substantial men of property, to attach themselves to some
powerful magnate, an earl, a bishop, or one of the richest barons, to
belong to some 'following' or 'meinie'. It is not enough to admit

[1] Palgrave, *Docs. Hist. Scot.*, 359–60; *Cal. Docs. Scot.*, ii, Nos. 1839, 1840.

[2] Ibid., 194–7, 299–301.

[3] Both William Fenton and his son John figure on the roll of forfeited landowners,
below, Appendix. *Coupar Angus Chrs.*, i, No. 71, mentions three generations of the
family, Sir William, his father John, and his son and heir John.

[4] Alan Murray, kinsman of Sir William Murray of St Fort, was no doubt Alan
Murray of Culbin, since he is said to have held lands in the sheriffdoms of Fife and
Forres, Palgrave, *Docs. Hist. Scot.*, 299, 307.

[5] Compare ibid., 195 with ibid., 313. For Thomas of Cremannan, cf. *Lennox
Cartularium, passim.*

[6] Palgrave, *Docs. Hist. Scot.*, 302.

that some of Bruce's supporters were his own vassals or lived within his sphere of influence and maintain that the rest were completely free agents who could make up their minds dispassionately whether to risk their lives and all they possessed fighting for Bruce, or stay peaceably at home content with an indefinite period of English rule. The point is important for two reasons. It may, indeed it must, explain the decisions taken by at least some of those who came out for Bruce, and also, perhaps more importantly, it must explain why many men did not come out. Thus John Cameron of Balnely was expressly said to be 'with' the earl of Atholl,[1] and the same was very probably true of his kinsman Cameron of Baledgarno.[2] Sir John of Leny was no doubt in the following of the earl of Menteith or the earl of Lennox. The Lennox men Sir John of Luss, Sir Duncan son of Anelf (Macaulay?), Sir Thomas of Cremannan, Sir Alexander Folkard and 'Coweyn' [Ewen] Mackessan of Garchell in Drymen[3] would certainly have been in the retinue of Earl Malcolm. It is noteworthy that Sir Alan Durward, holding Fichlie beside Kildrummy,

---

[1] *Docs. Hist. Scot.*, 308. Earl Malise of Strathearn's indemnification of Gilbert of Glencarnie the elder, June 26th, 1306 (Fraser, *Grant*, iii, No. 12) provides an excellent illustration of a lesser baron attaching himself to a great magnate. Whereas Gilbert has, contrary to the tenor of his charter of Glencarnie, rendered the earl personal service in the war of Scotland, adhering to the earl with his forces and his power, the earl declares that this service shall not form a precedent or redound to the prejudice of Gilbert and his heirs. It may be noted, similarly, that Walter Logan, lord of Hartside, who was sheriff of Lanark in 1301, had a grant of Luce from Robert Bruce in 1298 and called Bruce his lord. Logan figures on the roll of forfeited landowners in 1306. Cf. *Cal. Docs. Scot.*, iv, 387–8; *Kelso Liber*, No. 193; below, Appendix.

[2] *Rotuli Scotiae*, i, 27a, shows Robert Cameron of Baledgarno a tenant of the earl of Atholl (although for Baledgarno itself, in the Braes of the Carse of Gowrie, he was a tenant-in-chief of the Crown, ibid., 29a). Sir John Cameron, probably of Baledgarno, is among the knights mainperned in August 1297 by the earl of Atholl, Sir John of Inchmartin and Sir Alexander Menzies, *Cal. Docs. Scot.*, ii, No. 942. John of Inchmartin, who played a very prominent part in the war against England down to 1304, was also both a tenant-in-chief in his own right and a tenant of the earl of Atholl, Scottish Record Office, Register House Charters, No. 67; cf. *Coupar Angus Chrs.*, i, 160–1. His son David was executed in 1306, *Cal. Docs. Scot.*, ii, No. 1811; *Proc. Soc. Antiq. Scot.*, New Ser., vii, 173. For a charter in which are associated John of Strathbogie earl of Atholl, Alexander Menzies, John of Inchmartin, John Cameron, Laurence of Strathbogie, and Robert Cameron of Balnely, cf. J. A. Robertson, *Comitatus de Atholia etc.* (privately printed, 1860), 38.

[3] For Ewen Mackessan or MacCassen, of Garchell, cf. *Lennox Cartularium*, 22, 32, 46, 47, 82, 83; Fraser, *Lennox*, ii, 406, No. 209. This is probably the person appearing on the roll of forfeited landowners as 'Coweyn Mackassen in the county of Stirling', Palgrave, *Docs. Hist. Scot.*, 313.

Sir Thomas of Monymusk, adjacent to the Garioch and Sir Laurence of Strathbogie, whose name connects him with the earl of Atholl, and who had been with the earl in 1296 and 1297,[1] were all among the new king's earliest supporters. It is understandable that men should have come out with the lords to whose following they belonged; it is more striking when we find men supporting Bruce in opposition to their lord. This happened in 'English-speaking Lothian', which according to Dr Barron 'sent few volunteers to the standard of the new king'.[2] The tenants of Henry de Pinkney, an Englishman who was lord of Luffness and Ballencrieff in East Lothian, rose against King Edward in 1306,[3] but since the names of these daring men are not recorded Dr Barron ignores them, as he ignored the southerners who formed part of the heroic garrison of Stirling in 1304. Another man who seems to have tried to give a lead to his own leader was Sir Malcolm of Innerpeffray. Although he had served as King Edward's sheriff of Auchterarder and Clackmannan, he would almost certainly have belonged to the following of the earl of Strathearn, yet he joined Atholl, Boyd and the rest when they pursued the earl in the glens above Crieff trying to get him to do homage to King Robert.[4]

We hear of hardly any early supporters of Bruce coming from north of Inverness, from Lorne, Lochaber or Badenoch, from Buchan, or from Galloway west of Nithsdale. The earl of Dunbar had been a consistent adherent of the English king ever since 1296: his attitude must be part of the reason why we find so few men from East Lothian and the Merse supporting either the Guardians or Bruce. Those who did had in any case condemned themselves to many years of dispossession, a peculiarly difficult sacrifice for men and women of that time. For most of the eighteen years from 1296 to 1314 the country between Tweed and Forth was closely held by large English garrisons based upon the strongest castles in Scotland. For this reason alone, it is a quite untenable argument that the men of

---

[1] *Cal. Docs. Scot.*, ii, No. 742; mainperned by the earl of Atholl and others, 1297, ibid., No. 942.

[2] *Scottish War of Independence*, 227.

[3] Palgrave, *Docs. Hist. Scot.*, 306; cf. *Cal. Docs. Scot.*, ii, No. 857.

[4] For the part played by Sir Malcolm in Bruce's dealings with the earl of Strathearn, see Palgrave, *Docs. Hist. Scot.*, 320–1. His forfeiture is recorded ibid., 311 (misspelt Everph'me). Cf. *Cal. Docs. Scot.*, ii, No. 1858.

Lothian are to be judged on their performance as either pro-English or anti-patriotic. Much of the history of Scotland for the past two hundred years, political, economic and ecclesiastical, had been centred upon Lothian and Teviotdale. It is absurd to suppose that all this was swept away overnight under the onslaught of Edward I, simply because the population of Lothian spoke English or had an alleged (but wholly unverified) predisposition to accept English rule.[1]

After Methven Bruce fled to Drumalban, the mountain country dividing Perthshire from Argyll. He put his trust in a handful of loyal followers and in his own extraordinary powers of physical endurance, moral courage and knightly prowess. He believed, in this dark hour, that he had the blessing of one of the most celebrated of the ancient Scottish saints, Fillan of Glendochart. He no more forgot this holy man of the sixth century than his grandfather forgot Malachy O'Moore. His generosity many years afterwards not only to Saint Fillan and his shrine in Strathfillan but also to Inchaffray Abbey surely sprang from earlier events than his alleged veneration of Saint Fillan's relics on the eve of Bannockburn and the exhortation of the Scottish army by Abbot Maurice of Inchaffray.[2] It is in every way probable that as Bruce and his companions made their way westward from the field of Methven they were helped by the canons of Inchaffray, where Maurice had already been abbot since 1305.[3] To travel westward from Strathearn, as Bruce seems to have done, probably by Lochearnside and Glen Ogle into Glen Dochart, was to enter what might be called Saint Fillan's sanctuary. Here the chief men included Gilchrist and Henry of Balquhidder and Patrick (Macnab) lord of Glendochart,[4] heir of the ancient abbots of Glendochart who were Fillan's successors and custodians of his famous

---

[1] Yet this has been reasserted, without further evidence, by R. Nicholson, *Scotland: the later Middle Ages*, 85.

[2] *Inchaffray Chrs.*, xlv and n. 2.

[3] *Reg. Mag. Sig.*, i, Appendix I, No. 77, Abbot Maurice of Inchaffray a witness to a charter dating from the period when Alexander Abernethy was warden of Scotland between Forth and the Mounth and Matthew of Kinross was dean of Dunkeld. Abernethy was appointed warden at Michaelmas 1303 (*Cal. Docs. Scot.*, ii, No. 1694), but Matthew of Kinross was not dean of Dunkeld until 1304 (ibid., No. 1473, 1573). Abbot Maurice was active on Bruce's behalf at the time of his coronation, Palgrave, *Docs. Hist. Scot.*, 319.

[4] *Cal. Docs. Scot.*, ii, Nos. 1592, 1689. Patrick and Malcolm of Glendochart did homage in 1296 (ibid., 199, 200), as did Conan of Balquhidder (ibid., 200).

pastoral staff. We do not know how they received the new king of Scots; we know only that in later years Bruce granted the barony of Glendochart to one of the knights who were with him in 1306, Alexander Menzies of Weem in Strathtay.[1] This partial displacement of the Macnabs may mean that Patrick of Glendochart was Bruce's enemy.

At the head of Strathfillan, at a place called Dail Righ (Dalry), near Tyndrum, Bruce found his escape route barred by John Macdougall of Argyll, at whose hands he met his second defeat.[2] As a result Bruce and his men ceased to form an organized military force. The queen, the lady Marjorie (Bruce's daughter) and the other women of the party were given all the horses and sent across the Mounth, through the mountains of Atholl and Braemar, to Kildrummy Castle on Donside, in charge of the earl of Atholl, Neil Bruce (the king's brother), Alexander Lindsay and Robert Boyd.[3] Bruce himself and most of his men took to the mountains of Atholl and Breadalbane, little better than fugitives. It is impossible to construct anything like an exact chronology of their movements in the summer months of 1306. Fordun seems to put the battle of Dail Righ too late (August 11th).[4] It would be easier to understand Bruce's reported movements if Dail Righ were fought on July 13th (reading 'third of the ides of *July*' for Fordun's 'third of the ides of *August*'), or on July 30th (supposing Fordun's 'ides' to be a mistake for 'kalends'). For we have to account for the otherwise curious fact that Aymer de Valence, obviously pursuing either Bruce or some of Bruce's party, was in Aberdeen by August 3rd.[5] This would be understandable if he had news that the queen, Atholl and the others had already reached, or were heading for, Kildrummy. In

[1] *Reg. Mag. Sig.*, 1, Appendix II, Nos. 476, 652.

[2] Barbour, *Bruce*, 35ff. (at 'the hed of Tay'); *Chron. Fordun*, i, 342. Dail Righ means the king's meadow, but it is not certain, and seems a little improbable, that the place got its name from Bruce and his battle; it is surely older. Beside Dail Righ is the little Lochan nan Arm, 'tarn of the weapons'. The battle is wrongly located by F. M. Powicke, *The Thirteenth Century*, 716, at Dalry in Ayrshire.

[3] Barbour, *Bruce*, 44; *Cal. Docs. Scot.*, ii, No. 1829.   [4] *Chron. Fordun*, i, 342.

[5] *Cal. Docs. Scot.*, ii, No. 1810. A further contribution to the evidence for the events of the summer of 1306 is provided by *Cal. Inqu. Misc.*, i, No. 2029, which says that some time after the battle of Methven the earl of Strathearn sent his son with his own forces beyond the Mounth in aid of King Edward's expedition. John Sandal's Account Book (above, p. 216, n. 3) refers to an engagement by Loch Tay, presumably soon after Methven (fo. 16).

Barbour's account, which seems extraordinary, Bruce after Methven
made for Aberdeen by way of the Mounth, doubled back to Dail
Righ across the mountains, and only then – when he must have
known that the English were already in Aberdeenshire – sent the
ladies to Kildrummy. But both Barbour and Fordun agree that the
dispersal of Bruce's small party came after and not before the conflict at Dail Righ.[1]

Early in September Kildrummy fell to Valence and the prince of
Wales, the garrison being forced to yield when a traitor in their
midst set fire to the store of corn in the great hall.[2] On the approach
of the English army, the royal ladies had been sent hurriedly northward, in charge of the earl of Atholl.[3] Probably it was intended that
they should reach Orkney, for Bruce's sister Isabel, dowager queen
of Norway, was King Hakon V's sister-in-law, and Scoto-Norwegian
relations seem to have been friendly throughout the seventeen years
between the Franco-Scoto-Norwegian treaties of Paris (1295) and
King Robert's first major piece of diplomacy, the Scoto-Norwegian
treaty of Inverness (1312). But the party had only reached the
sanctuary of Saint Duthac at Tain when they were seized by Earl
William of Ross (a Balliol adherent) and sent to Edward I under
escort.[4]

A brief reign of terror followed the rout of Methven and the fall of
Kildrummy. Once again, the responsibility lay wholly with Edward
I. Indeed, we must accept that the slaughter and persecution, which
in their ferocity far exceeded anything previously seen in Edward's
reign, marked a new and deliberate policy of terrorizing the Scots
into submission. Simon Fraser was drawn, hanged and beheaded in
London, his head being put above London Bridge on a pole beside

[1] Barbour, *Bruce*, 45; *Chron. Fordun.*, i, 342.
[2] *Cal. Docs. Scot.*, ii, No. 1829; Barbour, *Bruce*, 59–60.
[3] Ibid., 57–8. Barbour says that Atholl stayed at Kildrummy. I have inferred that he
accompanied the queen from the penalty which King Robert afterwards imposed on
the Earl William of Ross of maintaining chaplains in the church of Tain to say mass for
earl of Atholl. See below, p. 438. Good sources say that the earl was taken 'in flight',
Flores Historiarum, iii, 134; *Proc. Soc. Antiq. Scot.*, New Ser., vii, 181. The omission
of the earl's name from the Kildrummy prisoners listed in Sandal's Account Book
confirms that he was elsewhere.
[4] Barbour, *Bruce*, 47; *Chron. Fordun*, i, 342.

that of Wallace.[1] Atholl, evidently captured at Tain, was the first
earl to be executed in England for 230 years. It was pleaded on his
behalf that he was King Edward's kinsman (his mother, a Kentish
lady named Isabel of Chilham, was a granddaughter of one of King
John's bastards).[2] Edward's response to this was an order that he
should be hanged from a higher gallows than anyone else, and then
decapitated and burned.[3] Neil Bruce was drawn, hanged and beheaded at Berwick, along with many others, including Sir Alan
Durward of Fichlie.[4] Christopher Seton, captured in Loch Doon
castle, suffered the same fate at Dumfries, where he had been art and
part in the murder of John and Robert Comyn.[5] His brother John,
taken at Tibbers in Nithsdale, was drawn and hanged at Newcastle
on August 4th, along with Bernard Mowat.[6] On the same day
fourteen other adherents of Bruce were hanged (without having
been drawn) at Newcastle, including two knights, David of Inchmartin (son of Sir John) and John of Cambo, and the king of Scots'
hereditary standard-bearer, Alexander Scrymgeour ('le Skirm-
ischur').[7] Alexander Scrymgeour, the son of Colin, Carun's son, a
Fife freeholder of Celtic descent, had been granted the constableship
of Dundee by Wallace in King John's name for the service of 'bearing the royal standard in the army of Scotland'.[8] He had served all
the Guardians in this capacity and his adherence to Bruce is therefore
especially noteworthy. Savage as these reprisals were, the peculiarly
maniacal quality of King Edward's vengeance has always seemed
most startling in his treatment of the women prisoners. Two of them,

---

[1] Fraser's capture and execution aroused enormous interest in southern England,
to judge from the widespread accounts which still survive. See, inter alia, Siege of
Carlaverock, 217–20. The remains of his body, together with the gallows on which
he had been hanged, were afterwards burned on King Edward's orders, Annales
Londonienses, 149. In this context the verb 'to draw' has its normal thirteenth-century
meaning of 'to drag to the place of execution by means of horses, usually on a hurdle'.

[2] Complete Peerage, i, 305.

[3] Chron. Guisb., 369; Flores Historiarum, iii, 134–5; Annales Londonienses, 149–50;
Scalacronica, 131.

[4] Chron. Fordun, i, 342; Flores Historiarum, iii, 135; Scalacronica, 131.

[5] Chron. Guisb., 369 (reading 'Lochdon' for 'Lochdor'); Chron. Lanercost, 204; cf.
Reg. Mag. Sig., i, No. 510.

[6] Cal. Docs. Scot., ii, No. 1811.

[7] Ibid.

[8] Highland Papers (SHS), ii, 125; Anderson, Diplomata, Pl. XLIII. Cf. G. G. Simpson, Handlist of the Acts of Alexander III, etc., Nos. 413, 418, 422.

it is true, got off lightly. The new queen of Scots, who to Edward's approval had rebuked her husband at their coronation for playing kings and queens like children, was confined in the manor house at Burstwick in Holderness. She was allowed two women companions, 'elderly and not at all gay'.[1] Christian Bruce, formerly countess of Mar and now widow of Christopher Seton, was sent to the Gilbertine nunnery of Sixhills in Lincolnshire.[2] Mary, King Robert's other sister, whose reported remarks were perhaps less to Edward's liking than those of the queen, and the Countess Isabel of Buchan, who had committed the unpardonable crime of crowning or enthroning Bruce, were lodged in cages of timber and iron, specially made for the purpose and placed within towers or turrets of Roxburgh and Berwick castles respectively.[3] There these two courageous ladies remained, forbidden communication with anyone save the English-women who brought their food and drink, exposed to the mockery (perhaps also, occasionally, the pity) of passers-by, treated for all the world as though they were beasts in a menagerie, save that they were allowed the convenience of a privy.[4] The countess was not released from her cage until June 1310, when Edward II allowed her to be removed to the house of the Carmelites in Berwick. In 1313 she was placed in the custody of Sir Henry Beaumont, who had married her husband's niece.[5] Mary Bruce also survived her ordeal. Still captive in Roxburgh Castle in 1310 (no longer, one hopes, in her cage) she was later transferred to Newcastle and freed at last after Bannockburn.[6] Bruce's daughter Marjorie, who cannot have been more than twelve years old, was at first ordered by King Edward to be kept in a similar cage in the Tower of London, and not to be allowed to speak to anyone, or be spoken to by anyone, save the Constable of the

---

[1] Palgrave, *Docs. Hist. Scot.*, 357.

[2] *Cal. Docs. Scot.*, ii, No. 1910.

[3] Palgrave, *Docs. Hist. Scot.*, 358–9; *Proc. Soc. Antiq. Scot.*, New Ser., vii, 175–6; *Flores Historiarum*, iii, 324; *Chron. Guisb.*, 367; *Scalacronica*, 130, 'the countess, . . . by command of King Edward of England, was placed in a little house of timber in a tower in the castle of Berwick, the sides latticed so that all there could gaze on her as a spectacle.' *Chron. Rishanger*, 229, says '[the countess] was placed in a little wooden house on the wall of Berwick castle, so that passers-by might gaze on her.'

[4] Palgrave, *Docs. Hist. Scot.*, 358; *eesement de chambre cortoise*.

[5] *Rotuli Scotiae*, i, 85b. See additional note below, p. 233.

[6] *Cal. Docs. Scot.*, iii, Nos. 131, 227, 244, 248, 340.

Tower.[1] For some unrecorded reason Edward revoked this horrifying piece of savagery, and Marjorie Bruce was sent to the Yorkshire Gilbertine nunnery at Watton.[2]

Long before King Robert had any news of the terrible punishments inflicted on his family and followers it had become obvious to him that he must flee the mainland and perhaps flee his kingdom altogether. Somehow, before all the escape routes were stopped up, a way must be found. The east-coast ports were in enemy hands. In the north also there were enemies as well as friends, the actively hostile earls of Ross and Sutherland to be set against the friendly but now fugitive bishop of Moray. The west, guarded by John of Lorne, was full of dangers. Only towards the south west was there any gleam of hope. The earl of Lennox was loyal and the men of Lennox were loyal to their earl. As long as John Balliol had been king, the Macdougalls were patriots and the Macdonalds pro-English. Now a minor revolution had occurred in west highland politics. One chief of the Macdonalds, Alexander, who had married John of Lorne's aunt Juliana, remained pro-English and therefore Bruce's enemy. But Alexander had brothers, Angus Óg ('young Angus') and, seemingly older and more important than Angus, Donald.[3] They were anti-Macdougall and therefore pro-Bruce. They seem to have had the people of Islay and Kintyre very firmly under their control. Moreover, one of the new king's most faithful supporters, Neil Campbell, had lands and influence in Kintyre. Beyond Kintyre lay Ireland, and there the horizon may have seemed

[1] Palgrave, *Docs. Hist. Scot.*, 359.

[2] *Chron. Guisb.*, 369; *Cal. Docs. Scot.*, ii, No. 1910.

[3] Donald of Islay occurs in three independent and unimpeachable pieces of record, viz., (1) *Cal. Docs. Scot.*, iv, No. 1822 (1306?), where John of Lorne is empowered to receive him into King Edward's peace; (2) *APS*, i, 459 (March, 1309), where Donald is named as present at Robert I's first parliament; and (3) *Melrose Liber*, ii, No. 376, where he witnesses an undated charter of Robert I, which may belong to the time of the St Andrews parliament. In view of this evidence, Donald can hardly be dismissed as a mere mistake for Angus, as he was by Barron, *Scottish War of Independence*, 364 (where 'Alexander' appears to be a slip for 'Angus'). Angus of Islay, to whom Barbour, *Bruce*, 53, gives the credit for helping King Robert in Kintyre in 1306, had already figured in record of 1301, when he was pro-English, Stevenson, *Documents*, ii, Nos. 614, 615. There is no evidence, and seems little likelihood, that one man used the names Angus and Donald indifferently; consequently, the view taken here is that Donald of Islay was an older brother of Angus, who died fairly early in King Robert I's reign and never found his way into the Macdonald genealogies.

not wholly dark. It is true that the earl of Ulster, Bruce's father-in-law, was a loyal adherent of Edward I. It is also true that theoretically all the chiefs and people of Ireland owed allegiance to the English king and might have been expected to show hostility to Bruce. But Ireland is a country where the expected often does not happen. Bruce, let it not be forgotten, was lord of Carrick, and as such lord of, or claimant to, considerable estates on the coast of Antrim and Derry, including Olderfleet (now Larne), Glenarm, and lands near Coleraine and Port Stewart.[1] Twenty-two years afterwards, it was from Olderfleet that Bruce issued a mandate which still survives.[2] One of his closest friends and allies, James the Stewart, by marrying Egidia de Burgh, had acquired the lands and castle of the Roe on Lough Foyle.[3] Ireland cannot have seemed in any sense a foreign or unfriendly country to Robert Bruce, married to an Irishwoman and inheriting more than a century of family connexions with Ulster. In late August, therefore, or early September, the new king and his small party, keeping no doubt to hill tracks and hidden glens and corries,[4] travelled by way of the Lennox and Loch Lomond to Bute. From there they sailed to the temporary sanctuary of the castle of Dunaverty, built on a rock jutting into the sea not far from the Mull of Kintyre, which Bruce had prudently taken seven months earlier. News of his attempt to break through the English cordon must have reached King Edward or his lieutenants well before September 22nd, by which date Sir John de Botetourt and Sir John Menteith were laying siege to Dunaverty and not finding the local population co-operative.[5] It is clear that they expected Robert Bruce to be inside the castle, but in this they were to be disappointed. Barbour may be right, and assuredly cannot be far wrong, when he says that Bruce stayed in Dunaverty no more than three days. Before his pursuers

[1] R. Greeves, 'The Galloway Lands in Ulster', *Dumfriesshire Trans.*, 3rd Ser., xxxvi; R. Frame, in *Irish Hist. Studies*, xix, 17, n. 60.

[2] Duncan, MS.

[3] Stevenson, *Documents*, ii, No. 401. It was from the mouth of the Roe that the Easter Ross family of Munro (Mun-rotha) are held to have migrated to Scotland about this time.

[4] Barbour, *Bruce*, 45–53. The rock called Clach nam Breatann, an ancient boundary mark above the Falls of Falloch, a few miles north of the head of Loch Lomond, is locally believed to have been one of Bruce's hiding-places at this period.

[5] *Cal. Docs. Scot.*, ii, Nos. 1833, 1834.

could reach him he had got clean away by boat, crossing the thirteen miles of open sea to the island of Rathlin and vanishing, for the next four and a half months, from the recorded knowledge of men in England and Scotland alike.

Additional Note (see above, p. 230).
The caging of Mary Bruce and the Countess of Buchan.

Sir Maurice Powicke, despite his admiration for Edward I, wrote of the 'peculiar ferocity' of the king's treatment of the two women, who were never tried for any crime, real or alleged (*The Thirteenth Century*, 716). Professor E. L. G. Stones (*SHR*, lii, 84) is disposed to give King Edward the benefit of the doubt in the matter of 'the Scottish female captives', as he calls them, whose cages, he surmises, 'may have been chambers of some size . . . complete with privies'. He reiterates Lord Hailes's objection to the chronicle accounts (*Annals*, ii, 12–13), namely that the cages were to be placed within turrets and therefore could not have been exposed to the public gaze. The detail of the king's instructions with regard to the privies seems to have been directed chiefly to ensuring that the prisoners could not escape through them, as they might have done through an ordinary castle garderobe. There is remarkable agreement among the chronicles that publicity was an element of the women's punishment, but even if they were all wrong on this point Professor Stones's defence of King Edward seems misconceived, since the essential cruelty of the king's orders emerges grimly enough from the wording of the official documents which, far from having been, as Professor Stones states, ignored in this work, are duly cited above, p. 230, n. 3.

10

A King in Search of
his Throne

THE story of how Robert Bruce returned to Scotland, of how after many disasters and setbacks he slowly won the initiative, of how by a wonderful mixture of patience, sagacity and daring he made himself master of all but one of the great fortresses held by the English, until he was powerful enough at last to meet the challenge of a full-scale invasion led by the king of England in person, is the story of one of the great heroic enterprises of history. If it were cast in the form of a romance it would possess at least one of romance's essential requirements, incredibility. And if Bruce had done nothing else he would find an enduring place in history as one of its greatest adventurers. But in fact he survived his adventure to become for fourteen years one of the best of medieval kings, prudent, conscientious, vigorous and patriotic. His failings, it is true, were far from trivial. But his most serious failing, the encouragement he gave to that dissipation of royal power which was one cause of the weakness of later medieval Scottish monarchy, was very much a failing of his time. Hardly any king in western Europe in the fourteenth century successfully averted or overcame the tremendous pressures making for the disintegration of central authority.

Consciously or unconsciously, Bruce modelled himself, politically speaking, on his great adversary Edward I, in the shadow of whose example he had grown to manhood. The things for which Edward is remembered in English history are the things for which Bruce is – or ought to be – remembered in Scotland: a jealous regard for the royal dignity and prerogatives, the use of parliament as the supreme organ of government, the definition and statutory declaration of the common law, the attempt to heal the wounds of a bitter civil war, the subjugation of a purely Celtic territory in the west – for Edward, Wales, for Bruce, the western highlands. In 1307 the accomplishment of these tasks lay far in the future. It was the product of an act of faith on Bruce's part, faith not only in himself but in the community of the realm of Scotland. His aims and achievements become credible and intelligible only when seen against the background of a long period of Scottish history. Three features of that history in particular were relevant to Bruce's *coup de force* and his policy as king. Firstly, there was the unbroken development of royal power and of the machinery of royal government since the days of Alexander I and David I. This gave to Bruce, enthroned at Scone with the help of the traditional representatives of the community, an immense advantage over his enemies within Scotland itself. Secondly, there was the long and prosperous reign of the king to whom Bruce referred over and over again in his charters as 'the lord Alexander, king of Scotland, of good memory, *our last deceased predecessor*'.[1] Finally – most importantly, yet at the same time most awkwardly for Bruce – there were the eight years of warfare during which the Scots had defied King Edward in the name of King John. John, it is true, had abdicated, he had been imprisoned and exiled and shifted about Europe like an object in an exhibition, until at last he settled down as an elderly *roi fainéant*. Nevertheless, down to 1304 the Scots had never ceased to look upon him as their rightful king, and even after 1304 the Comyns, Ingram de Umfraville, Alexander Abernethy, Adam Gordon, William Oliphant and many other leading men still believed that his claims or those of Edward Balliol were stronger than the claims of Bruce. Consequently Bruce must appeal to some other principle than dynastic legitimacy. He found it in the one overriding idea which had given continuity to Scottish politics since 1286, that idea of the community of the realm which had survived the Maid of Norway's death, the coming and going of Balliol, and experimentation with at least half a dozen assorted Guardians. And of course Bruce, however much his own genius and the death of Edward I bore him onward, could never have achieved success if many Scotsmen and Scotswomen had not shared this idea. Bruce, who could surely have lived honourably for the rest of his life in

[1] E.g., *Reg. Mag. Sig.*, i, Nos. 12, 13, etc.

········ Suggested route of Robert 1,
February 1307 to May 1308
Important strongpoints held by English
throughout these years underlined

0   20   40   60   80
Miles

Orkney

Caithness

Sutherland

L. Broom

Skelbo

Forres Duffus
Nairn   Elgin   Banff
Tarradale   Balvenie   Buchan
Inverness   Auldearn   Slioch   (23.5.08)
Castle Urquhart   (12.07)   Inverurie

G   Aberdeen
Barra   (Captured
Kisimul   Rum   June or July
Castle   Eigg   Castle   1308?)
        Tirrim   Inverlochy   The Mounth
Coll   M   Forfar (Captured 25.12.08)
Tiree   O   Brander   L. Tay
    R   (Aug. 1308?)   Dundee
Cairnburghmore   Dunstaffnage   Perth   Cupar
    Castle   N   Inchchonnel   St. Andrews
Dunchonnell   Law   Inchchonnel   (16-17.3.09)
    Castle   Inchmahome   Stirling

Islay   Jura   Dumbarton   Glasgow   Edinburgh
                    Rutherglen   Bothwell
        Arran   Berwick
    Rathlin   Brodick   Loudoun Hill
        (2.07)   Ailsa   Ayr (10·5·07)   Roxburgh
The Roe   Dunaverty   Ayr (13.5.07)   Tibbers
                Turnberry
Antrim   Glenarm   Lochdoon   Lochmaben
    Olderfleet   Dumfries   Caerlaverock   Lanercost   Corbridge
                    Carlisle   Hexham
        Glentrool   Buittle   Ne
        (April   (Summer   Burgh by Sands
        1307)   1308)   Skinburness

            Man

Scandinavia or on the continent, would have been mad to return to
Carrick in 1307 unless he knew already that under the right leadership
the people of Scotland would rise against the conqueror as they had
risen in 1297. What could one man, whose friends and family had
been butchered and jailed, who had hardly any money or troops,
hope to do against the immense wealth and resources of the king of
England, supported as he was by numerous powerful Scottish
lords? But one man at the head of a nation could work miracles.

No evidence has yet been discovered to prove where Bruce spent
the winter of 1306-7. Certain English writers of the fifteenth and
sixteenth centuries, who are followed, with strong supporting arguments, by Dr Barron, believed that he was in the Norwegian king's
dominions, perhaps in Norway itself, more probably in the Northern
Isles.[1] Walter of Guisborough and the Lanercost chronicle give no
support to this belief. Both say much the same thing, the one that
Bruce was lurking 'in the furthermost isles of that country' (where
'country' means either Scotland or the west),[2] the other that he hid
'in the outer isles of Scotland'.[3] By the end of January 1307 King
Edward evidently believed that Bruce's retreat was in 'the isles of
the Scottish coast' and 'the isles between Scotland and Ireland'.[4]
John Barbour believed that Bruce lay hidden in the small island of
Rathlin, a few miles off the coast of Antrim.[5]

The great fascination of this mystery (which historically is not
very important) lies in the fact that though unsolved it does not seem
quite insoluble. Dr Barron's main arguments for the Norwegian
theory, put briefly, are that certain English chroniclers (admittedly
writing two centuries later) state that he went to Norway, that
Bruce's sister Isabel lived at Bergen, as the presumably influential
widow of the late King Eric, that Bruce's wife and family were
caught at Tain, presumably on their way to Orkney, that the
bishop of Moray, one of his staunchest supporters, did in fact take
refuge in Orkney, and that Bruce's return to Carrick reveals an

[1] Barron, Scottish War of Independence, 252ff., citing a St Albans writer, as well as
Fabyan and Rastell; on all of which see T. F. Tout, EHR, xxix, 756.

[2] Chron. Guisb., 368.

[3] Chron. Lanercost, 205, in remotis insulis Scotiae. (Orkney and Shetland, of course,
were not part of Scotland at this date).

[4] Cal. Docs. Scot., ii, Nos. 1888, 1889.

[5] Barbour, Bruce, 55, 65.

ignorance of the state of affairs explicable only if he had been far
away. His grant to St Magnus' Cathedral at Kirkwall, cited by Dr
Barron, seems at first sight as significant as his grants to St Fillan. But
in fact it merely replaced an earlier grant made by some previous
king or kings.[1] In the absence of direct evidence, the appropriate
line of enquiry is surely to take into account opportunity, previous
conduct, and motive. Here there are three established facts. Bruce was
last heard of at or near his own castle of Dunaverty, in September
1306. The next definite news of him was that he had landed in
Carrick about the end of January or beginning of February 1307. In
1294, the last occasion on which Bruce had been driven from Scotland by his enemies, he had gone (or had the intention of going) to
Ireland.[2] It is easy to understand how a desperate man, hard-pressed
by his pursuers, might leave Scotland at the Mull of Kintyre with
the ultimate aim of reaching Orkney or Norway. It is very much
harder to believe that anyone returning from Orkney to Scotland
would land in Carrick. It becomes all the more extraordinary if
Dr Barron's main thesis is correct, that Bruce drew the bulk of his
support from the north, from Moray and Aberdeenshire. If he
really wintered in Orkney, why did he not make for the southern
shore of the Moray Firth? On the score of opportunity and past
conduct, therefore, the bare facts suggest Ireland and the southern
Hebrides more strongly than they suggest Orkney or Norway.

What of motive? The Norwegian theory is attractive on that
score, because of Bruce's family connexions with King Hakon, who,
incidentally, had given a safe-conduct to Wallace at a time when
Wallace and Bruce were friends.[3] Bruce had to make do at first
without the French alliance, and it was an early object of his policy
to make an alliance with Norway. But there were equally good
motives for going to Ireland, where he seems to have gone in 1294.
Dr Barron says that the Bissets of the Glens of Antrim, lords of
Rathlin, were 'warm adherents of Edward I',[4] but he does not give
any evidence to support this rather strongly worded description. At

---

[1] *Reg. Mag. Sig.*, i, Appendix I, No. 10: *ita tamen quod carte si quas habet episcopus
de dictis tribus celdris . . . vel de centum solidis ex donatione antecessorum nostrorum seu
nostra de cetero nihilum obtineant firmitatem.*

[2] *Cal. Pat.*, 1292–1301, 69.

[3] Palgrave, *Antient Kalendars and Inventories*, i, 134.

[4] *Scottish War of Independence*, 248.

the time of the battle of Falkirk in 1298 Thomas Bisset of Antrim had crossed to Arran with a force strong enough to overpower the islanders, intending 'as was commonly said' to support the Scots, of whom Bruce was then a prominent leader.[1] Only on hearing of Wallace's defeat did Bisset send messengers to Edward I to say that really he had come to fight for the English, and claiming the isle of Arran as his reward. In 1301, it is true, Hugh Bisset of Antrim was on the English side.[2] But what may be more to the point is that he was then in alliance with Angus Og and John Macsween against the Macdougalls of Lorne. In 1307, the Macdougalls were Bruce's bitterest foes, and the man in charge of operations against Bruce was Sir John Menteith, who had ousted Macsween from the lordship of Knapdale. In January 1307 Edward I commanded Hugh Bisset to join the hunt for Bruce with as many ships as he could find;[3] but this is far from proof that Bisset was loyal to Edward through the autumn of 1306 or even that he joined in the search for Bruce wholeheartedly. He opposed Edward Bruce's invasion of Ireland in 1315,[4] but ultimately, in 1319, Bisset openly joined Bruce.[5] The significant fact, surely, is that in 1306-7 a powerful English fleet operating from Ayr and Skinburness in Cumberland was unable to intercept Bruce. And whether or not the Bissets were his foes, Bruce as lord of Carrick would no doubt have maintained connexions with the estates on the Antrim coast which had belonged to his ancestors, some of which may still have belonged to him, while to the west of Bisset territory there was James Stewart's estate and castlery of the Roe on Lough Foyle. We do not know when the boy Andrew Stewart died, but in the autumn of 1306 Bruce may still have had him in his company. Most important of all is the fact that Bruce was supported in this critically dangerous period by the Macdonalds of Islay, Angus Ōg and Donald. The Macdonalds made their living partly by supplying galloglasses to fight in Irish wars.[6] Seen through their Hebridean eyes, Ireland must have seemed a very different country from the Dublin-ruled *dominium*

[1] *Chron. Guisb.*, 329.   [2] *Cal. Docs. Scot.*, ii, Nos. 1253-55.
[3] Ibid., No. 1888, cf. No. 1941.   [4] Barbour, *Bruce*, 248.
[5] *Cal. Docs. Scot.*, iii, No. 632. On the confused situation in Ulster, see R. Frame, *Irish Hist. Stud.*, xix, 29-30.
[6] A. McKerral, *SHR*, xxx, 7-8.

Hibernie over which King Edward believed he had full control.

So much for the facts which are not in dispute, and the various possibilities to which they point. The narrative of chroniclers closest in time to the events of 1307 strongly supports an Irish or Hebridean solution of the mystery and gives no hint of refuge in Orkney or Norway. Guisborough, whose facts may be correct though his dating must be wrong, says that Bruce returned to Kintyre from the isles 'about Michaelmas' (September 29th, 1306) with 'many Irishmen and Scots', and from Kintyre sent agents across to Carrick to uplift the rents of his earldom for the Martinmas term (November 11th).[1] (This is a detail which Guisborough can hardly have invented: Scottish rents, unlike English, were collected at Martinmas, and it is what we should expect of the penniless king, forced for so long to live on the generosity of his friends.) He goes on to say that in the following Lent (which in 1307 began on February 8th) Bruce sent a detachment under his brothers Thomas (who 'had always hated the English') and Alexander (dean of Glasgow) who were quickly captured.[2] The Lanercost chronicle says that on February 9th Thomas and Alexander Bruce landed in Galloway with eighteen ships, in company with Reginald Crawford, *a certain Irish sub-king*, the 'lord of Kintyre' (Malcolm MacQuillan) and a large following.[3] They were captured by Dungal Macdouall, who beheaded the Irish kinglet and the lord of Kintyre on the spot and sent the more important prisoners to Edward I for the same terrible, quasi-judicial punishment which had befallen Wallace, Fraser and so many others. Barbour's story, though much more elaborate and exciting, is not substantially different.[4] Some of Bruce's party, led by Douglas and Boyd, left Rathlin for Kintyre, whence they crossed to

---

[1] *Chron. Guisb.*, 370. Perhaps Michaelmas is a mistake for Candlemas, February 2nd, 1307.

[2] Ibid.

[3] *Chron. Lanercost*, 205. The Irish sub-king and the large force of Irishmen point to close links between Bruce and Ireland during the winter. Their presence also tends to support the suggestion now doubted that Malcolm MacQuillan was of the MacQuillans of Antrim. See *Flores Historiarum*, iii, 136, 327; *Proc. Soc. Antiq. Scot.*, New Ser., vii (1884–5), 184. The forms of Malcolm's surname here are Makayle and Makaillis (probably a mistake for Makaill'). Macaill, in the index to *Flores Historiarum*, is perhaps a variant reading in one of the MSS., although the editor does not say so.

[4] Barbour, *Bruce*, 65–74, 78–81.

Arran by night. There they seized valuable arms and equipment from a party which had come to reinforce the commander of Brodick Castle, John Hastings. (Hastings, having tried to get one third of the kingdom of Scotland in 1291 as a Competitor, had now got the earldom of Menteith, 'forfeited' by Earl Alan.[1]) Bruce then joined them and sent a spy across to Carrick to see how the land lay. If all seemed well, the spy was to light a fire on Turnberry Point. In fact he judged that the English were too strong to be attacked. Their leader was Henry Percy, who had usurped Bruce's earldom and now commanded the garrison in Turnberry Castle. But it chanced that someone else lit a fire, and misled by this Bruce and his men came over from Arran. Finding the situation desperate, they attacked the village of Turnberry at night, killing many of Percy's men in their sleep. The strongest confirmation of a Hebridean solution of the mystery come from Fordun, admittedly writing later in the century, but possessing important sources of information for Bruce's time which have not survived independently. Of King Robert's exile he says,

'He suffered these [hardships] alone for nearly a year, and at last, through God's mercy, with the help and by the power of Christiana of the Isles, a noble lady who wished him well, he returned to the earldom of Carrick, after much journeying in different directions, and after an infinity of toil, grief and adversity.'[2]

By Christiana of the Isles, Fordun can only refer to the lady usually known as Christian or Christina of Mar, daughter and apparently sole legitimate child of Alan Macruarie, lord of Garmoran.[3] As Alan's heir, Christina of Mar was a lady of many lands and islands of the west – Knoydart, Moidart, Arisaig, Rum, Eigg, Uist, Barra and Gigha. Christina had married Duncan of Mar, who was a younger son of Earl Donald of Mar and consequently a brother of Bruce's first wife and brother-in-law of Bruce's sister.[4] If family connexions meant anything, Christina had every reason for befriending Bruce

[1] *Cal. Docs. Scot.*, ii, No. 1771.
[2] *Chron. Fordun*, i, 343.
[3] *Cal. Docs. Scot.*, ii, 184, 200, where the homage is recorded in 1296 of Christian, wife of Duncan of Mar, of the county of Inverness ('widow', ibid., is an error). Ibid., 200, records the homage of Duncan, son of the earl of Mar, doubtless Christian's husband. Cf. *Inchaffray Chrs.*, 299–300.
[4] See Genealogical Table II.

in his time of need. And it can hardly be a coincidence that, just as Bruce granted to Inchaffray Abbey the church of Killin with the chapel of Strathfillan, so Christina of Mar granted to Inchaffray Abbey the lands of Carinish in North Uist with the chapel of the Holy Trinity of Uist – Teampull na Trianaide.[1]

On the strength of these facts and probabilities we may suggest the following outline of events in the winter of 1306–7. About the end of September 1306, Bruce and a few companions fled from Dunaverty to Rathlin. From there they may have visited parts of northern Ireland and almost certainly spent some time in various islands of the southern Hebrides. Towards the end of the year, Bruce sent agents to collect his Martinmas rents in Carrick. With the help of the Macdonalds, Christina of Mar, and friends in Ireland he gathered a force of Irishmen and Hebrideans, and about the beginning of February came to Kintyre. From there he crossed first to Arran and then to the Carrick shore near Turnberry. By this time he had divided his force, sending Thomas and Alexander Bruce to Galloway either from Kintyre or direct from Ireland. Their task may have been to divert attention from his own landing, or to put the Macdoualls and MacCans out of action. They met with complete disaster, and King Robert, who had already lost his brother Neil at Kildrummy, now lost two more of his brothers. Many years afterwards the English poet Robert Manning mourned the tragically short career of Alexander Bruce, the best scholar of his time at Cambridge, taken, badly wounded, from Galloway to Carlisle, and there, by King Edward's command, hanged and beheaded.[2]

How Bruce survived the next few months is a deeper mystery than where he spent the previous winter. This was the most perilous time of his career. He had landed in his own earldom, where the inhabitants might be expected to feel loyalty towards him. But all the castles in the country round about were in enemy hands, and the poorer people at least, if they were to come out against the

---

[1] *Inchaffray Chrs.*, Nos. 142, 143.

[2] *The Story of England by Robert Manning of Brunne* (ed. F. J. Furnivall, Rolls Series), i, 12–13. Cf. *Chron. Lanercost*, 205–6; *Chron. Guisb.*, 370. The heads of the Irish sub-king, Malcolm MacQuillan, Alexander Bruce and Sir Reginald Crawford were fixed to the three gates of Carlisle; Thomas Bruce's head was placed above the castle keep.

occupation régime, would need more assurance of protection than the sight of Bruce and a handful of desperate men. One local lady of good family, Christian of Carrick, King Robert's kinswoman and perhaps also his mistress,[1] brought him (says Barbour) forty men, and also news of the fearful toll taken by Edward I of the king's followers. 'The king of England' (so runs Barbour's well-imagined version of Bruce's response to these grim tidings) 'thought that the kingdom of Scotland was too small for him and me, so I will make the whole of it mine. As for good Christopher Seton, who was of such noble renown, it was a great pity that he should have died save where his valour might have been proved.'[2] At least Bruce could find consolation in the knowledge that to King Edward, already lying gravely ill at Lanercost, there could not remain many more days of butchery. Buoyed up by this knowledge, yet made desperate by circumstances, it was now that Bruce took a simple but momentous decision which changed the whole course and character of the war. He was the first of the Scottish leaders to accept the harsh logic of a situation in which the English would always have the upper hand in cavalry and siege machinery. For a great nobleman and a trained knight it was not only a revolutionary decision, it was proof of his genius and imagination. From the spring of 1307 to the short night which fell between the first and second days of the battle of Bannockburn, all Bruce's strategy was based on belief in the supreme virtue of guerrilla warfare. Speed, surprise, mobility, small-scale engagements, scorched earth and dismantling of fortresses – these were to be the hall-marks of his campaigns.

Bruce's plan of action in the months following his return is clear enough. Based on the hill country of Carrick and Galloway he would harass the enemy, spread panic among the English garrisons, recruit supporters until he was strong enough to break out towards the country north of Forth, where he could count on gathering many more followers and would have much more room to manoeuvre. The English commanders on the spot, under Aymer de Valence, were

[1] Barbour, *Bruce*, 81. That this lady, who was marvellously happy at Bruce's return, had at one time been his mistress may be suggested by the fact that Bruce had natural children called Neil of Carrick (killed at Neville's Cross, 1346) and Christian of Carrick.

[2] Ibid., 82.

John Botetourt, Robert Clifford and Henry Percy; with these
veterans were several prominent Scots lords, including John
Menteith, Ingram de Umfraville, John Macdougall of Lorne[1] – John
'Bacach', 'the lame', as he was known – John Moubray and the earl
of Atholl's son David. Their task was to hold Ayr and Turnberry,
keep open communication between these castles and the east, and
tempt Bruce into an engagement on favourable ground. Their
master, though a dying man, was astonishingly alert and impatient
to hear news of success. On February 11th he wrote to Valence and
the others expressing his amazement at not hearing of Bruce's
capture.[2] They are to tell the king at once what they are doing and
what their plans are; for he suspects from their silence that they have
acted timidly and wish to keep the king in the dark about it. Try as
they would, Bruce eluded them and slowly won the initiative. In
April he penetrated far into Galloway, hiding in the Glen of Trool,
a deep glen opening off the Cree valley, largely filled by the waters
of Loch Trool.[3] This is wild country, dotted with suggestive place
names – Murder Hole, Round Loch of the Dungeon, Loch Neldricken
('loch of the ambush'), Polmaddy ('wolf's burn') and so on. The
English made a raid in force into Glen Trool, were caught in a natural
ambush, and repulsed with heavy losses.[4] Bruce was now free to
move north, by-passing Ayr, and encountered Valence at Loudoun
Hill, a few miles east of Kilmarnock, about May 10th.[5] A skilful
choice of site forced Valence to fight on a narrow front, so that his
great superiority in cavalry and numbers was no advantage. Bruce
and his men set upon the leading ranks so fiercely that the rear fell
back in panic, and very soon Valence himself was fleeing to Bothwell. Three days later, Bruce struck hard at a force under Ralph de
Monthermer, earl of Gloucester, and chased him back into Ayr.[6]
Here at last was unqualified triumph, and the avenging of Methven.
It had an immediate effect on popular feeling towards Bruce. On
May 15th, within a few days of Loudoun Hill, a Scots lord on the

[1] *Cal. Docs. Scot.*, ii, Nos. 1957, 1961.
[2] Ibid., No. 1896.
[3] Ibid., No. 1942 (referring to April, not June); and see 512; Barbour, *Bruce*, 129.
[4] Ibid., 129–33.
[5] Ibid., 136–42. For the site, beside the farmstead of Allantonplains, cf. *Ayrshire Archaeological and Natural History Collections*, vi (1961), 241.
[6] *Chron. Guisb.*, 378.

English side (perhaps Alexander Abernethy) wrote an informative and highly revealing letter from Forfar.

'I hear that Bruce never had the good will of his own followers or of the people generally so much with him as now. It appears that God is with him, for he has destroyed King Edward's power both among English and Scots. The people believe that Bruce will carry all before him, exhorted by "false preachers" from Bruce's army, men who have previously been charged before the justices for advocating war and have been released on bail, but are now behaving worse than ever. I fully believe, as I have heard from Reginald Cheyne, Duncan of Frendraught and Gilbert of Glencarnie, who keep the peace beyond the Mounth and on this side, that if Bruce can get away in this direction or towards the parts of Ross he will find the people all ready at his will more entirely than ever, unless King Edward can send more troops; for there are many people living loyally in his peace so long as the English are in power. May it please God to prolong King Edward's life, for men say openly that when he is gone the victory will go to Bruce. For these preachers have told the people that they have found a prophecy of Merlin, that after the death of "le Roy Coveytous" the people of Scotland and the Welsh shall band together and have full lordship and live in peace together to the end of the world.'[1]

From May to September Bruce seems to have stayed in the south west, much more aggressive after Loudoun than before. On July 7th the English king died at Burgh-on-Sands, at the beginning of his sixty-ninth year. Towards the end of his life he had had second thoughts about the wisdom of his policy of savage repression, enunciated in the previous winter. On this, Walter of Guisborough has some illuminating comments. Many men went over to Bruce, he says, who had been outlawed by the English justices sitting in the previous year. For since according to English law the Scots were to be burned, drawn at horse-tails and hanged, so with one accord they joined Bruce, preferring to die rather than be tried by English law.[2] The Lanercost chronicler remarks gloomily 'despite the fearful vengeance inflicted upon the Scots who adhered to Bruce, the number of those willing to strengthen him in his kingship increased daily'.[3] These words are strikingly confirmed by a letter which the king addressed on March 13th to Aymer de Valence and all the

[1] *Cal. Docs. Scot.*, ii, No. 1926.
[2] *Chron. Guisb.*, 378.
[3] *Chron. Lanercost*, 207.

chief English officials and sheriffs in Scotland. 'As he understands that some have interpreted his recent ordinance for settling Scotland as too harsh and rigorous, which was not his intention, he commands it to be proclaimed that all who have been compelled to abet or give shelter to Robert Bruce under threat of force shall be pardoned.'[1] Barely a fortnight later Sir John Wallace, a brother of William, evidently captured while with Bruce's army, was sent to London to be drawn, hanged and beheaded.[2] In truth, it was too late for Edward to disavow any harsh intention in an ordinance which had decreed that all who were art and part in Comyn's murder should be drawn and hanged, that all found in Scotland without the king's leave should be hanged or beheaded, that all who took part in Bruce's rising should be jailed to await the king's pleasure, and even that the 'poor commons' of Scotland, though forced to join in the rising, should be held to ransom.[3] The view of Charlemagne as an epitome of the Christian king cannot have found much favour with the Saxons. It is easy to understand how the Scots likewise never came to share the belief that Edward I was a model of justice and magnanimity.

No concealment of the old king's death could hide for long the contrast between his masterful directing hand and the wilful *insouciance* of the new king, Edward of Caernarvon. The great expedition planned by his father had only reached Cumnock when, on August 25th, Edward II retired to England, not to show his face north of the border for three years. Valence remained in charge till shortly before October 12th,[4] and so long as he occupied the line of Clydesdale it is most unlikely that Bruce, reported in September to be raiding in Galloway,[5] would have left the south west. But on September 13th Edward II confirmed John of Brittany in the office of lieutenant of Scotland which he had been given in 1305 and in which Valence had superseded him for the emergency of Bruce's rising.[6] It seems that Valence, who is recorded as holding a guardian's court at Rutherglen as late as September 17th,[7] must have left Scot-

[1] *Cal. Docs. Scot.*, ii, No. 1909.
[2] *Chron. Lanercost*, 207; *Flores Historiarum*, iii, 327.
[3] *Cal. Docs. Scot.*, ii, No. 1908 (=Palgrave, *Docs. Hist. Scot.*, 361-3).
[4] P.R.O., E 101/373/23.
[5] *Cal. Docs. Scot.*, iii, No. 14.
[6] Ibid., No. 12. [7] Ibid., No. 13.

land early in the following month. Here again, vigorous direction was replaced by feeble fumbling. Since there was no immediate danger from England, King Robert could plunge into the bitter but fairly brief civil war without which his kingship would never be a reality. He first attacked his foes in Galloway, so fiercely that many of their peasantry took refuge, with their cattle, in the Cumberland forest of Inglewood.[1] Next it was the turn of John Comyn, earl of Buchan. It is not known whether his castles of Old Slains and Balvenie had yet been restored to him. Even without them, Earl John, strong in his command of a compact north-eastern earldom with its ring of castles at Ellon, Kinneddar, Dundarg, Old Slains and Rattray, was the most formidable obstacle to Bruce's conquest of Scotland.

Leaving a force under Douglas to recover, with brilliant success, Douglasdale, upper Clydesdale and the Forest as far as Jedburgh,[2] Bruce marched northward, probably about the last week of September. No doubt he gathered many recruits in the middle belt of counties, from the earldoms of Lennox, Menteith, Fife, Strathearn, Atholl and Angus. He would be anxious to perform notable acts of kingship, and one of these was almost certainly to bring about the promotion to the bishopric of Dunblane of Master Nicholas Balmyle, that key figure whose brief recorded appearances coincide with critical moments in the national struggle. Balmyle, already a canon of Dunblane, was elected by a committee of the chapter which included Bruce's friend, Abbot Maurice of Inchaffray, and Master William of Eaglesham, one of Bishop Lamberton's men and the colleague of William Frere and Baldred Bisset in 1301.[3] The new

[1] *Cal. Docs. Scot.*, iii, No. 14. For Douglas in Paisley Forest, September 1307, cf. P.R.O., E 101/373/23.

[2] Barbour, *Bruce*, 145-7. In this expedition Douglas, presumably in accordance with Bruce's firm policy, destroyed his own castle of Douglas. This was not the occasion of the famous 'Douglas Larder', when Douglas took his own castle by a stratagem, killed Clifford's English garrison and threw the bodies down the well. According to Barbour, *Bruce*, 85-90, this exploit was carried out early in 1307.

[3] Theiner, *Monumenta*, No. 386; Dowden, *Bishops*, 201; see above, p. 169. One of Nicholas's first achievements was to secure a reduction in the taxation due to the papacy on his promotion from either 160 or 100 merks to only 60 merks, on this occasion only, 'on account of the notorious desolation of the whole of (?) Scotland' by war; *Regestum Papae Clementis V*, Appendix I (Rome, 1892), 217, No. 67. I am grateful to the Rev. Charles Burns for checking this reference for me against the MS. register, and also against the printed volume, from which the entry is cited briefly in W. E. Lunt, *Financial Relations of the Papacy with England to 1327*, 469.

bishop-elect reached the papal court at Poitiers for his consecration shortly before December 11th. The patron of Dunblane diocese was not the Crown but the earl of Strathearn, a prisoner at Rochester. The pope's letter announcing Balmyle's consecration was addressed 'to Earl Malise *or another who may hold the place of the earl*'. We can be sure that Balmyle's appointment was King Robert's doing and had no support from the English. Bruce was short of good bishops. Wishart and Lamberton were in prison, Cheyne of Aberdeen, like the rest of his family, was still pro-English, so also were Dalton of Galloway (though a Bruce protégé), Farquhar Bellejambe of Caithness and Andrew of Argyll. Matthew Crambeth of Dunkeld was no doubt on Bruce's side, but had not many years to live. Besides him, the bishops on whose support Bruce could certainly or probably count were David Murray (Moray), Thomas of Dundee (Ross) and John Kinninmonth (Brechin). Balmyle's promotion to Dunblane was more than a reward for many years of service to the community of the realm, it was a most useful addition to King Robert's ecclesiastical councillors. It is a reasonable surmise that his election took place in the autumn of 1307, either at the king's suggestion or at least with his full approval.

The king's movements during the autumn and winter, though still not known in detail, have recently become much clearer thanks to the patience and skill of Dr Patricia Barnes in reading – deciphering would almost be the better word – a much-stained and worn letter sent to Edward II by Duncan of Frendraught, sheriff of Banff, probably in April, 1308.[1] Duncan's letter gave the English king news of Bruce's operations apparently since the previous autumn, and told him of an earlier attempt to get news through to the south, frustrated when Duncan's messengers were killed in an ambush. Using this letter as our chief guide, and reinforcing its information with the long-familiar contributions of Fordun, Barbour and other sources, we may suggest, however tentatively, the following course of events.

At the end of September Bruce led his army northward into the highlands, making for Comyn of Badenoch's castle of Inverlochy in Lochaber. This bold march across the mountains was, it seems, backed by a corresponding movement of galleys up Loch Linnhe.

[1] Text in *SHR*, xlix, 57–59.

In this way, John of Lorne felt himself threatened by land and sea and, knowing that no help would be forthcoming from the English, agreed to a truce. Inverlochy fell at an unknown date (October 8th, 13th or 21st are possible),[1] and the king's forces swept north through the Great Glen to take Inverness castle, which they razed to the ground, and burn Nairn. Castle Urquhart on Loch Ness was also destroyed. Bruce's audacity and speed took his enemies by surprise and the earl of Ross in particular seems to have been badly scared. Probably in November he sent a letter to Edward II which told of his plight.

'Be it known that we heard of the coming of Sir Robert Bruce towards the parts of Ross with a great power, so that we had no power against him, but nevertheless we caused our men to be called out and we were stationed for a fortnight with three thousand men, at our own expense, on the borders of our earldom, and in two other earldoms, Sutherland and Caithness; and he (Bruce) would have destroyed them utterly if we had not made a truce with him, at the entreaty of good men, both clergy and others, until Whitsun next (June 2nd). May help come from you, our lord, if it please you, for in you, Sire, is all our hope and trust. And know, dear lord, that we would on no account have made a truce with him if the warden of Moray had not been absent from the country, and the men of his province would not answer to us without his orders, for the purpose of attacking our enemies, so that we have no help save from our own men. Wherefore, dear lord, remember us and tell us what is your will on these matters of which we have given an account.'[2]

The warden of Moray was Reginald Cheyne lord of Duffus and Inverugie, and the earl's remark about his absence and the refusal of his men to give support suggests some lack of unity among King Edward's friends in the north. But considering their isolated position the determination with which they resisted King Robert is remarkable. Secured by his truce with Ross, the king pushed eastward in November to attack Elgin, unsuccessfully, and threaten Banff. At

[1] Inverlochy was taken on or about the feast of some virgin whose name is illegible in Duncan's letter. Ibid., 56, failed to take account of female saints whose feasts would have been familiar to a Scots letter-writer: Triduana, Findoca, Ursula and 11,000 (!) virgins, Kennere and Begha (October 8th, 13th, 21st, 29th and 31st respectively).

[2] Cal. Docs. Scot., iv, No. 1837 (full text, ibid., 399, where, among other corrigenda, substitute for nous ounes, nous oimes, 'we heard'; for a vuer, avuer, 'call up'; for afraunce, afiaunce, 'trust'; for de mene, demene, 'own').

this moment, when a decisive capture of the entire north of Scotland seemed within his grasp, Bruce was gripped by a serious illness. The strains and the rough living to which he had been exposed for the past year and a half were now exacting their price.

John Comyn earl of Buchan, David of Strathbogie earl of Atholl and John Moubray had by now mustered a respectable force and come to Duncan of Frendraught's assistance. Just before Christmas the king and his troops withdrew from the coastal lowlands south of Banff and took up a defensive position in boggy woodland at Slioch near Huntly. Winter weather sharpened the anxiety of Bruce's followers. Snow covered the ground and there was not enough food to fill the stomachs of 700 men. The king's sickness grew worse, no medicine was to be had, and they feared that he would not recover. On Christmas Day the earls' men came up and the archers of the opposing forces 'bickered' inconclusively. After a brief withdrawal, the earls returned more confidently on December 31st, only to find Bruce's force seemingly too strong to be attacked and in fact capable of retiring in good order, probably to the Garioch by way of Strathbogie (Huntly).

It is especially unfortunate that as Duncan of Frendraught's letter comes to deal with events of the first three months of 1308 its illegibility increases and we can glean only tantalizing fragments. The king evidently recovered sufficiently to attack the castle of Balvenie (doubtless before this date restored to the earl of Buchan) and destroy Cheyne's castle of Duffus after the interior had been fired. Striking still further west, Bruce took and destroyed the castle of Tarradale in the Black Isle and forced the earl of Ross and his son to withdraw either from that or some neighbouring strongpoint. William Wiseman, one of the king's northern supporters, seized the earl of Sutherland's castle of Skelbo near Dornoch. On Palm Sunday (April 7th) a second assault was made on Elgin castle but by the end of the month, through the timely intervention of John Moubray, the garrison had staved off the danger, at least for the moment.

A crucial problem in interpreting the patchy evidence of this period is the date, as yet uncertain, of the battle in which Bruce completely routed Buchan on the road between Inverurie and Old-meldrum. Fordun places the battle in 1308, that is the twelve-month

period running from March 25th, 1308 to March 24th, 1309. An
anonymous verse chronicle inserted in some texts of Bower's
Scotichronicon dates the event to the Ascension, 1308, a feast which
fell that year on May 23rd. This date would agree well with two
English official documents, the first[1] a letter of May 20th in which
Edward II urged the earl of Buchan, Duncan of Frendraught and
others to continue to defend the districts assigned to them until
August, the second an undated memorandum,[2] drawn up some
months later than the letter, from which it is clear that the English
knew they had lost their hold over the north of Scotland. The only
doubt which remains as to the date of Inverurie (apart from Barbour's placing it at Christmas, 1307, which is clearly wrong) turns
on tactical probability. If the battle was not fought till May 23rd we
have to accept the remarkable conclusion that Bruce was willing to
leave Buchan unsubdued in his rear while he doubled back to harass
the country west of Inverness and that then, after being repulsed
before Elgin castle, he was nevertheless still able to take his army
over the forty difficult miles eastward to Inverurie to tempt Buchan
from his lair and defeat him. He not only defeated the earl, he laid
waste the land of his earldom from end to end. Men still loyal to
Comyn were killed, homesteads destroyed, livestock slaughtered,
stores of corn burned. For fully fifty years, says the Aberdonian
Barbour, men grieved over the 'herschip' (harrying) of Buchan.[3]

After this the new king's hold over the Moray Firth hinterland
was unassailable. The earl of Buchan and his friends fled to the south.
The earl of Ross's position was now fraught with peril. Menaced by
the new king of Scots on the south and east, he was also defied in
the west, in Skye and the other islands supposedly subject to him,
by Lachlan Macruarie.

'We took the lands of the isles (the earl wrote to King Edward) from
our lord the king, your father, on whom God have mercy. We assigned
them to Lachlan Macruarie to answer to us for their revenues. Since he
refuses, may it please you, dear lord, to command him to answer to us

[1] Ibid., iii, No. 43.
[2] Ibid., No. 47 (August, 1308; J. R. Maddicott, *Thomas of Lancaster*, 109, n. 2).
[3] Barbour, *Bruce*, 156:
'And heryit thame on sic maneir,
That eftir that weile fifty yheir
Men menyt the heirschip of Bouchane.'

as justice requires. For we have answered to your chamberlain for the revenues of those lands. But Lachlan is such a high and mighty lord, he'll not answer to anyone except under great force or through fear of you.'[1]

Earl William came of good highland stock and might have known better than to expect a Hebridean chief to obey orders from the east without good reason. Whether or not he won an extension of the truce beyond June 2nd, the earl must have reckoned that Bruce was unbeatable. He duly submitted on the last day of October, at the royal castle of Auldearn near Nairn.[2] The terms of submission show that Bruce felt it was worth winning the earl to his side by magnanimity and shrewd concessions. Ross confessed his trespasses, now graciously pardoned by the king, and acknowledged that he had got his own lands back and in addition the burgh of Dingwall and the land of Ferincoskry (Creich) in Sutherland. Subjecting himself to the 'royal dignity', he promised to serve the king well and faithfully – a promise which he fulfilled with distinction.

The sureties for his change of allegiance and future good behaviour were David Murray, bishop of Moray, and Thomas of Dundee, bishop of Ross. As Dr Barron has made abundantly clear, Bishop Murray played an outstanding part in the national struggle.[3] He had been a fierce and persistent opponent of the English since the time when he was appointed bishop by Bruce and Comyn as joint-Guardians. Like Wishart of Glasgow, Murray had exhorted his flock that fighting for Scotland was as good a cause as fighting against the Saracens.[4] He is not known to have surrendered in 1304 and two years later he was one of only three bishops present at Bruce's coronation. After Methven he fled to Orkney and stayed out of Scotland for one year.[5] His lands were ravaged by the earl of Ross, and when he returned – to come briefly, it seems, into Edward II's peace – he threatened to excommunicate the earl unless the damage was made good. Now he had the great satisfaction of seeing how, in Barbour's words,

---

[1] *Cal. Docs. Scot.*, iv, p. 400.   [2] *APS*, i, 477.

[3] *Scottish War of Independence*, 295–8. Dr Barron was rightly puzzled as the result of Bain's error in transcribing the document printed *Cal. Docs. Scot.*, iv, 400 (=P.R.O. C.47/22/4, No. 77), where Bain omits a vital *ore* ('outside') between *un an* and *de vostre reaume.*   [4] Palgrave, *Docs. Hist. Scot.*, 330.

[5] *Cal. Docs. Scot.*, ii, No. 1907; P.R.O., C.47/22/4, No. 77=*Cal. Docs. Scot.*, iv, 400, where the first sentence of the third item should read: *Fete a sauoir que le Euesqe de Moref feut un an ore de vostre reaume Descoce encontre vestre fey.*

'The king than till his pes has tane
the north cuntre, that humylly
obeysit till his senyhory.
Swa that benorth the Month war nane
that thai ne war his men ilkane.'[1]

Bishop Thomas of Ross, if not so passionate a patriot as Murray, had been firmly attached to the Guardians and the community. For the next eighteen years these two bishops upheld the cause of King Robert in the prosperous and populous country round the Moray Firth.

Apart from the dean and the chanter (precentor) of Elgin cathedral, most of the witnesses to the submission were prominent landowners in Moray and Ross, who had supported the Guardians before 1304 and had been forfeited for supporting Bruce in 1306: William de la Hay, John Stirling, William Wiseman (sheriff of Elgin in 1305), John Fenton, and David and Walter Barclay. The most interesting name among the witnesses is that of Bernard of Linton, in his second earliest recorded appearance as 'Sir Bernard the king's chancellor'.[2] No doubt King Robert appointed a chancellor at his coronation, but he had not had much time for letter writing since March 1306. Yet in the struggle for Scottish independence the importance of written documents cannot be exaggerated, and in Bruce's re-establishment of royal authority the king's 'chapel' or chancery occupied a key position. In Bernard of Linton Bruce was lucky to find one of the really outstanding medieval royal chancellors. Almost nothing is known of his origins or early career, save that he was parson of Mordington near Berwick in 1296[3] and presumably took his name from one of the parishes named Linton in southern Scotland. The last chancellor of Scotland, Nicholas Balmyle, had been paid his salary from the revenues of Arbroath Abbey. King Robert went one better, and (circa 1311) made Bernard abbot of Arbroath, to hold both offices together.[4] The full measure of Abbot Bernard's

---

[1] Barbour, Bruce, 156.
[2] His earliest appearance is as witness to a royal mandate dated October 14th, 1308, Brit. Mus., MS. Add. 33245, fo. 49.   [3] Cal. Docs. Scot., ii, 207.
[4] It looks as though Robert I secured the supersession of Abbot John (who was pro-English, Cal. Docs. Scot., iii, No. 158) by Bernard of Linton either in 1310 or in 1311; cf. Arbroath Liber, i, No. 332. I am indebted to Professor Duncan for valuable notes on Bernard's appointment as abbot of Arbroath.

abilities will be seen when King Robert's charters are published. But if his reputation rested on nothing more than the Declaration of Arbroath of 1320 he would be sure of a place in history as the author of a masterpiece among political manifestos.

Within the course of a single year King Robert's position had changed out of all recognition. A wide belt of territory from the Ayrshire coast to the neighbourhood of Roxburgh and Jedburgh was under his control. Galloway was paying tribute. Between the Forth and the Mounth the adherents of Edward II were largely confined to defensible burghs and castles. North of the Mounth (save at Banff) the English had been expelled, and it would not be long before Bruce's authority was unchallenged. The last serious obstacle to be surmounted before he could concentrate all his energies on ejecting the English garrisons was the inveterate enmity of the Macdougalls, the ruling family of Argyll, and of the chiefs of Galloway, led by the Macdoualls and the MacCans. King Robert, himself born in the west and personally familiar with Argyll and the isles, never lost sight of the fact that a ruler of Scotland must have command of the western approaches.

To Alexander Macdougall, an old man by now, and to his son John Bacach, lying sick in Dunstaffnage through the winter of 1307–8, the outlook cannot have seemed very hopeful. In some ways their position resembled that of the earl of Ross. Old Balliol and Comyn men, they might fight for the community of the realm but they misliked Bruce. We have an undated letter written by John of Lorne to Edward II which, though gloomier and more prone to exaggeration, is parallel to Ross's letter already quoted and describes much the same pattern of events.

'I have received your last letter, dated March 11th, for whose contents I express my deep gratitude to your majesty (*vestre regalitati*). When it arrived I was confined to my bed with illness, and have been for six months past. Robert Bruce approached these parts by land and sea with 10,000 men, they say, or 15,000. I have no more than 800 men, 500 in my own pay whom I keep continually to guard the borders of my territory. The barons of Argyll give me no aid. Yet Bruce asked for a truce, which I granted him for a short space, and I have got a similar truce until you send me help. I have heard, my lord, that when Bruce came he was boasting and claiming that I had come to his peace, in order to inflate his own reputation so that others would rise more readily in his support. May God forbid this; I certainly do not wish it, and if you hear this from others you are not to believe it; for I shall always be ready to carry out your orders with all my power, wherever and whenever you wish. I have three castles to keep as well as a loch twenty-four miles long [Loch Awe], on which I keep and build galleys with trusty men to each galley. I am not sure of my neighbours in any direction. As soon as you or your army come, then, if my health permits, I shall not be found wanting where lands, ships or anything else is concerned, but will come to your service. But if sickness should prevent me I will send my son to serve you with my forces.'[1]

Historians have tended to assume that this letter was written in 1309, and because of the way in which Joseph Bain translated its opening words have believed that it was written shortly after March 11th.[2] It is, however, virtually certain that March 11th was the date of Edward II's letter to John of Lorne, now lost, to which John's own letter was a reply.[3] Consequently, the date at which John received the English king's letter would hardly have been before the beginning of April at the earliest, and might well have been towards the end of that month or even early in May. The reply seems to have been written not long afterwards – perhaps as early as the middle of April, perhaps as late as the middle of May. The contents of John of Lorne's letter make it most unlikely that it was written after Bruce's victorious incursion into Argyll which culminated in the battle of the Pass of Brander and the capture of Dunstaffnage Castle. In the first place, John seems to have already lost two of the three castles which he had had in his keeping.[4] Secondly, John would have had to

[1] P.R.O., C.47/22/6, No. 4, summarized unsatisfactorily, *Cal. Docs. Scot.*, iii, No. 80.

[2] *Cal. Docs. Scot.*, iii, No. 80 and pp., xiii–xiv; Barron, *Scottish War of Independence*, chap. 29; Colin MacDonald, *History of Argyll* (no date), 134.

[3] The crucial opening words, which Bain took to give the date at which John Bacach received Edward II's letter, run as follows: *Litteras vestras ultimo directas xi⁰ die mensis marcij percepimus, de quarum tenore vestre Regalitati multipliciter regraciamur.* It would be normal for the writer of a letter to identify his correspondent's last letter by its own date.

[4] Probably the three castles were Fraoch Eilean, Fincharn and Inchchonnell on Loch Awe. Dr MacDonald, *History of Argyll*, 135–6, holds that the loch twenty-four miles long, on which John Bacach kept galleys, referred to in his letter, was not Loch Awe but Loch Etive. The word used is *stagnum*, which seems rather more appropriate to an inland loch than a sea loch, although Adamnan, in his *Life of Columba*, used

be a master of the art of understatement, not to say downright mendacity, to describe the Brander campaign as a mere 'approach' towards his territories by Bruce. Dr Colin Macdonald, in his *History of Argyll*, is surely right to date the letter before the campaign of Brander, but since he believes that this campaign was not fought until 1309 he accepts 1309 as the year in which the letter was written.[1] Dr Barron, on the other hand, placing the Brander campaign in 1308, is nevertheless prepared to accept March 1309, as the date of John of Lorne's letter.[2] To overcome the biggest obstacle presented by this chronology, he supposes that a long interval may have elapsed between the battle of Brander and the fall of Dunstaffnage.

That an event of such importance as the Argyll campaign cannot be assigned beyond all doubt to a particular year is a striking illustration of the difficulties which face the historian of these early and critical years of Robert I's reign. On balance, the evidence seems to suggest that John of Lorne wrote his gloomy yet boastful apologia in April or May 1308. It is clear from the earl of Ross's letter that in the winter of 1307-8 Bruce already had a force numbering at least 3,000 men and probably considerably more, since the earl's own force of 3,000 was too small to withstand him. If by May Bruce had reduced all the northern castles save Aberdeen and Banff he could have gone south through the Great Glen, threatening the Macdougalls 'by land and sea', and granted – not asked for – a brief truce of the kind he had granted to the earl of Ross, knowing that Edward II would never send help. The refusal of the Argyllshire barons to support the lord of Lorne is significant and closely comparable with the refusal of the Moray landowners to support Ross.

---

stagnum for upper Loch Linnhe. Loch Awe is about twenty-two miles long, Loch Etive about eighteen; cf. *Chron. Bower*, i, 46: 'Loch Awe, 24 miles long, with three castles.'

Dr MacDonald believes that the word 'se' in Barbour's story of the battle of Brander must mean the salt sea. It is true that Barbour normally uses 'se' for 'sea' and 'louch' for 'loch', but here he may be using 'se' to mean inland water or else he may have been misinformed about the geographical details of the Pass of Brander. Of this he writes that 'a sheer crag, high and hideous, reached to the sea (raucht till the se) down from the pass', which is true only if by 'sea' we understand Loch Awe. Had John Bacach really been afloat on Loch Etive he could not have witnessed the course of the battle up in the pass. Moreover, *Rotuli Scotiae*, i, 58, shows him keeping the 'castle of Loch Awe'.

[1] *History of Argyll*, 133.   [2] *Scottish War of Independence*, 335-47.

They may have been jealous of the Macdougalls; they certainly did not want an English conquest of Scotland.[1]

By mid-August 1308 the truce had evidently expired, or was broken by Bruce. Fordun states definitely that the king 'defeated the Argyllsmen in the heart of Argyll within the octave of the Assumption of the Blessed Virgin (between 15th and 23rd of August), and our manuscripts of Fordun place this in the year 1308.[2] It is true that Fordun has no annal for 1309, but before we can assume that he meant to assign the Argyll campaign to that year we should have to possess stronger evidence than we do for believing that it did not take place in 1308. In his attack on Argyll the king followed the line taken by the modern road and railway to Oban. John of Lorne met him in the Pass of Brander, the narrow, treacherous pass where the southern flank of Cruachan (3,689 feet) falls precipitously into an arm of Loch Awe (118 feet). John himself, presumably still convalescent, kept to a galley on the loch.[3] His men were concealed along the hillside overlooking the track, lying in wait and aiming to do to Bruce what Bruce had done to the English in Glen Trool. The king was not to be caught so easily. He had many highlanders with him,

> 'Men that light and nimble were
> And light armour had on them there.'[4]

A party of these light-armed men were sent under James Douglas to scramble even higher up the slopes of Cruachan than the enemy. As the men of Lorne began to attack the main body of the king's army with arrows and stones and with boulders rolled down the steep hillside, Douglas's men rushed down upon them, punished them severely with a hail of shots from their bows, and finally used their swords at close quarters. Assailed from below, taken by surprise from above, the Argyllsmen broke and fled to the only bridge across the formidable River Awe, hoping to destroy it once they were over. Bruce's men forestalled them, pursuing them so hotly that the bridge had to be left intact. The king himself was able to cross with his main body

[1] By March 1309, Robert I's first parliament was attended by 'the barons of all Argyll and the Hebrides', including Gillespie MacLachlan, who less than three years earlier had been asking Edward I to grant him the lands of one of Bruce's first adherents (APS, i, 459; Palgrave, Docs. Hist. Scot., 318).   [2] Chron. Fordun, i, 345.   [3] Barbour, Bruce, 169-70.   [4] Ibid., 170.

and pursued his foes to Dunstaffnage, which he at once besieged. According to Fordun, Alexander Macdougall surrendered the castle after a siege 'of some time';[1] according to Barbour it fell to Bruce's vigorous assault 'in short time'.[2]

John of Lorne seems to have slipped down Loch Awe to his castle at Inchchonnell – if this is to be identified correctly as the 'Loch Awe castle' of contemporary record.[3] For by October 4th, 1308, Edward II had received news that John was sending men and ships to England and Ireland to obtain supplies and munitions with which to re-plenish the castle of 'Lochawa' which John had in his keeping.[4] The fact that Lochawe is the sole castle named no doubt means that Dun-staffnage had already fallen, along with two out of the 'three castles' of which John of Lorne, according to his letter to Edward II, had custody.[5] His father evidently came into Bruce's peace for long enough to attend the St Andrews parliament of March 1309.[6] But his submission cannot have been sincere. He soon left Scotland and was somewhere within easy reach of Berwick in October 1309.[7] He died in the English king's service about the end of 1310.[8] Alexander Macdougall's movements surely have some bearing on the question of whether the Argyll campaign was fought in 1308 or 1309. It would be understandable that Alexander should have gone to Bruce's first parliament virtually under duress, as the result of the battle of Brander and the fall of Dunstaffnage. It would be extraordinary if he had come to Bruce's peace before there had been any serious Argyll campaign, still more extraordinary if John Bacach had written his letter to Edward II within a month or so of his own father's appear-ance in the St Andrews parliament. On the strength of the scanty evidence we possess, the most probable course of events seems to be this.[9] In May or June 1308, Bruce turned from his successful Moray campaign to threaten Argyll. In mid-August, at the end of a short truce, he attacked the Macdougalls in strength, and as a result of his resounding victory on the slopes of Ben Cruachan Alexander Macdougall temporarily did homage to him, while John Bacach,

---

[1] *Chron. Fordun*, i, 345.   [2] Barbour, *Bruce*, 172.
[3] It is not easy to suggest any other castle which would fill the bill.
[4] *Rotuli Scotiae*, i, 58a.   [5] *Cal. Docs. Scot.*, iii, No. 80.
[6] *APS*, i, 459.   [7] *Cal. Docs. Scot.*, iii, 23.
[8] Ibid., No. 191.   [9] For a different reconstruction, cf. R. Nicholson, op. cit., 79–80.

after vainly trying to hold out in 'Lochawe Castle', fled to the English, to be joined by his father not later than the autumn of 1309.

Towards midsummer 1308, the king's only surviving brother Edward overran Galloway in a brilliant but savagely vengeful campaign.[1] The first phase of the reconquest of Galloway was evidently brief, and took the form of a devastating raid in which many Gallovidian natives were slaughtered or put to flight. Dungal Macdouall, who had much Scottish and Bruce blood on his hands, was driven out with all his kin, and many local chiefs were slain. Whether we prefer Barbour's version, which characteristically tells only of chivalrous warfare between brave knights – Edward Bruce on the one side against Ingram de Umfraville and Aymer de St John on the other – or the Lanercost-Fordun story of a ruinous harrying of the Galloway chiefs and peasantry, it is clear that Edward Bruce's summer campaign in 1308 was only a qualified success. The crucial battle was probably fought on the banks of the River Dee, not far from Buittle, mistakenly located by Barbour on the Water of Cree.[2] But Edward Bruce failed to eject the English garrisons from the castles marking a line of communication from which Galloway might ultimately be recovered – Lochmaben, Caerlaverock, Dumfries, Dalswinton, Tibbers, Loch Doon and Ayr. Barbour's statement that the reduction of these fortresses occupied an entire year must be read in the light of English record, which shows them still in English hands down to various dates between 1309 and 1313. Ayr Castle, for instance, probably under attack in June 1309, was in English hands as late as the following December.[3] The remaining south-western castles named above, together with Buittle, were also still held by the English in December 1309, their commanders being expressly ordered by Edward II not to take any truce from the enemy.[4] Unless subduing or putting to flight the native inhabitants may be taken as marks of lordship, it cannot be said that Edward Bruce succeeded before 1313 in justifying the title of 'Lord of Galloway' which his brother had conferred on him in or before March

[1] Barbour, Bruce, 161–6; Chron. Lanercost, 212 (which says that the leaders were Edward Bruce, Alexander Lindsay, Robert Boyd and James Douglas, and that their forces came from the outer isles); Chron. Fordun, i, 345.

[2] Barbour, Bruce, 162. His form 'Cre' is anachronistic, the fourteenth-century forms being Crith(e), Crich(e), etc., i.e. 'boundary'. The Dee would have been almost within sight of Buittle castle (Book IX, lines 533–5), the Cree far out of sight.

[3] Rotuli Scotiae, i, 66, 80a.   [4] Ibid., 80.

1309.[1]

Nevertheless, by the autumn of 1308 the three provinces in which loyalty to Balliol and Comyn would naturally die hardest, Buchan, Argyll and Galloway, had been overrun by King Robert's forces. In the north Banff still held out against him, but the castle at Aberdeen had been forced to surrender in June or July, so that one of the safest and most accessible North Sea ports was brought under the king's control. It was part of the logic of these events that Forfar, the first major English-held castle south of the Mounth to fall into Bruce's hands, was captured at the end of 1308.[2] The credit for this success belonged to a local man, Philip, forester of the royal forest of Plater or Platan beside Forfar, who, as Barbour tells us, hastened to the castle with his friends, climbed over the stone wall by means of ladders erected 'all privily', and because no proper watch was kept had little difficulty in seizing the castle and putting the garrison to death. This happened on Christmas Day 1308, after darkness had fallen. In accordance with his normal practice, the king had the castle dismantled and the well filled in.

From the autumn of 1308 we begin to have surviving written acts of government issued by King Robert, a sure sign that the king was turning from ceaseless campaigning to the hard work of settled administration. The earliest of these acts were dated at Inchmahome (September 28th), Dunkeld (October 5th) and 'Perth' (October 14th),[3] the first evidently issued on the king's return from the Argyll campaign, and the third confirming Barbour's statement that after the fall of Dunstaffnage the king passed towards Perth.[4] His success had begun to reap its own reward. Before March 1309 he had won over to his side James the Stewart, James's nephew Alexander Stewart of Bunkle (Berwickshire), Thomas Randolph the younger (son of the king's half-sister, and a landowner in Nithsdale and Berwickshire), and John Menteith (Stewart on his father's side), who gave up the empty title of earl of Lennox bestowed on him by Edward I, apparently for the actual lordships of Arran and Knap-

[1] APS, i, 459.
[2] Barbour, Bruce, 156; Chron. Holyrood, 179.
[3] Duncan, MS.
[4] Barbour, Bruce, 172.

dale.[1] The three Stewarts might have been expected to join or rejoin Bruce before long. Randolph, whose father had been closely
connected with the Balliols, had been with Bruce at Methven, but
changed sides after his capture. He held strong ideas about knightly
conduct, despised Bruce's policy of guerrilla warfare as being un-
worthy of a gentleman, and told the king as much.[2] He was kept
under constraint for a time until he had purged this contempt, but his
ultimate adherence to the king was to prove of inestimable value.
Another Lothian landowner, William Vieuxpont of Langton in
Berwickshire, had joined Bruce by the end of 1308, if not sooner.[3]

On March 16th and 17th, 1309, Bruce was able to hold his first
parliament.[4] Appropriately enough, it was at St Andrews, for among
its business was the composition of a reply to a letter from King
Philip IV of France, thus opening up the old North Sea lines of
communication which had been out of use for some five years.
King Philip spoke of his special love for King Robert, reminded the
Scots of the old alliance between them and the French, and asked for
Scottish help in a forthcoming crusade. To this the Scottish answer,
put briefly, was 'first things first'. They were delighted to hear of
Philip's affection for their king, they reminded him of the terrible
ravages which English invasion had made across the face of their
country, and they promised that when Scotland had recovered her
'pristine liberty' and was at peace, King Philip would find not only
the king of Scots but all the natives of his kingdom ready to join the
crusade with all their power.[5]

The resumption of Franco-Scottish relations was of fundamental
importance. It had in fact been set in hand as early as the previous
November by a French effort to secure a truce between Edward II
and the king of Scots.[6] But the most urgent task before the St
Andrews parliament seems to have been, as we should expect, the

---

[1] Cal. Docs. Scot., iii, No. 1786, ii, No. 423. Knapdale had been seized on behalf of
John Menteith by John of Lorne in 1301, ibid., ii, No. 1255. The history of Arran
is obscure in this period. It seems to have gone with the earldom of Menteith, but
perhaps because it had been Stewart property. John Menteith's son and heir emerges
in the middle of the fourteenth century as lord of both Knapdale and Arran, and the
probability is that his father was confirmed in these lordships by Robert I.

[2] Barbour, Bruce, 168.   [3] Rotuli Scotiae, i, 61b. See above, p. 152, n. 1.

[4] APS, i, 459; cf. ibid., 71. The parliament alleged to have been held by Bruce at
Scone Abbey, referred to in SHR, xxv, 315, n. 1, may perhaps have been the coronation assembly.   [5] APS, i, 459.   [6] Foedera, ii, 63; Rotuli Scotiae, i, 59–60.

solemn affirmation of Robert Bruce's right to the throne, and a
declaration of loyalty and support from a body of magnates and
prelates sufficiently representative to rank as the community of the
realm. It is much to be regretted that, apart from the reply to King
Philip and an original charter of confirmation issued at St Andrews
on March 16th,[1] our evidence for the proceedings at King Robert's
first parliament consists of copies made in the seventeenth century
of two original documents now lost,[2] and one brief abstract, made
in the eighteenth century and printed in the nineteenth, of a third
original which is likewise missing.[3] These precarious survivals combine to tell a consistent and inherently probable story, but as pieces
of historical evidence they necessarily lack the authority which
extant original instruments would possess. It seems that on March
17th, the day after the reply to King Philip's letter had been issued,
the clergy present at the parliament, or their representatives, describing themselves as fully and solemnly as possible as 'the bishops,
abbots, priors, and others of the clergy duly constituted in the realm
of Scotland', gave their authority to a bold and radical declaration
of right on behalf of Scottish independence and of Robert Bruce's
claim to be king of Scots.[4] In its reference to the competition for the
throne in 1291–2 we have for the first time a clear enunciation of the
belief that Balliol had been made king of Scotland by Edward I *de
facto* in defiance of a universal belief among the Scottish people that
Robert Bruce the Competitor had a better title. The declaration then
narrated the evils and disasters which had befallen Scotland by reason

---

[1] Duncan, MS.

[2] British Museum, MS. Harl. 4694, fos. 5–6, 35–6 (a manuscript of Sir James
Balfour of Denmilne, Lord Lyon King of Arms.)

[3] *APS*, i, 289, paragraph beginning 'In a MS. which belonged to Mr J. Anderson . . .'

[4] The view of the evidence expressed here differs radically from that hitherto
accepted, and must be explained carefully. Serious errors make the editorial comment
in *APS*, i, 289, misleading. Brit Mus., MS. Harl. 4694, fos. 5–6, 35–6, contains
copies of two separate versions of an identical document, whose text may be found in
APS, i, 460, cols. 1–2. Unlike the versions there printed the Harleian versions are
both dated at St Andrews: (1) *Datum in parliamento tento Apud Sanctum Andream in
Scotia xvii die Martij Anno Gratie Millesimo Trecentesimo octauo*, of which Balfour notes
'ther is onlie tuo sealls left of this declaratione, viz. Sigillum Episcopi St Andreae,
et Dunkeldensis. and .6. uthers broken from it;' (2) *Datum in parliamento tento Apud
Sanctum Andream in Scotia 17 die Martij Anno Gratie M⁰. CCC⁰. VIII⁰.* To which is
added (by Balfour or another?) *Sex sigilla cere viridis Episcoporum sunt appensa.*

of English invasion and the capture and imprisonment of King
John, until, through the working of divine providence, the people,
not wishing any longer to bear the calamities which had been
brought upon them through want of a captain and faithful leader,
had taken for their king Robert Bruce, grandson of the Competitor,
in whom the Competitor's right to the throne resided, and had raised
him to the throne. Having been made king of Scots, Bruce had
through Christ's mercy recovered and restored the kingdom, following the example of many former kings of Scotland by whom it had
been won and held, 'as is fully related in the ancient and magnificent
chronicles of the Scots, and as the warlike labours of the Picts against
the Britons and of the Scots against the Picts clearly testify.'[1] And
before concluding with a general affirmation of their loyalty to
King Robert, the clergy's declaration added this cautionary statement: 'If anyone, in opposition [to King Robert], should claim right
to the Scottish kingdom by means of documents sealed in the past
and containing the consent of the people, be it known that all this was
effected by irresistible force and violence, by manifold fears, bodily
torture and other terrors, which could well pervert the opinions
and minds of righteous men and strike fear into the stoutest hearts.'[2]

Apart from containing the earliest appearance of the powerful
myth that John Balliol was merely an English puppet, the declaration
is remarkable for two echoes. Its reference to the ancient chronicles
of the Scots and to the wars in which the Britons had been driven
out of Scotland by the Picts and the Picts by the Scots recalls the
case presented to Boniface VIII in 1301 by Baldred Bisset and his
colleagues, in rebuttal of Edward I's letter to the pope justifying his
overlordship in Scotland.[3] The phrase in which the declaration seeks
to explain the Scots' failure to defy the English claim of 1291 is not
merely an echo, it is almost a *verbatim* quotation, of the words used
in the bull *Scimus, fili* of 1299 and again in Bisset's pleading in 1301:
'the force and fear which can strike even the most steadfast' of the
earlier documents becoming 'the force, violence and manifold
fears which can strike even the most steadfast' of the later.[4] The

[1] *APS*, i, 460, col. 2, lines 2–6.
[2] Ibid. The 'documents sealed in the past' would no doubt have special reference
to the records of homages to Edward I in 1291, 1296 and 1304.
[3] *Chron. Picts. Scot.*, 280.
[4] Cp. ibid., 218, *per vim et metum qui cadere poterat in constantem* and ibid., 277, *per*

continuity of argument which links the documents of 1299 and 1301 to those of 1309 is proof that Bruce, in his first parliament, had available to him the documentation produced by the earlier struggles of the community of the realm. It suggests, indeed, that he had with him some of the actual men who were responsible for, or at least well-informed about, the preparation of these earlier documents. No doubt Nicholas Balmyle, who had been chancellor in 1301 and was now bishop of Dunblane, was present at the parliament. It seems that Matthew of Crambeth, bishop of Dunkeld, also attended,[1] and it is reasonable to posit the attendance of the bishops of Ross, Moray and Brechin and of representatives of the bishops of St Andrews and Glasgow.[2]

Parallel with this declaration by the clergy there was apparently a similar – perhaps an identical – declaration by the nobles.[3] According to the brief eighteenth-century abstract which forms the only surviving evidence of this declaration, the nobles, addressing themselves to the king of France, affirmed that King Robert was the true and nearest heir of King Alexander last deceased. This was done 'at the city of St Andrews in the year of grace 1308, in the third year of King Robert's reign',[4] that is, between March 25th, 1308 and March 24th, 1309. We need have no doubt that it belongs, like the clergy's declaration, to the St Andrews parliament. It was evidently sealed by six earls or their representatives and by Edward Bruce as lord of Galloway. Whether it bore any title or endorsement we do not know, but the document put out by the clergy is said to have had the significant title: 'Declaration made by the community of the

---

vim et metum qui cadere poterant in constantes with *APS*, i, 460, col. 2, *per vim et violentiam quibus non poterat tunc resisti et metus multiplices cruciatus corporum ac terrores varios qui sensus perfectorum et animos avertere poterant et cadere in constantes.* The elaboration of the 1309 document is partly due to its author's desire to employ the *cursus*; see below, p. 425. For the phrase itself, see above, p. 86, n. 1.

[1] Brit. Mus., MS. Harl. 4694, fo. 6.

[2] Ibid., fo. 36. It is hard to explain the affixing of seals by the bishops of St Andrews and Glasgow (the latter a prisoner in England, the former supposedly in Edward II's peace) except on the assumption that they were, with or without their knowledge and consent, 'represented'. Lamberton, indeed, may even have been present in person; *Foedera*, ii, 68, and see below, p. 374, n. 1.

[3] *APS*, i, 289, col. 1, at foot. There is obviously an error or a muddle in the list of signatories, but it may be suggested that seals were placed by Ross, Lennox and Edward Bruce, and by representatives of the 'communities' of the earldoms of Fife, Menteith, Mar and Buchan, as in ibid., 459.   [4] Ibid., 289.

realm of Scotland that Robert Bruce, grandfather of the lord Robert king of Scotland, was the true heir of King Alexander, and that he ought to have succeeded to the realm on his death.'[1]

This brings us to the vital question of the composition of the St Andrews parliament. The lords, knights and other laymen whom we know to have attended or to have been represented at this first parliament of King Robert were the following:[2] the earls of Ross, Lennox and Sutherland; the 'communities' of the earldoms of Fife, Menteith, Mar, Buchan and Caithness, whose heirs were in wardship; the communities of the other earldoms of the realm except Dunbar; Edward Bruce, lord of Galloway; James the Stewart; Alexander of Argyll; Donald of Islay; John Menteith; Gilbert de la Hay, constable of Scotland; Robert Keith, marischal of Scotland; Thomas Randolph, lord of Nithsdale; James Douglas; Alexander Lindsay; Alexander (?Fraser); William Wiseman; John Fenton; David Barclay; Robert Boyd; Edward Keith; Hugh, son of the earl of Ross; the barons of all Argyll and the Hebrides (among them Gillespie Maclachlan and three Campbells) 'and the inhabitants of the whole realm of Scotland acknowledging allegiance to Robert king of Scotland'. The church leaders present have already been mentioned, and to their number we must of course add the chancellor, Bernard of Linton.

This makes an impressive list, but in some ways the gaps in it are as striking as the names which are present. Ingram de Umfraville and his kinsman the earl of Angus; the earls of Atholl and Dunbar; Alexander Abernethy; John Moubray; Adam of Gordon; David of Brechin – these and several other men of the highest rank, many of whom could show a notable record in the war against England, were conspicuously missing. It was of the utmost importance to Bruce that he should actually enjoy the support of what could be called, without serious violence to the truth, the 'community of the

---

[1] Brit. Mus., MS. Harl. 4694, fc 35ʳ.

[2] The following list is derived from *APS*, i, 459 and 289; the name of John Fenton is added from the original letter (S.R.O., S.P. 3), where it appears, with that of Alexander Fraser, on one of the seal tags (No. 12), but was missed by the editors of *APS*. The tags themselves appear to have been cut from a draft of the final version of the document, since some of its phraseology may be read on tags 5 and 10. The document is not wholly legible, and probably some three or four names are lost. In particular, there is room for at least two names in the text on line 3 after *comit* [*is Rossie*] and on line 4 after *Alexander d*[*e . . .*].

realm'. The phrase 'the inhabitants of the whole realm of Scotland acknowledging allegiance to King Robert', used where all our reading of such documents from 1286 onwards might lead us to expect the simpler 'community of the realm', may well indicate some doubt on the constitutional point. The author of the rubric which is said to have been supplied to the clerical declaration was bolder or less scrupulous. One of the most remarkable proofs of the power behind the concept of the community is to be seen in the fact that in 1309 King Robert and his Scottish enemies both struggled to capture this concept and to appear to act on behalf of the community. As late as October 1309 'certain people in Scotland to whom the name "the community of Scotland" is given', who were presumably the not insignificant remnant of the old Balliol and Comyn party, petitioned Edward II to restore and confirm the terms which had been granted by Edward I in the peace he had made in 1304 with John Comyn of Badenoch and the rest of the community.[1] The request was allowed, but whether or not it impressed the English king is beside the point. The form of the petition is a forceful reminder that the idea of the community of the realm remained very strong, and that among the leaders of the Scottish nation King Robert had as yet no monopoly of it. Nevertheless, even if at his first parliament Robert Bruce could not claim with manifest truth to have the whole community behind him, it may be fairly said that the search for his throne was at an end.[2]

[1] *Rotuli Scotiae*, i, 77b.
[2] It was a mark of the king's achievement that by July 23rd, 1310 he had secured papal absolution from the sin of homicide, as a private man ('Robert de Bruyss, layman of Carrick, diocese of Glasgow'); H. J. Lawlor, in *SHR*, xix, 325–6.

11

The Turn of the Tide

IT is easy to regard the period from 1309 to 1314 as a mere prelude to Bannockburn, as though the Scots spent these years preparing themselves for an inevitable and decisive trial of strength with the English Crown. In truth, Bruce's famous battle was the least inevitable event in the whole war of independence. Bruce himself never seems to have been certain in his own mind that his crown and the independence of the Scottish kingdom would ultimately have to be vindicated in a single great trial by combat. An English observer in 1311 wrote that Bruce 'did not believe he was able to meet the [English] king's forces in a plain field',[1] an estimate which surely holds good for the whole period from Methven to the dramatic council of war held on the night of June 23rd–24th, 1314, between the first and second days of the battle of Bannockburn. Bruce's thinking was dominated by the principles summarized and made famous in later years in *Good King Robert's Testament*: dependence on infantry, scorched earth, guerrilla raids and sorties, and the systematic demolition of castles and fortifications; in short, caution in strategy, boldness in tactics. The English, in his view, must be so harassed and exhausted that they would come to feel that Scotland was not worth the effort and expense of conquest.

We must not exaggerate the success which Bruce had achieved by 1309, even while admitting that this success was extraordinary when we consider the almost ludicrous weakness of his position only two years before. The subjugation of Buchan, Ross and Argyll (a list soon to be augmented by Galloway), the resumption of communications with France, the winning over of many prominent nobles and lairds, the holding of a parliament at St Andrews – these

[1] *Cal. Docs. Scot.*, iii, No. 202.

were notable achievements, which bade fair to make 'King Hob' (as
the English called him in ridicule)[1] a much more serious exponent of
kingship than any but his most devoted followers of 1306–7 would
have believed. But in 1309 he had still not won over the whole of
Scotland. It is true that as the result of brilliant campaigns, his
Scottish enemies no longer had any base for concerted action outside Lothian, and even Lothian had come under heavy attack as
early as December 1308.[2] If Scotsmen still wanted to fight against
Bruce, they must now do so simply as individual members of the
English forces, and they were, indeed, described as 'English' by the
later Scottish chroniclers. But Bruce had to recognize – as we also
must recognize if we wish to grasp the significance of the years
before Bannockburn – that an unmistakable change had come over
the struggle with England since 1304. On the one hand there was
defeatism, bred of the memory of actual defeat in the field and of
material destruction and misery, and leading to a breakdown of
order and to opportunist shifts of allegiance. On the other, there
were the doubts entertained by many men of power and influence
as to the lawfulness of Bruce's claim to the throne, the open belief or
less articulate suspicion that he was a private man furthering a
private ambition.

At this point it is appropriate to offer a final criticism of the first
of the two main points made by Dr Evan Barron in his study of the
Anglo-Scottish war. This is the preponderant part which, Dr Barron
believes, was played by the north and the highlands, in contrast to a
supine or pro-English Lothian which contributed little or nothing.[3]
Whatever truth there is in this thesis can most easily be demonstrated during the years from 1306 to 1314. Once Buchan, Ross and
Argyll are got out of the way (and they are rather awkward ex-

---

[1] T. Wright, *Political Songs of England* (Camden Soc., 1839), 216:

'Now Kyng Hobbe in the mures gongeth
For te come to toune nout him ne longeth.'

The news of Bruce's rising and of his flight to the heather quickly reached Italy,
for Villani refers to Edward I's failure to subdue 'Ruberto di Busoo' who with his
followers had fled to the bogs and wild mountains of Scotland; G. Villani, *Historie
universali de suoi tempi* (Florence, 1570), 340–1.

[2] *Rotuli Scotiae*, i, 61 (for 'Landyan' read 'Laudyan', Lothian).

[3] It will be best to reserve for a final estimate of Bruce's achievement discussion
of Dr Barron's second point, namely that Bruce would never have succeeded had it
not been for the support of Celtic Scotland.

ceptions to Dr Barron's view) it is undeniable that King Robert's strength lay for many years in the country north of Forth and in the 'middle west' – Lanarkshire, Ayrshire, Lennox and the Firth of Clyde. In 1311, for example, we are told on good authority that Piers Gaveston was sent to occupy Perth by Edward II 'so that Bruce who at the time was on an expedition towards Galloway *should not return north of Forth to recruit an army*'.[1] But it was precisely in these regions that the English hold was weakest, not so much because of the exceptional hostility of the inhabitants as because of their remoteness from English bases and their excessively poor internal communications. Anyone attempting the recovery of Scottish independence in 1306 would have been obliged, if only for strategic and geographical reasons, to begin with the north and the west.

Dr Barron's depreciation of Lothian (from a patriotic standpoint) has force only if the whole long first stage of the war, from 1296 down to 1304, is ignored, and if the second stage is given undue prominence. Before 1304, as we have already seen, not only was the south-east – Lothian, Tweeddale, Teviotdale and the Forest – repeatedly the scene of major campaigns, but many south-eastern landowners were prominent on the Scottish side. Moreover, even after Bruce's revolutionary *coup de force*, it is not true to say that all Lothian men remained hostile or apathetic towards him until Bannockburn inspired or terrified them into patriotism. Between 1307 and February 1312 the following Lothian landowners had joined Bruce: William de Vieuxpont (Vipont) of Langton in Berwickshire; Sir Thomas Hay, Sir Robert Keith the marischal; and (in Keith's following) Godfrey Broun of Colston (December 1308); Geoffrey Fressingley (1308); Edmund Ramsay of Dalhousie (1309 or 1310); Peter of Pinkie and Aymer of Hadden (November 1310).[2] A series of fascinating documents from November 1312[3] throws a flood of light on the situation in Lothian a year and a half before Bannockburn, showing that it was a good deal more complex than Dr Barron's thesis would suggest. These documents show us the

[1] *Chron. Lanercost*, 214.

[2] *Rotuli Scotiae*, i, 61b; *Cal. Docs. Scot.*, iii, No. 245.

[3] Ibid. No. 186 (=P.R.O., Ancient Petitions 7743). It is clear from the original that Bain's dating is wrong, and that this belongs to 1312, and refers to the truce mentioned in *Rotuli Scotiae*, i, 111. Bain's summary is misleading and inadequate.

plight of the communities of 'King Edward's men' – presumably including both the genuinely English and the Scots loyal to Edward II – in the sheriffdoms of Edinburgh, Roxburgh and Berwick. On one side the Scottish king was treating them exactly as he was treating the indisputably English communities of Cumberland, Northumberland and County Durham, forcing them to pay him swingeing sums of blackmail for immunity from burning, devastation and worse. On the other side, the English garrisons, especially at Edinburgh, Roxburgh, Jedburgh and Berwick, were brutally ignoring these dearly bought truces or *souffrances de guerre*. They refused to contribute their own share of the cost of a truce, and when local landowners took refuge inside these castles in order to evade their responsibilities, they refused to allow these evaders to pay the proper share due from their estates. Finally, they seized the goods and cattle of Bruce's own supporters in their sheriffdoms, when these were being brought to market peaceably under the terms of the truce. In consequence, not surprisingly, the 'civilian population' (if they may be so called) feared reprisals by Bruce because the truce had been violated. Nothing in the record of this time is more ironical than to see King Edward II sternly rebuking his own sheriffs and garrison commanders for attacking the enemy and for making life harder for Edward's own supporters. Nothing is more illuminating than to read in these official records of 1312 explicit reference to the men in Lothian 'who adhere to the side of the aforesaid Robert [Bruce]'.[1]

A passage in the Lanercost chronicle describing the situation at the turn of the years 1311 and 1312 strikingly reinforces the impression given by these official records.[2] The writer states that the men of the earldom of Dunbar, who had hitherto been in the English king's peace, were forced to pay very heavily for immunity from Bruce's attacks. We have already seen that the earl of Dunbar had been consistently pro-English throughout the Anglo-Scottish war. His attitude will easily account for the fact that his earldom was loyal to Edward II, but though it consisted of a large group of estates in East Lothian and Berwickshire the earldom of Dunbar was not Lothian. It may be relevant to add that the two magnates who were prominent in these years as leaders and spokesmen of the English

---

[1] *Rotuli Scotiae*, i, 111: *illorum qui ex parte predicti Roberti se tenent*; P.R.O., Ancient Petitions 7743, para 2: *les gentz del enemiste*.   [2] *Chron. Lanercost*, 217.

party in Lothian were the earl of Dunbar himself and Sir Adam Gordon, who was a kinsman of the earls of Dunbar and held his principal estate, the village of Gordon in Berwickshire, as a member of the earldom. The Lanercost writer continues with these remarkable words:

'In all this fighting the Scots were so divided that often a father was with the Scots and his son with the English, or one brother was with the Scots and another with the English, or even one individual was first on one side and then on the other. But all or most of those Scots who were with the English were with them insincerely or to save their lands in England; for their hearts if not their bodies were always with their own people.'[1]

The men and women of south-eastern Scotland were, indeed, in an unenviable plight. If many of them remained in the increasingly ineffective 'peace' of King Edward, it would be unrealistic to attribute this to a lack of patriotic feeling. A few years later, when the triumphant Scots were raiding the English northern counties at will, many of the local inhabitants went over to the Scots. It does not occur to English historians (any more than it occurred to Edward II) to put this down to traitorous motives or lack of patriotism. They were prompted by stark necessity. No such necessity burdened the people north of Forth, where the majority were free to give effect to a patriotism which was neither more nor less pronounced than that which might be found in any feudal kingdom of comparable development.

Fourteenth-century patriotism was not a total, all-embracing patriotism, any more than fourteenth-century warfare was total warfare, but both, for all that, were real enough. We must not be too surprised, therefore, if we find hard-pressed Lothian gentry supporting the English, or impoverished young men from the surrounding countryside serving in the enemy garrisons of Linlithgow or Bothwell or even Perth and Dundee. Nor must we be too surprised if we find that a number of prominent men from districts well to the north or west of Lothian were conspicuously loyal to the English king and inveterate enemies of King Robert. Dr Barron has little to say on the point, but it is a striking fact that the hard core of

---

[1] *Chron. Lanercost*, 217. This is borne out by surviving letters of Sir John Graham referring to Eskdale in 1309 (*Melrose Liber*, Nos. 378–80).

Scots who fought consistently against Bruce, who either never submitted, not even after the tide of victory had turned decisively in his
favour, or submitted at the eleventh hour, was composed of men from
precisely those regions where the special strength of the patriots'
cause is supposed to have lain: Sir Dungal Macdouall of Galloway,
Sir Alexander Abernethy of Abernethy (Perthshire) and Inver-
arity (Angus), Duncan of Frendraught (on the borders of Aberdeenshire and Banffshire), his father-in-law and brother-in-law, the
elder and younger Gilbert of Glencarnie, from the highland parish
of Duthil in Inverness-shire,[1] and John Bacach Macdougall, lord of
Lorne.

The years from 1309 to 1314 were years not of orderly preparation
but of dour and confused struggle. The elimination of concerted
Scottish resistance to Bruce meant that the king's main efforts could
be directed towards clearing his kingdom of English garrisons and
re-establishing its independent position within the community of
North Sea countries. Save for the summer and autumn of 1309,
which he evidently spent traversing the west from Loch Broom in
the north to Dunstaffnage in Argyll,[2] and the autumn of 1312, when
he stayed for some weeks in Moray to witness the conclusion of the
treaty with Norway, King Robert's time was chiefly spent in the
centre and south of Scotland, or else beyond the Border, raiding
Cumberland and Northumberland.

The chief castles still in enemy hands after the end of 1309 were
concentrated in the south.[3] On the line of the Tay the English retained Perth and Dundee. North of this line they held only Banff,
which may have fallen to the Scots during 1310. Between Tay and
Forth the English position was surprisingly weak: Cupar, which
they still held in the spring of 1308, was lost not long afterwards,
and only the small castle of Muckhart, belonging to the bishop of

[1] Fraser, *Grant*, iii, No. 11. For a tradition concerning the lordship and name
Glencarnie (Glenchernich), whose seat was where Boat of Garten now is, see L.
Shaw, *History of the Province of Moray* (1775), 39n. The lands of Glencarnie were held
of the earls of Strathearn.

[2] A charter of August 8th, 1309, preserved at Cawdor Castle, is dated 'Loch Bren',
i.e. Loch a 'Bhraoin, now in Scots Loch Broom; another, of October 20th, 1309, is
dated at Dunstaffnage. See Map No. 9.

[3] *Rotuli Scotiae*, i, 80 and *Cal. Docs. Scot.*, iii, No. 218 are the chief authorities here.

St Andrews, remained in enemy hands, apparently as late as 1311.[1] On the crucially important line of the Forth, or immediately south of it, the first-class castles of Stirling and Edinburgh were English-held, and precariously linked by the minor strongpoints of Linlithgow and Livingstone. Already in 1309 the supply of these garrisons was proving difficult and dangerous. Food, stores and weapons were obtained from Berwick. Oddly enough, remote Banff and Dundee, because they could be supplied by sea, were easier to replenish than Stirling or Edinburgh. West of Stirling, English troops still controlled Kirkintilloch and Bothwell.[2] They must have felt increasingly isolated, though Bothwell, perhaps because of its exceptional size and strength, actually held out until the morrow of Bannockburn, when its Scottish commander, Walter, Gilbert's son, saw the light in time, handed Bothwell over to Edward Bruce, and survived to become the ancestor of the powerful Hamilton family. The still greater isolation of Ayr by December 1309 is shown by the fact that Edward II classed it along with Perth, Dundee and Banff as a castle whose commander was instructed to 'take what truce he could until Whitsun next (June 7th, 1310)'.[3] At what date Rutherglen and Dumbarton fell to the Scots is not known. Rutherglen, which was being besieged in December 1308, was apparently taken by Edward Bruce.[4] Dumbarton may have been handed over to Bruce when its keeper Sir John Menteith joined him, before the spring of 1309.

The castles of the extreme south west could be expected to hold out longer, at least until the English lost their command of the Solway Firth. In these regions, moreover, a higher proportion of the local people were Bruce's enemies. It was thus some years before the Scots regained Lochmaben, Caerlaverock, Dumfries, Dalswinton, Tibbers and Buittle. As late as the autumn of 1311 an enemy garrison held Bruce's own island fortress of Loch Doon in Carrick. Although they were besieged, an 'English' force under David of Strathbogie, earl of Atholl, was making a strenuous effort to relieve them.[5] Dumfries and Caerlaverock were probably the strongest of these castles. Dumfries was at last surrendered, to King Robert in person,

[1] *Cal. Docs. Scot.*, iii, No. 221.
[2] *Rotuli Scotiae*, i, 80.
[3] Ibid.
[4] Ibid., 60a; Barbour, *Bruce*, 190.
[5] *Rotuli Scotiae*, i, 106.

on February 7th, 1313, by his old enemy Dungal Macdouall.[1] With
a clemency and respect for military honour conspicuously absent
in Edward I's behaviour towards defeated garrisons, Macdouall
was allowed to go free, and lived for some time longer to fight for
the English king.

It was, of course, in the south east that the English position seemed,
if not impregnable, at least formidably entrenched. It was not merely
that they held, in addition to Edinburgh, three other first-class
castles – Jedburgh, Roxburgh and Berwick – as well as numerous
second- or third-rate strongpoints (Haddington, Luffness, Dirleton,
Yester, Dunbar, Selkirk and Cavers).[2] Even more useful was the
fact that the close, 'four-square' grouping of these castles, the
relatively good communications between them, and the proximity
of most of them to a North Sea coastline still dominated by English
maritime power, combined to make the whole English position
much less vulnerable in this area than anywhere else in Scotland.
Bruce knew that there was no easy short-cut to victory here. Every
single one of the major fortresses must be patiently invested, starved,
and, when the right moment came, seized by a mixture of stratagem
and daring. The methods of castle warfare used by the English were
simply not available to Bruce, for he was woefully short of heavy
siege engines and the skilled men to work them, and also of the food-
supplies needed to sustain prolonged sieges.

The tactics of Bruce and the bold young men – Douglas, Randolph,
Boyd and Edward Bruce – who under him were already forming a
band of famous captains, would have astonished and amused Edward
I. Castles must be surprised during the hours of darkness, and an entry
must be forced at the most suitable point on the walls by means of
rope ladders fitted with iron grappling-hooks. These simple but
ingenious scaling ladders, evidently light enough to be carried by
one or two men, may well have been used at Forfar and elsewhere
in the north. The first occasion on which they are recorded was the
attempt on Berwick, on the night of December 6th, 1312.[3] It is
characteristic of the audacity of Bruce and his captains that the first

[1] *Cal. Docs. Scot.*, iii, No. 304; cf. No. 279.
[2] Ibid., No. 218.
[3] *Chron. Lanercost*, 220.

big south-country stronghold to be attacked in earnest was the town nearest to the English border. The attempt was frustrated by the barking of a dog inside the walls, but in little more than a month Bruce was investing the town of Perth. Because of its strategic position, Perth (like Stirling) was of crucial importance to the English. Gaveston had been sent to hold and strengthen the town in February 1311,[1] during the campaign which Edward II conducted in southern Scotland between September 1310 and August 1311. The Perth garrison was large, with a high proportion of Scotsmen.[2] Since October 1311 at latest, they had been commanded by the Perthshire knight Sir William Oliphant. As the brave young commander of Stirling castle on behalf of King John and the Guardians, Oliphant had won great renown. He had been in an English prison from July 1304 until December 1308, when he was released on condition of fighting against Bruce.[3] He had already given a gloomy report of the situation at Perth as early as autumn 1311,[4] and by January 1313 things must have seemed wellnigh hopeless. The town was surrounded by a stone wall with turrets, and by a water-filled ditch (except on the east where the River Tay gave protection). On the night of January 7th–8th, 1313 – 'a myrk nycht' says Barbour[5] – the garrison failed to keep a good watch, believing from Bruce's movements that the Scots had lifted the siege. Carrying their ladders and light weapons, the Scots waded through the moat in the darkness. To the astonishment of a French knight in his entourage, their king himself led the way through the black, icy water, which at one point came up to his throat, and with the help of his own rope-ladder was the second man to scale the town wall. The men of Perth surrendered almost without a fight.

For some moments Bruce had clearly been in great danger; but it was during just such moments as these that he won not merely the castles but also the hearts of Scotland. In most ages of history, the Scottish soldier (unless extremely well-trained) has not possessed the gift which has been the conspicuous mark of his English counterpart: the capacity to hold on coolly and philosophically, through thick

---

[1] *Chron. Lanercost*, 214.
[2] *Cal. Docs. Scot.*, iii, 425–7.
[3] Ibid., No. 45; *Rotuli Scotiae*, i, 61b.
[4] Ibid., 105b.
[5] Barbour, *Bruce*, 158.

and thin, regardless of either leadership or conditions. On the other hand, no one has responded more heroically to the inspiration of an outstanding leader, a Murray of Bothwell, a James IV, a Montrose, a Moore. And it seems undeniable that a successful leader of Scotsmen must have above all the power to kindle both affection and imagination. It is not normally the mark of a good general that he fights alongside his men. But Bruce had to be more than a good general; he had to be a Joshua, a captain of his people, one who could not only draw on existing loyalty but awaken dormant loyalty and win over to himself the loyalty previously given to his enemies.

The English in Perth were allowed to go free. The leading Scots burgesses were slain, though if we may believe Barbour the number of those killed was small.[1] The example – if such it was – proved effective, for we hear of no more cold-blooded killings. Slaughter of this kind, though common enough in the period, was highly uncharacteristic of Robert Bruce. As we have seen, only a month after the fall of Perth (February 7th, 1313) Dumfries Castle was starved into surrender. The king had taken personal command of the attack upon Dumfries, Caerlaverock and Buittle during the previous July, perhaps because he felt that his brother had not done well enough in this task. It seems likely that after the surrender of Dumfries the other two castles also fell into Scottish hands, and the West March with them. There was no mistaking it now: the tide had turned.

Stirling, commanded by Sir Philip Moubray, a Scot, was the next big castle to be attempted. Edward Bruce laid siege to it from Lent nearly to midsummer 1313, without success.[2] Then, by an act of characteristic chivalry and folly, he committed his brother to a pact which threatened to ruin all Bruce's cautious strategy and to change the very nature of the war Bruce had chosen to fight. The hard-pressed Moubray asked for a year's respite in which help was to arrive or else his position be proved untenable. This extremely generous term was conceded by Edward Bruce. If no English army came within three miles of Stirling to do battle for the castle before Midsummer 1314, Moubray would surrender. Possibly, in view of Edward II's struggle with his own great lords, embittered as it was by their judicial murder of Gaveston in 1312, Edward Bruce may

[1] Barbour, *Bruce*, 160; but cf. *Chron. Fordun*, i, 346; *Chron. Lanercost*, 221–2.
[2] Barbour, *Bruce*, 191.

have thought that Stirling would be cheaply bought. Yet faced by so public a challenge neither the king nor the barons of England could ignore the threat to their honour and the opportunity of ending the Scottish war once for all. King Robert was virtually compelled to meet the enemy in a pitched battle, the one thing he had striven to avoid since June 1306.

The affair earned Edward Bruce a sharp rebuke from the king,[1] but was not allowed to interfere with his plans to reduce the remaining enemy-held strongpoints. Thwarted of Berwick and Stirling, Bruce turned to the two formidable strengths of Roxburgh – 'le Marche Mont (Marchmont)' in popular usage – and Edinburgh, 'le château des pucelles' or 'maidens' castle', clinging as stubbornly as lichen to its knob of volcanic rock. Well-guarded, these castles should have proved more than a match for ill-equipped besiegers. In fact, they fell within the space of a single Lent. On the night of February 19th–20th, 1314 (this was Shrove Tuesday and Ash Wednesday),[2] the Scots under James Douglas broke into Roxburgh castle and overwhelmed the garrison. Douglas and his men approached the walls at dead of night, crawling on their hands and knees, their body armour invisible under black surcoats. They carried the usual ingenious rope ladders, on this occasion apparently made by a man called Sim of the 'Ledows'.[3] Sim was the first man up. He made the way safe for the rest when he 'stekit upward with ane knyff' a sentry roused by the clatter as the grappling-hook of his ladder was lodged on the wall-head. Because it was Shrove Tuesday (Fastern's Eve) the garrison were relaxed, drinking and dancing. Taken utterly by surprise, many were killed or captured. Only their commander, a knight named Guillemin de Fenes from Bouglon in Gascony,[4] made any real resistance, shutting himself into a small turret. He surrendered the next day, however, and with his men was allowed to go freely to England.

[1] Barbour, *Bruce* 192.

[2] *Chron. Holyrood*, 180; Barbour, *Bruce*, 178–82.

[3] Ibid., 179, Sym of the Ledows. Ledhous (Leidhous, etc.) was the name of some lands beside Crossford in Lesmahagow parish, the next parish north of Douglas. Sim's name and special skill suggest that he may have been a lead miner.

[4] Barbour, *Bruce*, 181; *Chron. Lanercost*, 223; *Cal. Docs. Scot.*, iii, 406 and elsewhere passim; *Scalacronica*, 140, reading *de* for *et* before Burglioun. Bouglon is in dép. Lot-et-Garonne, arr. Marmande.

Edinburgh castle was taken three weeks later by Thomas Randolph, obviously determined not to be outdone by Douglas.[1] The folk-hero in this case was William Francis, a local man whose father had served in the castle and whom the king afterwards rewarded with forfeited lands in Sprouston, Roxburghshire.[2] As a youth, Francis had had experience of climbing out of Edinburgh castle after dark when, without his father's knowledge, he was paying visits to his sweet-heart in the town. On the night of March 14th, 1314 – once again, mercifully dark – a diversion was carried out at the East Port – 'the only place', says a contemporary, 'where an assault could be made'.[3] This sent the garrison rushing to the spot. Meanwhile, Francis and the other nimble leaders of the genuine assault party, rock-climbers before the art had been invented, inched their way in darkness up the steep and slippery north precipice, and swung their light siege ladders on to the masonry parapet. Up the ladders swarmed their followers, in numbers sufficient to overwhelm the astonished guards. The East Port was opened to admit the still larger force outside, and all was over. Most of the defenders fell in the fighting, but the commander, Sir Pierre Libaud (another Gascon), entered Bruce's service, only to be executed for treason soon afterwards. In accor-dance with his consistent policy, Bruce caused both Edinburgh and Roxburgh ('that fine castle', the Lanercost writer called it)[4] to be razed to the ground.

By their respective exploits at Roxburgh and Edinburgh, Douglas and Randolph set the seal on their already notable reputations. Already, in 1312, Bruce had demonstrated his confidence in Ran-dolph and shown the value he set upon his support by making him earl of Moray and granting him, with wide powers, the lands of an earldom which had been in the possession of the Crown since 1130. Bruce, of course, was a man of his time. The greatest prizes in his gift went to men who were his own kin, like his nephew Ran-dolph, or belonged to the circle of friends and allies of the Bruce family, like James Douglas and Walter Stewart, who had the greatest prize of all, the marriage of Bruce's daughter (and ultimate heir)

---

[1] Barbour, Bruce, 182–90; Chron. Holyrood, 180.
[2] Reg. Mag. Sig., i, Appendix II, Nos. 285, 373.
[3] Chron. Lanercost, 223, perhaps meaning 'east' port, not 'south'.
[4] Ibid.

Marjorie. But with the exception of his own brother Edward, who could hardly fail to be ennobled and honoured by Robert, all the men to whom Bruce granted high office, noble titles and rich estates proved their worth during the reign.

It is impossible to calculate the total of castles captured by Bruce between the early months of 1308, when he took Inverness, and the fall of Edinburgh six years later. On any showing, this must be reckoned one of the great military enterprises of British history. But the achievement appears even more remarkable when we set it in its context of activity in three other spheres – expeditions by sea to keep open an illicit Irish supply line and to threaten the Isle of Man; profitable raids south of the Border; and the resumption of commercial and diplomatic links with towns and countries of the continent.

By the summer of 1310, if not earlier, the Scots had been peaceably received in Ireland and allowed to buy not only corn, meat and other foodstuffs but also sorely-needed iron and steel weapons and armour.[1] Since these can hardly have been Irish-made they were presumably re-exports from England or the continent. Scottish access to Ireland was made possible by the superiority which Bruce now evidently enjoyed in Argyll, the isles and the seas between Galloway and Ulster. One of the most persistent lines of English strategy at this time was to encourage John Macdougall, the ousted lord of Lorne, to lead a naval expedition against the Hebrideans and Argyllsmen and try to win them over. To this end, Macdougall was appointed 'admiral and captain' of a special fleet in 1311, and given a base in one of the east-coast Irish ports, perhaps Dublin or Drogheda.[2] Here he could count on the support of dissident west highlanders such as John Macsween of Knapdale and his brothers Toirdelbach and Murdoch.[3] The corresponding Scottish naval movements are extremely obscure. King Robert himself made a western expedition in 1309,[4] and at the end of the following year he was reported to be planning an assault upon Man with a fleet from the Outer Isles.[5]

[1] *Rotuli Scotiae*, i, 86.
[2] Ibid., 99b; cf. 90a, 93b.
[3] Ibid., 90b.
[4] Above, p. 272, n. 2.
[5] *Rotuli Scotiae*, i, 96.

For the English, the defence of Man was complicated by being tied to the problem of Piers Gaveston, to whom the island had been given by Edward II a few weeks after his accession.[1] Little as the English barons liked the prospect of a Scottish occupation of Man, they liked scarcely less the thought of its providing a bolt-hole for King Edward's hated lover. In May 1311 Edward transferred the island to Sir Henry Beaumont,[2] but since he too incurred the suspicion of the king's opponents, the Lords Ordainers, the change was hardly for the better. At some date before April 1313, Man seems to have been seized in a baronial *coup*, but by the following year possession had been restored to Beaumont.[3] For his part, the king of Scots too had his views on the island's future. Whether he ever carried out his proposed expedition in the winter of 1310–11 is not known. John Fordun says that Bruce captured Man in 1314 (probably after Bannockburn)[4] and this is confirmed by a letter from Edward II in 1315, congratulating John Macdougall on 'recovering' the island for the English.[5] In the next year King Robert granted the lordship of Man to Thomas Randolph, who was reported in July 1317 to be making an attempt to win the island back for Scotland and for himself.[6] In this he must have been successful, for Man remained in Scottish hands from about 1317 until 1333. It may seem surprising that the Scots took so long to recover Man. It remains clear, nonetheless, that the English had lost their control of the western approaches during the earlier years of Edward II's reign. By the autumn of 1315 Scottish ships, mainly under the command of one Thomas Dun, had grown so bold that they were raiding English shipping at Holyhead.[7] In this period also, Thomas Dun helped Edward Bruce in Ireland.[8] Two years later a new galley was ordered to be fitted out in one of the ports of Devon or Cornwall to go into action against Dun, who was doing great damage to traders coming to the western

[1] *Chron. Lanercost*, 210.
[2] *Cal. Docs. Scot.*, iii, No. 481; cf. No. 277.
[3] Ibid., Nos. 307, 391.
[4] *Chron. Fordun*, i, 346.
[5] *Cal. Docs. Scot.*, iii, No. 420.
[6] Ibid., No. 562.
[7] Ibid., No. 451.
[8] For Thomas Dun's activities in Ireland in support of Edward Bruce's expedition, see Barbour, *Bruce*, 257.

harbours of England, and in the same year Thomas Randolph himself was said to be planning a raid upon Anglesey.[1]

From 1311 onward, the English in England itself came to learn what Bruce meant by 'defending himself with the longest stick that he had'. His idea of defence was attack, again and again at the same place or at many different places in rapid succession. He gave the enemy no rest. As early as 1307 Gallovidians and the cattle inseparably associated with them were sheltering from Bruce in Inglewood Forest, along with men from Liddesdale. Very soon there was no safety to be found in Cumberland, or indeed in any of the northern counties of England. It is true that between February 1309 and March 1310 (mainly owing to French exertions) some pretence of peace was maintained along the Border by a series of precarious truces. But after the collapse of Edward II's expedition of 1310–11 and his withdrawal from Scotland (August 1311) Bruce became far more aggressive.

Two students of this period, the late James Willard and Mrs Scammell, have examined the effect of the Scottish raids upon the north of England.[2] Willard's starting-point was the records of the central government, especially the exchequer. He showed that in 1307, for example, Northumberland paid its normal share of a national property tax: £916 18s. 11d. Two years later the county paid nothing, and in 1313 it was exempt. Much the same holds true for Cumberland and Westmorland. Working from the local north-country records as well as those of the central government, Mrs Scammell has been able to fill in the grim details behind these bare fiscal facts. The 'community' of Northumberland, like the 'community of Lothian', was forced to buy a truce from King Robert in 1311 and again from 1312 to 1313, each time for the colossal sum of £2,000. No one knew where the Scots would strike next – one month they poured across the fords of Solway to pillage and burn in Gilsland and the valley of the South Tyne; the next month they broke into Coquetdale and Redesdale, burning as far as Corbridge.

[1] Cal. Docs. Scot., iii, No. 562.
[2] J. F. Willard, 'The Scotch raids and the fourteenth-century taxation of northern England', University of Colorado Studies, v (1907–8), No. 4, 237–42; Jean Scammell, 'Robert I and the north of England', EHR, lxxiii, 385–403.

There was no organized resistance. The English either tried to buy
Bruce off or themselves resorted to burning to prevent the Scots
getting supplies. What the Scots wanted more than anything was
money, cattle and corn, the first two capable of being moved across
difficult country with relative ease. Where possible they obtained
what they wanted in the form of blackmail: for example, the men of
the earldom of Dunbar won temporary respite in 1313 for 1,000
quarters of corn.[1] If blackmail was not paid they overran the country
with fire and sword, though the killing of human beings was relatively uncommon and was not Bruce's object. In August, 1311, for
example, the Scots in upper Tynedale slew only those men who
offered resistance.[2] But in the following summer they penetrated
south of the Tyne, surprising a great throng of folk at Durham on
market day. Here they inflicted great destruction, burning the town
and killing many of the local people.[3] A few leading gentry of the
Bishopric at once acted on their own initiative, for the bishop,
Richard Kellaw, was away in the south attending parliament. They
met Bruce in person at Hexham (August 16th, 1312) and bought a
truce till midsummer 1313 for two thousand marks, 450 to be paid
at Holm Cultram abbey by September 29th, 1312.[4] Cumberland,
Coupland and Westmorland also bought a truce for the same period,
and since they could not raise the whole sum were forced to yield
hostages. On the approach of midsummer 1313, the Scottish king
notified the northern counties that if they did not buy a fresh truce
they would be raided. The mere threat was enough to bring promises
of payment from the county communities. But when Cumberland
had failed to pay by April 1314, instead of injuring the hostages, the
Scots under Edward Bruce established themselves at Rose Castle
and ravaged the surrounding countryside for some days.[5]

These raids and truce-bargains were extremely well organized and
far more profitable and effective than the wild ravaging of Wallace's
incursion in 1297. The Scottish staff-work was excellent, and
discipline, now under royal authority, was strictly maintained.

[1] *Cal. Docs. Scot.*, iii, No. 337.

[2] *Chron. Lanercost*, 216.

[3] Ibid., 220; *Historiae Dunelmensis Ecclesiae Scriptores Tres* (ed. J. Raine, Surtees
Soc.), 94.

[4] Ibid.; Duncan, MS.

[5] *Chron. Lanercost*, 224.

Estates which had obtained no immunity were systematically plundered. Estates which had paid for a truce were left in peace. Only in one case, the town of Hartlepool (where the Bruces had held lordship for over a century),[1] did the king appear to show vindictiveness. In 1315, the men of Hartlepool could not buy any truce from the Scottish king, and were forced to take refuge out at sea while their town was sacked (though not burned) by James Douglas.[2] In general, however, the English could have peace if they paid heavily for it. The effort proved too much for Northumberland, an ill-organized county which in any case was too vulnerable once the national defence system had broken down. After 1314 it 'ceased to negotiate as an entity'.[3] The palatinate bishopric of Durham was much tougher, but the price which it paid for immunity (some £5,000 between 1311 and 1329) was at least twice what it would normally have paid in taxes; and even then it was forced to allow the Scots free passage across the county to raid south of the Tees. By the time Edward II had gathered his large army in the summer of 1314 to meet the challenge of Stirling, the four northern counties of England were close to exhaustion, either devastated or impoverished or both. The money which they should have paid to the exchequer at Westminster had gone, with two- or three-fold increase, to fill Bruce's empty war chest. The men who should have joined Edward's army resented the appeals of a king who could not defend his realm. Some had no money left, some had been slain or put to flight, some had even gone over to the Scots. But this fact must not lead us to produce an English version of Dr Barron's thesis about Lothian. If for some years the northern counties contributed little to the English war-effort and actually contributed more to that of Bruce, we are not entitled to conclude that their patriotism was lukewarm. Given strong leadership and an adequate defence system the English borderers would once more give a good account of themselves, as they had done in the twelfth and thirteenth centuries.

The vigour and high morale infused into the Scots by their king were not enough. Scotland needed arms and armour from abroad,

---

[1] P.R.O., D.L. 36, iii, fo. 12, 3rd doc.; *Cal. Docs. Scot.*, i, No. 321; iii, No. 413.

[2] *Chron. Lanercost*, 230; cf. also *Cal. Docs. Scot.*, iii, Nos. 602, 631, 648, the last two referring to the capture of a Scottish ship at or off Hartlepool early in 1319.

[3] J. Scammell, art. cit., 386.

and allies in every quarter where English interests were vulnerable or where English influence might be damaging. It is doubtful if, during the whole course of the Anglo-Scottish war, there was ever any prolonged blockage of the lines of communication between Scotland and the continent. The chief single reason for this lay in the fact that Scotland's attraction for foreign merchants consisted in her wool, an annual crop which it was best to dispose of without delay. It was always in demand in the Low Countries because of its exceptionally fine quality. It did not occur to Edward I or his son to stop the trade in Scottish wool altogether, but naturally in the districts they controlled such profit as it made for the Crown went to English, not Scottish coffers. Of course they did try to place an embargo on trade with Scots 'rebels'. But the Flemings, and perhaps still more the German or 'Eastland' merchants, with their ancient, well-established contacts with Scottish ports, showed no reluctance to trade with independent Scotland whether it was under the Guardians or under Robert Bruce. In December 1302, for example, a ship freighted with clothing, armour and other goods for independent Scotland, probably bound for Aberdeen and almost certainly coming from the Low Countries or a Hanseatic port, was captured off Filey in Yorkshire.[1] Merchants of St Omer were buying wool, hides and deerskins in Moray in 1303 or 1304.[2] In October 1309, Edward II complained bitterly to the count of Flanders that the Scots and their 'accomplices' the German merchants had been getting great help and succour from the Flemish towns.[3] Men of Hainault were involved in the Scottish trade in 1312.[4] We hear of a ship from the Baltic port of Stralsund being in alliance with the Scots some time before 1312, and of German merchants who before January 1313 had seized an English ship bound for occupied Scotland, sold the cargo at Aberdeen and taken the hull itself to Stralsund.[5]

[1] *Cal. Docs. Scot.*, ii, No. 1479.

[2] Ibid., No. 1639 and 443.

[3] *Rotuli Scotiae*, i, 78b.

[4] W. Stanford Reid, 'Trade, traders and Scottish independence', *Speculum*, xxix, 217, citing H. J. Smit, *Bronnen tot Geschiedenis van den Handel med Engelond etc.* (The Hague, 1928), i, 214. The whole of Reid's article, and also that by Jas. W. Dilley, 'German merchants in Scotland, 1297-1327' *SHR*, xxvii, 142-55, should be read for a survey of the evidence on trade between Scotland and the continent in this period.)

[5] *Cal. Docs. Scot.*, iii, Nos. 252, 679.

It is true that our earliest record of formal relations between King Robert and continental powers, especially the Hanseatic, Flemish and other Low Country cities and principalities, comes from comparatively late in the reign. From 1321, for example, we have a royal letter to Lübeck and privileges issued in favour of Bruges;[1] from 1323 a letter to the count of Holland and Hainault.[2] It is not until 1316 that we have positive documentary evidence of the king negotiating with Genoese firms for the supply of weapons and ships.[3] All this was after Bannockburn, and admittedly nothing succeeds like success. But it would be a mistake to think that foreign merchant communities waited for results before investing in the Scottish enterprise. Moreover, ironical as it may seem, the Scots found some of their best friends among English merchants of North Sea ports such as Harwich, Norwich, King's Lynn, Hull and English-held Berwick. The temptation to smuggle contraband to Scotland overcame both patriotism and fear of the harsh penalties threatened against those who trafficked with the 'rebels'.[4]

The evidence, though patchy and slight, is conclusive. During the early part of Bruce's reign the Scots and their North Sea associates were able to keep trade routes open, and supplies of foodstuffs, weapons and armour, iron and steel, all absolutely essential to the war effort, were reaching Scottish ports. Presumably these imports were being paid for by exports of wool, hides and timber in sufficient quantities to imply a recovery of the fairly simple Scottish economy from the dislocation and destruction of the years before 1304 and of the period from 1306 to 1309. Of course, in these years Scotland must have been even shorter of luxuries than usual, and prior to Bannockburn Bruce certainly never had enough weapons and ships to equip his forces as he would no doubt have liked. But, so far as these matters are ever determined by purely technological considerations, the thin yet steady trickle of vital imports seems to have made the difference between success and failure.

The importance which Bruce attached to the resumption of continental alliances is shown by his readiness to receive envoys from

[1] Jas. W. Dilley, 'Scottish-German Diplomacy', *SHR*, xxxvi, 83.
[2] Ibid., 85.
[3] W. Stanford Reid, art. cit., 422.
[4] Reid, art cit., stresses the importance of smuggling for the Scots in this period.

the French kings, although the truces with England which were several times arranged through their influence were not much to his liking. There is record of truce negotiations of this kind, some of which may have been meant seriously to lead to a peace treaty, in 1308–9, in 1309–10, and in January 1312.[1] In January 1313, Abbot Maurice of Inchaffray, one of King Robert's most loyal and trusted supporters, was given an English safe-conduct to visit Edward II,[2] presumably to discuss a truce or a peace, and later in the same year representatives of King Robert (including Bishop Lamberton) and of King Edward appear to have been appointed to negotiate truce or peace in conjunction with the agents of the king of France and at his request.[3] There is no reason to believe that Bruce's attitude towards these negotiations was frivolous or cynical. But it is clear that he never allowed them to affect his military and strategic dispositions, and also that any serious peace talks would have to start from a recognition of his title to the Scottish Crown on the part of Edward II.

Long before there was anything which could be called a revived Franco-Scottish alliance (as distinct from friendly intercourse) Bruce had taken measures to preserve the good relations with Norway which had existed more or less continuously since 1295.[4] Scoto-Norwegian friendship had been threatened by a number of incidents. It seems that pirates from Scotland had kidnapped the seneschal of Orkney, a Norwegian knight, after he had collected the royal revenues and while the money was still in his possession. He had been held to ransom both for himself and for his money. In addition, there had been Scottish raids on Shetland. For their part, the Scots complained that an esquire named Patrick Mowat had been arrested in Orkney by a royal bailiff, beaten, chained, robbed of his goods and forced to ransom himself for forty merks. Still more serious was the affair of some Scots merchants, burgesses of St Andrews, who on arrival in Norway for the purpose of trading seem to have been treated as hostages. Their goods, worth £600, were seized, and they themselves suffered a lengthy imprisonment before

[1] *Rotuli Scotiae*, i, 59–60; 107–8.
[2] *Cal. Docs. Scot.*, iii, No. 300; cf. *Rotuli Scotiae*, i, 112.
[3] Ibid.; *Cal. Docs. Scot.*, iii, No. 346.
[4] *APS*, i, 461–4.

they were allowed to sail home empty-handed. These incidents may have an ugly look, but by the standards of international behaviour prevailing at the time none of them was atrocious. They can hardly have put Scoto-Norwegian relations in serious jeopardy, and for sheer horror cannot compare with an incident of 1316 which must have imposed a much greater strain upon relations between Norway and England.[1] Some English merchants from Berwick, having put in at a Norwegian port, invited aboard the provincial governor and ten other noblemen, who to save their hosts expense went unarmed and without servants. Instead of a second course, the merchants showered their guests with boiling water and hot cinders and then killed them with daggers and swords. Norwegian grievances against Scotland were probably less concerned with incidents, major or minor, than with the Scottish failure to maintain the terms of the treaty of Perth in 1266, by which the Scots kings were bound to pay a perpetual annuity to Norway of 100 merks. The agreement sealed at Inverness on October 29th, 1312, between King Robert in person and the envoys of King Hakon V, shows that both sides were anxious for a settlement and prepared to be sensible and statesmanlike. The Perth treaty was renewed without any alteration, and though nothing was said about past failures to pay the annuity its regular payment was promised in the future. The Scots agreed to pay 600 merks in final compensation for the kidnapping of the seneschal of Orkney; the Norwegians restored the goods taken from the merchants of St Andrews. The plundering of Shetland and the affair of Patrick Mowat were to be investigated by faithful inquest.

Among the few persons whom we know to have been involved in making the treaty of Inverness there are two clergymen, Farquhar Bellejambe bishop of Caithness and Bernard of Linton the chancellor, whose participation is worth noting. From the date of his appointment to the archdeaconry of Caithness in 1297[2] by King Edward I we have no evidence that Farquhar Bellejambe, who rose to be dean and then (1306) bishop of Caithness, played any positive part in political affairs or that he had supported the Guardians before the collapse of 1304. Nor does he seem to have come out in support of Robert Bruce in his early years, as the bishops of Moray and Ross

[1] *Cal. Docs. Scot.*, iii, No. 500.

[2] Ibid., ii, No. 927. Farquhar Bellejambe had been a canon of Aberdeen.

had done. In 1312, however, Bishop Farquhar was one of the two
Scots churchmen who took oath on behalf of King Robert for the
security of the Inverness treaty, and it is clear that by this time, if
not indeed earlier, the king had gained the allegiance of one more
Scottish bishop. As for Bernard of Linton, his importance to the
king has already been emphasized. It has recently been pointed out
by Professor A. A. M. Duncan that between March 1310 and June
1311 there is no evidence that King Robert made use of his great
seal to authenticate his written instruments.[1] Instead, he seems to have
used the privy seal only. The great seal was, of course, kept by the
chancellor, and used only on his own authorization. Now it was
about this time that Bernard of Linton was made abbot of Arbroath,[2]
and it can hardly be a coincidence that an abbot of Arbroath was
absent in Norway on the king's business (and his own) at some
unknown date within this general period.[3] As Duncan suggests,
therefore, it is in every way probable that Bernard of Linton was
sent to Norway to conduct the negotiations which led to the treaty
of Inverness. If so it would be a clear indication of the great store
which King Robert set by the continuance of Norwegian friendship.

If, in the spring of 1314, Robert Bruce, now in his fortieth year,
had taken stock of the situation in which Scotland found itself, his
feelings could surely have been summed up as a sort of anxious
satisfaction. Much, incredibly much, had been achieved in the vin-
dication of Scottish independence. Scarcely one castle was left with
a foreign garrison which could inflict serious harm on the surrounding inhabitants. Within the Scottish kingdom itself every province
from Galloway to Caithness, from the Outer Isles to Buchan
acknowledged Bruce as king. Beyond the Border, from Tweed and
Solway southward as far as Stainmore and the Tees, the English
had been made to feel the menace of a Scotland awakened and
revivified under a new ruler. Armies had been raised under a new
generation of young captains who were accustomed to victory
instead of defeat, and who showed a flexibility in tactics and a readi-

[1] In a memorandum whose gist will appear in Professor Duncan's forthcoming
volume of Robert I's acts.
[2] *Arbroath Liber*, i, No. 332.
[3] Ibid., No. 360.

ness to depend upon properly trained infantry which was in the sharpest contrast with the kind of warfare waged by the Guardians. Something like the accustomed machinery of government was once again in operation, and it is fair to infer that judicial activity and the collection of royal revenue had been resumed on a national scale. Three parliaments had been held, at St Andrews in 1309 and at Inchture[1] and Ayr in 1312, and probably there were others of which we have no record. King Robert and his subjects were now taken seriously by foreign kingdoms such as Norway and France, and by foreign trading cities and industrial principalities, such as the Hanse and Flanders. If, at this point, the king of England and his barons had been capable of far-sighted statesmanship, there was surely nothing to prevent a resumption of the happier relationship which prevailed between England and Scotland during the reign of King Alexander III. Alas, in Edward of Caernarvon England possessed one of the stupidest kings who have ever sat upon her throne, and among the ranks of his baronage and higher clergy (with the possible exception of Aymer de Valence, earl of Pembroke) one may search in vain for anything resembling statesmanship. Perhaps the nearest approach to peace had come in 1312 or 1313, after the collapse of King Edward's second Scottish expedition. The negotiations, though encouraged by Philip the Fair, had failed, and there seemed no possibility of the English king recognizing Robert Bruce's title to the throne of Scotland. The challenge of Stirling Castle was thus the occasion rather than the cause of a head-on clash between the forces of the two countries. Reluctantly perhaps, but methodically and with determination, Bruce began to prepare his troops for the greatest trial of strength they had yet faced.

[1] For the Inchture parliament the authority is a document in Duncan, MS.

12

Bannockburn

(i) *The preparations*

THE immediate objective of Edward II's invasion of Scotland in 1314 was the relief of Stirling Castle. It is clear, however, from the scale of his preparations, from the size of the army he raised, and from the language of his writs of summons, that the English king's real purpose was 'to put down and suppress the wicked rebellion of Robert Bruce and his accomplices in the king's land of Scotland'.[1] In short, the outcome was to be conquest and the final settlement of the 'Scottish Question'. His last expedition, in 1310 and 1311, had been a failure. It was undertaken in the face of almost universal hostility, or at least lack of co-operation, on the part of the English baronage. In 1314 the political scene augured better. Contemporaries say that many barons went over to the king's side because of disgust at the killing of Piers Gaveston.[2] Certainly Edward was well supported by the young earl of Gloucester, by the earl of Hereford, and by Aymer de Valence, since 1307 earl of Pembroke. Valence, superseded in his wardenship of Scotland in September 1307, was reappointed warden in March 1314 with wide powers.[3] The most prominent figure among the king's baronial opponents, Thomas, earl of Lancaster, had already begun to lose such respect as might once have been accorded him in virtue of his five earldoms, his doubly royal descent and his possession of the largest private estate in England. Both Lancaster and another leading opponent, Guy Beauchamp, earl of Warwick, had been formally though not sincerely reconciled with the king in October 1313.[4] The higher ranks

[1] *Rotuli Scotiae*, i, 118, 119b, etc.
[2] *Chron. Lanercost*, 219.
[3] *Rotuli Scotiae*, i, 119a.
[4] *Vita Edwardi*, 43.

of the baronage were, temporarily at least, no longer the stumbling block in the path of Edward's admittedly erratic ambition to complete his father's work north of the Border.

As early as November 28th, 1313, Edward had written to his remaining supporters in Scotland promising to have an army at Berwick before next midsummer.[1] This was in reply to a letter purporting to come from 'the people of Scotland'. In fact, it was sent by the earl of Dunbar and Sir Adam Gordon, evidently on behalf of the men of the earldom of Dunbar and its neighbourhood. They had been suffering greatly at the hands of English and Scots alike, and claimed to have paid £20,000 to Bruce in blackmail, though the figure is too large to credit. Edward's reply was perfunctory or absent minded enough to be addressed to 'archbishops' (among others), although Scotland had none. But it shows that already by the end of November Edward was taking the challenge of Stirling seriously. A month later (December 23rd) writs of summons for military service, naming a rendezvous at Berwick on June 10th, 1314, were sent to Thomas of Lancaster, seven other earls, and eighty-seven barons.[2] During February Edward again declared his intention to lead an army against the Scots in the summer, and already his advice was that the campaign would be largely an affair of infantry.[3]

Accordingly, from about March 9th onwards he began to issue the stream of orders necessary to raise and equip a large infantry force and also to supply a full-scale land and sea expedition.[4] Ships and sailors were demanded from practically every English port of any consequence. If the summonses were obeyed more than sixty vessels should have appeared, to serve under John Sturmy and Peter Bard as joint 'captains and admirals of the fleet'. Many of the ships' names are known to us from the enrolled lists, such as the *Christopher* of Westminster, the *Plenty* of Great Yarmouth, the *Welfare*, the *Valence* and the *Blithe*. The king hoped to raise considerable forces in Ireland and provided the necessary shipping to bring them over. The earl of

---

[1] *Rotuli Scotiae*, i, 114b.

[2] *Cal. Close Rolls, 1313–18*, 86.

[3] *Cal. Chancery Warrants*, i, 395 (February 26th), 398 (April 20th); cf. *Rotuli Scotiae*, i, 120a.

[4] See J. E. Morris, *Bannockburn* (1914), 40–1; and *Rotuli Scotiae*, i, 115ff.

10. The terrain of Bannockburn

Ulster (Robert Bruce's father-in-law) was put in command of the
Irish effort. Summonses were sent to many chiefs of the native Irish,
as well as to a fair selection of Anglo-Irish barons and knights. They
were assured that service east of the Irish Sea would not be made a
precedent. Several historians have cast serious doubts upon Irish
participation in the campaign.[1] The earl of Ulster at least appears to
have been with the English king at Newminster on May 29th, 1314,[2]
and it is hard to believe he would have come empty-handed. The
accounts available to Barbour fifty years later were that Edward II
had with him 'a great following from Ireland'.[3] Ireland was also
expected to provide bowmen and provisions.

About 5,000 infantry were called up from north and south Wales,
probably a mixture of spearmen and archers respectively. The total
is surprisingly small compared with twice that number of Welshmen
who had been on the Falkirk campaign of 1298. On March 9th
writs were sent to the midland and northern counties of England
demanding some 4,500 men armed with bows. On March 24th this
order was superseded by a more extensive call-up which demanded
the levying of over 16,000 foot from thirteen English counties. A
hundred crossbowmen and archers were called for from Bristol.[4] All
told (including the Welsh but excluding any estimate of Irish foot
and auxiliary groups such as masons etc.) the infantry required by
Edward II for his invasion amounted to some 21,640 men, who were
to gather at Wark-on-Tweed on June 10th.[5] Whether anything like
this number actually turned up is, of course, another matter. Desertion was common at all stages of a campaign, and often sheriffs were
simply unable to find the totals required. Lacking any documentary
evidence we are forced to fall back on estimates which are not much
better than guess-work. But at least we can try to make intelligent
guesses. Dr J. E. Morris, basing his estimates on his extensive knowledge of Edward I's Welsh campaigns and of English campaigns in
Scotland prior to 1314, suggested that Edward II may have succeeded

[1] Morris, op. cit., 35; *Complete Peerage*, xi, Appendix B, 11. M. McKisack, *The
Fourteenth Century*, 35, speaks of 'possibly, some Irish'.
[2] *Cal. Pat. Rolls, 1313–17*, 121; *Cal. Chancery Warrants*, i, 402.
[3] Barbour, *Bruce*, 194.
[4] Morris, *Bannockburn*, 40; *Rotuli Scotiae*, i, 120b.
[5] Ibid., 120b and 126–7.

in getting together some 15,000 foot.[1] Morris was in principle reluctant to accept the possibility of large concentrations of infantry
in Edwardian wars, but he was not aware that in 1296 as many as
60,000 infantry were in pay at Newcastle ready for the campaign
against Balliol.[2] Although it is virtually certain that nothing like this
number was actually employed in the 1296 campaign, the fact that
so large a force was collected at one time and place should put us on
our guard against modern writers who pour scorn on all large estimates. One recent account of the Bannockburn campaign, whose
inclusion in the *Complete Peerage* has unfortunately given it un-
deserved authority, proposes to reduce the infantry available to
Edward II in 1314 to a mere 5,000 all told.[3] This contrasts sharply
with Morris's experienced and intelligent guess-work, and indeed
hardly deserves serious consideration. But in any case, the actual
numbers of infantry in the English army are not of great historical
importance, for the battle of Bannockburn was a contest between
Scottish infantry and English cavalry: the English foot, contrary to
Edward II's surmise in February, played a very small part.

There are similar difficulties in estimating the cavalry, the really
important element in Edward's army. As Morris points out,[4] there
was no formal summons of the feudal host by parliamentary consent
and in consequence we have no marshal's roll to guide us, and no
later remissions of scutage. Nor have we any list of the valuable
trained war-horses brought to the campaign, such as survive for
several years between 1296 and 1314 when English cavalry was active
in Scotland. We are told explicitly by contemporary chroniclers that
all but three of the English earls refused to serve personally.[5] Taking
their cue, presumably, from Lancaster and Warwick, they sent the
minimum number of mounted troops required under their feudal
obligation of military service. In Morris's view this might have been
as few as sixty knights and men-at-arms from all these great noblemen together, a dismal performance by men bearing the proud
titles of Lancaster, Warwick, Arundel, Surrey (Warenne), and

[1] Morris, *Bannockburn*, 41.
[2] See above, p. 96, n. 4.
[3] *Complete Peerage*, xi, Appendix B.
[4] Morris, *Bannockburn*, 34.
[5] *Vita Edwardi*, 49–50; *Chron. Lanercost*, 224.

Oxford. (Norfolk, the king's half-brother, does not seem to have served either, but he was only fourteen.) The sheriffs were ordered to raise the feudal service due from the great ecclesiastical lords, the archbishops, bishops and abbots. If the bare minimum of service was rendered from this source it may have totalled some 150 mounted men. On the other hand, a large number of barons below the rank of earl were present willingly, and with them were Humphrey de Bohun earl of Hereford and Constable of England, Gilbert de Clare earl of Gloucester, and Aymer de Valence earl of Pembroke. These magnates may be expected to have brought with them vastly more than the minimum number of knights and men-at-arms which they owed by way of feudal service. The Scotch Roll preserves copies of letters of protection issued to Pembroke, Gloucester and the rest to cover some 890 mounted soldiers (knights, esquires and the more lightly armoured men-at-arms).[1] Morris thinks it not unreasonable to multiply this figure by 2½ or even 3 to arrive at the actual total of mounted troops present at the muster at Berwick on June 10th: some 2,000 or 2,500 men.[2]

To this provisional total we must add an even less certain figure of Scottish and Irish knights and of knights from Gascony and other continental countries. Their number was doubtless small, but there are no grounds for questioning Barbour's report that knights came to fight for Edward II from France, Brittany, Poitou, Guienne and Germany. The English king may have been a poor exponent of the art of government but he was not a poltroon. On the contrary, he was a tall, robust, athletic man of considerable physical courage. He was no general, but it is not true that he took no personal interest in the details of the campaign or in the men who were to fight under his standard. In August and October 1313, for example, he wrote no fewer than eleven separate letters to, among others, the *podestà* and city of Genoa and to both the emperors as well as to the empress of Constantinople, interceding for the release of one of his best knights, Sir Giles d'Argentan, who while going to fight at Rhodes had been captured by Christians and imprisoned at Salonika.[3] Sir Giles was

[1] Morris, *Bannockburn*, 34-5, makes the total of protections 830. My own count is about 890. The source is the Scottish Roll for 8 Edward II, P.R.O., C.71/7, m. 1, m. 5.
[2] Morris, *Bannockburn*, 35.
[3] *Cal. Close Rolls, 1313–18*, 76.

duly released and came home to fight his last battle at Bannockburn. Barbour, who mourned his death there, tells us that he was accounted 'the third-best knight of his day'.[1]

Chroniclers' estimates of the number of English cavalry vary, but possibly not so widely as is sometimes alleged. The *Life of Edward II*, certainly written by someone with first-hand or authoritative information about Scottish affairs, puts the total at 'more than 2,000';[2] a Scottish verse account seems to say 3,100;[3] Barbour himself, though he speaks absurdly enough of 40,000 horse, says that there were 3,000 'barded' or 'covered' horse,[4] and if this is the realistic part of his estimate, actually referring to all types of cavalry, it tallies well enough with the other versions. Even if the total was as low as 2,000, that would still represent a very respectable cavalry force, roughly equal to the English cavalry which fought at Falkirk. And Morris is surely wrong to say that 'the English went into battle unprepared and untrained'.[5] They were in fact led by men like Hereford, Sir Hugh Despenser, Sir Henry Beaumont, Sir Robert Clifford, Sir Maurice Berkeley, Sir Marmaduke Tweng, Sir Pain Tiptoft, Sir Giles d'Argentan and many others who were veterans of both Welsh and Scottish wars. In their ranks were Scots, such as Sir Ingram de Umfraville, who had not only fought on the Scottish side but had held the highest positions of command. Above all, in Aymer de Valence the English had a leader who knew Scotland inside out and enjoyed the rare distinction of having been in command against Bruce himself in two pitched battles, the first in open country at Methven, where he won, the second on a narrow site at Loudoun Hill, where he was beaten. If excuses must be sought for the English defeat in 1314, they cannot be found in lack of experience or training. It is surely more sensible not to look for excuses but to acknowledge that for every victory there must also be a defeat. King Edward had an excellent army at Bannockburn, but it made some grave tactical errors and ultimately it was outfought.

King Robert also had an excellent army, but vastly different in

---

[1] Barbour, *Bruce*, 234-5. He had fought at Methven, *Cal. Docs. Scot.*, v, No. 492.
[2] *Vita Edwardi*, 50.
[3] *Chron. Bower*, ii, 248.
[4] Barbour, *Bruce*, 194.
[5] Morris, *Bannockburn*, 49.

character and composition from the English. It was excellent above all else in *morale*. Its core consisted of men who had fought continuously for the past seven years under Bruce himself or under Douglas, Randolph and other famous captains. Almost always they had had the best of the fighting, and their king had gained a European reputation. But they were essentially an infantry army, armed with long iron-tipped spears, with axes, swords, and (to a less extent) with bows.[1] Before 1314 Bruce had not tried to recreate the old 'feudal host' of Scotland. Not only had it been discredited by Dunbar and other events of the time of Comyn ascendancy, but even if Bruce had felt it desirable to reintroduce such a force the necessary armour and trained, large-boned war horses were not to be had in Scotland. *Destriers* were not bred in Scotland, where in winter there was no fodder for animals with such large appetites.[2] All that Bruce had were some 500 light horse under the Marischal, Sir Robert Keith. The rest fought on foot. Despite Stirling Bridge (which was not a battle of the first rank) and Courtrai (which might have been a fluke) the possibility that an army of spearmen could defeat heavy cavalry had still to be convincingly demonstrated. Moreover, in point of numbers it is very doubtful if the Scots could come anywhere near to matching their foes. Unfortunately there is absolutely no reliable evidence on which to base an estimate of Scottish numbers at Bannockburn. Barbour believed that the Scots' strength was about one third that of the English.[3] If this were so, they would have had some 6,000 men against an English army of 2,500 horse and 15,000 foot. But we have no reason to accept or reject Barbour's belief; he may have put the ratio too low, to enhance his hero's merits. We have seen that in 1308 Bruce was thought to have had 3,000 men in Ross and 10,000–15,000 (surely a gross exaggeration?) in Argyll. The forces employed in Bruce's raids south of the Border were too strong to be resisted by the local population, but in view of the breakdown of the Border defence system this is not very significant. If we are to make guesses at all it might be safer to work from estimates which put the total population of Scotland in Bruce's day at about 400,000.[4] This in

[1] Above, p. 94, n. 2.
[2] *Chron. Lanercost*, 214.
[3] Barbour, *Bruce*, 194, 198: 100,000 English to 30,000 Scots.
[4] T. M. Cooper, Lord Cooper, in *SHR*, xxvi, 2–9; cf. the same author's *Supra Crepidam*.

turn, on a liberal calculation, might give us a figure for men of
fighting age of 80,000–100,000. No medieval country could ever
hope to raise, train and keep in the field more than a small fraction of
its able-bodied males. A tenth would probably be a generous
estimate, and this would allow Bruce not more than 10,000. To put
the strength of the Scots army at Bannockburn at between 7,000 and
10,000 would be no more than a guess, but probably not a wild
guess. Moreover, this would be a comprehensive figure, including
many who would take no part in the actual fighting. In terms of
effective participants, we may perhaps reckon on a light cavalry
force of 500 and four brigades or 'battles' of 1,000 to 1,500 each; say,
5,000–6,000 men. On the other hand, we can scarcely put the Scots
total any lower, for we know that the English cavalry was in fact
repulsed by mere foot soldiers, and it is hard to believe this could
have happened if the ratio of foot to horse had been less than 2 : 1.

The rendezvous appointed by King Robert was the Torwood.[1] This
was the ancient woodland stretching from the banks of the River
Carron west of Falkirk as far as the Bannock Burn, two and a half
miles south of Stirling. In the twelfth century it had been known by
the Gaelic name of Keltor (coille torr), 'wood of rocky outcrops'.[2] In
Bruce's time, the area was referred to by persons writing in French as
les Torres, and the Guardians had in fact dated one of their letters to
Edward I in 1299 'at the forest del Torre'.[3] It was a well-chosen
rendezvous, better than Wallace's position east of Falkirk in 1298.
There was good cover; to the west were hills and broken country; to
the north and east boggy 'carseland', that is, low-lying ground beside
a tidal estuary. Through the forest ran the high road from Edinburgh
to Stirling, on a line about 250 feet above sea-level, pioneered by the
Roman soldiers who built a marching way from the Antonine Wall
through to Strathallan and Strathearn. The enemy would have to
traverse this road, as William the Conqueror and Edward the Conqueror had done before them. Bruce was gathering his men in the
Torwood by the middle of May at latest, for on May 27th King
Edward, then at Newminster in Northumberland, wrote to his

[1] Barbour, Bruce, 197.
[2] G. W. S. Barrow, Acts of Malcolm IV, No. 46.
[3] APS, i, 454; cf. Stevenson, Documents, Nos. 632, 634; Cal. Docs. Scot., ii, No.
1432; Chron. Lanercost, 225.

sheriffs and recruiting officers to say that 'the Scots are striving to assemble great numbers of foot in strong and marshy places, extremely hard for cavalry to penetrate, between us and our castle of Stirling'.[1] He commanded them to urge the infantry forward as fast as possible, or else Stirling would have to surrender.

Bruce, however, did not mean to fight in the Torwood, and had not even decided whether to give battle at all. The English host left Berwick and Wark about June 17th.[2] Contemporaries described it as 'a very fine and large army', 'more than 2,000 armoured horse and a very large number of infantry', and wrote with amazement of the waggons carrying provisions and equipment: 'if they had been lined up end to end they would have stretched for twenty miles'.[3] The route taken was the same as Edward I's in 1298, up Lauderdale and over Soutra Moor to Edinburgh[4] – again on the general line, although not necessarily in the exact path, of a Roman road. Time was running short if the king was to keep his promise to be before Stirling by June 24th. The army was urged forward unsparingly during those warm midsummer days: 'short time was allowed for sleep, still shorter for meals'.[5] There was a brief halt at Edinburgh, reached about June 19th, and then on Saturday 22nd, when there would have been some nineteen or twenty hours of daylight, the whole army marched the twenty miles to Falkirk.[6] Fifteen miles and an army now lay between them and their goal. On this same Saturday the Scots were drawn up in the Torwood in four brigades, as for retreat.[7] Thomas Randolph, earl of Moray, led the vanguard, the brigade nearest to Stirling. The king, commanding the rearguard, covered the retreat at the extreme eastern end of the Scottish position. In between, side by side, were the other two brigades. One was nominally under the command of Walter the Stewart, the heir, though younger son, of James the Stewart. Since he was a mere youth, the actual command was held by James Douglas, Walter

[1] *Rotuli Scotiae*, i, 126–7.
[2] *Vita Edwardi*, 50.
[3] Ibid., where the writer also says: 'All who were present agreed that never in our times has such an army gone forth from England.'
[4] *Cal. Docs. Scot.*, iii, No. 365.
[5] *Vita Edwardi*, 51.
[6] Barbour, *Bruce*, 201, 204.
[7] Ibid., 200–1.

Stewart's cousin.[1] The fact that Douglas, who had already proved himself one of Bruce's most brilliant captains, should even nominally yield command to the hereditary Stewart of Scotland is a notable illustration of the conservatism of Scottish feudal society. But of course the arrangement did not prevent full use being made of Douglas's generalship. The other brigade was commanded by the king's brother Edward. Barbour gives us the composition only of the king's brigade.[2] It comprised the men of Carrick (although Edward Bruce was now earl of Carrick), the men of Argyll, Bute and the Isles,[3] many under Angus Macdonald of Islay, and 'ane mekill rout' of men from the 'playne land', presumably meaning the central lowlands and perhaps Fife and Strathmore. It is common-sense reasoning, not contemporary evidence, which suggests that Moray's brigade was made up of men from Moray and elsewhere in the north, Edward Bruce's of men from the south-west, including Galloway, and the Stewart-Douglas brigade of men from Strathclyde. During Saturday, as the English army made the last of its forced marches, the Scots withdrew from the Torwood to the next position chosen by Bruce, the wooded 'New Park',[4] a stretch of enclosed hunting preserve roughly one mile from north to south by two miles from east to west. At the point where the road entered it the New Park was set back half a mile north of the Bannock Burn, a fair sized stream which formed the only serious natural obstacle (apart from forest) between the Carron and Stirling. In the New Park they retained their order for retreat. The vanguard was now beside St Ninians kirk, only a mile or so from Stirling castle. Douglas and Edward Bruce were slightly to the south. The king's brigade halted at the 'entry' to the New Park. This was the point where the main road entered the woodland, on the edge of the higher ground overlooking the Bannock Burn from the north and west. Here, partly hidden by trees, King Robert and the men of his brigade took up their position towards evening on Saturday, June 22nd, and watched for the first signs of the great host which had now approached so near.

[1] Barbour, *Bruce*, 200, 226. It is strange that James Douglas was knighted only on the eve of Bannockburn, ibid., 221; presumably his promotion was to the rank of banneret.
[2] Ibid.
[3] Again strange, since Bute was in the Stewart's lordship.
[4] Ibid., 201–2.

(ii) The site of the battle

At this point our narrative too must halt. The battle of Bannockburn was a complex affair occupying two days. Its course cannot be understood unless we have some general knowledge of the terrain and some degree of certainty about the actual localities in which the successive phases of the conflict took place. At the risk of putting the cart before the horse it seems better to establish the site of the battle before resuming the story.

Historians have given serious consideration to four different sites. The so-called 'traditional' site, now marked by a statue, is at the Borestone, between Milton and St Ninians. The Reverend Thomas Miller and Brigadier-General Carruthers proposed a small but important modification of this site, which would place the main battle about half to three-quarters of a mile further east, on the Dryfield of Balquhiderock.[1] According to Dr Mackay Mackenzie's revolutionary hypothesis, the main battle was fought right down on the Carse of Stirling, in the vicinity of Upper Taylorton and Muirton two miles north-east of the traditional site and the same distance due north of Bannockburn village.[2] Recently, General Sir Philip Christison has put forward a case for locating the main battle in the triangle formed by the Bannock Burn, its tributary the Pelstream Burn and the 50 foot contour: that is, in what used to be called the Carse of Balquhiderock.[3] The Christison site is about half way between the traditional and the Mackenzie site.

These suggestions can be weighed only if we have in our mind's eye some idea of the surrounding terrain. The country east and south of Stirling is divided into three clearly-marked zones, radiating from Stirling Castle like three successive segments of a circle. First, in the north, is the great Carse of Stirling, flat, boggy ground which in 1314

[1] T. Miller, The site of the battle of Bannockburn (Historical Association, 1931); R. A. Carruthers, 'The site of the battle of Bannockburn', Chambers Journal (February, 1933), reprinted as an appendix to Barron, Scottish War of Independence.

[2] W. Mackay Mackenzie, The Battle of Bannockburn: a study in mediaeval warfare (1913); his hypothesis being first adumbrated in a paper in Proceedings of the Glasgow Archaeological Society for 1908–9. See also his sadly crotchety The Bannockburn Myth (Edinburgh, 1932), a reply to Miller.

[3] P. Christison, 'Bannockburn – 23rd and 24th June, 1314. A study in military history', Proc. Soc. Antiq. Scot., xc (1956–7, pub. 1959), 170–9; subsequently republished in a revised form as Bannockburn: the story of the battle (National Trust for Scotland, revised edn., 1962).

consisted in places, but apparently not everywhere, of a deep layer of peat lying on impervious clay.[1] This carseland is bordered on the north by the sinuous course of the tidal River Forth. The southern edge of the carse is clearly marked by a steep bank at the 50 foot contour, which follows a remarkably straight line south-eastward from Stirling. South-west of this comes the second or intermediate zone, some two to three miles wide, consisting of better-drained ground, firm though undulating, rising gradually from 50 feet to about 300 feet. Westward of this zone, sloping steadily upward from 300 feet, is broken country of poor soil, which rises without any break to the rough muirland and hills around the headwaters of the Carron and the Bannock Burn, 1,400 feet to 1,800 feet above the sea. It is vital for an understanding of the terrain as a whole and of the battle of Bannockburn in particular to realize that a considerable quantity of water drains off this hilly country through the intermediate zone and down into the carse, where in the fourteenth century it had somehow or other to make its way across peat and clay only a few feet above the level of high tide. In addition, a fair number of springs rise in the intermediate zone itself, and especially along its northern edge, at the foot of the bank marking the 50 foot contour. As a result, the carse was intersected by a large number of sluggish streams, some big, most of them little. These streams were known by the Celtic word *pol* ('pow' in later Scots) which in southern and central Scotland was widely applied to burns flowing sluggishly through carseland, often having deep peaty pools with crumbling, overhanging banks.[2] Today the Carse of Stirling is relatively well-drained farmland, interspersed with coal mines and railway tracks. The pows have largely disappeared, but their presence

---

[1] Authorities of the Geological Survey are quoted as saying that the peat had been removed from the Carse of Stirling long before 1314; but documentary evidence of the fourteenth and sixteenth centuries shows that peats were still being cut then in parts of the Carse.

[2] For this see W. J. Watson, *Celtic Place-Names of Scotland*, 204; where, however, the widespread use of *pol* to mean a sluggish stream in carseland throughout eastern and central Scotland is not brought out. Examples of *pol* or *pow* in this region, by counties, are: Aberdeen: Powis, now Den Burn, in Old Aberdeen; Mearns: Powburn in Laurencekirk; Angus: Pow Burn in Farnell, Powmyre in Airlie; Perth: Powgavie (formerly Polgavethin), Carse of Gowrie, Pow Water (formerly Polpefery), in Fowlis Wester etc., Carpow in Abernethy; Kinross: Pow Burn in Fossoway etc. Compare Powburn in North Northumberland, a sluggish tributary of the Breamish.

in former times is betrayed by place-names. In the parish of St Ninians alone (where the battle of Bannockburn was fought) one may still list Polmaise, Cockspow, Drypow, Powdrake, Powside, Powbridge, Pow Burn and the *Pel*stream Burn, while just across the Forth is the old estate of Powis.[1] Polmaise, indeed, which means 'sluggish stream in the plain', may well have been the ancient name of the Bannock Burn itself, for this stream is the largest of the pows between Stirling and the Carron. Not surprisingly, the entire Carse of Stirling was known in Bruce's time simply as *les Polles*, 'the pows',[2] the generic term for all these slow-running streams having become the colloquial name of a district, just as the district of the Torwood was known as *les Torres*.

Historians of Bannockburn have failed to grasp the fact that the carse was known as *les Polles* from the streams which intersected it, or else they have not seen the implications of this fact. On the contrary, most writers, especially Mackenzie and those who have followed him, not only supposed, quite mistakenly, that the *polles* were *pools*,[3] but have located these pools well to the north, in the 'buckle of the Forth', close to the tidal mouth of the Bannock Burn. Most modern sketch-maps of the battle are disfigured by a pimply rash of these imaginary pools. The point is important because the *polles* had their part to play in the battle and have been cited in various ways as evidence of where it was fought.

For an army approaching Stirling from the south-east, the choice of route was thus extremely restricted. The westernmost zone of moor and hills was quite impracticable. The northern zone, the *Pows*, was hardly less so, for although it was level enough it was boggy and intersected by countless streams of uncertain depth. These would be no obstacle to a man on foot, nor to small parties of

---

[1] All these are on the 1-inch Ordnance Map, except for Pelstream, taken from the article by General Christison, above, 302, n. 3.

[2] Stevenson, *Documents*, Nos. 632, 634; *Chron. Guisb.*, 303: *iuxta polles, ad polles*.

[3] Mackenzie, *Battle of Bannockburn*; Barron, *Scottish War of Independence*; J. D. Mackie, *SHR*, xxvi, 189–90. Sir Herbert Maxwell, in one of his rare flights of accuracy, saw that Barbour's *pollis* must be the Scots 'pows' or sluggish streams with which he was familiar in Galloway and elsewhere, and that the makeshift bridging would obviously be required for streams, not for pools, *SHR*, xi, 246, n. 1. But Sir Herbert did not realize that the whole region of the Carse was known as 'the Pows'; and in any case his own suggested site for the battle is quite unacceptable.

horsemen; but cumulatively they would reduce a large army with
its baggage train to helpless floundering. The advance therefore could
only be by way of the intermediate zone of undulating wooded
country; ideally, along the high road which naturally followed a line
through the middle of this zone.

The New Park was merely a northerly continuation of the Torwood, from which it was separated by the open cultivated ground of
the Bannock Burn valley. The park had been fenced in by King
Alexander III as late as 1264 – hence 'New Park' to distinguish it
from the older 'King's Park' just beneath Stirling Castle.[1] But despite
what is shown on the maps of many modern historians, the New
Park (as Miller made clear)[2] did not extend right across the intermediate zone from the hills on the west to the very edge of the carse
on the north-east. It is true that the high road ran into the park, at the
'entry', and then through the park to St Ninians kirk. But east of the
park were the lands of Balquhiderock, which were under cultivation
for corn in 1215[3] and can hardly have been swallowed up by forest
as a result of King Alexander's creation of the New Park fifty years
later. Like most estates on the edge of the intermediate zone,
Balquhiderock had a share of that zone, known as 'dryfield', and a
share of the peaty carse.

The terrain in the neighbourhood of the Scots position, as it would
appear to the English, may therefore be pictured as follows. On one
side the main road ran down out of the Torwood and over some
open country, to cross the Bannock Burn at Milton, and then up
across more open ground to enter fairly thick woodland near the
Borestone. On the other side, well to the east, there was a plateau of
open cornland, some half a mile wide, between the woodland and
the bank where the hard ground slopes steeply to the carse.

One further point must be insisted upon before this survey of the
terrain is complete. Few historians have given it serious thought, yet

---

[1] *Exch. Rolls*, i, 24, 38; cf. *Dunfermline Registrum*, No. 215 (1215) and F. W.
Maitland, *Memoranda de Parliamento*, 212 (1305), which show the king's serjeants
holding or claiming land, rights, etc., in Skeoch and in the Old and New Parks.

[2] See the map attached to his *Site of the battle of Bannockburn*.

[3] *Dunfermline Registrum*, No. 215. The ancient name of Balquhiderock would
hardly have survived continuously as a farm-name had this area been out of cultivation for a long stretch.

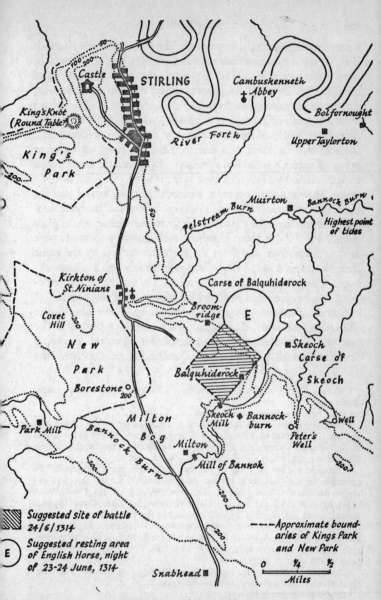

Castle

King's Knot
(Round Table?)

STIRLING

Cambuskenneth
Abbey

Bol fornought

Upper Taylorton

King's
Park

River Forth

Pelstream Burn

Muirton

Bannock Burn

Highest point
of tides

Kirkton of
St. Ninians

Carse of Balquhiderock

E

Broom-
ridge

Coxet
Hill

New

Park

Skeoch

Carse of
Skeoch

Balquhiderock

Borestone

Milton
Bog

Park Mill

Bannock Burn

Skeoch
Mill

Bannock-
burn

Well

Peter's
Well

Milton

Mill of Bannok

Snabhead

Suggested site of battle
24/6/1314

E   Suggested resting area
of English Horse, night
of 23-24 June, 1314

--- Approximate bound-
aries of Kings Park
and New Park

0   ¼   ½
Miles

11. The terrain of Bannockburn

it seems a point of crucial importance. The place where the Bannock
Burn crosses the intermediate zone and (flowing here between high,
steep banks in a miniature ravine) enters the carse was in 1314 an
inhabited locality with a long history behind it. It was called Bannok,
a name which must go far back into the Celtic past.[1] No doubt we
must not speak of Bannok as a 'village', with its implications of a
close-knit huddle of houses along a village street. Nevertheless,
Bannok was the name of a distinct inhabited place, an estate or
group of estates, a social and agrarian entity within the larger parish
of St Ninians. Moreover, Bannok was the name of a *place*, not of a
stream. The stream known as the Bannock Burn was named after the
place, not the other way round.[2] And even the name 'Bannockburn'
was itself coming to be applied in the fourteenth century to the place
called Bannok.[3] For about a century and a half the two names were
used as alternatives, but from the late fifteenth century the name
Bannok dropped out, being completely superseded by Bannockburn.[4] There is no reason to believe that the nucleus of this settlement is not represented today by the village of Bannockburn.

Bannok, *alias* Bannockburn, was large enough to have subdivisions.
The upland part was Ochtirbannok, 'high ground of Bannok'.[5] The
part where the Bannock Burn entered the carse was known as
Skeoch.[6] This tell-tale name shows that Bannok was associated by a

---

[1] Watson, *Celtic Place-Names of Scotland*, 195–6. Probably Bannok was a vestigial
district name.

[2] Ibid., *bannauc* or *bannog* meaning 'peaked', 'having peaks'.

[3] The canon of Bridlington (*Gesta Edwardi de Carnarvan*, ed. Stubbs, 46) and John
de Trokelow (*Annales*, ed. Riley, 124), both English writers, seem to be the earliest
to use the name Bannockburn apparently for the place. But see the story told in
Chron. Bower, ii, 247–8; cf. also *Cal. Docs. Scots.*, ii, No. 1636.

[4] Chronicles use Bannockburn for the place sooner than formal title-deeds. The
authorities for the statement in the text are as follows. (1) Scottish chronicles and
comparable sources: *Chron. Holyrood*, 180; *Chron. Fordun*, i, 342, 346; *Chron. Bower*,
ii, 243, 245, 246, 247–8, 251, 254, 255; *Chron. Pluscarden*, i, 237, 240; *Chron. Wyntoun*
(Laing), ii, 312, 403, iii, 336; *Glasgow Registrum*, No. 327. (2) Scottish record sources:
Dunfermline Registrum, No. 215; *Cambuskenneth Registrum*, No. 210; *Reg. Mag. Sig.*,
i, Nos. 464, 357, 759, Appendix II, Nos. 237–9, 580–1, 1643; ii, Nos. 1879, 1960,
3363, 3494; iv, Nos. 1799, 1973, 1630; vi, Nos. 1162, 1243; *Retours*, Stirling, Nos.
121, 215, 236, 255, 257, 261, 331, 361.

[5] *Dunfermline Registrum*, No. 215; *Cambuskenneth Registrum*, No. 210; *Reg. Mag.
Sig.*, i, Nos. 357, 759, and many other references passim.

[6] *Dunfermline Registrum*, No. 215.

cult dedication with an obscure saint called Skeoch, an Irishwoman of the sixth century.[1] Saint Skeoch was commemorated at a holy well near St Ninians called after her Tibbermasko, 'Saint Skeoch's Well'.[2] At Bannok there was a chapel dedicated to the Blessed Virgin and called 'the chapel of Skeoch *alias* Bannockburn'.[3] It may be guessed that originally this was dedicated to Skeoch herself. On the Bannockburn there seem to have been two mills, the first to be mentioned (1215) being the 'mill of Bannoc',[4] while we have later references to the 'mill of Bannockburn called "le mylne de Skeoch" or "Skeochmilne" '.[5] The mill of Bannok presumably stood at Milton, where the main road crossed the burn; Skeoch Mill is half a mile further downstream. There was plenty of cornland in the Bannock Burn valley to justify these mills: record of 1215 mentions corn tithes payable from Skeoch, Balquhiderock and Ochtirbannok.[6]

It has been necessary to demonstrate at such length the existence of an old-established locality of Bannok or Bannockburn because historians have assumed that the battle of Bannockburn was named not after a place but after the stream. It is at least reasonable to suppose that if a geographical name is given to a battle it bears some relation to the actual site. The naming of the battle of Bannockburn is illuminating. At first, as one might expect, the battle was not given any name at all. None of our three best early chronicle sources, the *Life of Edward the Second*, the Lanercost Chronicle and the *Scalacronica*, refers to the battle by name; even Barbour, whose account is much the longest we have, does not give it a name himself, although this is supplied in a chapter-heading added much later. Next, there seems to have been a tendency, at least among those far from the scene, to refer to it as the 'battle of Stirling', obviously taking the name of the nearest well-known place, and of the castle for whose possession the battle was fought. This was used in south-country

---

[1] J. M. Mackinlay, *Ancient Church Dedications in Scotland*, ii (Non-Scriptural), 503; cf. the same author's *The Influence of the Pre-Reformation Church on Scottish Place-Names* (1904), 25–6.

[2] *Reg. Mag. Sig.*, ii, No. 3494.

[3] Ibid., iv, No. 1630; *Retours*, Stirling, No. 121, etc.

[4] *Dunfermline Registrum*, No. 215.

[5] *Reg. Mag. Sig.*, ii, No. 1960, thereafter many references, e.g., *Retours*, Stirling, No. 236.

[6] *Dunfermline Registrum*, No. 215.

chronicles written at St Albans and London[1] and in letters written by Englishmen in the period 1314–1319.[2] But contemporary with this English usage we find, in Scottish sources only, that writers referred to the 'battle of Bannok', and events were actually dated '*ante* Bannok'.[3] It was possible, in Scotland, to write of the 'battle of Bannok' as late as the fifteenth century.[4] Almost, but not quite, as early to appear was the familiar 'battle of Bannockburn', invariably used in modern times. Two English chroniclers, John de Trokelowe and the canon of Bridlington, writing in the 1320's and 1330's respectively, already used this name,[5] and it occurs in an English inquest of 1357.[6] It was taken up by Scottish writers considerably later. John Fordun (1384–7) does not use it, but his fifteenth-century editors and continuators introduced it into their versions of his chronicle, and Andrew Wyntoun (c. 1420) speaks twice of the battle of Bannockburn.[7]

Lastly, we should note that some fourteenth-century writers tell us roughly where the battle took place, whether or not they give it a formal name. John de Trokelowe says that the battle was fought 'in the place called *Bannokesmora*' ('on the muir of Bannok').[8] A Welsh chronicle, the *Brut y Tywysogion*, in what is probably the earliest surviving reference to the battle, says it was fought in *y polles*,[9] that is, in *les Polles* or the Pows, the general name for the district of the Carse of Stirling. *Bannokesmora* would appear to be preserved today as Muir of Bannockburn, south of the modern village, an impossible site for the main battle. Alternatively this name might refer to the

---

[1] Trokelow, *Annales* (ed. Riley), 83; *Annales Londonienses* (ed. Stubbs), 231; *Annales Paulini* (ed. Stubbs), 276.

[2] *Cal. Docs. Scots.*, iii, Nos. 626, 627, 682. Cf. *Henry of Pytchley's Book of Fees*, ed. W. T. Mellows, Northants Record Society (1927), 91; 'Gilbert de Clare died killed in battle in Scotland at Stirling.'

[3] *Chron. Holyrood*, 180; *Chron. Fordun*, i, 342; *APS*, i, 682b.

[4] *Chron. Bower*, ii, 243, 245, 254.

[5] Trokelow, *Annales*, 124 (for *Baumkesburne* read *Bannukesburne*); *Gesta Edwardi de Carnarvan*, 46.

[6] *Cal. Docs. Scot.*, iii, No. 1636.

[7] *Chron. Fordun*, i, 346; *Chron. Bower*, ii, 246 etc.; *Chron. Pluscarden*, i, 237, 240; *Chron. Wyntoun* (Laing), ii, 312, 403.

[8] Trokelow, *Annales*, 86.

[9] *Brut y Tywysogion*, Peniarth MS. 20 (ed. T. Jones, Cardiff, 1941), 231; cf. Translation, T. Jones, *Brut y Tywysogion or The Chronicle of the Princes*, Peniarth MS. 20 version (Cardiff, 1952), 123, 219.

carse; but since it is unique, one cannot be certain what place was meant. The Chronicle of Meaux (c. 1406) says that the battle was fought 'in the field of Bannok near Stirling'.[1] The Oxfordshire clerk Geoffrey Baker of Swinbrook says merely that the battle took place in the district called Stirling; for him, even this name was outlandish.[2] Fordun, who writes of the 'battle of Bannok', implies that it took place when the English had got as far as Bannockburn, but it is not clear whether he meant the stream or the inhabited place. Walter Bower, who wrote an expanded version of Fordun's chronicle in the fifteenth century, tells an extremely interesting story in which Edward II's defeat is seen as a judgement for the cruel way in which the English treated Simon de Montfort.[3] The tale concerns a vision of a great battle 'at Bannockburn in Scotland', and an aged Scottish pensioner lodging at Glastonbury Abbey in Somerset explains to the abbot that 'Bannockburn is a place near to the royal burgh of Stirling in Scotland'.[4]

The evidence reviewed here shows that the battle got its name not from the stream (which would, in any case, be most unusual) but from the place at which it was believed to have been fought. If this is accepted, the site proposed by Mackenzie is ruled out of serious consideration. Had the battle really been fought around Muirton and Upper Taylorton in the 'buckle of the Forth', it could not have come to be known as the battle of Bannok or Bannockburn, for two much better-known places, Stirling and St Ninians, are closer to the Mackenzie site than the obscure settlement made famous by Bruce's victory. The Welsh report of a battle in *y polles*, which has been taken to support the Mackenzie site,[5] cannot be taken to do so. For this belief rests on false assumptions that *polles* were pools and that these pools were in the 'buckle of the Forth'. We are left with a choice from among the three remaining possibilities, the 'traditional', the Miller-Carruthers and the Christison sites. The 'traditional' site was successfully disposed of by Mackenzie, who in this has been followed by every serious student since he wrote. Consequently, we

[1] *Chronica monasterii de Melsa* (ed. Bond), ii, 331.

[2] *Chronicon Galfridi le Baker de Swynebroke*, ed. E. M. Thompson, 7.

[3] *Chron. Bower*, ii, 247–8.

[4] Ibid., 248: *Bannokburn . . . qui locus [al. campus] est . . . juxta burgum regium de Strivelyn in Scotia.*

[5] *SHR*, xxvi, 190.

must choose either the Dryfield of Balquhiderock or the Carse of
Balquhiderock. The narrative which follows is based upon a belief
that the main conflict, on June 24th, took place on the Dryfield. Sir
Philip Christison's arguments are, within their own limits, persuasive,
but they are best read in his own words and with the help of his
admirable plans. A different, though not widely different, view is
taken here. It is hoped that the reasons for this divergence will be
apparent from the evidence used and cited in the course of the narrative.

(iii) *June 23rd*

On Sunday, June 23rd, as we have seen, the Scottish army was
drawn up in four brigades among the trees of the New Park. The
vanguard, under Moray, was stationed by St Ninians kirk, at the
northern end of the park. The rearguard, commanded by the king in
person, was stationed at the 'entry'. Here it covered the main road,
not only at the point where it entered the wood but also from that
point down to the crossing of the Bannock Burn. The brigades of
Douglas and Edward Bruce were somewhere in between. Their
exact positions can only be guessed at, but Douglas was evidently
nearer to Moray. King Robert knew that the position he had chosen
was one of great natural strength. 'The enemy,' he said, 'are bound
to try to pass through the New Park, unless they go below us across
the marsh (i.e., the carse to the north). Thus, either way, we shall be
at an advantage. On foot, among the trees, we shall get the better of
mounted men; alternatively, the "sikes" (i.e., the pows or streams of
the carse) will put their cavalry out of action.'[1] But to make assurance double sure, Bruce used a device reminiscent of something he
had done at Loudoun Hill in 1307, when he had compelled Valence to
advance on a narrow front. At Loudoun his small force had stood
athwart a road with treacherous mires on either side, and he built a
triple earthwork to fill up the space between the bog and the road.[2]
Now, in a similar situation, he had the ground on either side of the
road honeycombed (the metaphor is Barbour's) with small pits or
'pots', covered with sticks and grass.[3] The modern analogy would be

---

[1] Barbour, *Bruce*, 199–200.
[2] Ibid., 137–8.
[3] Ibid., 202.

with a minefield, designed not only to cause casualties itself but to force the enemy to bunch at a single well-guarded spot.

Early in the morning the Scots heard mass.[1] Their day's meal was bread and water, for they kept the fast appropriate to the eve of Saint John Baptist. In good heart, they waited while Bruce sent Douglas and Keith with a party of horse to spy out the English advance. What these experienced soldiers saw disturbed them, but on their return Bruce ordered them to suppress their news of a vast and well-armed host, and instead to tell their men that the enemy was coming ill-arrayed. In truth, all was not well among the English ranks. Their mistakes began early. The cavalry pressed forward with a reckless impetuosity. All our detailed accounts give an impression of the total absence of any single directing hand. King Edward, it is clear, neither took effective command in person nor delegated the sole command to any of his veteran officers. On the contrary, with tactlessness remarkable even in a Plantagenet, the king appointed as constable for the occasion the young earl of Gloucester, Gilbert de Clare, his own nephew.[2] This act gave needless offence to the much more experienced earl of Hereford, Humphrey de Bohun, who was not only Constable of England by hereditary right but also, as lord of Brecknock, an old and bitter rival of the Clare lords of neighbouring Glamorgan. Yet these two proud and quarrelsome noblemen held joint command of the vanguard, the *corps d'élite* of the English host and – since the English were drawn up in the order for advance – the leading brigade among the ten into which the mounted troops were formed. Early on Sunday, the governor of Stirling Castle, Sir Philip Moubray – presumably armed with a Scottish safe-conduct – rode out to meet the English king. He had a much clearer idea than anyone in the English army of the strength of the Scottish position, and urged the difficulty of a direct attack through the New Park, where the Scots had blocked all the narrow paths. In any case, as Moubray explained, honour had been saved now that the English

[1] Barbour, *Bruce*, 199–200.

[2] *Flores Historiarum*, iii, 158. N. Denholm Young dismisses this as 'surely rubbish' (*Vita Edwardi*, 27) and prefers that work's explanation that the earls' quarrel over supremacy in leading the van arose because Hereford claimed in right of being Constable and Gloucester claimed by hereditary custom (*Vita Edwardi*, 53). There is no doubt that the two earls were jointly in command of the van, and neither explanation of their quarrel is flattering to King Edward's good sense.

king had come so near to Stirling by the appointed date: he would
not now be obliged to surrender the castle.[1] Moubray's advice, we
may guess, was 'Wait and see; the Scots may now retire and the
castle be relieved without bloodshed'.

Gloucester and Hereford never got to know of Moubray's good
advice. Beyond reach of effective orders from the king they pressed
on through the Torwood until, somewhere about Snabhead, they
could see, across the valley, a number of Scots scattered in front of
the New Park, apparently in the act of withdrawing.[2] The day must
now have been well advanced. Impatiently, the young knights and
esquires spurred their horses forward down the high road, crossed
the Bannock Burn, and rode as hard as they could up the hill towards the enemy lines. In the very front were some of Hereford's
retainers with their Welsh followers, presumably all mounted. It was
now that an unbelievable opportunity of glory came to Sir Henry de
Bohun, Hereford's nephew,[3] and endowed him with immortality.
In front of him was one of the enemy soldiers, separated from his
fellows, clad in mail, armed with a hand-axe, and mounted on a
small sturdy grey. His helmet, covered by a leather crest, was surmounted by a high crown. To vanquish the king of Scots himself in
single combat: such a feat of chivalry did not often come the way of
an ambitious knight. Henry de Bohun rode at Bruce, lance at rest.
Bruce pulled himself out of the path of the oncoming lance, so that,
in Barbour's memorable line, 'Schir Henry myssit the nobill
kyng'.[4] As he drew level, Bruce raised himself up in his stirrups and
with a mighty effort swung his axe downward so fiercely that the
blade pierced Bohun's helmet and split his head in two. Bohun's
body fell to the earth beside him, and Bruce was left holding the
stump of his axe-shaft, shattered by the tremendous impact. The
Scots, gathered at the edge of the wood and witnessing this extraordinary scene, exulted in their king's prowess, still more in his
safe emergence from the encounter. But their leaders rebuked him
severely for risking his life and their whole cause in this reckless
fashion. They were right, of course; but Bruce himself turned aside

[1] Scalacronica, 141.
[2] Vita Edwardi, 51.
[3] Ibid.; Barbour, Bruce, 211; cf. Morris, Bannockburn, 66–7.
[4] Barbour, Bruce, 211.

their rebukes, ruefully lamenting his broken axe-shaft. By rights, the incident ought never to have occurred; yet its effect on the highlanders, islesmen and others in the king's brigade can be imagined and the story, as it spread back through the rest of the army, would lose nothing in the telling. The Scots at the 'entry' surged forward to meet and repulse the oncoming English horsemen. The earl of Gloucester, well to the fore, was knocked off his horse in the mêlée. This was no minor skirmish, but a serious engagement in which Bruce's brigade took a full part and in which Edward Bruce's men may have joined also.[1] But after some fierce fighting at close quarters, in which the English van suffered sufficient casualties to make a lasting impression, the main body of cavalry withdrew south of the Bannock Burn, still intact. The Scots exultantly pursued them, but (the fact is a striking tribute to the discipline King Robert exercised over his army) they were recalled before any harm was done.

In the meantime, while Gloucester and Hereford were pressing forward impetuously to attack the Scots at the 'entry', another cavalry division under Sir Robert Clifford and Sir Henry Beaumont set off northward, towards the carse, in an attempt to by-pass the New Park altogether and force a way through to Stirling on the left flank of the Scots position.[2] Estimates of the strength of this division vary. Sir Thomas Grey, whose father, Sir Thomas Grey the elder, of Heaton on the Till, was one of its prominent members, puts it at 300;[3] Barbour says 800.[4] Probably Grey's figure is nearer the mark, for the cavalry, some 2,500 to 3,000 in all, were divided into ten brigades or squadrons which were presumably equal in numbers. On the other hand, Clifford and Beaumont, who had three bannerets under them,[5] may have commanded two of the ten cavalry brigades. It was obviously no mere patrol or raiding party, but a body of considerable fighting power. It has, indeed, been suggested that Clifford was carrying out a reconnaissance in strength;[6] his object,

---

[1] *Vita Edwardi*, 51; Morris, *Bannockburn*, 67.

[2] *Scalacronica*, 141; *Chron. Lanercost*, 225; Barbour, *Bruce*, 206ff. (who puts the episode before Gloucester's advance). *Vita Edwardi*, 51, confuses the separate advances of Gloucester and Clifford.

[3] *Scalacronica*, 141.

[4] Barbour, *Bruce*, 206.

[5] Ibid. Perhaps Barbour implies that Beaumont was one of the three bannerets.

[6] Barron, *Scottish War of Independence*, 504.

that is, was to find out whether there was a practicable route by which the whole army could reach Stirling without going into the New Park at all. This may have been the case, but the suggestion finds no support among contemporary writers. What most modern commentators seem to forget is that until the very last moment the English were confident that the Scots would not fight a pitched battle in daylight. Their tactics were based on this belief, and can only be explained in accordance with it. Gloucester and Hereford attacked Scots 'who seemed to be in retreat'.[1] Clifford, according to the Lanercost Chronicle, 'wished to ride round the [New Park] to prevent the Scots escaping by flight'.[2] Barbour's explanation is that Clifford was put in command of a specially selected squadron whose task was to force a way through to the castle and relieve it:[3] in other words, its purpose was the same as that of the vanguard, only the route was different. Grey attempts no explanation. He merely says that Clifford and Beaumont rode round the New Park in the direction of the castle. The lack of discipline and direction in the English army was such that we cannot really be sure what Clifford's intentions were. For all we know, the king may have been as little consulted about Clifford's advance as he was about Gloucester's, while it seems certain that between Gloucester and Clifford there was no liaison whatever.

Clifford's party probably crossed the Bannock Burn near the present village and headed straight for Stirling. As Grey and Barbour both emphasize, they kept to the open country well clear of the New Park and its trees. Whether this took them down on to the carse, just below the 50 foot contour, or whether they crossed the higher ground between Balquhiderock and Broomridge, is not clear. Barbour says that 'they completely avoided the New Park, for they knew well that the king [of Scots] was there. They went below the New Park, until they were below the church [St Ninians kirk], all in company.'[4] Whatever their route, they cannot have expected an attack. A large body of mail-clad knights on powerful horses, moving in close formation across open country, could feel confident that the Scots

1 *Vita Edwardi*, 51.
2 *Chron. Lanercost*, 225.
3 Barbour, *Bruce*, 206.
4 Ibid., 206–7.

spearmen would stay in the shelter of the wood. Indeed, they reached
a point beneath St Ninians kirk without being molested. Whether or
not they had crossed the boggy Pelstream Burn, they must by now
have been sure of winning through to Stirling.

Bruce, however, had seen Clifford's squadron riding off northward to make a circuit of the New Park. It was to provide against
just such a movement that he had stationed Moray near St Ninians
kirk, to guard the road and prevent an enemy break-through on the
Scottish flank. The way in which Bruce had arranged his brigades
shows, incidentally, that the idea of an English cavalry advance
right out on the carse never occurred to the Scots. It is easy therefore
to understand Bruce's sudden anger when he realized that Clifford
had drawn level with St Ninians without being challenged by
Moray.[1] Indeed, at this moment Moray was actually with the king,
apparently unaware of the English advance. In a terse, graphic
rebuke, the king told him that a rose had fallen from his chaplet; he
had been stationed to 'keep the way', yet the English had slipped
past him.[2]

Stung by the rebuke, angry with himself for a mistake that could
cost the Scots the whole battle, Moray rode furiously back to his
men. The situation was not quite hopeless. Clifford had still to advance across ground near enough to the wood for the Scottish footmen to reach it by a short march into the open. This is proved by
Beaumont's immediate reaction as he saw the bristling hedgehog of
spearmen coming out to meet the English knights. 'Let them come
on,' he cried, 'give them some ground. We must draw back a little.'[3]
Instinctively, he wanted the horse to have more room to manoeuvre.
Sir Thomas Grey took a more serious view. 'My lord,' he said to
Beaumont, 'give them what you like now; I'm afraid that in a short
while they will have everything.' 'Flee then,' retorted Beaumont,
'flee, if you're afraid.' 'Fear will not make me flee, my Lord,' was
Grey's answer as he put spurs to his horse and, with Sir William
Deyncourt, rode straight at the advancing line of spears. Deyncourt
was killed at once, Grey was pulled from his mortally wounded

[1] Barbour, *Bruce*, 207.
[2] Ibid., 204, 207, 'the way' being the high road leading past St Ninians kirk towards
Stirling.
[3] *Scalacronica*, 141.

horse and made prisoner. The battle that followed was fierce and exhausting. The spearmen sweated in the heat of the afternoon, and clouds of dust rose as the hooves of the heavy *destriers* churned up the dry earth. The whole object of Moray's schiltrom was to hold tightly together, presenting the mailed knights with an impenetrable hedge of spearpoints wherever they attacked. The horsemen for their part tried to rush the schiltrom, redoubling their efforts to find a weak point in its ranks so that they could pierce the whole formation and break it up. At Falkirk the cavalry had only been able to do this after archers had rained arrows and bolts down upon the infantry. Clifford had no archers, but at the same time Moray had a stiffer task than Wallace to keep his schiltrom unbroken. At Falkirk the schiltroms were static, dug in behind low palisades, whereas Moray's schiltrom was a freely moving group exposed and isolated on open arable. Training and discipline were to tell now, as never before on the Scottish side. Their own lances proving useless, the baffled knights hurled swords and maces, piling up a mountain of weapons inside the schiltrom. As at Falkirk, the Scots aimed their spears at the horses as much as at their riders. Most of the English casualties were no doubt caused by the unhorsing of knights encumbered with heavy armour. At last the impetus of the English attack was broken. The Scots, still holding together, pressed home their advantage, and the whole English squadron, or what remained of it, scattered and fled, some making for Stirling Castle, some (including Clifford) riding back the way they had come.

This hard fight between Moray and Clifford was the crisis of the whole battle, even though it involved relatively small numbers on both sides. Its critical character was understood by Douglas, Moray's colleague and friendly rival, and when the issue still seemed in doubt he implored the king to let him lead his own brigade to Moray's assistance.[1] With admirable coolness, Bruce held Douglas back. The day was late, admittedly, but there would be light for some hours yet. He could not be sure what further attempts the English would make. Bruce did, on the other hand, have confidence in his nephew's courage and soldierly skill. In the end, Douglas could contain his patience no longer, and led his men out of the wood, but only when all was over. The sense of chivalry for which he was famous made

[1] Barbour, *Bruce*, 209.

him halt, lest Moray and his sturdy spearmen should not enjoy all the glory earned by their exertions. Exhausted, soaked in sweat, Moray's men took off their helmets to feel the cool fresh air. Then they went to the king and reported their triumph, won with almost no casualties on the Scottish side. The rest of the army crowded round to congratulate them and salute the earl. His victory had in fact achieved two things of the utmost importance. It proved, firstly, that the schiltrom of spearmen in close formation could be used successfully as a mobile unit to attack armoured cavalry. Secondly, it stopped the English opening up a route to Stirling Castle; indeed, it seems to have stopped them making any but the most surreptitious contact with Moubray's garrison. It also greatly raised the spirits of the Scots and added enormously to the discomfiture of English *morale*. All our accounts agree that this second setback, coming after the repulse suffered by Gloucester and Hereford, spread gloom and confusion among the English.[1]

It was late in the day by the time Clifford and Beaumont regained the main body. No further attempts would be made before morning to penetrate the Scots position. Much the greater part of the English army had had no contact with the enemy, probably not even a sight of them. But all were exhausted by the heat and by hurried marches. Horses would have to be watered, and the men would need a meal and some rest. The aggressiveness of Bruce had alarmed the English into thinking that a night attack was not impossible, so proper sleep was out of the question. But a place had to be found where the army could rest and yet be ready to attack the Scots in the morning, if they were still there; a place, moreover, where men could bivouac and horses be given water. It was probably this last consideration that lay behind the dangerous decision to put all the cavalry and perhaps a part of the infantry across the Bannock Burn. Only Barbour and Grey describe this difficult and perilous manoeuvre. In modern English, what Barbour has to say is this.

'They bivouacked there that night, down in the carse, and made every man clean and prepare his weapons and armour to be ready for battle in the morning. And because there were "pows" [sluggish

---

[1] *Chron. Lanercost*, 225; *Scalacronica*, 142; Barbour, *Bruce*, 214, 219–20. *Vita Edwardi*, 51–2, speaks of the caution engendered among the English leaders because of their toil on June 23rd.

streams] in the carse, they broke down houses and roofing and carried
it off to make bridges by which to cross [the streams]. There are
also some surviving who say that nearly all the men in the castle,
knowing the difficulty the English army was in, came out after
dark [that is, about midnight], taking with them doors and windows.
In this way the English had before daylight bridged the pows, so
that everyone crossed over and had taken up a position on horseback
on the hard field.'[1] A translation of Grey's French gives this picture,
different in some respects, yet not incompatible or contradictory.
'The king's host left the road through the wood and came into a
plain in the direction of the River Forth, beyond Bannock Burn, an
evil, deep marsh with streams, where the English troops unharnessed
and remained all night in discomfort, being mortified and badly
troubled by the events of the previous day.'[2] It is possible that Grey's
words ought to be translated 'beyond Bannock Burn, an evil, deep,
boggy stream';[3] either way, it is clear that the cavalry at least did
cross the Bannock Burn during the night. On this point the Lanercost
Chronicle and the *Life of Edward II* confirm Barbour and Grey, for
the one states explicitly that the English had crossed the Bannock
Burn before the battle, and the other implies it.[4] The *Life of Edward II*
also confirms the impression of watchfulness, anxiety, and sleepless-
ness conveyed by Grey, for it says that when the English bivouacked
they got no rest, spending the night without sleep in constant fear
of a Scottish attack. And Barbour, with his account of pulling houses
down, making bridges across the numerous pows, and getting arms
and armour ready for battle likewise implies that the English spent a
sleepless night. No doubt the main purpose of the bridges was to
make sure that the heavy horses did not sink in the treacherous peat
through which the streams, including the Bannock Burn itself,
flowed. There was also the problem of transporting the king's household and tents and baggage across the carseland, for it cannot be

---

[1] Barbour, *Bruce*, 220–1.

[2] *Scalacronica*, 141–2.

[3] The MS. reads as follows: 'al ost le Rey . qy ia auoint gerpy la voy du boys .
estoint uenuz en un plain deuers leau de Forth . outre Bannokburn . un mauueis
parfound Ruscell' marras.' (Cambridge, Corpus Christi College MS. 133, fo. 205ᵛ,
col. 2). Since both *ruscell* and *marras* are masculine nouns, it is not clear which is
qualifying which.

[4] *Chron. Lanercost*, 226; *Vita Edwardi*, 54.

supposed that Edward of Caernarvon, however brave and athletic, was forced to bivouac like a common knight.

These few hours of darkness between Saturday and Sunday contained all the suspense and drama of the battle of Bannockburn. For while the English were groping and floundering about down in the carse, wet, uncomfortable and depressed, their infantry drinking themselves into an unreal cheerfulness with cries of 'Wassail' and 'Drinkhail',[1] the Scots were actually proposing to withdraw altogether from their strong position in front of Stirling, and find a fresh base somewhere in the Lennox, a country too wild for the English army to reach them.[2] So powerful and deep-seated was Bruce's inclination to avoid pitched battles and wage guerrilla warfare, an un-knightly policy which only harsh and bitter experience had taught him. But Grey says that during the hours of darkness a Scots knight in English service, Sir Alexander Seton, disgusted by the lack of leadership and dispiritedness among the English barons and knights, made his way to Bruce's camp and gained an audience of the king. 'My lord king, now is the time, if ever you mean to win Scotland. The English have lost heart; they are discomfited, and expect nothing but a sudden and open attack. I swear, on my head and on pain of being hanged and drawn, that if you attack them in the morning you will defeat them easily without loss.'[3] Barbour makes the debate take place in a public assembly after Moray's victory.[4] Although this artistically more satisfying story of Barbour's is probably largely invention, there is no reason to doubt the gist of what he says. The king asked his leaders if they should fight or not. With one voice their answer was 'Good King, as soon as day comes tomorrow order yourself and your army for battle. We shall not fail for fear of death, nor flinch at any suffering till we have made our country free.'

(iv) *June 24th and after*

Both the days on which the battle of Bannockburn was fought were apparently warm and sunny. Unless the night was cloudy, there

---

[1] *Chronicon Galfridi le Baker*, ed. Thompson, 7.

[2] *Scalacronica*, 142.

[3] Ibid. For Seton see additional note below, p. 332.

[4] Barbour, *Bruce*, 214-5.

would have been no real darkness,[1] only some five hours of dusk blurring the sharp outlines of the landscape: across the Forth, the Ochils rising steeply out of the plain beyond the tower of Cambuskenneth Abbey and the abrupt bluff of the Abbey Craig; to the west, the rock of Stirling, and beyond it, in the far distance, the highland hills. At about a quarter past three by modern reckoning, the first light of Monday, June 24th, would have begun to spread into the sky over the Firth of Forth. Within an hour or so it would pick out more and more distinctly to English eyes the trees of the New Park, where the Scots waited, hearing mass and eating a spartan breakfast.

When Barbour says that the English bivouacked 'down in the carse' and Grey tells us that they debouched into 'a plain in the direction of the River Forth, beyond Bannock Burn', we may conclude that the English cavalry got what rest they could somewhere in the area bounded by the Pelstream Burn, the Bannock Burn and the 50 foot contour. On the previous evening and during the night they had come down from the high ground by the Roman road, probably on a wide front, on to the Carse of Skeoch. At St Peter's Well in Bannockburn village, at another well beside what is now Bannockburn railway station, and also in the Bannock Burn itself, the horses could have been watered with little difficulty. We may then imagine the cavalry brigades picking their way slowly and uncertainly north-westward along the carse, negotiating the pows on bridges improvised out of beams and planks removed from the houses of Bannok. The Bannock Burn itself was probably too wide to be crossed in this way. There would have been delay while the various units, still spread out on a wide front, waited their turn at the few existing fords. Even when they reached a resting-place, horses were kept bridled, and the men had their arms in readiness.

Neither Barbour nor Grey gives any support to the belief that the fighting on Monday took place here, where the English rested, in the boggy Carse of Balquhiderock. From this area the Scots position in the New Park would have been invisible. Before daybreak, says Barbour, the cavalry had reached the 'hard field',[2] and it was upon

[1] Information kindly supplied by Professor H. A. Brück, Astronomer-Royal for Scotland, per litt., June 14th, 1962.
[2] Barbour, Bruce, 221.

this 'hard field' or 'plain hard field'[1] – surely the firm ground between Balquhiderock and Broomridge – that he says the battle was fought. If the leading English brigades were not far above the 100 foot contour, where in daylight they could see the Scots, then it is true that several of the rear brigades, even though huddled altogether 'in one schiltrom', as Barbour says,[2] must still have been down on the carse, below the 50 foot contour. But at the outset, just before the fighting began, the opposing armies were in sight of each other. Baston, the Carmelite friar brought to glorify an English triumph in verse but compelled by the Scots who captured him to versify in the opposite sense, speaks of the battle on the *arida terra Strivelini*,[3] the dry arable of Stirling, which recalls the name 'dryfield' by which the ground above the 50 foot contour was known in earlier times.[4] Moreover, Grey, Barbour and the *Life of Edward II* agree that the battle was begun simply by the Scots advancing out of the 'wood' or New Park. If all the English had still been down on the carse, the Scots would have had to march more than half a mile before even coming in sight. Nor is there anything in contemporary accounts to suggest that the Scots were on appreciably higher ground,[5] as they had been at Stirling Bridge. What contemporaries do say or imply, without exception, is that the battle field was extremely constricted, indeed fatally so for the English. Admittedly, Barbour's phrase 'the great straitness of the place'[6] would apply to the Carse of Balquhiderock. But if in 1314 it was taken for granted that no one in his senses would fight a heavy cavalry action in carseland, the phrase fits the Dryfield of Balquhiderock quite as well, if not better.

The nearest we are ever likely to get to Robert Bruce's words at Bannockburn is the speech attributed to him by his friend Bernard of Linton, abbot of Arbroath and chancellor. It is hardly to be doubted that Bernard was at the battle, for he was one of the king's closest councillors and in any case, as abbot of Arbroath, he would have been responsible for ensuring that the famous relic casket known as

---

[1] Barbour, *Bruce*, 222 (lines 447, 457).
[2] Ibid., line 437.
[3] *Chron. Bower*, ii, 252.
[4] T. Miller, *Site of the battle of Bannockburn*, 6 n., 15 n.
[5] As suggested by Barron, *Scottish War of Independence*, 464.
[6] Barbour, *Bruce*, 221.

the Brecbennoch of Saint Columba (now the Monymusk Reliquary) was present, suitably attended, in the midst of the army.[1] According to Abbot Bernard, Bruce addressed his men early on the Monday morning, presumably just before battle was joined.

'My lords, my people, accustomed to enjoy that full freedom for which in times gone by the kings of Scotland have fought many a battle! For eight years or more I have struggled with much labour for my right to the kingdom and for honourable liberty. I have lost brothers, friends and kinsmen. Your own kinsmen have been made captive, and bishops and priests are locked in prison. Our country's nobility has poured forth its blood in war. Those barons you can see before you, clad in mail, are bent upon destroying me and obliterating my kingdom, nay, our whole nation. They do not believe that we can survive. They glory in their warhorses and equipment. For us, the name of the Lord must be our hope of victory in battle. This day is a day of rejoicing: the birthday of John the Baptist. With Our Lord Jesus Christ as commander, Saint Andrew and the martyr Saint Thomas shall fight today with the saints of Scotland for the honour of their country and their nation. If you heartily repent of your sins you will be victorious, under God's command. As for offences committed against the Crown, I proclaim a pardon, by virtue of my royal power, to all those who fight manfully for the kingdom of our fathers.'[2]

And Barbour tells us that the king also proclaimed a general remission of death-duties (reliefs and wardship) in respect of every man who might be killed in the battle.

At daybreak, King Robert gave the order to attack. The honour of leading the army went to the brigade of Edward Bruce, which had probably been stationed at the eastern edge of the New Park, half way between the Borestone and St Ninians. Next, on Edward Bruce's left, came Moray's brigade, so slightly to the rear that to English eyes the brigades seemed to be side by side. The Stewart's brigade, commanded by Sir James Douglas (both men newly knighted by the king,) came out of the New Park on Moray's left, likewise slightly to the rear, so that the three schiltroms marched forward in echelon by the right. Once out in the open, in full view of the enemy, the Scots halted: every man knelt, saying the Lord's

---

[1] *Arbroath Liber*, i, Preface, p. xxiii; F. C. Eeles, 'The Monymusk Reliquary or Brecbennoch of St Columba', *Proc. Soc. Antiq. Scot.*, lxviii (1933–4), 433–8.
[2] *Chron. Bower*, ii, 249–50.

Prayer and commending his soul to God. King Edward had watched the infantry emerging from the wood. Even at this late hour he could not believe they would invite a pitched battle. 'What!' he exclaimed, 'will those Scots fight?' And then, still incredulous as he saw them kneeling to pray, he said: 'Those men kneel to ask for mercy.' 'You are right; they ask for mercy, but not from you. They ask it from God, for their sins.' According to Barbour, the answer was spoken by Sir Ingram de Umfraville, who among those present shared with King Robert alone the distinction of having once been a Guardian for the community of the realm of Scotland.[1]

Sir Ingram's opinion of the fighting qualities of Bruce's troops was too high for the liking of the younger men with Edward II. Apparently both he and the earl of Gloucester had advised the English king to postpone the battle, Gloucester for a whole day, Umfraville suggesting a feigned withdrawal beyond the English tents and baggage, so as to lure the Scots to destruction by tempting them with plunder. The earl was absurdly accused by the king of cowardice; Umfraville's advice, on the other hand, if correctly reported by Barbour, was surely disastrous, and King Edward did right to reject it. Honour and the tactical situation alike demanded that the English did not now refuse battle, even in pretence. They were in a tight corner and must get out of it as best they could.

The anonymous eye-witness whose story is given in the Lanercost Chronicle reported that the first actual fighting was a brief exchange of shots between archers on both sides, in which the Scots had the worst of it.[2] But there is no question that the first major clash came when the English vanguard, under Gloucester, charged the leading Scottish schiltrom across the short stretch of intervening ground. The movement was a spectacular failure. The mailed knights made no impression on the 'impenetrable forest' or 'dense hedge' of spears; the air was filled with the screams of dying horses and the sharp report of breaking spear-shafts. Soon after battle was joined the Scots killed the earl of Gloucester. Impetuous to the last, he was cut off from his household knights and esquires and borne down by the sheer press of spearmen. His was only the first name, though the noblest, on what was to prove a long and costly casualty list of

English chivalry. Sir Pain Tiptoft, Sir Edmund de Mauley, Steward of the King's Household, the veteran Sir Robert Clifford, and Sir John Comyn, lord of Badenoch, son of the Guardian whom Bruce had killed in 1306, all seem to have been in the vanguard with Gloucester, and like him fell before the Scottish onslaught.[1]

While Edward Bruce was successfully holding the English vanguard, and perhaps forcing it to give ground somewhat, Moray and Douglas brought up their brigades and launched a general attack on the remaining nine English divisions, which were bunched in one single mass, 'all in a schiltrom' as Barbour puts it.[2] Again the Scots went for the horses as much as their riders, and by dint of keeping together in tight formation, as Moray's men had done the previous afternoon, all the Scottish schiltroms presented an impenetrable barrier to the lances and swords of the knights. Even making every allowance for the poetic effect at which Barbour strove, his impression of appalling tumult, no doubt gained from authentic tradition and eye-witness accounts, is surely true. He describes the clash of spears on the knights' helmets and 'birnies' (coats of mail), the shrieks of disembowelled horses, the panic stampede of riderless animals, and the grass made red with the outpoured blood of man and beast. The carnage was doubtless not so great at first as it had been at Falkirk, but it must be remembered that in cavalry actions casualties were not expected to be very heavy. Courtrai, in 1302, where the Flemish foot had virtually wiped out the French feudal host, had shocked Europe; and now Bannockburn was bidding fair to rival Courtrai.

Not until the English had taken great punishment was it possible for them to bring out on one flank a body of archers to harass the Scottish schiltroms by steady shooting against which they had little or no protection. Here, of course, was a cardinal error on Edward II's part. His archers should have been available in large numbers from the start, and their shooting should have been integrated with the short rushes of the cavalry. But in fact the larger part of the English bowmen seem to have been in the rear, and could only be brought up to the front with difficulty because of the narrowness of the battlefield. King Robert must have anticipated some such move,

[1] *Chron. Lanercost*, 226; *Vita Edwardi*, 53-4.
[2] Barbour, *Bruce*, 231.

and to meet it he had held in reserve the only cavalry force in his army: some five hundred knights and men at arms, on light horses, under the marischal, Sir Robert Keith. Keith was sent to scatter the archers and prevent them from shooting steadily. In fact he did better: his charge was so fierce that the whole body of archers broke and fled, and many who tried to get back into the English ranks further in the rear were set upon and beaten up by men of their own side.[1] On which flank this took place matters little: from now on, the archers were no longer an element in the battle, which became solely a dour and strenuous contest, in the growing heat of a mid-summer morning, between the spears and Lochaber axes of the Scots on foot and the lances, swords and maces or clubs wielded by mail-clad knights. The greater part of the infantry on the English side do not seem to have been engaged at all, and it may well be that most of them remained south of the Bannock Burn. The Scots evidently had sufficient numbers to occupy the English cavalry along virtually the whole width of the available ground between Bal-quhiderock and Broomridge; Barbour speaks of the three schiltroms of Edward Bruce, Moray and Douglas as 'all fighting very nearly side by side'.[2] King Robert seems to have known better than any of the English leaders how dangerous their archers might have proved if put to better use. Once Keith had routed them, he felt that the Scots were on top, the battle was theirs. He could not contain his jubilation; now, he told the officers of his brigade, was the moment; if only some extra pressure could be put on the English, defeat would quickly follow. There was evidently room to bring up his own bri-gade, presumably on the right flank of the three already engaged.[3] The highlanders, islesmen and others serving under the king's own standard, chafing with impatience (as one may imagine) at not yet having taken any part, now rushed upon the enemy in a rage.

> With all thar mycht and all thar mayne
> Thai layd on, as men out of wit;
> And quhar thai with full strak mycht hit,
> Thar mycht no armyng stint thar strak;

[1] Barbour, *Bruce*, 229.
[2] Ibid., 227.
[3] Ibid., 229. Once Bruce's brigade or 'battle' was fully engaged (Barbour says) all four 'battles' were fighting on one front, ibid., 231.

> Thai to-fruschit thame thai mycht our-tak
> And with axis sic duschis gaff
> That thai helmys and hedis claff.[1]

This, as the racy, excited, irresistible flood of his verse makes clear, was for Barbour the climax of the battle. No other source denies or contradicts him here. We accept his judgement or abandon any attempt at a detailed account. All four schiltroms, the whole effective strength of the Scottish army, was now engaged, fighting along one front. The English vanguard ceased to be a distinct unit; the entire English army now formed one huge schiltrom, packed so close that if one man fell he had no room to rise but was trampled under foot. Where men had once fought silently and grimly, saving their breath, emotions now inevitably got the better of discipline. The Scots were exultant, the English were beginning to be desperate. They had fought, and continued for some while to fight, stoutly; but they were fighting with the wrong tactics, the wrong weapons, and on the wrong ground. Amid the clash of arms and the groans of the wounded, battle cries 'hideous for to hear' sounded on every side. As the knights began to yield, the Scots shouted: 'On them, on them, on them, they fail!'[2] The Scots archers took courage, and added a cruel rain of arrows to the mêlée.

For the English, the battle was now past saving. In front of them the Scottish schiltroms still remained intact, a steadily advancing engine of destruction. Behind them were the gorge of the Bannock Burn and the treacherous carse with its innumerable pows, and on their flank the Forth itself, too wide and deep to be forded in safety. At this moment, there appeared in the rear of the attacking Scots a great mob of unarmoured, untrained lesser folk – yeomen, servants and labourers – bearing hastily improvised banners and armed with homemade weapons.[3] King Robert had kept them strictly apart from his fighting men, setting them to guard the supplies in a hollow, probably to the north of Coxet Hill.[4] Now, unbidden and having little or no effect upon the outcome, they streamed across the open ground with shouts of 'Slay, slay, on them hastily.' No blame

[1] Barbour, *Bruce*, 230.
[2] Ibid., 232.
[3] Ibid., 233.
[4] Ibid., 203, line 426; cf. 233, line 230. They were within the New Park.

if some of the hard-pressed English had really believed they were a second Scottish army, arriving vigorous and fresh when they themselves were near to exhaustion. King Robert himself could hardly have welcomed an undisciplined rabble who might kill English lords and knights indiscriminately so that their valuable ransoms would be lost. But in any event, the surviving English leaders knew that the end had come.

The earl of Pembroke and Sir Giles d'Argentan were with the king, the latter in his personal bodyguard.[1] At all costs Edward must be got safely off the field. His death would have been a national disgrace, but his capture would have been far worse. His ransom alone would, economically speaking, put Scotland back on her feet, while the terms of his release could hardly have been less than unconditional recognition of Bruce's claim to the Scottish throne and of Scottish independence. King Edward had carried himself with notable courage, and protested as he was led from the field; but he was got away only just in time. As it was, he had one horse killed under him and had to be given a fresh mount, while the Scots captured Sir Roger Northburgh along with the king's shield which he had in his keeping.[2] Five hundred knights went with the king, not crossing the Bannock Burn, where the fighting was fiercest, but riding towards Stirling along the edge of the carse, in the vain and dangerous hope that they would find refuge in the castle. As soon as King Edward was out of immediate danger, Giles d'Argentan, 'the third best knight' in Christendom, declaring that his honour would not allow him to flee, returned to confront the schiltrom of Edward Bruce and plunged, gallantly but quite suicidally, into the forest of spears.[3]

In other circumstances, the king of England's personal presence should have been an enormous asset. Now it was to prove calamitous. His withdrawal was the signal for general flight, which, utterly uncontrolled as it was, turned defeat into stark disaster. Men fled in every possible direction, north-west to Stirling Castle, north to the River Forth in which most of those trying to cross were drowned, south-east to the Bannock Burn. It was here, in the gorge north of

[1] *Scalacronica*, 142; Barbour, *Bruce*, 196.

[2] Barbour, *Bruce*, 234; *Scalacronica*, 142–3; Thomas Walsingham, *Historia Anglicana* (ed. H. T. Riley), 141.

[3] *Scalacronica*, 143; Barbour, *Bruce*, 235.

Bannockburn village, and presumably also in the peat-bordered stretch below the gorge, that the beaten army suffered its most terrible casualties.

> Bannokburn betwix the brais
> Of hors and men so chargit was,
> That apon drownit hors and men
> Men mycht pass dry atour it then.[1]

In more laconic fashion, Grey, the *Life of Edward II*, and the Lanercost Chronicle all bear out Barbour's account. The English, says Grey, 'recoiled upon the ditch of the Bannock Burn, tumbling over one another'.[2] The Lanercost account says 'a further misfortune befell the English, for since, a little while before, they had crossed a big ditch called the Bannock Burn, into which the tide flows,[3] and now, thrown back in confusion, they wished to retreat, many noblemen and others with their horses fell into this ditch because of the great press of men behind them. Some got away only with difficulty, but many never extricated themselves, so that "Bannockburn" was on English lips for many years afterwards.'[4] The *Life of Edward II* has the same story, though it does not mention the Bannock Burn by name: 'While our people fled, a certain ditch entrapped many of them, and a great part of our army perished in it.'[5]

It is usually hard enough for a general to plan a battle so that it goes the way he wants it to go; it is only rarely that even the best of generals can steer the course of events after a successful battle so that he may reap the maximum advantage. Robert Bruce had won a brilliant victory, which rightly takes first place among the few decisive battles in the history of Scotland. It cannot tarnish the brilliance of his achievement to add, as a matter of historical fact, that in the battle's aftermath the English escaped more cheaply than they

[1] Barbour, *Bruce*, 235.
[2] *Scalacronica*, 142.
[3] Although Mackenzie took this as evidence for his suggested site of the battle, it is not certain that the writer meant that the tidal reaches were in the battle zone, or that he was correctly informed, and it is possible that many of the English troops fleeing after the battle were drowned or bogged down in this part of the burn.
[4] *Chron. Lanercost*, 226.
[5] *Vita Edwardi*, 54.

deserved. This was due largely to circumstances beyond Bruce's control. True, the English lost all their supplies and baggage and nearly all their arms and armour, amounting to an immensely rich haul for the Scots. King Edward lost his shield (which King Robert courteously returned to him)[1] and also his seal and all his personal equipment, clothing and other possessions, save what little he could carry with him. It is true also that casualties were heavy, proportionately heaviest among men of noble rank, that is barons, knights and esquires. One earl was killed: Gloucester, whom Bruce mourned as a cousin, and over whose corpse, decently laid in a nearby church, he made a night's vigil. It was then sent to King Edward at Berwick, along with the body of Clifford, who after Gloucester was the most high-ranking magnate to be killed.[2] Besides these and Tiptoft, Mauley and Comyn, at least thirty-four barons and knights are recorded as having been slain, including William, lord of Hingham (Suffolk), hereditary marshal of Ireland; Edmund Hastings, the younger son of John Hastings the Competitor; and John Lovel the Rich.[3] The family of Vieuxpont suffered heavily, losing an English and a Scottish representative, while Clifford was a Vieuxpont on his mother's side.

The English king, however, got away, and his escape was not due merely to good luck. When he reached Stirling Castle, its commander Moubray either told him that he was free to enter, in which case he would be taken by the Scots, or else (for the same reason) he raised the drawbridge and shut the gate against him.[4] Edward and his party thereupon turned about and made off through the King's Park, crossed the rear of the Scottish army, until, regaining the Torwood, they sped along the high road in the direction of Linlithgow.[5] Large numbers of the English followed the king to Stirling and scrambled vainly about the castle rock. But Bruce judged them too

[1] T. Walsingham, *Hist. Angl.*, 141.

[2] Ibid., 142; Barbour, *Bruce*, 240.

[3] *Annales Londonienses*, 231, to whose list add the name of John de Grey from *Gesta Edwardi de Carnarvan*, 46. Cf. Brit. Lib., MS. Cott. Cleop. D iii, fo. 56ᵛ.

[4] Ibid., 46–7; Barbour, *Bruce*, 236; *Vita Edwardi*, 54.

[5] Barbour, *Bruce*, 236–7. *Scalacronica*, 143, actually says that the king's party rode round the outside of the Torwood (i.e., to the west), before reaching the plain of Lothian. But they would scarcely have had time for such a lengthy detour. *Chron. Lanercost*, 227, says that the king's party included Hugh Despenser the younger and Sir Henry Beaumont.

dangerous to be left in his rear, and kept a strong force to overpower them. Consequently, he ordered no serious pursuit of the English king. Instead, Douglas was allowed only sixty horse, with which he gave chase as best he could.[1] He had no real hope of doing more than harass a party nearly ten times as strong. Barbour tells how the English halted briefly at Winchburgh to feed their horses, Douglas's troop following suit a short way off. Then away they rode again through Lothian, the Scots maintaining such a hot pursuit that the English lords and knights, in Barbour's expressive phrase, 'had not even leisure to make water'. If any of them did lag behind they were quickly captured. At last Edward reached the castle of Dunbar. It says much for the sorely-tried loyalty of Earl Patrick that he received Edward hospitably and saw him safely on board the boat which took him to Bamburgh, and so to the comparative security of Berwick. Most of the five hundred knights reached Berwick by land.

A sizeable body of cavalry, under the earl of Hereford, fled to Bothwell Castle on the Clyde.[2] The constable, Walter, Gilbert's son, though a Scot, had hitherto been on the English side. He admitted Hereford and his party, which included Robert de Umfraville earl of Angus, Ingram de Umfraville, Maurice, lord of Berkeley, John lord of Segrave, and Anthony de Lucy.[3] Once inside, he made them all prisoners, having presumably decided to go over to Bruce if the English were defeated. Profitable ransoms were obtained for these rich and important magnates. The earl of Hereford was so great a prize that in October Bruce was able to exchange him for his queen, his daughter the lady Marjorie, his sister Mary, and Robert Wishart, bishop of Glasgow, now very old and blind.[4] On the other hand, Bruce behaved with conspicuous generosity towards some of his prisoners. Sir Marmaduke Tweng, for example, an old veteran of the English wars in Scotland, surrendered personally to King Robert and was allowed to go home to Yorkshire free of ransom.[5] Ralph de

[1] Barbour, *Bruce*, 237, 241–3.

[2] Ibid., 237; *Chron. Lanercost*, 228.

[3] Ibid., *Vita Edwardi*, 55.

[4] Barbour, *Bruce*, 245; *Cal. Docs. Scot.*, iii, No. 393. It was intended that the young earl of Mar, Bruce's nephew, should be repatriated at this time, but when he reached Newcastle he refused to go any further and chose to remain with King Edward, to whom he was closely attached, *Chron. Lanercost*, 229, and below, 385.

[5] Barbour, *Bruce*, 240–1.

Monthermer, who had been styled earl of Gloucester before the
succession of his step-son Gilbert de Clare, was likewise liberated
without any ransom.[1] Such remarkable treatment for a man of the
highest rank suggests that there must be some kernel of truth in
Barbour's romantic tale of Earl Ralph saving Bruce from Edward I
in 1305 or 1306.[2] Sir Philip Moubray, after surrendering Stirling
Castle, was allowed to change sides and came into King Robert's
peace. The castle itself was razed to the ground. It is not the hero-
worshipping Barbour but a hostile English writer who tells us that
the bodies of Gloucester and Clifford were restored to their families
without any conditions or demands, and that Bruce's behaviour
towards the English captives was so humane and courteous that he
completely won their hearts.[3]

The humanity, coolness and resolve which distinguished the
Scottish king's actions were not wholly absent on the other side.
They had always been noteworthy in the career of the earl of Pembroke, in a period when these qualities were conspicuously lacking
among the English baronage as a whole. Now, after Bannockburn,
they were seen at their best. Pembroke succeeded, apparently on
foot, in shepherding a large body of half-naked Welsh infantry, perhaps several thousand in all, across the hundred miles of difficult
country between Stirling and Carlisle.[4] He may at first have had
Maurice of Berkeley with him,[5] and he would certainly have been
accompanied by men accustomed to command. They were unable
to prevent the Scots through whose country they passed attacking
and killing large numbers. Nevertheless, by far the greater part of
this big Welsh contingent won through to safety, and the fact remains a remarkable tribute to Pembroke's courage and powers of
leadership. It was probably one of this Welsh party which gave the
news of Bannockburn to some monastery in his own country,
perhaps Valle Crucis, whose chronicle contains what seems to

[1] T. Walsingham, Hist. Angli., 141, 'because of some close friendship with the
Scottish king, which some time before had chanced to develop at the English king's
court'.

[2] Above, p. 198.

[3] T. Walsingham, Hist. Angli., 141-2.

[4] Chron. Lanercost, 228; Barbour, Bruce, 238; Annales Londonienses, 231.

[5] Barbour, Bruce, 238, mentions only Berkeley and ignores Pembroke, but Berkeley
seems to have been captured at or near Bothwell.

be the earliest report of the battle that we have.[1]

If the Scots had had more horses at their disposal, if they had been rather more prepared than they were for such a resounding victory, if the earl of Dunbar had behaved like his counterpart at Bothwell, then it is possible that the peace would have been won with the war, and Robert Bruce, who was now recognized as king of Scots throughout his own kingdom, might have gained the same recognition south of the Border. As it was, he had won the independence of Scotland, though the English were not yet prepared to admit the fact. In addition, he had triumphantly vindicated his claim to the Scottish throne and his revolutionary bid for leadership of the community of the realm. By the tests of the age, legality by hereditary right, legality by the acceptance of the people, and legality by God's judgement in a trial of battle, King Robert had now attained to a position of unshakeable authority.

[1] T. Jones, *Brut y Tywysogion* (1952), 48–9 and 62–3.

Additional Note (see above, p. 319).
Sir Alexander Seton.

Professor Duncan has drawn attention to an important agreement or 'band', unfortunately preserved only in late and poor sources, made between Seton, (Thomas?) Hay of Lochwharret (Borthwick) and Neil Campbell of Lochawe, probably *c.* 1308–10, in the presence of the abbot of Cambuskenneth (*SHR*, xlv, 199). The three knights swore to defend the liberty of the kingdom and Robert lately crowned king against all mortal men, French, English and Scots 'until the very end of their lives'. Thomas Hay had joined Bruce by Christmas, 1308 (*Cal. Docs. Scot.*, iii, No. 245). We may accept that the band was really made, and its language gives fascinating evidence of continuity between Wallace (above, p. 124) and Bruce, between the community of the realm in the time of the Guardians and in 1320, when the Declaration of Arbroath was composed in its name (below, p. 428). The band exemplified the part played in the independence struggle by the class of lairds or middling nobles (NLS, MS. Adv. 35.3.7, p. 318; Mackenzie, *Writers*, iii, 210).

13

War and Peace

FOURTEEN years separated Bannockburn from the Treaty of Edinburgh, which brought to an end the Scottish war begun by Edward I. By that time Edward of Caernarvon had been murdered and Robert Bruce was a sick man, within a year of his own death. The king of Scots' consistent objective during this period was to win from England recognition of his own position and a full renunciation of the English Crown's claims to suzerainty over Scotland. The efforts of Edward II and of most of the leading men of the community of the realm of England were directed towards avoiding or postponing these admissions. It is said that this was the price King Robert had to pay for his victory. Bannockburn, it is argued, was a mistake, because the English were bound to seek revenge. The reasoning seems curious; of the heads-I-win-tails-you-lose variety. It cannot seriously be maintained that the English would have been more ready to conclude a peace if Bruce had remained a *guerrillero*. As for the Scots, the effect on their morale if Bruce had lost Bannockburn or declined a pitched battle can easily be guessed.

There is no doubt whatever that Bruce had no wish to prolong the war. He would gladly have made peace at any time if his not very extravagant terms had been met. But he was confronted by a peculiar difficulty, arising from the historical structure of medieval England. The wealth of the country, its trade, its food production, its industries and its manpower, were all concentrated in the south and the midlands. To Englishmen south of Humber and Trent the Scottish war seemed immensely remote. It mattered little to them if Bruce extracted blackmail from the northern counties year after year and raided as far as Lancashire and Yorkshire. It is true that Bannockburn made a profound impression throughout England: it was, after

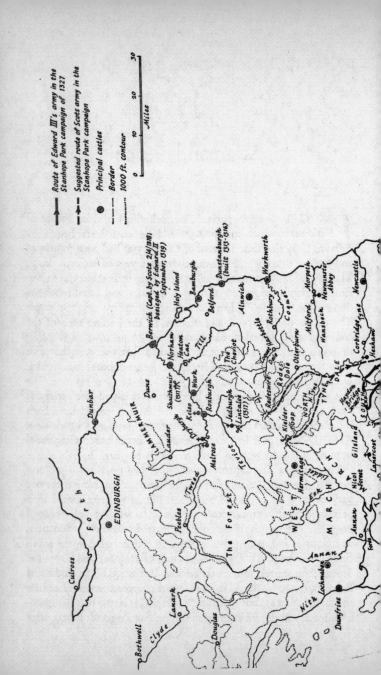

Route of Edward III's army in the Stanhope Park campaign of 1327

Suggested route of Scots army in the Stanhope Park campaign

● Principal castles

Border

1000 ft. contour

0   10   20   30
Miles

Culross
Forth
EDINBURGH
Bothwell
Clyde
Lanark
Douglas
Peebles
The Forest
Tweed
Melrose
Teviot
Ettrick
Dryburgh
Kelso
Roxburgh
Jedburgh
Lintalee (1317)
Duns
Smailmuir (1317)
LAMMERMUIR
Lauder
Lauderdale
Dunbar
Berwick (Capt. by Scots 24/1381; besieged by Edward II September, 1319)
Holy Island
Norham
Heaton Cas.
Wark
Bamburgh
Belford
Dunstanburgh (built 1313-1316)
Alnwick
The Cheviot
Warkworth
Coquet
Redesdale
Rothbury
Otterburn
NORTH TYNE
Mitford
Morpeth
Wansbeck
Newminster Abbey
Newcastle
Kielder Gap
Corbridge
Tyne
Hexham Bridge
SOUTH TYNE
Haydon Bridge
Hexham
Gilsland
Lanercost
Esk
Liddel
Hermitage
Nicol Forest
WEST MARCH
Annan
Nith
Lochmaben
Dumfries
Annan

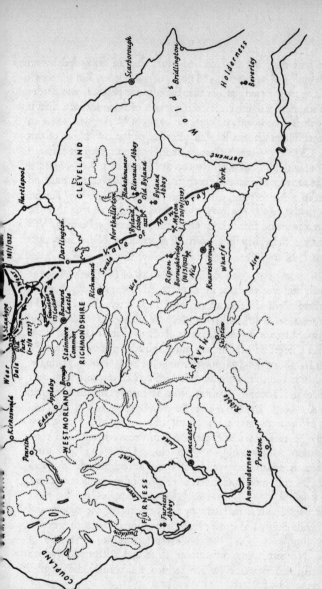

12. Southern Scotland and Northern England to illustrate the Scottish Raids, 1311–1327

all, the first time for six hundred years that an army led by an English king had been destroyed north of the Border. But the shock induced heart-searching rather than a desire for peace. It was harder for the southern English to learn the lesson of Bannockburn than it was for their descendants to learn the lesson of Yorktown. It was an additional but much smaller difficulty that of the two popes of this period, Clement V was a Gascon strongly predisposed in Edward II's favour and John XXII, who succeeded Clement in 1316, regarded Bruce as a sower of discord whose struggle was preventing England from taking her proper part in the crusade against the Turks.[1] Although the fact is not easy to explain, it remains true that the Scots gained more from the support given them by Boniface VIII before 1302 than they lost from the opposition of his successors between 1305 and 1323.

After Bannockburn, the Scottish raids south of the Border became so regular and frequent that they amounted to the virtual subjection of England north of Tees and involved the selective devastation of a still larger area. Northumberland suffered heavy depopulation and was reduced to a miserable anarchy. Ruffians such as Jack the Irishman and Gilbert of Middleton, and English garrison commanders (e.g., at Bamburgh) did as much harm as the Scots. Not surprisingly, many men in Northumberland and northern Cumberland went over to Bruce and became 'Scottish', just as many Lothian men had previously been 'English'. The Scottish leaders had three chief objects in view: revenue in blackmail; the recovery of Berwick, now the only Scottish town and castle left in enemy hands; and plain terrorization. All three objects were achieved, though it took time. A conservative estimate would put Bruce's total income in blackmail at £20,000, mostly received over a period of some ten years.[2] Berwick fell in 1318. And throughout northern England the mere rumour of a Scottish raid sent peasants fleeing to the woods and moors while clergy and gentry made joint efforts, as best they could, to buy immunity. Only in the exceptionally strong castles of Carlisle, Norham, Newcastle upon Tyne and Richmond (which never fell), and Berwick (which resisted stubbornly) did English *morale* remain high.

[1] On Clement see *EHR*, lxxxiii, 303ff.
[2] Jean Scammell, *EHR*, lxxiii, 402.

No two raids were exactly alike, but they followed a pattern which was to become only too familiar. The leaders were usually Sir James Douglas – the 'Good Douglas' – and Thomas Randolph earl of Moray, whose audacity and skill grew with each new expedition. The raiders were mounted on sturdy light horses, 'hobins', strong in wind and limb and sure of foot, and from their hobins the men themselves derived their popular (and most misleading) name of 'hobelars'. They wore little armour, but took with them the weapons appropriate for fighting on foot in schiltrom formation. They lived rough and ate sparingly, every man carrying an iron plate or 'girdle' on which he could bake himself oaten bannocks at the bivouac fire.[1] We are not told how the large sums of blackmail were transported, but presumably coin could be stowed in leather bags slung over spare horses. Often the Scots were satisfied with promises that the money would be paid later at some convenient point close to the Border, taking hostages, however, to guarantee payment. A number of sumpter horses must have accompanied the raiders, for we have the significant story of how the Scots were overjoyed to find so much iron when they raided Furness in 1316, since iron was scarce in Scotland.[2] Most of the booty consisted of cattle and prisoners who would simply have to transport themselves; but the practice of driving off great numbers of animals had the consequence that whereas the raiders could strike with lightning swiftness when they were on their way south they were bound to be slower on the return journey.

Tough, brisk, grimly businesslike, these Scottish hobelars were exponents of a type of warfare not seen in Britain since the Danish raids of the ninth century. Set beside their highly professional operations, King John's cavalry at Dunbar and Wallace's spearmen at Falkirk seem to belong to a different era. It is hard to believe that some of the men accompanying Moray and Douglas had fought in

[1] Le Bel, *Chroniques*, 47–8.

[2] *Chron. Lanercost*, 233. In one of those graphic touches by which Barbour creates the illusion of having been present at the events he describes, he says of the Scots withdrawing from Stanhope Park (over Wolfcleugh Common?) in 1327:

'And tynt bot litill off thar ger
Bot gyf it war ony summer [sumpter]
that in the mos wes left liand.'

(Barbour, *Bruce*, 358.)

the armies of 1296, 1297 and 1298. We know of few such men for
certain, since most of those who have left their names in record have
done so because they were captured, killed or executed. But Robert
Baird of Strathaven, noted for his bitter hostility to the English,
Sir Gilbert Hay of Errol whom Bruce made Constable before March
1309, and Sir Robert Keith the Marischal, all of whose military
careers span the whole period from the Guardians to Bannockburn
and after, were perhaps not untypical of that class of lairds and lesser
nobles from which the patriotic cause drew so much of its strength.

The Scottish raids not only reached a new peak of effectiveness
after 1314, they were also much bolder and penetrated much further
south into the richer lowlands such as the Vale of Mowbray,
Amounderness and even Holderness. In August 1314, Edward Bruce,
James Douglas and John de Soules (great-nephew of Sir John de
Soules the Guardian)[1] devastated Northumberland, passed through
County Durham to raid in Richmondshire, and returned by Swale-
dale with enormous plunder, burning Brough, Appleby and Kirkos-
wald.[2] In a second raid the same year, King Robert seems to have
resumed the lordship of Tynedale held by Alexander III, for its men
did him homage.[3] Douglas and Moray raided in County Durham in
the summer of 1315, and on July 22nd of that year King Robert laid
siege to Carlisle.[4] Against the defenders' seven or eight stone-
lobbing engines the Scots had only one, of little use. They built a
'sow' or shelter for the sappers undermining the fortifications, and an
assault tower or 'berefrey', which sank in the soft earth when they
tried to wheel it up to the wall. On the 30th they made a general
assault, using the same stratagem of a diversionary attack by which
Edinburgh had been won, but this time it did not succeed. They
withdrew hastily on August 1st, leaving their siege equipment
behind them and suffering casualties at the hands of some of the
garrison, ably commanded by the sheriff of Cumberland, Sir Andrew
Harcla (of Harcla, now Hartley, near Kirkby Stephen). Six months
after this setback, King Robert and Sir James Douglas failed in their
second attempt to capture Berwick.[5]

[1] *Dumfriesshire Trans.*, 3rd Ser., xxvi, 186.
[2] *Chron. Lanercost*, 228–9.
[3] Ibid., 229. Confirmed by evidence discussed in *Arch. Æliana*, 5th ser., ii, 149–52.
[4] *Chron. Lanercost*, 230.
[5] Ibid., 232.

The summer of 1316 saw the raiders once again in north Yorkshire and also, for the first time, in Furness.[1] Thereafter, the attempted conquest of Ireland under Edward Bruce diverted large numbers of Scots until 1318.[2] Edward Bruce and the earl of Moray led a small but well-trained and well-equipped force which crossed from Ayr to Larne in May 1315. The veterans of Bannockburn had little difficulty in defeating the first local opposition under the Anglo-Irish lords of Ulster. Making a truce with the garrison of Carrickfergus, they pressed southward as far as Dundalk, and then returned to Connor in Antrim. After consolidating their hold on eastern Ulster, the Scots again marched south and won a series of victories over the chief English magnates and officials, including the justiciar, Edmund Butler. In May 1316, a year after he had left Scotland, Edward Bruce was crowned king of Ireland at Dundalk. Carrickfergus fell to the Scots in the following September, and that same autumn Edward Bruce and Moray crossed over to Scotland and succeeded in persuading King Robert to join them in Ireland at the head of large reinforcements. But instead of crowning Edward Bruce's triumphant career with final success, this combined expedition of the two royal brothers in the winter of 1316-17, dogged by pestilence and famine, foreshadowed the eventual – and inevitable – collapse of the Scottish attempt to set up an independent kingdom across the Irish Sea. In the reign of Robert Bruce, the Irish episode forms a digression, remarkable only for the display of the king's powers of leadership during the slow retreat from Limerick, the southernmost limit of his march. Although (as the author of the *Life of Edward II* realized) the Scottish expedition was undertaken partly with the aim of using Ireland as a base from which to attack Wales and England, it proved to be a diversion of manpower and resources which King Robert could ill afford. Early in 1317 he returned home and thereafter, although he paid two more visits to

[1] *Chron. Lanercost*, 233.
[2] No attempt has been made in this book to deal at length with Edward Bruce's attempt to win the crown of Ireland and his brother's supporting expedition. The Bruces' intervention in Ireland has been comprehensively discussed by Robin Frame, in *Irish Hist. Studies*, xix (1974), 3-37. See also R. Nicholson, *Scotland: the later Middle Ages*, 92-6, 118-9, 121-2; J. F. Lydon, in *Historical Studies* (ed. G. Hayes-McCoy, London, 1963), a paper which I did not 'too lightly dismiss' (R. Nicholson, *EHR*, lxxxi, 559) because in fact it appeared too late for me to use in the first edition of this book.

Ulster, he concentrated on direct invasions of England across the
Border.

Not that in Scotland 1316 and 1317 were years of military in-
activity. Douglas won great honour in February 1316, in a sharp
fight on Skaithmuir near Coldstream.[1] A strong party of horsemen
from Berwick, including several Gascon knights, had been out
raiding the Merse and Teviotdale to replenish their empty larders.
Douglas was in Selkirk Forest when he heard of the raid, and promptly
gave chase. The raiders turned about to meet him and in the fight
which followed, reckoned the hottest encounter Douglas ever took
part in, most of the Berwick men were slain, including Raymond de
Calhau, apparently a nephew of Piers Gaveston. In this period also,
Douglas inflicted heavy casualties on another raiding party, sent by
the earl of Arundel, at Lintalee, south of Jedburgh.[2] In yet a third
fray of the same kind, this time near Berwick, he routed a squadron
of English knights and killed its leader, Robert Neville of Raby, the
'Peacock of the North'.[3] The reputation of 'Monsieur James',
north and south of the Border, now stood very high, and it is not
surprising that when King Robert and Moray went to Ireland in the
autumn of 1316 Douglas was made warden or lieutenant of Scotland.[4]

North-country Englishmen, despairing of help from their king,
collected a fleet in the Humber and on their own initiative attempted
an invasion of Fife, probably in 1316 or 1317.[5] They landed either at
Inverkeithing or Donibristle and were half-heartedly challenged by a
party under the sheriff of Fife and, if Barbour is right, Earl Duncan
also.[6] One sight of the English invaders put such fear into the party
that they turned back from the coast. Five miles away, at Auchtertool,
a manor belonging to the see of Dunkeld, they were met by the
bishop himself, William Sinclair, a brother of Sir Henry Sinclair of
Roslin, one of Bruce's Lothian adherents. Indignant at their cowardice, the bishop, already in armour and mounted, put the knights to
shame by seizing a lance and riding off to do battle with the enemy.
His example was infectious, and very soon the English were driven

[1] Barbour, *Bruce*, 270–3; *Scalacronica*, 143.
[2] *Scalacronica*, 143; Barbour, *Bruce*, 287–91.
[3] Barbour, *Bruce*, 287–91; *Scalacronica*, 143.
[4] Barbour, *Bruce*, 278. Moray was at Lauder on Dec. 6th, 1316; S.R.O., Reg. Ho.
chrs., No. 83.   [5] Barbour, *Bruce*, 292–6; *Chron. Bower*, ii, 259.
[6] Barbour, *Bruce*, 293; see below, p. 391.

back in confusion, many of them being killed, and many others, trying to escape in too small a boat, drowned.[1]

The year 1318, which closed with the ominous defeat of the Scots at Dundalk and the death in battle of Edward Bruce, began with striking Scottish successes east of the Irish Sea. On the night of Saturday and Sunday, April 1st and 2nd, Douglas's men scrambled over the town walls of Berwick and got possession of the town after some fierce and confused street fighting in which Sir William Keith of Galston distinguished himself.[2] The entry had been contrived by an English burgess of Berwick, Peter of Spalding, who had charge of a section of the wall.[3] Barbour's story is that he was related by marriage to Keith the Marischal[4] and sent a message to Keith saying he would admit the Scots at his part of the wall on a pre-arranged date. Keith reported his treachery to the king, who decided to risk the possibility that a trick was being played, and assigned the task of taking Berwick to Moray and Douglas jointly. Berwick Castle was starved into surrender about eleven weeks later.[5] The loss of Berwick was a severe blow for the English, and it was followed by the capture of three lesser castles in Northumberland, Wark on Tweed, Harbottle in Coquetdale and Mitford.[6] In May 1318, a big raiding party swept south into Yorkshire, burning Northallerton and Boroughbridge. At Ripon the inhabitants shut themselves in the minster, and the Scots accepted an offer of a thousand marks as the price of not burning the city. Six citizens were delivered up as hostages to ensure payment. More than two years later three-quarters of the debt was still outstanding. Eventually the hostages' wives petitioned the king to intercede on their behalf with the

[1] Barbour, Bruce, 295.

[2] Ibid., 297ff. Keith of Galston was afterwards to bring the body of Douglas home from Spain, ibid., 376.

[3] Ibid., 298; Chron. Lanercost, 234–5; Scalacronica, 144. According to John of Tynemouth, Peter was bribed with £800 by Douglas, but afterwards executed on a false charge of plotting against the king's life (Stevenson, Illustrations, 5).

[4] Lord Hailes (Hailes, Annals, ii, 77n.) proposed over-ingeniously to substitute 'the Marche Earl' (i.e. Patrick earl of Dunbar) for 'the marschall' of Barbour, Bruce, 297, on the grounds that (1) Keith lived far from Berwick; (2) was not likely to have been sheriff of Lothian; (3) Grey (Scalacronica, 144) says that Spalding and the earl of March helped to procure the fall of Berwick. But in an undated charter of this period Keith is styled warden of Berwick, and he may well have had some interest in the burgh; Melrose Liber, No. 372.

[5] Barbour, Bruce, 302, says 'six days', but see ibid., 464–5. [6] Chron. Lanercost, 235.

archbishop of York, as lord of Ripon, to compel their heedless and callous fellow-citizens to pay off the ransom. After leaving Ripon, the raiding party burned Knaresborough, scoured the neighbouring woods for cattle, and returned home by Skipton in Craven.[1]

Affairs had now gone so ill for the English that in 1319, for one brief and unsuccessful campaign, King Edward and Earl Thomas of Lancaster actually joined forces and besieged Berwick, where they were repulsed by Walter the Stewart, to whom Bruce had committed town and castle.[2] The English king, however, had a respectable-looking force of some eight thousand men which Moray and Douglas were afraid to confront in open battle. Instead, they took their hobelars to Boroughbridge, by the West March, and began to ravage Yorkshire in the usual way. It was rumoured that Douglas intended to kidnap the queen, then at York, and she was removed to Nottingham. The mayor and citizens of York and its archbishop, the good and kindly William Melton,[3] raised such men as they could (chiefly inexperienced townsmen and clergy) and went out to do battle with the marauders, as Archbishop Thurstan had done in 1138. The Scots met this motley company a few miles east of Boroughbridge, at Myton-on-Swale, and made short work of them in a most unequal contest. Though the affair hardly earned any glory for Douglas and Moray, the 'chapter of Myton' (as it was called in irony, from the great numbers of clergy slain or put to flight) did cause Edward II to raise the siege of Berwick and retreat south of the Trent. In consequence, Douglas carried out the most savage raid yet seen on the west side of the Pennines, waiting till after the harvest, about November 1st, and then burning all the corn and seizing large numbers of men and animals in Gilsland and Westmorland.[4]

At Christmas the English secured a truce for two years.[5] The inter-

---

[1] *Chron. Lanercost*, 235-6; *Cal. Docs. Scot.*, iii, Nos. 707, 858.

[2] Barbour, *Bruce*, 304-10.

[3] For Archbishop Melton's handling of the situation caused by the war see Rosalind Hill, 'An English archbishop and the Scottish War of Independence', *Innes Review*, xxii, 59-71.

[4] Gilsland suffered severely from the Scottish raids. A schedule of assized rents due from the Gilsland farms of Wetheral Priory for the Whitsun and Martinmas terms, 1327, shows rents in arrears for periods of 2, 9, 10, 12 and in one case even 20 years. Yet the schedule also proves that after a few years' truce recovery could begin and that the district cannot have been totally depopulated. (Dean and Chapter of Carlisle, MS. Cartulary of Wetheral Priory, schedule bound in at the end of the volume.)

[5] *Chron. Lanercost*, 240.

val was to prove the decisive turning-point in King Edward's reign and life. In future, there would be no possibility of his leading a concerted attack upon Scotland with even a majority of the baronage behind him. In the meantime Moray and Douglas grew in strength, King Robert himself surmounted the most serious political crisis of his reign, the Soules conspiracy, while the community of the realm of Scotland met reiterated fulminations from the papacy with the famous letter addressed to Pope John XXII in 1320, usually called the Declaration of Arbroath.[1]

The conflict which broke out in Wales in 1321 between Humphrey de Bohun earl of Hereford and other marcher lords on the one hand, and the king's favourites, the Despensers, on the other, foreshadowed the disorder and upheaval in which Edward II's reign came to its end six years later. The king's relations with Lancaster had gone from bad to worse, a fact of which the Scots took full advantage. At the end of 1321 Lancaster entered into secret negotiations with Douglas and Moray in which Lancaster was quaintly referred to as 'King Arthur'.[2] Lancaster had little to offer in return for Scottish help. It is doubtful if Bruce took these negotiations very seriously. It was obviously in his interest, from a short-term point of view, to encourage civil war in England, but he is said to have remarked about Lancaster's overtures: 'How will a man who cannot keep faith with his own lord keep faith with me?' Certainly the negotiations were not allowed to hinder military plans. Barely had the two-year truce expired than Douglas and Moray were over the Border (January 6th, 1322) and plundering Tees-side. While Moray stayed at Darlington, Douglas raided Hartlepool and Cleveland and Walter Stewart (by now a hardened veteran) went to Richmondshire and sold immunity to its inhabitants at a heavy price.[3]

All this time Lancaster, although he was present in south Yorkshire with a sizeable force of armed men, did not lift a finger against the Scots. King Edward's immediate concern was to deal with Lancaster and his other baronial enemies, Hereford among them. He failed to prevent the two earls joining forces, but succeeded in driving them from the position they had taken up at Burton on Trent (March

[1] Below, pp. 424–30.
[2] *Cal. Docs. Scot.*, iii, No. 764 (summarizing *Foedera*, ii, 463, 472, 474). On this see J. R. Maddicott, *Thomas of Lancaster* (1970), 301–3.   [3] *Chron. Lanercost*, 241–2.

10th) to block the royal army's passage of the river. The earls retreated northward, meaning to join the Scots. Their plan was utterly frustrated by a brilliant and unexpected move on the part of Andrew Harcla. While the Scots were in Teesdale Harcla raised the levies of Cumberland and Westmorland, by-passed Moray, and took up a position covering both the ford and the bridge at Boroughbridge, where Lancaster would have to cross the River Ure. In the battle that followed (March 16th) Harcla's tactics were a deliberate and masterly imitation of Bruce's at Bannockburn.[1] Hereford was killed on the bridge, Lancaster, after a night's delay, was taken prisoner and soon afterward executed. The Scots prudently retired north of the Border. This copybook victory, which he had not deserved, brought out the worst in Edward II. His capacity for learning and forgetting nothing might have been the envy of a Restoration Bourbon. Boroughbridge led directly to the aggrandizement of the Despensers which in turn led to Edward II's downfall in 1327.

One immediate result was that it gave Edward II sufficient confidence to lead another expedition into Scotland. It proved to be his last. It was entirely fruitless and for the king personally nearly ended in a worse disaster than Bannockburn. The expedition, which crossed the Border about the beginning of August, followed a particularly provocative Scottish incursion led by Bruce himself. On July 1st, 1322, the king of Scots progressed down the west side of Cumberland, plundering as he went, crossed the Duddon Sands into Furness (which bought immunity with only partial success) and finally crossed the sands of the Kent estuary to burn Lancaster and Preston. The entire Scottish party was back over the Border in less than four weeks.[2] Edward II's answer was to march through Lothian as far as Edinburgh, but Bruce had ordered all cattle to be removed and food stocks destroyed. The main Scottish army was withdrawn to Culross, north of the Forth. The English sacked Holyrood Abbey but early in September famine forced them to withdraw, with very heavy loss.[3] The story went that in the whole of fertile Lothian they had found only one lame cow, straying in the cornfield of Tranent, of which the earl of Surrey remarked: 'This is the dearest beef that I ever saw;

[1] J. E. Morris, *Bannockburn*, 94–5; *EHR*, xix, 711–3.
[2] *Chron. Lanercost*, 246 (for Lenyn read Leuyn, i.e. River Leven).
[3] M. R. Powicke, in *Speculum*, xxxv, 561.

surely it has cost a thousand pounds and more!'[1] On their way south they attempted the sack of Melrose Abbey, but part of the army was surprised by Douglas, who in his usual way had been lurking in the Forest and rushed down amid shouts of 'Douglas! Douglas!' inflicting severe casualties.

The English king's retreat was the signal for Bruce to launch an exceptionally bold and dangerous raid, for which he had recruited a great host of men from north and south of Forth as well as from Bute, Argyll and the western isles. They entered England over the fords of Solway and presumably followed the familiar Eden valley route into north Yorkshire.[2] Knowing that Edward II was retiring southward, they struck out boldly across the North Riding towards the Hambleton Hills, apparently making for the region of Sutton Bank ('Blakehoumor') where they had never been before.[3] They were at Northallerton about October 12th, when Edward was still lodging in Rievaulx Abbey, fifteen miles to the south east.[4] Learning of the English king's whereabouts, Bruce moved swiftly towards Rievaulx, to find his direct route blocked by a considerable English force under the earl of Richmond, John of Brittany. Richmond was evidently occupying the western edge of Scawton Moor, overlooking Sutton Bank and Roulston Scar, a steep and partly rocky hillside, up which only a rough path gave access to the summit.[5] The only other way to Rievaulx was round by Helmsley, some fourteen miles. If they delayed, the king would certainly escape. Douglas and Moray at once began a fierce attack straight up the hillside. Sir Ralph Cobham, 'the best knight in England', was taken prisoner, and with him Sir

[1] Barbour, *Bruce*, 330.

[2] *Foedera*, ii, 496, shows that by September 27th, 1322, men were fleeing from the North Riding into County Durham with their cattle.

[3] *Chron. Lanercost*, 247; *Foedera*, ii, 497 (from which it appears that the encounter upon 'Blakehoumor' was not fortuitous). For the identification of 'Blakehoumor' see A. H. Smith, *Place-Names of the North Riding of Yorkshire*, 197, where the references to *Yorkshire Lay Subsidy* (Yorks. Arch. Soc., 1897), 56, and to *Yorkshire Deeds* (Yorks. Arch. Soc., 1924), iv, 85, certainly refer to a locality in the region of Old Byland. The account in the text is based on the assumption that when contemporary sources use the name Byland they mean Old Byland; and that in Barbour, *Bruce*, 332, line 368, 'Bilandis abbay' is a mistake arising from confusion between Old Byland (close to Rievaulx Abbey) and [New] Byland Abbey.

[4] *Cal. Docs. Scot.*, iii, Nos. 790, 791; *Chron. Lanercost*, 247; *Scalacronica*, 149.

[5] Barbour, *Bruce*, 332 and *Chron. Lanercost*, 247, agree on the nature of the terrain, and their accounts will fit only Sutton Bank and Roulston Scar.

Thomas Uhtred, better than the best, for he had held his ground longer than Cobham. At the critical moment, King Robert ordered his highlanders and islesmen to climb the precipitous cliffs to one side of the path so as to take the English on the flank. Before long, Richmond and his knights, assailed by Douglas and Moray on their front and unable to break the wild highland charge across the top of the high ground, gave way and fled in confusion. Richmond himself was captured, and with him a noted French lord, Henry de Sully, butler of France. Many others were killed or made prisoner. The Scots failed to achieve their main objective, for King Edward had just enough warning to make his way first to Bridlington and then to York.[1] For the second time in eight years, he was forced to abandon his personal possessions and equipment, silver plate, jewellery, horse trappings and harness.[2] It was only by the merest good luck that he eluded his pursuers, who followed hot on his heels to the very gates of the city. Nationally speaking, the affair was not a disaster like Bannockburn: but for the king the humiliation was far greater.

Baulked of their prey, the Scots – or a large party of them – coolly crossed the Yorkshire Wolds to Beverley, where they levied blackmail as usual. They returned to Scotland on November 2nd. Richmond, a close friend of Edward II and apparently the object of Bruce's special dislike, was not ransomed for two years. It was not Bruce's intention to antagonize the French, and consequently, after giving a hospitable welcome to Sully and the other lords from France who had been captured with Richmond, the king of Scots sent them home free of ransom. Before returning to France, Sully assisted in the negotiations which led eventually, in May 1323, to the conclusion of an Anglo-Scottish truce intended to last for thirteen years. This truce, to be discussed in more detail shortly, was the nearest the English had come since Bruce's coronation to making a firm peace with the Scots. It was a measure of the success which King Robert had achieved after seventeen strenuous years. But neither Bannockburn nor the rout near Old Byland had taught Edward of Caernarvon good sense or moderation, and he began the truce negotiations with a letter that referred only to the 'people of Scotland' and ignored

[1] *Gesta Edwardi de Carnarvan*, 79–80 (which says wrongly that Edward was at Byland Abbey instead of Rievaulx); *Chron. Lanercost*, 248.
[2] Ibid., *Cal. Docs. Scot.*, iii, No. 791; *Foedera*, ii, 498.

their king altogether. Bruce's own comment on this letter as expressed to Henry de Sully the go-between, shows both dignity and a sense of humour in the face of such an exasperating opponent.

'Robert, by God's grace king of Scotland, to the most noble Henry, lord of Sully, knight, his good friend, affectionate and loving greeting. You will recall, my lord, how it was stated in our letters sent to the king of England, and how also we informed you by word of mouth, that we desired and still desire at all times to negotiate with the king of England on a final peace between him and us, saving always to us and to our heirs our realm free and independent, and also the integrity of our allies. If the English king had been agreeable, we were willing to make a truce until Trinity (May 22nd). Regarding this, my lord, we have received your letters and transcripts of letters from the king of England declaring that he has "granted a truce to the people of Scotland who are at war with him". To us this is a very strange way of speaking. In earlier truces, even though the English king has not deigned to call us king, we have at least been named as the principal on one side, as he has on the other. But it does not seem advisable to us to accept a truce in which no more mention is made of us than of the humblest man in our kingdom, so that we could demand no more than any other if the truce were to be infringed wholly or in part.'[1]

The long delay between Bannockburn and the peace treaty was not due solely to the pride of Edward II and the indifference of the southern English to the sufferings of their fellow-countrymen in the north. Peace would have come much sooner if King Robert had enjoyed the support of the papacy and the king of France, an advantage from which King John and the Guardians had benefited greatly down to 1302. Philip the Fair died in the year of Bannockburn. It was a misfortune for the Scots as well as the French that his long reign was followed by the three short reigns of Louis X, Philip V and Charles IV. Although Charles IV did not die until 1328, a year before Bruce's own death, his reign lasted only six years, and his brothers ruled for still shorter periods. From 1303 until the outbreak of the petty 'war of Saint-Sardos' in 1323, relations between France and England, although hardly cordial, were never so bad as to lead to open war and thus incite the French kings to support the Scots. And after the Saint-Sardos affair had been settled (1325) the English

[1] Foedera, ii, 511.

queen Isabella and her lover Roger Mortimer, from whom Bruce might have some hope of obtaining peace, became as obnoxious to the French as they were to Edward II. Consequently, although as early as 1309 Philip the Fair had recognized Bruce as king of Scots, there was no strong pressure from Paris to persuade Edward II to follow suit. All that Bruce could achieve was the formal renewal of the Franco-Scottish alliance in 1326.

With the papacy the position was rather different, for here Bruce had to contend with outright opposition and, indeed, the most stringent condemnation. John XXII was not naturally predisposed to favour the English kings, as Clement V had been, but he wished for peace among the powerful monarchs of western Christendom so that they might join forces in a crusade against the Turks. Neither the pope nor anyone else in the fourteenth century would have denied the reality of patriotism as a political force, or refused to acknowledge that it might be the motive of a just war. But the age of Bruce saw nothing especially sacred in patriotism or nationalism in themselves. In the minds of most men trained in law, philosophy or politics, patriotism could never transcend loyalty and obedience to lawfully constituted authority. Everyone would have agreed that defence of the realm was a fundamental duty and a legitimate *casus belli*. But to fight for one's *nation* or for one's *country* simply because one belonged to it and wished to preserve its integrity was quite a different matter, and might, indeed, be unlawful rebellion. To the ordinary man, it is true, the concept of patriotism, or of a racialism and xenophobia more primitive than patriotism, was clear and compelling. Members of the ruling class knew how to exploit it when necessary. Edward I, for example, in his summons to parliament in 1283, had inveighed against the wickedness of the Welsh nation (*lingua Walensium*) whose men had taken the lives of English people.[1] Bishop Sinclair of Dunkeld's reported words, when he shamed the cowardly knights of Fife in 1317, were 'Whoever loves his lord *and his country*, follow me!'[2] But Robert Bruce could never have justified himself and his cause before the bar of contemporary opinion if his aim had been nothing more than 'Scotland for the Scots'. Philip the Fair, admittedly, had praised the Scots in 1299 for bravely defending

[1] Stubbs, *Select Charters* (9th edn), 460; cf. ibid., 480, anti-French propaganda, 1295.
[2] Barbour, *Bruce*, 294.

their 'native land' (*defensionem natalis patrie*) but this defence was coupled with firm loyalty to King John.[1] Similarly, King Robert, once he had been, and could manifestly be seen to have been, chosen by the community of the realm of Scotland, was at pains to emphasize that his war with Edward II, even his fearful incursions beyond the Border, were in defence of his kingdom and of that same royal dignity of Scotland which had inhered in the monarchy of Alexander III and had been so carefully preserved by the Guardians.

It was difficult, naturally, to persuade the pope to accept this. Down to 1304, the Scots had acknowledged John Balliol as king. He had never been formally deposed by the Scots, and the parliament of 1309 which affirmed Robert Bruce's right had not been clearly a full and representative assembly of the community of the realm. What was worse, Bruce himself had begun his reign by murdering his chief rival in church. Even if Pope John had been utterly impartial and not in the least disposed to listen to English propaganda, he could scarcely be blamed for being in no hurry to recognize Bruce's title, even although Bruce, as a private person, had been absolved in 1310 from the sin of killing John and Robert Comyn.

The record of Pope John's attempt in 1317 to compel the Scots to observe a two-year truce with the English contains the clearest statement of Bruce's position and, incidentally, what Lord Hailes called 'the best original portrait of Robert Bruce which has been preserved to our times'.[2]

In August or September 1317, after much difficulty, the two cardinals who were Pope John's legates in England managed to send two envoys to King Robert personally.[3] They were honourably received and the king listened attentively to the papal proposals for peace. Then, after taking the advice of his councillors 'like a wise man', the king declared that he did indeed desire to have a firm and lasting peace. But without the advice of his whole council and other lords, he could not say definitely whether he would hold talks with the cardinals so long as they continued to address him merely as 'Governor of Scotland'. Bruce's ironic remarks at this point are best put into direct speech. 'We cannot,' he told the envoys, 'say anything in reply to the cardinals' letters which are not addressed to us as king. There are several Robert Bruces who, in company with the other

[1] *Cal. Docs. Scot.*, ii, 536.   [2] Hailes, *Annals*, ii, 74.   [3] *Foedera*, ii, 340.

barons, are "governors of the kingdom of Scotland". We will in-
spect and have read out to us the pope's open letters [which bore only
a general address], but we will not open the pope's sealed letters, for
they carry no royal title and are not addressed to us.' But the king's
councillors assured the envoys that the king would gladly negotiate
with the cardinals if they addressed him correctly.

The envoys reported to the cardinals that even the official news of
Pope John's coronation had been kept out of Scotland because the
relevant bulls did not use Bruce's royal title. To Bruce himself they
tried to excuse the pope's omission of his title by explaining that as
long as a case was *sub judice* the papal see did not wish to say or write
anything which might prejudice one or other of the parties. They
thereby laid themselves open to the king's unanswerable retort that
if the papal see did not wish to prejudice one party [Edward II]
by calling Bruce king it was not clear why it should prejudice the
other party [himself] by not doing so. 'Especially,' Bruce added,
'since I have possession of the kingdom, my royal title is acknowledged throughout the kingdom, and foreign rulers address me as
king. Our father the pope and our mother the church of Rome seem
to be showing partiality among their own children. If you had
brought letters such as these to other kings you might have had a
rougher answer.' The reply was firm, but the king's tone was friendly
and his expression remained unclouded. King Robert knew how to
administer a stinging rebuke, but mercifully he was not afflicted by
the sudden convulsive rages to which the Angevins, especially
Edward I, were notoriously prone.

The pope's two-year truce should have run from 1317 to 1319, but
it was not observed by the Scots, who captured Berwick in defiance
of it. They ignored excommunication, a general interdict imposed on
all Scotland, and a prohibition of all Bruce's adherents, and their
relatives to the second degree, from holding ecclesiastical office.[1] The
two-year truce which Edward II was fortunate to obtain at the end of
1319 was duly observed, but it brought a firm peace no nearer.[2]
Lancaster's treasonable negotiations in 1321 and 1322 were too much
the intrigues of a slippery customer bent on his own selfish policies to

[1] *Cal. Papal Letters*, ii, 191-2, 199.

[2] For important but abortive negotiations at Bamburgh in March-April, 1321 see
P. A. Linehan, 'Anglo-Scottish relations in a Spanish manuscript', *BIHR*, xlviii,
106-22.

be a constructive step towards peace. The next negotiations were held at Lochmaben on January 3rd, 1323, between Bruce himself and Sir Andrew Harcla, who since his victory at Boroughbridge had been earl of Carlisle. These also were a piece of private enterprise, undertaken without Edward II's knowledge. Consequently, they were held to be as treasonable as those of Lancaster, and Harcla, like Lancaster, was accused of furthering his own ambition, even of seeking a marriage alliance with the Bruces. Harcla may have been ambitious, but it is much easier to excuse his treason than Lancaster's. The rout near Old Byland had convinced men in the north of England that Edward II was incapable of defending them. Yet he would not adopt the only alternative policy and treat for peace. A contemporary observer on the spot, who seems to have heard his last speech from the scaffold, said that Harcla, realizing that Edward II could not rule, judged that it would be better for the communities of both kingdoms that each king should possess his kingdom freely and peacefully, without homage, rather than that every year there should be so much slaughter, burning and depredation, so many people made captive and so much land laid waste.[1] Harcla's mistake was to put into action, too soon and on his own initiative, thoughts which must have been in the minds of many contemporaries. At least his trial and the horrors of his execution (March 2nd, 1323) were not in vain if they helped to pave the way for the thirteen-year truce which was concluded two months later.

Harcla's abortive peace negotiations are worth looking at briefly, for they show better than the thirteen-year truce the way King Robert's mind was working on the terms of a final settlement. Unfortunately, the surviving texts of the Bruce-Harcla treaty represent two different versions, and it is not certain which was meant to be binding. According to the best text, preserved at Copenhagen,[2] the two kingdoms would be distinct and separate, each having its own king 'of its own nation', and governed according to its own laws, customs and rules. The earl promised the king and the community of the realm of Scotland to do everything in his power to implement the treaty and to secure King Robert and his kingdom in their independent status. For their part, King Robert and the whole com-

[1] *Chron. Lanercost*, 248; cf. ibid., 251.
[2] *Proc. Soc. Antiq. Scot.*, iii (1857–60), 458–61; also in Duncan, MS.

munity of the realm promised to promote and maintain the common advantage of the English kingdom. Twelve arbiters, six from each country, would be appointed to settle differences of detail and interpretation between the king and the earl. If the Scottish king brought an army to England under the terms of the treaty he would not harm the earl's property, nor would the earl harm the king's property in the [unlikely] event of his taking an army into Scotland. If Edward II could be persuaded to accept these terms within a year, Bruce would (1) pay him 40,000 merks, in ten annual instalments; (2) found a monastery in Scotland with an income of 500 merks *per annum*, for the souls of those killed in the war; and (3) give the English king the right to choose a wife from his own family for Bruce's male heir, provided that Bruce and Harcla and the twelve arbitrators deemed this desirable in the interests of both kingdoms. If, however, Edward II did not accept the terms within a year, Bruce would not be bound by these last three conditions. Finally, neither king would be forced on the conclusion of peace to receive back into his own kingdom anyone who had fought against him, or to restore his lands.

The other version of the treaty survives in copies kept in England.[1] They presumably represent a text originally in Harcla's possession, and used against him at his trial; but it is possible that they are not to be regarded as final and definitive. The chief difference between the 'English' version and the Copenhagen version is that the former seems to have envisaged the twelve arbiters becoming a body of regents or guardians who would decide matters for the common good of both realms; moreover, the great lords would be sworn to carry out the decisions and commands of the twelve. Nothing was said about Bruce bringing an army into England. It must be remembered that this agreement was made only seven months after the parliament of York, in which the Ordinances of 1310–11 had been annulled. It is tempting to suggest, therefore, that Harcla took back with him to England a slightly watered-down version of the agreement which kept silent about Scots military intervention in England but gave prominence to a baronial body that might seem attractive to those who sympathized with the Lords Ordainers and

---

[1] The best version of these is probably that found on an Exchequer Memoranda Roll (P.R.O., E.159/96, m. 70), summarized *Cal. Docs. Scot.*, iii, No. 803. This is printed in Stones, *Documents*, No. 39, which see for the various chronicle versions.

wished to revive the Ordinances. But it would be unwise to exaggerate the differences between the two versions of the treaty. The points of overwhelming importance – the independence of Scotland, the generous price offered for Edward's acceptance, the marriage alliance and the refusal to rehabilitate men of either side who had forfeited their estates in Scotland or England – all these were present in both versions.

Bruce's generosity was undoubtedly the most remarkable single feature of the treaty. In 1189, William the Lion had paid 10,000 merks for his independence, but this was after his defeat in war and fifteen years of subjection. In 1266, Alexander III, after a single battle, militarily quite inconclusive, had paid Magnus of Norway 4,000 merks plus a perpetual tribute of 100 merks a year in return for Norway's surrender of any title she might have to the Isles. Now, after a bloody war of nearly thirty years, during the last half of which Bruce had won victory after victory, he was prepared to pay nearly £27,000 in return for the English Crown's renunciation of all claim to suzerainty over Scotland. This was an appreciably larger sum than that ultimately accepted by the English in 1328.

The thirteen-year truce was concluded at Bishopthorpe, near York, on May 30th, 1323, and confirmed by Bruce at Berwick on June 7th.[1] It touched on hardly any points of fundamental importance for a final Anglo-Scottish peace, but it lessened friction on the Border and produced a reasonably calm atmosphere for the serious peace talks of 1324 at York. These talks, however, foundered on the question of suzerainty, for Edward II still refused to concede points which involved what he called 'the manifest disinheritance of our royal crown'.[2] Under the truce, no new fortifications were to be built in the border counties of either country, there were to be special wardens to control crossing of the Border, to settle disputes, and to report unresolved disputes to the two kings. Sensible provisions were made to protect the shipping, Scottish and foreign, trading to Scotland, most of which had to run the gauntlet of the English coast.

One important clause provided that Edward II would not hinder the Scots from obtaining absolution from the pope and the lifting

[1] *Foedera*, ii, 521, 524.
[2] Ibid., 595.

of the sentences of excommunication and interdict. Yet in the very
next year (1324) Edward II sent a powerful mission to the papal
curia, headed by the bishop of Winchester, John Stratford (afterwards archbishop of Canterbury), whose chief purpose was to
secure the continuation and if possible the intensification of the papal
sentences against the Scots. With staggering effrontery, the English
king demanded, among other things, that no one in Scotland should
be made a bishop in the Scottish church, 'for it is the prelates of
Scotland who encourage the nobility, gentry and people (*status*) in
their evil acts'.[1] In particular, he asked that John of Egglescliffe, an
Englishman who had been made bishop of Glasgow in 1318 through
English influence (and who, of course, had never been able to set
foot in Scotland) should not on any account be translated to a see
outside Scotland. The pope's reply to these demands, remarkable in
view of the fact that Scotland was under an interdict and her king excommunicate, was that since no Englishman could enter Scotland the
people would have no bishops, a state of affairs he could not tolerate.[2]
The pope did, however, agree to Edward's request that when a new
bishop was appointed in Scotland the papal bull authorizing the
sovereign to deliver to the new bishop the temporalities of his see
should be addressed to Edward 'and not to any other person', a
practice which Edward quite mistakenly claimed had always been
followed in the past.

In 1325 the English king got his way. Pope John rejected Bruce's
plea that he and his kingdom should be freed from excommunication and interdict, and duly received Edward II's profuse thanks.[3]
But at least Bruce had been able to obtain papal recognition of his
royal title. Late in 1323, the earl of Moray went to the papal curia
and in the pope's presence argued most shrewdly the case for
recognizing Bruce as king of Scots. On January 13th, 1324, the pope
wrote to Edward II to explain, half-apologetically, that he had
decided to address Bruce as king in future, for to do so 'could not
diminish your right and honour, nor add to Bruce's', but would
help to bring peace nearer.[4] What King Robert made of Edward II's

[1] *Foedera*, ii, 541ff.
[2] Ibid., 542, *Responsiones Papae ad articula*, 2, 3.
[3] *Foedera*, ii, 613.
[4] Ibid., 541.

dishonourable behaviour during these years we are not told. From his point of view the truce was of very little value unless it quickly led to a peace settlement. It is only surprising that Bruce agreed to a truce for as long as thirteen years, when he must surely have counted upon a peace treaty being concluded long before that period had ended. And, as though his intrigues at the papal curia were not sinister enough, Edward II took another step in 1324 (July 2nd) which must have appeared to the Scottish king in the worst possible light. Edward Balliol, son and heir of King John, who since his father's death in 1313 had been living on the Balliols' ancestral estates in Picardy, was commanded to come to England and given a safe-conduct to do so.[1]

It was some compensation for all this English activity that in 1326 Bruce was able to renew formally the alliance with the king of France. The negotiations seem to have been conducted on the Scottish side by the earl of Moray, Master James Ben (Lamberton's successor in the see of St Andrews), Master Adam Murray and Master Walter of Twynholm (Abbot Bernard's successor as chancellor). Their mission to the French court resulted in the treaty of Corbeil (April 1326) whereby each country undertook to give military aid to the other against the king of England.[2] The revival of the formal Franco-Scottish treaty must be seen in the light of the little war of Saint-Sardos, which, although it did not break out until the summer of 1324, originated in an outrage committed in October 1323. When Charles IV embarked, in the spring of 1324, on action which would surely lead to war with England, he must have regretted the absence of any firm commitment on the part of the Scots. Even so, and in spite of the truce of Bishopthorpe, it was apparently believed in English government circles that the Scots would intervene if there were to be an Anglo-French war. The papal nuncio in London, Hugh of Angoulême, wrote to John XXII at Avignon on May 22nd, 1324: 'He who acts as king of Scotland (Robert I) has held his solemn council in a certain castle called Berwick. Although what was discussed is not known, it is generally believed that if there should be war, which God avert, Bruce will

---

[1] *Foedera*, ii, 558; repeated August 20th, ibid., 567.

[2] *APS*, xii, 5-6. See R. Nicholson, *Scotland: the later Middle Ages*, 117.

come to Charles IV's aid by every means in his power.'[1] It is a matter of great interest that Robert I decided against intervention at this moment; but he was soon embarking on the negotiations which led to Corbeil, and the initiative may have been as much French as Scottish.[2]

In the event, final peace was to come only after further warfare and under a new king of England. Edward II was deposed on January 20th, 1327, and Edward III, fourteen years of age, was crowned on February 1st. The Scots chose the very day of Edward's crowning to mount a dangerous assault upon Norham Castle, which might well have succeeded had not a Scotsman in the garrison got wind of the attack and warned the castle commander. This dramatically-timed assault was surely meant as a reminder to the new English government that if they chose to supplant one king by another they must face the consequences, one of which was that the thirteen-year truce was between Robert I and whoever was lawfully king of England. It was no more than a reminder, for it was not followed by any further hostile acts, but it succeeded in its purpose. The new rulers of England were a council of regency, of which the chief was Henry earl of Lancaster, brother of the executed Earl Thomas, and in whose counsels the queen-mother Isabella and her lover Mortimer had a considerable, though indefinable, influence. One of their first acts (February 15th) was to ensure that the truce was kept on the English side of the Border.[3] Then they proceeded to confirm the truce unilaterally (March 6th).[4] There is evidence which suggests fairly strongly that the English government sincerely desired peace, though it is true that in April troops were collected in the north. The Scots seem to have suspected English intentions,[5] and it is likely that King Robert's patience was close to exhaustion. There is no question that Bruce had ample ground for holding that the English had broken the truce since 1323, for (as Barbour says and as con-

---

[1] Vatican Archives, Instrumenta Miscellanea 944. I am indebted to Fr Charles Burns for providing me with information about this letter, together with a photostat.

[2] Chron. Lanercost, 258–9.

[3] Foedera, ii, 689 (Cal. Docs. Scot., iii, No. 907).

[4] Ibid., 696 (Cal. Docs. Scot., iii, No. 914).

[5] Chron. Fordun, i, 351.

temporary English records confirm)[1] Scottish and other ships had been seized on the high seas, cargoes stolen, and Scots people (including women and pilgrims) massacred, all without redress. But this does not explain why the Scottish king chose the summer of 1327 as the right moment to mount an invasion of England. It is possible that Moray and Douglas, who, as in the old days, actually led the raid, were in favour of a much more aggressive policy than their ageing and gravely ailing master. Yet Bruce's illness, so serious at this time that one hostile reporter declared that he could not last another year, did not prevent him crossing to Antrim, apparently at the invitation of certain Irish leaders. By an agreement forced upon Sir Henry Mandeville, the seneschal of Ulster, at Glendun on July 12th, 1327, King Robert secured food supplies delivered free at Larne, and compelled the pro-English gentry of Ulster to remain inactive until Whitsun of the following year.[2]

The main force of Scots crossed the Border on June 15th, probably through the Kielder Gap and down the North Tyne.[3] Besides Moray and Douglas, they had as leaders Earl Donald of Mar (a strong sympathizer with the deposed Edward II),[4] James Stewart, younger brother of Walter the Stewart who had died in 1326, and Archibald Douglas, Sir James's younger brother. They ravaged Weardale and another unidentified valley which Barbour calls 'Cokdaill' (Cockdale). The young king of England left York on July 10th with a large army, including many Hainaulters in the following of John of Hainault, to whose niece the king was betrothed. One of these Hainaulters, John le Bel, has left a graphic account of the campaign. On the 18th the English, then at Durham, could see

[1] Barbour, *Bruce*, 343; *Cal. Docs. Scot.*, iii, Nos. 853, 887, 888, 889, 965. On October 2nd, 1323, Edward II ordered the wardens of the truce on the Marches to arrest all Scots residing in England, ibid., No. 827. It was alleged in April 1326 that there had been 'unofficial' Scottish attempts to surprise the castles of Carlisle, Norham, Wark on Tweed, Dunstanburgh and Alnwick, ibid., Nos. 882, 883. Edward II seems to have made some attempt to discuss points of the truce with Robert I in June, 1326, *Foedera*, ii, 631.

[2] *Cal. Docs. Scot.*, iii, No. 922; R. Nicholson, *EHR*, lxxvii.

[3] *Chron. Lanercost*, 259. *Chron. Fordun*, i, 352, speaks of two incursions, one on June 15th, one in August. The place of entry in June is suggested (1) by Le Bel's remark that the Scots came in so quietly that no one in Carlisle or Newcastle got wind of them, Le Bel, *Chroniques*, i, 46; (2) by the fact that Weardale was their first objective.

[4] See R. Nicholson, 'The last campaign of Robert Bruce', *EHR*, lxxvii, 233–46.

smoke from the fires kindled by the raiders and set off in pursuit.
For two whole days they marched across boggy moorland, probably
by way of Blanchland,[1] but the Scots never came in sight. We might
have some chance of explaining the odd failure of the two armies
to make contact if we could identify the place Barbour had been
told of when he wrote:

> The Scottis men all Cokdaill
> Fra end till end thai heryit haill.[2]

For it seems clear that it was the Scots' decision to move to this
valley from Weardale that misled the scouts of Edward III. It may
be suggested, tentatively, that 'Cokdaill' was the valley of the little
River Gaunless, a large part of which is occupied by the ancient
parish of Cockfield.

At all events, the failure of their intelligence caused the English
army to make a grave blunder. Its leaders decided on a forced march
to the Tyne to cut off the Scots' retreat, and the cavalry reached
Haydon Bridge on the evening of the 20th. That night it came on to
rain heavily, and the rain continued for a week, sending a spate down
the burns and rivers, making the going difficult and living conditions utterly wretched. Morale sank very low. It was not until the
31st, when the English army was probably somewhere in East Allendale,[3] that an esquire, Thomas Rokeby, who had gone out to look
for the Scots, reported that he had found them nine miles away. He
had been captured, but joyfully released because the Scots were as
pleased to hear the whereabouts of Edward III as he would be to hear
of theirs. The English camped that night at Blanchland, and on
August 1st marched to the Wear, beyond which, on the south side,
the Scots were drawn up in a very strong position on the slope of a
hill. Moray and Douglas refused to leave this position to do battle
on more open ground, and deadlock might have been reached had

---

[1] Edward III lodged the second night 'in the mean hall of an abbey which was there',
Le Bel, *Chroniques*, i, 50. Only Blanchland will fit.

[2] Barbour, *Bruce*, 345. The suggestion that this was the Gaunless valley would fit
in with Grey's statement that Archibald Douglas's party fell upon and massacred a
large gathering of peasants *near Darlington* (*Scalacronica*, 154).

[3] Ibid., says that the English army marched to Haydon Bridge by way of 'Anandre-
dalle', clearly not Annandale but Allendale. East Allendale would lie on their natural
route south-eastward from the neighbourhood of Haltwhistle, where they forded the
Tyne, to Blanchland.

not the Scots, during the night of the 3rd, suddenly decamped and, apparently crossing the Wear, taken up a second position in Stanhope Park, one of the bishop of Durham's hunting preserves.[1] On the night of the 4th, Douglas audaciously raided the king's own quarters, inflicted heavy casualties and very nearly succeeded in capturing Edward himself. But the alarm was quickly raised and the king's personal servants put up a stout defence, his chaplain being among those killed. On the 5th the English were led to expect a night attack and prepared themselves accordingly. Their intelligence, however, must still have been extremely inefficient, for during this same night the entire Scottish force, doubtless much smaller in numbers than the English, but all well-mounted, slipped away unnoticed from Stanhope Park across a treacherous moss, and by the morning they were out of reach, well on their way to the Border. King Edward wept with mortification, and it cannot have been much consolation for him to write from Stanhope on August 7th that 'his enemies had stolen away by night secretly, as if vanquished'.[2] Once again, energy, discipline and experience of the countryside had scored, and an English king had been put to shame in his own land.

In this campaign the Scots had been twisting the English lion's tail. The reverse suffered in Weardale amounted to a military defeat and must have been deeply humiliating. It led at once to Edward III's withdrawal to York. This was bad enough, but King Robert followed up the Scottish success with a massive incursion into Northumberland.[3] In August and September he mounted an elaborate

[1] There is an unusually serious conflict of evidence among the most nearly contemporary authorities for the Stanhope Park affair. This probably reflects a genuine confusion and uncertainty on the part of the eye-witnesses from whom our accounts, directly and indirectly, are derived. The conflict is impossible to resolve, and the account in the text can be no better than an approximation, based on Le Bel, *Chroniques*; Barbour, *Bruce*; *Scalacronica*; *Chron. Lanercost*; *Cal. Docs. Scot.*, iii, Nos. 929, 933.

W. M. Mackenzie's notes (Barbour, *Bruce*, 482ff) are valuable, but his argument that the Scots were always on the north bank of the Wear needs modifying in view of the clear implication in Le Bel, *Chroniques*, i, 62, that when the English first approached they found the river between them and the Scots. Since the English were coming from Blanchland, they can hardly have been on the south side of the river, while the Scots were strongly positioned on a steep hillside, presumably the hill opposite Stanhope.

[2] *Foedera*, ii, 712.

[3] See R. Nicholson, *EHR*, lxxvii, 233–46.

siege of Norham Castle, while Douglas and Moray made less sustained attempts to capture Alnwick and Warkworth. The entire
countryside of Northumberland was ravaged. Marcher districts
which were relatively fortunate bought a truce till the following
Whitsun (May 22nd, 1328) for a large sum of money. These included
the Palatinate of Durham (except for Norhamshire), Richmondshire and Cleveland in the North Riding, probably Cumberland
and Westmorland, and possibly Allertonshire. It was believed that
the king of Scots was now bent upon the outright annexation of
Northumberland. It seems more likely that Bruce meant only to
terrorize the enemy into agreeing to make peace. But colour was
given to the rumours of annexation by the serious efforts he made to
capture Northumbrian castles and by the fact, which appears to be
authenticated, that he began to grant lands in Northumberland to his
supporters by charter.[1]

All this aggressive activity on the Scottish side, coming on top of
the Stanhope Park fiasco, the dismissal of the Hainaulters, and the
growing insecurity of the queen-mother and Mortimer, at last compelled the English government to begin negotiations for a firm and
final peace. It was idle for Isabella and Mortimer to issue any further
writs for military service, although they did so in the first week of
October, more for form's sake than from any real hope of saving
the situation.[2] On October 9th, two experienced English envoys,
Henry Percy lord of Alnwick and William of Denum, a well-
known common lawyer, were appointed to treat for a final peace.[3]
They sought out the king of Scots while he was still engaged on the
siege of Norham. At Berwick on October 18th Bruce sent a reply
containing six points which he required Edward III to grant under
his great seal.[4] These six points, intended to form the basis of a

[1] *Rotuli Scotiae*, 221b. Compare Barbour, *Bruce*, 361:

    'The landis of Northumbirland,
    That next Scotland thar wes liand,
    In fe and heritage gaf he
    and thai payit for the selys fee.'

with the record of the king's grant of part of Belford (formerly a Graham, before
that a Muschamp barony) to a Scrymgeour, September 4th, 1327, Duncan, MS.

[2] *Rotuli Scotiae*, i, 221-3.

[3] The essential guide here is E. L. G. Stones, 'The Anglo-Scottish negotiations of
1327', *SHR*, xxx, 49-54.

[4] Ibid., 51, 53-4; cf. Stones, *Documents*, No. 40.

final peace, were as follows. (1) King Edward and his baronage must acknowledge that Robert I and his heirs for all time to come should have the kingdom of Scotland free, quit and entire, without rendering any kind of homage. (2) King Robert's son and heir [David, born on March 5th, 1324] would be married to King Edward's sister [Joan of the Tower, born on July 5th, 1321], who would receive as dower a sum to be agreed on. (3) No person in the faith of the king of England or of his adherents might demand land or tenements in Scotland, nor might any person in the faith of the king of Scots demand land or tenements in England. (4) King Robert and his heirs would give military aid to the king of England against all, saving the alliance between the kings of Scotland and France. Similarly, the king of England and his heirs would give military aid to King Robert and his heirs in Scotland against all, 'as good allies'. (5) King Robert would pay £20,000 within three years of peace being made, giving reasonable security. (6) It would be ordained by the king of England and his council and by King Robert and his council that the sentence of excommunication pronounced at the papal curia against King Robert and his people should be formally repealed as soon as possible, and that King Edward would give aid and counsel to put this into effect.

If the king of England would inform the nobles of Scotland under his great seal that he was willing to confirm all six points and treat on these lines for a final peace, King Robert would command his envoys to go to Newcastle upon Tyne under sufficient safe-conducts from the English king, to negotiate with the English representatives.

On October 30th King Edward, then at Nottingham, agreed that negotiations should be started at Newcastle on the basis of a marriage between David Bruce and Joan of the Tower and a Scottish payment of £20,000.[1] The question of a military alliance and the peculiarly difficult problem of the 'disinherited' – the lords whose lands in either kingdom had been forfeited because of their allegiance during the war – were to be discussed by the envoys. If King Edward were satisfied on these points he would admit Robert Bruce's independent title to the kingdom of Scotland. It will be noted that the English reply was couched in language which still made it appear that King Edward III was a magnanimous victor and Robert Bruce a

[1] SHR, xxx, 51.

defeated rebel humbly suing for peace. But despite this form of words it was a great advance on anything that had gone before. The six points were sufficiently acceptable to the English to form the core and substance of the treaty of peace concluded in March 1328. The envoys negotiated at Newcastle during November and part of December. They must then have broadened their discussions to take in other matters on which one side or the other (or both) felt strongly, such as the limits of the Scottish kingdom, Scottish security in the Isle of Man, English security in Ireland, the restoration to Scotland (for cancellation) of all muniments showing or tending to show that the English Crown enjoyed a feudal superiority over Scotland, and any other documents touching on the liberty of Scotland.

The striking feature of these six points of October 1327 is their similarity to the chief points of the abortive 'treaty' made between King Robert and Andrew Harcla in 1323. According to the terms of the Harcla treaty the two kingdoms were to be separate and independent; indeed, the very same words were used, for in the Harcla treaty Robert was to 'hold' the kingdom of Scotland *francement, entierement et quitement*, and to 'have' his kingdom *frank et quit*, while in the points of October 1327 he was to 'have' the kingdom of Scotland *frank*, *quit* et entier'. Again, by the Harcla treaty King Robert agreed to let the king of England provide a wife from any suitable member of his own family for Bruce's male heir. In 1327 this offer was repeated, naturally more specifically, since by this date a son had been born to Bruce and his queen. In 1323 the Scottish king was prepared to pay 40,000 merks (nearly £27,000) for the recognition of independence. In 1327 this offer was admittedly reduced, but not by very much. The remarkable thing is that the Scottish proposals remained so generous. If Edward II and the Dispensers had accepted peace on Bruce's terms in 1323 the English would have fared better than they did five years later, when Isabella and Mortimer and the young king, Edward III, at last agreed to bring the war to an end.

The negotiations at Newcastle must have been largely successful. In February 1328 Scottish representatives came to York, where King Edward was holding the third parliament of his reign. In this parliament, on March 1st, the English king issued letters-patent, endorsed 'by the king himself and council in parliament', which at long last gave the Scots what they had been striving to obtain in some thirty years of warfare.

'Whereas we,' King Edward declared, 'and some of our predecessors, kings of England, have attempted to gain rights of rule, lordship or superiority over the kingdom of Scotland, and terrible hardships have long afflicted the realms of England and Scotland through the wars fought on this account; and bearing in mind the bloodshed, slaughter, atrocities, destruction of churches, and innumerable evils from which the inhabitants of both realms have suffered over and over again because of these wars; and having regard also to the good things in which both realms might abound to their mutual advantage if joined in the stability of perpetual peace, and thus more effectually made secure, within and beyond their borders, against the harmful attempts of violent men to rebel or make war; *we will and concede for us and all our heirs and successors, by the common counsel, assent and consent of the prelates, magnates, earls and barons and communities of our realm in our parliament that the kingdom of Scotland shall remain for ever separate in all respects from the kingdom of England, in its entirety, free and in peace, without any kind of subjection, servitude, claim or demand, with its rightful boundaries as they were held and preserved in the times of Alexander of good memory king of Scotland last deceased, to the magnificent prince, the lord Robert, by God's grace illustrious king of Scots, our ally and very dear friend, and to his heirs and successors.*'[1]

The letter, having thus concurred by implication in the Bruce doctrine that John Balliol had not been rightful king of Scots, went on to renounce any right the king of England and his predecessors might have sought in the Scottish kingdom, to cancel any obligations or agreements made by any of the kings or inhabitants of Scotland concerning the subjection of Scotland or of any of its inhabitants, and to declare null and void any documents which might subsequently be discovered relating to such agreements. It is virtually certain that the letter was not made public on March 1st, for an alternative version of the same date was prepared which spoke of the boundaries of Scotland *at the time of Alexander III's death*, thus explicitly including Man and the Hebrides within the Scottish kingdom.[2]

---

[1] Stones, *Documents*, No. 41a. (My italics.)

[2] See *SHR*, xxix, 27–8 and n. It must be emphasized that the main body of the treaty itself refers to the possibility of revolt 'in the Isle of Man or in the other isles of Scotland' (Stones, *Documents*, No. 41c) thus implying, as Professor Stones noted, English recognition of Scottish possession of Man and the isles.

The final version (as given above) was presumably not decided upon until the peace treaty was concluded sixteen days later. Its ambiguity might be manipulated in England's favour, though a fair and reasonable interpretation would surely have left the boundaries of Scotland as they stood in March 1286. The question of boundaries was a minor point when set beside Bruce's main achievement. His representatives at York had the immense satisfaction of knowing that the king of England in parliament had at last admitted the independence of Scotland in unambiguous terms. Moreover, by admitting Bruce's claim to be king, Edward III had acknowledged Scottish independence twice over, for it was abundantly clear that Bruce's title did not derive in the slightest degree from any English judgement, whereas John Balliol's title, however soundly based in law, had been established by a court one of whose chief purposes was to make manifest Edward I's sovereignty over the Scottish realm.

As a final demonstration of Bruce's achievement, the treaty of peace was concluded, not in England, nor even upon the Border, but on Scottish soil, at Edinburgh, which for perhaps a century and a half had enjoyed some claim to be regarded as the principal town and castle, if not the capital, of Scotland. An imposing delegation had been sent north from York by Edward III.[1] It was led by Henry Burghersh, bishop of Lincoln and treasurer, William Ayermin, bishop of Norwich, Sir Geoffrey le Scrope, chief justice of King's Bench, Henry Percy of Alnwick and William de la Zouche of Ashby. These commissioners had had experience of Scottish affairs, including the peace negotiations of 1324, and it may be noted in addition that Percy and Zouche were themselves interested parties, being two of the 'disinherited' with claims to land in Scotland. They reached Edinburgh on March 10th, with full powers to conclude and proclaim a final peace and to command its observance by subjects of the English king. Bruce had once more been laid low by sickness since his strenuous campaigning of the previous summer. He was confined to bed, and it was in fact 'in a chamber within the precincts of the monastery of Holyrood in Edinburgh where the lord king was lying' that the peace was concluded, after a bare week of final discussion, on March 17th.[2]

---

[1] E. L. G. Stones, 'The English mission to Edinburgh in 1328', SHR, xxviii, 121-32.
[2] SHR, xxix, 48.

Naturally enough, since the king himself was present, there was an impressive gathering of notables on the Scottish side. Many of the traditional spokesmen and leaders of the community of the realm were present in a properly constituted parliament, to conduct or approve the last negotiations and to witness the sealing of the documents which brought the long war to its close.[1] We can hardly doubt that Bruce himself, even on his sickbed, dominated the scene. The force of his personality, his strength of character, the magic of his name and reputation, would have ensured as much, even if he played little or no part in the actual business. But there were men with the king who would be accounted great in any age and company. Thomas Randolph and James Douglas, the two men who apart from Bruce had done more than any others to win the war and spread the fame of Scotland among the nations of Christendom, were both present. If they were unmatched in feats of war, their experience of negotiation and statecraft could be equalled by that of Bishop Lamberton of St Andrews, who could look back over thirty years of service to the national cause. Besides Lamberton there were six other bishops, John Lindsay of Glasgow, William Sinclair of Dunkeld, John of Pilmour of Moray, Maurice of Dunblane, Roger of Ross and Simon of Wedale of Galloway. Besides Randolph there were five earls, Duncan of Fife, the doyen of the earls of Scotland, Patrick of Dunbar or March, Murdoch of Menteith, Hugh of Ross and Donald of Mar (a future Guardian).[2] Geographically, these six earldoms were broadly representative of Scotland, but the list – for various reasons – shows notable omissions, e.g. Buchan, Angus, Atholl, Strathearn and Lennox. Only one other Scots magnate, Sir Robert Lauder, justiciar of Lothian, appears by name in the official records of the treaty,[3] but the writ of summons called for all the magnates,[4] and we can tell from charters and other royal acts issued at Edinburgh at this time that members of the king's household in attendance included the chancellor, Abbot Bernard of Arbroath,

---

[1] The text of the brieve of summons to this parliament has survived and appears in Duncan, MS.

[2] Statements about those present are taken from the records of the Treaty of Edinburgh and from charters and other acts of the king dating from this parliament, Duncan, MS.

[3] Stones, *Documents*, 170.

[4] Duncan, MS.

Gilbert Hay the constable, Robert Keith the marischal, and Andrew Murray of Petty and Bothwell, the pantler (the son of Wallace's colleague); while of the unofficial baronage there were present Sir Alexander Seton – whose role at Bannockburn had been so crucial – Sir Alexander Fraser of Touch Fraser (the king's brother-in-law), Sir Robert Menzies, Sir David Barclay, Sir David Lindsay of Crawford, and Sir William Muschet of Cargill and Kincardine-in-Menteith, and no doubt this list is very incomplete.

The terms of the final treaty show clearly that it was based on Bruce's six points of October, which in turn had derived from the abortive Harcla treaty of 1323. But there were some notable differences which prove that although both sides were keen to reach agreement their negotiations cannot have been easy and were not, in the end, entirely successful. Some matters of great moment were passed over, apparently being insoluble. The main provisions of the treaty were contained in five formal documents, all dated at Edinburgh on March 17th, 1328.[1] The main substance was published in two indentures, one in Latin and one in French. Next, there were two notarial instruments in which King Robert bound himself to pay the £20,000 he had previously offered. Finally, there were King Robert's letters-patent on the subject of the marriage settlement. It will be convenient to summarize these main provisions in the order of the six points of October 1327, as given above.

(1) King Edward's solemn renunciation of all claims to lordship, suzerainty, or sovereignty over Scotland, made in the York parliament on March 1st, was embodied *verbatim* in the text of the Latin indenture. (Perhaps this was the reason why this indenture was written in Latin and not in French.)

(2) A marriage was contracted between David Bruce and Joan of the Tower. They were to wed as soon as this could duly be done, having regard to their tender age. King Robert promised to make available to Joan before the following Ascension Day (May 12th) a dower of landed estates worth £2,000 a year, guaranteed for the term of her life. Should Joan die before the marriage could be solemnized, the English king would be free to arrange a marriage between David and someone else of the English blood-royal. Simil-

arly, if David were to die before the marriage, King Edward would be free to arrange a marriage between Joan (or some other suitable princess) and the heir-male of the king of Scots.

(3) No part of the final treaty dealt with the vexed question of the 'disinherited'. In the previous October, Bruce had very wisely proposed that no one dispossessed because of the war, on either side, should be reinstated. But on the English side the pressure exerted by certain disinherited lords, notably Henry Beaumont (who had married an heiress of the earldom of Buchan), Henry Percy and Thomas Wake of Liddel, was evidently very strong. Presumably this question was among those discussed, to no avail, at Newcastle in November and December 1327. In view of the presence of Percy and Zouche, we may guess that the subject was again raised at Edinburgh in the following March. But it is pretty certain that Bruce was determined not to risk the peace being wrecked by the bitter feuds which old property disputes might so easily beget, while it seems clear that on the English side there were several lords, both Scots and English, selfish enough to press their claims regardless of the public interest.[1]

(4) There was to be a military alliance between England and Scotland, saving the Franco-Scottish alliance of 1326. If their French allies drew the Scots into war, the English would be allowed to make war in return, notwithstanding the terms of the treaty. The bare proposals of 1327 were modified by two provisions showing where English and Scottish anxieties lay. If anyone in Ireland made war against the king of England, the Scots were not to help him. Likewise, if anyone in Man or the Hebrides made war against the king of Scotland, he was not to be helped by the English.

(5) King Robert bound himself to pay to King Edward £20,000 'for the sake of peace'. The money was to be paid at Tweedmouth in three annual instalments. It has been suggested that this sum may represent approximately the amount taken by Bruce from the northern counties of England in blackmail.[2] But since the king had been prepared to pay nearly £27,000 for the recognition of independence as early as 1323, the suggestion can hardly be accepted. However un-

[1] It should be made clear that these lords were not under threat of total disinheritance merely on the score of their allegiance. The choice before them was to swear allegiance *either* to the English king and recover their lands in England *or* to the Scottish king and recover their lands in Scotland.

[2] Jean Scammell, *EHR*, lxxiii, 402.

just or illogical it may seem, it was not uncommon for one party to a dispute to pay to have its lawful rights acknowledged by the other party. The two sums offered by Bruce at different times may be seen simply as the price he was prepared to pay to silence for ever the ancient quarrel between English and Scottish kings over feudal superiority. Had the English observed the terms of the treaty of Edinburgh – and Bruce had every reason to believe they would – then the sum of £20,000, large as it was for a poor country like Scotland, would surely not have been too great a price to pay for the permanent healing of this old sore.

(6) The English king and his council would do all they could to have the papal sentences of excommunication against Bruce and his subjects lifted. This Edward proceeded to carry out in good faith, and the sentences were in fact repealed by a bull of October 1328.

So much for the points in the treaty which can be compared with the preliminaries of October 1327. With one notable exception, all Bruce's six points had been incorporated in the final settlement. The heart of the matter was the English renunciation of sovereignty and – as a *quid pro quo* – the marriage alliance, which Edward III regarded as vital, because otherwise the future David II would undoubtedly have found a bride at the French court. As a corollary of the renunciation, King Edward agreed to restore to the Scots all documents touching on English claims to superiority. As a guarantee of the marriage, King Robert agreed to pay the impossibly large sum of £100,000 if by Michaelmas 1338 the marriage between David and Joan had not been solemnized. The point of this arrangement was that David Bruce would not reach the age of fourteen – the legal age for giving his consent to the match – till March 1338, and at any time before that date the Scots might repudiate the contract (or so the English feared).[1] Bruce was therefore given the fairly generous period of ten years, plus six months grace, in which to have the marriage solemnized. In fact, however, the Scots had no intention of defaulting on this part of the agreement. The English queen-mother travelled north with her daughter early in July 1328, and on July 12th Joan of the Tower and David Bruce, though minors, were married at Berwick on Tweed, in the presence of a great gathering of magnates of both realms.

[1] *SHR*, xxix, 30-1.

The king of Scots himself was either too ill or (more probably) too punctilious to travel to Berwick for the wedding, but Isabella and Mortimer took the opportunity, nevertheless, of reopening discussions on the subject of the disinherited. It seems that at this point the English government had the sensible idea of restoring to the Scots the Stone of Destiny and the Black Rood of Saint Margaret, looted by Edward I more than thirty years before.[1] Probably this action was meant as a softener to persuade the Scots to make concessions to the dispossessed lords who claimed estates north of the Border. Unfortunately, both the Black Rood and the Stone of Destiny remained at Westminster. It is said that the London mob prevented the stone's removal. But despite this it may have been on the occasion of the wedding that the Scots – perhaps because of the king's illness – imprudently conceded (though not as part of the formal peace treaty) that Beaumont, Percy and Wake should get their Scottish estates back.[2]

Thus, within a year of his own death, Robert Bruce at last achieved the object for which he had fought so long: peace between Scotland and England on the basis of mutual independence. The Treaty of Edinburgh of March 17th, 1328, was formally ratified on the English side at the parliament of Northampton on May 4th. It was a remarkably fair, honourable and statesmanlike settlement, considering the length and bitterness of the struggle which it brought to an end. It has been rightly said that 'it would indeed have been well for both countries if the agreement of 1328 had governed their relations for the rest of the middle ages'.[3] But with how much greater force might it be said that if Edward I had chosen to abide by the spirit of that earlier agreement, the treaty of Birgham, which he ratified at Northampton in the summer of 1290, the later agreement, which his grandson ratified at Northampton thirty-eight years afterwards, would never have been necessary, and there would have been no occasion for the dark years of carnage and destruction, and the breeding of hatred between two nations who for the past century had been learning, not without success, to be friends.

[1] *SHR*, xxiv, 33; *History*, xxxviii, 56–8. On the English failure to restore the Black Rood (despite the report in *Chron. Lanercost*, 261), cf. E. L. G. Stones, *SHR*, xxxviii, 174–5.

[2] *SHR*, xxix, 34–5; Stones, *Documents*, No. 42.

[3] *History*, xxxviii, 61.

14

Good King Robert

HAD Robert Bruce done no more than defy the power of
Edward I, restore the monarchy and win the battle of Bannockburn, he would still be reckoned among the Titans. But his fame
among contemporaries and with posterity has always rested on a
broader and more profound achievement. He was known to later
generations of his countrymen as 'Good King Robert'. The epithet
has been most sparingly distributed among Scottish sovereigns.
Contrary to what might be supposed, the title 'good' was not
bestowed automatically upon every king of Scots who defeated the
English. Its attribution to Bruce sprang from a popular, instinctive
feeling that he had achieved a *rapport* with the community of the
realm which was closer, more securely established than any comparable relationship experienced by his predecessors or successors,
even by James IV at the height of his popularity. Much of this
instinctive feeling must have been derived ultimately from a direct,
personal knowledge of Bruce which is denied to us. We see him
only through the opaque and sometimes distorting glass of record
and chronicle. We may be disappointed, even disillusioned, to see
the hero and champion of his people acting very much as a man of
his time: a conservatively feudal prince, an exponent of a particularly
brutal and destructive form of warfare, a dynast prepared to use his
country's resources in furtherance of family aggrandizement in
Ireland, a begetter of bastards, an accessory, if not a principal, in a
deed of plain assassination. But the feet only seem to be made of clay
if we choose to idolize the man. Record and chronicle, which show
us the defects and shortcomings of the king, also give abundant proof
of his courage, prudence and magnanimity. Perhaps, indeed, it was
above all the king's humanity which won the affection of his

people, the humanity so remarkably exemplified in the story Barbour tells of how once, in Ireland, retreating in perilous circumstances, Bruce halted the entire army to give protection to a poor laundress in labour, until she could be safely delivered of her child.[1] The stature and the statesmanship of King Robert I appear enhanced rather than diminished when we see him grappling with political difficulties and often failing to find an easy or brilliant solution. He had to manage rough and unruly noblemen who did not all go in awe of him; he had to manage churchmen who, however much they might be his loyal supporters, owed allegiance to the Church and to its own monarchy the papacy. Above all, he had to manage the community of the realm, impalpable, inarticulate, yet always a force to be reckoned with; wayward to lead, yet impossible to drive. King Robert's problems in government can best be understood, his success best measured, if we look in turn at his relations with the clergy, the nobles, and the community as a whole.

(i) The clergy

In 1324, as we have seen, Edward II complained to the pope that it was the prelates of Scotland who were chiefly responsible for encouraging the nobles and people to make war upon the English. Beyond any question, the part played throughout the war of independence by the Scottish bishops was crucial. But it would not be true to say that Bruce always had the Church behind him. Only three bishops attended his coronation. Of these, Wishart and Lamberton were old hands at the game, former Guardians, while David Murray was deeply involved in the national cause, and belonged to a family which, perhaps more than any other, was identified with the fight to preserve Scottish independence. It was to be some years before Bruce could count on the support of a majority on the bishops' bench, equal to that enjoyed by the leaders of the nation between 1296 and 1304.

Down to 1302, thanks to a benevolent papacy (especially under Boniface VIII, 1294–1303), the Scots had normally been able to secure the consecration of bishops favourable to the patriotic cause: Matthew Crambeth (Dunkeld, 1288), Thomas of Dundee (Ross, 1296), William Lamberton (St Andrews, 1298), John Kinninmonth

[1] Barbour, Bruce, 285–6.

(Brechin, 1298), David Murray (Moray, 1299). But King Robert found it extremely hard to persuade a hostile papacy to confirm the episcopal appointments that would have met with his approval. True, in 1307 he seems to have got Nicholas Balmyle made bishop of Dunblane. But even on an interpretation of the evidence which is most favourable to Bruce, he cannot be allowed an attendance of more than five bishops at his St Andrews parliament in the spring of 1309. His biggest difficulty was in connexion with the two bishoprics of St Andrews and Glasgow, which were pre-eminent both ecclesiastically and politically, and together made up nearly half the population of Scotland.

Robert Wishart, who had already held his see for thirty-four years, was imprisoned in irons in 1306, and the English kings made strenuous efforts to have him deprived of his office by the papacy. In 1308 Wishart, escorted by the bishop of Poitiers, was allowed to go to the papal curia to answer the charges against him. Two years afterwards he was still at the curia, and in January 1311 Edward II argued the case against his return to Scotland in a bitterly-worded letter.[1] Some months later, King Edward requested the pope to remove Wishart from his see and put in his stead Master Stephen Segrave.[2] Pope Clement V, to his credit, neither suspended nor deprived Wishart, but he would not use his influence to have him set free and restored to his diocese. The bishop returned to English custody until after Bannockburn, when, much aged and going blind, he came home to Scotland (along with the royal ladies) in exchange for the earl of Hereford. He died on November 26th, 1316, indisputably one of the great figures in the struggle for Scottish independence, the statesman of the period 1286 to 1291, the patron and friend of Wallace and Bruce, the persistent opponent of Plantagenet pretensions, an unheroic hero of the long war.

For most of the years during which the English had possession oɩ the bishop, King Robert had possession of his diocese. He could not afford to see its organization fall apart and its rich revenues dissipated. By April 1309 he had appointed a high-ranking governmental commission to take charge. Bernard of Linton the chancellor and, with

---

[1] *Cal. Docs. Scot.*, iii, No. 194; *Foedera*, ii, 126. Unless otherwise noted, statements about episcopal appointments and careers are based on Dowden, *Bishops*.

[2] *Cal. Docs. Scot.*, iii, No. 207.

him, Master Stephen of Dunnideer, a canon of Glasgow who was
already king's chamberlain, were made vicars and lieutenants of the
see on Wishart's behalf. Dunnideer, formerly associated with Bishop
Lamberton, had also been parson of Laurencekirk, a parish owned by
the Wisharts, although the living was in the patronage of St Andrews
cathedral priory.[1] Soon after Wishart's death, the king tried to get
Dunnideer promoted to the Glasgow see, but under pressure from
Edward II the appointment was refused by the pope. Dunnideer,
having vainly sought a reversal of this decision, died at Paris in 1317.
In this or the following year Edward II succeeded in getting an
English Dominican, John of Egglescliffe, 'elected' bishop of Glasgow.
He was never in possession, and by March 1323 had been 'translated'
to Llandaff. Meanwhile, King Robert's candidate for the see was a
nobleman, Master John Lindsay, perhaps grandson of Philip Lindsay
who had been chamberlain to Alexander III. Although his election
(c. 1317) was not at first recognized by the papacy, Lindsay was
treated in Scotland as bishop-elect, and eventually, with the bettering
of relations between Bruce and Pope John XXII, he was consecrated
in 1323. Thus, for fifteen years there was no consecrated bishop in
possession of the see of Glasgow; only from 1314 to 1316 and again
from 1323 to 1329 did King Robert have a bishop in this large and
important diocese on whose co-operation and loyalty he could
depend.

At St Andrews the situation was rather different; less dramatic, but
still for a time troublesome. William Lamberton shared imprisonment with Wishart in 1306, but he was clearly not regarded by
Edward II as an incorrigible recidivist. Possibly he had friends, such
as the earl of Pembroke, in high places. In August 1308 he made his
peace with the English king and in return was given a partial freedom,
so long as he remained within the diocese of Durham.[2] By stationing
himself on the Tweed, Lamberton could now be in direct contact
with at least that part of his own diocese which was still in English
hands. For the next four years the bishop seems to have enjoyed the
confidence of both King Edward and King Robert. At the end of
1308 he took part in truce negotiations involving the English,

[1] *Glasgow Registrum*, No. 258; *St Andrews Liber*, 120, where for 'Domdouyr' read
'Donidouyr'.

[2] *Cal. Docs. Scot.*, iii, No. 50. See M. Ash, in *The Scottish Tradition* (ed. Barrow),
44–55.

French and Scots.[1] Again, at the turn of 1309–10 he acted as an 'English' envoy in truce negotiations, along with John Lindsay the future bishop of Glasgow.[2] In February 1310 he was present at a court held in King Robert's name in Fife.[3] In this same year he had been able to hold one synod at St Andrews on June 11th, and was proposing to hold another one at Holyrood.[4] In July 1311 the English king was informed that Lamberton was in Scotland and gave him leave to remain there. He was again Edward II's agent in 1312, and even in the following year, when he went to the court of Philip IV, it seems to have been as much on Edward II's as on Robert I's behalf. By now, the English garrison in Berwick did not view him with much favour and actually threatened him with violence. In fact, Lamberton seems to have returned definitively to the Scottish fold in the spring of 1312, when he came to the Scottish king's camp during the successful siege of Dundee.[5] Bruce was obviously ready to receive him back into favour, and there is no suggestion that Lamberton, in his collaboration with the English, ever betrayed Bruce. For the rest of his life the bishop was busy and prominent in public affairs and in the administration of his great diocese, from which in 1319 Edward II vainly tried to oust him. The culminating point in his episcopate came on July 5th, 1318, when, in the presence of King Robert himself and a vast concourse of magnates, clergy and people, he consecrated the now completed cathedral church of St Andrews, begun his by predecessor Arnold as long ago as 1162.[6] Lamberton died in 1328. In politics, his role from 1299 to 1304, and again in 1306, was of crucial importance. He seems to have been a moderate, conscientious man and an able diplomat. A patriot was who not for nothing the nominee of Wallace and the secret confederate of Bruce, Lamberton was also a notable churchman who has left abundant record of a busy and respected episcopate.

[1] *Foedera*, ii, 68. In view of its date (March 4th, 1309), we might infer from this safe-conduct that Bishop Lamberton was present, or thought to be present, at the St Andrews parliament. On August 15th, 1309, Lamberton was at Durham, Raine, *North Durham*, Appendix, No. 488.

[2] *Rotuli Scotiae*, i, 80.

[3] *Lindores Liber*, No. 10 (February 19th, 1310).

[4] Raine, *North Durham*, Appendix, No. 489; the details are given in the original document, Durham, Dean and Chapter Muniments, Misc. Charter No. 1351.

[5] Duncan, MS.

[6] *Chron. Bower*, ii, 271.

The remaining ten dioceses presented similar problems. At Dunkeld Matthew Crambeth may have lived long enough to attend the St Andrews parliament in 1309, but must have died soon afterwards. In 1311 William Sinclair (of a prominent Lothian family) was elected to succeed him and was consecrated in 1312. But Sinclair cannot have been an effective bishop in independent Scotland until 1313 at the earliest, for in February of that year we find Edward II giving him a grudging safe-conduct to go to Scotland to be installed, but only as far as Berwick and on condition of not holding any converse with the enemy.[1] Sinclair must have eluded the English and soon became one of Bruce's staunchest supporters: 'my bishop', the king used to call him. Henry Cheyne of Aberdeen was appointed in 1282 and lived until 1328, when he was surely a very old man. He might have been expected to prove a stumbling-block, for he had never shown opposition to English rule. Like the other prominent members of his family (the elder and younger Reginald Cheyne of Inverugie in Buchan) the bishop had often been active on behalf of the English government. But after the fall of Aberdeen in 1308 Cheyne's position cannot have been easy. His decision to change sides may not have been taken for some years, but on April 7th, 1312, he attended King Robert's parliament at Inchture,[2] and for long afterwards he remained loyal to the king.[3] As far as we know, Bruce could always count on the support of John Kinninmonth, the bishop of Brechin. By contrast, the bishop of Argyll, a Dominican friar named Andrew, although appointed under the Guardians in 1300, was possibly a protégé of the Macdougalls and therefore Bruce's enemy. At all events, he remained in the protection of England, at least until 1314.[4] Nothing seems to be known of the political leanings, in Bruce's early years, of Alan of Galloway, bishop of Sodor and

[1] *Cal. Docs. Scot.*, iii, No. 301.

[2] Duncan, MS.

[3] *Aberdeen Registrum*, i, 44–5, of date December 5th, 1318, records a remission of rancour and restoration of revenues to Bishop Cheyne of Aberdeen, purporting to have been granted at the Scone parliament of December 3rd, 1318. This parliament did in fact meet, but the remission cannot be authentic as it stands, for one witness is Murdoch earl of Menteith (not earl before 1320). One would expect the remission to have been granted in 1312 or earlier, and there is no evidence that Cheyne incurred the king's displeasure thereafter.

[4] *Cal. Docs. Scot.*, iii, No. 355. By November 1314 Bishop Andrew had come into King Robert's peace, *APS*, i, 289, last item in col. 2.

Man. By the date of his death in 1321, and probably by 1314, Bishop Alan was firmly in the king's peace. Finally, the bishop of Galloway, Thomas Dalton, although he had originally owed his appointment to the king's grandfather, the Competitor, remained hostile to Bruce for several years.

Gradually the situation began to shift in Bruce's favour. It would be safe to say that almost all the new episcopal appointments made during his reign were of men approved, if not actually nominated or suggested, by the king. In Moray, for example, on David Murray's death in 1326, there was elected in his place John of Pilmour, son of a Dundee burgess and nephew of a Cistercian monk from Coupar Angus, who had served the king in 1321 as an envoy in peace negotiations.[1] Dalton of Galloway was succeeded in 1321 by the abbot of the royal abbey of Holyrood, Simon of Wedale, whose consecration was blocked until 1327.[2] Nicholas Balmyle died some time between 1319 and 1322, and his successor at Dunblane was the king's old friend Abbot Maurice of Inchaffray. Presumably Roger, an Augustinian canon of Abernethy, chosen to follow Thomas of Dundee at Ross in 1325, was *persona grata* with the king. It is remarkable that all these new bishops were regular, not secular, clergy, but it seems impossible to say whether the reason for this lay in the troubled conditions of Bruce's earlier years.

The bishops formed only a tiny minority of the clergy as a whole, but they had constant and direct dealings with the Crown, and if they were able and conscientious and possessed strong personalities their influence among the clergy and people of their dioceses might be very great indeed. For administration they depended on the services of highly trained, experienced clerks, many of whom were university graduates. Since a century was to elapse before there was any university in Scotland, there was a good chance that her educated clerks would rid themselves of any undue insularity. After a period spent in a bishop's *familia* or household such clerks would normally be promoted to the various offices of diocesan administration,

---

[1] *Cal. Docs. Scot.*, iii, No. 718; *Moray Registrum*, 14 and Nos. 117, 277. It is possible that Bishop Pilmour himself had, like his uncle and namesake, been a monk of Coupar and is to be identified with the envoy of 1321. The bishop was an envoy to the Roman Curia in 1329, presumably to negotiate for the rite of anointing to be included in David II's coronation, *Exch. Rolls*, i, 211.

[2] Dowden, *Bishops*, 360–1; G. Donaldson, *Dumfriesshire Trans.*, xxvii, 132.

especially those of archdeacon – the chief administrative officer of the diocese – and of Official, that is, president of the archdeacon's or the bishop's ordinary court of jurisdiction. The same class of educated clerks might also find preferment as dignitaries of cathedral churches, as deans, sub-deans, chancellors, treasurers, and chanters. All these offices, often lucrative in themselves (especially the archdeaconries), might be regarded by the ambitious, able or merely well-connected clergyman as rungs on the ladder leading upward to the higher office of bishop.

In the Scottish Church during the war of independence this class of educated clergy was relatively small. Its members formed a close-knit, interconnected group, moving easily from diocese to diocese, often holding several offices simultaneously in different dioceses, exerting an influence out of all proportion to their numbers. Their common experience of long years of study at one or more of the great continental universities must have given the graduates among them a genuine *esprit de corps*, perhaps a sense of superiority. They were familiar with Paris and Cologne, and there seems to have been a strong Scottish connexion with Bologna, the centre of legal studies. This connexion dated from long before the outbreak of the war with England and continued into the fourteenth century. Among Scottish clerks found at Bologna University in the late thirteenth century[1] were Robert, bishop of Ross (Thomas of Dundee's predecessor), Hervey of Dundee, bishop-elect of Caithness, Ralph of Dundee, Master Michael of Dundee, Thomas of Dundee, bishop of Ross, Alpin, archdeacon of St Andrews (possibly the Master Alpin who was treasurer of Scotland under King John), John of Berwick (parson of Renfrew), William of Twynholm, and most famous of all, Master Baldred Bisset. With the exception of the Franciscan philosopher Duns Scotus, Bisset was surely the most remarkable of all the Scottish clergy of this period below the rank of bishop. He seems to have spent a good many years at Bologna and to have been a professional jurist of some distinction.[2] We have already seen the outstanding part he played in 1301, when the Scots were

[1] Based on Sarti and Fattorini, *De claris archigymnasii Bononiensis professoribus* (2nd edn, C. M. Foroliviensis and C. A. Ravennas, 1888–96), ii, 307–31.

[2] Ibid., 327–30; G. C. Trombelli, *Memorie istoriche concernenti le due canoniche di S. Maria di Reno e di S. Salvatore insieme unite* (Bologna, 1752), 71; R. J. Brentano, *York Metropolitan Jurisdiction*, 126, 144, 159; *Nat. MSS. Scot.*, ii, Pl. XII.

pleading their case against Edward I before Pope Boniface.

With such a background, it would not be surprising if the educated Scottish clergy of Bruce's day displayed a high *morale* and possessed a keenly-developed sense of their own liberties and privileges. They were well aware of the special status of the *Ecclesia Scoticana* within the western church as a whole, consisting as it did of a group of bishoprics directly dependent, *nullo mediante* in the historic phrase of the bull of 1192, upon the papacy. These self-confident clergy formed perhaps the biggest single obstacle to English pretensions north of the Border, and Edward I and his son were entirely justified, from their own point of view, in attempting to anglicize the Scottish Church, even though it cost them much energy and money.

If the earlier years of the struggle had produced outstandingly able clergy such as Robert Wishart, Nicholas Balmyle and Baldred Bisset, the clerical hero of Robert I's reign was unquestionably the chancellor, Bernard of Linton, better known as Abbot Bernard of Arbroath, least well known of all as Bishop Bernard of Sodor and Man, a see to which he was unaccountably promoted in 1328 and held until his death in 1331. It is generally supposed that Bernard was the principal author of the Declaration of Arbroath of 1320. He must have been perfectly familiar with the manifesto supporting Bruce's claim to the throne published at the St Andrews parliament of 1309, even if he was not actually its author. It would hardly be rash to guess that Bernard had some hand in the production of one puzzling version of this manifesto, which survives in an original and is dated 'in a general Scottish council held in the church of the Friars Minor of Dundee on February 24th, A.D. 1309, in the fourth year of [King Robert's] reign', i.e., February 24th, 1310, by modern reckoning.[1] Like the clerical version of the manifesto dated at St Andrews in March 1309,[2] this 'Dundee' version purports to come from 'the bishops, abbots, priors and remaining clergy holding office in the realm of Scotland', and its text is identical with the St Andrews document. We may assume that 'general Scottish council' meant a provincial council of the Scottish Church, and not a national general council, but it has been objected that no such assembly could have

[1] S.R.O., State Papers, No. 4 (written in a chancery hand of the earlier fourteenth century).

[2] British Museum, MS. Harl. 4694, fos. 5–6, 35–6; see above, p. 262, n. 4.

met in the Greyfriars of Dundee at a date when both castle and town
were in English hands, certainly not to approve a document so
seditious from an English standpoint.[1] If the objection is sound, the
dating clause is fictitious; we should have to suppose that the version
was produced at some later date, or elsewhere, and for some unknown
reason deliberately ante-dated or given the wrong place of issue. But
it is conceivable that during the Anglo-Scottish truce which prevailed at Dundeè and elsewhere during the early part of 1310 a
group of Scottish clergy did in fact hold a council at Dundee, to
which, despite its possible incompleteness or irregularity, they gave
the name *concilium generale Scoticanum*.[2] The opportunity would then
have been taken to re-issue the St Andrews manifesto in an effort to
prove that it had the full support of the Scottish Church. In any
case, we know that the manifesto – an enormously useful and vitally
important document – was re-issued considerably later than 1309.
For we possess, also in the original, another text of the manifesto
which, instead of emanating vaguely from the prelates and clergy,
purports to have been issued by the twelve bishops of Scotland. They
are all named, and the document apparently bore their seals.[3] It
seems to be authentic. It cannot be earlier than 1312 (for William
[Sinclair] appears as bishop of Dunkeld) nor later than November
1316 (for Robert Wishart appears as bishop of Glasgow). In fact,
it can hardly be earlier than 1314, since one of the bishops named,
Andrew of Argyll, seems to have been in exile in England until
March of that year, and was presumably not reconciled with Bruce
until after Bannockburn.[4] It may, therefore, be taken as reasonably
certain that at some date between Bannockburn and Wishart's

[1] D. Hunter Marshall in *SHR*, xxiii, 280–93. In *Coupar Angus Chrs.*, No. 105
(1325), *concilium Scoticanum* is the equivalent of *concilium provinciale*, both referring to
a provincial council of the Scottish Church.

[2] A laborious search of all the surviving record might throw some light on the
question of which clergy were available to meet at Dundee on February 24th, 1310.
Bishop Lamberton of St Andrews and his Official, Master William of Eaglesham,
were evidently present at a justiciary court at Lindores on February 19th, 1310
(*Lindores Liber*, No. 10), and Bishop Lamberton held synods at St Andrews and
(possibly) at Holyrood in this year (Raine, *North Durham*, Appendix, No. 489).
Bishop Murray of Moray was at Elgin on March 23rd, 1310 (*Moray Registrum*, Nos.
135–6).

[3] S.R.O., State Papers, No. 5, in a chancery hand closely similar to but not identical
with that of the 'Dundee Declaration'.

[4] Above, p. 375, n. 4.

death a provincial council of the Scottish Church was held, partly to signalize the full reconciliation of the entire bench of bishops with the king. At this council, the St Andrews manifesto was evidently issued in the names of all the bishops, with the fullest solemnity and publicity. Whatever their private feelings may have been, the bishops of Scotland were now ranged solidly behind King Robert I.[1] It can hardly be doubted that Abbot Bernard played a principal part in the process by which, in the face of severe penalties of excommunication, the clergy came to present a united front of patriotism to the papacy, to England, and to the other nations of western Christendom.

(ii) *The nobles*[2]

It cannot be said too often that Scotland in the thirteenth and fourteenth centuries was an intensely feudal and conservative kingdom. This fact more than any other governed the relations of King Robert with the nobility. Before these relations can be properly appreciated, we must clear away two myths which threaten to entangle the main thread of Scottish political history between 1286 and 1329. The first myth has already been encountered: the belief, derived at best from a mere quarter-truth, that the war of independence was fought and won by the common people in defiance of aristocratic apathy or hostility. The story of the struggle as it has been unfolded in the foregoing pages should give ample proof of the absurdity of this belief. At every stage of the struggle save in 1297 the Scottish nobility, as was only to be expected, occupied a leading place. Even in 1297 many of the nobles were deeply involved in the national rising, although for nearly a year most of the historic names were in the background, and the giant figure of Wallace bestrode the stage. But from 1298 to 1304, for good or ill, the nobles were back in command. When Bruce made his revolutionary bid in 1306, he was supported by a few earls, a fair number of great barons, and a considerable following of the lairds or gentry. It is one thing, and true enough, to say that the noble class was rent asunder by feuds and factions difficult or impossible to heal. It is quite another,

---

[1] Since *Aberdeen Registrum*, i, 44–5, is not authentic it cannot be evidence of any rancour borne by Robert I against Bishop Cheyne after *c.* 1312.

[2] Most of this section is based on *Reg. Mag. Sig.*, i; Duncan, MS., and standard works such as the *Scots Peerage*. To these sources references are given only where necessary for clarity or because of conflicting evidence.

and certainly false, to say that the nobility as a whole lacked the will
and effectiveness to conduct the war against England.

The second myth that needs to be demolished is that the war of
independence, and particularly the reign of Robert I, saw the overthrow of so many of the old aristocratic families that a virtually new
ruling class came into being, composed of 'new men', adventurers
even, who gambled on Bruce's victory and were consequently
showered with lands and favours. Like so many of the conveniently
simple and picturesque accounts which find their way into history
books, this generalization is not wholly untrue. But, by over-
simplifying, it seriously distorts the truth. It can be corrected only by
stating the relevant facts. The first fact of real importance is that
throughout his reign, even after November 1314,[1] King Robert
held fast to the principle that there should be no disinheritance of
men and women claiming property by hereditary right, provided
that they were prepared to swear allegiance to him and come into
his peace fully and without any reservations. From 1314 this meant
that they could no longer be English landowners as well. For the
first time since the eleventh century men and women of this class
must choose to be either Scots or English: they could not be both.
The 'disinherited' whom King Robert wisely wished to exclude
from the peace terms in 1328 were those who wanted to have it
both ways, to enjoy their Scottish lands and yet be subjects of the
English king or vice versa. The second fact of significance is that the
king's dealings with regard to property and the services rendered by
its holders were informed by a spirit of conservatism and restoration.
There were undoubtedly changes, but the remarkable thing is not
that change occurred but that the changes which took place were
not very much more radical in their character.

It will be as well to start with the earls of Scotland, whose ancient
history and special position we have already seen. In 1286 the earldoms numbered about thirteen. There were no more than this at the
time of King Robert I's death in 1329, for though the king created –
or rather revived – the earldom of Moray in 1312, he virtually

[1] The date of the Cambuskenneth parliament in which it was enacted that all who
were against the king's peace should be forfeited, APS, i, 464. Barbour, Bruce, 246,
says that a year's grace was allowed to those concerned, and although the act as we
have it mentions no period of grace, Barbour's statement seems borne out by the
dates at which several magnates changed sides after November 1314.

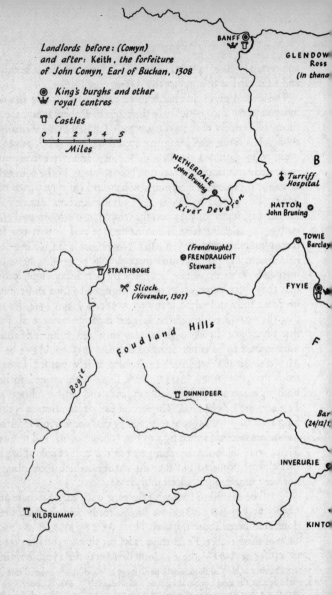

Landlords before: (Comyn)
and after: Keith, the forfeiture
of John Comyn, Earl of Buchan, 1308

◉ King's burghs and other
♛ royal centres

♜ Castles

0 1 2 3 4 5
Miles

BANFF

GLENDOW
Ross
(in thana

NETHERDALE
John Bruning

B

✝ Turriff
Hospital

River Deveron

HATTON
John Bruning

TOWIE
Barclay

(Frendraught)
◉ FRENDRAUGHT
Stewart

♜ STRATHBOGIE

FYVIE

⚔ Slioch
(November, 1307)

F

Foudland Hills

Bogie

♜ DUNNIDEER

Bar
(24/12/1

INVERURIE

♜ KILDRUMMY

KINTO

13. Buchan and Formartin showing chan

landlordship in the reign of Robert I

suppressed the earldom of Buchan. The part played by the earls of Caithness and Sutherland in Bruce's reign is almost unrecorded. At the date of the St Andrews parliament in March 1309, William earl of Sutherland, previously a supporter of the English crown, was evidently in King Robert's peace, perhaps through the influence of his powerful neighbour the earl of Ross. The earldom of Caithness, held jointly with the Norwegian earldom of Orkney, was in wardship. In 1320, Earl Magnus of Caithness was included among the magnates of Scotland who addressed the Letter to Pope John XXII. Presumably the earl was in King Robert's peace then, but nothing is known of his activities, and he died before the end of the reign. Earl William of Ross, an auditor for Balliol in the competition for the throne, began the reign of Bruce as a firm opponent. He was won over as early as 1308 and became one of the king's staunchest supporters. The earl's elder son Hugh (who succeeded to the earldom in 1323) was held in special favour by the king. Royal grants and confirmations of lands and offices made him before the end of the reign one of the richest magnates of the kingdom, and next to Thomas Randolph unquestionably the greatest potentate in the north. The sheriffdoms and burghs of Dingwall and Cromarty, the burgh of Nairn, vast estates in the Black Isle and elsewhere in Easter Ross, baronies and thanages in north-eastern Scotland, the Isle of Skye – all these came within the lordship of Earl Hugh, and as a final mark of favour he was given in marriage Maud Bruce, one of the king's sisters. His younger brother John (who died childless) was given in marriage Margaret Comyn, niece and co-heir of John Comyn, last earl of Buchan, and with her came half the earl's lands. Hugh of Ross was certainly no *novus homo;* his descent was direct in the male line from Farquhar MacTaggart, hereditary lay priest of Applecross, whom King Alexander II had made earl of Ross about 1225.

John Comyn earl of Buchan, constable of Scotland, another of Balliol's supporters in 1291, died childless at the end of 1308. He was an irreconcilable enemy, but the king had no intention of exterminating the Comyns root and branch. Nevertheless, the ancient earldom of Buchan, whose lands were overrun and harried by Bruce and his brother Edward in 1308, was virtually dismembered during the next twenty years. As we have seen, half went to Margaret Comyn, one of Earl John's two co-heirs, daughters of his brother Alexander, and to her husband John of Ross. The other half escheated to the crown because Margaret's sister, Alice Comyn, wife of Sir Henry Beaumont, had become irretrievably English. This half seems to have been sufficient to enable the king to grant away large tracts of land in Buchan to faithful followers. The biggest share went to the Keiths. Sir Robert Keith the marischal was given Aden and many other estates in the heart of Buchan; his brother (and heir) Edward had grants of much land in what are now the parishes of Methlick, Monquhitter, New Deer, Ellon, Longside and Foveran. Sir Gilbert Hay of Erroll (who held the constableship of Scotland which had been Earl John's) was granted the lands, and presumably also the castle, of Slains, with which his family was to be so closely associated for many centuries. Archibald Douglas got Crimond and Rattray with its harbour, Sir John de Boneville got Collieston, and Hugh of Ross, Sir Walter Barclay and Sir Philip Meldrum had grants of similar size and value. Not one of these men appears to have been in any sense an upstart or adventurer. Comyn's loss, to be sure, was their gain, but they had not started from nothing. What is more, the infeftment for military service of the king's constable and marischal in this strategically important coastal province forcibly recalls what King David I had done in the south west nearly two centuries earlier, when he planted his Stewart in Renfrew and North Kyle and his Constable in Cunningham.

The history of the earldom of Mar provides a striking illustration of the king's patience and of his reluctance to admit failure in his efforts to win the nobles to his allegiance. The links between Bruce and the Mar family were very close. Young Donald of Mar, who had a clear expectation of succeeding to the earldom at his father's death about 1302, was the king's nephew and had been his ward. He may have fallen into English hands at Methven or Kildrummy; at all events, he was brought up at the court of Edward of Caernarvon, to whom he became strongly attached. He was brought to Newcastle in 1314 to be returned to Scotland along with other exiles, but refused. He did not rejoin the Scots until after King Edward's deposition. With great generosity, Bruce not only restored his earldom but allowed him to take a leading part in the invasions of England during the summer of 1328 and also to intrigue in England against Isabella and Mortimer on behalf of the imprisoned Edward of Caernarvon.[1]

The case of Robert de Umfraville earl of Angus was even more remarkable. Neither his father Earl Gilbert (who had sponsored Balliol in 1291 and who died in 1307) nor Robert himself had ever shown the least inclination to join forces with the Scottish patriots. They were emphatically Englishmen, lords of Coquetdale and Redesdale in Northumberland, with an inherited distrust of aggressiveness north of the Border. Although the earldom of Angus had been theirs by marriage since 1243, the only member of the family who ever looked like striking roots in Scotland was Sir Ingram de Umfraville,[2] who after many years of loyalty to the cause of John Balliol came into King Robert's peace (perhaps reluctantly) from about 1314 until 1320. Earl Robert died in 1325, leaving as heir a young son Gilbert who was completely in the power of the English king. Despite the obvious Englishness of the Umfravilles, Bruce forbore to confiscate the earldom until the very end of his reign. Then, convinced at last that they would never become Scots, he granted it to Sir John Stewart of Bunkle, grandson of Sir John Stewart of Jedburgh who fell at Falkirk.[3]

King Robert was also personally related to the earls of Atholl. John of Strathbogie earl of Atholl had married as his first wife Marjorie, daughter of the elder Earl Donald of Mar, so that for some years Atholl and Bruce were brothers-in-law. Earl John, a Bruce supporter in the Great Cause, had played a strenuous part in the national struggle down to his capture and execution in 1306. It might have been expected that his son and heir David of Strathbogie would have become one of Robert Bruce's firmest adherents. But his wife was a daughter of the murdered John Comyn of Badenoch, and he gave his allegiance, for what it was worth, to the English king. Down to 1312 he was active in the war against Bruce, who, as usual, was in no hurry to have the earldom forfeited. Earl David changed sides before October 1312, his earldom was restored to him, and he was even given the office of constable of Scotland. This was a signal

[1] R. Nicholson, *EHR*, lxxvii, 234.

[2] For his relationship to the earl of Angus, cf. Hodgson, *History of Northumberland*, II, i, 31, n. (b).

[3] First recorded as earl in a charter of June 1329; but Barbour, *Bruce*, 359, and *Scalacronica*, 155, call him earl of Angus in their accounts of the Stanhope Park campaign in 1327.

proof of Bruce's anxiety to win over yet another Scottish earl, for he had only recently granted this office, provisionally at least, to Gilbert Hay of Erroll, whose loyalty and good service had been conspicuous from the very beginning of the reign. Though Earl David played a notable part in the capture of Perth,[1] the king's generosity was sorely misplaced. There was bad blood between the earl and the king's brother Edward Bruce, who had seduced the earl's sister Isabel and had then deserted her for a daughter of the earl of Ross. Earl David chose to take a treacherous revenge. On the very eve of Bannockburn he attacked the Scottish supply depot at Cambuskenneth Abbey, killing the officer in charge, Sir William of Airth, and many of his men, and carrying off stores of food.[2] This act could not be forgiven. His earldom lands were granted to Sir Neil Campbell and to the king's sister Mary, whom Sir Neil married after her release from captivity in 1314. Stratha'an in Banffshire, which he held of the earl of Fife, was given to Earl Malcolm of Lennox. His patrimony of Strathbogie in Aberdeenshire was granted to the prominent Berwickshire magnate Sir Adam Gordon, no doubt as part of the price of winning him over. Earl David was dead by 1327, leaving a line of Strathbogie 'pretender' earls of Atholl recognized only in England. The earldom passed first to the Campbells, then to the Stewarts. In November 1314, in the parliament which approved the forfeiture of David of Strathbogie, the constableship of Scotland was restored to Gilbert Hay. This time the office was granted heritably, and it has been held by the Hays of Errol ever since.

Malise earl of Strathearn, an auditor for Balliol in 1291, had done homage to Bruce in 1306, evidently under compulsion. Speedily reconciled with Edward II, he served against Bruce until the fall of Perth in January 1313. Barbour says that he was in the Perth garrison when the Scots captured the town, that he was brought to King Robert by his own son, the younger Malise, who was already on Bruce's side, and that because of the son's loyalty Bruce gave the father back his earldom. This story may well be true. At least it is not contradicted by the evidence of record,[3] which shows the younger Malise of Strathearn in receipt of English pay down to January 1310,

[1] *Scalacronica*, 140.
[2] Barbour, *Bruce*, 239–40, apparently meaning the night of June 23rd–24th.
[3] *Scots Peerage*, viii, 249; 251 and n. 2.

but not thereafter. As for the elder Earl Malise, all we know for certain is that he disappears from English record at the end of 1310, and he seems to have died about 1313. His son, recognized as earl, was definitely in King Robert's peace in March 1317,[1] and he seems to have remained a loyal adherent. Here again, therefore, we see a family of ancient Celtic descent successfully retaining its hereditary earldom throughout the Anglo-Scottish war.

At the end of the thirteenth century, the two earldoms to the south-west of Strathearn, Menteith and Lennox, were also held by old families of partly Celtic descent and strongly Celtic tradition. Walter Stewart, earl of Menteith in right of his wife Mary, had supported Bruce in 1291. His son Earl Alexander had taken an active part in the war under Balliol and the Guardians. Alexander's son Earl Alan had come out in support of Bruce at his coronation. He surrendered to the English, was deprived of his earldom, and died, probably in captivity, some time between November 1306 and March 1309, leaving as heir a young son of the same name, evidently in English hands.[2] The younger Alan died too soon to succeed to the earldom, which for most of Bruce's reign was in custody, at first on young Alan's behalf, afterwards on behalf of his sister Mary.[3] Eventually, perhaps in 1323, the king granted the earldom, on its resignation by Mary of Menteith, to her uncle Sir Murdoch of Menteith, brother of her father Earl Alan. Murdoch of Menteith had been with the English until 1317, possibly until 1320, the year of the Soules conspiracy against Bruce. He is said to have got wind of the plot and told the king. For this he got lands which had belonged to the conspirators, and it may be that the earldom also was in the nature of a reward.[4] At all events it remained in the possession of the old family of Menteith, although not in the direct line of descent. Lennox, the neighbouring earldom to the west, presented a more straightforward case. Earl Malcolm, who had sponsored the Bruce claim in 1291, was an old and tried friend. The king indeed owed his

[1] Duncan, MS.

[2] This is shown by *Cal. Docs. Scot.*, iii, No. 410, and by a document discovered by Professor Duncan in the MS. Morton Cartulary (omitted from the printed edition). His forthcoming work will contain a note on this point.

[3] Based on evidence provided by Professor Duncan. *Scalacronica*, 144, says that Murdoch of Menteith became earl of Menteith through his niece's resignation.

[4] *Reg. Mag. Sig.*, i, Appendix II, Nos. 263, 384, 514; *The Scottish Tradition*, 40.

very survival in the dark days of 1306 to the loyalty of the earl and his followers. Malcolm of Lennox played a full part in King Robert's reign, and had several grants of land and office, notably the hereditary sheriffdom of Clackmannan and the sheriffdom and castle of Dumbarton, which his ancestors had previously held but which King Alexander II had prudently annexed to the crown.[1]

Carrick was not one of the ancient earldoms, yet it represented in part the older and larger lordship of Galloway of the twelfth century. Robert Bruce had held it since 1292 by inheritance from his mother, and it was only to be expected that he would settle it on a member of his family. His brother Edward and his nephew Thomas Randolph might both be thought to have some claim upon it.[2] For Randolph, however, other awards had been made or were in store, and by October 1313 Edward Bruce had become earl of Carrick. At first sight this looks a poor exchange, for early in the reign Edward Bruce had been given Balliol's more ancient title of 'lord of Gallo- way'. But down to 1313 the lordship of Galloway can hardly have been more than an empty title, whereas the earldom of Carrick, secure in Scottish hands, was an honour with tangible profits. More- over, the lordship of Galloway, if historically greater, was technically inferior to any earldom. On Edward Bruce's death in 1318 the earl- dom of Carrick came back into the king's hands. It was given first (1328) to his son, young David Bruce, and afterwards to David's cousin Alexander Bruce, the bastard son of Edward and Isabel of Strathbogie, daughter of Earl John of Atholl.

The earl of Dunbar (or March) Patrick IV, had supported Bruce the Competitor in the Great Cause. From 1296 until his death in 1308 he had given his allegiance faithfully to the English crown. His son and heir, Patrick V, at first followed suit, though from 1309 onwards his loyalty was maintained at great and increasing sacrifice. It was to this Earl Patrick that Edward II owed his escape after Bannockburn, and it seems to have been not much later, certainly before the Ayr parliament of May 1315, that the earl came over to the patriots.[3] His earldom and estates, including those held of him

[1] *Lennox Cartularium*, 1–2.

[2] See Genealogical Table II.

[3] *Melrose Liber*, Nos. 416, 417. It has been denied that this was a parliament, and perhaps it should be called a council, although *Chron. Bower*, ii, 256, says *parliamentum statuit apud Ayre.*

by tenants still in rebellion, were restored, and thereafter his loyalty to Robert I never wavered.

So far we have passed under review twelve earldoms, in only two of which had the king, by the end of his reign, installed an earl who did not belong to the family which had held the earldom before 1286. Considering the upheavals to be expected from almost thirty years of continuous warfare, some of it civil war, this was a most remarkable feat of conservation. Bruce's sole innovation among earldoms was his creation, probably in the summer of 1312, of an earldom of Moray in favour of Thomas Randolph.[1] Even here, neither earldom nor earl can be considered an upstart or raw intruder. The earldom consisted of most of what the crown had held in Moray since David I's time, including the Red Comyn's lordships of Badenoch and Lochaber.[2] But this was more or less equivalent to the lands and rights of the old mormaers of Moray shorn of the earldom of Ross, and the province would almost certainly have grown into a normal earldom had it not escheated in 1130 on the death of Angus, daughter's son to King Lulach. As for Randolph himself, his father was of an old-established landowning family in Nithsdale, while through his mother he was a potential heir to the earldoms of Fife and Carrick. Even if he had not been one of the king's two indispensable lieutenants, his candidature for earl's rank would have seemed perfectly legitimate. He progressed from 'lord of Nithsdale' (c. 1306–12?) through 'earl of Moray and lord of Annandale' (1312) to 'earl of Moray, lord of Man and Annandale' (1313).

Fife, which in many ways gave the king his most intractable problem among the earldoms, has been left to the last. By common consent it was the senior earldom of Scotland, and its holder had the unchallenged privilege and duty of placing a new king of Scots on the seat of royalty at Scone. Without this ceremony, indeed, a king's title might be called in question. The young Earl Duncan (a posthumous child) was about sixteen years old when his elder sister Isabel crowned Robert Bruce.[3] He was brought up a ward of the

[1] *Reg. Mag. Sig.*, i, Appendix I, No. 31; *Moray Registrum*, No. 264. The latter, undated, text may be the original version, and Randolph appears as earl of Moray in October 1312, *APS*, i, 463.

[2] *Moray Registrum*, No. 264; cf. Stevenson, *Documents*, ii, 190.

[3] Evidence contained in a memorandum kindly sent me by Professor Duncan.

English Crown. It was a momentous decision on his part to wrench himself from English tutelage in 1315, to leave behind his childless wife, the young Marie de Monthermer, and to come into King Robert's peace. For the king his change of allegiance was crucial. The earl appears to have met King Robert's representatives at Crichton in Midlothian on August 23rd, 1315.[1] He agreed to surrender his earldom to the king, in order to receive it back on certain conditions. Failing any lawful heirs which Earl Duncan might subsequently beget, it was to be entailed upon the king himself and any of his lawful heirs to whom he chose to assign the earldom, in such a way that the persons of king and earl of Fife should always be distinct, and the arms of the earldom always distinct from the royal arms. If the king were to die without a lawful heir to whom the earldom could be thus assigned, it would revert to Earl Duncan's cousin Alan, son of Earl Alan of Menteith.[2] This tailzie or entail was made in order to ensure that there would always be a holder of the earldom of Fife, because, as the agreement frankly stated, 'the earl's wife is detained [by the English] and he might die without heirs of his body' and, further, because 'kings of Scotland ought to be made (i.e., inaugurated) by whoever is earl of Fife'. On these terms the premier earl of Scotland, at the age of twenty-five or thereabouts, was restored to his earldom with all its lands and honours intact. He was also confirmed in possession of the three baronies of Kinnoull, Oneil and West Calder, which belonged ancestrally to the earls of Fife though not as part of the earldom.[3] In this case, reversion was in favour of Thomas Randolph who, like Alan of Menteith, had some claim of inheritance from the former earls of Fife. The agreement with Earl Duncan is a remarkable instance of the king's anxiety not to offend the great nobles by disinheriting one of their number, and it shows the importance which he and his council attached to the observance of ancient constitutional custom.

The pattern revealed in King Robert's treatment of the earls was repeated with variations in his dealings with the lesser nobles and the gentry. We find the same patient conservation and restoration, the same reluctance to overthrow ancient rights or to offend feudal

[1] National Library of Scotland, MS. 72, fo. 10r (this appears in Duncan, MS).
[2] The exact relationship is unknown, but see *The Scottish Tradition* (ed. Barrow), 40.
[3] *Reg. Mag. Sig.*, i, Appendix I, No. 68.

susceptibilities. The king might, to be sure, display a sense of humour in this delicate process of rewarding both the faithful and the prodigal. The fate of the barony of Manor in Tweeddale is a case in point.[1] It had belonged since Alexander III's time to the family of Baddeby. Alexander Baddeby, who held it in the early years of Robert I's reign, was forfeited for adhering to the English, and in the St Andrews parliament of March 1309 the barony was granted to the king's retainer (*valletus*) Adam the marischal. Baddeby returned to Scottish allegiance probably after Bannockburn, and in April 1315 the king divided the barony in two, leaving half in possession of the faithful Adam and re-granting the other half to his former enemy Baddeby. This generous arrangement did not satisfy Baddeby, however, and in 1323 he petitioned for the restoration of the whole. To this King Robert replied: 'I have given Alexander Baddeby half of Manor of my own grace. It is open to him to choose between resting content with that arrangement or surrendering his half to me and submitting the whole matter to the judgement of my court.'[2] Baddeby declared himself perfectly content with the king's gracious award.

Undoubtedly there was forfeiture of property among the noble and gentry class, but much the largest part of the total of forfeited estates consisted of lands, lordships and privileges held by a very small minority of irreconcilables. It is not often realized what an enormous amount of property was placed at the king's disposal through the forfeiture of only six men: John Balliol, John Comyn of Badenoch, John Comyn earl of Buchan, Alan la Zouche, William Ferrers and Enguerand de Guines. The last three were not Scotsmen, but they had inherited (or in the third case married into) very large Scottish estates. Enguerand de Guines, husband of Christian Lindsay, who succeeded to the great French lordship of Couci in 1311, never became King Robert's man. After forfeiture, he himself (but not his widow and family) passed from the Scottish scene for good. This meant that the king could grant away lands in Berwickshire and East Lothian as well as the baronies of Skirling, Durrisdeer, Staplegorton and Westerkirk.[3] Yet Staplegorton did in fact descend to

---

[1] J. W. Buchan and H. Paton, *History of Peeblesshire*, iii, 544; *Reg. Mag. Sig.*, i, Appendix I, Nos. 95, 96.

[2] Ibid., No. 96.

[3] *Cal. Doc. Scot.*, ii, No. 1452; Duncan, MS.

John Lindsay, the future bishop of Glasgow, as heir of Philip Lindsay, and although their exact relationship is obscure we can be sure that John Lindsay was a close kinsman (perhaps, indeed, the son) of Enguerand de Guines from the fact that he displayed the arms of Couci as well as Lindsay.[1] It is true that John Lindsay resigned the barony, but this was because he was a clergyman. Westerkirk remained in the hands of the Soules family (who had held it as tenants of de Guines) until William de Soules forfeited it in 1320.[2] Durrisdeer went first to James Stewart (a younger son of James the Stewart who died in 1309) then to his sister Gelis and her husband Sir Alexander Menzies. In any event, the forfeiture of de Guines cast no blight on the fortunes of the Lindsays as a great landowning family. Pro-Bruce heirs of other anti-Bruce Lindsays might inherit despite forfeiture, as when in 1321 Sir John Lindsay (nephew of the Philip Lindsay mentioned above) received Wauchope and lands in Annandale as heir of his father Simon Lindsay, who had been forfeited as 'the king's rebel and enemy'.[3] And of course there were some Lindsays, like Sir Alexander of Barnweill in Ayrshire, who had been active in support of the Guardians and had then been 'out' with Bruce from the beginning.[4]

In the same way, there was nothing vindictive in the king's treatment of men and women who bore the names of Balliol and Comyn. Although John Balliol and his son Edward and their kinsmen Alexander Balliol of Cavers and Richard Balliol of Yetholm suffered forfeiture, Sir Henry Balliol, submitting to Bruce, was able to get Branxholm (forfeited by Richard Lovel of Hawick) 'saving the land granted by the king to Walter Comyn'.[5] The widow of Edmund Comyn of Kilbride was provided for 'until she can recover her rightful dower according to the assize of the land'.[6] The respectable, if never dominant, place occupied in the north of Scotland during the later middle ages by families of this name proves that Bruce pursued no clan vendetta against the kinsmen of the Red Comyn and the earl of Buchan. In truth he had no need to, for the

[1] Dowden, Bishops, 311–2; Duncan, MS.
[2] Duncan, MS.
[3] Ibid.
[4] Above, pp. 118, 222.
[5] Reg. Mag. Sig., i, No. 24.
[6] Ibid., Appendix I, No. 6.

lands and lordship of Comyn of Badenoch by themselves gave plenty
of scope for royal generosity. Thus, in Nithsdale Thomas Randolph
got the lordship of the whole dale, temporarily at least,[1] to go with
his ancestral barony of Morton, while Walter the Stewart and Robert
Boyd divided Dalswinton between them. Elsewhere, James Douglas
got Bedrule, Walter son of Gilbert got Machan in Clydesdale,
Malcolm Fleming got Kirkintilloch, and the Red Comyn lordship of
Badenoch was included in Thomas Randolph's earldom of Moray.

The forfeiture of John Balliol meant the redistribution of three
groups of property – first, his lordship of Galloway, secondly his
inherited third share of the Scottish lands of Earl David, brother of
King William the Lion, and lastly his similar inheritance from the
old Moreville and de Quinci lands in Lauderdale, Cunningham,
Fife and East Lothian. The rest of Earl David's estates had passed to
Bruce himself and to Edmund Hastings, a forfeited English lord,
while the remaining Moreville–de Quinci lands had fallen to two
other English lords, Alan la Zouche and William Ferrers, and to the
earl of Buchan. Thus the whole of this vast feudal complex was
available for regranting, or was already in Bruce's possession. The
lordship of Galloway, as we have seen, went to Edward Bruce, who
died without lawful issue in 1318. Perhaps from policy the king let
the lordship lapse, but in 1325 he made a grant of its historic *caput*,
Buittle in Kirkcudbright, to James Douglas, with jurisdictional
liberties which just stopped short of the 'four pleas of the Crown'.
Moreville–de Quinci property ranged widely, in every sense, em-
bracing lordship of large tracts like Lauderdale and Cunningham,
respectable burghs like Irvine and Lauder, and collieries like that
known as 'Wawayne's Pot', in the East Lothian coalfield. It would
take too much space to give an account of the redistribution of all
this land, but it is worth noting that the two men who seem to have
received the largest single shares were both very close to the king.
The faithful James Douglas got the constabulary of Lauder, while
the king's young grandson, Robert Stewart, born in 1316, was
granted 'all the king's lands in Cunningham',[2] that is, whatever
property in Cunningham was available through forfeiture after

---

[1] Appears as lord of Nithsdale in March 1309, *APS*, i, 459, and in February 1310,
Lindores Liber, No. 10.

[2] Duncan, MS.

deducting estates already given to others, such as Kilmarnock, given to Robert Boyd.

It should not be thought that the forfeitures of men like Balliol, Comyn, Guines, Ferrers and Zouche were untypical of the transfers of property under King Robert I. On the contrary, if a generalization is permissible, it would be roughly true to say that the king forfeited only those non-Scots who had no intention of becoming his subjects and only those Scotsmen who proved irreconcilable enemies. The second class was small and (if we except the Comyns) did not represent any significant amount of property. The chief Scottish baronial families which either never made their peace with the king or came into it only temporarily included the Macdougalls of Lorne, the Macdoualls of Galloway, the Lovels of Hawick, the Siwards of Tibbers and Aberdour (Fife) and the Moubrays, whose lands were widely scattered across southern and central Scotland. Conversely, King Robert had no objection to rewarding Englishmen with lands in Scotland if they left the English king's faith and came into his own. Thus, his brother-in-law, the Yorkshire knight Sir Christopher Seton, who was executed in 1306, was regarded as virtually a Scotsman, held land in Annandale,[1] and had a chapel founded at Dumfries in his memory. The English burgess of Berwick on Tweed, Peter of Spalding, without whose help the Scots would probably not have captured the town in 1318, was given an estate in Angus which put him in the knightly class.[2] At the surrender of Edinburgh Castle its Gascon commander, Pierre Libaud, became Bruce's man and was granted considerable estates in Lothian, though he soon lost them and his own life by turning traitor. One interesting grant of this type was that made to Sir William Blount 'in renunciation of any claim on which he might base a demand against the king by reason of the treaty made between the king and the late Andrew Harcla, earl of Carlisle'.[3] Admittedly, the Lanercost Chronicle calls Blount 'a knight of Scottish nationality'[4] (he was perhaps one of the Blounts of Esbie) but when he fled to Bruce, at the time of Harcla's downfall in 1323, he was thoroughly anglicized

[1] Palgrave, *Docs. Hist. Scot.*, 302.
[2] Duncan, MS. (May 1st, 1319).
[3] *Reg. Mag. Sig.*, i, Appendix I, No. 80. King Robert died in debt to Sir William Blount, *Exch. Rolls*, i, 285, 404.
[4] *Chron. Lanercost*, 250.

and one of the earl of Carlisle's 'special cronies'.[1] Like Spalding, Blount was given an estate in Angus, far from the Border where the memory of his treachery might have made life impossible for him.

If we turn from those who lost land to look at those who gained it, a study of the confused welter of detail reveals a few facts of over-riding importance. One is that the men whom the king rewarded with really large grants of land and power were very few in number and were almost entirely his own close relatives. In other words, they were the men who would almost certainly have benefited even had there been no war and no forfeitures. Besides Edward Bruce and Thomas Randolph they included Sir Neil Campbell, who married the king's sister Mary and whose son John became earl of Atholl, and Sir Alexander Fraser of Touch-Fraser and Cowie, second cousin (once-removed) of Sir Simon Fraser, who married Mary Bruce on Sir Neil's death about 1316. Campbell and Fraser had been with the king throughout the early desperate days when he had taken to the heather. Merely to be given a lady of the royal house in marriage was itself a mark of special favour. It put a noble-man into a small and distinguished class to be the king's brother-in-law. But it did not automatically bring lands and privileges. In contrast with Hugh of Ross (married to Maud Bruce and showered with favours) Andrew Murray, the son of Wallace's colleague and grandson of Andrew Murray of Petty, does not seem to have had any really notable grants from the king, although he became the third husband of Christian Bruce when she was already the widow of Earl Gartnait of Mar and Sir Christopher Seton. As heir of his father and of his uncle (Sir William Murray 'the Rich' of Bothwell) Sir Andrew Murray of Bothwell was in his own right one of the the most powerful nobles in the kingdom. He was marked out as one of the leaders of the community of the realm by his descent, his wealth and his marriage to a Bruce, and understandably became Guardian of Scotland in 1332 after the disaster of Dupplin.

By far the most favoured of the king's kinsmen were the Stewarts. James the Stewart died in July 1309, ending his days – in the spirit of 1286 or of 1297 – as a firm and public supporter of the 'royal dignity' and the community of the realm. Since his eldest son Andrew had died, his heir was his second son Walter, who is said

[1] *Chron. Lanercost,* 250.

to have been 'but a beardless lad' in 1314.[1] Yet in 1315, nine years
before the birth of his son, the king took the momentous step of
giving to Walter Stewart in marriage his daughter Marjorie, then
his only legitimate child. The royal house of Stewart was thus in a
very real sense the creation, or at least the legacy, of Robert Bruce.
The marriage of his eldest child to Walter Stewart must be seen in
the light of the close friendship between the families of Bruce and
Stewart which is abundantly illustrated between the date of the
Turnberry Band of 1286 and the field of Bannockburn, and may go
back much further. With his wife (who was a few years his senior)
Walter Stewart received the barony of Bathgate and other lands. He
also got three-quarters of Comyn's barony of Dalswinton. His son
Robert (born in 1316) had a grant of most of Cunningham as well
as five forfeited baronies in Roxburghshire. The Stewart's kinsmen
figure prominently among beneficiaries of Robert I's charters. The
Stewarts of Bunkle (descended from James the Stewart's brother
John who fell at Falkirk) having acquired Kimmerghame, Garleton,
Elvingston and Ethie Beaton, ended the reign holding the earldom
of Angus. Other branches of the family got forfeited lands in Ayrshire, Dumfriesshire and Aberdeenshire. If the Comyns had
dominated the pattern of landownership in the thirteenth century,
the Stewarts bade fair to succeed them in the fourteenth.

Among the king's closest relatives, at least one of his bastard sons,
his namesake Sir Robert Bruce, was well provided for. In 1321 he
was granted the small border barony of Sprouston (forfeited by the
heirs of the de Vesci family) to be held 'in regality' as it had apparently
been held under Alexander III by the lord de Vesci. About the same
time he had a grant of the great and strategically important border
lordship of Liddesdale, forfeited by William de Soules. The regalian
privileges of Sprouston, absurd though it may seem in the case of a
small country parish, meant that the king's officers had no right to
enter for any official purpose. The lord was answerable solely to the
king, and possessed his own justiciar, chamberlain, chancellor and
coroner. There is very little evidence of any tendency under the two
Alexanders to initiate or encourage the growth of such regalities, and
Sprouston scarcely makes an impressive regality, however it is
regarded. It is Robert I's use of the precedent of the regality that

[1] Barbour, *Bruce*, 197, 'bot ane berdlas hyne'.

gives interest to its existence in Scotland before 1286. For it cannot well be denied that a few of King Robert's grants gave a fillip to the process by which the crown lost power through excessive delegation, even to the point of dissipation. Some of the king's predecessors had done much the same, it is true. William the Lion had even proposed to grant away the whole of Lothian to Otto of Brunswick.[1] But in the twelfth century, when royal government was comparatively ill-developed, delegation of power was quite a different matter from what it might become in the fourteenth century, by which time centralized government had made great advances and there were signs of the beginning of an organized state in the modern sense. It must be emphasized that in Robert I's time there was no opening of the floodgates to let in the excesses of bastard feudalism or the overmighty subject. On the contrary, military feudalism seems to have undergone a fairly rigorous overhaul in the interest of more efficient service to the crown, while there is good evidence of the king's successful defence of his prerogative. Nevertheless, his creation of the earldom of Moray as a true 'regality' in which his nephew Thomas Randolph was to exercise all the powers of the crown and be answerable only to the king was an unfortunate reversion to the old 'palatinate' concept familiar in Norman England. Palatinates were little more than confessions of failure by the crown to exercise direct control throughout its dominions. The regality of Moray was echoed, perhaps anticipated, on a smaller scale in the regality of Annandale, created when the old Bruce lordship of Annandale was made over to Randolph about 1312. Even the more restricted jurisdictional liberties given to James Douglas by the 'Emerald Charter' and the charter of Buittle contrast markedly with the policy generally pursued by Edward I and Philip the Fair of controlling and restricting feudal privilege. In this respect Robert I, a vastly stronger and more effective ruler than Edward II, showed himself hardly different in kind. As long as he himself reigned, no Scottish feudatory would try to act the part of Thomas of Lancaster, Hugh Despenser or Roger Mortimer. But the fact remained that King Robert could not, even if he wished, resist the overwhelming pressures – paralleled in contemporary England, France and Germany – towards fragmentation of royal power.

[1] *Chronica Magistri Rogeri de Houedene* (ed. Stubbs), iii, 308.

A second fact to emerge from a study of the nobles who either made or improved their family fortunes under Bruce is that besides the king's close relatives there was a small group of specially trusted, specially favoured men, who though not personally related to the king were obviously his intimate counsellors, prominent in every department of the royal service, military, diplomatic and judicial. Some had been his companions in adversity in 1306 and 1307. Among them, rivalled only by Randolph as the recipient of royal favour, Sir James Douglas stood supreme. Alone with Randolph he shared the duties and honour of guardianship of the realm in Bruce's time. No other man save Randolph had grants of land and power to compare with his. He had, of course, a charter of Douglasdale and Carmichael, his own inheritance.[1] He was granted numerous forfeited estates, Buittle in Galloway, Lauderdale, Cockburn, Bedrule, Staplegorton, and half of Westerkirk. He was also given the royal burgh and castle of Jedburgh with the lands of Bonjedward. In two cases the service was reduced to a nominal honorific *reddendo*: Douglasdale (which must have been held for military service) and Buittle would in future render only gilt spurs annually. The 'Emerald Charter' (1324) gave him wide powers of justice in all his lands in recompense for over four thousand merks he had forgone when three French knights he captured at Byland in 1322 were repatriated free of ransom by the king.

The other members of this small group of key men were Sir Robert Keith the marischal, Sir Gilbert Hay the constable, Sir Robert Boyd, Sir Alexander Seton, Sir Robert Lauder and Sir John Menteith. Keith had been marischal since King John's time, his family having held the office for over a century. He was active on behalf of the Guardians until the general submission of 1304. For the next five years he had submitted to the English Crown, but at Christmas 1308 he joined Bruce and thereafter became one of the king's indispensable commanders and administrators. We have seen something of his rewards in grants of land, which removed the main centre of his family's interests from Keith in East Lothian to the north east of Scotland. But he was perhaps not unknown in the

---

[1] It is not certain, but seems probable, that Carmichael, like Douglasdale, was the inheritance of the lords of Douglas, *Origines Parochiales*, i, 151; *Reg. Mag. Sig.*, i, No. 77 and Appendix I, No. 35.

north as early as 1305, when Edward I's Ordinance made him one of the two justices between the Forth and the Mounth. After his reconciliation with King Robert, Keith evidently retained or resumed this very same office, for in February 1310 he is to be found presiding over a court at Lindores in Fife as 'justiciar between Forth and the Mounth'.[1] His commission was afterwards extended, and by October 1312 he was justiciar from Forth to Orkney.[2]

Sir Gilbert Hay of Errol and Sir Robert Boyd of Noddsdale in Cunningham had been with the king since the start of his reign, and both outlived him by a few years. Hay got the hereditary constableship, to which he had no substantial claim by inheritance, and considerable grants of land in Aberdeenshire. As a mark of special favour, his estates were exempted from the duty of paying relief and from liability to wardship at his death.[3] But he was not in any sense a *novus homo*: his family had held the barony of Errol for knight service since the early years of William the Lion's reign. Robert Boyd probably owed rather more to royal favour, for the grants he got from Robert I undoubtedly enabled the Boyds to rise from the position of fairly modest knightly tenants in Cunningham to holding one of the most powerful lordships of south-western Scotland. Robert Boyd himself was given a good deal of forfeited land, West Kilbride, Ardneil and Kilmarnock in Cunningham, Trabboch in Kyle, and parts of Dalswinton and Bridburgh in Dumfriesshire and of the Glenkens in Kirkcudbrightshire.

Sir Alexander Seton must hold a rather special place among those who were rewarded.[4] Pro-Bruce in 1310, he became his enemy until the night of June 23rd-24th, 1314, and his defection from the English at that critical moment was of decisive importance. Like Hay and Keith, he was already by descent and inheritance a baron of some consequence in eastern Scotland, one of his ancestors having been given Seton in East Lothian by William the Lion for knight-service. His rewards were substantial, though not spectacular: Tranent, Myles, Elphinstone and Falside in East Lothian (all these were out of old de Quinci land), burghal status for Seton itself, and the East Mill of Haddington together with land beside the burgh. Seton's near

---

[1] *Lindores Liber*, No. 10.
[2] S.R.O., Lindsay Collection, Box 19, No. 6.
[3] Duncan, MS.   [4] Above, p. 332.

neighbour, Sir Robert Lauder, was one of the very few men rewarded by King Robert with substantial grants of land and high office who really seems to have been raised from obscurity. He was among those who benefited from the redistribution of Pierre Libaud's forfeited lands, getting Cowden in Dalkeith from this source. He also received Pencaitland and Nisbet in East Lothian and Larbert Mill in Stirlingshire from forfeited estates. The chief proof of the trust reposed in him by the king, apart from his fairly frequent appearance as a witness to royal charters, is the fact that Robert I had made him justiciar of Lothian by 1321, and employed him as an envoy in the peace and truce negotiations of 1323. He was one of the magnates who took oath to maintain the truce of 1323, and had the distinction of being the only person to take oath on the king's behalf as surety for the general provisions of the Treaty of Edinburgh in 1328.[1]

Perhaps it will never be possible to free Sir John Menteith from the infamy which gathered about his name and memory in later generations because he handed over the fugitive Wallace to King Edward I. At the time of Wallace's capture, in 1305, Menteith had been in King Edward's service for some two years. Not to have surrendered Wallace would have meant publicly defying his acknowledged king and lord at a time when in Scotland itself not a single other Scotsman of note was resisting the king of England. Menteith joined Robert Bruce before March 1309, perhaps some while before. It is doubtful if he then suffered from any stigma of treachery, popular or otherwise. He became a close counsellor of the king, who confirmed him in his strong position as a lord of the Firth of Clyde region, and probably made it still stronger by granting him Glenbreackerie in Kintyre and the Ailsa Craig.[2] He was frequently named as a witness to the king's charters, acted as an envoy in the peace negotiations of 1310, put his seal to the Declaration of Arbroath in 1320, as 'tutor of the earldom of Menteith', and was one of the magnates who took an oath to maintain the thirteen-year truce of 1323, his name being

[1] Foedera, ii, 521, 524; Stones, Documents, 170. Cf. The Scottish Tradition, 54-5.

[2] The identification of 'Aulisay in Kintyre' (Eulisay, Aulesai) with Ailsa cannot be taken as proved, but is suggested by the forms for Ailsa found in Dean Monro (Monro's Western Isles of Scotland, ed. R. W. Munro, 1961, 46, Ellsay) and in Charters of the Abbey of Crosraguel (Ayrshire and Galloway Archaeological Association, 1886), i, 38, Ilysay; ibid., no. 4, mentions the old castle on Ailsa. See Chron. Bower, i, 45.

given third among the barons after the Stewart and Sir James
Douglas.[1]

At the end of Robert I's reign, the nobility of Scotland, with a few
notable exceptions, was still the old nobility, the nobility of the
thirteenth, even of the twelfth century. If the families remained the
same, can this also be said of their relationship to the Crown, and of
the terms by which they held their land? It is not an easy question to
answer. There is evidence that in the field of tenure and service King
Robert was as much of a conservator and restorer as he was in
respect of the feudal lords themselves. Yet there was some change and
innovation which was neither haphazard nor sporadic. A study of the
charters of land granted to noblemen and gentry leaves an inefface-
able impression of a deliberate royal policy of strengthening, while
at the same time modifying feudal military service. One result of this
policy was a sharp divergence, for the first time since the twelfth
century, between Scottish and English development. At a time when
the formal enfeoffment for knight service or some form of military
serjeanty was being abandoned in England, and forces were being
raised either by commissioners of array in the shires or by private
indenture, the king of Scotland adhered to the older practice of
attaching military service permanently and hereditarily to the holding of land. Since Robert I, of all men, was the least likely to be
negligent, ultra-conservative or merely inept in the matter of military
service, we must conclude that in his view the twelfth-century
model – with certain modifications - was best suited to the conditions
of Scottish society even in the fourteenth century.

The explanation, surely, lay in the king's own experience of
Scottish warfare. Because of the relative poverty of the country, the
'feudal host' of Scotland, which had failed at Dunbar, could not
maintain a place in Scottish military organization comparable with
the place once held by its counterpart in English military organization. Robert I could without regret shift the emphasis away from
knight service, in the old sense of heavy-armed cavalry, and place
it instead upon knights who would normally fight on foot, and still
more upon bowmen, who constituted a vitally important arm in
which Scotland had been conspicuously deficient. Knight service was
therefore restricted to an even more select minority of landowners

[1] *Foedera*, ii, 524.

than it had been in the previous century. The typical grant – among those which actually mention the service required – stipulated for the service of an *architenens*, a bowman.

There is positive evidence that knight service was converted into archer service. The barony of Manor in Tweeddale, for example, had formed one knight's fee in the thirteenth century. Robert I, regranting it in 1309, asked for ten archers.[1] When the barony was divided into two in 1315, one half was granted for the 'services used and wont' under Alexander III, but since the barony had never been divided before 1315 it looks as though the very common formula 'services used and wont' was here no more than a royal safeguard. Again, an estate in Whitsome (Berwickshire) was held of King John for half a knight's service. Robert I divided the estate in two and demanded the service of half an archer from each half.[2] The barony of Cessford in Roxburghshire had almost certainly been held for knight service under the Alexanders. Robert I regranted it (in two parts) for a total of five archers.[3] Bridburgh in Nithsdale had also probably been a knight's fee: Robert I got archer service from it.[4] The barony of Tranent in East Lothian had been a knight's fee and remained so; but Robert I, in regranting its component members, stipulated for one archer's service from the part forfeited by William de Ferrers.[5] Longforgan rendered knight service in the twelfth century, and when a third part of it (ex-Balliol) was granted out by King Robert the *reddendo* was the service of half an archer.[6]

Regardless of the extent to which knight service was converted into it, archer service for hereditary tenure increased unmistakably in Robert I's time. Significantly, we find the great tenants in chief themselves subinfeudating for archer service.[7] The king's eagerness

---

[1] *Reg. Mag. Sig.*, i, Appendix I, No. 95; Buchan and Paton, *Peeblesshire*, iii, 544; Duncan, MS.

[2] *Reg. Mag. Sig.*, i, Nos. 7, 8; *Rotuli Scotiae*, i, 22.

[3] *Reg. Mag. Sig.*, i, No. 11; and Appendix II, No. 286 and n. Cessford was an estate comparable to Eckford, Caverton etc., held by knight-service, and it seems probable that all these estates contributed to the castle ward of Roxburgh.

[4] Duncan, MS; Fraser, *Southesk*, ii, 478.

[5] *Reg. Mag. Sig.*, i, Nos. 56, 58, 71 and Appendix I, No. 45.

[6] *Lindores Chartulary*, No. 1; Duncan, MS.

[7] J. A. Robertson, *Comitatus de Atholia* etc. (1860), 9–10, a grant by David of Strathbogie earl of Atholl to Robert Menzies of the thanage of Cranach for one archer (c. 1312–14).

to secure bowmen is shown by his grants of hereditary annual pensions or 'money fiefs' in return for archery. Occasionally he even put on a feudal basis the ancient pre-feudal service of 'a man on foot with spear and sword'.[1] But if the charters are to be taken at anything like their face value, knight service was not a thing of the past by 1329. It was, indeed, too deeply embedded in the framework of Scottish feudal society and its landed estates to be eradicated, but there is nothing to suggest that Robert Bruce wished to eradicate it. Probably its incidence was often reduced, for in Scotland the increased financial burden of equipping and maintaining a heavily armed cavalry soldier and his *destrier* must have been relatively greater than in England, where it was already felt to be oppressive. It seems likely that when King Robert's charters speak of *servitium militis* they refer not to any precise technical requirement but to a vaguer obligation that the tenant holding by this service will furnish one or more trained warriors possessing the best available weapons and horses.

Between 1306 and 1329 there was a marked tendency for knight service to be confined to the rich, and in the case of fees answering for more than one knight the tendency became an absolute rule. Thus great magnates like Randolph, James Douglas, Walter the Stewart and his son Robert, and substantial barons like Robert Boyd, Edward Keith, and Malcolm Fleming, are to be found holding fiefs for which the service was one or more knights. Fractional knights' fees tended to be the characteristic holding of men of rather less wealth and standing. There is a remarkable conservatism in at least some of the surviving knight service grants. For example, Thomas Randolph was granted Annandale for ten knights, the very service required when William the Lion confirmed this lordship to Robert Bruce before 1174. Loudoun in Ayrshire, which had formed a single knight's fee in the twelfth century, was granted to Duncan Campbell for one knight's service. Robert Stewart was granted the lordship of Cunningham for three knights' service, a figure which may be compared with the two knights for which (we may infer) Irvine, the *caput* of the honour of Cunningham, had been held in the thirteenth century.[2] James Douglas got Lauder and Lauderdale for

---

[1] *Reg. Mag. Sig.*, i, Appendix I, Nos. 100, 101, 102.
[2] *Cal. Docs. Scot.*, ii, No. 824 (6).

the services used and wont, which appears to mean that he owed six knights, since in 1296 one sixth of this fief owed one knight.[1] William the Lion had granted Lenzie in Dumbartonshire to William Comyn for one knight's service. When Robert I gave this same barony, then known as Kirkintilloch, to Malcolm Fleming, the same service was required. It is not clear whether this evidence points to a genuine conservatism or means that the concept of knight service was in process of becoming merely honorific.

The truth may be that wherever estates were broken up or re-grouped it was easier for the king to innovate and introduce archer service. When, however, ancient estates were regranted or confirmed with their boundaries intact it was perhaps harder to impose fresh services and customs. This would explain grants which have an obviously antique flavour. For example, Hugh, afterwards earl of Ross, got the old thanage of Glendowachy (the north-east extremity of Banffshire) for the service of eight horses for carting once a year from each arable unit of the estate. When Henry Butterwambe was given land at Clunie near Dunkeld, his *reddendo* was put in language of the period 1180–1250: 'one serjeant, horsed and in an haubergel'.[2] It would also explain many of the knight-service grants, in which the service would have been simply a survival from earlier times. But the king, as we know, could on occasion impose knight service on a newly-created fief, for he required eight knights' service from Randolph's earldom of Moray. In view of the fact that the ancient earldoms were probably never held in return for knight service, this suggests strongly that for King Robert knight service was not purely ornamental or honorific but real and desirable.

This impression of a strengthening – one might fairly call it a revival – of military feudalism under Robert I is decisively confirmed if we look at the king's dealings with the barons of the west high-lands and islands. In the west the typical unit of military service was not the mounted knight nor the bowman but the 'birling' or galley of twenty, twenty-two, twenty-six or forty oars. Hebridean chiefs

---

[1] *Cal. Docs. Scot.*, No. 824 (2).

[2] *Reg. Mag. Sig.*, i, Appendix I, Nos. 5, 81. Another good illustration of the con-firmation of a holding of ancient type is seen in Robert I's charter (Loch Broom, August 8th, 1309) to William, thane of Cawdor, of the thanage of Cawdor in feu-ferm for 12 merks a year, *The Book of the Thanes of Cawdor* (Spalding Club, 1859), 3–4.

had served with birlings for generations before Bruce's time, but prior to the reign of Alexander II none of them had held his land as a fief in return for a fixed amount of military service. Indeed, down to the end of the thirteenth century most of them still held by Celto-Scandinavian tenure, and contributed to a general levy with ship service assessed on the quantity of productive land on their estates. Robert I brought many (perhaps all) of these men into a direct feudal relationship with the Crown by confirming or regranting their estates as fiefs in return either for fixed numbers of birlings of a stated capacity, or else (but much more rarely) for knight service.

This feudalized Hebridean and Argyll ship service is proof of the vitality and flexibility of military feudalism under Robert I. It was also bound up with the whole problem of the west, to which the king had always shown himself particularly sensitive. South of Skye, where the earl of Ross was installed in power, the western seaboard had no lord of earl's rank nor, indeed, any single dominant lord, for Comyn of Badenoch and Lochaber had been killed in 1306 and John of Lorne put to flight two years later. The king would have to woo, to cajole, to placate, and yet withal to overawe the leaders of the native aristocracy. He began with a solid advantage: he virtually inherited the support of the Campbells and of the Macdonalds, the ruling family of Islay and Kintyre. The precise origin of the Campbells is not known. There is no doubt that their greatness as territorial lords dates from King Robert's reign. But they were certainly not landless adventurers. Colin Campbell (possibly with his son and heir Neil) had been one of the auditors for Bruce the Competitor in 1291, along with the clerical Master Neil Campbell, clearly a kinsman.[1] In 1296, Colin's son Sir Neil was bailie of the crown lands of Lochawe and Ardskeodnish (i.e. Kilmartin parish);[2] probably he had an hereditary claim to these lands, and had been compelled to hold them of the crown at farm by King John's ordinance. They were confirmed to his son Colin in 1315 as a free barony, for a birling of forty oars.[3] Sir Neil Campbell was one of that small band of noblemen without whose help in 1306 and 1307

[1] Palgrave, Docs. Hist. Scot., Illustrations, No. II, p.v.; Foedera, i, 767 (where Nicolaus and Colinus were perhaps father and son, but probably refer to the father only); Chron. Rishanger, 365. On the Campbells, see W. D. H. Sellar, Scottish Studies, 17 (1973), 109–25.

[2] Rotuli Scotiae, i, 32a.   [3] Duncan, MS.

·Robert Bruce would hardly have survived, let alone recovered the kingdom. Until his death about 1315, Sir Neil was one of the king's most trusted counsellors. His kinsmen shared in the family's rise under the new régime, being given large tracts of land forfeited by John Macdougall of Lorne. Donald got part of Benderloch for one ship of twenty-six oars, Dugald the isle of Torsa and many other lands, Duncan the lands of Duntrune. Other Campbells who supported Bruce in his early years included Thomas, whose son Duncan was confirmed in his fief for a birling of twenty-two oars, and Sir Arthur, who was granted land in Benderloch, together with the Macdougall strongholds of Dunollie and Ardstaffnage, for the quarter of a knight's service.

Thus, by a drastic revolution, those baronial neighbours whom (as he told Edward II in 1308) John of Lorne could not trust swept in to take possession of his lands, and laid the foundations of Campbell dominance between Loch Fyne and Loch Creran. Not that all families dependent on the Macdougalls succumbed. John Macdonleavie (or Maclay) seems to have been an adherent of John of Lorne in 1304;[1] Robert I confirmed to James Macdonleavie seven and a half old merklands in Kintyre for one twenty-six-oared birling.[2] No doubt, also, there was some sheer opportunism, as men shifted their allegiance in order to scramble for the lands of those who fell from power and favour. Thus Gillespie Maclachlan, a prominent baron of Argyll in 1293, petitioned Edward I for land in 1306, apparently the barony of Strath Eachaig in the parish of Dunoon, whose owner, Molbride the younger, had joined Bruce.[3] Yet within three years this same Gillespie attended Bruce's first parliament as one of the loyal barons of Argyll, and at some point in the reign got a charter from the king either granting or confirming to him the estate of 'Shirwachthyne', now Shirvan in Kilmichael Glassary.[4] The relative lawlessness of the west was also apt to throw up from time to time a buccaneering predator who played solely for his own hand. Such may have been Lachlan Macruarie, the bastard son of Alan

[1] *Reg. Mag. Sig.*, ii, No. 3136 (1304; or 1302, cf. *Proc. Soc. Antiq. Scot.*, xc, 204).
[2] *Reg. Mag. Sig.*, i, Appendix I, No. 105.
[3] Palgrave, *Docs. Hist. Scot.*, 318; see Appendix below.
[4] *APS*, i, 459; *RMS*, i, Appendix II, No. 654. In 1296, Gillespie Maclachlan had sent in his homage in common with the other freeholders; *Cal. Docs. Scot.*, ii, 209, 'Gilascope fiz Rouland' of the county of Perth.

Macruarie, lord of Garmoran, and half-brother of King Robert's relative and protector Christina of Mar. A sinister figure, Lachlan flits in and out of the record of the Anglo-Scottish war, always in the background, always a troublemaker. He defied in turn and with impunity King John, King Edward I, the Guardians and the earl of Ross. At last, in 1306, he appeared before the English king at Ebchester in County Durham to petition for the lands (probably in the west) of Patrick Graham. Soon afterwards he disappears from history, surely regretted by no one save his own followers. His brother Ruairi seems to have stepped into his brogues, but only on condition of becoming King Robert's feudal vassal. By an arrangement which proves the extent of Macruarie power, Christina of Mar surrendered Glenelg, Knoydart, Moidart and the islands which made up the lordship of Garmoran to her half-brother Ruairi Macruarie. The conditions were that if Ruairi had no male heir, the lordship would revert to Christina's son, another Ruairi, who was required to marry one of his uncle's daughters. The service for his archipelagic lordship was to be only one birling of twenty-six oars. In view of the king's debt to Christina the whole settlement seems curious. Yet it put Garmoran into the hands of the man whom its warriors probably already regarded as their chief, and it brought that chief into direct feudal dependency on the Crown.[1]

Rewarding Angus Óg and his family and strengthening their position was an obvious and straightforward step. Angus's motive in supporting Robert Bruce may have been partly his inherited enmity towards the Macdougalls, but his conduct rose above mere opportunism. His father had been linked with the Bruces in the Turnberry Band of 1286. The Macdonalds' control of Islay and Kintyre was of crucial importance in 1306-7, and so too, in all probability, were their connexions with northern Ireland. We may surmise that Angus had an older brother who attended the St Andrews parliament of 1309, for it is virtually certain that he is to be identified with the 'Donald of Islay' recorded as being present. He and Angus after him must have been confirmed in possession of Islay and the Macdonald

[1] *Reg. Mag. Sig.*, Appendix I, No. 9. It may be noted that according to the *Annals of Ulster*, ed. B. MacCarthy (1893), ii, 433, *Annals of Loch Cé*, ed. W. M. Hennessy (Rolls Series, 1871), i, 595, and *Annals of Clonmacnoise*, ed. D. Murphy (1896), 281, one 'MacRory, king of the Hebrides' fell at Dundalk in 1318, probably Ruairi Macruarie, Lachlan's brother.

lands in Kintyre, though no charters to this effect are recorded. Robert I made over to Angus the Comyn lordship of Lochaber, and he had a charter of the adjacent districts of Morvern ('Cenel Badin')[1] and Ardnamurchan, probably his own inheritance. His nephew Alexander of Islay got the Isles of Mull and Tiree, formerly in Macdougall hands.

The result of the king's west highland policy may be summed up as follows. Skye and Wester Ross were under Earl Hugh; Garmoran was converted into a fief held for ship-service; what is now the county of Argyll was parcelled out among friends and supporters, in particular, Angus Óg Macdonald, John Menteith and the Camp-bells. Robert Bruce knew the highlands and the west from long personal experience. He succeeded with the chiefs doubtless because he understood them and possessed the gifts which they admired. He captured their imagination by bold encounters such as the battle of Brander and by gestures which appealed to their sense of tradition and prophecy, such as having himself, in 1315, borne across the *tairbeart* or isthmus between Knapdale and Kintyre, from East Loch Tarbert to West Loch Tarbert, in a galley with the sails hoisted.

> And quhen thai that in the Ilis war
> Herd tell how the gud Kyng had thar
> Gert schippis with the salys ga
> Out-our betwix the Tarbartis twa,
> Thai war abasit all utrely.
> For thai wist throu ald prophesy
> That he that suld ger schippis swa
> Betwix the seis with salys ga,
> Suld wyn the Ilis swa till hand,
> That nane with strynth suld him withstand.[2]

Above all, King Robert grasped the strategic and, by implication, the political importance of the highlands and islands. He was the first king since David I to be able to take islesmen with him on an invasion of England. He used their birlings constantly to keep open com-

---

[1] *Reg. Mag. Sig.*, i, Appendix II, Nos. 56–8. For Cenel Badin (Cineal Bhaodain), one of the most ancient district names in the Highlands, cf. Watson, *Celtic Place-Names of Scotland*, 122.

[2] Barbour, *Bruce*, 269–70. In general, see Barrow, *Kingdom of the Scots*, 362–83.

munications with Ireland, and to menace and then re-conquer the
Isle of Man. In his days the highland nobility were not, in the main,
disaffected. Anticipating in the wildest terrain of his realm the alleged
ambition of his descendant James I a century later, King Robert made
'the key keep the castle and the bracken-bush the cow'.

The king handled the nobles conservatively, but with consummate
skill and a strong sense of justice. Before concluding this review of
the relations between Crown and nobility in his reign we should
note one innovation. Almost certainly, it strengthened the solidarity
which undoubtedly existed by the end of the reign between the
king and the nobles as a class. Robert I's charters granting or confirming landed estates of major importance made regular use of the
formula *in liberam baroniam*, 'in free barony'. The adoption of this
novel standard formula was not accidental and can hardly have been
a trivial matter of chancery procedure. It must be seen as part of a
deliberate policy of defining and stereotyping feudal rights as well
as obligations. Baronies had existed since the twelfth century, but
under Robert I it is clear that only a feudatory who held explicitly 'in
free barony' had the rights of jurisdiction which custom ascribed to
the true baron: the right to hear all suits arising among the lord's own
tenants (saving appeal to the sheriff court) and 'pit and gallows', the
graphic phrase covering a very full competence in criminal cases
where the crime had been committed within the barony or concerned
its men and property. It may happen that a new term introduced to
denote old customs and institutions will itself produce, through
regular use, a fresh and standardized concept of these customs.
Before Robert I's time, the concept of 'barony', though familiar,
had been vague and ill-defined. King Robert gave it a new precision.
He emphasized, on the one hand, the doctrine that barony, like
regality, stems only from the Crown. On the other hand, he did not
whittle away feudal privileges as such. The nobles surely welcomed
not only this new certainty but also the security that went with it.

(iii) *The community of the realm*

In an unavoidably brief review of King Robert's relations with the
community of the realm as a whole, it may be useful to look at the
reign in terms of the king's elementary duties towards the community

and of the community's obligations to the king. We shall look in turn, therefore, at the succession question, at royal administration, legislation, parliament and taxation. Finally, we must try to judge the importance of the personal element in Robert I's kingship, and the degree of national unity to which Scotland attained at the close of the reign.

It was not much use restoring the monarchy if the king could not ensure its perpetuation. In this matter Bruce was dogged by ill luck. His first marriage, to Isabel of Mar, cannot have lasted more than six years or thereabouts, and so far as is known the only child born to Isabel was Marjorie, who would have been about ten or eleven years old in 1306 and hardly more than twenty when she died. Bruce's second marriage, to Elizabeth de Burgh in 1302, was marred by eight years of enforced separation when the queen was a prisoner of the English. There were, nevertheless, four children of this marriage, two boys and two girls. Of the sons, one died a child and the other, David, born as late as March 5th, 1324, was the king's sole surviving male heir of the body.

It must have seemed an urgent necessity from the very start of the reign that the succession should be settled. But the first formal provision was not made till the Ayr parliament of April 27th, 1315.[1] This was a month before Edward Bruce's expedition to Ireland to win for himself and his heirs the crown of Ireland offered him by the king of Tyrone with the support of various Irish underkings and chiefs. It was also shortly before the marriage of Marjorie Bruce and Walter Stewart. The tailzie, or entail, of the Scottish crown published in the Ayr parliament provided, with the consent of Marjorie Bruce, that if the king died without a male heir the crown should go to his brother Edward, 'as a man of great prowess in warlike actions for the defence of the rights and liberties of the Scottish realm'. This drastic and possibly unjust reversal of the succession policy laid down by Alexander III in 1284 is a measure of what the conservative community of the realm had suffered in the intervening years. Not only would it upset the principle of

---

[1] *APS*, i, 464–5. For its status as a 'parliament', see above, p. 389, n. 3. An impressive list of those present is given in *APS*, i, 290. Seals were affixed to the document recording the tailzie of the Crown by 'the prelates, earls, barons and greater men (*maiores*) of the community'.

seniority, it would contemplate a union of the crowns of Ireland and Scotland about which many Scottish magnates might well have deep misgivings. Marjorie would succeed only if both Robert and Edward Bruce died without male heirs. If she died before marriage, the reversion would pass to the king's nearest heir by lineal descent, but in the same breath it was provided that Marjorie should marry, with her father's consent. If on the king's death the heir to the throne were a minor, Thomas Randolph earl of Moray would be Guardian of both child and kingdom, until such time as the community of the realm (or its greater part) deemed him fit to rule. Randolph was likewise to be Guardian if Marjorie died a widow, leaving an heir under age. Finally, if the king and Edward and Marjorie were all to die without leaving any heirs, Randolph was to be Guardian until the leaders of the community could take counsel among themselves on the choice of a new king.

There was clearly deep-seated rivalry between the rash, ambitious and arrogant Edward Bruce and Thomas Randolph; perhaps, indeed, between Edward Bruce and his brother, for Barbour, in a phrase he uses elsewhere of King Robert and King Edward I, says that Scotland was not big enough to hold both the Bruces.[1] Randolph's guardianship offset Edward Bruce's irresponsibility. Moreover, in September 1316, after Edward had been crowned king of Ireland, Randolph was specially secured by King Robert and the Scottish magnates in his possession of Moray and the Isle of Man, the security being made 'by the consent of Edward, by God's grace king of Ireland', and for good measure bearing his seal.[2]

The death of Edward Bruce at the battle of Dundalk on October 14th, 1318, made fresh arrangements necessary. By this date Marjorie also was dead, but in her fatal fall from her horse in March 1316 she had given birth to a son, Robert Stewart. The new tailzie, promulgated in the parliament held at Scone on December 3rd, 1318,[3] provided for Robert's succession should the king die without male heirs. Once again, the guardianship of kingdom and heir (if a minor) was committed to Randolph or, if he died, to Sir James

<hr />

[1] Barbour, *Bruce*, 247. Edward is defended by R. Frame, *Irish Hist. Stud.*, xix, 6–8.

[2] National Library of Scotland, MS. 72, fo. 93, Morton Cartulary (omitted from the published edition). I am grateful to Professor Duncan for telling me of this important state paper.

[3] *APS*, i, 465–6.

Douglas, until the time when the community or its wiser majority should deem the heir fit to govern. 'Randolph and Sir James', so runs the act, 'took this guardianship upon themselves with the approbation of the whole community.'

After David Bruce had passed his second birthday, surviving the most dangerous period for any child of the period, it was necessary for the leaders of the community to do him homage and swear fealty. Although the tailzie of 1318 did not require renewal, it was no doubt thought advisable to confirm it by a second parliamentary declaration, and the renewal of the Franco-Scottish alliance in April 1326 may have been the prime factor in this decision. At all events, the Cambuskenneth parliament of July 15th, 1326, witnessed the publication of a tailzie which was probably a simple re-issue of that of 1318, no doubt with the name of the lord David taking precedence of the vaguer 'male heirs of the king's body lawfully procreated'.[1] It might have been better for Scotland if David Bruce, who was born too late, had never been born at all. It is true that Robert Stewart made no very effective king when he did eventually succeed to the throne in 1371. But he was then nearly as old as King Robert I was when he died, and he had deteriorated markedly. In 1329 he would have begun to reign at thirteen, on the brink of manhood, not on the brink of senility.[2]

Providing for the succession was only one primary duty to the community of the realm. The country looked to the king to give good and abundant governance, by proper administration of justice, by making and confirming good laws, and by the frequent holding of parliaments. King Robert claimed to be the immediate successor of Alexander III. In the administrative field he worked, in the main, to restore Alexandrian government. The early years of his reign are veiled by a deep obscurity which could only be cleared if we possessed vastly more evidence than we do. A few hard but unconnected facts stand out, like mountain peaks rising above a sea of mist. Among the major offices under the crown, a chancellor and a chamberlain, as we have seen, had been appointed by 1309. If the

---

[1] *APS*, vi, Pt. 2, 628, 664; cf. ibid., i, 546. For other record of the Cambuskenneth parliament of July, 1326, see ibid., i, 475–6.

[2] For vigorous apologies for David II see Bruce Webster, *TRHS*, 5th ser., xvi, 115–30; R. Nicholson, *SHR*, xlv, 59–78; *Scotland: the Later Middle Ages*, chaps. 6 and 7.

appearance of Keith the Marischal early in 1310 as 'justiciar from Forth to the Mounth' is anything to go by, we may infer that something like the Alexandrian system of justiciarships – as modified in Edward I's Ordinance of 1305 – had already been restored. It was certainly fully restored by the middle of the reign. There were possibly subordinate justiciars also, such as John, son of Adam Bruning, who acquired a good deal of land in the north east in the later years of the reign.[1] Desperate circumstances, however, called for novel measures, and the same document which shows us Keith holding his justiciarship shows us Randolph acting as 'the king's lieutenant from Forth to Orkney'.[2] These special positions of responsibility were created because of military necessity. The best example is the king's appointment, when he crossed to Ireland to help his brother in 1316, of Sir James Douglas and Walter the Stewart as 'wardens in his absence'.[3] 'Lieutenants' would perhaps be a better description of their position.

There is evidence that the system of sheriffs and sheriffdoms was continued with relatively little upheaval from 1306 into the years when King Robert had control of the north and west, and eventually into the period when he was master of the entire kingdom. Only one new sheriffdom was created in the reign: Argyll, which seems to have come into existence between 1315 and 1325.[4] It is not clear how much of the sheriffdom of Perth was carved away to form the new sheriffdom, but its creation was clearly an implementation, if only in part, of the sensible ordinance of 1293. The king's interest in the western approaches led not only to this sheriffdom but also to an extraordinary development of Tarbert, between Knapdale and Kintyre, as a royal castle, seaport and burgh. Under King Robert the sheriff remained the crucial figure in royal administration, as he had been in the thirteenth century. As soon as surviving record allows us to see the king governing at all, we find typical governmental activity, often involving the sheriff, in every part of the realm. Brieves or writs were 'retoured to the chapel' – returned to the chancery or writing-office – as in King Alexander's day. Free-

[1] *Reg. Mag. Sig.*, i, No. 84; Appendix I, No. 67; Appendix II, Nos. 43, 69.

[2] *Lindores Liber*, No. 10. Cf. *Historiae Dunelmensis Scriptores Tres*, Appendix No. 94, which shows that Thomas Randolph was acting as lieutenant of Robert I in 1314. As early as 1309, Randolph was warden this side (north?) of Forth (*St And. Lib.*, xxxi).

[3] Barbour, *Bruce*, 278.　　　　[4] Information from Professor Duncan.

holders were served heir to their fathers or other lawful predecessors;
inquests were held by local juries into unlawful dispossessions, or to
determine an estate's rightful boundaries by the ancient process of
'perambulation'. As far as administration and procedure go, it is
clear that under Robert I what were called in the Treaty of Perth of
1266 'the laws and customs of the realm of Scotland' remained
substantially in force.

It seems likely that the 'king's chapel', the royal writing-office, was
the first of the organs of royal government to be restored to pre-war
vigour.[1] Since 1296 there had been no single hiatus of more than two
years during which a writing-office under the control of the Scottish
government had ceased to function, and no doubt there were available to Robert I at or soon after his enthronement a number of clerks
with chancery experience. Already in the earliest surviving records
of the reign we find the essential points of continuity. The king is
once again *Rex Scottorum;* once again, he addresses 'all his good men',
omnibus probis hominibus suis; once again he is styled, round the circumference of the great seal, 'king of Scots under God's governance',
Deo rectore rex Scottorum. But if Bernard Linton, the new chancellor,
took care to restore the time-honoured forms of Alexander III's
reign, he also introduced fresh practices. For one thing, there was a
notable increase in the use of letters-patent, a more informal means of
communication than the older charter. For another, a new type of
charter, the inspection, came to be used to confirm the titles of
holders of old rights, property and privileges. The inspection recited
the older title-deeds at length, instead of merely referring to them
as had been the case with the typical charter of confirmation before
1286. If in Bernard's time the handwriting of royal clerks showed a
change for the worse, that was the fault of a new fashion characteristic of the period as a whole. Whatever the exact reasons, it is
undeniable that the handwriting of Bruce's chancery was faster and
uglier than that used by the clerks of Alexander III. The biggest
innovation of the reign was probably the acceptance of the fact that
the king's chapel could no longer travel with the king wherever
he might go. It seems likely that it was given a more or less fixed
headquarters, possibly located at Arbroath Abbey. This innovation

[1] A. A. M. Duncan, 'The *acta* of King Robert I', *SHR*, xxxii, 1–39; see also T. M.
Cooper, *Supra Crepidam* (1951), 48–59.

meant that very much greater use had to be made of the privy seal, which would normally be kept by an official in the king's company. The privy seal could thus be used to authorize the king's immediate commands, while the great seal remained with the chancellor.

Robert I's reign marks a turning point in the development of written instruments of government. Under Abbot Bernard's direction, the chapel was strengthened and became more flexible. At least some classes of royal 'out-letters' had been systematically enrolled since the turn of the twelfth and thirteenth centuries. In the disturbance of the years from 1296 to 1306, and fundamentally because of Edward I's attempt to conquer Scotland, most of these archives were lost. Under King Robert, rolls began to be kept once more, and a small portion of these are still extant. It was especially important to enrol copies of the grants which the king made to loyal supporters of property forfeited by enemies, and most of the surviving enrolments are in fact concerned with forfeited lands.

There was a similar mixture of continuity and novelty in legislation. The principal statement of the laws of 'Good King Robert' was promulgated in the parliament which met at Scone on December 3rd, 1318, and on the days following.[1] A few of the enactments were obvious, not to say platitudinous: the 'fredomis of haly kirk' (Chapter I) and the promise of equal justice to rich and poor (Chapter II) were repetitions, almost verbatim, of laws passed by William the Lion in the twelfth century. Other enactments were novel only because they were necessitated by a period of prolonged warfare. Thus goods and money were not to be exported without royal licence (Chapter XXIV), provision was made for the punishment of soldiers who broke the law while serving in the army, and careful rules were drawn up to regulate the way in which the army obtained food and other necessaries (Chapters IV and V). The 'assize of arms' (Chapter XXVII) might have been issued at any period, but obviously had a special relevance in 1318. By it, every man whose goods were worth ten pounds or more must have a stuffed leather jacket, a basnet, a mail coat, an iron hat and 'gloves of war'. Poorer men, possessed of goods worth one cow, must have a good spear or a good bow with a sheaf of two dozen arrows.

[1] *APS*, i, 466ff.

In the field of property law there was appreciable reform. It is, admittedly, not easy to be sure whether any particular law was an innovation or not. For example, Chapter XXV, which laid down the principle that no one may be ejected from a freehold without the king's brieve (i.e. the brieve of right) was based on a ruling of English law which became established under Henry II. Although the laws of William I and the two Alexanders make no mention of it, there is a remarkable piece of evidence which proves that it was well-known in Scotland before 1296.[1] But it seems certain that the procedures of the old-established possessory actions of novel dissasine and mortancestry, borrowed from Henry II's laws early in the thirteenth century, were altered in favour of the dispossessed pursuer. Thus, by Chapter XIII the action to recover property of which the pursuer had been dispossessed could in future lie not only against the sitting tenant (who might, of course, be innocent and unaware that he had dispossessed anybody) but also against the original perpetrator or perpetrators of the act of dispossession, wherever they could be found. Anyone caught ejecting a freeholder by force of arms would be very severely dealt with. Sitting tenants, however, got some protection from Chapter XIX. This provided that a pursuer trying to recover land, whether by a brieve of right or by brieves of novel dissasine or mortancestry, must state the whole of his case first, before the tenant need make his defence in court. Mortancestry – the recovery of a lawful inheritance from feudal superiors who might try to withhold it – also figures in Chapter XXIII, which extends the 'ancestors' from whom one could claim an inheritance to include grandfathers and grandmothers, along with parents, brothers, sisters, uncles and aunts.

Very few of the statutes of 1318 touch upon criminal law, which suggests, therefore, that it underwent little change. There was a provision against interfering with tracker dogs hunting for criminals (Chapter VII) and anyone found guilty of this offence was to be treated as conniving at the original crime. No one save those lords who had such a privilege granted in the past was to take 'theft-boot'

[1] P.R.O., S.C.1/18/147 (Ancient Correspondence), a letter discovered by Mr G. G. Simpson, shows Alexander of Islay telling King Edward I that 'many people say that according to the law of England and Scotland no one ought to lose his heritage unless he be first impleaded by writ and named in the writ by his own name'.

(compensation for theft, payable by the thief or his kin) on pain of severe penalties. Here, no doubt, the object was to discourage still further the private subject's participation in criminal justice. There were a few other miscellaneous laws, some too technical to be summarized briefly, others, of more or less importance, which are interesting if only because of their variety. Thus the great nobles are strictly enjoined to keep the king's peace – a more realistic measure in 1318 than it would have been before Bannockburn (Chapter XX); conspirators and rumour-mongers are to be punished (Chapter XXI) – had there been already some presage of the Soules plot of 1320? – and the owners of cruives or fish-traps in salmon rivers are not to make the meshes so small that smolts and fry cannot pass freely up and down stream (Chapter XI). The old law enforcing a close season for salmon fishing was re-enacted.[1]

The statutes of 1318 were of course by no means the whole of King Robert's law-making. They say nothing about Galloway. In 1324, the king renewed for the benefit of the men of Galloway a provision apparently first made by Alexander III about 1285.[2] This extended to Gallovidians the option of having an accusing jury if suspected of crime, instead of being arrested and charged by a serjeant of the peace merely on his word alone. The privilege had been made standard practice for the rest of southern Scotland in 1245, when Galloway had been excluded, 'having its own special laws'. The laws and liberties of Galloway as they existed before 1234 had been granted to the province in 1296 when Edward I restored Thomas of Galloway. Whether these included a reversion to the practice of individual serjeants making arrests and summarily hanging red-handed criminals is not clear. By about 1304 or 1305 the Galloway men were petitioning King Edward to abolish 'accusation of serjeants' (surdit de sergaunt) but we do not know whether he did so or not. Thanks to King Robert, from 1324 a Gallovidian could enjoy 'English law', and 'thole the good and faithful assize'[3] of his neighbours instead of submitting to the arbitrary and perhaps tyran-

[1] APS, i, 752.
[2] Reg. Mag. Sig., i, Appendix I, No. 59; on this cf. W. C. Dickinson, 'Surdit de Sergaunt', SHR, xxxix, 172.
[3] Persons undergoing a trial in a civil action in Scotland were said to 'thole an assize'.

nical proceedings of an individual royal or feudal officer. Gradually
thereafter whole districts of Galloway were permanently freed from
the burden of being subject, and giving hospitality, to serjeants, and
were allowed to adopt the jury system.[1] The king also had available a
standard form of commission appointing the chief of a clan in
Galloway 'in accordance with the laws and customs of Galloway
hitherto in use'.[2]

There are three surviving formularies which contain texts of many
official documents of King Robert I.[3] Several of these constitute
legislation or quasi-legislation. For example, at an unknown date,
most probably early in 1320,[4] the king took stringent measures to
control the spread of a serious disease of sheep, variously
called scab, 'pilsoucht' or 'pluk'. Local juries were to find out what
sheep were infected in their own districts. Infected beasts must be
slaughtered within eight days of notice given, on pain of a heavy
£10 fine. There was an absolute prohibition on the movement of
livestock, and any sheep found to have been moved from one pasture
to another were to be forfeited to the Crown. In another semi-
legislative act, the king provided a standard form for the reception
of his former enemies into his peace. After Bannockburn former
enemies must have been summoned to return to the king's faith and
peace, and in the Cambuskenneth parliament which met in November 1314, those who had not yet done so were declared disinherited
(perhaps with one year's grace).[5] This decree was not absolute,
however, for after its promulgation many men of note were reconciled and restored to favour. We know of individual issues of 'remission of rancour' by the king. Gilbert of Carrick, for instance,

---

[1] SHR, xxxix, 172–3.
[2] Duncan, MS.
[3] This passage is based on information and material generously supplied by Professor Duncan. The formularies are the Ayr and Bute MS. formularies edited by
Lord Cooper (Register of Brieves, ed. T. M. Cooper, Stair Society, 1946) and an
unpublished formulary in Edinburgh University Library, MS. 207, studied by
Professor Duncan.
[4] The date is determined partly by the available evidence on when this disease,
which spread from the south, reached Scotland; partly by evidence suggesting that the
king's enactment shortly preceded the parliament of August 1320. Chron. Lanercost,
240, reports the onset of the disease in northern England early in 1320; Chron.
Fordun, i,349, says that almost all beasts in Scotland died in the severe winter of 1320–1
(following on the disease?).
[5] See above, p. 381, n. 1.

chief of the Kennedys, had incurred the royal wrath because his son-in-law Arthur had surrendered Loch Doon castle to the English in 1306, thus letting the king's brother-in-law and great friend Christopher Seton fall into enemy hands and be executed. Gilbert had been granted a remission of rancour by 1309.[1] Henry Cheyne, bishop of Aberdeen, was evidently granted remission of rancour – presumably for opposing the king between 1306 and 1312 – but unfortunately the surviving letter of remission cannot be authentic as it stands.[2] The formularies show that by a routine letter men who wished to become King Robert's subjects could have their property restored and enjoy a remission of rancour incurred by 'trespasses committed in war against the king and his royal dignity'.

Legislation was closely linked to the holding of parliaments. In addition to the assembly at his coronation, we have record of some sixteen parliaments held by King Robert. It is more than likely that our record is incomplete, for an average of one and a half parliaments a year seems low for the early fourteenth century. Edward II, in a disturbed reign of twenty years, held at least twenty-six parliaments. This is not the place for a disquisition on parliament under Robert I, but we may note some of the more important types of business which parliaments were summoned to deal with. Parliament was obviously the proper occasion for approving and promulgating major acts of state, such as the declaration of the king's right in the St Andrews parliament of 1309, the ratification of the Franco-Scottish treaty in July 1326, and the ratification of the final peace with England (Edinburgh, 1328). The succession settlements of 1315, 1318, and 1326 were all made in parliament. It was in parliament that the estates announced their consent to major measures of taxation. Parliament was the supreme secular court of justice, terminating numerous lawsuits of whose record probably only a very small fraction survives. In 1320, for example, the 'Black Parliament' gave judgement on the Soules conspirators; in 1323 a Scone parliament settled the lawsuit Abbot of Dunfermline v. John Campbell; in a parliament of 1325 sentence of forfeiture was passed on Ruairi of Islay; and in 1327 parliament confirmed an agreement between Randolph and Sir William Oliphant. Connected

---

[1] *Reg. Mag. Sig*, i, No. 510.
[2] *Aberdeen Registrum*, i, 44–5.

with parliament's judicial role is the fact that more charters and like documents were issued for private subjects in or about the time of parliament than at any other period of equal duration. Not that such charters were any more valid than others, but at parliament one might secure more witnesses of good standing, and there were doubtless more skilled lawyers and clerks available in time of parliament than at other times. Long before the reign of Robert I, parliament, or its thirteenth-century ancestor (often called a *colloquium*), had become the most solemn occasion for expressing the will and opinion of the community of the realm. Under King Robert this position was immensely strengthened.

The men who were summoned to parliament by the king represented in themselves or by proxy the estates of the realm which with the king made up the community. In his first parliament (1309) there were bishops, earls and barons individually and lesser clergy and 'communities' of the earldoms presumably by some form of representation. At the Inchture parliament of April 1312, there were very probably present, in addition to the magnates, burgh representatives, who received an assurance that all the king's dealings with burghs would be through the chamberlain.[1] At various parliaments between 1312 and 1326 the higher ranks present were named and the description of the assembly was then rounded off with some such phrase as the 'remainder of the community' or 'the whole community of the realm'. Unless these words are to be regarded as a mere flourish, we must presume that some form of representation of men below baronial or knightly rank was in force. The Cambuskenneth parliament of July 1326 used to be taken as marking the first appearance of burgesses in parliament. This view would not now be generally accepted, and, indeed, the attendance of certain burgh representatives at the parliament early in 1296 which ratified the French treaty, even if they were there only to underwrite Scotland's financial obligations, is proof that burgess representation as such was already thirty years old in 1326. Moreover, it is now certain that the burghs were represented in the Edinburgh parliament of February and March 1328. The summons to this parliament has miraculously survived, and it is worth quoting the list of those called: 'bishops, abbots, earls, barons, freeholders and six

[1] Duncan, MS.

sufficient persons of the various burgh communities specially empowered for the purpose'.[1]

The burgesses coming to parliament were only one example of the extremely close links between the burghs and the Crown which emerge in the reign of Robert I with a force and clarity not to be found in record of earlier times. The king obviously set great store by the burghs, and the burgesses looked to him for protection and encouragement. Surviving evidence leaves a strong impression of the important part the burghs played in the war with England, but it does not fill in the details. Perhaps some were more to the fore than others in the national struggle, burghs such as Inverness, Aberdeen, Dundee and Berwick, which early or late or throughout the long war made a notable contribution. Perhaps also the fierce and sometimes bitter rivalry between neighbouring burghs tended to throw one town into the arms of the English if its rival were firmly committed to Bruce. Perth and Dundee might offer a possible instance, but this is mere surmise which might be confirmed or wholly contradicted by fuller evidence. The overriding picture is of burghal solidarity in the patriotic cause.

King Robert therefore favoured the burghs, readily confirming the ancient privileges or granting fresh ones. But he expected a good price in return. The towns formed a vital source of Crown revenue. Hence the burgesses summoned to the Cambuskenneth parliament in the summer of 1326, and to the Edinburgh parliament a year and a half later. By an indenture drawn up on the earlier occasion,[2] the community of the realm contracted to pay the king for the remainder of his life a tenth of rents and income from land and property held directly as well as from land held by tenants. The contribution, which was clearly intended to be exceptional, was to be paid throughout the realm, burghs and private liberties being included along with the rest of the country. The tenth was to be reckoned according to what was called the 'old extent', the valuation of land current in Alexander III's reign. If land had been wasted by war, allowance would be made after an inquest had been held by the local sheriff. In return for this sizeable grant, the king promised to forego other irregular sources of income, especially prises, that is

---

[1] Edinburgh Univ. Lib., MS. 207, fos. 146–7.
[2] APS, i, 475–6.

summary or arbitrary seizure of goods and chattels, sometimes without payment. It was provided that money from the grant would pass through the king's Chamber or financial office. The grant would cease immediately the king died, or if he granted any exemptions, and would be without prejudice either to the king or to the community of the realm: the *status quo* would simply be resumed. The tenth was confirmed at the Edinburgh parliament of February–March 1328. This assembly witnessed the conclusion of the final treaty of peace with England, with its heavy stipulation of a payment 'for peace' of £20,000. To raise so large a sum in only three years a fresh effort was called for, and the king obtained a further tenth of income from the community, although the burghs compounded for their share with an annual payment of five hundred merks. The money was, in fact, paid off on time, but only with the help of loans.[1]

The best illustration of royal policy towards a burgh is to be seen in the difficult case of Berwick on Tweed. Down to 1296 the richest – and to traders perhaps the best-known – of Scottish mercantile centres, Berwick, having lost most of its native population by slaughter or flight, was carefully built up by Edward I and thoroughly anglicized, even though it was not transferred from one country to the other. Steadily shrinking to little more than a beleaguered garrison town during the years after Bannockburn, Berwick was recaptured by the Scots in April 1318. It is striking testimony to the favoured economic position the town enjoyed that King Robert not only repaired the castle but also repaired the town walls to a height of ten feet[2] and set about restoring Berwick's predominance as a Scottish trading community. By a long and important charter granted in 1320, the king confirmed to the mayor and burgesses the old boundaries of their burgh.[3] The Berwick community was to enjoy all the usual customs and privileges of a free burgh, to go toll-free throughout the realm and to have a monopoly of buying and selling wool, woolfells and hides in the sheriffdom of Berwick. The burgesses were to have a merchant gild and, by a

[1] *Exch. Rolls*, i, 110–11.

[2] Barbour, *Bruce*, 322; *Reg. Mag. Sig.*, i, Appendix I, No. 17.

[3] Duncan, MS (also in *Percy Chartulary*, ed. M. T. Martin, Surtees Society, 1911, 437–440).

somewhat uncommon privilege, one of their number would act as
king's coroner within the burgh. There was to be a market every
Monday and Friday, and a fair during the summer months when
foreign merchants came to trade. The annual farm which Berwick
was to render to the king in return for all this was 500 merks. King
Robert followed up this charter of privileges by measures designed
to encourage men of substance from all over Scotland to take up
residence in Berwick on favourable terms. He made a grant for
the cleansing of Berwick after its decay and partial destruction, and a
contribution was levied from Scotland north of Forth for the re-
stocking and maintenance of the burgh.[1]

In the relations between Robert Bruce and the community of the
realm as a whole, the year 1320 is an obvious landmark. It was in
1319 and 1320 that Pope John XXII's fulminations against Bruce and
his supporters were at their loudest and most menacing. Four leading
bishops, St Andrews, Dunkeld, Aberdeen and Moray, were cited to
appear at the papal *curia* by letters dated November 18th, 1319.[2]
They ignored the summons and were eventually excommunicated
(June 16th, 1320) along with the king of Scots himself.[3] In the face of
this powerful papal offensive, mounted as it was with all possible
encouragement from Edward II, the Scots were forced to close their
ranks and give every appearance of unity in defence of their independence. They did so in a manner similar to that adopted by
Edward I and his barons when they came under the censures of
Pope Boniface VIII in 1301. The barons of England had answered the
papal claims to acts as special guardian or protector of Scotland with
a lengthy historical letter which purported to come from the Lincoln
parliament of January 1301. The barons and community of the realm
of Scotland answered Pope John in 1320 with a comparable letter,
dated 'at the monastery of Arbroath in Scotland, April 6th'.[4]

This famous letter, better known as the Declaration of Arbroath,
tells us nothing, in itself, of the circumstances in which it came to be
drafted, or written out in its final form, or sealed. It simply presents
itself as a collective letter to the pope, sealed with the seals of all

---

[1] *APS*, i, 681b; *Reg. Brieves*, 56; Edinburgh Univ. Lib., MS. 207, fo. 143ᵛ. The
farm actually levied was only 400 merks (*Exch. Rolls*, i, 311–2).

[2] *Cal. Papal Letters*, ii, 191.   [3] Ibid., 199.

[4] *APS*, i, 474–5 (with facsimile); Cooper, *Supra Crepidam*, 61–71. For the English
procedure in 1301, see *The Ancestor*, vi (1903), 185–90.

those individuals who are named among those responsible for sending it, and endorsed, significantly, in one version, with the words
'A letter addressed to the lord supreme pontiff by the community of
Scotland'.[1] It seems to be the general opinion among historians that
the letter originated in some actual assembly which met at Arbroath
Abbey in April 1320 to decide upon an adequate reply to papal
condemnation. This opinion, unsupported by the surviving record
of formal royal acts, is presumably based on the account given by
Walter Bower.[2] Bower's words justify the notion of an assembly of
magnates, though not of a parliament of which certain modern
historians rashly speak. But might it not be that Bower simply put
two and two together and assumed, with the text of the letter in
front of him, that there must have been some such assembly? It is
not impossible that there was a gathering of the nobles at Arbroath in
April 1320, but it seems more likely that the assembly (a notably
well-attended council) actually met about the end of March at
Newbattle Abbey in Midlothian. The author may well have been
Bernard of Linton, abbot of Arbroath and chancellor of Scotland.[3]
Arbroath formed the chancery's headquarters during Abbot Bernard's long tenure of office. The final version of the letter may thus
have been prepared at the abbey during April and this would explain
why it was formally dated at Arbroath. The substance of the letter
was probably discussed and agreed in the Newbattle council, and it
would then have been necessary for the chancellor to take temporary
possession of the seals of some forty to forty-five lay magnates and
have them attached, in orderly rows of red and green wax, to the
'fair copy' despatched to the pope and to the 'file copy' kept in
Scotland (which still survives, though fragile and sadly damaged).

[1] See facsimile, APS, i, facing 474.
[2] Chron. Bower, ii, 275, magnates regni fecerunt convocationem suam.
[3] Cooper, Supra Crepidam, 53–5. The Declaration of Arbroath has recently been
the subject of several important studies: James Fergusson, The Declaration of Arbroath
(1970), which examines the different stages in the make-up of the text, and also
discusses the history of printed editions; A. A. M. Duncan, 'The Making of the
Declaration of Arbroath' in The Study of Medieval Records, ed. D. A. Bullough and
R. L. Storey (1971), 174–88, which deals with the assembly which authorized the
letter and the technical details of its production; A. A. M. Duncan, The Nation of
Scots and the Declaration of Arbroath (Historical Association, 1970), which discusses
motivation; and G. G. Simpson who reviews this literature and makes some important suggestions in an article in the SHR (forthcoming).

Sir Edward de Maubuisson and Sir Adam Gordon carried it to the papal court.[1] It reached Pope John in time for him to date his reply (which, incidentally, was a remarkable feat of evasion) on August 28th, 1320.[2] Of course, it is not suggested that the Declaration of Arbroath was thought up by Abbot Bernard or by any other individual on his own, still less that its final version and despatch to the papacy were in any sense unofficial or lacking in authority. Behind it there must have been fairly lengthy consultation among the leaders of the community, prelates and lay magnates alike, and the king must have been privy to these consultations even if he did not take part in them.

Whatever its precise origins, however we look at it, the letter is a masterpiece. The Latin in which it is written, terse yet rhythmic, is the work of an accomplished stylist. It wastes scarcely a word, yet it succeeds in summarizing, in much less space, almost everything of importance in the long *processus* of Master Baldred Bisset of 1301. It adds a brief account of how the people of Scotland came to make Robert Bruce their king in 1306. With admirable conciseness, it states the essence of the theory underlying the community of the realm. It is especially interesting to see that the early history given in Master Baldred's process has been appreciably altered. No longer do we hear of the Scots coming from Egypt to Ireland, and so to Scotland. Instead, the Scots are now said to have come from Great Scythia to Spain, by way of the Pillars of Hercules, and thence to their future homeland. The change was perhaps introduced in order to make the conversion of the Scots to Christianity by the apostle Andrew, brother of Peter, sound more plausible.[3] For one of the very few reasonably early statements recorded about Saint Andrew was that he had preached to the Scythians. There was a stubborn tradition that the Picts had come from Scythia, and the letter of

[1] Cooper, op. cit. The community's letter was apparently accompanied by letters from King Robert and Bishop Lamberton in which papal privileges granted to Scotland were recited, and complaints made about the appointment of John of Egglescliffe to the see of Glasgow, *Cal. Papal Letters*, ii, 427.

[2] Ibid., 428; Theiner, *Monumenta*, No. 433; G. Donaldson, *SHR*, xxix, 119–20.

[3] The bull *Scimus, fili* of 1299 (*Chron. Picts-Scots*, 219) says, with an approach to accuracy which was possibly accidental, that 'By God's gift the Scottish kingdom was, by means of the venerated relics of Saint Andrew, converted to the unity of the Catholic faith.' This is a not inaccurate description of the part played in Scotland by the cults of Peter and Andrew in the century following the Synod of Whitby.

1320 seems to be an early example of the confusion of Pictish with Scottish origins. In any event, the use made of the evangelizing work of Saint Andrew and his relationship to Saint Peter is note-worthy both in the documents of 1301 and in the Arbroath letter. The main difference is that in the Arbroath letter the point is made extremely skilfully and tactfully, with an obvious appeal to papal feelings on a sensitive subject: 'Our Lord Jesus Christ, after His passion and resurrection, called the Scots to His most holy faith among the very first, even though they were settled at the outer-most ends of the earth. Nor would He confirm them in that faith save by the most gentle Andrew, first of His apostles by calling[1] (though second or third in rank), brother of the Blessed Peter, whom He wished always to be their patron. The holy fathers, your pre-decessors, mindful of these events, have bestowed many favours and privileges on the Scottish realm and people, as being the special concern of Saint Peter's brother.'

The Arbroath letter went in the names of eight earls (Fife, Moray, March, Strathearn, Lennox, Ross, Caithness, Sutherland), Walter the Stewart, William de Soules the butler, James Douglas, Roger de Moubray, David Brechin, David Graham, Ingram de Umfraville, John Menteith, tutor of the earldom of Menteith, Alexander Fraser, Gilbert Hay the Constable, Robert Keith the Marischal, Henry Sinclair, John Graham, David Lindsay, William Oliphant, Patrick Graham, John Fenton, William Abernethy, David Wemyss, William Muschet, Fergus of Ardrossan, Eustace Maxwell, William Ramsay, William Mowat, Alan Murray, Donald Campbell, John Cameron, Reginald Cheyne, Alexander Seton, Andrew Leslie, Alexander Straiton, the remaining barons and free-holders, and the whole community of the realm of Scotland. The omission of the clergy (save in so far as they formed part of the community) must have been deliberate. Perhaps the English barons' letter of 1301 was used as a model. The bishops were omitted from that letter pre-sumably because its purpose was to request the pope not to inter-vene in a strictly temporal domestic affair. But in England the pre-lates and clergy stood more apart in society than they did in Scot-land. Their exclusion from the Arbroath letter may rather be ex-

[1] *Chron. Bower*, ii, 286, *primum apostolum vocatione*, has a better text here than the 'original', *APS*, i, 475a, which omits *vocatione*.

plained by the fact that the leading Scottish bishops were in the act of ignoring a summons to the *curia* to answer for their transgressions. Their case was *sub judice* and they themselves were already guilty of contempt of court.

After dealing with early history and recent events, the letter reaches its crucial passages, which form a declaration of the independence of Scotland and a clear statement of the constitutional relationship between the king and the community.

'At length it pleased God, who alone can heal after wounds, to restore us to liberty from these innumerable calamities, by our most serene prince, king and lord, Robert, who, for the delivering of his people and his own rightful inheritance from the enemies' hand, did, like another Joshua or Maccabeus, most cheerfully undergo all manner of toil, fatigue, hardship and hazard. The divine providence, the right of succession by the laws and customs of the kingdom (which we will defend till death), and the due and lawful consent and assent of all the people, made him our king and prince. To him we are obliged and resolved to adhere in all things, both upon account of his right and his own merit, as being the person who hath restored the people's safety in defence of their liberties. But, after all, if this prince shall leave these principles he hath so nobly pursued, and consent that we or our kingdom be subjected to the king or people of England, we will immediately endeavour to expel him as our enemy, and as the subverter both of his own and our rights, and will make another king who will defend our liberties. For so long as there shall but one hundred of us remain alive, we will never consent to subject ourselves to the dominion of the English.'[1]

Adroitly adapting[2] some noble words which the historian Sallust puts into the mouth of a colleague of Catiline, the passage concludes: 'For it is not glory, it is not riches, neither is it honour, but it is liberty alone that we fight and contend for, which no honest man will lose but with his life.'

It is fascinating to compare 1258, 1295, 1306 and 1320. If in 1295 we see the community of Scotland coming of age, politically and constitutionally, in 1320 we see it reaching full maturity.

There is a certain irony in the Declaration of Arbroath considered

---

[1] This translation is taken from the edition of the Declaration of Arbroath published in Edinburgh at the Revolution of 1688, printed in *Miscellanea Scotica, etc.* (Glasgow, 1820), iii, 126 of the first print.

· [2] The adaptation, as Lord Cooper pointed out, was chiefly due to the requirements of the *cursus*.

as the utterance of a united realm. A cynical observer might wonder, on examining the list of baronial names, whether some of the magnates had been deliberately chosen to seal the document as a test of their loyalty and future intentions. To be sure, there are the men whose names occur again and again in company with Robert Bruce or performing his service, men such as Thomas Randolph earl of Moray, the earl of Lennox, Walter Stewart, James Douglas, John Menteith, Gilbert Hay, Robert Keith, Donald Campbell and one or two more. But considering that the list contains only thirty-nine names in all, the number of nobles named in it who within the year had been convicted or suspected of lese-majestie and treason seems at first sight alarmingly large. These men mostly belonged to the old Balliol party, and some had not long been in King Robert's peace. They gathered round the (to us) somewhat colourless figure of William de Soules, the hereditary butler, great-nephew of Sir John de Soules. Apparently their intention, however improbable it may sound, was to put Soules on the throne; he was at least the son of one of the competitors for the throne in 1291. Barbour says that the plot was disclosed by a lady (whose name he evidently did not know).[1] This is not incompatible with the more explicit and probably reliable statement of Sir Thomas Grey that the disclosure was made by Murdoch Menteith, who returned to Scotland from his long sojourn in England expressly for the purpose of reporting the conspiracy.[2] There is a suspicion that Murdoch himself was one of the plotters,[3] whoever the unknown lady may have been. We have already seen how the king rewarded Murdoch for his part in the affair.

Of the noblemen whose names are included in the Declaration of Arbroath, William de Soules, David Brechin and Roger Moubray were convicted of treason before the judges in the parliament which met at Scone on August 4th, 1320. Moubray had in fact died before parliament met, and his corpse was brought before the judges on a litter. This was done apparently because conviction and sentence involving perpetual disinheritance could only be pronounced and carried into execution on the body of the convicted person,[4] but on the intervention of the king, Moubray's corpse was spared mutilation

[1] Barbour, *Bruce*, 338–9.   [2] *Scalacronica*, 144.
[3] Stevenson, *Illustrations*, 10 (John of Tynemouth).
[4] *APS*, i, 415; W. C. Dickinson, *SHR*, xlii, 84–5.

and allowed decent burial.[1] Patrick Graham and Eustace Maxwell, who also figure in the Declaration, were accused with the rest but acquitted. The earl of Strathearn does not seem to have been involved, but the countess of Strathearn, either his wife, or, more probably, his mother, was accused, convicted and condemned, like Soules himself, to perpetual imprisonment. The other conspirators were the shifty opportunist Gilbert Malherbe of Stirlingshire,[2] John Logie (whose custody while a minor Gilbert Malherbe had been prevented from enjoying by the elder earl of Strathearn),[3] and a squire named Richard Broun. They were sentenced to be drawn, hanged and beheaded. Sir David Brechin, a brave and gallant knight who had distinguished himself in 'Balliol' or English service against Bruce before Bannockburn, though not himself a plotter, had been privy to the plot and had failed to report it.[4] For this he too was condemned to hanging and beheading at Perth, a sentence which so disgusted Sir Ingram de Umfraville that he left Scotland for good. Thus four out of the thirty-nine sponsors of the Declaration were lost to King Robert's service within a few months of its date of issue, and two more had come under suspicion of treason. In view of the fact that there must have been in 1320 numerous barons in Scotland of proven loyalty whose names could have been given in the Declaration of Arbroath, men such as Andrew Murray of Bothwell, Robert Lauder or Robert Menzies, it looks very much as if the authorities responsible for the document deliberately cast their net wide, and tried to bring into the leadership of the community men associated for years with opposition to the Bruce régime. If this was indeed done it was surely a sound move, politically speaking, even though it did not wholly succeed. The letter to Pope John remains, in spite of flaws, a most impressive piece of work. Certainly we shall find no clearer statement of Scottish nationalism and patriotism in the fourteenth century. Equally certainly, no finer statement of a claim to national independence was produced in this period anywhere in western Europe. In this respect, the conservative community of the Scottish realm stands out in advance of the age.

[1] *Chron. Fordun*, i, 349.   [2] Above, p. 150.

[3] *Cal. Docs. Scot.*, iii, No. 410; cf. Palgrave, *Docs. Hist. Scot.*, 302, for Gilbert Malherbe's demand for the wardship of the son of Malise Logie in 1306.

[4] Barbour, *Bruce*, 339–41. John of Tynemouth says that Alexander Moubray was in the plot but fled to England; Stevenson, *Illustrations*, 10.

15

In Search of Robert Bruce

IT is easy to strip away the legend surrounding some notable figure from the distant past, but clearing away the legend does not necessarily reveal the man. Nothing that has been stated as a fact about Bruce in the foregoing pages, nor any speech or writing attributed to him, is legendary in quality. But it must still remain doubtful whether we have come much nearer to the king's true personality. To some extent our view of Bruce will always depend on how much credence we give to Barbour. If we choose to ignore Barbour altogether, as we may, we shall be left with a jejune assortment of glimpses in record and chronicle, and a few authentic utterances. These might carry more weight than Barbour, but they would not add up to a portrait. Barbour is far from being legend, but we need to remember that for him Bruce was the hero of a work of art. Consciously or unconsciously, he emphasized the chivalrous qualities in Bruce, and in Douglas, his other hero. More seriously than this, he over-emphasized the chivalrous qualities of the age in which Bruce and Douglas lived. It was an age in which a king of England was murdered with a red-hot iron plunged through his rectum into his bowels, in which two knights at the court of Philip IV, because of an affair with the king's daughters-in-law, were flayed alive – one of them having been extradited by Edward II for the purpose, much to the indignation (may it be said to their credit) of ordinary English people. It was, though not of course uniquely, an age of horrors and brutality, of intrigue and squalor. Much of this Barbour passes over. He writes of the miseries, but he dwells on the splendours.

Nevertheless, on the score of general reliability Barbour must be reckoned a biographer, not a romancer. How much would we feel we knew of Dr Johnson were it not for Boswell? It would not be absurd to ask a similar question with regard to Bruce and Barbour. Of course, Barbour lacks the pages of dialogue recalled *verbatim*, the mass of convincing detail, which constitute the chief reason for reading Boswell and believing his portrait to be a very close approach to truth. But Barbour, though only a boy when Bruce died, was a most careful and exact recorder, especially of names, personalities, incidents and points of detail. We shall not be on unsafe ground if we accept Barbour's portrait of the king, even though we must correct it by more reliable evidence wherever that is necessary and possible. He shows us a man at once humane and kingly, generous and firm of purpose. Barbour was not often embarrassed by the need to excuse or explain away some act which detracted from his hero's stature. The execution of the burgesses at Perth in 1313 was played down by Barbour in the words 'bot thair wes few slayne', which were vague enough not to be untrue.[1] The apparent fact that the king singled out the Scots for deterrent punishment, letting the English go free, is actually contradicted by Barbour's statement 'that thai war kynde to the cuntre he wist, and had of thame pite'.[2] The king's refusal to intervene to save Sir David Brechin's life clearly troubled Barbour, and he passed rapidly on from this sorry business to tell an anecdote of Bruce's unusual generosity towards Sir Ingram de Umfraville.[3] In these somewhat pathetic evasions or discomfitures of Barbour lies one of our surest pieces of evidence of Bruce's essential goodness.

The king's sense of humour comes out even in dry official documents, but is best remembered in his reply to the nobles who rebuked him for risking his life in the encounter with Sir Henry de Bohun at Bannockburn.[4] His immense courage is attested by the whole of his career. Patience, on the other hand, he was forced to learn, yet once learned it became his most dominant characteristic. Men trusted his word and his judgements, so that decisions and laws made by him were respected and, in after years, invented in order to be respected. In a period when there were virtually no professionals,

---

[1] Barbour, *Bruce*, 160.
[2] Ibid.
[3] Ibid., 340-1.
[4] Ibid., 212.

generalship was not of a high order. But modern military experts agree that Bruce's handling of Bannockburn was masterly. The secret of his success here lay in the fact that behind his tactical brilliance and superlative gifts of leadership Bruce had an exceptionally good grasp of strategy: he always knew what should take priority. Directly or indirectly, Barbour's portrait gives us these qualities. His terms of reference forbade him to write of shortcomings, such as the evident rashness and hot-headedness of Bruce's earlier years. Barbour hardly brings out Bruce's ambition, yet it cannot be doubted that from young manhood Bruce was determined to play a leading part. The truth about his submission to Edward I in 1301-2 has now been established in sufficient detail to disprove all the old charges of treachery and double-dealing, yet the fact remains that Bruce did change sides two years in advance of his colleagues. Nothing but frustrated ambition will easily account for his conduct. Barbour also fails to mention, presumably because word and concept were alike lacking in his time, one of Bruce's greatest gifts, the imaginative quality of his mind which allowed him to be revolutionary in more than just the political sense.

Finally, we must return to Robert Bruce's kingliness. It was suggested earlier that the key to much of his conduct may be sought in the background, at once aristocratic and royal, in which his grandfather was brought up and lived out his long career. There is an unmistakable assurance about the manner in which Bruce assumed kingship even though he reached the throne by a revolutionary *coup*. Even his flight in the heather did not snuff out his claims to royalty, though the news of it inspired mocking ballads in England[1] and became common gossip as far away as Italy.[2] The *regia dignitas* of Scotland was never in safer hands than those of King Robert I. Barbour convincingly makes the magnates gathered at his deathbed mourn their lord as a great exponent of kingship and kingliness: 'for better governour than he mycht in na cuntre fundyn be.'[3]

Let us look at two brief letters of which King Robert was at least the official author. They have not been mentioned earlier, and one was scarcely known at all until Professor Duncan recently

---

[1] T. Wright, *Political Songs of England*, 216.
[2] G. Villani, *Historie universali de suoi tempi* (Florence, 1570), 340-1.
[3] Barbour, *Bruce*, 368.

brought it to light. The first was addressed to Edward II at some unknown date, the second to the kings and people of Ireland, probably in 1315, preparatory to Edward Bruce's expedition.

To the most sincere prince, the Lord Edward, by God's grace illustrious king of England, Robert, by the same grace king of Scots, sends greetings in Him by whom the thrones of rulers are governed.

Since while agreeable peace prevails the minds of the faithful are at rest, the Christian way of life is furthered, and all the affairs of holy mother church and of all kingdoms are everywhere carried on more prosperously, we in our humility have judged it right to entreat of your highness most earnestly that, having before your eyes the righteousness you owe to God and to the people, you desist from persecuting us and disturbing the people of our realm, so that there may be an end of slaughter and shedding of Christian blood. Everything that we ourselves and our people by their bodily service and contributions of wealth can do, we are now, and shall be, prepared to do sincerely and honourably for the sake of good peace and to earn perpetual grace for our souls. If it should be agreeable to your will to hold negotiations with us upon these matters, let your royal will be communicated to us in a letter by the hands of the bearer of this present letter.[1]

The king sends greetings to all the kings of Ireland, to the prelates and clergy, and to the inhabitants of all Ireland, his friends.

Whereas we and you and our people and your people, free since ancient times, share the same national ancestry and are urged to come together more eagerly and joyfully in friendship by a common language and by common custom, we have sent over to you our beloved kinsmen, the bearers of this letter, to negotiate with you in our name about permanently strengthening and maintaining inviolate the special friendship between us and you, so that with God's will your nation may be able to recover her ancient liberty. Whatever our envoys or one of them may on our behalf conclude with you in this matter we shall ratify and uphold in the future.[2]

Does either of these letters give us the real Bruce? Are they, in the most personal sense, authentic, or are they both merely the products of an embryonic 'foreign office' with an eye on the main chance? In view of the extremely personal quality of royal govern-

---

[1] *The Liber Epistolaris of Richard de Bury*, ed. for the Roxburghe Club by N. Denholm Young (Oxford, privately printed, 1950), 325–6, No. 463.

[2] Duncan, MS., from Edinburgh Univ. Lib., MS. 207, fo. 150ᵛ. The letter was published in advance of Professor Duncan's edition by R. Nicholson, *SHR*, xlii, 38–9.

ment in the fourteenth century, it would probably be wrong to put these letters too far from the king himself. At the very least they show two aspects of his policy, and give examples of his method of approach. There is no reason to suspect Bruce's sincerity in his professions of peace towards England, so long as it was peace between independent monarchies and not simply submission. And it seems typical that he should write direct to the only person who could take the initiative on the other side. The letter to Ireland is a very different matter. The invasion of Ireland is the only really large question-mark hanging poised over Bruce's career. Some English historians dismiss it as nothing more than deliberate trouble-making, and dwell upon the horrors and miseries that followed from King Robert's perilous and futile march to Limerick and from the Scots' whole sojourn in Ireland between May 1315 and October 1318. One or two even contrive to suggest that this unique and shortlived Scottish invasion ended a halcyon period of Anglo-Irish harmony, and introduced a note of altogether unusual barbarity into the history of a nation which had hitherto been ruled and protected by the English Crown with motherly solicitude.[1]

The question must nevertheless be asked, was Bruce's motive plain aggression, the sort of aggression upon which successful revolutionary nationalism so often embarks? The affair hardly admits of any simple explanation. A powerful resurgence of Celtic tradition and Irish national feeling would have caused an explosion regardless of Scottish intervention. Behind the obvious propaganda appeal of Bruce's letter lay important truths.[2] Scotland and Ireland did share in part a common ancestry and culture, and the Irish did yearn to be free of foreign rule. The example set by Bruce in his own kingdom was bound to be infectious, and it was understandable that some of the Irish leaders should fancy that an answer to all their pent-up

[1] Cf., e.g., A. L. Poole, *From Domesday Book to Magna Carta* (1951), 317: 'The beginnings of a settled state . . . survived for a century until Edward Bruce with his army, flushed with his [sic!] victory at Bannockburn, entered Ireland and began the process of disintegration which reduced most of the country once more to chaotic independence.'

[2] The phrases in King Robert's letter find a contemporary echo in the protest against English rule sent to the pope by certain Irish kings and notables in 1317, *Chron. Bower*, ii, 267, 'the kings of lesser Scotia [i.e., Scotland] have all taken the origin of their race from our greater Scotia [i.e., Ireland], retaining in some sort our language and our ways of life.'

aspirations lay in Edward Bruce and a few thousand veterans of
Loudoun Hill, Brander and Bannockburn. Edward Bruce remains
the most sinister figure in the affair, if a man so apparently lacking in
intelligence can be called sinister. He is praised for his bravery, his
gallantry, but this was offset by his overweening ambition and
almost total irresponsibility. 'He aspired to the title of king',[1] he
thought that Scotland was too little for his brother and himself. Why
not, therefore, win glory and a crown in Ireland? But the notion that
he could lead a successful national revolt in Ireland and rule there as
king on the same footing as his brother ruled in Scotland was preposterous and foredoomed to extinction. The killing of Edward
Bruce and most of his army at Dundalk in 1318 was described by a
certain Irish commentator as 'the best thing that had ever been done
for the Irish people since the expulsion of the Fomorians'.[2]

The idea that Robert I hankered after a conquest of Ireland or even
an Irish kingdom subordinated to his own can be rejected, yet some
disquiet remains. There can be little doubt that King Robert had an
acute awareness of the dangers of a hostile, of the value of a friendly,
Ireland. The military and economic importance of Scoto-Irish relations has appeared plainly enough in the course of this book. King
Robert, descended from a line of lords of Carrick whose trade and
interests had flowed across the North Channel, never forgot Scotland's Irish frontier. In the very last years of his life, when suffering
from a crippling illness, he crossed to Ulster twice, in 1327 to ensure
that Edward III got no help from Ireland, in the summer of 1328 for
some reason as yet unknown. It was certainly an essential part of
Bruce's policy to exercise a major influence at least in northern Irish
affairs. It would in any case be a serious mistake to sentimentalize the
relations of the two peoples in this period. They made use of each
other when it suited them, and since under Robert I the Scots were
better organized the advantage probably lay on their side.[3]

To the modern Scottish mind, largely protestant or post-protestant,
there is one element in Robert Bruce's nature which has seemed un-

[1] Stevenson, *Illustrations*, 3.

[2] *Annals of Loch Cé* (ed. W. M. Hennessy, Rolls Series, 1871), i, 595; cf. *Annals of
Ulster* (ed. B. MacCarthy, 1893), ii, 433.

[3] For comment on Scoto-Irish relations between 1315 and 1329, see R. Nicholson,
'A sequel to Edward Bruce's invasion of Ireland', *SHR*, xlii, 30–40 and R. Frame,
'The Bruces in Ireland, 1315–18', *Irish Hist. Stud.*, xix, 3–37; see below, p. 446.

familiar and unattractive and has consequently been omitted from standard and popular works, or played down. This element is the king's piety and devoutness, especially his devotion to certain saints of the church. Perhaps he was in no way exceptional in this respect among the kings of his time. But one is left with a strong impression that religious feeling at this level had a much more dominant place in his life than in that of Edward II, even if it meant less to him than it had done to Henry III. Certainly no picture of the king would be complete if it did not take this into account. Bruce seems, for example, to have felt a special devotion towards Saint Fillan, one of the most renowned of the Scoto-Irish saints. He granted Fillan's chief church and sanctuary (Killin and Strathfillan) to Inchaffray Abbey, evidently with the intention that a daughter-house of Inchaffray should be founded at Strathfillan, and this daughter-house he endowed with land in Glendochart.[1] The story goes that he venerated Saint Fillan's arm bone on the eve of Bannockburn and invoked the saint's help; and in the year of his death his natural son Robert Bruce of Liddesdale made a gift of £20 towards the fabric of Saint Fillan's church. Robert I is the first king known to have invoked Saint Andrew publicly as the nation's patron, and in thanks for his great victory he granted the cathedral priory of St Andrews an annual endowment of a hundred merks, afterwards exchanged for the patronage of the church of Fordoun in Kincardineshire.[2] Saint Cuthbert attracted his love and reverence, just as he had inspired the devotion of the twelfth-century kings of Scots.[3] Saint Thomas the Martyr of Canterbury, in whose honour William the Lion had founded the splendid abbey of Arbroath, was invoked along with Saint Andrew, Saint John Baptist, and the saints of Scotland (doubtless including Columba) at the outset of the battle of Bannockburn. It must be remembered that Bernard of Linton, who tells us this, was abbot of Arbroath and would watch over Saint Thomas's interests with special care. But there is little doubt of King Robert's reverence for the martyr, for he granted very numerous charters to his abbey and, only a few days before he died, wrote on its behalf to Edward III to ask for the restoration of Haltwhistle parish church, given to

---

[1] *Inchaffray Chrs.*, 44–5.
[2] *Chron. Bower*, ii, 271–2.
[3] Raine, *North Durham*, Appendix, Nos. 79, 80.

Arbroath 150 years earlier.[1] He did not forget Saint Malachy, whose wrath his grandfather had tried to placate in 1272. In the Cistercian abbey of Coupar-Angus – the daughter of Melrose, the daughter of Rievaulx, the daughter of Clairvaux where Malachy had died – the king provided for a candle and a lamp to burn perpetually at the altar of the Blessed Malachy.[2]

The king's observance of his religious duties was occasionally linked to his strong sense of fitness and justice. In 1306 Earl William of Ross had evidently seized Earl John of Atholl in the sanctuary of Saint Duthac at Tain, where he had taken refuge with the royal ladies after their flight from Kildrummy. Since Ross had handed Atholl over for execution, one condition of his being received into King Robert's peace was that he should maintain at his own expense six chaplains to say masses for Earl John at St Duthac's church.[3] The king's brother-in-law Sir Christopher Seton, perhaps the man he loved best of all among his friends, was hanged at Dumfries after his capture at Loch Doon. When his widow, the Lady Christian Bruce, founded a chapel of the Holy Rood at Dumfries in memory of Sir Christopher, the king arranged that £5 towards its upkeep should be paid by the barony of Caerlaverock, temporarily forfeited by Sir Eustace Maxwell who was an adherent of the English.[4] Sir Neil Bruce, hanged in 1306 like Atholl and Seton, had been taken in Kildrummy. By a charter granted in 1328, the master and brethren of the hospital of Turriff, a house formerly under the patronage of the king's enemy the earl of Buchan, were required to find a chaplain to celebrate masses for Neil Bruce's soul.[5]

The clearest evidence of Bruce's religious devotion is provided by the long drawn-out-and surely painful pilgrimage which he undertook in the last few months of his life to the shrine of Saint Ninian at Whithorn in Galloway.[6] He was at Girvan in southern Carrick on February 6th, 1329. From there he was borne slowly southward to Inchmichael (the present Lochinch), where he stayed for over a

[1] *Cal. Docs. Scot.*, iii, No. 984 (Cardross, May 3rd, 1329).
[2] *Coupar Angus Chrs.*, No. 100 (February 8th, 1319).
[3] Duncan, MS.
[4] Ibid.
[5] Ibid. (October 16th, 1328).
[6] G. Neilson, *The Scottish Antiquary*, xiii (1898), 49–54. Houses were built at Inchmichael in 1329, presumably for the king's stay, *Exch. Rolls*, i, 152.

month, and so by way of Glenluce and Monreith to Whithorn, reached by April 1st. Some four days at least were spent at Whithorn, seeking the intercession of Saint Ninian – who in Bruce's time was perhaps just approaching the height of his popularity among the Scots – before the royal party returned, with rather better speed than on their outward journey, to the king's house at Cardross.

About three years before his death, King Robert, who had caused every royal castle in Scotland to be destroyed save Berwick and Dumbarton, began to build a house for himself where he could find some comfort and relaxation and watch his son grow from infancy to childhood. He chose for the site of this house the village of Cardross, on the north shore of the Firth of Clyde and on the right bank of the River Leven, immediately opposite the burgh of Dumbarton.[1] In some ways it was a remarkable choice. The Crown had virtually no demesne land in the Lennox, and the king had to go out of his way to acquire the necessary ground at Cardross by compensating the two existing landowners. The earl of Lennox, from whom he bought about two hundred and eight acres, received instead the lands of Leckie near Stirling.[2] Sir David Graham, who seems to have owned the bulk of the Cardross property, was given Old Montrose in Angus, an exchange which gave rise to the historic association between the names of Graham and Montrose.[3]

The king's house at Cardross has long since vanished, and only archaeological investigation could now reveal its size and character.[4] It was not a 'castle', as it is sometimes called locally, but a *manerium*, which in Scotland meant a dwelling-house. There is no evidence of fortification of any kind, although a stone wall was built beside the king's chamber. The house was planned on a reasonably generous scale, with a hall, queen's chamber, chapel, kitchen and larder. The roofs were thatched. In 1328 there was an apartment called the 'new

[1] The position of the medieval village of Cardross is indicated today by the remains of the parish church in the Levengrove Park, and by the name Kirkton, still applied to the area a little to the west of the ruins. The modern village of Cardross four miles to the west dates from a much later period.

[2] *Reg. Mag. Sig.*, i, No. 90. A ploughgate would be 104 Scotch acres of arable, but might well have included a much larger area of uncultivated ground.

[3] *Hist. MSS. Commission, 2nd Report*, Appendix, 167; Duncan, MS.

[4] The following passage is based on *Exch. Rolls*, i, 56, 118, 123–36.

chamber' (perhaps the same as the 'king's chamber') which evidently
had plastered and painted walls and glazed windows. Beside this new
chamber was constructed the 'new gate'. Apart from the house itself
there was a garden, for which we read of seeds being bought, and a
park for the king's hunting, under the charge of Gillis the hunter and
various parkers, William, Gilchrist and Gilfillan. A special building,
surrounded by a hedge, housed the royal falcons. Material for the
manor house was in fact brought considerable distances. A hundred
'large boards' for repairs to Cardross park were shipped from Tarbert
on Loch Fyne in 1326, and two years later 400 boards were brought
as far as Lamlash in Arran, presumably en route for Cardross. The
large quantities of provisions bought by the constable of Cardross,
Adam, Alan's son, show that the king lived and entertained com-
fortably and hospitably, though not lavishly. A fishing coble in the
Leven, which was attached to the estate, may have helped here. In
addition to hunting and falconry, Bruce seems to have taken an
interest in sailing and boat-building. He kept ships at Cardross (as did
his nephew Thomas Randolph) and we read of eighty stones of iron
being bought for their repair in 1328. The king had more than one
ship, but we read most of his 'great ship', and of at least one occasion
when she sailed to Tarbert and back. At one time this ship was drawn
up out of the water into the burn beside the house, and her tackle and
equipment were carted and carried 'into the manor house', presumably into its precincts or outbuildings.

The site of this house is now unknown. The belief which prevails
locally and for the time being is that it stood on Castlehill, about half
a mile west of the River Leven. It is here that it has been thought fit
to commemorate publicly Bruce's close connexion with this part of
Cardross parish, now within the burgh of Dumbarton. Public com-
memoration is only right, and perhaps it does not matter greatly
what site is chosen for it. But it must be pointed out that the belief
that Bruce died at Castlehill rests not just upon insufficient, but upon
positively invalid evidence. This consists chiefly of two erroneous
assumptions, first, that the royal residence must have been a 'castle'
because no king would live in anything else, secondly, that the old
name Castlehill obviously marks the site. In fact, the mound at
Castlehill, which requires investigation, could not possibly be the
site of King Robert's *manerium*. The contemporary evidence,

whose implications were stated many years ago by David Murray,[1] points to a site closer to the River Leven. There is still beside the river, half-way between Dumbarton Bridge and Dalchurn, the farm of Mains of Cardross. By all analogy, the 'mains' (='demesne', *dominium*) of Cardross would be at or close to the lord's dwelling. We recall that the king's great ship was drawn up out of the river (*ab aqua*) in a burn beside the house. Not only does this prove that the house cannot have been far from the river, but the only burn of any consequence between the mouth of the River Leven and Dalchurn is that which rises above Dalmoak and enters the river just north of Mains of Cardross. In 1362 the lands of 'Pelanysflat' – the last ele-ment denotes level arable or meadow – lay between Dalchurn and the king's park of Cardross.[2] An undated eighteenth-century map by Thomas Kitchin shows 'Pilinflait' south of Dalchurn and slightly north-east of Dalmoak, suggesting that it was situated just to the north of Mains of Cardross.[3] Between Mains of Cardross and Dum-barton Bridge the ground has been enormously disturbed, partly by changes in the line of the River Leven, partly by industrial and road building. But it seems certain that the exact position of the house in which Bruce died is to be sought either at Mains of Cardross or somewhere in the half mile which separates the farm from the modern railway bridge over the Leven.

The king's choice of Cardross as the home of his last years raises a larger question, which has been postponed from an earlier stage of this study. Whether or not Bruce was bred in the Gaelic tradition, he certainly chose to die in a strongly Gaelic district. It might be thought that this would lend support to Dr Barron's thesis by confirming the links between 'Celtic Scotland' and the patriot king. As we look back at Bruce's record as nobleman and king and at his relations with the community of the realm, we may be better placed to judge the truth of Dr Barron's claim that 'the War of Independence was the achieve-ment of Celtic Scotland and especially of the northern part of Celtic

[1] D. Murray, *Old Cardross* (Glasgow, 1880); also in letters in *The Glasgow Herald*, June 12th and 15th, 1928. Cf. Eunice Murray, *The church of Cardross and its ministers* (Glasgow, 1935), 6–8.

[2] *Reg. Mag. Sig.*, i, No. 117.

[3] The copy I have consulted is in Dumbarton Public Library, Murray Collection, iii.

Scotland, and that Teutonic Scotland – Lothian – had neither lot nor part in the Scots' long struggle for freedom'.[1] As far as Bruce himself is concerned, his decision to make a home for himself at Cardross certainly seems additional evidence of his love of the west, of his belief – against the current of fourteenth-century Scottish history – in the importance of the western approaches, the gateway to Ireland, the sea lanes which formed the only adequate communication with the powerful and potentially dangerous lords of Islay, Lorne and Garmoran. Whether the decision also drew Robert Bruce in towards a society which – given different terminology – he would have recognized as 'Celtic Scotland' is another matter. If this book has attempted anything, it has been to demonstrate that the most stubborn, persistent, tenacious resistance to foreign domination came from the old Scottish kingdom of the twelfth and thirteenth centuries, fed by a tradition of deep-rooted loyalty to the Crown and by a sense of political nationhood expressed in the term 'community of the realm', which was employed over and over again in a great variety of contexts, yet almost always with the same meaning. This does not seem to have been a monopoly of either 'Celtic' or 'Teutonic' Scotland. Indeed, these terms belong to a discredited phase of ethnological study that projected into a society so complex as thirteenth-century Scotland sharp divisions of race and culture which might perhaps have had some justification when applied to the country a thousand years earlier.

For historical reasons largely unconnected with racial factors the essential 'heartland' of the feudal kingdom of Scotland, as it was built up by the kings of Scots from the first to the third Alexander, stretched on the east from Dornoch to Berwick and Roxburgh, on the west from the Great Glen to Ayr. It is instructive to apply this fact to the events of 1286–1329. The least consistent support for the community of the Scottish realm during this period, and the most consistent support for the English kings, came from areas outside this heartland: Caithness, the Outer Isles, Garmoran, Islay, Lorne, Galloway and the Isle of Man. The heartland itself showed more consistent support for the community and less for English rule. Yet even if this rough and ready conclusion is acceptable, there were

---

[1] Barron, *Scottish War of Independence*, lxxx B.

notable exceptions to warn us of the danger of giving too much weight to any broad generalization. The clash between Macdougall and Macdonald, for example, was strictly irrelevant to the Scots' long struggle for freedom, yet it proved of immense importance to Robert Bruce. The division of ancient Galloway into two parts was another irrelevance, but in the end it too played a vital part in Bruce's success. The prolonged and effective English occupation of most of Lothian and part of Teviotdale makes difficult any direct comparison between this region and the rest of Scotland. The biggest single weakness suffered by the community of the realm was not the threat of Teutonic defection from a Celtic Scotland towards which it felt hostility, but the dilemma of a disputed succession from which the war itself had arisen. Even Robert I did not solve this problem of schism, as was to be made painfully clear a few years after his death, when many Scots who had been identified with the national movement did homage to Edward Balliol as king, and later, after the catastrophe of Halidon Hill, an even greater number submitted to Edward III.

Even on Dr Barron's own showing, the preponderance of 'Celtic' over 'non-Celtic' elements is hardly demonstrable, from surviving evidence, in political or military terms. He makes the family of Murray an ancient Celtic house, yet they sprang, in the male line, from a twelfth-century Flemish adventurer. His heroes, rightly enough, are men like Alexander Pilche, the Inverness burgess, William Cresswell the chantor of Moray, the Wisemans, Fentons, Barclays and many more. But in what sense were these men more representative of Celtic Scotland than (say) Duncan of Frendraught, Gilbert of Glencarnie, Lachlan Macruarie, John Macdougall, Dungal Macdouall or Donald MacCan? Where do such men as Robert Keith, Simon Fraser, William Wallace, Alexander Lindsay, John de Soules, James Douglas and Thomas Randolph fit into the racial pattern which makes Celtic synonymous with patriotic, non-Celtic synonymous with unpatriotic or even quisling? I can see no other common factor which would link these men to one another or to Dr Barron's northern heroes but that they were Scotsmen and patriots. The truth is that the composition of Scottish society at the outset of the war was too complex to be patient of any such crude and over-simplifying analysis.

Robert Bruce died at his house in Cardross on June 7th, 1329, at the age of fifty-five. For at least two years he had been suffering from a serious illness. The existing evidence is apparently insufficient to enable medical experts to determine its character with certainty.[1] In two independent English accounts, the Lanercost chronicle and Sir Thomas Grey's *Scalacronica*, which are generally well-informed and which may without hesitation be trusted to give at least the popular belief, the king is said to have contracted leprosy and died of it.[2] In another independent account, Jean le Bel says that in 1327 the king was a victim of *la grosse maladie*,[3] which is usually taken to mean leprosy. The difficulty here is to judge how much, if any, meaning these statements possess, in view of the ignorant use of the term 'leprosy' by fourteenth-century writers. Almost any major skin disease might be called leprosy. Moreover, it cannot be proved, though it may be thought probable, that Bruce died of the disease he was known to have contracted. Our earliest mention of this disease is to be found in an original letter written by an eye-witness in Ulster at the time the king made the truce with Sir Henry Mandeville on July 12th, 1327. The writer of this letter reported that the Scottish king was so feeble and struck down by illness that he would not live till the following August, 'for he can scarcely move anything but his tongue'.[4] Yet Bruce recovered sufficiently to play a not inactive part in the northern English campaign of the late summer. He was present, though evidently confined to bed, at the Edinburgh parliament of March 1328, and was even able to cross once more to Ulster in August.[5] He was obviously ailing gravely when he made his pilgrimage to Whithorn in the following year, yet the significant fact from the point of view of the seriousness of his illness is that he was able to go through with it. The Scottish historians do not speak of leprosy, but this could be explained by a natural reluctance on their

---

[1] Cf. W. P. (afterwards Sir William) Macarthur, 'Some notes on old-time leprosy: the case of King Robert the Bruce,' *Journal of the Royal Army Medical Corps*, xlvi, 321–30, esp. 326 and n. 1.

[2] *Chron. Lanercost*, 259, 264; *Scalacronica*, 159.

[3] Le Bel, *Chroniques*, i, 33, 48.

[4] *SHR*, xlii, 34.

[5] Ibid., 36, and references there cited, to which should be added the notice of a mandate issued by Robert I at Larne ('Wlringfrith') on August 13th, 1328 (ibid., xxxii, 38), from the Dudhope muniments.

part to attribute to a hero-king a disease regarded with superstitious dread and loathing. On the other hand, Barbour writes of the king's illness without trying to minimize its seriousness, and his explanation is that 'it began through a benumbing (of the king's body) brought on by his cold lying' during the months of wandering from 1306 to 1309.[1] There does not seem to be any evidence as to what the king himself or his physicians believed his illness to be. Nor is there any sign of an attempt in his last years to segregate the king, even moderately, from the company of friends, family, courtiers or foreign diplomats.[2]

He had always wished to take part in a crusade, to fight the 'Saracens' in the Holy Land or elsewhere. On his deathbed he asked that his heart should be taken from his body, embalmed, and carried to the Holy Sepulchre by a warrior able to do battle with the enemies of God. The honour was given, either by the king himself or by the nobles who were with the king when he died, to the faithful Douglas. The king's body, with the heart removed, was borne to Dunfermline, where most of the Scottish rulers since King Edgar had been buried. It was laid beneath the middle of the choir in the abbey church, and over it was placed a 'fair tomb' which the king had ordered to be made in Paris. Douglas, with many Scottish knights, sailed from Montrose to Flanders early in 1330, and from there to Spain, armed with letters of protection from Edward III and a letter of commendation from the same king to King Alfonso XI of Castile and Leon. King Alfonso, based on Seville, was conducting a campaign against the Moors of Granada who were strongly reinforced by contingents from Morocco. Sir James Douglas was given the command of a division of the Christian army – perhaps, as Barbour says, consisting of all the knights from England, Scotland and other foreign lands. Bearing Bruce's heart, Douglas went into battle at Tebas de Ardales on March 25th, 1330. Deceived by the Moorish tactics of making a feint attack, the Scots found themselves cut off from the main body and helpless against a superior force of Moorish cavalry. Douglas himself, Sir William Sinclair, and Robert and Walter Logan were

---

[1] Barbour, *Bruce*, 362.

[2] In this connexion, too much should not be made of the fact that Queen Elizabeth died at Cullen (October 26th, 1327) and that young David Bruce was established in the bishop of St Andrews' house at Inchmurdo.

among the slain. The heart of Robert Bruce and the bones of the
Good Sir James were brought back to Scotland by Sir William
Keith of Galston, the former to be buried at Melrose Abbey,[1] the
latter in the parish kirk of Douglas, where in after years Sir James's
natural son, Archibald the Grim, erected a noble alabaster tomb. In
accordance with the terms of the tailzie of 1326, the earl of Moray
assumed the office of Guardian of Scotland.

[1] Barbour, *Bruce*, 376 and notes, esp. 490–1; A. A. M. Duncan, in *SHR*, xxxii,
18–22.

On October 18th, 1331, Thomas Randolph earl of Moray granted to the perpetual
chaplains of his own and other chapelries in Elgin Cathedral the patronage of the
parish kirk of Alvie in Badenoch ('Lochalueth'), and the surplus income from this
small Highland church, together with the revenues from Birnie and Altyre, was
assigned by Bishop John Pilmour to the chapelries in Elgin Cathedral to augment
the chaplains' salaries, on condition that each chaplain should celebrate a requiem
mass once a week for the soul of the most noble prince, the lord Robert, of good
memory, king of Scotland, and for the health during his life and soul's weal after
death of Thomas Randolph (*Moray Registrum*, 291–3).

Additional Note (see above, p. 436).
Robert I and Ireland.

Dr Frame's important paper in *Irish Historical Studies*, xix, argues persuasively that
the Scots intervention in Ireland was 'in the mainstream of Scottish policy, not
regarded as a temporary diversion of it' (ibid., p. 15). I believe that he is right to see
Robert and Edward Bruce working in harmony rather than rivalry, and I accept
his more favourable view of Edward's character and motives. Some slight support
is provided for Dr Frame's view of the importance for Robert I of the idea of a
'Scottish' kingdom of Ireland by Brit. Library Add. Chr. No. 3320, a much-corrected
draft of letters-patent issued by the counts of Blois and Flanders referring throughout
to Robert I as 'by God's grace king of Scotland and Ireland'. Nevertheless, I remain
not wholly convinced that even all the varied evidence discussed by Dr Frame
proves that the Irish question was central to Robert I's political strategy, at any rate
for more than a few years.

Appendix

Scottish landowners forfeited by Edward I in 1306 for supporting Robert Bruce, with the names of those who petitioned to have their lands

This list is based on the roll printed in Palgrave, *Docs. Hist. Scot.*, 301–318; cf. ibid., 319. It will be noticed that a good many names of forfeited land-owners occur more than once; either because they held lands in more than one sheriffdom or because their lands were sought by more than one petitioner. It has been thought best to keep the entries in the order in which they appear on the roll. This is not a complete list of those known to have been Bruce's supporters in 1306. (S) after a petitioner's name indicates a Scotsman.

Forfeited landowner	Lands	Petitioner
HAY, Gilbert de la	(Errol?)	Hugh Despenser
CARRICK, earl of (Robert Bruce)	Annandale	earl of Hereford
ATHOLL, earl of	Atholl	earl of Gloucester
SETON, Christopher	in Annandale	Robert Felton
CLOSEBURN, Stephen of	(Closeburn?)	John Cromwell
LOGAN, Walter	?	John Cromwell
CAMERON of BALEDGARNO John	Baledgarno	Hugh, son of earl of Ross (S)
FRASER, Richard	Touch Fraser	John de Luk
FRASER, Alexander	Cornton	John de Luk
FRASER, Thomas (brother of Simon Fraser)	?	Thomas Grey
BICKERTON, Walter	Kincraig, Fife	Thomas Grey
FRASER, Alexander, son of Andrew Fraser	?	Thomas Grey

Tenants of Henry Pinkney	in Luffness and Ballencrieff	Henry Pinkney
RANDOLPH, Thomas	Stichill	Robert Hastings
SOMERVILLE, John	?	Robert Hastings
SOMERVILLE, Thomas	Linton, Roxburgh. Carnwath	Robert Hastings
LOGAN, Walter	?	William Mulcaster, John Bisset
FRASER, Richard		Alexander Balliol (?S)
MENZIES, Alexander		Alexander Balliol (? S)
CRAWFORD, Reginald	in Ayrshire	Robert Haustede
LENNOX, earl of	Lennox	John Menteith (S) Aymer de Valence
STRATHEARN, earl of[1]	Strathearn	Aymer de Valence
SOMERVILLE, John	Clifton, Roxburgh	John Weston
WEMYSS, Michael	in Midlothian	John Weston
SOMERVILLE, William	in Midlothian	John Weston
FRASER, Alexander	in Midlothian	John Weston
LINDSAY, Alexander	in Midlothian	John Weston
RANDOLPH, Thomas	Garlies in Minnigaff, Kirkcudbright Morton in Nithsdale, Dumfriesshire	Thomas Paynel
SOMERVILLE, John	Hedgeley, Northumberland	Robert Hastings
LOCKHART, Simon	Lochwood, Ayr The Lee, Lanarkshire	Robert Hastings
LOVEL, Hugh	(Hawick?)	Robert Bures
FENTON, William	?	Duncan of Frendraught (S)

[1] Subsequently restored.

ROSSIE, Walter of	in Angus	John Lutton
DEMPSTER, Andrew the	in Angus	John Lutton
ATHOLL, earl of	Stratha'an, Banffshire Strathbogie, Aberdeen	Alexander Abernethy (S)
MURRAY, William	St Fort, Fife	Alexander Abernethy (S)
MURRAY, Alan (cousin of preceding)	(Culbin?)	Alexander Abernethy (S)
CARRICK, earl of	Lands north of Forth	Alexander Abernethy (S)
BALCASKIE, Thomas of	Balcaskie, Fife	Alexander Harcaz
BOYS, Thomas de	?	John Autry
VALOGNES, Adam de	? in Angus	John Autry
SIWARD, John	in Mearns	Richard of Denmuir (Fife) (S)
ARBROATH (ARBUTHNOT?), Duncan of	?	Richard of Denmuir (Fife) (S)
NEUTROBRE, Richard of	in Angus	John Comyn (S)
BEN, Robert	?	John Comyn (S)
CAMERON OF BALNELY, John	in Perthshire	Simon Warde
CUNNINGHAM, Robert of	in Ayrshire	Edmund de Beyville
RIEL, Henry of	?	John Wigton
COMLONGAN, laird of	in Ayrshire	John Wigton
ASKELOC, Roland	in Ayrshire	John Wigton
KIRKCONNEL, Thomas of	in Dumfriesshire	Henry Malton
KIRKCONNEL, Robert of	in Dumfriesshire	Henry Malton
BOYS, Walter de	?	Adam Swinburne
CORRY, Nicholas	?	Adam Swinburne
CALDECOTE, Robert son of Geoffrey	in Galloway	Adam Swinburne
COCKBURN, Peter	in Peeblesshire	Michael Witton
SOMERVILLE, Thomas (nephew of Simon Fraser) and his son and heir	(in Roxburgh and Lanark?)	Walter de Moncy

CARRICK, Gilbert, son of Roland of	in Ayrshire	Gilbert Elsfield
RANDOLPH, Thomas	?	Maurice le Brun
MACCULIAN, Malcolm	in 'the isle of Kintyre'	John Ferrers
FRASER, Richard	Arkelton, Dumfries	John of Bristol
GRAHAM, Patrick	(in West Highlands?)	Lachlan Macruarie (S)
DALLAS, Thomas of	Dallas, Moray	Alexander Seton (S)
WISTON, Walter of	in Lanarkshire	Henry Prendergest (S)
MURRAY, Austin	in Lanarkshire	Henry Prendergest (S)
NESBIT, Robert	in Lanarkshire	Henry Prendergest (S)
INCHTURE, Robert of	in Perthshire	Henry Prendergest (S)
SLEGH, Andrew, of Aberdeen	in Aberdeen	William le Jettour
BISHOP, Andrew, burgess	in Aberdeen	William le Jettour
CHAPEU, Adam, burgess	in Aberdeen	William le Jettour
RATTRAY, Eustace of	in Perthshire	John Thirlwall
CAMPBELL, Neil	(in Argyll?)	John Dovedale
ALYTH of the BRAE, Walter	in Perthshire	Adam Brunyng (S)
COKYN, John	?	Adam Brunyng (S)
INNERPEFFRAY, Malcolm of	in Perthshire	Adam Brunyng (S)
FOLKARD, Alexander	in Lennox	Walter Gylling
ANELF, Duncan, son of (Macaulay?)	in Lennox	Walter Gylling
LUSS, John of	in Lennox	Walter Gylling
DUNDEE, Master Ralph of	(in Angus or Argyll?)	John Hayward
WISHART, John	Conveth in Mearns	John Hayward
ANGUS, Laurence of	(in Angus?)	John Hayward
HAY, Gilbert de la	Errol	John de la Mare

MURRAY, William, of St Fort	Kinninmonth	John de la Mare
BLAIR, Brice	in Ayrshire	William of Cambou
LOVEL, Hugh	Enoch and 'Domcroy' in Nithsdale	John Daniel
ST MICHAEL, John of	in Roxburghshire	John Alegate
MELVILLE, William	in Roxburghshire	John Alegate
FORBES, John	?	Robert Chival
MURRAY of DRUMSERGARD, John	in Lanarkshire	Robert Chival
CAMPBELL, Donald	(in Argyll?)	Stephen Deepham
INCHTURE, Robert of	in Perthshire	William de Stroir
STOIL, Roger	?	William de Stroir
FRASER, Thomas	?	Robert de Repples
AUCHTERGAVEN, Donald of	in Perthshire	Richard Wollaston
CREMANNAN, Thomas of	in Lennox	Nicol de Boys
LENY, John of	in Menteith	Robert de Sapy
MACKESSAN, Coweyn (Ewen?)	(Probably Garchell in Drymen, Stirlingshire)	Alexander the queen's chandler
(FRASER)	'Ughtrothere-strother' (Crawford Priory, Fife)	Thomas Grey
HAY, John de la	in Inverness-shire	Oliver Avenel
KEITH, Bernard	in Ayrshire	Thomas and Herbert de Borehonte
LINDSAY, Alexander	Barnweill, Ayr	Roger de Borehonte
SOULES, John de	Old Roxburgh	Richard Lovel
CARMUNNOCK (?) Thomas of	?	Geoffrey Segrave
CUNNINGHAM, Robert of	in Ayrshire	Geoffrey Segrave
KNOCKDOLIAN, John of	in Ayrshire	Geoffrey Segrave
MONTGOMERY, John of	(Ayrshire or Renfrew?)	Geoffrey Segrave
GRADEN, Peter of	in Berwickshire	Randolf de Charron

STRATHBOGIE, Laurence of	in Caithness and Sutherland	Cristyn of the Aird (S)
PILCHE, Alexander, burgess	in Inverness	Cristyn of the Aird (S)
LINDSAY, James, son and heir of Walter	Thurston, E. Lothian	Thomas Convers
FRASER, Alexander	Drip, Stirling	William Montfichet
DURWARD, Alan	Fichlie, Aberdeenshire	William Montfichet
FORBES, John	?	William Comyn (S)
DALLAS, Thomas of	in Moray	earl of Sutherland (S)
TROUP, Hamelin of	in Banffshire	William de Hustweit
BARCLAY, Walter, of Kercock	in Perthshire	Gilbert Peche
MONYKEBBUCK, Walter of	in Aberdeenshire	Gilbert Peche
WAUCHOPE, Robert·	in Fife	Richard de Lisle
FENTON, John, son of William	in Midlothian	Geoffrey of Ledes
MONYMUSK, Thomas of	Forglen, Banff	Thomas de la Greve
CARRICK, Maud of	in Cumberland	Henry Touke
BOTHWELL, Eustace of	in Cumberland	Henry Touke
MENZIES, William, son of Alexander	Shielswood and Harden	John de Lisle
LOGAN, Walter	?	John de Lisle
FRASER, Alexander	?	John de Lisle
HATTELE, Alexander of	?	John de Lisle
NESBIT, Robert	?	John de Lisle
MURRAY, Austin	Wiston, Lanark	John de Lisle
MOWAT, William	Kinnettles, Angus	John de la Mare
MOLBRIDE the young	Strat (Strath Eachaig?)	Gillespie MacLachlan (S)
[BOYD, Robert	Coronerships of Ayr and Lanark	Dungal Macdouall (S)][1]

[1] Granted by the King, perhaps without petition.

Tables

I. THE SUCCESSION, 1290–1292

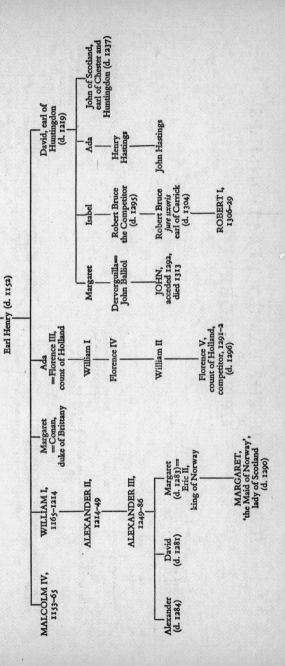

II. SOME OF THE FAMILY RELATIONSHIPS
OF KING ROBERT I

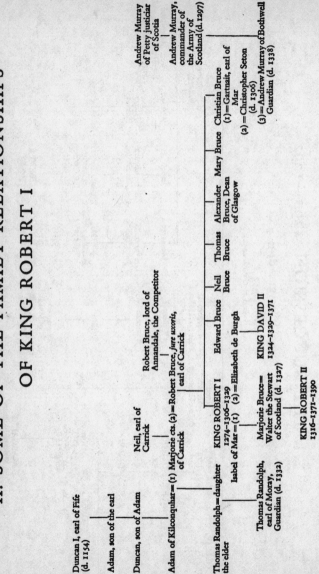

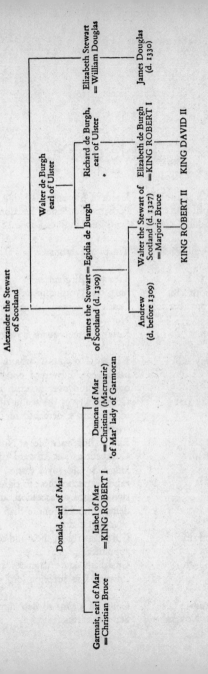

Table of Dates

1292	November 7th	Bruce the Competitor resigns claim to seek the Scottish throne to his son and heirs.
	November 9th	Bruce the Competitor's son resigns earldom of Carrick to his own son, the future king.
	November 10th–14th	Count Florence V of Holland presses his claim to Scottish throne.
	November 17th	Court pronounces judgement in favour of Balliol.
	November 30th	King John enthroned and crowned at Scone.
	December 22nd	Edward I gives judgement in case of Roger Bartholomew.
	December 31st	Edward I repudiates all promises and obligations made during the interregnum.
1293	January 2nd	King John declares null the Treaty of Birgham and all Anglo-Scottish agreements made during the interregnum.
	After September 29th	King John protests against Edward I's claim to hear appeals; withdraws his protest, and submits as Edward's liege vassal.
1294	June	War between Edward I and Philip IV over Gascony. King John and Scottish magnates summoned for military service overseas.
	September	Revolt in Wales.
	Before December	Scots obtain absolution from Pope Celestine V from oaths taken under duress.
1295	July 5th	Stirling parliament; election of council of twelve.
	October 23rd	Franco-Scottish treaty.
1296	March	War between Edward I and John Balliol.
	March 30th	Capture and sack of Berwick.
	April 27th	Battle of Dunbar.
	July 2nd–10th	King John submits to Edward I, renounces French treaty and abdicates, resigning kingdom of Scotland to Edward I.
	August 28th	Berwick parliament; Edward I receives homages and fealties of some 2,000 freeholders in Scotland.

	c. September 29th	Edward I commits government of Scotland to John earl Warenne.
1297	Before May	Disturbances in west highlands, Aberdeenshire and Galloway.
	May	Wallace slays sheriff of Lanark. Wallace and William Douglas attack the justiciar at Scone. Robert Bruce, earl of Carrick, heads revolt in Carrick.
	June–July	The Stewart, the bishop of Glasgow and Bruce confront Clifford and Percy at Irvine and capitulate.
	Summer	Rising in Moray under Andrew Murray.
	August 22nd	Edward I sails for Flanders.
	c. August 31st	Murray and Wallace join forces at Stirling Bridge.
	September 11th	Warenne's army destroyed at Stirling Bridge. Wallace and Murray liberate Scotland.
	October–November	Wallace raids northern England.
	November 3rd	William Lamberton elected bishop of St Andrews.
1298	Before March	Wallace appointed Guardian.
	Late February–Early March	Scots magnates and their followers with Edward I in Flanders leave him at Aardenburg and sail to Scotland.
	March 14th	Edward I returns from Flanders.
	July 1st	English army, assembled at Roxburgh, advances into Scotland.
	July 22nd	Battle of Falkirk.
	Between July and December	Wallace resigns guardianship; Bruce and Comyn the younger of Badenoch elected joint-Guardians.
1299	July	John Balliol transferred from England to papal custody near Cambrai.
	August	Scots magnates raid The Forest. Bishop Lamberton made chief Guardian with Bruce and Comyn.
	Before December	Scots take Stirling castle.

1300	May 10th	Rutherglen parliament. Ingram de Umfraville appointed Guardian *vice* Bruce, resigned.
	July–August	Edward I's campaign in Galloway.
	October 30th	Truce for seven months.
1301	Beginning of year	John de Soules elected sole Guardian.
	May 7th	Edward I's letter to pope, defending his policies in Scotland.
	May–June	Scottish delegation at papal curia defending Scottish independence.
	Summer	John Balliol transferred from papal custody to his own castle of Bailleul-en-Vimeu.
	July–September	Edward I and Edward of Caernarvon campaign in south-western Scotland.
	c. September 24th	Edward I takes Bothwell castle.
1302	January 26th	Truce for nine months.
	c. January 26th (before February 16th)	Bruce submits to Edward I and comes into his peace.
		Bruce marries Elizabeth de Burgh.
	July 11th	Battle of Courtrai.
	Autumn	Scottish delegation at Paris.
1303	February 24th	Battle of Roslin.
	May	Edward I's expedition to Scotland.
	May 20th	Peace between France and England, excluding the Scots.
1304	February 9th	Comyn and other Scots magnates submit to Edward I.
	March	St Andrews parliament; Scots freeholders submit to Edward I and have their lands restored. Robert Bruce of Annandale, father of the future king, dies in England.
	May–July	Siege of Stirling castle.
	June 11th	Secret band between Bruce and Bishop Lamberton.
	July 20th.	Fall of Stirling.

1305	February	Westminster parliament; new constitution ordered for Scotland.
	May	Scottish parliament to advise on new constitution.
	August 3rd	Wallace captured.
	August 23rd	Wallace executed.
	September 15th	Westminster parliament; Ordinance for the Government of Scotland promulgated.
1306	February 10th	Bruce murders Comyn at Dumfries.
	March 25th	Bruce enthroned and crowned at Scone.
	March 27th	Bruce undergoes second inauguration ceremony with assistance of Isabel of Fife, countess of Buchan.
	June 19th	Battle of Methven.
	August 11th (really July?)	Battle of Dail Righ.
	September	Bruce flees from Dunaverty to Rathlin.
1307	February	Bruce returns to Carrick.
	April	Ambush at Glen Trool.
	c. May 10th	Battle of Loudoun Hill.
	July 7th	Death of Edward I.
	December 25th–31st	Encounter at Slioch near Huntly.
1308	May 23rd	Battle of Inverurie (?).
	c. June 24th	Galloway campaign.
	August 15th or later	Battle of Brander.
	October 31st	Earl of Ross submits.
1309	March 16th–17th	St Andrews parliament.
	August–October	Bruce on western expedition.
1310– 1311	September– August	Edward II's campaign in Scotland.
1312	August	Bruce raids northern England.
	October 29th	Scoto-Norwegian Treaty of Inverness.
1313	January 7th–8th	Bruce takes Perth.
	February 7th	Bruce takes Dumfries.

	June 23rd	Edward Bruce gives one year's respite to Stirling castle.
1314	February 19th–20th	Douglas takes Roxburgh castle.
	March 14th	Randolph takes Edinburgh castle.
	June 23rd–24th	Battle of Bannockburn.
	November	Cambuskenneth parliament; forfeiture of Bruce's opponents.
1315	April 27th	Succession to Scottish throne settled on Edward Bruce, failing male heirs to Bruce.
	May	Edward Bruce's expedition to Ireland.
1316	May	Edward Bruce crowned king of Ireland at Dundalk.
1316–		
1317	Winter	Bruce in Ireland.
1318	April 1st–2nd	Capture of Berwick.
	October 14th	Death of Edward Bruce.
	December 3rd	Succession to Scottish throne settled on Robert Stewart, failing male heirs to Bruce.
1319	July	Edward II besieges Berwick.
	September 20th (?)	Battle or 'Chapter' of Myton.
	December 25th	Two-year truce.
1320	April 6th	Declaration of Arbroath (letter of Community of the Realm of Scotland to Pope John XXII).
	August 4th	Scone parliament; trial of Soules conspirators.
1322	March 16th	Battle of Boroughbridge.
	August–September	Edward II's last expedition to Scotland.
	October	Bruce leads raid into north Yorkshire.
	October 20th	Battle of (Old) Byland.
1323	January 3rd	Bruce–Harcla 'treaty'.
	May 30th	Thirteen-year truce.

1324	January	Papacy recognizes Bruce's title as king of Scotland.
1326	April	Franco-Scottish treaty of Corbeil.
	July 15th	Succession to Scottish throne settled on David Bruce, remainder to Robert Stewart.
1327	January 20th	Deposition of Edward II.
	February 1st	Coronation of Edward III. Scots break truce with attack on Norham.
	June 15th	Scots raid Co. Durham.
	July 18th	Edward III and his army at Durham.
	July 31st	Edward III in Allendale.
	August 1st–5th	English and Scots confront each other at Stanhope Park.
	c. August 7th	Edward III withdraws to York.
	August–September	Bruce invades Northumberland.
	October–December	Peace negotiations.
1328	March 17th (May 4th	Treaty of Edinburgh ratified at Northampton).
	July 12th	Marriage between David Bruce and Joan of the Tower.
1329	June 7th	Death of Bruce.
1330	March 25th	Death of Douglas in Spain.

Index

Where appropriate Scottish counties are abbreviated to the name of the county town. Dates following office holders refer to the period of office.